Y0-DUR-082

Learning to Teach in the Elementary School

THE MACMILLAN COMPANY
NEW YORK • CHICAGO
DALLAS • ATLANTA • SAN FRANCISCO
LONDON • MANILA

IN CANADA
BRETT-MACMILLAN LTD.
GALT, ONTARIO

Learning to Teach in the Elementary School

MARGARET G. McKIM
CARL W. HANSEN
WILLIAM L. CARTER

Teachers College
University of Cincinnati

New York
THE MACMILLAN COMPANY

First Printing

Library of Congress catalog card number: 59-5986

The Macmillan Company, New York

Brett-Macmillan Ltd., Galt, Ontario

Printed in the United States of America

to KATIE

who helped to make this book come true.

Preface

This book is designed to give concrete help to student teachers and to teachers who are in their first years of full-time classroom responsibility. It is focused upon the problems you will face in guiding the classroom experiences of boys and girls and in becoming an effective member of a school faculty. Many of these problems are essentially the same whether you are working with an experienced cooperating teacher or responsible for your own classroom. Much of this volume, therefore, is addressed to all beginners. However, at points where the situation faced by either a student teacher or a first-year teacher is unique because of the special nature of his assignment, sections or paragraphs have been addressed to these special problems. The authors believe that the book will be useful to those who are members of student-teaching seminars, or of general methods courses which include classroom participation as part of their experiences, and that it will continue to serve as a resource to teachers employed in a full-time classroom position.

Underlying the decisions regarding what problems to stress and how much detail to include is the basic assumption that your major concern as a beginning teacher is to translate your professional education into successful classroom practice. Accordingly, although a conscientious effort has been made to include the full range of professional problems you are likely to meet as a beginner, the chapters comprising the heart of the book stress problems of how to teach. These chapters are not, however, mere condensations of more extensive texts on methods in specific teaching fields. The emphasis is rather upon basic educational principles. The illustrations of these principles in operation have been chosen from many fields and many grade levels. Your responsibility will be that of making the applications to your particular classroom situation.

The elementary school classroom envisioned in this volume is one in which there is pupil-teacher planning and a problem-solving approach to learning, with the maximum development of each individual as an ultimate goal. No two teachers, however, work under exactly the same conditions. Nor will any two personalities work with children in exactly the same way. Although the authors have striven for consistency in their interpretation of educational principles, they have endeavored through their choice of illustrations to recognize the wide variety of situations in which you, as a beginning teacher, may find yourself. No single type of curriculum design has been advocated. Every effort has been made to select illustrations that are applicable to many types of classrooms and to include problems of concern to teachers in both large and small school systems. The authors trust that their interpretations of the realities which teachers face in elementary schools today have been sufficiently unbiased to make it easy for you to apply what you read in this book to the classroom setting in which you find yourself.

You will be able to put this volume to more effective use if you understand its organization. The focus of the chapters and of the major sections within each chapter is upon those professional problems with which every elementary teacher must deal again and again. Chapters are arranged according to the general sequence in which these problems are likely to be met by the beginner entering upon his first extensive classroom experience. Part I provides an over-all view of what is entailed in becoming an effective member of the teaching profession. Part II deals with problems of getting acquainted with a new school and a new group of boys and girls. Part III is devoted to classroom problems—guiding pupils toward self-discipline, planning for and with pupils, helping learners understand their world, developing fundamental skills, fostering growth in creative expression, utilizing the school community as a source of learnings, evaluating and reporting progress, and achieving effective classroom administration. Part IV discusses those problems associated with securing a teaching position and with growing as a member of the profession. Part V, the final chapter, is addressed to cooperating teachers on the assumption that those who work with student teachers will welcome a discussion of their problems within the covers of a book designed to help their students.

Each chapter, and to some extent each major section within each chapter, is written to stand by itself. It is not necessary to begin with the first chapter, therefore, if your immediate concern lies in some other area. The table of contents, the index, and the cross references within each chapter should make it possible for you to use the materials in this volume in whatever order is suited to your special problem or pattern of problems. The authors hope that its flexibility in this regard will render the book readily adaptable to the particular needs of student groups or of individuals.

Even though the problems about which the chapters are centered have been discussed in concrete detail, this book is not merely a "how-to-do-it" handbook. Neither this, nor any other single text will provide detailed answers to all classroom problems. The *Books You Should Know* at the end of each chapter may aid you in securing additional insights. More important, however, is that you learn to think for yourself. The effectiveness of the experiences provided for boys and girls depends, in the final analysis, upon the good judgment of their teacher. This volume will serve its purpose if it helps you face your classroom problems with a greater depth of professional insight and with an ever-increasing sense of personal security.

Margaret G. McKim
Carl W. Hansen
William L. Carter

Cincinnati, Ohio

Acknowledgments

Many people have helped to make this book possible. Special thanks are extended to the teachers and teachers-to-be with whom the authors have worked either in cooperative student-teaching relationships or in college classes, both graduate and undergraduate. Their insights, personal experiences, and problems are reflected on every page. Although it is impossible to mention them by name, their contribution is testimony of the classroom teacher's role in the deepening of professional insights into the art of teaching.

The authors' colleagues in the University of Cincinnati have given generously of their time in discussing special problems, in appraising parts of the manuscript, and in suggesting items for bibliographies. They are especially indebted to Professor Robert D. Price, Assistant Dean of Teachers College, for his thoughtful help in the planning of this volume and to Professor Agnes Ann Manney who read the entire manuscript critically.

Colleagues in the schools of Cincinnati and of Hamilton County, Ohio, have been equally generous in sharing their insights into practical school problems and the needs of beginning teachers. Particular thanks are extended to Miss Helen A. Bertermann and to Miss Rebecca A. Montgomery, of the Cincinnati Public Schools who read the entire manuscript. Mrs. Mildred J. Crouch and Mrs. Shirley B. Ohlhauser of the Cincinnati Public Schools, and Miss Opal Shifflet of the Wyoming, Ohio, Public Schools, all of whom served on the faculty of the University of Cincinnati Summer Demonstration School, were most helpful in arranging for pictures and in supplying details for the extensive units described in Chapter 7.

The technical problems of preparing a manuscript for publication are many. The authors are grateful to Mrs. Mary H. Swift for invaluable editorial assistance, and to Mrs. Dorothy Nicholson for intelligent and conscientious typing. Thanks are due to Mr. D. Arthur Bricker and Mr. Gilbert H. Corlett of the Cincinnati Public Schools, and to Mrs. Audrey B. Norris of the schools of Hamilton County, Ohio, for their special assistance in securing photographs. The pictures are reproduced with the permission of the Cincinnati Public Schools, the St. Bernard Public Schools, the Public Schools of Hamilton County, Ohio, and the Summer Demonstration School of the University of Cincinnati. Specific credit is given to each school system and to each photographer under the appropriate picture. Appreciation is also extended to the publishers and authors who gave permission to quote from their publications.

Table of Contents

Teaching as a Profession

PART I

Appraising Your Assets for Teaching

CHAPTER 1

Make it thy business to know thyself, which is the most difficult lesson in the world.[1]

A self-accepting person knows his weaknesses. He knows which faults he can alter, and learns to live with the others. He feels that despite his limitations he is a person to be approved. He feels that he is doing what can reasonably be expected of him. He approves himself without feeling that he is perfect.[2]

A teacher cannot make much headway in understanding others or in helping others to understand themselves unless he is endeavoring to understand himself. If he is not engaged in this endeavor, he will continue to see those whom he teaches through the bias and distortions of his own unrecognized needs, fears, desires, anxieties, hostile impulses, and so on.[3]

No matter how long you have been preparing for teaching or how extensive your experiences with children, you will be a rare individual if you do not face your first opportunity to take full-time responsibility for a class with some trepidation. Will my pupils like me? Will they work with me? Will I be able to help them learn? How satisfied will I be that I have chosen wisely in deciding upon teaching as my life's work? These are the kinds of questions that all beginning teachers ask themselves.

It is often said that teachers are born, but it is the rare individual who seems, from birth, to have a gift for working with children. It is perhaps closer to the truth to say that teachers are developed. Experi-

[1] Miguel de Cervantes, *Don Quixote,* Pt. ii, Ch. 42.

[2] Lee J. Cronbach, *Educational Psychology,* p. 563. New York: Harcourt, Brace and Co., 1954. Used by permission of the publisher.

[3] Arthur T. Jersild, *When Teachers Face Themselves,* pp. 13-14. New York: Bureau of Publications, Teachers College, Columbia University, 1955. Used by permission of the publisher.

ences from early childhood—with other children, with your parents and other adults, with everyday events—have combined to make you the person you are today. Throughout your years in the elementary and secondary school, your teachers have contributed to your store of knowledge, to your skills, to your ability to think, and to your attitudes toward your chosen profession. Academic courses at college have deepened your understanding of the cultural heritage and the world in which you live. Professional courses have developed and clarified your insights into your responsibilities as a teacher. You bring this accumulation of attitudes, knowledge, skills, and insights with you as you step inside your own classroom for the first time.

Student teaching and your first years on the job are late steps in the long process of preparing to become a teacher. You need have few apprehensions about your ability to take these steps successfully if you have been building toward them wisely—heeding the counsel of those persons who know you best—and capitalizing upon the available opportunities for growth. There is, however, much to be learned in this, your first venture in full-time responsibility for a group of boys and girls. Whether or not your chosen profession offers all the satisfactions for which you have hoped depends, to a large extent, upon you. Are you aware of your own assets? You will want to capitalize upon them in your work with boys and girls. Have you made a clear-eyed, objective appraisal of your potential liabilities? You must be prepared to compensate for these in your classroom work. How well do you know yourself? What must you do to make yourself a successful teacher?

WHAT PERSONAL ASSETS DO YOU BRING TO THE CLASSROOM?

You will bring to the classroom your innate personal equipment and what you have been helped to make of it over the years of living—physical stamina, intellectual ability, special talents, personal appearance, voice. For no two people is this personal equipment the same. None of the extensive research concerning the characteristics of an effective teacher has uncovered a definite pattern of talents and capacities that results automatically in success on the job. You do not, therefore, have to make yourself into a different person in order to become a good teacher. What *is* important is that you learn to use your unique personal equipment as effectively as possible in the interests of the maximum growth of the boys and girls under your care.

How do you appraise your physical stamina? Teaching can be exhausting. The most rigorous combination of college classes, committee chairmanships, and a part-time job rarely equals the physical demands of the classroom. There will be few opportunities during the school day to relax completely. There will be no half-day off to rest unless serious illness demands it. You will probably be on your feet for longer periods than those to which you have been accustomed. Even with conscientious efforts to encourage active participation on the part of your pupils, you will be making more use of your voice than ever before. There will be as much "required" reading as was ever demanded by a full schedule of college classes. You will be repeatedly exposed to colds, influenza, mumps, measles, chicken pox.

People differ in their physiological requirements. Even though you have received a clean bill of health in a recent physical examination, it is important to identify just what your own physical limitations are. Are you a person who needs more than the usual amount of sleep in order to be fresh, bright, and cheerful? If so, it might be well to take another look at your college program and extra-class activities. It is far better to postpone an elective course or to resign from a committee than it is to drag yourself into the classroom day after day fatigued by midnight study or long hours in committee sessions. Do you know your own nutritional needs? The days that you try to teach after an inadequate breakfast or lunch can become unbelievably long and wearisome. How long can you keep going without a chance to relax? A few teachers seem to be human dynamos who draw strength from the stimulation of an active group of youngsters, but most find that they cannot operate at full power all day long. The typical elementary school schedule does not allow many free periods away from the children, but you can, for their sake as well as your own, learn to plan a program in which there is an appropriate alternating of active and quiet work—periods in which you are giving active leadership to the entire group and work sessions where you can talk with youngsters individually, times when you need to be on your feet and times when you can sit for a few minutes. It is not an indication of weakness to recognize one's personal need for such adjustments. Teaching ceases to be fun if the physical demands of the classroom become unbearably heavy.

If you are a person whose physical resistance tends to be below normal, you should take particular precautions to avoid the fatigue that often invites trouble. You will soon find that your teaching will lose its effectiveness for your pupils and its satisfactions for you if it is interrupted by a series of absences for illness. Consult your family physician, if necessary, for appropriate medical advice. Plan your personal living to provide the rest and relaxation consistent with the professional job you have to do.

But is a hermit-like existence all that you can anticipate when you begin to teach? By no means. The old adage that a change is as good as a rest has sound psychological foundations. Every teacher needs to make sure that he does not allow his preoccupation with professional responsibilities, challenging and stimulating though these may be, to cut him off from other types of activities which he finds personally satisfying. Certainly you will need to arrange your schedule so that you are not harassed by more demands than you can handle. Work for balance in your activities. Broadly interpreted, health is emotional as well as physical. Do not sacrifice completely your recreational and social life. Children deserve to be working with teachers who have buoyancy, enthusiasm, and a zest for living.

How flexibly do you deal with new ideas? A candid analysis of classroom activities indicates that there are dozens of times a day when the quality of pupils' learning depends upon their teacher's ability to sense the implications of a situation quickly and accurately. Your boys and girls will become confused at the most unexpected points; you will have to set them straight. They will phrase their questions vaguely and leave you wondering exactly what they mean. They will grasp only part of an explanation and arrive at conclusions incomprehensible to anyone not intellectually agile enough to follow their reasoning. They will contribute anecdotes from their out-of-school life that can have major bearing upon their classroom work if you but sense the relationships. They will ask an appalling number of questions, many of which appear only distantly related to the immediate topic under discussion. You will have to decide how to deal with these.

Not all people can think with ease and facility on their feet. Some see the far-reaching ramifications of a situation instantly; others need time to marshal their thoughts. Some grasp what another person is trying to say from a minor cue; others must have the point fully spelled out. Some can follow several threads in a discussion at once; others become confused when they try to deal with more than one idea at a time. You are not likely, during your student-teaching experience, to make many fundamental changes in the way you think. You can, however, recognize your own characteristic ways of reacting to new ideas.

Once you are aware of these you can prepare more intelligently for the classroom situations you will inevitably face.

Whether you think quickly or slowly on your feet, you owe it to your pupils to make careful plans. Experienced teachers never neglect this, even though they are going over much the same ground for the umpteenth time. Teaching is far more complicated than merely getting along companionably with a group of boys and girls and answering their questions glibly. You must make each minute count. The more skillfully you learn to think through every detail of the work on which you are about to embark, the better prepared you will be to handle your pupils' questions and comments in ways that will result in maximum growth. Experienced teachers will tell you that their planning is usually much more thorough than merely mapping out a single course of action. They plan alternate illustrations upon which they may draw if the ones they first use prove inadequate. They identify points at which pupils might become confused and plan how to give more help if it seems to be needed. They think about the applications to out-of-school life that their pupils are likely to make and the relationships to previous lessons that they may identify. No matter how adept you are in handling emergencies, you will be a more skillful teacher if you learn to prepare yourself for the unforeseen.

But suppose you are a person who needs time to grasp the full implications of a new idea or to sense the importance of a question. If this is true, you would do well to recognize the fact and to come to your classroom carefully prepared to use techniques that will give you a chance to catch your breath. You will contribute far more to the development of accurate information and clear thinking if you are prepared to say frankly to your boys and girls, "Let's not guess; we'll need to look that up," than you will by vague acceptance of an incorrect fact or an illogical conclusion. Likewise, you will stand a much better chance of helping the pupil who is confused if you will question him until you are sure you have understood his difficulty than you will by launching into a hasty explanation that misses the point.

On the other hand, you may be a person who enjoys the matching of wits in a good argument. In this case, you would do well to take a second look at the way you handle new ideas. You may recognize in yourself a tendency to respond too readily—to jump to a conclusion regarding what a pupil is trying to say without hearing him out, to advance a solution to a problem without giving the child who is in difficulty a chance to think, to pull the entire class off on a tangent because of the implications you happen to see in a question, to be impatient with the youngster who thinks slowly. If you have a tendency to make snap decisions, it may be important for you, also, to develop techniques that will give you time to think about the implications of the situation you face.

Nothing is more satisfying to a teacher than to watch boys and girls acquire new skills and concepts. Your first classroom situation is the time and place to discover the detail with which you, yourself, must prepare in order to guide their learning competently. It is your opportunity to develop the techniques you need to manage the give-and-take of class discussion effectively.

What impressions will your personal appearance convey? "I'm not sure that older children will listen to me. Some of them will be taller than I am." "Won't a man my size frighten fourth-graders?" "I feel so odd asking sixth-graders to sit down. After all, I don't look much older, myself." Children give their respect and their love to teachers of all ages, sizes, and shapes. What you reveal about yourself through your dress, your grooming, your voice, and your manner makes the difference. If a petite young woman adopts a very youthful dress and hair style and tries to joke and tease like a ten-year-old, her pupils are apt to respond in kind. If her clothing, hair style, and manner suggest maturity, she will be regarded as an adult. If a large man gives the impression from his dress and grooming that he is engaged in manual labor and uses a blustering voice and manner, his pupils may be intimidated. If he wears the clothing they associate with professional people and his manner is gentle, they will turn to him readily. First impressions are important. Before you step into your new classroom, give some thought to your personal appearance.

What should you wear? If you think back to your own school days you will realize that you noticed your teacher's clothing. You looked forward to the days when Miss Simpson wore a dress which you particularly admired or when Mr. Jones donned a tie that was your favorite. On the other hand, you may also remember at least one occasion when you were so fascinated by a teacher's jangling bracelet or the extreme style of her dress that you could scarcely keep your mind on your work. Bright colors, attractive and youthful styles, and costume jewelry belong in today's classrooms. However, although you would not deny your pupils the fun of seeing you dressed for a tea (or for a picnic) once in a while, you should, for the most part, choose garb suited to the activities in which you will be engaged. You will need to be active in playground games, to help mix paints, to stretch to write on the blackboard, to kneel to work beside a youngster. This calls for attractive, informal business attire and comfortable, well-fitting shoes.

You will want to pay particular attention to your dress the first day you arrive. It is a wise precaution to dress attractively but conservatively until you have an opportunity to ascertain the custom in your particular school. (For women this means hose, and for men a coat and tie, even in warm weather.) For your first few days in the classroom you would not choose your most youthful garb. Certainly, clothing that identifies you immediately as a college student (socks, saddle shoes, athletic sweaters, or whatever is the current campus craze) is inappropriate, even though you are merely walking down the hall to the laboratory school which you have visited countless times. Above everything else, choose for your first day the costume in which you feel most at ease and poised. Use your dress to contribute to your feelings of competence and security.

If you expect your boys and girls to appear with clean hands, manicured nails, combed hair, and clean clothing, you can do no more than set them a good example. Good grooming is, perhaps, partly a matter of habit, but it conveys to others a definite impression about the way you regard yourself. So, in the case of women, does the choice of cosmetics. You may not possess a large wardrobe, but you can at least make sure that your boys and girls will be working with someone who is fastidious about personal cleanliness, who is conservative in the use of cosmetics, whose clothing is spotless, and whose shoes are polished.

Have you listened to your voice lately? Your pupils are a captive audience. If you speak too rapidly to be easily understood, lisp, employ a harsh, shrill voice, or speak in monotonous tones, you are creating an annoyance which they must endure day after day. Perhaps even more important, the quality of your voice can have a definite effect upon your pupils' behavior. If you sound competent, assured, and secure, they will accept your leadership; if you sound uncertain, dubious, and hesitant, they are likely to feel doubtful. If the edge in your voice indicates that you are becoming increasingly tense and irritated, their behavior may reflect your irritation. You can arouse them to a fever pitch by the excitement in your tone or you can help them to become relaxed and calm by your serenity. Few of us can appraise our own voices accurately. In fact, it is a common experience not even to recognize one's own voice in a recording. Seek help in evaluating the quality and volume of your voice and in eliminating undesirable mannerisms. Many a teacher has discovered that with a little practice he can make a decided improvement in his ability to use his voice effectively in achieving his purposes in the classroom.

"Yes," beginners sometimes say, "I know how to dress, but how shall I *behave* if I want the children to respect me?" The personality to which your boys and girls will be responding is made up of many things—voice, posture, dress, grooming, poise, assurance, friendliness. You cannot don a new personality as you would a new costume. You can, however, be your normal, competent, adult self. From your vantage point, the gap between your age and that of your pupils may seem negligible, but from theirs it is very great indeed. If you are so unwise as to try to adopt the mores and manners of your pupils in order to be accepted by them, they will recognize that your behavior does not ring true and will respond accordingly. Dress like the adult you are; speak with the assurance of your twenty-odd years of living; walk, stand, and sit with poise. Have confidence in your own leadership ability and you will convey this confidence to your boys and girls.

HOW BROAD IS YOUR ACQUAINTANCE WITH YOUR CULTURAL HERITAGE?

You have chosen a profession that calls for depth and breadth of understanding. You will be responsible for helping pupils to grow in understanding their world. Yours will be the challenge of opening to them the doors to creative expression—literature, art, music, drama, dance. You will be helping them to gain command of problem-solving skills—reasoning, communicating, observing, listening, calculating. You will be providing the experiences they need to develop physical coordination and skill in games. You will be the one to help them grow in their ability to work cooperatively with their fellows.

A total of some sixteen years in school (and some twenty years of living) no matter how wisely invested, has taken you only a short way along the road toward becoming an educated person—a road which you have obligated yourself to travel for the remainder of your life. As you begin to think about guiding the growth of the boys and girls under your care, it is appropriate to inventory your cultural accomplishments. What have you to offer? What are the resources at your command to help yourself grow as your pupils grow?

Where are the strengths in your academic background? Not until you face thirty or more eager youngsters—be they five, eight, or a dozen years old—will you have any notion of the extent to which your academic background will be taxed. Children will respond to the subject matter you are trying to teach with questions that explore the most minute details. They will push logical discussions to conclusions you have never dreamed of. Nor will your pupils' zeal for information be confined to the topics listed in the course of study. They will bring their outside world to school. Eager voices will report on last night's television production. Grubby hands will present you with leaves to classify, snakes to name. Young scientists will come bearing their latest ventures in developing miniature rockets. Budding musicians will ask for help in transcribing a new song to paper.

What has been the pattern of your college work? Where do your strengths lie? Even in areas in which you are well schooled, you may find yourself turning for further information to a variety of technical and nontechnical resources, but here, at least, you have depth of background upon which to draw. Do not count, however, on teaching only those subjects in which you feel most secure. Your pupils have a right to expect guidance from you no matter what direction their interests take. Where is your background the most limited? At these points you would be well advised to embark early upon an extensive reading program. Do not count on keeping only a page ahead of your class. Their questions will not fall into such an orderly pattern. Read your pupils' books first. These will acquaint you with the background materials from which their questions will come. Do not, however, stop at this point. The simplified statements in children's texts have a host of meanings back of them. You will have to read carefully at the adult level if you are to enrich and expand upon these materials. It is not uncommon for teachers to say that they have never learned as much about a topic as they did the first time or two that they taught it. This is your time to grow. Make the most of it.

How good is your grasp of the basic generalizations and problem-solving techniques of the various subject fields? Even if your major has been geography, you are not likely to have mastered the details of topography, climate, and ways of living for every country to which you and your pupils may have reference. If, however, you have learned to think as a geographer thinks, you will have some basic principles to guide you as you and your pupils begin to read about an unfamiliar land. You will not know all the answers to the questions that alert second-graders can pose about living things, but if you have learned to think clearly and objectively, you can help them to discover many answers for themselves. Your sense of historical perspective should alert you to glaring errors of fact and point the direction for further reading. Your grasp of the principles of science should allow you to indicate the general direction of an answer to a pupil's question even as you plan with him for further reading or for experimentation. You bring as a major strength to your classroom your grasp of basic principles and your ability to think logically within the boundaries of a subject field.

How well do you know available resources? Your pupils will think no less of you if you propose that you and they stop to search for an answer. They have a right to expect, however, that you will be able to turn to appropriate resources. One of your first steps upon entering your classroom should be to survey the available teaching aids—texts, reference books, globes, maps, pictures, models. Marshal your own resources, too. You possess college texts and notes that can be helpful. Besides, you have access to library facilities. If you are near your college campus, you will have, in your professors, expert help to which you can turn. You bring ten more years of intellectual maturity to a problem than do your pupils. Given a chance to catch your breath overnight, you can at least put yourself in a position to give intelligent leadership as your pupils plan how to explore a topic with which you are relatively unfamiliar. One of the challenges of teaching is to help your pupils grow in their ability to solve problems. You need not be able to supply all the answers yourself if you can direct them to the resources which will help them to find the answers for themselves.

What special talents and training do you bring to the classroom? Beginners who feel reasonably competent in their ability to give leadership in areas where it is possible to go to the library to locate the necessary information often feel much more hesitant in attempting to give guidance in areas such as art, music, or creative writing. It is a rare individual who brings to the classroom exceptional talent and special training in every area in which he is expected to guide the growth of a group of boys and girls. You may be inclined, at first thought, to say modestly that you have no real talent at all. Actually, this is equally rare. Some persons would even say that the individual who is completely lacking in talent does not exist, although they would acknowledge that in many cases potential ability has been given little chance to develop. Perhaps by the standards of the Metropolitan Opera, Broadway, or the National Art Gallery, your talents are modest. Nevertheless, you will have something special to contribute—a good singing voice, skill in games, love of poetry, a flare for dramatics, talent in arranging flowers or planning bulletin boards. Pupils deserve the stimulation that comes from their teacher's special enthusiasms. It is important that you recognize the points at which you can make a unique contribution to their lives.

Need your pupils have a less stimulating program than they deserve in areas in which you have no unusual interests or abilities? This will not happen if you recognize your deficiency and take steps to compensate. Undoubtedly your professional courses in college have equipped you with techniques which you can use to release your pupils' creative abilities in fields where you, yourself, are not particularly talented or in which you are not an exceptional performer. A choreographer, for example, does not have to be a talented dancer. The director of a play probably is not a gifted actor. Yet each of these makes a vital contribution to those who have special talents and gifts. Do not hesitate to use the skills and abilities which you have, limited though they may be, to develop special talents in your boys and girls. The most important talent you possess is your ability to guide children—your skills in helping them to set goals, in freeing them to undertake new ventures, and in helping them to evaluate their own performances.

It is possible, and very exciting, to learn while your pupils learn. If you put your mind to it, it is not very difficult to acquire enough skill to be able to use your piano once in a while. As you and your youngsters work together to develop a play, you will discover that your sensitivity to the elements of a good dramatic production will increase. Your skill in oral reading will improve rapidly if you work at it. You should expect that your first experiences in taking full-time responsibility for a classroom will make a marked contribution to your professional insights and skill. If you are truly interested in becoming an effective teacher, use these experiences to contribute to your personal growth as well.

How broad is your general experience background? Your college preparation is only a small part of the total breadth of preparation you bring to the classroom. The reading you have done, the jobs you have held, the trips you have taken, the longer life you have lived—all these and more are assets not to be taken lightly. City children will be enthralled with tales of life on the farm. Your contacts with foreign students at college can help enrich discussions of other lands. Your summer work experiences may allow you to speak with authority in areas where your pupils have limited background. Beginning teachers are sometimes reluctant to talk about themselves and their lives, but you have, in the wealth of your experiences, an important means of clothing your pupils' reading with reality. In appraising your assets for teaching, count on your background of experience.

You will not be the only one in your classroom with a wealth of experience to offer. It is not uncommon for a teacher to find himself in a situation where many of his pupils have traveled more extensively than he. Nor is it uncommon for creative children to have developed special interests and talents far beyond their teacher's level of attainment. What help can you be in such situations? You can utilize your teaching skill to enable the youngster with the special background to make his unique contribution to the group. Your most effective role may be that of guide—one who comments on interesting and important contributions and keeps the discussion pointed toward outcomes that are worth while. If you are an intelligent listener, your general experience background and your additional years of living will enable you to achieve profitable learnings for all.

You would not be meeting your full obligations to boys and girls if you were not, right now, making plans to extend your own experiences. At least, you can find time for the daily paper, a weekly news magazine, the programs on television most likely to broaden your understandings, an occasional travel magazine. It may be far more important for your pupils' total growth to take time for such enriching experiences than to collect and grade that extra set of papers. In the longer view, begin to weigh a summer of travel against a summer in college classes. Or, if your travel has been extensive, weigh another trip against employment for the summer.

Teachers cannot afford to live in ivory towers. You owe it to your pupils to be able to acquaint them with history, the arts, the scientific advances that are part of their cultural heritage. You have an obligation, also, to help them explore the realities of the world around them. This you cannot do unless you, yourself, are closely in touch with that world.

HOW DO YOU MEET PROBLEMS OF EVERYDAY LIVING?

Teaching is a profession calling for mature ability to make decisions. You will be entering into many new kinds of relationships with people —pupils, colleagues, supervisors, parents. There will be complex classroom activities to coordinate. You will have reports to file and a variety of other administrative details to handle promptly and systematically. There will be days when everything goes smoothly and days when one emergency arises after another. How well prepared are you to meet the problems of this complex new environment?

Beginners bring to their classroom work varied backgrounds of experiences in handling difficult situations and making decisions. Some will have been fully responsible not only for their own personal lives but for managing a home as well. Others will have lived under the family roof with parents ready and willing to be consulted whenever a problem arises. Some will have learned from a series of successful attempts to assume responsibilities in home, school, and college that the most complicated task usually works out satisfactorily. Others may have grown to doubt their ability to make a sound decision when faced with even the simplest problem. Most feel more competent in some areas than they do in others.

Your own attitude toward your competence as a person will make a difference in the way in which you approach your responsibilities as a teacher. It is only human to be optimistic and resilient in areas in which we feel secure and to tend to become panicky, discouraged, and perhaps defensive if difficulties arise in situations in which we already have some doubts regarding our ability. Experiences stretching back to early childhood have taught you to react as you do to the problems you face. You will not relearn new ways of behaving overnight. You can, however, identify the situations which, for you, pose the most difficult hurdles. Self-understanding is a first step toward more mature behavior.

Where are your strengths in working with people? The fact that you have chosen teaching as a profession indicates that you find satisfaction in working with people. Not until you begin to teach, however, are you likely to realize just how many types of human relationships a teacher is expected to handle competently. Children may view you as a purveyor of information, an aid in solving problems, a friend, a counselor, a parent substitute. Parents may look to you for advice and counsel or may regard you as a public servant whose methods, dress, and manner can be openly criticized. You will be part of a team—a member of the school faculty with definite obligations to those who have administrative responsibilities. You will be a colleague, sharing with other persons joint responsibility for the welfare of boys and girls. You will be a learner looking to persons with supervisory responsibilities who will help you grow. Some roles you will be well equipped to handle; others may be roles in which you have had little experience; still others may represent roles about which you have developed anxieties. Take a look, before you begin to teach, at your areas of strength and your areas of inexperience in working with people.

What have been your relationships with children? Some beginning teachers bring broad and varied experiences with children to their classroom work; others have had only limited contacts with boys and girls. What has been your experience in working with youngsters?—companion? playmate? playground leader? It is not unusual for beginning teachers to discover that they must learn new ways of behaving in order to assume leadership in the classroom. Are there youngsters with whose background you are not familiar? The middle-class teacher, for example, often has to make an extra effort to understand the values, attitudes, and behavior of the youngster from the lower class. Are you aware of differing attitudes toward certain types of children?—some to whom you are likely to be drawn? some you are apt to mother? some you tend to reject? It is a rare teacher who does not find that he has to guard against a tendency to accept from some children behavior that he would not accept from others. Learning to work with and to understand children takes time. You will bring much to the lives of boys and girls through your youth and your generous desire to be of help. You can make your contribution even more significant if you are sensitive to the points at which your present skills and understandings are the most limited.

What have been your previous relationships with adults? Have you been in a variety of situations under democratic leadership where older persons treated you as a colleague? If so, you are well prepared for your role as a member of a school faculty. Not all young people, however, have had this experience. Have older persons tended to make your decisions for you? This may mean that you have some lessons to learn in carrying your share in cooperative relationships. Are you, by any chance, still struggling with an adolescent urge to prove to your elders that you are completely competent without their help? or with an adolescent feeling that grown-ups really don't understand and the less shared with them the better? It will be difficult for supervisors to assist you unless you, yourself, can change such attitudes. Have you been accustomed to having the spotlight at home?—to being given lavish praise for a job well done? to having an attentive audience whenever you speak? Your colleagues will welcome you as one with interests similar to their own, but they will not assume that you need any special recognition. You will be an asset to a school faculty with your new ideas, your eagerness to learn, your enthusiasm. Before you assume your responsibility as a teacher, analyze your ability to work with others on a professional level.

How effective are your skills as a group member? Even persons who have had a number of years of experience with children have not always had the opportunity to develop the skills they require for classroom leadership. It is important for you to know the areas in which you may need more experience. Have you worked with large groups? There are techniques for giving leadership to a class of thirty or more that are not of as crucial importance if one is working with a group of five or six. Did your experience with large groups call for democratic planning, or were you merely giving orders? If the latter, you may have some discussion skills to develop. Can you operate as the resource person or the harmonizer in situations where someone else has the leadership? This is an important technique in working with pupil committees. Have you had experience in adjusting your leadership skills to the age group to which you are now assigned? If not, do not be surprised to find that you have some additional lessons to learn. Learning to teach is, in large measure, a matter of learning to work with groups. This is your year to examine, test out, and refine your skills.

How readily do you assume leadership responsibilities? You are stepping into a situation where your pupils will be looking to you for leadership—in approaching a new problem, in situations involving behavior, in emergencies. They sense reluctance and hesitation readily. Have you tended to stay in the background, hoping that someone else will act? If so, this is a behavior pattern you will have to overcome from your first day of school. Do you hesitate to say anything which implies criticism of another person lest you lose his friendship? In the classroom you must learn to speak frankly when pupils disregard agreed-upon rules. Are you, on the other hand, someone who goes ahead impulsively and thoughtlessly? This can sometimes result in decisions that disregard the feelings of others. You are about to have some challenging experiences in defining and learning how to accept an effective leadership role. You can make a marked contribution to your own growth by learning to evaluate yourself in action.

How skillfully do you handle complex situations? Teaching is not an easy task for someone who dotes upon calmness and order. The very fact that thirty or more individuals are looking to you for guidance, for leadership, and for a friendly expression of interest in their concerns makes it inevitable that there will be days when your attention is demanded in a dozen directions at once. Furthermore, if you meet individual needs, there will be aspects of your program where your boys and girls work on independent projects or in small groups. As if this much confusion were not sufficient, there will be records due in the office, announcements to make, special events for which your carefully planned program must be adjusted. Can you handle a multitude of demands with calmness and good humor?

In spite of your most thorough preparation, some days will be confused. There will inevitably be situations causing you to revise your carefully laid plans. Do you become flustered when you must make adjustments? irritable with your pupils or your colleagues? You can prepare yourself to some extent for such days by learning to consider ahead of time just how your plans might best be adjusted if an emergency arises. You can also, for the sake of your colleagues, your pupils, and your own nervous system, learn to recognize the situations most likely to cause your temper to become frazzled and to take whatever steps are most helpful in restoring your serenity. It is sometimes far wiser, on the day when it seems that one more ounce of confusion cannot be borne, to switch to a quiet work period than to proceed with an activity as planned.

How methodical are you? You are joining one of the most creative professions, but it is also a profession in which there must be meticulous attention to detail. You will not be able to stroll in late in the morning, to take a few extra minutes to wind up a discussion if your class is due in the library, to hand in records and reports to the office at your convenience. There will be attendance records to maintain accurately, cumulative records to keep up to date, your own grade book to keep systematically. If you and your pupils are not going to waste time, you will need to see that books are in order, supplies are stored neatly, desks and notebooks are well organized. Effective teachers are good classroom administrators. Reliability is one of their important characteristics.

Promptness, orderliness, and reliability are, in part, habits. Yet the person who has not developed these traits may be revealing something more basic about the way he handles his problems. If you are a person who is never quite on time, who never quite completes all the details of the task for which you volunteer, who always ends up in eleventh-hour confusion, it might be well to ask yourself why. Are you, without realizing it, putting off the jobs in which you don't quite feel secure? Are you late partly because you are reluctant to face a new situation? Does working in disorder and confusion provide you with a convenient excuse for not doing the job well? Do you tend to put your energy only on those things *you* consider important, disregarding the needs of others? Whatever your answer, you are now in a situation where many people other than yourself will be inconvenienced by your shortcomings. If you value your professional reputation, you will be well advised to set up a firm work schedule to guarantee that your responsibilities will be met promptly and methodically.

How objective are you when things go amiss? Perfectionists usually have an unhappy time in teaching. The very nature of your responsibility in trying to give leadership to thirty lively youngsters makes it inevitable that some things will go wrong. Your pupils will misunderstand you at the most unexpected places. They will forget information that seemed to be completely mastered yesterday. They will ask questions to which you do not know the answers. The more complex the project you undertake, the greater will be the possibilities for trouble. An objective understanding of these inevitable sources of confusion will make your work easier.

How good is your sense of humor? You cannot work week after week with a roomful of live-wire youngsters without some very amusing occurrences. Sometimes one pupil will upset the entire class; sometimes you will make the error. It will be tragic, indeed, if you view such episodes as evidence of your ineffectiveness as a teacher or as proof that your pupils are uncooperative and disinterested. Your year will be much more satisfying if you come to your work prepared to enjoy the humorous entanglements in which you will inevitably find yourself.

How sensitive are you to the needs of others? Not all of the disruptions in your day will be of your own making. Billy may be so enthralled by his new baseball glove that he completely ignores your arithmetic assignment. Your entire group may vent upon you their resentment of the rain that prevented their trip to the park. One of your colleagues, with his mind upon his own teaching, may forgetfully take your time in the visual-aids room. Your principal or your cooperating teacher may ask for the reports he needs without regard for your plans for the evening. You will have to learn to view these as normal occurrences in a situation where people must work together, not as personal affronts or attempts to throw as many barriers as possible in the way of your doing a good job.

Can you take responsibility for your own mistakes? It is important for a teacher to develop depth of insight into the motives of others and generosity toward their inadequacies. It is equally important for him to accept responsibility for his own errors—to look frankly at his shortcomings. The administrative organization of almost all school systems today is developed upon the assumption that teachers want to improve. In your student-teaching experience, your cooperating teacher will be expecting to help you to analyze your lessons and to develop more effective teaching techniques. As you step into your first position, your principal and probably a supervisor will be prepared to offer similar service. It will not be easy for them to help you if you cannot accept the fact that you may occasionally be wrong. Have you tried to analyze your reactions when you make a mistake? Do you typically try to justify your actions? blame someone else? become so upset that persons who could help you spend all their time trying to reassure you? Have you learned to admit frankly that you did a poor job and to proceed cheerfully to figure out how to do it better the next time?

How patient are you? You have not joined a profession whose secrets can be acquired overnight. Some of the skills you will be trying to master are very complicated indeed. Unless you are a most unusual learner it will take time to coordinate the thousand and one techniques that must operate smoothly together. Furthermore, just as you think everything is proceeding satisfactorily, some seemingly minor incident will cause the entire situation to take on a different aspect. How quickly do you become discouraged? Can you work toward a skill, day after day, even though it may take you weeks to master it?

How willing are you to take a chance? Teachers who want each day to unfold smoothly under their complete control sometimes bar themselves and their pupils from experiences that can be highly stimulating and educationally challenging. Are you going to be willing to try something new for the sake of your own growth as well as that of your pupils, or will you feel compelled to protect yourself from possible failure by staying with the routine and the familiar? There will probably never again be as much help available to you as there is during your student-teaching experience and your first few years on the job. This is your chance to learn from the mistakes you make. Are you sufficiently secure in your own feelings of competence to profit from it?

WHAT ARE YOUR ATTITUDES TOWARD YOUR CHOSEN PROFESSION?

Do you have a clear understanding of the social significance of your profession and of the contribution it can make to our present social order? Just how do you view your role as a teacher? Your attitude toward the profession of teaching will have a major influence upon the ways in which you approach your classroom responsibilities. What you believe about your function as a teacher will condition the steps you take to prepare yourself as a contributing, worth-while member of the profession. How seriously have you thought about these matters?

How do you view the social significance of your profession? The school is an institution which society has established to meet one of its needs. As such it is always close to the people and will at one time or another be subject to criticism. The articles and books you have read, your contacts with schools and teachers, the opinions of other persons —all these have helped to build your attitudes and beliefs about teaching. Have you tried to think through carefully just what you believe and feel about your chosen profession?

Why did you choose to become a teacher? Did you see in teaching an opportunity to make a vital contribution to the lives of boys and girls and through them do your share in developing our democratic ideals and in preserving our cultural heritage? Did you choose to teach because you like to help people and find the warmth of their response satisfying? Is teaching a second choice, elected reluctantly because you were not able to complete the work in some other specialized field? Is it merely an extra string to your bow, a guarantee of an income if plans for marriage and a family do not work out? Perhaps you are saying honestly that there was a bit of all these influencing your decision. This may well be true, but which one predominates now?

What is your attitude toward professional education? Do you regard teachers as members of a corps of competent persons equipped with specialized skills and knowledge or have you tended to deprecate professional training—to regard teaching as "largely common sense"? If your attitude has been the latter, you may well find yourself having to rediscover, on the job, principles regarding how children learn which should have long been part of your professional equipment. Have you stopped recently to take stock of the professional skills, know-how, and knowledge you will bring to your first classroom? These are to be valued highly as you make your initial contribution as a member of the teaching profession.

Each teacher takes into the classroom his expectancies regarding the roles he will play. He may see himself as a dispenser of information whose major responsibility is to inspire his pupils to learn. He may view himself as a hero to his pupils—someone surrounded by an adoring group. He may act as a benevolent adult—someone who takes responsibility for pupils' welfare, does things for them. He may serve as a counselor and guide. The role or roles you assume depend upon many things—your previous experiences with teachers, the satisfactions you have found in your relationships with people, the roles your pupils expect of you. Whether or not you are conscious of the roles you are playing, they will have a decided effect upon the way you work with boys and girls. You would do well, as you plan for your first contacts with boys and girls, to take time to examine the concept of an "ideal" teacher which you will take into your classroom.

Teaching will achieve greater status as a profession as there is increased public recognition of the contributions teachers are making to the lives of boys and girls. This will come about, in part, as more and more teachers speak with assurance of the social significance of their work and demonstrate in action the quality of their professional competence. Will you be able to make a positive contribution?

How dedicated are you to the task of becoming an effective member of your profession? Master teachers have never ceased to grow. In their zeal to give the most effective leadership in the classroom, they work constantly to develop a better understanding of boys and girls, better ways of helping them to learn, and broader insights into world affairs. They continually seek new ways of doing—new ways of enriching not only the lives of their pupils, but, equally important, their own lives, too. They are contributing members not only of the school community, but also of the larger community—the home, the church, and an ever widening circle of personal and professional friends. In short, they are professional people—adjusted, alert, curious, ever anxious to improve. If you approach your first classroom experience with the same attitudes, this will be a most significant year for your over-all professional growth.

This book is based on the premise that you are anxious to learn—that you want to improve yourself as a person and that you are ready to become a professional individual who can make an effective contribution to the lives of boys and girls. It is organized around the major problems you are likely to meet as you grow into the profession of teaching. Its aim is to help you to think about these problems, not to provide you with ready-made answers. The truly competent teacher knows what he wants to achieve and why. This should be your goal as you embark upon your new venture.

BOOKS YOU SHOULD KNOW

Books about personal and professional growth:

Bernard, Harold W. *Mental Hygiene for Classroom Teachers.* New York: McGraw-Hill Book Co., 1952. Pp. 472.

Bruce, William F., and Holden, A. John, Jr. *The Teacher's Personal Development.* New York: Henry Holt and Co., 1957. Pp. vi + 346.

Highet, Gilbert. *The Art of Teaching.* New York: Vintage Books, 1955, Pp. xviii + 291.

Jersild, Arthur T. *When Teachers Face Themselves.* New York: Bureau of Publications, Teachers College, Columbia University, 1955. Pp. x + 169.

Menninger, William C. *Self-Understanding: A First Step to Understanding Children.* Chicago: Science Research Associates, 1951. Pp. 49.

Redl, Fritz, and Wattenberg, W.V. *Mental Hygiene in Teaching.* New York: Harcourt, Brace and Co., 1951. Pp. 454.

Richey, Robert W. *Planning for Teaching.* Second Edition. New York: McGraw-Hill Book Co., 1958. Pp. xv + 550.

Vander Werf, Lester S. *How to Evaluate Teachers and Teaching.* New York: Rinehart and Co., 1958. Pp. vi + 58.

Books on teaching in the elementary school:

Adams, Fay. *Educating America's Children.* Second Edition. New York: The Ronald Press Co., 1954. Pp. x + 628.

Baxter, Bernice; Lewis, Gertrude M.; and Cross, Gertrude M. *The Role of Elementary Education.* Boston: D.C. Heath and Co., 1952. Pp. x + 374.

Brogan, Peggy, and Fox, Lorene K. *Helping Children Learn.* Yonkers-on-Hudson, N. Y.: World Book Co., 1955. Pp. x + 380.

Burrows, Alvina T. *Teaching Children in the Middle Grades.* Boston: D. C. Heath and Co., 1952. Pp. xvii + 280.

Caswell, Hollis L., and Foshay, Arthur W. *Education in the Elementary School.* Third Edition. New York: American Book Co., 1957. Pp. xviii + 430.

Gans, Roma; Stendler, Celia B.; and Almy, Millie. *Teaching Young Children.* Yonkers-on-Hudson, N. Y.: World Book Co., 1952. Pp. x + 454.

Herrick, Virgil E.; Goodlad, John I.; Estvan, Frank J.; and Eberman, Paul W. *The Elementary School.* Englewood Cliffs, N.J.: Prentice-Hall, 1956. Pp. xiv + 474.

Klausmeier, Herbert J., and others. *Teaching in the Elementary School.* New York: Harper & Brothers, 1956. Pp. xvi + 614.

Lambert, Hazel M. *Teaching the Kindergarten Child.* New York: Harcourt, Brace and Co., 1958. Pp. xi + 339.

Mehl, Marie A.; Mills, Hubert H.; and Douglass, Harl R. *Teaching in the Elementary School.* Second Edition. New York: The Ronald Press Co., 1958. Pp. vi + 518.

Otto, Henry J.; Floyd, Hazel; and Rouse, Margaret. *Principles of Elementary Education.* Revised Edition. New York: Rinehart and Co., 1955. Pp. xv + 455.

Thomas, R. Murray. *Ways of Teaching in Elementary Schools*. New York: Longmans, Green and Co., 1955. Pp. xiv + 558.

Books on student teaching in the elementary school:

Adams, Harold P., and Dickey, Frank G. *Basic Principles of Student Teaching*. New York: American Book Co., 1956. Pp. ix + 372.

Burr, James B.; Harding, Lowry W.; and Jacobs, Leland B. *Student Teaching in the Elementary School*. Second Edition. New York: Appleton-Century-Crofts, 1958. Pp. ix + 459.

Lindsey, Margaret, and Gruhn, William T. *Student Teaching in the Elementary School*. New York: The Ronald Press Co., 1957. Pp. viii + 214.

Michaelis, John U., and Grim, Paul R. *The Student Teacher in the Elementary School*. Englewood Cliffs, N.J.: Prentice-Hall, 1953. Pp. x + 433.

Wiggins, Sam P. *The Student Teacher in Action*. Boston: Allyn and Bacon, 1957. Pp. xii + 217.

Wingo, G. Max, and Schorling, Raleigh. *Elementary-School Student Teaching*. Second Edition. New York: McGraw-Hill Book Co., 1955. Pp. 452.

Thinking Professionally About Educational Problems

CHAPTER 2

The children in Mr. Young's sixth grade come with many questions regarding the local election campaign. The course of study in this school system indicates that the social studies program is to cover old-world backgrounds. How much time should Mr. Young take to study the election?

Miss Stanton's fourth-graders are very much incensed about what they consider to be arbitrary treatment by the safety guards. What should be her aims as she and the children talk through this problem? How much of the time set aside for reading activities is she justified in using for this discussion?

In a Parent-Teacher Association meeting, a mother states very decidedly that kindergarten children would have a much better start in first grade if the teachers would make more use of reading readiness workbooks. Is she right?

In another Parent-Teacher Association meeting, a father praises a European educational pattern where only the intellectually elite are given college preparatory programs. What factors should be considered in deciding whether American schools should move in this direction?

In her fifth-grade classroom, a student teacher discovers two twelve-year-olds who read fluently only if they have third-grade books. What is the justification for asking her cooperating teacher rather than Miss Johnson in the third grade to teach these youngsters?

Situations such as these illustrate the problems faced by teachers in present-day schools. It is easy to express an opinion about them, but it is not nearly so easy to arrive at a sound professional solution. Every profession requires its membership to be equipped with techniques for solving new and complicated problems. The profession of education is no exception. From your first day in the classroom you will meet situation after situation for which there is no ready-made answer. Even if you are working in a school system where there is a detailed course of study, there will be countless day-by-day decisions in which only your professional judgment can determine what is best for your pupils. You have chosen a profession which demands persons who can think clearly and independently about professional problems—who know the reasons for their procedures and can explain these reasons to others.

Through your years of college you have been exploring the foundation areas upon which teachers draw in making professional decisions. You know something of the traditional role of the school in American democracy. You have studied the changes taking place in our modern, industrialized society and the implications of these changes. Your courses in educational psychology and human development have deepened your understanding of the boys and girls with whom you will be working—their needs, the way they grow, and the way they learn. Your first full-time classroom experience will provide a major opportunity to think through in detail how the large issues and general principles derived from such background studies actually affect day-by-day decisions. You will discover that learning to teach is more than acquiring a "bag of tricks" useful in keeping a class interested, busy, and cooperative. Unless you learn to think as a professional person, such a "bag of tricks," no matter how amply stocked, is not likely to give you the help you will need as you face one new problem after another, day after day on the job.

This chapter examines briefly what is involved in decision-making in education. It is intended to help you to identify some of the fundamental issues with which teachers are dealing today and to become aware of the direction of their proposed solutions. It aims to assist you in thinking about the skills that *you* must develop if you are to become a professional person—a person able to make competent decisions regarding professional problems.

WHAT IS EXPECTED OF SCHOOLS IN AMERICAN DEMOCRACY?

America has a long and proud tradition of faith in education. Early in our national history the principle was established that elementary schooling should be free for the children of all of the people. The public schools in this country, therefore, have been delegated a major responsibility for producing citizens who are competent and willing to make their contribution so that our democratic way of life may flourish. The public schools have also been delegated a major responsibility for equipping future citizens to live in our modern, industrialized society.

How the schools can best discharge these obligations poses many problems. What you believe about the meaning of democracy; about the attitudes, skills, and knowledge which individuals must have to lead effective and satisfying lives; and about the place the school should occupy in our national life will influence your professional decisions. These decisions you cannot avoid if you are to be an effective teacher.

Schools in America have an obligation to help young people grow in the ways of democracy. Democracy is a term that means different things to different people. For some, it refers rather strictly to the processes through which those nations classified as democracies are governed and to the rights and responsibilities of their citizens. For many, democracy is more than a form of government; it is a way of life. Those who accept the latter definition believe that the most effective and satisfying personal values can be achieved only when we extend democratic concepts and ways of working to every aspect of living—to family life, to classrooms, to church and club groups, to professional organizations, to our relationships with friends and neighbors, and to fellow citizens whom we have never met.

Certainly, the schools in a democracy are responsible for acquainting youth with the processes of their government and with their rights and responsibilities as citizens. Our democratic tradition has established a legal pattern which respects the rights of the individual but which also protects the welfare of the group. We have a form of government under which we relinquish some of our personal freedoms for the sake of orderly ways of living together. It is a form of government which allows us to establish for ourselves the rules under which we live and provides ways of changing these rules when they no longer prove satisfactory. Under our Constitution we are guaranteed the right to vote; equality under the law regardless of political affiliation, race, social or economic status; freedom to participate in the religion of our choice; freedom of speech and the right to be heard whether we belong to the majority or to the minority.

Helping prospective citizens to understand the basic forms of their government is a far bigger job than merely teaching courses in civics or American history. It will be your responsibility to identify the ways in which boys and girls can become familiar with democratic government in action. What lessons in democracy are there when six-year-olds learn to abide by school policies? What understandings might be developed when fifth-graders rebel against a school regulation that keeps them from crossing a busy street to the candy store at recess? What learnings should come to the safety guards who act as an arm of a law-enforcing body? What may we hope to teach through student-council activities? These are only a fraction of the experiences through which youngsters meet democratic government in action. A well-informed, sensitive teacher makes the most of them.

Teachers who believe that democracy is more than a form of government—that it is a way of life—need to analyze carefully what this means in practice. Sometimes discussions in social groups indicate that the definitions on which we are operating are somewhat limited. Occasionally there is a hint that the speaker is thinking only about a majority vote. ("If we were to try to be democratic about it, the children would vote to take a holiday, and then where would we be?") Sometimes the speaker seems to be thinking of equality in the sense of making sure everyone is treated exactly alike. ("The talents of our children are being wasted if we try to be democratic and teach everyone exactly the same thing." "Colleges should be more democratic about parking privileges. Why should the faculty have reserved parking? Make it first come, first served.") Sometimes it sounds as though the speaker thinks it is undemocratic to take any leadership responsibility whatsoever. ("I know it's not democratic, but how else could you get an orchestra playing together?") Or that democracy means the right of the individual to do exactly what he chooses, regardless of the group. ("You can't be too democratic with children, you know, or you'll have some of them climbing out of the windows.") Or that it is a matter of letting pupils think they have made decisions, even when this is not actually the case. ("We work it out democratically in my room, but, of course, I always know where they're going to come out.")

Obviously, what we mean when we talk of democracy as a way of life is more significant than the quotations in the preceding paragraph imply. Analyzing what democratic ways of working actually do mean for daily living is one of the most challenging and significant tasks that you as a teacher will face. It is a lifetime job. In your classroom, situation after situation will arise where you will stop to wonder what is the democratic thing to do.

What are some of the values held by those who think of democracy as a way of life? For one thing, we have in our democratic tradition a belief in the unique worth of the individual. We hold that we should be able to establish ways of living and working together that will allow each person to develop to his own maximum potentiality while he makes it possible for others to do the same. What it means to recognize the unique worth of each individual poses a number of challenging problems. For example, what type of school curriculum will actually make it possible for each boy or girl to develop to his own maximum potentiality? What system of grouping and promotion will be most satisfactory?—should we segregate the very able or the very slow? retard youngsters not up to grade level? promote those who are advanced? How do we go about helping an individual to reach his own goals and still teach him that he has an obligation to assure the same opportunity to others? How do we help children and youth to develop respect for those who differ—in race, religion, economic status, talents, interests?

If such problems sound complicated when stated in theoretical terms, they become even more so when they arise in the classroom setting. Sixth-grade John refuses to work with the subcommittee which is to locate information about industries in modern England, but he volunteers to do an independent report on the effects of the Industrial Revolution. What democratic values should be taken into account in appraising his proposal? Fourth-grade Jeanne is a talented musician. Is it undemocratic to release her from her arithmetic lesson to take private music lessons? First-grade Belinda loves to paint and makes a dash for the only easel every free-choice period. What should she be helped to learn about the ways of democracy? In choosing characters for a play, fourth-graders ignore Andy, who lisps. Should this be talked through, and if so what issues should be raised? In planning to exchange Christmas gifts, several youngsters argue that everyone should be allowed to spend just as much money for a gift as he wishes. Is it undemocratic to veto this proposal? These problems all have at their base the fundamental issue of what it really means to respect the unique worth of each individual. They are typical of the practical situations you will face as you try to determine your own attitudes and decide what attitudes your pupils should develop.

In our democratic tradition, too, is the belief that each individual has both a right and an obligation to contribute to the solution of problems in which his well-being and that of his group are involved. In our government, we do this through universal franchise. Those who see democracy as a way of life extend their faith in the cooperative solution of problems to clubs, to committees, to classrooms, to family groups. What it means to involve those concerned in the solution of a problem is, in itself, a difficult question. Certainly the effective solution of many of the problems we face in today's complex world calls for more than a majority vote. There are many times when we must rely upon the advice of an expert. We must help young people to develop bases for deciding when to look to an authority for help and how to appraise the competence of the persons to whom they turn. Furthermore, there are often varying degrees of maturity and insight among the persons concerned with a common problem. We must develop techniques of cooperative problem-solving that will enable each individual, expert or uninformed, mature or immature, to make his appropriate contribution. We must also perfect the skills needed if the members of a group are to work effectively together—leadership skills; techniques for communicating with others, for identifying issues and resolving conflicts, for arriving at consensus. In addition, there are problems of how to safeguard the rights of the minority—of deciding when the will of the majority should be accepted and when a minority has a right to dissent, of using minority voices to best advantage in working toward more effective solutions of common problems.

As you begin to think about helping boys and girls to operate as effective group members you will uncover a number of challenging points to ponder. What does this mean for pupil-teacher planning? Should the pupils (who certainly are vitally concerned) have a share in deciding classroom procedures? To what extent? What happens if the pupils' proposal runs counter to your well-laid plans? Suppose it runs counter to a board of education rule? What leadership role should you play? Mr. Smith is helping his class perfect a song for the school assembly. Miss Adamson is working to develop more proficiency in basic arithmetic processes. Miss McCabe's pupils are trying to decide how to decorate their classroom for Halloween. If each teacher is to be democratic, will his procedures be exactly like those of his colleagues? Miss Simonds' sixth-graders come bursting in with a proposal that they build and launch a rocket. Is it undemocratic for her to ask them to stop to examine the difficulties involved? Mr. Sampson sets up an exhibit of all his Mexican souvenirs and then asks his pupils to think about the social studies unit they should start with first. After a brief discussion (in which he points out how much more interesting it will be to study Switzerland later in the winter), they vote to study Mexico. Has he been democratic?

In our democratic society we also believe in freedom of inquiry and a research approach to the solution of problems. We do not accept without proof the pronouncements of the so-called "expert." Our books do not distort the evidence in order to support a political faith. We value our laboratories and our research workers, and we expect them to be able to pursue their investigations without coercion or fear of reprisal. We face a very important task in helping boys and girls to develop a healthy respect for methods of scientific investigation and of rational thinking. Still more crucial, we must teach them how to use these methods in the solution of new problems.

Teachers who wish to develop in their pupils respect for a scientific approach to the solution of problems face some challenging questions in deciding how to teach. When should classroom time be devoted to activities in which pupils use an experimental approach to solve a problem, when to reading for answers in a textbook? What authority role should the teacher play? What teaching techniques seem most likely to help pupils develop the problem-solving approaches of the various subject disciplines?—to acquaint a pupil with the research techniques of the scientist? the economist? the historian?

Pupils learn what they experience. This is an obvious but often forgotten principle of education. It means that we must *teach* what we want pupils to learn—that we must provide experiences so that they will learn. If we want to insure that boys and girls will grow in their understanding of democracy, we must make certain that they experience democracy in action. One of your most important professional decisions will be to determine for yourself what it means to practice democracy in your own classroom.

Schools in America must equip young people to live in this modern world. The pupils in the classrooms of 1960 will be in leadership positions in the year 2000. Deciding what attitudes, information, and skills will prepare them to cope successfully with their world would be relatively easy in a simple and static culture. However, we are living in an extremely complex society and in a world that is changing rapidly. How to equip the young people of today to live intelligently in the world of tomorrow is a matter of grave concern to those who teach in America's schools.

You do not need an extended analysis to remind you of some of the problems which the pupils whom you are now teaching will have to face. Radio, television, and jet propulsion have made us next-door neighbors to the entire world. Whether our democracy as we know it will exist when the youngsters we teach have grown up may depend on how successful we are in building international understanding, in learning to communicate with other nations, in developing techniques for the cooperative solution of international problems. How best to equip children and youth to make their contribution to international understanding poses some major problems for educators. What should we emphasize in studying other cultures? Should political ideologies other than our own be examined in our schools? What should be our attitude regarding the teaching of foreign languages? These are only a few of the questions which require professional decisions. How we, as teachers, answer them will help to determine the course of our national life in the years ahead.

Through the agencies of radio, television, and the press, children and youth today are exposed to widely divergent and conflicting value systems. They see a western marshal use his gun to stop a criminal. They hear newscasts reporting the number of cars owned by the current singing star and the failure of the local bond issue for new school buildings. They read of the fourth marriage of the actress who is their current heroine. In this complex and contradictory milieu families do not exert the same kind of stabilizing influence they once did. You may be astounded to discover how many of your pupils come from broken homes, how many mothers are working, how many youngsters have no regular church affiliation. Teachers belong to the one agency that touches the lives of all children. Is the teaching of values a task we must assume? Perhaps it would be more accurate to ask whether we can escape it even if we wish to do so. How is it best accomplished? —by teaching religion in the public schools? by developing reading skills through stories with morals? Is it an emphasis that should permeate all our teaching? How? Whether you are conscious of it or not, these are professional questions that you answer time after time by the way in which you deal with day-by-day problems in your classroom.

The vast communication network that links farm to city and east coast to west poses another type of problem for our schools. Never before has it been possible for a single television personality to touch the lives of so many, for advertisers to come into such a large number of homes, for news analysts to make their opinions so widely felt. How are we going to equip young people to cope with the bids being made for their attention, their time, and their money? Should we teach observation and listening skills as well as reading skills? Should we be concerned about developing skills of critical evaluation in reading? Should there be training in propaganda analysis? consumer education projects to help in the interpretation of advertisements?

If present predictions are borne out, the pupils you teach will face job opportunities and working conditions very different from those of today. We read much about the need for top-flight scientists, but our society will also require many persons in professions calling for expertness in human relationships—teachers, physicians, nurses, psychologists, social workers, personnel executives. On the other hand, with increased automation it seems likely that machines will take over many of the routine tasks once assumed by the less well-educated. In all probability most people will have more leisure time than ever before. Does this mean that we should be paying increased attention to the creative arts? to the development of personal interests and hobbies? Questions such as these may seem to require the use of a crystal ball, but they must be answered. You will be associated with colleagues who face seriously their professional responsibility to find the answers.

Perhaps the most challenging phenomenon of all is that our pupils will live in a world of rapid change. Certainly, we want to equip them with the knowledge that will render them effective in their chosen professions and in their daily living, but what we teach as fact today may have to be reinterpreted tomorrow. Even basic physical and chemical principles may be rewritten as new discoveries are made in the physical sciences. In the biological and social sciences there are many problems still unsolved. If the speed of our transition from telegraph to radio to television, or from the model-T to the jet plane, is any indication of the changes to come, our pupils will be called on to weigh new evidence, appraise new principles, and solve new problems beyond our boldest predictions. What kind of classroom situation will provide a learner with existing knowledge and still prepare him to meet new challenges? How can we teach so that our pupils leave us equipped to locate new information and arrive at new generalizations for themselves? How do we prepare our slower learners to secure competent advice when they face situations with which their training in school has not equipped them to deal?

As you listen to discussions of educational problems and read professional literature, you will discover that serious attention is being given to the question of what role the school should play in preparing boys and girls to live effectively in tomorrow's world. Some teachers argue that the schools have all they can do to equip children and youth with the traditional and established elements of our cultural heritage —reading; spelling; writing; calculating; and basic scientific, historical, political, economic, and social facts and principles. Others hold that this is not sufficient, that too many important applications of basic principles to present-day problems will be left to chance. They maintain that it should be possible to focus more directly on the pupil's present world without sacrificing essential elements of the cultural heritage. Again, you will find teachers who believe that the major responsibility of the schools should be to develop the problem-solving skills and techniques for acquiring new information essential in a world of rapid change. Occasionally, you will read a plea that teachers make a blueprint of the future world they desire. These are not points of view to accept or reject on the grounds of prejudice or bias. They should be the basis for thoughtful reading and study as you meet the day-by-day situations that reflect these larger issues.

Schools in America are expected to meet the needs of all children and youth. In America it is taken for granted that the schools shall serve all children. It is our tradition that all boys and girls be given an opportunity to climb the same educational ladder. We do not sort out, at an early age, the college-bound student from the one destined for industrial and service occupations. We have extended compulsory attendance age limits to sixteen years of age—to eighteen years in some states. All this presents many problems in actual practice. How do you provide a worth-while education for all boys and girls—the bright and the slow, the well-adjusted and the emotionally disturbed, the privileged and the underprivileged, the healthy and the physically handicapped?

Teachers in the elementary school are deeply concerned about the ways in which they can meet this challenge. You will find them experimenting with schemes for grouping learners in classes and in subgroups within a class in an effort to provide the best possible educational environment for every boy and girl. This is not nearly as simple in practice as it sounds in theory. How many years can a child be retarded before he is such a social and physical misfit that both he and his classmates suffer? How much should we accelerate those youngsters whose skills and reasoning ability are ahead of their age group? Inasmuch as not all the capacities and potentialities of a given individual develop evenly, would it be better to group by ages and then to vary the educational offering for individuals? These are problems for which there are no categorical answers. There are democratic values to consider as well as psychological implications. Can it be argued that the unique worth of each individual is being honored when all children in the same class read the same texts, when lessons are geared to the understanding of the pupil of average ability? On the other hand, should able pupils not have the opportunity to learn to work with those who think more slowly? And does the less talented child not need to be in some situations where he learns to acknowledge the contribution of his more able colleagues? Whatever the basis for setting up class groups in your school, you will still find yourself working with a range of abilities in your room and trying to decide how to meet your obligation to help each pupil grow. Your psychology courses have taught you to expect this, but the first class you actually work with closely will show you how complicated the task really is. As one beginning teacher phrased it, "I'd heard about individual differences all the way through college, but I didn't realize what it would mean to meet forty sets of individual differences until I began to teach."

WHAT IS THE DIRECTION OF OUR EFFORTS TO SOLVE EDUCATIONAL PROBLEMS?

Many important educational problems are solved on a day-by-day basis in the classroom, but back of these decisions are major theoretical considerations. Some relate to the curriculum design—the pattern that indicates the scope of the experiences to be provided for boys and girls, the areas of study under which these experiences are to be grouped, and the sequence in which they are to be studied from grade to grade. Others refer to methodology—to the ways in which teachers guide the learning experiences of boys and girls. Thoughtful teachers have always worked toward improved curriculum designs and methodology. Problems related to these two major areas of concern are under serious consideration in many school systems today.

What kinds of educational programs are resulting from our efforts to define the functions of schools in American society, to translate these general objectives into specific goals, and to decide what teaching procedures will best achieve these goals? Although there are many areas of agreement, there are no absolute answers. This will not surprise you if you stop to think of the major problems about which value judgments have to be made—what it means to teach the ways of democracy, how best to equip young people to live in tomorrow's world, what it means to meet the needs of all the pupils in our schools. Serious educators may, with good reason, disagree on issues such as these.

Many types of curriculum designs exist today.[1] Class discussions

[1] The following references provide more detailed analyses of existing types of curriculum design: Florence B. Stratemeyer, Hamden L. Forkner, Margaret G. McKim, and A. Harry Passow, *Developing a Curriculum for Modern Living,* Second Edition, pp. 85-112. New York: Bureau of Publications, Teachers College, Columbia University, 1957; Hollis L. Caswell and Arthur W. Foshay, *Education in the Elementary School,* Third Edition, pp. 247-279. New York: American Book Co., 1957; J. Galen Saylor and William M. Alexander, *Curriculum Planning,* pp. 245-305. New York: Rinehart and Co., 1954.

and school visits prior to student teaching will have taught you that schools are operating today under a variety of curriculum designs. You may be placed as a student teacher or first-year teacher in a school system using a curriculum design very similar to that under which you, yourself, went to school. On the other hand, the pattern may be very different. Whatever the design, it represents a thoughtful decision regarding how best to meet the educational needs of boys and girls. It is important for you to become thoroughly familiar with the values held by the persons with whom you are teaching and with the decisions they have made regarding the curriculum design they feel to be most effective for their situation. It is important, also, if you are to grow into a teacher with a broad professional outlook, that you be able to identify the values that lie back of other proposals for curriculum designs—proposals that your colleagues have not accepted. It is all too easy to classify a position you do not understand as "traditional," "progressive," "subject-centered," thereby brushing aside a thoughtful educational proposal with an emotionally laden label.

The curriculum design with which the majority of beginning teachers will be most familiar from high school and college days, and perhaps from elementary school also, is the one in which *separate subjects*—history, geography, composition, literature, physics, chemistry—are the centers about which classroom work is organized. When the separate subject design is used, aspects of the subject are usually assigned to grades. Problems near at hand and present-day are dealt with in the primary grades—community helpers, family life. Older pupils go farther back in time and farther afield. Typically, a topic is repeated in more complex form about every three or four years—American history, for example, in fifth, eighth, and eleventh grades. Typically, too, subject lines are adhered to more firmly as pupils grow older, with separate teachers for each subject and opportunities to specialize common at the upper grades in the high school. Separate subjects are the traditional way of organizing the essentials of our cultural heritage. They encompass, however, more than groupings of knowledge; they also represent ways of thinking and of solving problems. Problems of historical research demand procedures different from those of the science laboratory. A sociologist has ways of working different from those of a mathematician. Those who plan the school curriculum by designating aspects of various subjects for specific grades make this choice, in part, because they feel that the best equipment young people can take into the world is a thorough understanding of the traditional fields of knowledge that are their cultural heritage and the ability to use skillfully the ways of thinking and solving problems that are unique to these subject areas.

Persons who feel that there are more effective bases than separate subjects for organizing the experiences of children and youth sometimes claim that teachers of subjects tend to follow textbooks too closely and give too little help in applying knowledge from basic subject areas to present-day problems. This could be a danger, especially if the textbook contains an extensive amount of material to be covered. However, it would not represent good teaching. If you are working under a curriculum design organized around separate subjects, you will find your colleagues particularly concerned about helping pupils to see the values the subject has for their lives today. You will find them planning with pupils and developing problem-solving activities that will encourage boys and girls to think for themselves. You will discover, also, that teachers of separate subjects are much concerned about helping pupils see interrelationships among subject fields. Good teaching has many common elements, regardless of the curriculum design.

Next most popular, country-wide, are the patterns in which related subjects are pulled together into *subject fields* or *groups of related subjects*—history, geography, and civics may be grouped as social studies; nature study, physics, and chemistry become general science; and so on. As with the sequence where subjects are taught separately, younger pupils tend to work with the near at hand. In fact, the experiences considered appropriate and worth while for primary children are so similar from one curriculum to another that it would be difficult to tell by walking into a kindergarten or a first grade just what the design for the school system is. Subject fields are more frequently the organizing centers for learners' experiences at the elementary than at the secondary or college levels. However, if you have had a course in Problems of Democracy in high school, or have taken courses in Survey of Western Civilization, Survey of Science, or Survey of Mathematics in college, you have had experience in working broadly within a subject field. What are seen to be the advantages, as against teaching within the boundaries of individual subjects? Persons who feel that subject fields are the most appropriate bases for organizing curricular experiences value highly, among other things, the opportunities this plan provides for helping pupils to see interrelationships among separate subjects. In developing a problem related to an aspect of American history, for example, a teacher can draw upon as much background as is needed from geography and political science.

Educators who object to the grouping of subjects into related fields do so on several bases. On the one hand, some fear that the thoroughness with which a separate subject would be studied may be lost. In a sense, this may be true. If you elected the Survey of Western Civilization in college rather than European History, you probably explored historical backgrounds more broadly but not as deeply at all points. You did not, however, necessarily learn any less thereby; you simply acquired a different set of understandings. On the other hand, some educators maintain that even the subject-field type of curriculum does not provide sufficient opportunities to explore extensively with their pupils. The courses of study in school systems where the curriculum design is built around groups of related subjects are developed so as to overcome, at least partially, this criticism. For example, helping pupils to understand newspaper articles reporting a plan to prevent the pollution of the local river may call not only for geographical and historical background, but also for concepts from such fields as bacteriology and chemistry. Actually, if you are working under such a curriculum, you will find your colleagues concerned about challenging your pupils to explore each problem they undertake as thoroughly as their maturity allows. It is not a proposal that allows for superficial learnings. You will also find your colleagues concerned about helping pupils to draw extensively upon areas of knowledge not encompassed by the subject field. Charts are often included in courses of study, for example, showing the points at which the suggested work in such fields as the natural and the social sciences can be correlated.

Very different from the curricular patterns in which subjects or subject fields are designated as centers for study are those in which an attempt has been made to study *broad areas that cut across subject fields*—areas which would allow for the organization of knowledge from many fields around the types of problems pupils actually will face in life. In these patterns, subjects are drawn upon as extensively as needed, but the problems designated for study are grouped under such areas of living as homemaking, earning a living, recreation, communication, conserving goods and resources, transportation, housing. Problems related to simpler aspects of each area are assigned to the elementary school grades, more complex problems to the upper grades. In some high schools a series of appropriate units are assigned to a "core" block of two or more periods, and subject electives are provided for the rest of the program. If your college methods courses have been consolidated into one large time block within which you and your instructor have been free to take up topics in the order you felt most crucial, you have had some experience with such a core. It is quite possible, also, that you have had experience with a certain number of units of work that focused on problems of daily living even under a curriculum design developed around fields such as social studies and science. For example, there may have been a unit on transportation proposed for the fourth grade or a study of the national election inserted into the old-world focus of a sixth grade. Why advocate a curriculum that is so different from the pattern under which most teachers have received their training? Those who have given this type of proposal their thoughtful support see many advantages. Among the most important are the greatly increased opportunities to provide experiences through which boys and girls can learn to bring information from all needed subject areas to bear on the day-by-day problems they actually face.

If your schooling has been under a traditional curriculum pattern, you probably will be voicing many of the typical questions that are raised regarding a curriculum proposal that departs radically from this pattern. How will such a plan ever lead to a thorough knowledge of anything? How will the pupil who has studied conservation, communication, transportation, homemaking, ever get along in college? On the other hand, if specific topics are definitely assigned to the various grades, what have you really gained? Won't these topics be just as far removed from pupils' lives as blocks of work selected from subject fields? Actually, you will need to examine courses of study carefully to realize how broad and deep the activities developed under this type of curriculum design can be. If you are teaching under such a design, you will realize that your colleagues take great pains to explore each area under discussion in as much detail as is appropriate to their pupils' maturity and to make sure that the total experiences for the year contribute to a balanced program. You will also find that there is considerable effort expended to keep the potential contributions of subject areas in mind, to use time lines to provide historical perspective, to develop needed scientific principles. You will discover, too, that the total curriculum plan provides a number of opportunities for upper-grade pupils and for high school youth to explore specific subject areas under the guidance of specialists.

In contrast to educators who would assign specific subjects, topics, or units to each grade are those who feel that the most useful understandings will be built only when a teacher is completely free to work with the *problems or concerns of a group.* Under such a curriculum design, it would not be possible in advance to say for certain exactly what the year's activities of a group would be. Teachers would be responsible for studying the needs, the strengths, the weaknesses, the experience backgrounds, of their pupils and for deciding cooperatively with them the areas for study for the year. The teachers most likely to be working in situations where such freedom exists will be those in college laboratory schools or in public school systems noted for their experimental approach to curriculum design. In some schools there may be available rather elaborate studies of typical problems faced by pupils of various ages as guides in providing for a well-balanced program. In others, teachers may be expected to draw upon their total professional background in deciding what areas for study will prove the most effective learning experiences for their classes.

Educators who want to give teachers maximum freedom of choice are deeply concerned about equipping future citizens with a broad foundation of knowledge. They feel, however, that intelligent teachers can make the most effective choice of exactly what areas of study are most likely to contribute to maximum growth. This certainly would not mean that minor and incidental problems in which pupils happen to express an interest would necessarily be developed into elaborate units regardless of their potential educational values. Teachers would evaluate carefully possible topics for study. Nor would opportunity be lacking to explore subject fields extensively. At both upper elementary and high school levels, there would be science laboratories, art studios, social science seminars, writers' clinics, to which pupils with special interests or concerns could be referred. Obviously, such a program demands extremely competent and sensitive teachers with great depth of subject matter background and broad understanding of the present-day world.

This brief sketch will not have done much more than help you identify the curriculum design under which you are working and perhaps start you thinking about how and why it contrasts with the one under which you went to school. You will have to do much more studying before you will be able to decide where you stand, and why. Particularly, you are going to need broad reading and experience to understand the values to be achieved through those curriculum patterns that are unfamiliar to you. We would not be human if we did not tend to prefer ways of working similar to those which provided us with our most satisfying experiences and to have trouble recognizing the potential values of procedures with which we have had little experience. If you wish to grow as a professional person, however, do not accept any one answer too quickly. Keep studying and keep asking *why*.

There are many common emphases in methodology. A first look at contrasting proposals for organizing the experiences for pupils often suggests that teaching methods differ widely. Sometimes the terms we use to describe differing curriculum designs add to the confusion. Occasionally we talk about "subject-centered" designs as opposed to "child-centered" ones, as though those who teach within subject frameworks have little concern for the pupils they teach and those who are working in terms of the needs of pupils don't care at all what information is learned. Sometimes "subject" and "experience" curriculums are contrasted in such a way as to give the impression that those who teach subjects draw on no concrete experiences and that those who work from the experiences of children never have them read for information. Actually, although there are differences in emphasis, depending on which values are considered to be most important, there is much agreement on what represents a sound educational program for boys and girls regardless of the curriculum design.

In the first place, all teachers today try to provide *purposeful learning experiences*—to help pupils to see the purpose of what they are learning in school. This is just as important to the teacher of a college preparatory course in high school physics as it is to the teacher whose pupils want to learn enough about electricity to do a good job of wiring a model log cabin. This is a point at which psychological research in the area of motivation has made a major contribution. Early studies were largely concerned with extrinsic motives—gold stars, honor rolls, grades. Recently there has been much more emphasis on understanding how the learner views the situation. In your own case, for example, you defined the way you would work in a college class in terms of the way you sized up the value of the class to you, the grade you hoped for and the instructor's requirements that would have to be met to earn it, the relative importance of other classes and other grades, and probably the importance of social engagements and campus leadership responsibilities. Your pupils will likewise define the way they work with you in terms of the goals they understand. You will hear much discussion of the role of interest in learning. Interest is important, but this alone can hardly guarantee all the learnings for which schools are responsible.

The basic question is how to make the work more meaningful or purposeful, how to tie what you are teaching to problems in the pupil's world. No matter what your grade level or your teaching field, you will need to develop skill in helping your pupils to establish vital purposes for what they learn.

Every teacher who cares about his subject field works seriously and conscientiously to secure *maximum carry-over to life outside of school.* There is not much point to spending hours studying the battles of the War Between the States if one cannot bring generalizations from this study to present-day tensions. Neither is there much value to acquiring ways of manipulating numbers in arithmetical processes if one cannot apply basic understanding of the structure of the number system intelligently to a new mathematical process. Perhaps one of the most important contributions of psychological research to teaching lies in the evidence that *how* we teach is crucial in determining what is learned. This is the problem of transfer of learning. We cannot be certain that a series of lessons in grammar and punctuation will result in polished writing unless we aim for this. A course in American history will not guarantee a more intelligent voter unless we deliberately and carefully teach toward this goal. No matter what you are teaching, you will find your cooperating teacher or supervisor anxious to help you learn how to work so that your pupils will arrive at concepts and generalizations that can be applied to new situations.

Occasionally articles stressing the importance of pupils' applying what they learn are interpreted to mean that the authors are concerned only with the knowledge needed to handle day-by-day problems. Actually, all teachers are concerned with *sound scholarship.* The group rigging the lighting system in the log cabin would be held to as accurate thinking about electricity as would the pupils in the physics laboratory. There are differences of opinion, of course, as to what learnings are most important. In some school systems Latin requirements may be giving way to modern languages, or extensive studies of the Western world may be curtailed to make room for acquaintance with the Far East, but whatever the area chosen for study, teachers are concerned that each pupil be challenged to extend himself to the limits of his ability. No matter what the focus of your work, you will need to learn how to hold for your pupils standards as high as their maturity will allow.

Whether your curriculum design is organized around topics that allow all subject areas to be drawn upon as needed or planned so that each teacher works within a separate subject field, you will find concern that pupils be helped to develop *awareness of interrelationships among subject fields.* It is impossible for any teacher today to do a good job if he concentrates only on health, or history, or arithmetic. A health problem related to good nutrition has science implications. Realistic arithmetic problems touch on consumer education and economics. The history of the early explorers does not make much sense without the application of geographical principles.

You will also find that teachers under all curriculum designs stress the development of *competence with fundamental skills.* It may surprise you to realize how broadly the word "skill" is interpreted. Your cooperating teacher or your supervisor will urge you to work toward higher levels of ability in reading, language, and numbers, but he will also be thinking about listening skills, observing techniques, and group-process skills. He will be helping you to analyze your lessons to see whether you are teaching effective problem-solving techniques—to think about how to handle a situation when a pupil says, "The mountains would be about a mile high, I guess," or states blithely, "There are, too, men on Mars; I saw it on television." Furthermore, he will want you to recognize the variety of skills a pupil may need for competence in a single subject area. In arithmetic, for example, there are specialized skills not only in mathematical processes, but also in reading —skills peculiar to the reading of problems and to the interpretation of charts, graphs, and tables. Similarly in science or history, there are specialized vocabularies with variant meanings and specialized techniques for finding additional information and evaluating data. You will not be a teacher very long before you find that the teaching of skills is an important aspect of your work in every field or area.

Because each human being has his own unique pattern of strengths, weaknesses, and experience background, you will find your colleagues giving much thought to achieving the *maximum development of each individual,* whether they are following the topics in a single, adopted text or are free to choose with their pupils the points of focus for their studies. You, too, will be expected to bring all your previous training to bear in identifying the needs of your pupils, and to develop a program flexible enough to allow you to give help both to the pupil who grasps ideas slowly and to the able learner. In most classrooms, this will mean learning to utilize small groups and individual projects for part of your work as well as to individualize your attention when you are working with the class as a whole.

Whatever the pattern of your course of study, you will soon realize that the teachers with whom you are working are thinking about *democratic values*. They will not count it a waste of time to stop to discuss better ways of settling an argument, to talk out the reason for a school rule, or to listen to a student-council report. They will be involving pupils in planning and using teaching techniques that allow pupils to develop effective skills as leaders and group members. You will find that those responsible for your supervision are as concerned about the democratic atmosphere in your room and the interpersonal relationships you develop as they are about any other aspect of your teaching.

There are, then, many points of agreement regarding the direction in which we should be moving in order to provide effective learning experiences for boys and girls. There is no room for complacency, however. A wide gap exists today between the best and the poorest of American schools. Furthermore, each turn of events on the national or international scene is a challenge to re-evaluate present practices. Each educational advance suggests a host of new problems. If you want to become a professional person, you will equip yourself to do your share to assure the continued improvement of educational programs and practices.

WHAT SKILLS ARE NEEDED FOR THE EFFECTIVE SOLUTION OF EDUCATIONAL PROBLEMS?

Whether or not you will make a sound contribution to the development of better educational experiences for boys and girls—either in your own classroom or as a member of a curriculum committee—will depend upon the effectiveness of your problem-solving skills. Just as a research chemist must be able to use the scientific method or an historian must be skilled in the techniques of historical research, so teachers need to acquire those skills basic to the effective solution of educational problems.

Sometimes you will hear, even from professional people, comments which suggest that we do not always use effective problem-solving procedures in the field of education. You may hear someone talk about "the pendulum swinging" as if we tended to go from one extreme position to another. A teacher may describe his procedures as "middle of the road"—a position which seems to imply that he does not deem his colleagues to be as sound as he in their points of view. You may even hear some well-meant comments about the "gap between theory and practice" which, in effect, means that you have not been taught very much that is practical. On the other hand, your colleagues may ask "What does the college believe?" as though, to be up to date, one must accept the philosophy of the prevailing authority.

If we are realistic, we must admit that some of our educational practices are determined by factors other than thoughtful, impartial study. In some school systems, what teachers consider to be a desirable program has to be balanced against what they feel must be taught for the purposes of standardized tests. There are situations where the quality of the educational program is conditioned by the classroom space available, the textbooks adopted, or the salaries which teachers can be offered. In some places the concerns of special community groups will determine what is taught. Although such factors need to be reckoned with, lasting gains in terms of better programs for boys and girls will be made only as more teachers become skilled in analyzing and solving educational problems. You will have experiences that help you to develop such skills every time you plan a lesson, consider your next move when a problem of behavior has arisen, or analyze your role as a playground leader or club sponsor.

Teachers must be able to analyze the educational potentialities of complex situations. One of the most important skills for you to acquire is the ability to analyze complex situations for yourself. Beginning teachers are often baffled and frustrated when they seek help on their classroom problems. Typically, instead of saying "Do this" or "That's right" or "That's wrong," principals and supervisors say "Let's study the situation." This is a much slower process, but it is at the heart of a professional solution to an educational problem. There are few black or white answers in the field of education; there are many shades of gray.

To creative teachers, the fact that educational problems are rarely simple is one of the most challenging aspects of the profession. Consider, for example, Mr. Bantam, who is planning a sixth-grade science unit on how sound is produced and transmitted. Certainly, he wants his pupils to end up with accurate information about sound—but is this all? Whether he realizes it or not, he is also teaching attitudes. He may be turning able youngsters toward or away from science as a career. By the way he teaches, he may be encouraging independent exploration and building appreciation of the scientific method, or he may be developing the attitude that the word of experts (in this case, Mr. Bantam and the authors of the textbook) is to be accepted without question. He must think about the reading skills he is teaching and the discussion techniques and skills in cooperative problem-solving he plans to develop. Even in conveying accurate information about sound, he must decide whether he will be satisfied if his pupils can give back the exact words of the textbook or will take steps to assure that they can use their information accurately. All these decisions, and many more, will influence his lesson plans—how he will present the problem to his class, whether he will let pupils experiment, how he will use his textbook, whether he will lecture, what time he will allow for present-day applications, on what bases he will evaluate pupil growth.

Even a problem seemingly as simple as working with a third-grade reading group has many facets. As Miss Antonio makes her plan, she needs to consider what special reading skills she wishes to stress—word-analysis techniques, ability to locate accurate information, skill in summarizing what has been read, oral reading skills. She, too, is building attitudes—reading interests, feelings of competence, ease before an audience, habits of reading critically. If certain youngsters are having special problems, she may find herself helping others in the group to develop attitudes of sympathy and tolerance. All these considerations combine to determine how Miss Antonio plans her reading lesson and works with her group.

Problems of developing effective interpersonal relationships in the classroom call for just as careful an analysis. Three of Mr. Jackson's fourth-grade boys habitually interrupt in group discussions. There must be causes for this behavior and as Mr. Jackson and his supervisor sit down to consider next steps they analyze the situation to see what these might be. Perhaps the boys simply lack discussion techniques and need specific instruction regarding how one behaves in a group. It could be that they lack basic respect for other individuals and need to be helped to develop this attitude. Possibly being the center of attention is satisfying basic needs—needs for affection, for group status, for the satisfaction of intellectual curiosity. It could even be that Mr. Jackson, as discussion leader, is allowing more freedom than he realizes and the boys are simply following his cues. Once Mr. Jackson has decided what the undesirable behavior means and what his goals should be, he will have a sense of direction in deciding what to do next. All three youngsters could respond to the same approach, but it is possible that the behavior stems from a different cause in each case. If so, the procedures used to effect changes in behavior must differ.

These examples are no more complex than many of the everyday problems teachers face. Deciding what to do in any situation involves thinking of the attitudes and values the pupils will be acquiring, the ways of working they will develop, the attitudes that will be built toward other persons in cooperative or authority roles, precisely what information or skills they will learn. Whether or not the day's activities are as effective as they should be will depend on how positively they contribute to all the potential learnings in the situation. How good a science teacher is Mr. Bantam, for example, if his pupils pass with flying colors tests over the facts in the book and never apply scientific ways of working to their own solutions of problems? How well has Miss Antonio done if her pupils analyze words with great skill and never take home library books to read? How good is Mr. Jackson's discipline if his boys behave only when his eye is on them? One of the most important contributions that your student-teaching experiences can make to your eventual success as a teacher is to help you to develop more sensitive insights into the classroom problems you face.

Teachers must be able to translate goals into behavior. Beginning teachers often fail to achieve desired goals because they do not define exactly what they are after. You will have to learn to translate your general objectives into specific behavior. Watch three student teachers helping their fourth-graders learn a ten-word spelling list. Ruth Gladstone goes at it by giving a pre-test, helping the children to identify the words difficult for them, and then analyzing the sight and sound elements in each word with them. Dave Martino tells his class to write each word ten times for homework; he has no discussion of how to study and gives no help in analyzing words. Sam James decides that the children will do better if they are interested and plans a spelling bee where those who miss a word go to their seats. Each of these plans hints at the teacher's conception of the characteristics of a good speller.

You will need to translate goals into behavior if you wish to teach information effectively. What would you accept as evidence that your teaching in a fifth-grade unit on safety has been a success? Do you want your pupils to be able to list the exact points in the textbook? If they can write their own stories about safety, or make posters, is this the evidence you seek? Do you expect changes in behavior on the playground? In what ways?

Behavioral goals are equally important in developing group relationships. At the beginning of his student teaching Bob Anderson was very enthusiastic about the responses he was securing in his class discussions. When his supervisor visited he found a very lively discussion indeed —but everyone was trying to outshout everyone else. Comments such as "You're crazy" or "Oh, shut up" were frequent; unfounded opinions were defended heatedly even in areas where ample evidence was available. Do these suggest behaviors that relate to good discussion techniques? How clearly has Bob defined the democratic value of respecting the unique worth of each individual? If you would have your lessons effective you must learn to make your goals precise.

Teachers must be able to use effectively research regarding human growth and development. The solution to almost every educational problem calls for answers to three questions: (1) What are our goals (in terms of our best insights into the needs of individuals, the needs of our democratic society, and the potential learnings in a given situation)? (2) What do these goals mean specifically in terms of behavior? (3) What are the most efficient and economical means of reaching these specific goals? Research in human growth, development, and learning makes a major contribution to this third step.

Once in a while you will hear comments which indicate that the contribution of educational psychology to good teaching is not very clearly understood. A parent sometimes is heard to say, "I used all the psychology I knew and then I spanked him." A beginning teacher may be advised, "At first, forget your psychology and show them you are in control." A leader persuades a group to do something about which they are not too happy and reports, "All it took was a little psychology." Or a mother hears a psychologist talk at a Parent-Teacher Association meeting and wonders whether the speaker would "take a look at Sammy." Actually, of course, our insights into human behavior make a much more basic contribution to effective teaching than a bag of tricks for persuading people to do as we wish or a crystal ball for understanding deviate behavior.

As you work with your pupils, try to identify the situations in which you can apply what you know about maturation and readiness; about basic needs and developmental tasks; about motivation and the nature of learning; about individual differences; about transfer of learning; about the effects on behavior of broken homes, social class structure, family patterns of permissiveness and authoritarianism; about group dynamics and democratic social climates. These are among the research areas on which you will draw over and over again as you face the realities of teaching.

Many a beginning teacher (and many an experienced teacher, too) has described to a supervisor the way he handled a class situation or a problem with an individaul child and then has asked, "Was I right?"

As you learn to analyze the situations you face, to spell out your goals precisely, and to apply appropriately what you know about the ways in which children grow and learn, you will become better and better able to answer this question for yourself.

Teachers must be able to use research techniques in solving new problems. As you study more closely the research underlying modern classroom procedures, you will discover that many of our ways of working are deduced from basic psychological studies. For example, our general knowledge from laboratory studies of the effect of the learner's purpose on the way he works suggests that it is important to provide for pupil-teacher planning so that pupil purposes will be clear; what we know about transfer of learning suggests that the way we teach will make a crucial difference in what our pupils actually learn; what we have learned from research in child-study laboratories has helped to define our concept of readiness for learning. If our progress toward better educational programs is to be continuous, teachers must become more and more skillful in testing basic educational principles in the classroom setting.

In recent years serious thought has been given to the possibilities of involving teachers in classroom research. Typically, in the past the research pattern was designed by college professors, research bureaus, or doctoral candidates, and if teachers had any share, it was largely to carry out instructions. Today there are many school systems in which individual teachers, the members of an entire school faculty, or the faculties of several schools are engaging in research projects. You may well find the teachers in your building testing out a proposal for an individualized reading program; comparing the results of a spelling program built around words pupils actually need with those of a program which follows the adopted text; investigating ways of gearing learning activities more effectively to pupils' experience backgrounds; studying how to help children develop more effective problem-solving techniques. One of the most exciting advances in the field of education is our realization that teachers themselves can make an important research contribution to better programs for boys and girls.

Research involves complicated techniques for identifying and clarifying a problem, advancing hypotheses, collecting and analyzing data, drawing conclusions, and testing them further as necessary. An effective research project calls for a high level of skill at all these points. In your first years of teaching you probably will not find yourself involved in much extensive research. You can, however, learn to approach your classroom problems with a scientific point of view. You can learn to make hypotheses as to why a procedure worked well or failed and to test your hypotheses. You can use objective techniques for studying pupils to collect concrete evidence of the success of your teaching. You can also learn to withhold judgment and study a situation rather than saying too quickly and glibly, "I believe in this" or "Of course, I don't hold with that at all." Teaching offers endless possibilities for growth for those who choose to take a scientific approach to educational problems. Every day suggests a new hypothesis to test and new types of data to be collected.

DEVELOPING YOUR OWN EDUCATIONAL POINT OF VIEW

Philosophies of education, like philosophies of life, keep on growing. No one has the insights at twenty that he will have at forty. No one at sixty, if he has maintained his interest in professional problems, will think exactly as he did at forty. To all the richness of experience which comes through dealing creatively with professional problems must be added the challenges of a changing world. Who knows but that new evidence in psychology, psychiatry, and medicine in the next quarter of a century may change our ways of looking at human nature? Certainly, few teachers in 1930 dreamed that developments in the physical and social sciences would soon cause them to reappraise their attitudes about the world in which they live in the light of the atomic age. As a beginning teacher, you are taking early steps in the lifelong process of building a sound professional point of view. How can you guarantee that your student-teaching experience and your first years on the job contribute to this goal as richly as possible?

Do not expect "snap" answers. Your expectations of what it means to learn to teach will help to determine how much you grow. If you are looking for pat answers and simple solutions, you will not move very far in the direction of solving professional problems effectively for yourself, and you may find student teaching and your first years under supervision in a classroom of your own very frustrating, indeed. Learn to think about the situations you face. Even responsibilities that seem routine and simple merit a careful analysis. You will grow in your ability to solve professional problems for yourself to the degree that you make yourself work at it.

If you are expecting to do a perfect job every day and to receive nothing but praise from your cooperating teacher or supervisor, you are also in for disappointment and frustration. The more complex the teaching responsibilities you undertake, the more likely it is that something unforeseen will go awry in spite of your most careful planning. This is part of the challenge of teaching. If you want to grow, take on the difficult tasks and welcome opportunities to analyze your mistakes. Even your most experienced colleagues, you will discover, face each new day as a challenge and an opportunity for professional growth.

Keep asking *why*. Preparing yourself day after day to give leadership to thirty or more boys and girls offers unparalleled opportunities to develop skill in educational planning. Make yourself think by asking *why* as you develop your lesson plans. It will be a temptation at times to adopt blindly the procedures of a colleague or even, in despair, to recall how Miss Hannabell did it when you were in the fourth grade. However, you will find that the time you spend thinking through goals and outlining your plans in detail will pay off in feelings of security as you teach. There is nothing more difficult than trying to give a class a sense of direction if you yourself are not sure where you are going.

Ask your cooperating teacher or your supervisor *why* also. If your first full-time experience in the classroom is as challenging as it should be, you will discover that you cannot always identify in practice principles that seemed quite clear in college classes. Because each new group of boys and girls poses a different teaching problem, your cooperating teacher and your colleagues will almost certainly be using some teaching techniques you did not talk about in your methods courses. Perhaps you will find yourself in a classroom where both curriculum and teaching methods are quite different from those you remember from your own school days. You may be tempted to reject those practices that do not look familiar. "After all," you may be saying, "I had an excellent education, and my teachers did not go in for all of this." It is strange that the very person who extols the virtues of progress in medicine and points with pride to how much better protected is the health of his children today sometimes argues vehemently for a return to the "good old days" in education. Actually, in most cases, there will be good reasons for the procedures you are now observing and for the suggestions of your supervisors. You should feel a professional obligation to ask for help in interpreting what you have seen. The persons supervising your work can spell out the reasons back of their objectives and procedures if you will let them know where you are puzzled.

It is equally important, however, that you do not feel compelled to accept completely everything you see. There are genuine differences of opinion as to what learnings are of most value for boys and girls. You will not grow if you reject too quickly ideas that are unfamiliar, but neither will you grow if you bend all your efforts into making yourself a carbon copy of your cooperating teacher or of the colleague next door. Keep on ferreting out explanations, but at the same time match your best thinking against that of the experienced teachers working with you.

Keep yourself up to date. Teachers do not grow unless they actively seek new ideas. It is a common complaint of beginning teachers that they have far too little time to sleep, let alone to read and think. To some extent this is true, but your first years of teaching should also be years of thoughtful study. You must continue to grow in your insights into human nature and the society in which we live—two of the foundation areas upon which all teachers draw. If you have never stopped to think what you mean by "democracy," this is the time to do so. You will be vague and uncertain about many of the steps you take in developing effective human relationships in your classroom if your goals in teaching democratic relationships are not beginning to clarify. Your preoccupation with college classes may have left you woefully ignorant of what is going on in the world today—even of the television which your pupils watch so avidly. If you are going to help your boys and girls understand what is happening in the world around them, you may have to set yourself a definite reading program. You will also find that you will need to continue to examine basic psychological principles. No matter how rich your college background in this area has been, your firsthand experiences with youngsters will deepen and sharpen many of your concepts. This is your year to dip back into books on human relationships in the classroom, on the influence of social class backgrounds, on meeting the emotional needs of pupils, on working with the exceptional child.

It is also important for you to grow in your sensitivity to the major educational problems which concern the members of your profession. In many schools, student teachers are invited to participate in faculty meetings, workshops and other in-service projects, Parent-Teacher Association meetings. As a beginning teacher you will be expected to make such activities part of your professional life. You may wish you could decline these invitations under the pressure of your college classes, campus obligations, or the weight of all your new responsibilities in your first year in a classroom of your own. If you are anxious to become a top-flight teacher, however, you will arrange your schedule to include such professional meetings. They offer priceless opportunities to learn firsthand the types of problems that are receiving the attention of educators today. This is your chosen profession and these, your colleagues-to-be, are anxious to help you feel that you are an accepted, full-time member of it.

BOOKS YOU SHOULD KNOW

Cole, Lawrence E., and Bruce, William F. *Educational Psychology*. Revised Edition. Yonkers-on-Hudson, N. Y.: World Book Co., 1958. Pp. 720.

Counts, George S. *Education and American Civilization*. New York: Bureau of Publications, Teachers College, Columbia University, 1952. Pp. xiv + 491.

Cronbach, Lee J. *Educational Psychology*. New York: Harcourt, Brace and Co., 1954. Pp. xxvii + 628.

Jersild, Arthur T., and associates. *Child Development and the Curriculum*. New York: Bureau of Publications, Teachers College, Columbia University, 1946. Pp. xi + 274.

Research for Curriculum Improvement. 1957 Yearbook of the Association for Supervision and Curriculum Development, N.E.A. Washington, D.C.: The Association, 1957. Pp. x + 350.

Rugg, Harold, and Withers, William. *Social Foundations of Education*. Englewood Cliffs, N.J.: Prentice-Hall, 1955. Pp. x + 771.

Saylor, J. Galen, and Alexander, William M. *Curriculum Planning for Better Teaching and Learning*. New York: Rinehart and Co., 1954. Pp. xiii + 624.

Stratemeyer, Florence B.; Forkner, Hamden, L.; McKim, Margaret G.; and Passow, A. Harry. *Developing a Curriculum for Modern Living*. Revised Edition. New York: Bureau of Publications, Teachers College, Columbia University, 1957. Pp. 740.

Teachers for Our Times. Washington, D.C.: American Council on Education, 1944. Pp. xix + 189.

Getting Acquainted

PART II

Becoming Part of a New School

CHAPTER 3

Gets along well with others.

Accepts suggestions graciously and readily.

Is dependable; is prompt and accurate in completing reports.

Assumes his share of the responsibilities of the school without prodding.

Is loyal to school policies which are honestly conceived and fairly administered.

Refrains from talking disparagingly of his associates and his school.

Is discreet about discussing school problems in public.

Statements such as these are typical of the comments which appear on the appraisal forms of applicants for teaching positions. They illustrate one type of information which school systems need to determine probable teaching success. Those who employ you want to know how effective you are likely to be as a member of a school faculty. Part of your success as a teacher will depend on how well you can work with others. You will be joining a complex organization in which your cooperativeness, your conscientiousness in abiding by the regulations that facilitate effective working conditions, and your professional loyalty will be extremely important to the welfare of everyone.

A crucial first step for any new teacher is to become acquainted with the school in which he is going to work. You will need to understand the personnel structure in your building—the responsibilities carried by your colleagues and the cooperative relationships that will be expected of you. You will also want to become thoroughly familiar with the school organization and with the special policies and rules that will affect your classroom procedures. If you are a student teacher, you will have the added responsibility of working effectively within the framework that has been jointly established by your college and the school in the interests of your maximum growth.

Varied means are used to help new teachers to become acquainted with the over-all philosophy and organization of the school system and with the policies and procedures of their particular building. In many school systems, some types of information will be available in printed form. The course of study, for example, will indicate the general curriculum design and will often provide specific help on matters of time allotments to particular subject areas, school services available on a system-wide basis, sources of special supplies and materials, and policies with regard to evaluating and reporting pupil progress. There may also be a personnel handbook which describes the administrative and supervisory structure of the school system and covers system-wide policies relating to teacher and pupil personnel. In addition, there may be a handbook covering special policies and procedures peculiar to your building. You should inquire whether such printed materials exist and, if they do, read them carefully, not once but many times.

Handbooks and courses of study can never cover completely the thousand and one contingencies which a beginning teacher will face. The people with whom you work will be your best resources when immediate problems arise which touch upon school organization and policies. When you are a student teacher, your cooperating teacher will undoubtedly be the one to take major responsibility for orienting you to the school. When you step into your first full-time teaching position, this will be one of the functions of your principal. You must be sufficiently sophisticated about problems of school administration, however, to know what questions to ask.

DEVELOPING EFFECTIVE RELATIONSHIPS WITH YOUR COLLEAGUES

No matter how large or how small the school, you will be a member of a team which must function smoothly in the best interests of boys and girls. This team includes not only your principal and your fellow teachers but the nurse, the school secretary, the custodial and lunchroom staffs, and in many school systems a host of persons who serve on a system-wide basis—psychologists, attendance officers, social workers, research personnel, supervisors. You will need to know the functions of all persons who contribute to the welfare of your pupils and to identify carefully your own responsibilities in helping to secure effective working relationships.

In most school systems, there will be a special program of events—some professional, some social—to help new faculty members feel at home. Student teachers may be included in some of these. It is probable, also, that the cooperating teacher and the principal will have some special plans for helping student teachers to get acquainted. Arrangements may be made for you to tour the entire building and to spend some time visiting other classrooms. You may be asked to work for a morning or two in the principal's office or to assist the school librarian or the nurse. Your cooperating teacher may ask you to accompany him as he goes to the office to requisition supplies, confers with the school nurse, checks a set of books out of the library, requests some visual aids, or carries out lunchroom or playground duties. These are all valuable opportunities to get the "feel" of staff relationships and school policies.

Student teachers sometimes need to be reminded that the persons with whom they are working are thinking of them as prospective colleagues. They will be deciding how it would be a year from now to have you next door and across the lunch table every day. Normal tact and good judgment are all that is needed to make a favorable impression. However, an occasional student, in his zeal for information and his anxiety to sound sophisticated about school affairs, has betrayed woeful ignorance of the complexities of school administration and insensitivity to human relationships. "All I want to know," said Jim Sampson in his first conference with his principal, blissfully unaware that in many schools the principal has major responsibilities for classroom equipment, "is why there is such atrociously poor equipment in the science room."

Determine your obligations to your principal. In most schools the principal is the person with delegated legal responsibility for the welfare of the pupils and the staff. He is expected to give supervisory assistance to his teachers. He is responsible to the central administration in his system or to the state department of education for accurate records of such matters as pupil attendance. He is in charge of the budget and supplies for his building and responsible for decisions regarding the use of space and equipment. He is the person whom parents consult when problems arise involving home-school relationships. A principal may employ a democratic approach with his faculty in the solution of many school problems, but this in no way changes his ultimate responsibility. There are many points at which he must count upon the good judgment, promptness, and conscientiousness of his faculty. The ease with which you fit into a new school on your first job will depend, in part, upon how sensitive you become to the professional obligations teachers owe to their principals.

Because your principal must be certain that all classrooms are manned when school opens each day, you will probably find some plan for teachers to check in when they arrive. Frequently the student teacher's name is added to this list so that the office has a complete record of everyone at work in the building. There will also be a definite arrangement for teachers to notify the principal if they are ill. In the case of student teachers, the cooperating teacher is often the one to be called. This is a point you should clarify at once, even though you have never had a day's illness. Principals and cooperating teachers are not inclined to be generous in the case of beginners who straggle in to school late or who fail to let the appropriate individual know when they are ill. From your point of view as a student teacher, these may seem to be minor matters when your cooperating teacher is at hand to take charge of the classroom, but your principal will have visions of attempting, a year from now, to keep forty lively youngsters in their seats while he makes a last-minute call for a substitute.

As the person responsible for the administrative details of the school, your principal will be involved in considerable record-keeping. He will not only have to report attendance at stated intervals, but he may be in charge of ordering school supplies, requisitioning special materials, and keeping account of sets of textbooks supplied by the board of education. It is important that teachers facilitate his work by ascertaining what reports they must submit and by being prompt and meticulously accurate in filling them out. In a student-teaching situation these will be matters for which the cooperating teacher will probably take major responsibility, but a student teacher should welcome the chance to learn how to complete each of the forms in use in his building. If, as a student teacher, you have an opportunity to work for a few days in the principal's office to discover just how varied his administrative responsibilities are and how easily one or two careless errors on the part of teachers can complicate things, by all means capitalize upon it.

Because of your principal's ultimate responsibility for the welfare of the children in his building, there will be certain types of emergencies which should come to his immediate attention. Accidents to children in the classroom or on the playground are usually reported at once, even though the school nurse is on duty. Problems calling for unusual disciplinary action should normally be reported. In some states corporal punishment cannot legally be administered unless the principal or some other witness is present. Situations in which a teacher senses severe emotional disturbance on the part of a child or a parent probably should be brought to the principal's attention. Typically, also, permission for a child to be sent home during school hours is given by the principal. It can be very important, not only for the sake of the pupil but for your own legal protection, that you ascertain early in the school year the situations in which your principal should be promptly involved.

Your principal will probably want to be consulted before you and your class make plans for an activity not usually considered part of the regular classroom routine. Field trips, walks around the block, activities involving special use of playground, lunchroom, or auditorium facilities, parties and programs to which parents are invited, are types of experiences about which he should be informed. The exact list will differ from school to school. It is your responsibility to determine just what is the custom in your building. It can be embarrassing to you and disturbing to your pupils if, in a planning session, you make promises which you discover later cannot be fulfilled. Know when to say "We must check about that."

Most teachers, realizing their principal's over-all concerns about the school program, take pains to let him know what is going on in their classrooms even though no special regulation demands it. The principal certainly will be at hand to give support in the case of an unusual disciplinary problem (although he will be hoping that you will be able to handle most situations for yourself), but he is much more interested in knowing boys and girls as friends. He will welcome invitations from pupils to see work of which they are particularly proud. He will be anxious to aid in interpreting your program to parents and to work with you on your classroom teaching problems. In order that he may do this, you have an obligation to let him know what you are doing. You should expect to have him drop in once in a while to see you work.

Identify the cooperative responsibilities you will share with your colleagues. Among the many rewards as a member of the teaching profession are those that accrue from one's associations with colleagues. You will find them interested in your work, anxious to be of help, and willing to share materials and equipment.

As a student teacher, your closest associations will, of course, be with your cooperating teacher. Some of the steps you can take to make this relationship a pleasant and profitable one will be discussed in a later section of this chapter. There will be others on the school staff with whom you will develop friendly, but only casual, relationships. However, there will be some with whom you will share definite responsibilities for your pupils. You will need to ascertain just what your obligations are in each situation.

It is particularly important for you to discover what your relationships should be with other teachers who are working with your class. If special teachers of art, music, or physical education come to your classroom, you should know what your responsibilities are in preparing your pupils for this special work and what, if any, your duties are while such teachers are in charge of your class. You will also need to know how much help on problems related to your regular classroom program can be expected from special teachers. If you are teaching in the primary grades, where the help of specialists is not always readily available, you will want to find out whether and when such assistance might be given. If you are the specialist, you will, of course, need similar information from the point of view of your teaching assignment.

In many schools teachers are assigned responsibility for all-school activities—the student council, the safety patrol, the office helpers, the school paper. Their work can be facilitated if you, as a classroom teacher, know what they are doing. In some cases, you may need to adjust your classroom schedule so that your youngsters are free to go about their special work with these teachers. In others, classroom discussions may be needed to help your boys and girls understand the work of the special group.

In most schools, there are supervisory responsibilities which faculty members share—lunchroom and playground duties, duty in the halls as children enter and leave the school. You will need to discover what the general standards of behavior are in halls, playgrounds, and lunchrooms and to cooperate by helping your boys and girls to abide by them. You will probably find that whenever a pupil near you deviates from the expected standards of behavior, there are steps you should take even though supervisory responsibilities have not been specifically assigned to you. This, however, is not always the case. You should ask what is expected of you in situations where you seem to be the person nearest the source of trouble.

In many schools, one or more teachers will assume special service responsibilities to their colleagues. There may be an audio-visual aids representative, a teacher responsible for science equipment, someone who keeps up to date the file on desirable field trips. Such persons can be very helpful to a beginning teacher. You will need to know who they are, when they can be most easily consulted, and what special requisition slips or record cards they need from you to facilitate their services.

It can also be enlightening to you to become well acquainted with those teachers who have worked with your boys and girls in previous years. These persons can tell you about helpful procedures that they used with individuals who may be troubling you. They may, in the case of youngsters who are learning slowly, be able to lend materials more appropriate than those in your own room. You will discover, also, that among the faculty as a whole there is a generous give-and-take in the interest of better experiences for boys and girls. Your youngsters may be invited to read to the kindergarteners. You may ask the fifth-graders to be an audience for your special science program and, in turn, be invited to theirs. Third-grade Bobby may take his arithmetic paper to the sixth-grade mathematics class to be praised for how neatly he makes his numbers. One of your most pleasant, and most challenging, responsibilities to your colleagues is to take your part in enterprises such as these.

Ascertain the assistance available from other professional personnel. Depending upon the size of the school system in which you are working, its financial support, and the concern its administrators have for providing special assistance to teachers and children, you may find a number of other professional personnel available to help you. Supervisors, librarians, psychologists, attendance officers, visiting teachers or social workers, special remedial teachers, nurses and physicians, would fall into this category. These special personnel will be working on a variety of schedules. A school nurse may be in your building regularly. There will probably be an attendance officer ready to give help in cases of excessive absence. If there is a local library, there may be assistance from a librarian on a regular basis. In a system of some size, there will probably be an elementary supervisor who will supplement the work of the principal in helping teachers with their classroom problems. This person may visit regularly or may come only on call. Psychologists, social workers, and special remedial teachers are likely to be carrying a heavy case load and to be available only upon request. It is important for you to ascertain which of these special personnel serve in your school system and upon what basis their assistance can be secured.

As a student teacher, you will probably learn to take some responsibility for securing help from the persons who are regularly in your building. You will need to know their schedules and the procedures involved in requesting their assistance. In the case of the school nurse, there may be special referral forms to file. If there is a librarian regularly available, you will want to be sure how long a period your class may spend in the library, what types of help the librarian will have time to give, and how you can best assist.

Referral of pupils for special psychological study usually is done only after consultation with the principal and, in some instances, with parents as well. Your cooperating teacher will undoubtedly take the leadership in this. It can be a worth-while experience for you, however, to be included in the conferences regarding such a problem. As you already know from your college work in mental hygiene, psychologists and social caseworkers do not solve problems for children merely by interviewing or testing them. If there is a youngster in your classroom who is receiving special help, you may have an excellent opportunity to discover, firsthand, what the role of the teacher may be in working with such cases.

Ascertain your cooperative relationships with nonprofessional personnel. Among the most valuable members of a school staff are its nonprofessional personnel—the school secretary, the engineer, the custodian, the lunchroom helpers. These are persons who can make many positive contributions to the lives of your pupils. They can also be very helpful to you in locating needed materials or in providing special services. Make sure that you meet these people and that you can call them by name.

Persons on the nonprofessional staff have a heavy work load of their own. You will need to ascertain just what help you can request of them and under what circumstances. There may, of necessity, be rather strict limitations on the amount of additional stencil cutting that can be done by the school secretary, although there may be mimeographing or dittoing equipment if you can prepare your own copy. This is something you will need to check before you breeze in with a test you would like to use at 10:00 or assure your pupils that there will be no trouble mimeographing their proposed school paper.

You will need to inquire, also, whether there are certain services you should assume in the classroom to facilitate the work of nonprofessional personnel. There may, for example, be regulations regarding the purposes for which children should be given permission to use the office telephone. In many schools it will be customary to pick up waste paper and align desks before going home in order to speed the custodial care. There will be policies regarding behavior in the lunchroom. You should be prepared to help your boys and girls understand their responsibilities toward those who share in making their classroom and school a clean and pleasant place in which to live.

Teaching is a cooperative affair. You will need to know your own responsibilities and to discover the persons who can give you help. On the other hand, you should be equally aware of the ways in which you can be of assistance.

ADJUSTING TO THE SCHOOL ORGANIZATION AND POLICIES

People cannot live and work effectively in a social structure without agreements to govern their conduct. A school, with from a hundred to a thousand or more boys and girls, their teachers, their principal, and other professional and nonprofessional personnel, is a complicated social structure. In most schools, every effort is made to develop an organization and policies that facilitate the work of teachers and make a positive contribution to the learning experiences of boys and girls. Even so, the resulting pattern can be quite complex. Innumerable details of day-by-day classroom management will depend upon your familiarity with the over-all policies of the system of which your school is a part, the general organization in your building, and the specific regulations by which the teachers are asked to abide. Even though you have a cooperating teacher at hand to advise you, you will save yourself many awkward moments if you will become acquainted with the policies of your school as quickly as possible. You will be grateful, too, for all the sophistication you can develop regarding the administrative organization of a typical school when you face, as a beginning teacher, the problem of fitting smoothly into a new setting.

Orient yourself to the purposes and policies of the total school system. Often beginners become frustrated with regulations that to them seem unreasonable. Some of these may be aspects of policy over which a principal has little, if any, control. If your school is part of a larger school system, certain decisions will be made on a system-wide basis. Regulations regarding the certification of teachers, tenure, reporting of pupil attendance, and even certain aspects of the curriculum, will be established by law for the entire state. In some cases, considerable flexibility within the general framework of the over-all policy is possible at the building or classroom level; in others, few, if any, adjustments can be made. You will be more intelligent about procedures in your school if you know which of them reflect system-wide policy and what adaptations are permissible in your classroom.

Among the policies usually established on a system-wide basis are those regarding the *general curriculum design* and the *over-all organization for instruction.* Textbook policies are likely to be system-wide, as are policies with regard to school budgets and the amount of money available to teachers for the purchase of special classroom equipment. Usually in matters which concern effective classroom instruction considerable latitude is allowed to the individual school and to the classroom teacher. You are likely to find your cooperating teacher and your colleagues staying within the general framework of the course of study, but making whatever adjustments are necessary to meet the needs of pupils more effectively. In all probability, too, there will be a variety of textbooks available, and the principal or an elementary supervisor will try to be of assistance if additional materials are needed. These are policies about which you should inquire specifically, however, as you begin to think about your own lesson plans.

The procedures required in *recording* and *reporting progress*—the type of report cards and the type of cumulative record—will be the same for every school in the system. So will any general policies regarding acceleration or retention of pupils. In matters of recording and reporting pupil progress, however, there may be adjustments unique to a particular building. In Wilson School the teachers have developed a system of parent conferences. In Valley Lane, there is an unwritten understanding regarding how letter grades are to be assigned in the case of a child who is being considered for retention. In Fifth Street, the teachers file in the cumulative records a special list indicating each pupil's recreational reading. You will want to inquire carefully regarding the reporting and evaluation procedures in your particular school.[1]

Personnel policies will also operate on a system-wide basis. These would include regulations regarding absence for illness, leaves of absence, visiting days, attendance at conventions, salary increments, and appraisal. In some school systems there will also be extensive plans for involving teachers in curriculum revision and for providing in-service education activities. These may not concern you directly as a student teacher, but the more you can learn about typical employment conditions, the more competent you will be when you apply for a position of your own.

[1] See Chapter 11 for a more complete discussion of reporting and evaluation procedures.

There are other types of *general regulations* established on a system-wide basis in which few adjustments can be made at the building level. The calendar for the year, the vacations, and the special holidays are determined by the central office. So, usually, are the dates upon which report cards are to go home and the dates upon which certain types of administrative information from principals are due. There may also be a system-wide program of intelligence and achievement testing. If there are special services, such as those of an audio-visual aids exchange, there will be established procedures for their use to be followed by all teachers.

The course of study for your school system, the personnel handbooks, and any special bulletins regarding salary schedules, retirement policies, and absences, will be helpful guides to system-wide policy. In addition, your cooperating teacher, your colleagues, and your principal will be glad to answer questions. These persons know how difficult it is for a newcomer to grasp the details of a complex organization. They would much rather have you ask than have you make errors in judgment because you concealed your ignorance.

Determine how the organization of your school should be reflected in your classroom procedures. An understanding of the details of the organization of your particular building will probably have a much more direct effect on the ease with which you manage your day-by-day teaching responsibilities than will your knowledge of system-wide procedures and policies. There will be the physical plant with which to get acquainted but, even more important, there will be a time schedule and a plan to facilitate the use of special personnel and equipment.

You may be responsible for going with your pupils to special parts of the building—music or art rooms, the library, the gymnasium, the nurse's office, the lunchroom, rest rooms. Get acquainted with the *physical layout* of your building. Find out, also, which stairways and doors your pupils are to use in case of fire drills—you will have no time to ask when the siren sounds. If you are in charge of your pupils' outdoor play, you will need to know how the playground space is allotted. You should also investigate the plans for the sharing of special rooms—the library, the visual-aids room, the auditorium, the primary playroom. Many teachers will be wanting to use these facilities; you and your youngsters will face some disappointments if you do not take the proper steps to reserve them.

You will need to identify any aspects of the *time schedule* peculiar to your building. In some schools there will be staggered schedules for lunch and recess. If so, you must have your pupils ready when their turn comes. If there is a bell schedule, you must know what it signifies. You can make life very difficult for a special teacher who may have your boys and girls for only a forty-minute period if you consistently send them late. Check, too, on special times for entering the school in the morning and for dismissal. John Anderson first became fully conscious of the warning bell when he started his pupils down the hall five minutes before dismissal, only to have them sent back by the principal.

The importance of determining your responsibilities with regard to other persons who work with your boys and girls was mentioned in the preceding section. It is very likely that there will be definite *schedules for special personnel.* In some schools the schedules of art and music teachers are planned so that they have free periods to come to classrooms to give special help when requested or to work with pupils who have special talent. There may be librarians in attendance upon certain days only. In all likelihood there will be times when you will be able to send individual children for books and other times when your class will go as a group. You will enable these special persons to give much more effective help to your boys and girls if you know precisely the schedules into which your youngsters' classroom program must fit.

If there is a program of *school-wide activities* in which your pupils are likely to be involved, you will want to know what it is. Student council may meet during school hours. Safety patrol boys and lunchroom helpers may have to leave their rooms early and report late after their duties are performed. Clubs may be meeting on an early-morning or late-afternoon schedule. You can plan appropriate classroom activities more readily if you have clearly in mind the times when only part of your group will be present.

Make sure you know special school regulations. In addition to becoming acquainted with the general organization in your building for the effective use of facilities, time, and personnel, you will need to become thoroughly familiar with a number of specific regulations. It may seem to you, at first, that there is an unnecessarily large number of directives and special forms; but when you stop to consider their purposes, the necessity for most of them will be readily apparent to you.

There will be special procedures to be followed in keeping track of *pupil personnel.*[2] You will be given a special attendance book and asked

[2] See Chapter 12, pages 480-482, for a more detailed discussion of the teacher's responsibility for attendance reports.

to mark it in specific ways. Tardiness, as well as absence, must be indicated. Once a month a statistical summary will be due in the principal's office. In all probability there will be a designated procedure for reporting absences during each half-day. Notes may be required from parents when a pupil is absent and, if he has been ill, perhaps a permission slip from the school nurse before he re-enters class. Children who are tardy may need permission from the office to enter class. When you realize that there are legal regulations regarding school attendance which school personnel are expected to enforce, you will understand the importance of such routine procedures.

Another crucial set of regulations will be concerned with the *safety of pupils*. Some of these will relate to the movement of classes. You should learn immediately the complete fire-drill procedure—not only exit assignments, but also the regulations regarding whether doors are to be closed, the sequence of classes in going down stairs and outdoors, talking in line, and whether you, as the teacher, are to lead the line or bring up the rear. Have clearly in mind, also, an alternate route in case you find your regular exit blocked. If yours is a small school, pupils may be encouraged to move through the halls quietly but informally on entering and leaving school or moving to other rooms. If, however, large numbers of youngsters must be on the move at once, you may discover that there are definite rules to be followed. For the sake of your pupils' reputations as good citizens, as well as your own, be prepared to remind them of the rules occasionally. You will also need to know what other safety regulations have been established for the protection of individual youngsters. What types of games are permissible on the playground? Are the children to be allowed to enter the classrooms early if the teacher is not present? Who takes care of an ill child if the school nurse is not in the building? May pupils be kept after school or must they be on their way before traffic guards go off duty? May children be sent alone on errands throughout the building, or do they travel in pairs? What are the regulations regarding bicycles? When may a parent take his child out of school during school hours?

Some safety regulations will be established, at least in part, for the *legal protection of teachers*. Permission notes from parents will probably be needed if you wish to take your class on an excursion. Accidents are usually reported on special forms. There may be definite restrictions regarding how much first aid can be offered. Health authorities may have to be called if the pet hamster decides that Jeanie's finger would be good for dessert. The details of any corporal punishment may need to be witnessed and reported. If the situation is one where parents might raise any question later regarding negligence on your part it is foolhardy, indeed, not to have complied fully with whatever regulations your board of education has established for your protection.

In most schools there will be policies with regard to *securing supplies and equipment.* Few school systems have unlimited resources. You will probably find that you are expected to plan carefully with the children so that paper and other materials are used economically. When additional supplies are needed there are likely to be special requisition forms to be filled out. Inquire before you assume that you will be able to raid the art room for all the materials you want for a special project. You may be in a school with a "petty cash" fund which can be used by teachers for emergency supplies, but do not assume this, either, without checking. In his first few weeks of student teaching William Smith made anything but a favorable impression on his principal when he purchased a dollar's worth of crepe paper to decorate his bulletin boards and casually presented his bill. "This is a small matter," you are probably saying. True, but Will's principal was left wondering what more serious violations of regulations this young man might commit in his zeal to have everything just right for his pupils.

Each school will have other types of *special regulations* and *unwritten agreements.* Some will be stated in a building handbook, but others you may discover only by listening and by being sensitive enough to know when to ask questions. Parents or visitors may be requested to report to the office before they come to your classroom. It may not be permissible for children to bring money for a party. There may be rules regarding accepting gifts from pupils. In some schools, also, for the sake of their own personal budgets, teachers have agreed that they will not become involved financially in sponsoring elaborate parties for children. Janie Smith learned this too late when she enthusiastically volunteered ice cream and two chocolate cakes for a Christmas party her class was planning and then discovered that cookies and juice were the agreed-upon limit. Again, you may be tempted to say, "What difference does it make?" It does make a difference, however, when a half-dozen other classes beg their teachers to let them have the same.

Discover the procedures used to keep teachers informed. No matter how carefully the school calendar is planned ahead of time, there are day-by-day problems about which teachers must be kept informed. Some will concern teachers only—requests from the office for special information, deadlines after which materials cannot be ordered, dates when certain reports are due, notices of meetings, days upon which normal schedules will be interrupted for meetings of the Parent-Teacher Association. Some will involve pupils—dates when the dental clinic is open, rules regarding riding bicycles, special assemblies, notices to be taken home to parents. You will not want to be the person to whom the principal has to make an emergency call or the one whose boys have to be summoned specially for a meeting of the safety guards. Nor will you want to discover at 8:45 that all your plans must be adjusted for an assembly when you could have learned about it yesterday by taking a few more seconds to read the bulletin board.

In every school there will be some device for keeping teachers informed. It may be through the office bulletin board, a mimeographed "flyer" that is in your mailbox every morning, a system of sending a pupil messenger with a note, a series of announcements made at faculty meetings, or a combination of these. Discover early what the system is in your building and make a habit of checking regularly and reading carefully. This is just as crucial when you are a student teacher as it will be when you have a classroom of your own. Your cooperating teacher will be there to remind you, true; but he should not have to be responsible for this. Furthermore, he has other things on his mind, and even with the best intentions, he will sometimes forget you. You can save yourself many frustrating adjustments by checking for yourself.

If you are the least bit absent-minded you will not only read notices carefully, but you will establish some foolproof method of remembering them. In Sarah Greene's room announcements for children were written the first thing in the morning on part of the blackboard labeled *Special Events*. John Wilson wrote reminders about special dates in red on his school calendar. Andrea Gander tacked such notices on a corner of her bulletin board and read them just before her children were dismissed. Joanna Smith fastened them to the outside of her plan book. Ronald McGhee designated pupils to serve as checkers of special notices. You may, at first, be frustrated by these interruptions of your work, but such announcements are essential if life in the school community is to run smoothly.

ASSUMING YOUR ROLE AS A STUDENT TEACHER

As a student teacher, you will face some special problems in becoming part of the school to which you may be assigned. You will be a responsible member of two groups—a school faculty and a college student body. You will be both a teacher and a learner—entrusted with the welfare of boys and girls, but expected to grow in your effectiveness in working with them. You will be sharing a classroom with another teacher who also has a double responsibility—responsibility for the growth of the boys and girls entrusted to your joint care and responsibility for your growth as well. You will be under the supervision of two persons—your cooperating teacher and your college supervisor. All this sounds very formidable. Yet student after student reports that student teaching is the high point of his college experiences, that the friendships he formed with his cooperating teacher and his college supervisor are among those he cherishes most deeply. You can make this true for yourself if you display sensitivity in working with the persons responsible for your supervision and show poise, maturity, and good judgment as the representative of your college.

Each teacher-education institution has its own way of assigning student teachers to schools and its own pattern for the development of student-teaching experiences. In all probability your cooperating teacher will be given freedom to plan your classroom experiences in ways best suited to your needs and to those of the boys and girls with whom you are working. There will probably be, however, college policies regarding such matters as dates upon which your work begins and ends, observance of school and college vacation periods, types of special reports due to college authorities, and group and individual conferences with your college supervisor. It will be your responsibility to ascertain just what the plan is in your college and to be quite clear as to the regulations governing your joint responsibility to the school and to the college.

Regardless of the plan under which the student-teaching program develops, there are certain ways of working that characterize effective relationships between a student teacher, his cooperating teacher, and his college supervisor, and certain kinds of behavior typical of the student teacher who is a worthy representative of his college. This section is designed to help you think about some of the most important of these.[3]

Develop effective working relationships with your cooperating teacher. The person with whom you will establish the closest working relationships during your student-teaching experience will be your cooperating teacher. If you are typical of most students, you will come to this new relationship with some apprehension. This apprehension will

[3] Chapter 15 contains detailed suggestions for the kinds of experiences that would be helpful to you and the ways in which cooperating teachers may supervise your work.

be compounded of many factors. In part, it will reflect your very natural concern about whether you will do a good job and be rated as an able teacher. Your anxieties will also reflect preconceived notions about supervision, based on previous experiences in working with adults. Then, there will be all the vague feelings that have been built up by the comments previous student teachers have made—comments that may have been positive or negative, bubbled at the end of a highly satisfactory experience or wailed on the dreary day when everything seemed to go wrong, as it does on occasion for even the most skillful teacher. To top all of this, you may have been the recipient of well-meant but misleading advice from a student who worked with your particular cooperating teacher last year—a student completely unlike you in temperament, background, and skill in working with people. You will embark upon your relationships with your cooperating teacher with more security if you can replace these vague concerns and apprehensions with some positive thinking regarding the help he will expect to give you and how you can best contribute to making the working relationship a pleasant one.

Perhaps it will be most important to your peace of mind to realize that your cooperating teacher will expect you to grow gradually into full-time teaching responsibilities. You will not be regarded as a finished product sent out by your college to demonstrate the latest theories. Each cooperating teacher will have his own way of moving a student into his teaching responsibilities. It is entirely likely that in the beginning you will be given considerable time to observe, thus enabling you to become acquainted with the children and to get the "feel" of the classroom organization. It is probable, too, that your cooperating teacher will gradually give you responsibilities that will help the children to look to you as a teacher. These are likely to be of short duration and in areas where you feel secure. As you move into more extensive teaching responsibilities, there is apt to be a period of time when your cooperating teacher will be planning with you rather closely and perhaps be doing some cooperative teaching with you—each of you being responsible for certain aspects of the program. You will probably be consulted regarding which activities you would prefer to take over first and how rapidly you wish to assume new responsibilities. By the end of your student-teaching experience you should be fully responsible for your pupils, but you need not begin your work apprehensive about this ultimate goal.

Many student teachers raise questions regarding how much originality they will be permitted to use. Will you be expected merely to follow your cooperating teacher's plans, or may you teach as you wish? Situations differ, of course, but most cooperating teachers expect their students to think for themselves. In fact, cooperating teachers often speak appreciatively of the wealth of new ideas students bring to their rooms. For your own security in your first year on the job, your cooperating teacher will want to be sure that you have had ample experience in making your own plans and in locating your own materials. It will be expected, of course, that you will use good judgment in pursuing your own ideas. A person with common sense will not normally upset the daily routines in a classroom just to do things differently. Nor does one proceed counter to the general policy of the school. You should realize, also, that each teacher has developed his own philosophy of education and his own particular strengths in working with pupils. Your cooperating teacher is there to share with you his techniques as a master teacher. It may be far more important to your all-round growth as a teacher to learn all that your cooperating teacher has to offer than to use your student-teaching experience merely to test out your own ideas.

Although you will be urged to think for yourself, you will not be expected to do everything perfectly. Your cooperating teacher is there to help you learn. You should look forward to a frank, critical analysis of your work and to advice regarding how to improve. Cooperating teachers have worked out many ways of giving this help. The joint planning sessions that are often characteristic of the early part of the student-teaching experience will provide opportunities for you to check your thinking against that of a more experienced person. As you begin to take over more responsibilities for planning, your cooperating teacher will undoubtedly want to see your plans in writing and will react to them critically but sympathetically.[4] For extensive activities, such as units of work, these may be requested in detail several days ahead of the time when you plan to initiate the unit. The exact form in which your plans should be written will depend on what your cooperating teacher feels he needs to be helpful to you. Be sure to inquire about this and to be conscientious in supplying whatever type of plan is requested. It is often far more helpful (and certainly more satisfying) to rework your plans after a critical reaction from an experienced teacher than it is to plunge blindly into difficulty. Most cooperating teachers use conferences with their students as another means of giving help. Such conferences may be for the purpose of planning ahead or of re-

[4] Chapter 6 contains a more detailed discussion of planning.

viewing a lesson just completed (and frequently for both). In many situations, cooperating teachers also use notes as a means of helping students. These may vary from brief memos to logs that are running commentaries on your day. If you are to grow from your student-teaching experience, you will welcome all such efforts to help you.

Although a student will ordinarily be given enthusiastic support in trying out his own ideas, the cooperating teacher is the person legally responsible for the boys and girls in his classroom. Naturally, your cooperating teacher will assume this responsibility and will count on your understanding and cooperation. Both of you must put the welfare of boys and girls first. In some classrooms this may mean that your cooperating teacher will continue rather actively to give special remedial help or other assistance needed by the children even when you have assumed major responsibility for the day's program. After all, the presence of an inexperienced person in the classroom can scarcely be justified if the lives of boys and girls are not enriched thereby. Once in a while your plans may have to be adjusted because of school policy or special considerations regarding community relations. Occasionally, student-teaching responsibilities will have to be assumed more slowly if it becomes apparent that the student is having unusual difficulty in establishing effective rapport with pupils or in planning appropriate lessons.

What can you do to make it easy for your cooperating teacher to help you? Perhaps most important, you can welcome criticism graciously. Your cooperating teacher will certainly compliment you for jobs well done, but your greatest progress will often be made by tackling complex situations rather than by doing simple things well. No one is more difficult to help than the defensive student who feels compelled to explain and justify every mistake he has made (unless, perhaps, it is the student who dissolves in tears at the slightest hint of criticism). A cooperating teacher who is sensitive to human relationships can hardly be as helpfully critical as he should be if he faces someone who says, mournfully, "I was terrible, wasn't I?" or who eagerly asks "Well, did I do any better today?" You will make it far more easy for your cooperating teacher to analyze your work if you will engage in some objective self-analysis. "I've been trying to figure out what happened in that reading group. Do you think they lost interest because I drew out the introduction too long?" "It seemed to me that they settled down much better today except for the group in the corner. Did you notice whether I seemed to forget about them?"

You can also make it much easier for your cooperating teacher to be helpful if you will become sensitive to minor clues to suggestions regarding how to proceed. Because they have genuine respect for all that their students are able to accomplish, cooperating teachers are sometimes reluctant to be flatly critical, even if it is apparent that the student is objective and anxious for help. Learn to listen for and to think carefully about suggestions voiced casually in the course of discussions. "I wonder if we are challenging that better reading group?" "Don't you think perhaps the play period was a little noisy today?" "Have you watched Sandy when he gives an incorrect answer? Should he be given a little more reassurance?"

It is important to realize that most cooperating teachers have a high regard for their student's recent college work and are genuinely modest about what benefits will come from experience in their classrooms. You will help your cooperating teacher to provide rich experiences for you by reacting enthusiastically and generously to the opportunities extended. After all, one does not go out of one's way to give assistance which the student seemingly does not recognize as valuable. "This is a difficult group," said Miss Jackson. "I think it would help you to have a chance to observe some of the problems rather carefully before you begin." "If you say so," said Mary Smith, "but frankly, I've never learned anything much from observing. I have to try out everything for myself." "Would it be of help if we planned to talk about that over lunch?" asked Miss Gordon. "It certainly would," said Janice Michaelson. "Are you sure you have time?"

You should remember, too, that there are many justifiable differences in philosophy of education and many effective ways of teaching. If you are to learn from your cooperating teacher, you will need to ask questions, to understand why certain procedures are used and why certain pupils are dealt with as they are. A blind attempt to pattern your work after procedures you do not understand will not help you to grow and often, because you do not know what you are doing, will lead straight to disaster. You must learn, however, to phrase your questions so that you demonstrate respect for what your cooperating teacher is trying to do. Many a student teacher has cut himself off from further help by seeming to have little or no insight or by seeming to be downright critical.

You can do much to make your presence in the classroom a pleasure by being sensitive to the little things that make it easier for two people to live and work together. Basically, it is your cooperating teacher's room. Be sensitive to, and maintain, his standards of housekeeping.

Unless you have permission, think twice before taking your cooperating teacher's texts or going into the drawers of his desk. With some cooperating teachers the books and equipment will be shared as common property, but with others the student will be expected to use books and a desk assigned to him. Think twice (in fact, think several times) before reading notes from parents or other confidential materials left on your cooperating teacher's desk unless you are invited to do so. Be thoughtful, also, about joining in conversations, unless you are invited, if parents or other teachers come by. There may be problems which it is better that you do not hear discussed. It can be embarrassing to all concerned to have to explain this to you. Be sensitive, also, to points at which you can be of extra help—errands you might run, papers you might grade, records you could complete. Because he knows of your heavy college load, your cooperating teacher may not always ask you to take on extra tasks, yet these can often provide valuable learning experiences for you. Furthermore, your willingness to go beyond the line of duty can add much to your reputation as a professional person.

It would be unrealistic, of course, not to point out that some student teachers will find themselves with cooperating teachers whose procedures are quite dissimilar to those just described. Many factors are involved in the assignment of student teachers. It could be that you and your cooperating teacher are both, to some degree, victims of an administrative policy in which students are assigned without regard for the preferences or other responsibilities of the teachers with whom they are placed. If this is the case you as well as your cooperating teacher are facing a particularly difficult adjustment problem. Rebelling against the situation will not help. Do your best to fit in and to learn as much as you can within the limitations of the situation in which you find yourself. In making this adjustment, your college supervisor can often be of considerable help. Seek his advice.

Assist your college supervisor in working effectively in your situation. Provisions for the supervision of student teachers differ from one teacher-education institution to another. You may have rather brief and infrequent visits from your college supervisor or he may be easily available for help. Even under the most favorable circumstances, however, he still will not know all the details of your situation and the day-by-day problems you are facing. If he is to be of maximum assistance to you, you must assume definite responsibilities in acquainting him with your work.

You have a major obligation to help your college supervisor to understand the policies and the ways of working which are unique to your classroom. Students are sometimes reluctant to do this. They recognize that the procedures which seem to fit best in their particular situations are not always those that were discussed favorably in their college classes. Yet out of a sense of professional loyalty they feel that they must not say anything to a supervisor which would in any way seem critical of their cooperating teachers. Then, when the supervisor arrives for a visit, they find themselves the prey of conflicting emotions—feeling an obligation to carry out plans approved by the cooperating teacher, but fearful lest the college supervisor not approve. Actually, the theme of most of your college classes has been that methods are effective only when they meet the demands of the particular situation. Your college supervisor will not be appraising you on some arbitrary scale that takes no account of the situation in which you are working. He will want to know how effectively you can operate under the circumstances in which you find yourself.

It follows from what has just been said that student teachers who meet together in college seminars must be tolerant, understanding, and careful in making comparisons among different kinds of teaching situations. Sally Johnson's slow fourth-graders are obviously not going to produce the creative writing that Jane Anderson's able youngsters will do. Betty Smith's first-graders, most of whom are very immature, are not going to be reading at the level achieved by Wanda Raleigh's advanced group. John Ames will not be likely to achieve the same quality of group work from his fifth-graders, who have had few experiences of this sort, as Sam Ellis, whose youngsters have grown up in the group work tradition. Jeannette Barnes, whose cooperating teacher believes in considerable observation at the start, may not seem to be taking over the class as rapidly as her roommate whose cooperating teacher tends to turn over the reins early and assist from the side lines. You must trust your college supervisor to understand such differences and to appraise your work in the light of the situation you face, not that which is faced by your friends.

Obviously, the same attitude toward criticism which will make it easy for your cooperating teacher to aid you will also facilitate the work of your supervisor. If he is to be helpful, he should see your trouble spots as well as the work you do best. You may wish to use his visit as an opportunity to teach your hospitality committee how to greet a stranger, but you would not, of course, warn your entire class that your reputation hangs on their good behavior. Unless some special circumstances warrant it, you would not make an emergency adjustment in your normal schedule in order to do something you think will be more interesting to your supervisor. As a matter of fact, such adjustments quite often prove very disturbing to the children and result in a much less effective day than would have developed had the regular schedule been followed. Accustom yourself, too, to the idea that no day will go completely to your satisfaction. Because your college supervisor visits infrequently, you will probably be more conscious of his presence than you will that of your cooperating teacher. Every dropped pencil will land with the thud of a crowbar. Minor infractions of rules will suddenly loom as potential discipline problems. Remember, however, that your supervisor knows children, too. The most telling demonstration of your strength as a teacher often comes in the poise and insight with which you handle an unforeseen emergency.

Depending upon his own previous experiences with supervisors, your cooperating teacher may also be understandably concerned about your supervisor's visit and anxious for you to be at your best. The student teacher is often in the most effective position to help his cooperating teacher and his supervisor work together for his own interests. It is important that you relay promptly any information pertaining to the student-teaching program. You can also make a welcome contribution to your cooperating teacher's professional growth by sharing bibliographies, teaching aids, and other appropriate materials provided in your college classes. If your college supervisor has made a special plea that the regular classroom program not be adjusted because of his visits or that he be asked to cancel his plans to visit if the time he has chosen is inconvenient, you should be the one to reassure your cooperating teacher on this point. It is important, also, to share with your cooperating teacher the gist of any conferences with your supervisor. If your supervisor has been present on a rugged day, resist very carefully the temptation to report your conference with him in terms that bolster your own ego by shifting the responsibility to your cooperating teacher or by implying that your supervisor is hopelessly unfeeling. ("Well, Dr. Jones certainly didn't think much of *our* plans for that social studies unit," or, "I'm *so* discouraged. He never seems to like *a thing* I do.") You should expect, also, that your cooperating teacher and your supervisor will at times want to confer regarding your work. Do not become overanxious if they step out of the classroom to talk. One or the other will bring you up to date later. In all probability, your supervisor will try to arrange some three-way conferences to include you and your cooperating teacher. These provide excellent opportunities to clarify plans for your further growth. Do not hesitate to raise questions that concern you at these times. Above all, be sensitive to your cues. "Don't you think," said Josephine Wand's college supervisor, "that Mrs. McCrea could be more helpful to you if you would give her more detailed plans as she has requested?" "No," said Josephine, "I don't think that would help at all."

You have a professional obligation, also, to share with your college supervisor problems in your personal and professional relationships with your cooperating teacher that present real difficulty to you. It is not unusual for two persons who are sharing responsibilities for the first time to misunderstand each other. It is not unusual, either, for a student teacher to have difficulty understanding the reasons behind the procedures in the new classroom to which he must adapt himself. You may have some hesitancy in raising questions regarding personal and professional relationships between yourself and your cooperating teacher. Your college supervisor, however, is the proper person with whom to discuss such problems. It is not wholesome to worry about them alone until they develop out of all true proportions, nor is it professional to air them to casual friends.

Be an effective representative of your college. As a representative of your teacher-education institution, you stand in a unique position to promote or impair school-college relationships. When the student-teaching program is cooperatively developed between a college and a public school system, the professional manner in which the student teachers conduct themselves as members of the school faculty is often the deciding factor in keeping the door open for successive groups of students. Much will depend, of course, on the contribution you make to the lives of pupils and the effectiveness with which you work with your cooperating teacher, but there are other things to keep in mind.

If yours is not a full-time teaching assignment, you should make every effort to arrange a college schedule that will allow ample time to meet your student-teaching responsibilities. Sometimes this may mean applying for a scholarship or a loan in order to reduce the hours given to a part-time job. Often one extra class or the chairmanship of one more committee makes the difference between being able to undertake the full round of professional opportunities offered to you in student teaching and having to slight aspects of your work, to plan sketchily, and to be unable to do anything over and above your specific assignment. Student teaching is not just another course. It is the culmination of your pre-service preparation.

It is important that you learn to divorce your professional life from your personal life. You will have as colleagues individuals who have learned to manage homes and families and to handle personal problems without allowing these to influence negatively their work with boys and girls. Requests for an afternoon off because one is chairman of a sorority tea or for a long weekend because of the senior prom in a neighboring college will not reflect to your credit. Neither will the off-again, on-again romance that has a student dripping sweetness one day and snapping at children the next. Certainly, in the case of a genuine emergency, those who work with you will be anxious to help. If you are uncertain of the professional move in such cases your college supervisor or your college advisor should probably be consulted before anything is said at school.

Be meticulously careful, also, about abiding by the regulations which govern the activities of all teachers in your building. Your principal and the other members of the school faculty are not thinking of you as a student. They are appraising you as a professional person. They will have no assurance regarding how responsible a staff member you will be if your behavior during student teaching does not give evidence of it.

Last, but by no means of least significance, interpret your college work professionally. You will come to your student-teaching assignment after three years or more as a college student. It will be unusual, indeed, if you have not, in all this time, engaged in some "gripe" sessions. Yet, from your vantage point now, as someone who has had classroom experience, you will realize that the best of teachers have some dull days and that a good teacher continually appraises his work and seeks to improve. You will realize also that on all faculties—school and college alike—there will be wide differences in teaching methods and in the types of contributions made by individuals to the lives of children and youth. Few of your college experiences were black or white, marvelous or terrible; most had strong points as well as points at which your particular needs were not met. It is a mark of maturity on your part to recognize that this is so. You can do your professional reputation a grave disservice by sweeping and thoughtless comments regarding your training.

MAINTAINING A PROFESSIONAL ATTITUDE ON THE JOB

Being a member of a school faculty, whether as a beginning teacher or as a student teacher, is a very exciting business. Around the lunch table, in the office, and in the halls you will be involved in the give-and-take of faculty discussions—arguments about teaching procedures, concerns about recent requests from the principal, comments on the adequacy of supplies and equipment. In your classroom there will be thirty to forty youngsters whose records reveal fascinating information—good grades and poor ones, high IQ's and low, confidential reports from psychologists or home visitors. As you become acquainted with parents you will pick up hints of broken homes, of overprotection, of neglect, of anxiety to have children succeed. Among your acquaintances and friends there will be some who treat you as an authority on schools and schooling—critics and friends of modern education anxious to involve you in discussions and folks who are just curious about what's happening in the local situation. What is the professional attitude toward the information you are acquiring?

Be discreet in discussing school affairs. One of the distinctive characteristics of any occupational group that has attained the right to be called a profession is the reluctance of its members to discuss the professional problems of the group with outsiders. One of the first things you must learn if you are to be professional about your work is to be discreet in discussing school affairs.

You will unquestionably hear your colleagues disagree with each other and you will hear criticisms of existing school policies. This is often a sign of a healthy professional climate in a school. Genuine cooperation is not possible unless the individuals who are working together feel quite free to express their points of view. Teachers can often disagree on major issues and still have the greatest respect for each other. Often, too, a teacher will support a new administrative policy wholeheartedly, even though he states quite frankly that it adds a major complication to his already crowded day. Better ways of working are eventually developed in schools where individual concerns and differences of opinion are aired freely. These concerns and differences should not, however, be discussed with persons who are not fully acquainted with the total setting in which the problem arose.

You will probably attend faculty meetings in which proposed changes in school policy are being discussed—a new system of reporting to parents, a possible redistricting that would send children on a certain street to another school, an experimental reorganization of classes in order to focus on the needs of the talented pupil. There are established channels for conveying such information to the public at the point at which lay persons need to be involved. Unnecessary anxiety on the part of parents and others can often be aroused if such proposals are discussed prematurely.

Teachers are human beings. They have their bad days and their good, their moments of discouragement and their times of elation. These feelings are likely to show once in a while. It is indeed a very mature and poised person who, over the year, never speaks critically of a school policy, exaggerates his feelings about a child, or expresses general weariness regarding the entire profession. Your ability to refrain from repeating such comments in gossip sessions is a mark of your professional attitude toward your colleagues and of your own understanding of people.

By the same token, you should think carefully about what you say about your own work and to whom you say it. Oscar Wilson regaled his church youth group with tales of his two "problem children." With his flair for the dramatic, Oscar told some very good stories, indeed—so good that he convinced two of the school board members that his discipline left much to be desired. Sandra Cain made a habit at the faculty lunch table of calculating how many hours of student teaching were left. Sandra's unfortunate bid for attention from her colleagues was taken to mean that she had few deep professional interests. When you cannot speak enthusiastically about your work, it is well to choose your listeners carefully if you speak at all.

You may occasionally find yourself in situations where you feel you have cause to be genuinely concerned about the quality of the work of one of your colleagues. Your pupils come back from a session with a special teacher complaining about an assignment or fussing because they were asked to start over and go through the halls more quietly. The rising tide of confusion from the classroom across the way suggests that the beginning teacher at work there is still struggling with techniques of good classroom control. What do you do in such situations? In dealing with critical comments and unfortunate comparisons from pupils, remember that there are many effective ways of teaching and that different persons can have different values and standards and yet achieve effective results. A teacher has an obligation to help his pupils realize this and to help them evaluate their own behavior in the light of the situation that confronts them. No professional teacher joins sympathetically in the discussion in such a way as to destroy the status of a colleague in pupils' eyes. If the situation is one about which a teacher feels strongly that something should be done, the professional move is to talk with the person designated to handle such problems—

the principal or, in some cases, the supervisor. As a student teacher, of course, you would rarely be the person to take such a step except possibly when you find yourself sharing responsibilities with a substitute teacher whose procedures seem unusually disturbing to the children. Certainly, criticisms of a colleague which one would hesitate to make in the privacy of the principal's office should never be expressed in casual conversation with other faculty members.

Hold information about pupils strictly confidential. To work intelligently with pupils, you must know them well. This means that you must have access to cumulative records with all the special information about home and family problems that such sources of data contain. This entails the responsibility of handling such records carefully and of keeping the information they contain strictly confidential.

Day-by-day events in your classroom result in other kinds of information regarding pupils which should be treated professionally. Entertaining your colleagues at lunch with Willie's latest exploit may make Willie's life still more difficult by giving others who work with him a false impression. Talking about a youngster's reading problem in a bus or corner drugstore can arouse many family anxieties if you are overheard by an aunt or a grandmother. If you feel the need of special help in handling a youngster with a difficult problem, it is far wiser to turn to the persons designated to give such help and to protect the child's reputation in the eyes of others.

Parent contacts will pose other problems of professional ethics.[5] Certainly, you would ascertain school policy and think carefully before you revealed exact scores on intelligence or achievement tests. You would be most hesitant to show a parent all the grades in your grade book. You would be careful, also, not to refer to the achievement of a neighbor's child for the purpose of comparison or to attempt to answer questions regarding the work of another teacher. Obviously, too, home and family problems revealed to you by parents should be treated in strictest confidence.

Occasionally teachers find it desirable to use their work with an individual pupil as the basis of a case study for a college class. Student teachers, particularly, may find themselves eying eagerly the wealth of data available to them. There are ethical steps to follow in using such data. Permission should always be sought from responsible authorities, and every effort should be made to disguise not only the pupil, but

[5] This is so important an aspect of teaching that a section in Chapter 11, pages 456-464, is devoted to it.

the school as well. There is always a risk that such papers will be mislaid or will be read by persons who do not treat them as confidential. You have a professional responsibility to make sure that the information they contain cannot be identified and reflect negatively upon a pupil, his parents, or his teachers.

Your professional treatment of information about pupils should extend to the total population in the school. Overgeneralized statements regarding your pupils indicate your own insensitivity to individual differences and often convey an unfortunate impression to those who do not know the situation. ("Our dear little raggedy tykes. They're *so* slow.") Sometimes, in a well-meant effort to praise a new situation, a student teacher makes statements that are derogatory regarding previous experiences. ("This is much more relaxing than Pine Dell School. Everything there was *so formal.*") Sometimes, too, a student teacher who speaks ethically about his own experiences misquotes his friends glibly. ("I'm so glad I was placed here instead of in Rose Hill. From what my friends say, they have *terrible* discipline problems with those children.") Such sweeping generalizations reflect professional credit on neither the originator nor the person who relays them.

Interpret your profession ethically. Teaching is an honorable profession, but you may get an entirely different impression if you listen to some teachers apologize because they are teachers. ("And what do you do?" "Oh, I'm *just* a classroom teacher.") A few try to conceal their profession completely, perhaps because of stereotyped memories of their own classroom days. ("I bought some shoes with comfortable heels, but I do hope they won't make me look like a teacher.") Certainly if teachers themselves do not speak proudly of their profession they can scarcely expect others to do so.

In your day-by-day contacts with friends and casual acquaintances you will face many situations which will tax your judgment regarding how to interpret your profession. The most difficult of these are likely to be occasions in which well-meaning acquaintances try to involve you in discussions about the profession in general. "When are you people going to teach some phonetics again?" asks the father of a friend. "Judging by my secretaries, the spelling in our schools has grown steadily worse." "I've been wondering," says Jean's mother, "what you do in *your* school about group work; it seems to me that Jean wastes far too much time on this sort of thing." "What do you think about that article describing the teacher who turned everything she taught into a game?" asks an acquaintance at the dinner table. It is easy to talk professionally and enthusiastically about your own work, but how do you handle questions such as these?

You will recognize, of course, that the statements just cited may represent a bias on the part of the speaker that will not easily be changed regardless of the arguments you advance. Teaching, just as any other profession, has its prejudiced as well as its thoughtful critics. Sometimes it is best to pass over critical questions as briefly and as tactfully as you can.

There will be times, however, when you will be drawn into discussions you cannot avoid. You have an obligation to prepare yourself to offer the professional explanation where such exists. There is, for example, a sound theoretical answer to the phonetics question. If you are not sure what the explanation is, you have an obligation to say so. Many times a speaker helps to substantiate a criticism by vaguely seeming to agree or by being so concerned about justifying the teachers in his own school that he unwittingly destroys the reputations of others. "Well, I suppose there are many places that don't teach phonetics, *but of course in our school. . . .*"

You have a professional obligation, also, to refrain from commenting on a specific situation about which you know nothing. When Jean's mother asks about group work she offers the listener a tempting opportunity to demonstrate what he knows about good teaching. This can be done, however, only at the expense of the professional reputation of a teacher whom Jean's mother may have badly misinterpreted.

You should *not* feel compelled to defend procedures that seem obviously to be examples of poor teaching. One probably would have to visit the classroom of the teacher who "turned everything she taught into a game" to be sure that this was not the version of a reporter who chose to dramatize a small part of the total program. One would be justified, however, on the basis of such a newspaper article to say, "This probably is not a fair picture. But if it were, it would not represent good educational practice." Vaguely supporting comments, such as "Oh, pupils learn so much faster when they are interested," do not help to build respect for the soundness of the speaker's professional training.

Every profession grows through research and the testing of new ideas. Every profession has some of its hypotheses disproved when all the evidence is in. Every profession revises its basic theories in the light of new evidence. Every profession has its inadequate practitioners. And every profession has its critics—just and helpful or unjust and destructive. We have many problems to solve but we have accomplished much. Speak proudly and intelligently of these achievements. Identify problems and research frontiers where we do not have all the answers just as proudly and intelligently.

Give serious thought to the codes of ethics by which your colleagues abide. The problem of what it means for a teacher to be ethical in all aspects of his professional relationships is one that concerns every member of the profession. You have been reading illustrations of the types of situations calling for ethical behavior faced by teachers in the normal course of their daily work. Now, read thoughtfully the code of ethics adopted by the National Education Association as a guide to every aspect of a teacher's professional life.[6]

CODE OF ETHICS

WE, THE MEMBERS of the National Education Association of the United States, hold these truths to be self-evident

—That the primary purpose of education in the United States is to develop citizens who will safeguard, strengthen, and improve the democracy obtained thru a representative government;
—That the achievement of effective democracy in all aspects of American life and the maintenance of our national ideals depend upon making acceptable educational opportunities available to all;
—That the quality of education reflects the ideals, motives, preparation, and conduct of the members of the teaching profession;
—That whoever chooses teaching as a career assumes the obligation to conduct himself in accordance with the ideals of the profession.

As a guide for the teaching profession, the members of the National Education Association have adopted this code of professional ethics. Since all teachers should be members of a united profession, the basic principles herein enumerated apply to all persons engaged in the professional aspects of education—elementary, secondary, and collegiate.

FIRST PRINCIPLE: *The primary obligation of the teaching profession is to guide children, youth, and adults in the pursuit of knowledge and skills, to prepare them in the ways of democracy, and to help them to become happy, useful, self-supporting citizens. The ultimate strength of the nation lies in the social responsibility, economic competence, and moral strength of the individual American.*

[6] *Code of Ethics of the National Education Association of the United States,* adopted by the Representative Assembly, Detroit, Michigan, 1952. Washington, D.C.: The Association. Quoted by permission.

In fulfilling the obligations of this first principle the teacher will—

1. Deal justly and impartially with students regardless of their physical, mental, emotional, political, economic, social, racial, or religious characteristics.
2. Recognize the differences among students and seek to meet their individual needs.
3. Encourage students to formulate and work for high individual goals in the development of their physical, intellectual, creative, and spiritual endowments.
4. Aid students to develop an understanding and appreciation not only of the opportunities and benefits of American democracy but also of their obligations to it.
5. Respect the right of every student to have confidential information about himself withheld except when its release is to authorized agencies or is required by law.
6. Accept no remuneration for tutoring except in accordance with approved policies of the governing board.

SECOND PRINCIPLE: *The members of the teaching profession share with parents the task of shaping each student's purposes and acts toward socially acceptable ends. The effectiveness of many methods of teaching is dependent upon cooperative relationships with the home.*

In fulfilling the obligations of this second principle the teacher will—

1. Respect the basic responsibility of parents for their children.
2. Seek to establish friendly and cooperative relationships with the home.
3. Help to increase the student's confidence in his own home and avoid disparaging remarks which might undermine that confidence.
4. Provide parents with information that will serve the best interests of their children, and be discreet with information received from parents.
5. Keep parents informed about the progress of their children as interpreted in terms of the purposes of the school.

THIRD PRINCIPLE: *The teaching profession occupies a position of public trust involving not only the individual teacher's personal conduct, but also the interaction of the school and the community. Education is most effective when these many relationships operate in a friendly, cooperative, and constructive manner.*

In fulfilling the obligations of this third principle the teacher will—

1. Adhere to any reasonable pattern of behavior accepted by the community for professional persons.
2. Perform the duties of citizenship, and participate in community activities with due consideration for his obligations to his students, his family, and himself.

3. Discuss controversial issues from an objective point of view, thereby keeping his class free from partisan opinions.
4. Recognize that the public schools belong to the people of the community, encourage lay participation in shaping the purposes of the school, and strive to keep the public informed of the educational program which is being provided.
5. Respect the community in which he is employed and be loyal to the school system, community, state, and nation.
6. Work to improve education in the community and to strengthen the community's moral, spiritual, and intellectual life.

FOURTH PRINCIPLE: *The members of the teaching profession have inescapable obligations with respect to employment. These obligations are nearly always shared employer-employee responsibilities based upon mutual respect and good faith.*

In fulfilling the obligations of this fourth principle the teacher will—

1. Conduct professional business thru the proper channels.
2. Refrain from discussing confidential and official information with unauthorized persons.
3. Apply for employment on the basis of competence only, and avoid asking for a specific position known to be filled by another teacher.
4. Seek employment in a professional manner, avoiding such practices as the indiscriminate distribution of applications.
5. Refuse to accept a position when the vacancy has been created through unprofessional activity or pending controversy over professional policy or the application of unjust personnel practices and procedures.
6. Adhere to the conditions of a contract until service thereunder has been performed, the contract has been terminated by mutual consent, or the contract has otherwise been legally terminated.
7. Give and expect due notice before a change of position is to be made.
8. Be fair in all recommendations that are given concerning the work of other teachers.
9. Accept no compensation from producers of instructional supplies when one's recommendations affect the local purchase or use of such teaching aids.
10. Engage in no gainful employment, outside of his contract, where the employment affects adversely his professional status or impairs his standing with students, associates, and the community.
11. Cooperate in the development of school policies and assume one's professional obligations thereby incurred.
12. Accept one's obligation to the employing board for maintaining a professional level of service.

FIFTH PRINCIPLE: *The teaching profession is distinguished from many other occupations by the uniqueness and quality of the professional relationships among all teachers. Community support and respect are influenced by the standards of teachers and their attitudes toward teaching and other teachers.*

In fulfilling the obligations of this fifth principle the teacher will—

1. Deal with other members of the profession in the same manner as he himself wishes to be treated.
2. Stand by other teachers who have acted on his behalf and at his request.
3. Speak constructively of other teachers, but report honestly to responsible persons in matters involving the welfare of students, the school system, and the profession.
4. Maintain active membership in professional organizations and, thru participation, strive to attain the objectives that justify such organized groups.
5. Seek to make professional growth continuous by such procedures as study, research, travel, conferences, and attendance at professional meetings.
6. Make the teaching profession so attractive in ideals and practices that sincere and able young people will want to enter it.

This is the statement of the professional organization to which a majority of the teachers in this country belong. It is the code of ethics by which your colleagues live and which they are pledged to support actively when cases of unethical behavior come to their attention. You have an obligation to accept and support this code—or one similar, proposed in your state—when you become a member of the teaching profession.

BOOKS YOU SHOULD KNOW

Eye, Glen G., and Lane, Willard R. *The New Teacher Comes to School.* New York: Harper & Brothers, 1956. Pp. xii + 376.

Staff Relations in School Administration. Thirty-third Yearbook of the American Association of School Administrators, N.E.A. Washington, D.C.: The Association, 1955. Pp. 242.

Whitelaw, J.B. *The School and Its Community.* Second Edition. Baltimore: Johns Hopkins Press, 1951. Pp. 96.

Yauch, Wilbur A. *Helping Teachers Understand Principals.* New York: Appleton-Century-Crofts, 1957. Pp. xii + 98.

Getting to Know Your Pupils

CHAPTER 4

A parent asks, "Why should Susan be doing so poorly in school? Kathy is a year and a half younger, and she reads better and seems to enjoy school so much more." What would you tell this mother who is disturbed by the fact that her daughters are so unlike?

Ralph has no difficulty analyzing three-syllable words for himself in reading, but in his spelling he mixes up the letters so badly that it is almost impossible to guess what he means. How could a student have difficulty with one phase of work in a subject and find a related phase so easy?

Sixth-grade Sally has come to school several times wearing lipstick. Whenever she gets a chance, she combs her hair. How early should one expect adolescent preoccupation with personal appearance to develop?

"He's a dope! Do we *have* to have him on our team?" Upon what bases do intermediate-graders accept or reject one another?

"It made such a difference to see Ronald's home. I can understand so much better now why he seems so listless in school, and I believe I've discovered at least one interest that might challenge him." How important is it for a teacher to make home visits?

"I'm always amazed to see the help I get if I involve my pupils in planning. Inevitably I uncover interests I did not suspect, and today they revealed an appalling lack of background. It didn't occur to me that their travels within the city would be so limited." Does your experience with pupils justify this faith in pupil-teacher planning?

These illustrations point to one of the fundamental concerns of classroom teachers today. How does one get to know about the pupils he is to teach? No matter how well informed you are in academic fields, or how good your theoretical command of psychological and sociological principles, your classroom efforts are not likely to be completely successful if you are insensitive to the needs, strengths, weaknesses, and experience backgrounds of your pupils.

The first few weeks in the classroom are very important in setting the stage for the year's work with a group of boys and girls. This is the time to begin to acquire the information about pupils which is essential background for effective teaching. When you are in charge of your own classroom, you will have to collect much of this information as you teach, but as a student teacher you are likely to be given early opportunities to observe your class without interruption. This chapter aims to help you decide what to look for, how to study your pupils in action, how to interpret available records, and how to get acquainted with the community.

WHAT SHOULD YOU LOOK FOR?

In spite of their previous work in psychology, beginning teachers do not always realize what information about their pupils is likely to be of most use until they actually begin to work with them. Your first temptation probably will be to classify your group in general terms. "They're sweet"; "they're noisy"; "they're bright"; "they're slow"; "they're cute." You will need to look more sharply than this at individuals and at specific aspects of behavior if the information you collect is to be of help to you.

What should you look for, particularly, as you try to get acquainted with your pupils? It is an easy generalization to say that you should study the "whole child," but this is too vague to be of much help. Furthermore, you are not going to have the time or facilities to make the detailed study of each pupil that will reveal the complicated interrelationships among intellectual, physical, social, and emotional aspects of growth that we refer to when we talk about the growth and development of the "whole child." Few teachers ever do. These, however, are the aspects of development that experienced teachers keep in mind as they study their classes. They look at physical and intellectual traits; but they also look at individual needs and experience backgrounds, at the dynamics of social relationships in the classroom, at their pupils' own concepts of themselves, and in so far as they can, at how these are interrelated in the development of individual pupils.

Survey intellectual skills. As you listen to faculty lunchroom conversations, you will hear comments that suggest that teachers tend early in the year to size up the intelligence levels of their classes—"I have the 'low' fourth grade this year." "There is an unusual range of ability in my class." "I have a very cooperative bunch, but they certainly aren't brilliant." It is only natural for teachers to be concerned about the intelligence of the pupils in their classes since they do have the job of guiding their learning experiences. Actually, however, labeling an entire class as "bright" or "average" or "dull" will not help very much in your teaching. What should concern you more is the significant behavior that suggests how each pupil's intelligence is functioning and how to adjust your teaching methods to give each individual precisely the help he needs.

Certainly, through your observations early in the year, you will identify those youngsters who seem to learn quickly and those who seem to have more than ordinary difficulty when faced with intellectual tasks. These rough discriminations will give some guidance as to how to think about adjusting your teaching procedures. You should soon, however, begin to supplement your general impressions with a more careful look at specific aspects of intellectual growth. Pupils who display unusual facility with language do not always show the same aptitude with number and spatial relationships, and vice versa. Whether such differences represent truly discrete factors of intelligence or are the result of environmental influences, they are realities to be reckoned with as you plan your teaching. Sue may read well, make thoughtful and well-stated contributions in a social studies discussion, and write charming poems, but the world of numbers may be a complete mystery to her. Randy may have developed a number system with base twelve just for the fun of it, yet he may panic utterly when asked to write three logically connected sentences. Such examples are extreme, but they do exist. You will not help either child if you overlook the possibility that these may be genuine deficiencies or say to either one's mother "Any youngster this able has no excuse for having any trouble if he will just put his mind to his work."

You will want to survey your pupils' academic progress in specific skill areas. Their scores on a reading comprehension test may easily show a range of three or four years. So may their scores on tests of arithmetic achievement, spelling, or any other area you choose to mention. This will be true even of pupils with similar intelligence quotients. Furthermore, even within a single skill area an individual may display uneven development. This fact is often forgotten as the beginning teacher plans his work for and with children. In the opening paragraph of this chapter you read about Ralph who was experiencing difficulty in spelling even though he could read fluently. Ralph is going to have a hard time overcoming his spelling problem if you call him lazy or careless because you know how well he handles words when he reads. There may also be situations where your best calculator cannot solve arithmetic problems or where the youngster who speaks fluently is hopelessly inadequate when he is asked to put his thoughts on paper. You will not be able to identify all such patterns of strengths and weaknesses in the first few weeks of teaching, but this it not too soon to begin to train yourself to take a careful diagnostic look at individual performances.

There are other aspects of intellectual growth that your observations may help you to identify. Typically, intellectual maturity results in increased capacity for sustained attention, although other factors—physical, emotional, and the nature of the task itself—are also involved. It will be of value both in teaching and in achieving effective interpersonal relationships in your classroom to be aware of the typical span of attention, how it varies with the tasks at hand, and what the differences among individuals seem to be. With intellectual maturity there should come more accurate concepts, a more realistic awareness of cause-and-effect relationships, greater ability to cope with the remote in time and space, although these aspects of growth are conditioned by experience backgrounds, interests, and degree of motivation. The more you can learn of the level of reasoning of which your pupils are capable, the more effective your teaching will be.

As a student teacher, you would do well not only to attempt to assess the intellectual abilities in your group, but also to study the ways in which your cooperating teacher goes about meeting individual needs. What are the bases for establishing smaller groups for special help in the skill areas? How are provisions made for individuals who are having unusual difficulties? During independent work periods, what kind of help is given to individuals, and how does it seem to be related to their needs? How does the classroom schedule seem to reflect attention spans, and what are the typical adjustments if pupils grow restless before the period is up or are still working intently when it is time to stop? How is the introduction of a new topic managed so that the pupils' experience backgrounds and present levels of thinking are revealed? What adjustments are made if concepts are inaccurate and experience background meager?

No teacher finds it easy to adapt instruction to individual differences. However, the more you know about the individuals in your class, the easier it will be for you to plan a realistic program for them. If you know your pupils, you will not make the mistake of treating all youngsters with high IQ's as good readers or good achievers in arithmetic, nor will you assume that they all have good work habits. Neither will you waste your breath trying to hold the attention of your class long after you have lost your audience or plunge into a new lesson blissfully unaware of your pupils' dearth of background experiences.

Assess the ways in which your pupils are facing developmental tasks and seeking to satisfy basic needs. Knowing a pupil's mental age and IQ does not tell you what he is ready to learn. Human beings are dynamic, goal-seeking organisms. Your boys and girls will come to your classroom with needs and purposes of their own—needs and purposes stemming from their general levels of maturity as well as their particular backgrounds of experience. If the learning activities you provide are to be effective and the interpersonal relationships you develop are to be sound, you must become sensitive to the goals your pupils, themselves, are seeking.

Of all the analyses of changes in behavior with maturity, those concerned with *developmental tasks* may be among the most valuable to you in developing insights into the behavior of your pupils. Lists of developmental tasks are the result of psychologists' efforts to identify those major growth achievements which a youngster's own stage of development sets for him as he learns to live in our modern society. They suggest some of the techniques for getting along with people and the values, attitudes, and skills pupils must achieve at their present stage of maturity if they are to live effectively in their world. One of the best known of such lists proposes the following as the developmental tasks of middle childhood:[1] learning physical skills necessary for ordinary games; building wholesome attitudes toward oneself as a growing organism; learning to get along with one's age mates; learning an appropriate masculine or feminine social role; developing fundamental skills in reading, writing, and calculating; developing concepts necessary for everyday living; developing conscience, morality, and a scale of values; achieving personal independence; and developing attitudes toward social groups and institutions.

How can such a list help you in getting to know your pupils? It will suggest many insights as you think about your boys and girls in the light of it. Ten-year-old Jimmy puts in long hours pitching and catching

[1] Robert J. Havighurst, *Human Development and Education,* pp. 25-41. New York: Longmans, Green and Co., 1953.

a baseball. You can hardly persuade him to put it down when school begins. His preoccupation will be more understandable (although you will still pry him loose from his ball and glove during school hours) if you realize that in one form or another all boys and girls in middle childhood face the task of learning the physical skills necessary for ordinary games and that in our country, for boys, this probably includes baseball. In first grade, John flatly refuses your help in buttoning his overshoes, insisting that he can do it by himself. His behavior may be less trying to your patience if you recognize it as one of many steps along the road to achieving personal independence—another developmental task of middle childhood. Jerry, on the other hand, is at your side constantly for help. With this same developmental task in mind, you may become concerned about this immaturity and plan how to help him take a next step toward more mature behavior.

"Middle childhood," the focus of the list of developmental tasks just cited, represents a wide age span. Even a little more maturity can make a difference in a pupil's behavior. This is important to remember, particularly if your previous experiences have been with another age group. A seven-year-old boy may willingly read the part of the mother in a class dramatization, but Steve, who is eleven and in the fifth grade, may balk at the suggestion—and rightly so. Steve has developed new insights into an appropriate masculine role. In first grade, boys may work willingly with girls. By fifth grade, objections may be voiced to having anything to do with "those silly girls," although if you watch closely you will observe some nudging, teasing, and jostling that indicates that adolescence is not far off. These are not changes that take place in neat steps on each birthday. They come about gradually and not necessarily at an even rate in any one individual. You will need to identify what the unique pattern is for each of your pupils.

You will also want to become sensitive to the ways in which your pupils are seeking to satisfy *basic psychological needs.* Depending upon the particular texts you may have read, you will identify these needs in such terms as *security* or *affection* in relationships to other individuals; *status* or *belonging* in a group; *independence, achievement,* or *self-respect* in one's concept of oneself. These are needs that each of us, at his own maturity level, strives to satisfy.

As you study your class you will soon discover that the ways in which individual pupils of the same age seek satisfactions for their basic needs can be extremely varied. You must use as much, if not more, caution in categorizing the motives for an individual's behavior as you would in classifying his intellectual ability. Billy's hand is always in the air; so is Ray's. Both are likely to respond with a wisecrack if you call on them. "They are just bidding for attention," you say. But is it that simple? As you watch the two boys in other situations you realize that Billy is always at your side. You seem to be his main source of status, recognition, and affection. On the other hand, Ray seldom seems to want your individual attention. Typically he is with his pals, sometimes annoying them but for the most part the center of an admiring group. Certainly, these two youngsters will need very different treatment if they are to be helped.

As you collect evidence about individuals, you will find, also, that some have many resources for satisfying their needs whereas others seem to have only one or two techniques, and sometimes these are not very constructive. Marcella dissolves in tears when she misses a couple of spelling words. This seems incomprehensible until you study her background. Then you discover that she has been accelerated; that she is small for her age and not mature enough socially to be accepted by her classmates; that her mother tends to praise her lavishly for a good paper and to withdraw her affection when school marks are low. Good grades seem to be Marcella's one sure way to her mother's affection and to status in the class. Ben seems to be in everybody's hair. Groups reject him because he destroys their work; you have to extract him from so many difficulties that you seem always to be scolding; he is known on the playground as a bully. It is hard to understand how one youngster can cause so much unpleasantness until you discover that he has few academic skills through which to secure status in the group or praise from you; he is the youngest child in a family whose members have many social obligations and is rarely noticed in their busy world; in school, you realize with a twinge of conscience, getting into trouble is the only technique that guarantees Ben a place in the spotlight for at least a minute or two. How to help such youngsters find alternative and more satisfying outlets is a major problem.[2]

As a student teacher, it will be important for you to become sensitive to the ways in which your cooperating teacher helps pupils to satisfy basic needs. This is particularly so in the case of youngsters who are facing difficult adjustment problems. Roberta is not going to develop self-reliance very quickly if you succumb to her appeals for help while your cooperating teacher is trying to encourage her to work things out

[2] See Chapter 5, pages 162-170, for a discussion of possible steps to help pupils with emotional problems.

for herself. Neither will Anthony be readily weaned from his clowning bids for attention if he finds in you an appreciative audience after his attempts to get a smile from your cooperating teacher have failed.

Because you literally teach the "whole child," the success of your lessons as well as your relationships with individuals will depend on your growing sensitivity to the causes of behavior. Youngsters who are preoccupied (even though not conscious of it) with meeting needs for status, for affection, for security, may not give their full attention to legitimate classroom activities. Needs for recognition from you, for status in the group, for a feeling of achievement, are powerful motives if they can be harnessed to the work at hand.

Study pupils' experience backgrounds. Depending on where you are placed for your student teaching or for your first full-time teaching assignment, you may have major adjustments to make in understanding pupils' environmental experiences. Children in our schools come from vastly different family, social, and economic backgrounds. A teacher cannot close his eyes to such differences.

One of the greatest threats to your success as a teacher may be your tendency to reject youngsters whose ways of living you do not understand. You may meet language patterns, ways of expressing emotions, values, attitudes toward other people, taboos, very different from those characteristic of your own background. The greater the disparity in social class backgrounds, the more important it will be for you to set yourself the task of learning to know your pupils, their homes, and their community. This is a point at which your principal, the school nurse, the attendance officer or home visitor, can be very helpful to you. What you can read about social classes is often not enough to counteract the stereotypes you may have developed. To understand, you must see the handicaps under which some mothers manage to send their children to school neat and tidy; listen to the aspirations expressed by parents who did not themselves have a chance; face the realities of the home that offers all conceivable economic resources but leaves the child in the care of servants a good share of time.

Your boys and girls may have differing attitudes toward the value of an education. The belief, widely held by teachers, that to be successful in school is the best assurance of success in later life is not always shared by pupils. The child who comes from a home where there is no tradition of education or respect for it cannot be expected to be as highly motivated to learn as the one who comes from a home where schooling is cherished. Attitudes toward education—whether positive or negative—are factors with which you must reckon in your classroom work.

In appraising your pupils' experience backgrounds it can be helpful to inquire about the stability of your community. Have your boys and girls grown up in the community and in the school? or are there a large number of transients? Teachers have particularly difficult problems to face in communities where families have found it necessary to change residences frequently because of shifting industrial demands. Youngsters from these families, report cards in hand, who stream through the principal's office to register are likely to show the effects of inconsistent schooling, regardless of the best efforts of all who have worked with them. A mobile student body is not uncommon in America today. If yours is a class made up largely of transient pupils, you must be prepared to give help with some of the special problems they face.

It is also important for you to know the breadth of the out-of-school experiences which your pupils bring to school. Some will not have traveled more than a few blocks from their homes (except by means of television). Others will have visited many parts of our own country—perhaps even Mexico or Europe. In some homes children will have been encouraged to pursue hobbies, taken on trips to points of historic interest, art galleries, and museums. Still others, perhaps equally favored economically, will have had few such opportunities. The richness or poverty of your pupils' experience backgrounds will help to determine the nature and extent of the firsthand experiences you must provide if you are to be successful in the development of new concepts and generalizations.

As a student teacher you should observe carefully the ways in which your cooperating teacher is adjusting the general requirements in the course of study to the maturity, needs, and experience backgrounds of your class. You may find certain areas—perhaps language skills and reading—stressed more heavily to make up for home and community deficiencies. Excursions, motion pictures, and other visual aids may be used more frequently than you might have expected in order to supplement meager home and community experiences. In other situations the problem may be how best to capitalize on the wealth of experience backgrounds that exist, or how best to adjust the school program in the light of pupils' after-school activities in dancing schools, art classes, recreation centers. It is important to note, also, the ways in which adjustments are made for individual differences in backgrounds and the place that is given to individual hobbies, talents, and interests.

"Start where your pupils are" is a fundamental principle of good teaching.

Seek an understanding of the social interrelationships in the classroom. As you work with a group of pupils, you will discover that the patterns of leadership and friendship which develop in your group are important. You cannot neglect social relationships even though your goal is to teach pupils how to multiply, read, or speak distinctly.

Life with your pupils will be more satisfying and exciting if you sense the cluster of values of the peer group and view these manifestations with the objective eye of the social psychologist. These will not always coincide with your standards of behavior. There will be times when you will wonder if you can stand a blaze of bright pink shirts, a rash of secret notes in code, a series of inane jokes, an outbreak of babbling in artificial languages, an epidemic of nicknames, or a fad for backhand slants in writing. Yet, within reasonable limits, you must see such phenomena for what they are and accept them.

It will be important to identify friendship roles and group-process roles in your class. Friendships may perhaps be the easiest to see, especially if pupils are permitted to sit near their friends or if noon and recess periods allow time for clusters of friends to form. Leadership and other group-process roles will take more study. Youngsters who are the most vocal may be readily identified, but these may not always be the leaders. You should begin to analyze the quality of pupils' comments—to decide which ones make the contributions that move the plan ahead, which plead their own special interests, which argue seemingly for the sake of disagreeing with their friends, which play the follower's role. Such observations will not only alert you to the leadership strengths in your group, but also to the youngsters who are going to need your help.

An understanding of status roles will also be valuable. Leaders will be recognized rather readily. Other types of status roles may be more difficult for you to identify or to understand. Some youngsters will have a hidden link to the group—the first-grader with the pretty curls; the third-grader who owns a baseball; the boy whose mother is a cub-scout leader; the youngster with particular talent in whatever represents the latest peer-group fad. Achieving status in a group is a basic psychological need. As you take over responsibility for your class, it is important to have some preliminary "hunches" as to why your pupils seek status in the ways that they do.

You will also need to sense your roles in the class group. Are you a giver of information? judge? organizer? mother substitute? pal? Many factors will help to determine what your roles will be. Perhaps most important will be your own experiences which have contributed to your concept of the ideal teacher. You will also have roles assigned to you by your pupils out of their previous experiences with teachers and other adults. First-grade Jerry may have been told often by his older brother that teachers will certainly make him mind. Fourth-grade Claire may expect criticism. Susannah may be quite sure teachers will as easily succumb to her teasing as her mother does. The role your cooperating teacher plays will also affect the way your pupils view your leadership. "We knew Mrs. Cross wouldn't let us," said one third-grader candidly, "but we thought you wouldn't be so strict." If you are to be successful, you will not become a carbon copy of your cooperating teacher, or change, chameleon-like, with the expectations of your pupils. You are yourself, and to ring true you must not assume a role you do not fully accept. You do, however, need to take an objective, analytical look at the roles you have assumed. Many beginners are startled to realize just what roles they are playing and why. Some reject these roles as immature and adopt more sensitive ones wholeheartedly when they have taken an impartial look at themselves.

Because you will be sharing the classroom with another person during your student-teaching experience, it is important for you to become sensitive to the ways in which your cooperating teacher is building toward better interpersonal relationships in the classroom. As you watch the group process at work, analyze the leadership of your co-operating teacher as well as the reactions of pupils. What leadership techniques are being used? What devices are employed to help the overly aggressive child? the shy child? the youngster who fails to stick to the point? How is help being provided for the youngster who is clowning? the child who is belittling others? the one using aggressive techniques to achieve group status? How are small groups being helped to develop more effective working relationships? How do these vary from one type of learning situation to another? When you assume responsibility for these boys and girls you will want to be sure that your leadership contributes consistently to their skills and insights in human relationships.

Seek to understand how pupils view themselves. Among the teacher's most baffling problems is that of the pupil who fails to live up to his potentialities. The way you appraise a youngster's talents, strengths, weaknesses, and status in a group may be quite different from the way he views his own capacities and competencies. Yet each individual behaves in terms of his own concept of himself—a concept built through a host of experiences at home, in other classrooms, on playgrounds, in community groups.

It can be particularly helpful to become aware of how individuals view their own capacities to learn. Third-grade Joanne, a very able child intellectually, gives up helplessly whenever she meets an unfamiliar word in her reading. Actually, she has considerable skill in word analysis, but it takes her teacher's supporting presence to encourage her to use it. Sixth-grade Bobby fully expects to write a very poor spelling paper. He, like many pupils who present remedial problems, is quite sure that spelling is a skill he cannot master. Fourth-grade Jerry has been told since he was three years old that he cannot carry a tune. Convincing youngsters like Joanne, Bobby, and Jerry that they are able to learn is an important first step in remedial teaching, and often a very difficult one. On the other hand, you will be surprised and delighted to find in your room children of average or less-than-average intellectual ability who do exceptional work. Across the aisle from Joanne is Maxine, no more able intellectually, but very sure of her reading skills. No matter how hard the job, Maxine is willing to try. Mistakes do not shake this youngster's faith in her own ability. Theresa does not approach Bobby's intellectual capacity, but she has learned through repeated successes that mastering a spelling list is not particularly difficult. Linda does not have exceptional musical ability, but her family has always encouraged her to sing; she does not hesitate when asked to lead the group in a song just learned in music class. Successful achievement involves more than academic aptitude. How the pupil views his own capacities and the faith he has in his own ability to achieve are of definite significance.

You should also be alert to the ways in which pupils themselves view their relationships to their peers. Competent Susan, in fifth grade, prefaces her suggestions (when she can be persuaded to contribute to a group planning session) with "This won't work, but. . . ." When invited to take the chairmanship of the games committee for a class party she refuses to act, saying "Oh! The other kids have better ideas." Here is a potentially able leader who will need to be provided with many successful experiences in working with others before she makes the contribution of which she is capable. Even before he hears why his teacher has asked him to come to the desk, Andy says belligerently, "I didn't do anything; the kids always blame me." Whether or not your observations confirm the fact that Andy is rejected and the scapegoat of the group, this is reality for Andy. If he is to learn to make a more positive contribution to his peers, he must be helped to view himself as someone who is accepted by them. Anne, whom you judge to be one of the most attractive youngsters in the class, begins a paragraph on *Things I Like About Me* with "There aren't many things I like about me. Particularly I don't like the way I look. I am too fat and I wish I had curly hair like Sandy. I wish I had sweaters like the rest of the kids, too." Here are strong feelings of being different from the group. On the other hand, Barby, whose appearance does not impress you particularly and whose clothes are often bedraggled, assumes that people will like her and want to work with her. The effectiveness of your help as your pupils face problems of learning to live and work together will depend on how sensitive you are to the ways they see themselves relating to their peers.

You will often glean valuable cues regarding the next step with the youngster who is having difficulty in conforming to school regulations if you can determine how he sees himself in relation to adults in authority. Joe is overheard bragging, "I've been in the principal's office more than any boy in this school, I bet." Joe is the terror of the school, in his own eyes. You will have to provide experiences to change this attitude if he is to become a responsible school citizen.

As you become better acquainted with your class, you will realize that your cooperating teacher is adjusting the ways in which he works with individual youngsters in order to build more positive self-concepts. Shy little Anita may be allowed to report without any correction of her English usage, since it is very important to build her self-confidence before a group. Aggressive Ronnie, who is quite sure that everyone will stop to listen no matter how carelessly he speaks, may be checked for ungrammatical usage much more rigorously. Every effort may be made to convince John that his attempts to be cooperative are appreciated, since John does not typically view himself as a contributing group member. Not so much praise may be given to Riva whose every move tends to be a cooperative one. This is not unequal treatment of individuals on the part of your cooperating teacher; it is recognition of differing needs. If your pupils are to be given consistent help, you must become aware of why your cooperating teacher is treating individuals as he is and plan to give similar support.

Self-concepts are built out of repeated experiences—failing or passing grades on report cards many times over, rejection or acceptance by the group time after time, support and approval or criticism by the family in situation after situation. You will not change a child's concept of himself merely by admonishing him that he can do better work or saying reassuringly, "Of course they like you; you're just imagining things." He will need many satisfying experiences before he begins to view himself in a different light. To provide such experiences, you must learn to see his world through his eyes.

Become aware of physical needs and problems. Beginning teachers sometimes become so engrossed in their teaching that they forget that pupils with physical bodies are sitting in front of them. Actually, there are many times when the effectiveness of pupils' learning depends upon the teacher's sensitivity to factors related to physical needs and growth patterns. In getting to know your pupils, part of your attention should be directed to their physical development and to the adjustments needed in the classroom to provide a healthful environment. You must become aware of the factors in the classroom that contribute to good health—lighting, temperature, ventilation, size of desks. You must also identify classroom routines established for health purposes—regulations regarding leaving the room and getting drinks, breaks in the schedule to provide for physical activity. Part of your responsibility as a teacher will be to insure that your classroom contributes positively to pupils' physical well-being.

In any classroom there will be some youngsters with physical handicaps. In spite of her glasses, Jo Anne may need a seat near the front of the room when work is to be copied from the board. Jerry's hearing loss may make it necessary for him to see your lips. Tim is malnourished and tends to become irritable toward the close of the day. Maria's family of eight sleep in two rooms; she is likely to doze in the early afternoon. Steve has a mild cardiac condition that limits his activity on the playground. You must have such physical conditions clearly in mind if these youngsters are to profit from your teaching.

Elementary teachers also need to become sufficiently familiar with a pupil's typical behavior when he is well that they can identify signs of illness. Childhood diseases can blossom quickly, and the youngster who was bounding with energy at 9:00 can be running a fever by 10:30. You will not be expected to diagnose the illness; this is a physician's responsibility. However, you are the adult in the best position to sense that something is amiss and to take appropriate steps to guard the child's health as well as the health of the other pupils in your room.

Even experienced teachers find that they sometimes have to guard against allowing a pupil's physical appearance to influence their expectations regarding his behavior. It is a temptation to mother a youngster struggling with a physical handicap, to expect mature behavior from a large child, to excuse immature behavior from the smallest youngster in the room. Yet maturity and size are not necessarily related. The tallest boy in your class could be the youngest. He could also be a child who is maturing more slowly than the typical pupil of his chronological age, who will be one of the last of his age group to reach adolescence. By the same token, the doll-like, well-coordinated little girl could be one of the pupils who is physically most mature. This you will learn only as you consciously try to relate a pupil's behavior to what you know about individual differences in rates of maturity.

Each youngster is unique. Physically, socially, emotionally, intellectually, and in his concept of himself he will present his own individual pattern of development and his own unique constellation of learnings from previous home, community, and school experiences. Yet you will understand him better as an individual if you view him in the light of all that you know about his age group—their physiological maturity, the developmental tasks they face, the level of reasoning of which they are capable, the types of social relationships that are most typical. You face a never-ending task in getting acquainted with your pupils. It is one of the most important responsibilities you will assume if you are to help them learn.

USING DAY-BY-DAY OPPORTUNITIES TO STUDY PUPILS

The experienced teacher has trained himself to be aware of the hundreds of day-by-day behavioral clues that suggest that his pupils are learning successfully or encountering difficulty. He can do this, in part, because he has met such behavior before and knows how to interpret it. He has also developed specific skills in observing his pupils, in collecting new information about his class as he teaches, and in using a variety of classroom tests, special assignments, and other work products to provide the missing pieces of the puzzle. Beginning teachers often marvel at the adeptness with which the experienced teacher senses an individual's need for assistance, provides just the right challenge for an able pupil, or settles an argument almost before it begins. "It will all come with experience, I suppose," is commonly the beginner's resigned plaint. Experience will help, of course, but you can do much to train yourself to make the most of the opportunities to learn about your pupils in your day-by-day classroom activities.

Make classroom observations profitable. Classroom observations are one of the fundamental approaches to becoming acquainted with pupils. When you are in your own classroom you will have to learn to take time during the busy day to acquire objective information about your boys and girls. As a student teacher, your opportunities to observe will be somewhat more numerous, particularly at the beginning of your assignment. Make the most of them.

Some of your first observations should be devoted to getting to know your pupils. Map out the seating arrangement and then, as you identify names, enter them in the correct space. It can be helpful to jot down, also, characteristics that distinguish individuals. Physical traits may be the most obvious in the beginning, but you can take some early steps toward a more insightful understanding of individuals—to say nothing of winning friends—if you make note of Susan's comment about her kitten, Jerold's excitement as he tells about feeding his baby sister, Jonathan's zeal for planes. Few steps you can take in your early days in the classroom, either as a student teacher or a beginning teacher, will contribute as much to your own security as becoming able quickly to let your pupils know that you recognize them as individuals.

By the time you are sure of pupils' names, you will also have gained some helpful insights into individual backgrounds, interests, strengths, and weaknesses. To become well acquainted with your boys and girls, you will have to be more thorough than this. You will not, obviously, learn everything there is to know about a child in a few weeks. You can, however, make your early observations more profitable by setting up a systematic plan. Do not trust your memory to retain what you have observed. The preceding section has suggested the areas in which it is desirable to collect information, both for individuals and for the class as a whole—intellectual skills, ways of meeting basic needs, experience backgrounds, social interrelationships, self-concepts, physical needs and problems. If you will devote a page in your notebook to each child and strive conscientiously to enter descriptions of pertinent behavior for each area, you will discover that it does not take very long to amass a considerable amount of information about each child. Without some such systematic plan for observation you may never "see" some pupils. A blank page in your notebook for Billy or Susan means that you should shift your attention and observe one or the other for a while.

Collecting effective anecdotal records is an art. The records you make should be exact descriptions of behavior. Interpretations such as "Jack was unusually stubborn today" or "Joanna is getting along much better with the girls in her committee" will not be nearly as useful to you as specific descriptions of what Jack or Joanna actually did. Obviously, however, you are not going to be able to write voluminous notes, especially if you are busy with other aspects of your job. One device which teachers have found useful is to jot down at least a phrase or two at the time of the incident to help them remember what occurred. Then, at the end of the day, they round out the story. Look, for example, at the reminders (in parentheses) that Elaine Adams wrote and what finally went into her notebook as evidence of intellectual development for Roger, an able fourth-grader:

(Encyclopedia)

Reported accurately on encyclopedia article on Indian life. No problem with difficult words. 9/10

(Multiplication)

Tried out two-digit multiplication on his own "for fun." Process correct. 9/20

(Library)

Asked librarian for science books with "more information." Took sixth-grade book. Had him read a little aloud for me. Comprehends. 9/21

It is not always necessary to write notes, even brief ones such as those of Elaine Adams, in order to collect accurate observational data as class work proceeds. Symbols can sometimes be employed. For example, plus can be used to indicate a contribution that helps to move a discussion ahead, zero to indicate one that is of relatively little value but at least bears on the topic, and minus to indicate one that pulls the discussion off the track. With a little practice you will discover that you can enter such ratings on your seating chart as a discussion proceeds. A survey of your tallies will tell you which children contributed the most frequently and what the typical quality of their contributions was.

The validity of the picture of a child resulting from a series of observations depends upon the skill of the observer. Experienced observers have developed a number of techniques for increasing the accuracy of their observations. One technique is to make accurate records of exactly what happened, as illustrated by Elaine Adam's anecdotes. It is important, also, to delay judgment until a pupil has been observed in a variety of settings. In the reading group, fourth-grade Anna's responses are monosyllabic. She seldom volunteers an answer and you are left with the general impression that she is either a slow learner or has limited reading skill. Then you talk with her alone about her recreational reading and discover that she enjoys and comments intelligently on books well beyond her grade level. Shyness and limited ability to express herself fluently in a group seem to be the more accurate interpretation of her behavior. Andy is a source of constant turmoil during music. Anyone observing him at this time only would classify him as a troublemaker, disinterested, and unwholesomely aggressive. Yet when Andy is at work with books, his behavior is quiet, cooperative, and highly motivated. The more varied the circumstances under which evidence is collected, the better rounded the interpretation is likely to be. No isolated bit of behavior should be the basis of your final judgment.

Closely akin to the fault of interpreting behavior on the basis of too little evidence is that of allowing a "halo" effect to color your observation. We all have our likes and dislikes. Certain children will inevitably impress us more than others, either positively or negatively. There are many reasons for this, but whether we make allowances for our prejudices is the point at issue. A skilled observer will try his best not to let his biases distort his appraisal of an individual. Bobby may be the most intriguing curly-haired, rosy-cheeked cherub you have ever seen, but this should not keep you from noting objectively that he interferes with other children, gives very little leadership, and tends to use his charm to appeal for adult support. Jill may be one of the most cooperative youngsters in the room. Whenever there are plants to water, boards to wash, or books to arrange, she is on the spot. Her comments on matters pertaining to good housekeeping sound mature and wise. This should not blind you to the fact that in situations calling for complex reasoning, she displays very limited ability.

It is helpful to check on an impression of a single individual by looking at others with the same trait in mind. During her first week with an able sixth grade after previous experiences with fourth-graders of limited ability, Sarah Colby talked long and enthusiastically about how easily Robin learned and how well he reasoned. Soon she discovered several other pupils who grasped ideas with equal ease but who did not make their presence felt as quickly as did vocal and out-going Robin. Jacqueline Anderson's first impression was that Peter's English usage was incredibly poor. Then, as she listened to Peter's friends, she realized that she was dealing with a common problem stemming from limited home experiences. An understanding of the typical characteristics of pupils of the age with which you are working is one of your safeguards against misinterpreting the behavior of individuals.

How do you manage to collect all the observational evidence you need and still carry out your regular classroom responsibilities? Experienced teachers do not try to collect all their data in the early months of the school year; they space their observations over the entire year. Neither do they rely on observations alone as a guide to knowing their pupils. Cumulative records, written assignments, class discussions, and a variety of tests and inventories will all help you to make a general appraisal of the strengths, weaknesses, and experience backgrounds of your pupils.

In collecting precisely the evidence you need, it is helpful to learn to concentrate on one aspect of behavior for a specific period of time, and perhaps only for one or two youngsters. You cannot keep an eye on everything and everybody. As you review the information accumulating in your notebook about individuals, you may identify gaps or a series of anecdotes that are baffling to interpret. These may send you back to observe particularly what part Carl takes in a group discussion, to check on your impression that Mabel doesn't really think before she answers a question, to see whether Johnny is really wasting as much time as your anecdotes about his work habits suggest.

With a little experience you will be able to sense rather accurately which activities most readily yield certain kinds of information. Sharing periods, for example, can give many insights into the interests of individual pupils, their poise before a group, their command of oral English. Discussion sessions, in class or small-group settings, can be analyzed for group roles—leaders, followers, clowns, compromisers, special-interest pleaders. Independent work periods are good times to appraise specific skills. Planning sessions or discussions where new concepts or generalizations are being developed often reveal the reasoning powers of individuals. Recreation time can be used to size up physical skills.

Your colleagues have also learned how to use noon hours, recess breaks, and early morning periods to become better acquainted with individuals. One of the reasons experienced teachers arrive at school in good time is to have materials on the board, books out, and other administrative chores done before their pupils come. Then they are free to listen as individuals burst in with their special concerns. Six-year-old Jeannie may come clutching a favorite book; second-grade Earl bears a rock he intends to add to his collection; fifth-grade Bobby carries a simple barometer his father has helped him construct. In one classroom Katie Johnson uses the time before the morning bell rings to talk about recreational reading; across the hall James Wilson is discussing a television program with a group of would-be scientists; in the music room Sadie Simonds is helping some fourth-graders put their new song on paper. Your opportunities to learn about your pupils are endless if you are a good listener.

Many teachers plan deliberately to include in their programs special activities that will easily yield information about their pupils' backgrounds. In the early fall, a get-acquainted bulletin board may be used for snapshots of homes and families, stories about summer activities, descriptions of other members of the family, articles on *How I Help at Home* or *Where I Study.* In the primary grades, and often in the intermediate grades, too, sharing periods can be times when pupils relate interesting events from home and community experiences. Sharing tables, corner museums, special-interest bulletin boards, can all be used to stimulate pupils to bring their out-of-school worlds to the classroom.

Student teaching is an opportunity to learn to teach, but it can be frustrating to be asked to become acquainted with individuals and with classroom procedures before one tries one's hand. Student teachers sometimes say impatiently, "I can't learn by watching; I have to try things out for myself." For this reason, most cooperating teachers plan so that students have opportunities to participate as well as opportunities to observe. You can, however, be participating vigorously even while you are observing. The first few weeks are not too early to begin to project some long-term plans. As you observe, consider the implications of your observations for planning future experiences for your pupils. Test out your growing insights into pupil needs, too, by trying to foresee your cooperating teacher's next move. What would *you* have said in answer to Billy's question? How would you have handled the group in the corner quarreling about the encyclopedia? How close are your decisions to those your cooperating teacher actually makes? Observation can be a very active and dynamic process if you choose to make it so.

Collecting information as you teach. Many a lesson has failed because the teacher assumed competencies that the pupils did not have. The skillful teacher draws upon all his background information about pupils in planning his lessons. He has also developed techniques for assessing the present status of his group and for judging how effectively he is teaching as his lesson proceeds.[3]

The devices that you may incorporate as part of a lesson to help you appraise the present status of your class will vary with the problem at hand. Sometimes it will be as simple as saying "Before we go on, let's make sure we all remember how to . . . ." At other times you may plan one or two general discussion questions designed to reveal what your youngsters know. "This is Lincoln's birthday, and I have an interesting story for you. Before we hear it, let's find out what we know about him." "Several of you were asking about sharing your library books with the class. How many have ever made a book report?" Occasionally you will need to set up even more elaborate means of analyzing present competence. For example, in deciding how and when to introduce a new topic, it is sometimes wise to allow a day or more for probing previous backgrounds. Alicia Raziek used an informal inventory test when she was planning to introduce division with common fractions to her fifth grade. Her test on the multiplication of fractions revealed that only eight of her twenty-nine pupils achieved perfect scores. Accordingly she spent another week on multiplication before she introduced division. What happened to the eight pupils with the perfect scores? They were given enrichment opportunities while the rest of the class polished their knowledge, understanding, and skill with multiplication of fractions.

Experienced teachers have many ways of assessing the effectiveness of pupil learning as their lessons proceed. It is helpful to insert questions into a demonstration or explanation to make sure that your pupils have understood. Pupils who have incorrect answers may be encouraged to identify themselves if you ask "How many agree?" or "How many have a different answer?" rather than approving or disapproving the first answer you hear. It can also be revealing to take a few seconds to explore with a pupil the reason for his incorrect answer. Many a beginner has missed an opportunity to clear up genuine confusion by saying, reprovingly, "Now, you aren't thinking" or by supplying the correct answer himself (or eliciting it from a pupil) and then proceeding to the next point in his lesson plan without further explanation. You will not help your learners to achieve maximum growth if your zeal

[3] Because effective teaching is vitally related to understanding pupils' needs and competencies, help on how to study the present status of your class is also included in Chapters 6, 7, 8, and 9.

to carry out your lessons as originally planned blinds you to opportunities to discover individual difficulties.

Skillful teachers often use independent work sessions to examine the work in progress, talk with individuals, and give special help. Sometimes such a survey will give evidence of a common error, suggesting a point at which teaching was not effective or a new problem on which help is needed. If you are capitalizing fully on the opportunities offered by independent work sessions to know your pupils better, plans for future lessons will frequently stem from surveys of present status.

Use class time to collect special information. You will want to supplement your observations and your insights from the give-and-take of class discussions with concrete evidence from a variety of pupil work products. Teachers who feel that there is not enough time to know their pupils well have probably overlooked some of the opportunities for collecting data that actually exist in their classrooms.

One of your most fruitful sources of evidence is to be found in your pupils' written work. Although you will often want pupils to correct their own work and to analyze their errors, you will certainly want to take sets of papers home from time to time. In the quiet of your own room you will be able to substantiate your classroom observations by analyzing the types of errors. Those common to the majority of the class may well become the focus of later lessons. Those made by only one or two pupils may be set aside until the opportunity for individualized work presents itself. Often in examining pupils' written work, it is helpful to consider factors other than the specific skill you have been stressing. Sixth-grade Bill handed in acceptable exercises in percentage until he came to a set of problems that called for careful reading. He missed the point of these completely, as did several others. Dora Shores correctly assumed that reading skill might be involved and then spent some time with this small group concentrating on how to read arithmetic problems.

Classroom tests represent another source of special information. At the elementary school level, the distinction between tests and day-by-day written assignments is shadowy. Primary teachers, for example, use very few devices they would classify as tests. Nevertheless, they collect many pieces of concrete evidence regarding pupil progress and needs—a set of original stories to judge handwriting and English usage; a work sheet of arithmetic problems; a series of questions related to the main concepts developed in a unit of work; some word-analysis activities from a reading group. Tests can be used at many points in the teaching process—for preliminary surveys, for checks on progress, for an indication of pupil competence at the end of a block of work. Whenever they are employed they should be analyzed for evidence of progress and new needs. Common difficulties should be made the focus of additional teaching. There ought to be few, if any, times when you give a test merely to secure an additional set of marks for your grade book.[4]

It is important to collect concrete information about aspects of growth other than the acquisition of knowledge and skills. Inventories can contribute to your understanding of pupils' homes, interests, and out-of-school activities. For example, both interests and how pupils use their time may be revealed in a question asking which television programs they watch regularly. Something of the educational background of children's parents can be deduced from a question about the kinds of reading matter in the home. The richness or poverty of a youngster's out-of-school experiences may show up in a diary of week-end activities. You need not prepare an elaborate device to have a useful interest inventory. A mimeographed sheet, asking for the information you wish and providing ample space to write, can yield much information if you will take time to convince your pupils that you are genuinely interested in their responses: *What games do you like to play the best? What chores do you do at home? What do you usually do between the time school ends and supper?* Primary teachers often collect similar evidence informally through sharing periods and through conversations with individuals.

You will find your colleagues experimenting with a variety of projective techniques to secure evidence regarding pupils' personality needs and their attitudes toward themselves. Pupils may be asked to write their autobiographies. Topics such as *Things I Like About Myself, Things That Make Me Mad, If I Were a Teacher,* when used as the basis for creative writing have yielded helpful information. Free-response or open-ended questions have proved valuable—*I enjoy television because . . . , I wish . . . , I think that reading . . . , I think school . . . .* Youngsters have been shown pictures suggesting family relationships, peer-group behavior, or individual problems and asked to write or to tell a story explaining them. Classes have been asked to add the endings to unfinished stories involving human relationships (sometimes drawn from actual classroom occurrences). Teachers have

[4] See Chapter 11, pages 436-451, for further discussion of the construction and use of classroom tests.

also learned to be alert to the psychological implications in children's pictures, in their written expression, and in their dramatic play. You would not, of course, plunge into data-collecting in areas that touch closely on social and emotional adjustment without careful planning. Such activities may be very disturbing to pupils unless the ground is prepared carefully and the discussions handled with sensitivity.

Sociograms will also be helpful to you in becoming acquainted with your pupils. The evidence for these, too, needs to be collected thoughtfully and with due regard for the feelings of individuals. Usually the safest data, from the standpoint of pupils' mental health, are collected when there is a genuine need for a new work pattern or seating arrangement. If desks are to be rearranged each child may be asked to list one person he would like to have seated near him. Committees may be needed for a class project and pupils asked to indicate the persons with whom they would most like to work. With first or first and second choices in hand, you are ready to construct your sociogram. It will be helpful to you in doing this to make first a master chart of where the choices fall. This is easily done by placing the children's names in the same order across the top and down the left-hand side of a sheet of squared paper and then entering the choice of each child listed down the left-hand side, under the appropriate name at the top. Part of Sarah Wilson's master sheet appears below, with first-choice votes indicated. Betty and Jim are the two popular children thus far.

	Alex	Betty	Jim	Helen	Kay	Marian	Sam
Alex							1
Betty			1				
Jim		1					
Helen		1					
Kay		1					
Marian			1				
Sam	1						

There are several ways that Sarah can show this information on the chart that is her sociogram. One of the simplest, and most easily read, is a system in which circles representing each child (or circles and squares, if you wish to distinguish girls from boys) are placed so that first-choice votes are always the same distance apart. Since Betty has the largest number of first-choice votes, her circle makes a convenient starting point. After the symbols for Jim, Helen, and Kay are arranged around Betty, those of children who chose any of these three can be entered, and so on. Arrows can show the direction of the choice. Thus, the portion of Sarah's sociogram that included these youngsters looked as follows:

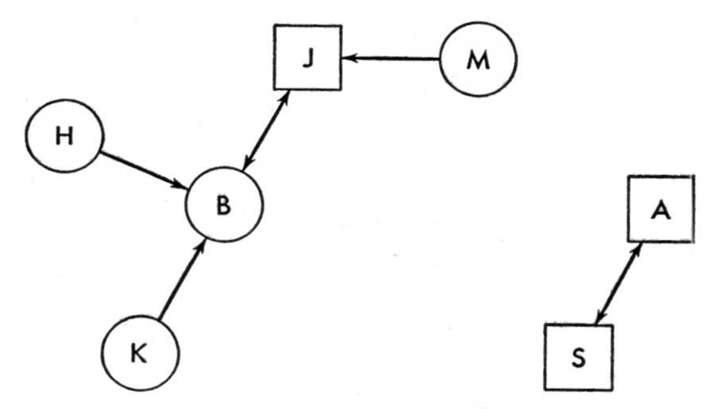

Had Sarah also collected second-choice votes, she would simply have used arrows and another color to indicate these. Space relationships cannot be held exact for both first and second choices.

If you do not want to break faith with your pupils, you must follow through with the actual changes in seating or set up the proposed committee structure which was your reason for collecting the data for your sociogram. It is important to recognize, also, that the emotional climate in some groups will make data-collecting for sociograms unwise, even though a genuine reason for asking pupils to express a preference among their classmates presents itself. In such situations, and in the primary grades where reading and writing skills may hinder data-collecting, very similar evidence can be obtained through observation. If pupils are allowed to sit near friends, who sits where? What are the typical clusters at noon, at recess, before school starts? Who walks home with whom? Which youngsters play together? Which sit together for lunch?

Many teachers use, in addition to the types of specific evidence suggested thus far, data collected in individual conferences. Although such conferences are not easy to work into an already full schedule, they can be arranged. For the week before each report period Sally Gerrard and her class planned their schedule to include some quiet work sessions so that she could sit down with each pupil for ten minutes, go over his notebooks where samples of his work were filed, and talk with him about his progress. Ruth Anderson's second-graders spent part of their reading time in individualized reading activities. During these periods, pupils came back to Ruth in turn to talk about their books and in some cases to read a page or two aloud. Ronald McClay was accustomed to having each pupil write a note to his parents giving his own views on his progress. Ronald did not do this, however, without conferring with each youngster regarding what he planned to write.

Tests, creative activities, and other pupil work products need to be saved. After all, the key to a pupil's progress and difficulties lies in the picture of his growth as indicated by a series of activities, not a single paper. Experienced teachers have developed a number of ways of saving such evidence.[5] In some classrooms, pupils keep notebooks in which they file samples of their own work—a creative writing collection, a spelling notebook, a notebook containing all the written work connected with a unit. Sometimes a folder is maintained for each child, and he and his teacher together decide on typical pieces of work to file. Teachers also use a variety of class charts to record both group and individual progress—a bar graph of books read, a check-off sheet for number combinations mastered. These accumulations will need to be sorted, eventually, and samples selected for inclusion in pupils' cumulative records. For most of the year, however, effective teachers plan so that much of their data-collecting and their recording is an integral part of their on-going classroom activities.

STUDYING CUMULATIVE RECORDS

In every school, there will be a backlog of information about boys and girls in the school records. Whether this information is meager or detailed, you will want to examine it. Cumulative records can be very helpful to you in meeting pupil needs if interpreted properly and used wisely.

Cumulative records typically contain information of many types. You will probably find *personal data,* such as name of child and date of birth, address, name of father and mother or guardian, sex, race or

[5] These means of saving evidence are described more fully in Chapter 11, pages 433-436.

nationality; *administrative data,* such as list of other schools attended, attendance record, date entered school, date of transfers; *test and achievement data,* including scores on standardized aptitude and achievement tests, results of interest and personality inventories, semester grades by subjects or areas; and *behavior reports.* Cumulative records imply just what the name says—records which have been kept over a long period of time and which reveal growth, progress, and trends in development.

Teachers sometimes disagree regarding when to examine cumulative records. Some prefer to wait until they have become acquainted with the pupil, feeling that data in the record might possibly color their impressions of him. Others think that records should be examined as early as possible, feeling that the more they know about a pupil before they meet him, the more quickly they can get acquainted with him. Although teachers must always take precautions lest a child's previous history influence unduly their reactions to him, it would seem that this could be done without refusing to use all the help in getting to know him that is provided in the cumulative record. Professional judgment has been utilized in selecting pertinent information to include in these records. You must learn to be equally professional in using them. If you know how to interpret them, there is no reason for not studying them prior to meeting your class.[6]

Study personal and administrative data. Data regarding date of birth, parents or guardian, school attendance, and transfers will probably not be difficult to interpret, but you may miss significant information if you neglect this part of the record. It may seem obvious to suggest that you check on a pupil's age, but unless you do this you may find yourself assuming that the large youngster in your room is the most mature or treating as immature the one who is small. Age may give a false impression of intellectual ability. You may be exasperated with Don's inability to grasp number relationships when he talks so intelligently about common-sense matters, until you realize that he is two years retarded and has therefore had more time than his friends to amass worldly wisdom. Equally exasperating may be fourth-grade Willie's immature outbursts of enthusiasm that seem so out of keeping with his academic progress until you discover that he has just turned eight.

It is also helpful to check on the data regarding a pupil's family. Is

[6] Read Chapter 11, pages 456-464, also in relation to the problem of interpreting cumulative records.

he living with both parents or does he come from a broken home? Is he perchance living with a grandmother or an aunt? Do both parents work? How many brothers and sisters does he have, and what is his position in the family? Are his parents American or foreign-born? If the latter, how long has the family been in this country? These are the kinds of data that will help you construct a tentative picture of a youngster's family group, to be checked, of course, by some firsthand investigation of your own as time permits.

Records of schools attended, and the attendance record while in the present school, are likewise worth examining. You will find some pupils who have grown up in the school (as, indeed, their parents may have). Others will have a history of transfers within the city or perhaps from state to state. Sometimes, but not always, the latter are struggling with inadequate academic backgrounds. Sometimes, too, the pupil who has moved from place to place is finding it difficult to make friends. Do not assume, however, that growing up in the school means continuous school experience. You may discover a history of illness in the early grades. A spotty record—a few days in school and then a day out with a cold—can sometimes be even more of a handicap in acquiring a good foundation in reading and numbers than an illness lasting for several weeks. You may also find a history of truancy or, in the case of youngsters in underprivileged areas, of absence because there was literally not enough clothing to send every child in the family to school on a cold day. Such attendance data provide a valuable setting against which to look at achievement test data and teachers' marks.

Use caution in interpreting intelligence and achievement test data.[7] The intelligence and achievement tests which have been given to your pupils will usually be recorded in their cumulative records. Depending on the guidance policies in your particular school, these data may be rich or meager. Intelligence tests are not always administered every year. Sometimes a readiness test is given in the kindergarten or first grade and a group intelligence test used at the beginning of the second grade and perhaps again in fourth and sixth. System-wide achievement tests are sometimes administered on a similar time schedule and individual teachers encouraged to order additional tests to secure whatever information they want in the intervening grades. In other schools, there may be a yearly testing program. Whatever the information available, you must draw upon all that you have learned about standardized

[7] See also Chapter 11, pages 447-450, for a discussion of interpreting the scores of standardized tests.

tests if you are to make proper use of the intelligence and achievement test data.

There are many cautions you should heed in interpreting a single test score, whether it be an IQ or a grade score from an achievement test. The perfect evaluative instrument is yet to be constructed. We are sometimes far too prone to accept a test score as valid once it is in black and white on a pupil's record. You will do well to ask how old the child was when he took the test. Research indicates that there is great variability in the intelligence test scores for children under six; research also indicates that the greater the time lapse since the test was taken, the less the score can be trusted. Look, also, to see what type of test was used. We know that group intelligence tests give less stable results than individual tests. We know, too, that the population groups upon which the tests from different series are standardized will differ somewhat and, therefore, that grade scores or IQ's will not be exactly comparable from test to test. There is also evidence that the structure of a test, its time limits, and the way in which the pupil records his responses can, at times, influence his performance. Many of your questions about the nature of the tests which your pupils have taken will be answered if you can locate a sample of the test and read its accompanying manual. You cannot, of course, know the conditions under which the test was administered. Yet this factor, too, has its effect on the accuracy of the test score.

In attempting to interpret a pupil's score on any particular test, it is also important to remember that his skill in one area can influence his performance in another. Sixth-grade Joan's IQ surprises you; you are sure she is more able intellectually. Then you realize that she is a slow, cautious reader and that the group intelligence test had a short time limit. Fourth-grade Alan's arithmetic achievement test shows a pattern of high computation and low problem-solving scores that puzzles you until you note his low score in reading comprehension. Randy's high score on a language achievement test seems impossible in view of his atrocious English usage until you stop to think that all he had to do was to identify the correct answer—a task well within his intellectual grasp. You will need to look at the pattern of the pupil's scores, then, not solely at the score on one individual test.

In spite of your previous training in interpreting test scores cautiously, you may be tempted to make unsound quantitative comparisons. You may find yourself thinking of Ray, with a recorded IQ of 110, as being distinctly superior to Sally, whose IQ is listed as 104,

Yet what we know about the reliability of intelligence tests indicates that these scores could easily be reversed on a retest. Grade scores on achievement tests are, if anything, even more difficult to compare on a mathematical basis, since the grade level at which the pupil is working makes a difference in interpreting the score. If third-grade Susan has a grade score of 2.0 on a reading achievement test, this is likely to be evidence that she will have serious trouble with a third-grade book. However, a grade score of 5.0 in reading does not necessarily indicate that sixth-grade John will be greatly handicapped comprehending his regular classroom texts.

If this is your first experience in using test scores in a practical situation you may have to guard against being unduly impressed by a very high test score or, conversely, unduly worried by a low one. If you find in your room a youngster with an IQ of 130, you would do well to remind yourself that four or five pupils out of one hundred will have a similar record. You may also need to stop to think that a grade score of 7.0 on a reading test does not mean that fourth-grade Jeanne is capable of comprehending all seventh-grade books. It simply says that she did as well on this test as the average seventh-grader. Likewise, a distribution of achievement test scores for your class indicating that a third to a half of your pupils are under their actual grade placement should not be taken to mean that you have a more than ordinarily retarded group. By the very nature of their standardization, achievement tests are scored so that such a distribution is likely to occur.

Above everything, withhold judgment until you have seen your pupils in action. Standardized tests are valuable aids to teachers. They provide an opportunity to check standards from one community against norms that are nationwide. Often they help to counteract the halo effect that has developed because of a pupil's appearance or behavior. A test score should never be accepted as valid in the face of overwhelming evidence that it is inaccurate as indicated by a pupil's day-by-day performance.

Interpret teachers' marks thoughtfully. Even more difficult to interpret than standardized test scores may be the marks given to your pupils by preceding teachers.[8] A letter grade, be it an *A, B,* or *C,* or an *E, S,* or *U,* is an attempt to communicate information regarding a pupil's progress to his parents, to the pupil himself, and to others who are interested in his welfare. To interpret a letter grade you must know

[8] The discussion of reporting pupil progress in Chapter 11, pages 456-460, will provide additional help on the problem of interpreting letter grades.

the meaning it has in your particular school. Sometimes you will even need to discover what the letter grade meant to an individual teacher. An *A* could indicate that a youngster is working up to his full capacity, whatever that capacity is; it could mean that he is one of the top achievers in the room, even though he has never worked up to capacity; or it could represent a compromise somewhere in between.

No matter what else you learn from teachers' marks, they will give you clues to your pupils' probable concepts of themselves as scholars. Some will have been told by one low grade after another that their work is unsatisfactory or mediocre. Others will have been told time after time that they are good students. For some pupils, expectations of failure or success may have been built for specific areas of growth; every aspect of other pupils' performances may have been rated poor or good. As you try to understand your pupils' attitudes toward school, toward special subjects, toward their chances of improving, it is well to keep such background information in mind.

In some school systems teachers have realized the difficulties in attempting to convey through letter grades information about individuals, each of whom has his own complex combination of strengths and weaknesses. Consequently, you may find copies of supplementary letters that have been written to parents, lists of books the pupil has read, descriptions of special help he has been given, and possibly selected samples typical of his work. Such material can be very helpful to you in assessing your pupils' present needs and should be examined with care.

Interpret reports of behavior cautiously. School systems vary in the extent to which reports of behavior are included in cumulative records. If such reports are to be helpful they must be accurate, and this means that negative comments as well as positive ones will have to be recorded. Some teachers feel very strongly that a negative statement should never be allowed to remain in a permanent record, arguing that the risk, however slight, of having such information fall into the hands of a person who will misinterpret it is not worth taking. On the other hand, vague comments such as "Sally is adjusting better in her group relationships" or "John is showing much more mature work habits this year" scarcely merit the time it takes to file them.

The summaries you find in the cumulative record will have been made from much more detailed anecdotal records collected under a variety of circumstances over a full year. When they are well written, these summaries give concrete evidence, not merely the teacher's interpretation. As you examine them, you should keep carefully in mind what you have learned about how behavior changes with maturity and with altered circumstances. You are reading a description of a child as he was a year ago in a particular class and under a particular teacher. With these precautions in mind, you will find that behavior records can provide important insights about your pupils. Consider, for example, what you can learn about sixth-grade Ralph that marks and test scores alone would not have told you:

Ralph has made many positive contributions to the class this year, especially to the projects where sketches and models of gadgets or mechanical devices were needed. He constructed a radio and demonstrated its workability to the class during the study of "Newer Means of Communication." During library periods he usually read from periodicals like *Popular Mechanics*. However, most of these contributions were on an individual basis. When he was first made chairman of a class committee in the fall, Ralph tended to tell the others what to do and to grow very impatient if children did not share his enthusiasms. His first committee rebelled and asked to be disbanded. This spring, he served as a committee member to develop a bulletin board showing progress in transportation and was well accepted because of his concrete contribution. He still needs help in learning to lead a group.

If the boys and girls under your guidance are to achieve maximum growth, you must use, objectively and professionally, all the data that you can acquire about them. You will, however, withhold judgment until you see your pupils face to face. They deserve a fresh start with you. On the other hand, you should not waste their time and yours collecting anew information readily available in cumulative records.

GETTING ACQUAINTED WITH THE COMMUNITY SETTING

Your pupils bring their out-of-school worlds into the classroom—lack of sleep because they have watched late television; week-end picnics; father's concerns about what the weather will do to crops; conversations overheard in front of the corner bar; experiences in clubs and youth centers; church school contacts. If you are to know the boys and girls in your classroom, you must become acquainted with the homes and community from which they come.

Take time to get acquainted with the school community. For some teachers, the school community will be the one in which they, themselves, grew up. Others will be hundreds of miles from home, or much closer geographically but just as remote in terms of the differences in cultural background. If you are starting to teach in a new community, take steps to get acquainted with it.

One helpful procedure is to walk through the school neighborhood. What are the homes like?—single dwellings, apartments, or tenements? well-kept or shoddy? What places to play do you see?—playgrounds? yards equipped with play materials? mainly streets and alleys? What centers for community life are there?—churches? community recreation centers? settlement houses? What is the social and economic climate of the immediate school community?—urban and industrial? residential? tenement? What contacts with nature will there be?—parks? gardens? places to keep pets or raise flowers?

It can be helpful to take part in community activities and to become acquainted with other people interested in boys and girls. Who leads the scout or guide movements? How active are the church programs? Who are the people working in the youth centers or settlement houses? Do law-enforcement agencies sponsor recreational programs? These people can add much to your insights about your pupils' out-of-school life.

You will also want to become familiar with community resources. If your pupils are accustomed to visiting the local museum, feeding the ducks in the nearby park, watching the boats on the river, acting as sidewalk superintendents in a rapidly expanding housing area, you will want to know about this. Such activities help to build experience backgrounds upon which you can draw to make your lessons meaningful. Consider, for example, the insight displayed by Sally Johnson, teaching in an underprivileged area, who helped her pupils to develop pictures of signs of spring that included Mother's new spring hat, playing marbles, policemen without overcoats, windows open so that fresh air could come in, a robin in the park, green grass and leaves on a small plot in front of the school.

Take special pains to make contacts with parents. Conscientious teachers make a definite effort to become acquainted with the parents of their pupils. A youngster's house and the street on which he lives may tell you something of the physical setting from which he comes, but the emotional climate depends largely upon his parents. In your own classroom, you will be responsible for using whatever channels seem most profitable to get to know parents. As a student teacher, however, you should not undertake independent parent counseling without first consulting with your cooperating teacher. Even experienced teachers typically involve their principals in difficult problems of parent-pupil-teacher relationships.

By all means attend meetings of the Parent-Teacher Association, school open houses, special community meetings. Stay for the social hours, mingle with the parents, and take the trouble to seek out those who seem hesitant or retiring. These meetings give you an opportunity to match parents with children. They also reveal something of the attitudes of parents toward education in general and the school in particular. In addition, such meetings give insight into the leadership role being assumed by the school—the interpretations being made of aspects of the school program, the guidance being given in problems of understanding children's growth and needs, the help provided in interpreting popular articles concerning education.

It may be that a system of parent conferences is in operation in your school. Certainly, individual parents will be requesting your help. Conferences are one of the teacher's most important means of getting to know parents and of sharing information about youngsters. In your student-teaching experience you may be a relatively passive observer. But, as you listen, try to identify the parent's attitude toward the child. Is it one of acceptance or rejection? Are there anxieties about aspects of the youngster's development? Do you get hints that immature behavior is being explained away or that the standards held are too high? Try also to identify attitudes toward the school and toward modern educational practices. These may help you to understand some of the child's reactions. Does it seem likely that his school activities are being approved or criticized around the family dinner table? Do the parent's comments suggest that the help given at home will reinforce school experiences or might there be an effort made to counteract what is considered to be an unwise school procedure? Are the educational objectives of the home basically those of the school?

In some schools, home visitation is regular procedure. There may also be casual opportunities to walk home with a child who is ill, to accompany a committee to deliver a set of get-well cards, to take home books and assignments for a convalescent. You will be interested in the furnishings of a home and in the housekeeping, but, more important, be sensitive to the emotional climate. What seem to be the relationships among family members?—between parent and child? among siblings? between children and other adults in the home? What is the evidence that the child has an accepted position in the home?—a place for his toys? playthings in the yard? a room of his own? books of his own?

What is the evidence that the child is a contributing member of the family?—does he open the door for you? help to entertain you? have regular chores? take responsibility for younger children?

In all parent contacts, it is important to remember that you are in a position of professional responsibility. You may find yourself the recipient of confidences about family problems that would make interesting tidbits at the faculty lunch table. Parents will not trust you twice if information shared in confidence comes back to them distorted through another source. You may find yourself listening to criticisms of the school administration or of another teacher. These you must learn to handle with professional dignity. There will also be parents who, in a well-meant effort to understand and help their own youngsters, comment on the behavior of other pupils, or ask for comparisons of academic work. You must learn to keep your conversation focused on Johnny, not to include his pals, fascinating though the information you are gathering about them may be. Above all, you may find yourself tempted to share with a parent your reactions to the school, its faculty, your cooperating teacher, and your pupils. This a professional person never does. If you belong in the teaching profession, you have made your choice primarily because of a deep love of people and a desire to be of service to them. Your sensitive understanding of the needs, aspirations, and values of others must extend beyond boys and girls to their parents and to your professional colleagues.

BOOKS YOU SHOULD KNOW

Cunningham, Ruth, and associates. *Understanding Group Behavior of Boys and Girls.* New York: Bureau of Publications, Teachers College, Columbia University, 1951. Pp. xviii + 446.

Detjen, Ervin W., and Detjen, Mary F. *Elementary-School Guidance.* New York: McGraw-Hill Book Co., 1952. Pp. 266.

Driscoll, Gertrude. *How to Study the Behavior of Children.* New York: Bureau of Publications, Teachers College, Columbia University, 1941. Pp. viii + 84.

Froehlich, Clifford P., and Darley, John G. *Studying Students: Guidance Methods of Individual Analysis.* Chicago: Science Research Associates, 1952. Pp. xviii + 411.

Havighurst, Robert J. *Human Development and Education.* New York: Longmans, Green and Co., 1953. Pp. ix + 338.

Heffernan, Helen (Editor). *Guiding the Young Child.* Prepared by a Committee of the California School Supervisors Association. Boston: D.C. Heath and Co., 1951. Pp. x + 338.

Helping Teachers Understand Children. Prepared by the staff of the Division on Child Development and Teacher Personnel for the Commission on Teacher

Education. Washington, D.C.: American Council on Education, 1945. Pp. xv + 468.

Hymes, James L., Jr. *A Child Development Point of View.* Englewood Cliffs, N.J.: Prentice-Hall, 1955. Pp. ix + 145.

Jenkins, Gladys G.; Shacter, Helen; and Bauer, William W. *These Are Your Children.* Expanded Edition. Chicago: Scott, Foresman and Co., 1953. Pp. 320.

Jersild, Arthur T. *In Search of Self.* New York: Bureau of Publications, Teachers College, Columbia University, 1952. Pp. 141.

Kough, Jack, and DeHaan, Robert F. *Teacher's Guidance Handbook: Part I, Identifying Children Who Need Help.* Elementary and Junior High Edition. Chicago: Science Research Associates, 1955. Pp. 145.

Langdon, Grace, and Stout, Irving W. *Teacher-Parent Interviews.* Englewood Cliffs, N.J.: Prentice-Hall, 1954. Pp. xii + 356.

Lee, J. Murray, and Lee, Dorris May. *The Child and His Development.* New York: Appleton-Century-Crofts, 1958. Pp. xiii + 624.

Moustakas, Clark E. *The Teacher and the Child.* New York: McGraw-Hill Book Co., 1956. Pp. 256.

Olson, Willard C. *Child Development.* Boston: D.C. Heath and Co., 1949. Pp. 417.

Prescott, Daniel A. *The Child in the Educative Process.* New York: McGraw-Hill Book Co., 1957. Pp. 502.

Rasey, Marie I., and Menge, J.W. *What We Learn from Children.* New York: Harper & Brothers, 1956. Pp. 164.

Willey, Roy D. *Guidance in Elementary Education.* New York: Harper & Brothers, 1952. Pp. xiii + 825.

Meeting Classroom Problems

PART III

Guiding Pupils Toward Self-Discipline

CHAPTER 5

"I know I let Jimmy get away with too much, but he's so cute—just like my kid brother."

"I made them wait until they were all listening, but I felt so mean. . . ."

"There are times I could just die they're so funny, but I suppose you should never let it show."

"They're darling, but they are so wiggly."

"I do ask them to take turns, but I seem to be nagging so much if I keep at it all the time."

"What puzzles me is just where I should draw the line. How do you decide when it's too noisy?"

"That's all well and good with most children, but Barnie just lies down and kicks."

"And Art! You'd almost think he enjoyed being scolded. It doesn't seem to matter what you try."

"All I do is keep order. These kids have no ambition. They don't want to learn."

If student teachers and beginning teachers were asked their one big concern, a majority would answer "Discipline." So would principals, supervisors, and experienced teachers, and with good reason. Discipline, interpreted in its narrowest sense, implies that unless there is at least minimum respect for the teacher and willingness to work with him, little learning can take place. Construed in its broader and more positive sense, there is the implication that there must be mutual respect and understanding, growing self-control, and good judgment if pupils and teachers are to work together in a happy classroom atmosphere.

Guiding pupils toward self-discipline is not the clear-cut problem that it appears. Basically, it is a matter of helping boys and girls to develop the skills in human relationships, the work habits, and the self-understanding and self-control that they need in order to live and work harmoniously with others. As the person responsible for guiding this learning process, it is important for you to know what you want to accomplish. Then, you must utilize basic learning principles effectively in helping boys and girls to achieve your objectives. Your responsibilities do not end with this, however. You must know how to establish a classroom atmosphere that forestalls the restlessness, the inattention, and the seeking after excitement that often occur in situations where leadership is vacillating. You will also face the very baffling problem of helping the youngster who is struggling with serious emotional difficulties. Teaching children to achieve self-discipline is a full-time responsibility. It is an integral aspect of everything you do.

WHAT ARE WE WORKING FOR?

"Good discipline" has many meanings. To some it implies order, quiet, obedience. ("Miss Johnson has excellent discipline. You can hear a pin drop in her room.") To some, it is synonymous with punishment. ("All that child needs is a little discipline! One good spanking would solve a lot. You can't reason with youngsters of that age.") Others are thinking of increased self-control. ("Today Sally carried out our plans completely without once being distracted. Hasn't she grown!") Current articles with exaggerated discussions of "undisciplined" youth in our schools have added to the confusion. Not infrequently situations which are actually the result of ineffective classroom leadership or just plain lack of common sense are given publicity as examples of "modern methods" or "present-day psychology." "I want to be a modern parent," a mother is quoted as saying, "but we just can't afford to let him destroy *all* our furniture." Before teachers can develop effective human relations in the classroom, they must know exactly what they are working for.

Disciplined citizens certainly are needed in a society which values respect for the unique worth of individuals, willingness to contribute one's best to the cooperative solution of problems, and ability to abide by the rules through which citizens govern themselves. This is not the kind of discipline valued in a dictatorship where decisions are made by those in control and the common man does as he is told. Citizens in a democracy must be able to discipline themselves. They need to learn self-control—to be able to make their own decisions and govern their own actions in ways that will promote the happiness and well-being of themselves and of others.

Self-control is too all-inclusive a term, however, to be of much help in meeting day-by-day problems in the classroom. It is an ultimate objective and probably—if we are completely honest—achieved by few adults in all aspects of their lives. Most of us engage in undisciplined behavior once in a while—we exceed the speed limit, treat someone we love to a fit of temper, put off a job that we know very well should be done now. In between the newborn baby and the relatively mature, disciplined adult are long years of growth and learning in which parents, teachers, community members, and the world itself combine to help shift the source of authority and control from outside agents to the individual himself. To identify your part in the process, you must be able to spell out behavioral goals for the age group with which you are working—in terms of pupils' person-to-person relationships, their relationships to those in leadership roles, their response to authority, their work habits, and their inner security and sources of satisfaction.

What kinds of person-to-person relationships are desirable? Beginning teachers report many perplexities as they assume responsibility for helping thirty or more boys and girls to learn to live and work together. What behavior do you allow and when do you call a halt? When is a buzz a healthy sign and when does it signify lack of control? What do you do or say in situations where your leadership is obviously needed? Such questions will become less puzzling if you will take time to ask yourself what kinds of relationships with each other are desirable for the age group with which you are working.

Respect for other individuals is certainly one basic goal. With young children this will be expressed in a willingness to take turns, to share with other children, to find means of settling differences other than loud talk, grabbing, or punching. There are problems of learning how to treat the child who is different and of understanding that other individuals have needs and purposes of their own. For some kindergarteners and first-graders there will be social amenities to learn—please, thank you, pardon me. With older pupils situations calling for respect of others will have widened to include a much larger social group. There will be out-of-class responsibilities on the playground and in the halls as well as in-class demands for mature behavior toward others. Older groups are expected also to be able to go through halls without disturbance, to need little supervision in lavatories, to arrive at school and to travel from class to class on time. There will be an increasing number of independent contacts with other adults to manage—the custodian, the engineer, the school secretary, the principal, other teachers, visitors to the school.

We need citizens who are experienced in the ways of cooperative problem-solving. In first grade this means learning to take turns in a planning session, being willing to give up one's proposal if outvoted, carrying through a relatively independent part of a cooperative task. Older pupils need to develop more varied controls in discussion situations—giving the speaker full attention, taking one's turn without yelling for the floor, disagreeing in terms other than "That's crazy," helping to work out a compromise, cooperating on a group project without wasting time, leading a group without bossing, presenting facts rather than persisting in an undocumented opinion, giving in without slamming one's desk and flouncing out of the room.

Conscientiousness in meeting one's obligations to other individuals and to the group is another essential characteristic of the good citizen. Everybody is ready to share but Benny. Has he the right to hold things up because he is absorbed at the science table? If Andy agrees to work with the group making the map, should he shirk his obligation and read a book instead? When Bill volunteers to open the Lost and Found Office in the morning, may he dally on the playground if he feels like it? Should one look at a neighbor's paper in order to secure a good grade on a spelling test? What's the thing to do, copy the poem and pretend it is one's own or tell where it came from? What is one's responsibility in reporting accurately the details of a disagreement with another child? in telling the teacher if a classmate misbehaves? Pupils who are growing in self-discipline demonstrate increasing ability to make such decisions for themselves.

Meeting obligations to others also involves respecting their property rights. With kindergarteners and first-graders this means learning which classroom materials may be used by all and which are the property of individuals. It calls for the development of a sense of responsibility in returning borrowed materials. It means protecting the table and the floor when painting; using materials economically; handling library books and other school property carefully. Older pupils should be expected to display a similar sense of responsibility extending to other parts of the school building, the playground, the property of persons living or working in the school neighborhood.

Person-to-person relationships in a democracy do not conform to a stereotyped and rigid code. Pupils must be able to adjust to the demands of a wide variety of situations. For example, respect for the other fellow means that he is given strict attention during a report or discussion. Others do not talk while he is talking, nor do they draw pictures, read, or walk over to sharpen a pencil. On the other hand, in a work period where several projects are under way in small groups, a quiet buzz of conversation may be appropriate; it is usually permissible to move about the room quietly; another group can be interrupted briefly if one needs help. It is quite all right to cheer loudly on the playground, but other ways of showing enthusiasm must be found if a class is working next door. We have fun on our own part of the playground but we don't run full tilt through a kindergarten group. Often the beginning teacher attempts to achieve what he remembers to have been the atmosphere of the class he observed a year ago, but fails to sense that the situation he faces is not at all the same. He allows during discussions or times when pupils are making reports the quiet buzz and the moving around that were reserved for the work period the year before. He tries to achieve with a fourth-grade arithmetic class the self-government to which he was accustomed in his sixth-grade social studies situation. You will have to learn to analyze each new situation. The behavior desired will never be exactly the same for any two groups.

What is meant by democratic leadership? Teachers should expect to receive and (much more important) to give the same courtesies in person-to-person relationships as do their pupils. Teachers, however, have also been delegated leadership and authority roles in their classrooms. These roles must be assumed if pupils are to feel secure and the work is to proceed. Psychological research, in the past twenty years, has revealed much about the effects of varied types of leadership on the behavior of individuals.[1] Although many questions are still unanswered, important clues for teachers have come from these studies. In a laissez-faire situation where leadership is not assumed, or in situations where leadership is assumed in a vacillating fashion—sometimes helping and sometimes just letting things happen—group morale tends to be low. Pupils bicker among themselves, waste time, and in general accomplish very little. On the other hand, authoritarian leadership typically results in order and in a high work output. When authoritarian leadership is benevolent and understanding pupils are quite often happy under it, but they do not usually take much responsibility for their own standards

[1] For a pioneer study, see Kurt Lewin, Ronald Lippitt, and R.K. White, "Patterns of Aggressive Behavior in Experimentally Created Social Climates," *Journal of Social Psychology*, 10:271-79 (May, 1939).

of behavior. Under authoritarian leadership which is resented, some children are likely to be made scapegoats and become targets for the antagonism that the group members dare not direct against the leader. Explosions are very likely to occur when the leader is called away and the restraint is removed.

Democratic leadership aims for gradually increasing self-control and self-direction. This does not mean that the leader behaves in exactly the same way in all situations. The democratic leader does, however, have certain characteristics which are considered to be typical:

He takes responsibility in unifying the group and securing suggestions.

He makes sure everyone has a share in plans.

He secures consensus and calls for votes as needed.

He gives help where his background makes him a source of assistance, but he does not impose his way upon the group.

He helps to build standards through group evaluation sessions and opportunities for individuals to talk things out rather than by imposing his standards on them.

He helps to secure good working conditions—calling for order, delegating responsibility, taking responsibility himself, as the occasion demands.

Teachers who want to give democratic leadership face a major problem in deciding exactly what is demanded of them and of their pupils for each new situation they face. Certainly, you must consider the maturity of your boys and girls. First-graders will not be ready for the degree of self-direction that can be allowed to sixth-graders. It is important, also, to appraise pupils' experience backgrounds. The type of leadership needed by children who have had few opportunities to assume responsibility for their own behavior will differ from that required by a group who have been relatively self-directing for several years. It is obvious, too, that different parts of the day and different types of activities will require different kinds of leadership. Learning a new arithmetic process, planning a class party, taking a spelling test—each calls for distinct and different ways of behaving from leader and group. The variation of patterns of leadership and followership appropriate in a democratic setting are infinite. Among your most challenging classroom problems will be that of deciding what your leadership functions should be.

In a classroom where pupils are being helped to grow in ability to think things through, evaluate, and make suggestions, events are not as securely under the teacher's thumb as they are when there is a benevolent dictator in charge. Pupils' comments may startle you until you stop to think what is back of them. "Don't you think you could work better if you had more room?" asked Miss Carson. "No," answered first-grade Penny, "I can reach things this way." Is this insubordination or a first step in thinking for oneself? "What would you think of making masks for our Halloween party?" asked the art teacher. "I think it would be sort of silly," said sixth-grade Jane. Is this a dare or a cue that Jane could be helped to use a little more tact in expressing herself in a discussion?

What understandings of the role of authority in a democracy are needed? Citizens in a democracy do not do exactly as they please. We obey traffic signs when we drive. We follow the rules of our employer regarding the times for arrival at and departure from work and for coffee breaks. We live under laws voted by our representatives; we cooperate with persons who have been appointed to enforce these laws. We have orderly and systematic ways of changing our laws. Furthermore, we are subject to penalties of various sorts if we disregard our rules of living. Modern concepts of discipline do not neglect or treat lightly the importance of helping children and youth to grow in their willingness to abide by laws, rules, and regulations; in their feeling of obligation to cooperate with those who enforce these rules; and in their respect for the orderly procedures whereby rules are changed.

In the school community there are many situations in which pupils must learn to abide by regulations established to govern the conduct of all school citizens. Fire-drill rules must be followed unhesitatingly. Procedures to facilitate coming in from the playground or passing in the halls must be obeyed. There will be safety precautions, library rules, attendance regulations, times when notes from home are required. Primary children must be helped to become acquainted with the policies and rules that govern their school life and must learn under supervision to abide by these. Older pupils should be expected to take increasingly independent responsibility for behaving as law-abiding school citizens and for helping others so to behave.

There will also be important lessons to learn regarding responsibility to persons in authority positions. Primary youngsters must identify these persons—their own teacher, the principal, other teachers with special supervisory responsibilities, nonteaching personnel, safety guards, and other children with delegated responsibilities. They must be helped to understand what roles such persons play in the school community and to learn to accord them the cooperation that is their due. Older pupils can be expected to assume increasingly independent responsibility for their behavior in working with school personnel in authority positions. They must also develop increased understanding of how to serve in an authority role—as a line leader, a person responsible for primary games, a safety guard. What is the mature step to take, for example, if a playmate won't heed when you've asked him politely to cooperate? Do you shove? threaten? shout? give up and let him break the rule if he chooses?

Living in the classroom also offers some valuable learnings in the ways in which citizens in a democracy govern themselves. Even kindergarteners can, with help, decide upon classroom policies with regard to getting wraps, cleaning up at the end of a work period, getting drinks. They can learn to abide by these policies once they are established and to participate in discussions regarding what to do if an agreed-upon way of proceeding does not seem to be serving its purpose. Older pupils can be given a larger share in establishing the policies that govern classroom living and can be expected to take increasingly independent responsibility for abiding by these agreements without constant supervision.

The school community offers an unparalleled opportunity to help boys and girls to learn, through firsthand experience, the importance in a democracy of regulations that assure orderly living. If disciplined citizens are our goal, it is important for teachers to appraise thoughtfully the potential learning experiences in situations where pupils must live and work together in school populations ranging from less than one hundred to over two thousand and in class groups of under twenty to over forty.

What work habits do we want? A disciplined person is efficient in the way in which he carries out a responsibility. He displays self-control and good judgment in performing the tasks he has undertaken. Helping children and youth to develop effective work habits is another important goal in building toward self-discipline.

The individual with disciplined work habits can set up and carry out plans for himself. He is able to outline his own goals clearly, and he can lay out a series of proposed steps to reach these goals. He knows how to budget his time and energy in order to keep several responsibilities moving ahead simultaneously. He is able to settle himself to work without undue procrastination and waste of time. With first-graders good work habits mean the ability to state precisely one's part of a simple plan—"I am going to paint our horse brown"—and to go ahead with it without being distracted by or distracting somebody else. Older groups can reasonably be expected to make more elaborate plans, to work steadily for longer periods without disturbing others, to abide by the class schedule without constant supervision in matters of being ready on time and cleaning up.

A person with good work habits can set up efficient working conditions for himself. He makes certain that needed equipment is available; he has an orderly way of storing his materials and a suitable place to work; he is sensitive to matters of ventilation, light, or noise. First-graders begin by helping to get paper for their groups and by deciding how to keep track of crayons, where scissors should be kept, when pencils should be sharpened, how to care for paint brushes. They plan how they can provide a quiet atmosphere when reading groups meet. Before pupils enter junior high school, they should be expected to take responsibility for arriving with needed equipment in good working order, for contributing to a quiet atmosphere in the room without undue reminders, for carrying out agreed-upon plans in independent work periods.

Growing self-discipline includes increased ability to work for long-term goals. The four-year-old spends his nickel for candy; the six-year-old disciplines himself to set several nickels aside until he can buy the toy he wants. First-graders need to see the results of their efforts fairly soon (or if it is an elaborate project, to be able to check off one step at a time), whereas fourth-graders can reasonably be expected to work toward a goal through a time span of several weeks without losing interest or tending to give up. By the time they reach college age, many persons are working toward goals four to eight or ten years in the future. Even for adults, however, intermediate goals are often highly desirable as aids in attaining ultimate objectives.

A disciplined person can evaluate his own efforts. He does not have to wait to be told he has done a good job, nor does he set his standards merely in terms of another person's evaluation. How well disciplined is the sixth-grader, for example, who asks "Will spelling count?" when he is taking a social studies test? Or, for that matter, the college student who says "Will there be any questions on our supplementary reading?" If we are to send out into the world young people with a sense of obligation to contribute their best to the job at hand, we have a major responsibility in helping them to grow in their ability to hold high standards for themselves and in the self-discipline necessary to achieve these standards.

What sense of personal worth is needed? Persons who are mature in their self-control—who are disciplined—have developed socially acceptable ways of satisfying their own basic needs. They have feelings of adequacy and self-respect. Studies of the school adjustment of delinquent children show that in addition to lack of affection at home they tend to be rejected by their teachers. Sociograms often show them to be isolates or to be actively rejected by their peers. Means of demonstrating their loyalty to the school as safety guards or office helpers are usually denied them, since these jobs go to "responsible" people. And report cards, those very important pieces of evidence of what the teacher thinks of you, often tell them month after month and year after year that they can't achieve the goals their teachers seem to hold most dear.

Every human being has a basic need to be accepted as a person—to be considered of worth both by the adults who are close to him and by his peers. Boys and girls need to be in classrooms where there are teachers who can give them genuine affection and a feeling of being accepted. This acceptance is even more important when one has acted in an undisciplined fashion. Jimmy needs to know that he still has his teacher's basic respect and affection even while he is being set straight as to why baseballs should not be thrown in the classroom. Sixth-grade Bob, who is already on the point of truancy, is caught smoking in the lavatory. He is not going to come any more willingly to school if he feels that his act has made him unwanted. One of the most difficult tasks you may face will be to show that you accept a pupil as a person even though you cannot condone his behavior.

Pupils need to feel that they belong in their class groups—that they have a worth-while contribution to make.[2] This does not necessarily mean a leadership position. There are many avenues to status in a group. The clown—even a third- or fourth-rate clown—has high status, as many a beginning teacher has discovered. It is even better to be a class enemy than not to be recognized at all. Children who achieve their group status by tormenting others or by undue amounts of clowning are not, however, learning status roles that are conducive to effective interpersonal relationships. One of your major challenges as a teacher will be to discover ways of helping all children—able or slow,

[2] For a helpful discussion of children's behavior in social groups, see Ruth Cunningham and associates, *Understanding Group Behavior of Boys and Girls*. New York: Bureau of Publications, Teachers College, Columbia University, 1951.

physically attractive or unattractive, outgoing or shy—to develop wholesome and constructive ways of achieving acceptance and status in their peer groups.

Recognition by others and status in a group are not sufficient bases for a sense of personal worth. Each person also has to respect himself—to accept himself in spite of his shortcomings. He needs to be objective about his weaknesses and inadequacies, but he also needs to recognize objectively those areas in which he is competent. He needs a sense of achievement. As a teacher, you will face a major responsibility in providing the kinds of classroom experiences that will help boys and girls to develop adequate self-concepts. The more difficulty a youngster is having in achieving the controls that result in self-discipline, the more important this may be.

Present-day goals in discipline, then, are much more inclusive than achieving a quiet and obedient class. They are even more inclusive than teaching those behaviors which make one acceptable in society. Basically, helping children and youth to achieve self-discipline is a matter of helping them to develop those mature ways of meeting their own personality needs which are the foundation for their behavior toward others.

HELPING PUPILS GROW IN SELF-CONTROL

Opportunities to help pupils grow in self-discipline permeate every aspect of the school day. As a matter of fact, it is impossible for a teacher to refuse to capitalize upon these opportunities—to postpone a lesson in self-control as he might set aside a spelling test. Every step you take, all day long in the classroom, makes its contribution. It either helps the pupil to assume more self-control, teaches him to obey blindly, or points out to him that how he behaves really doesn't matter. You as a teacher cannot be neutral where discipline is concerned. Whatever you do teaches *something*.

Discipline is learned. How does one go about making a positive contribution to pupils' growth toward self-control? Basically, it is as much a teaching problem as is a language or social studies lesson. Self-discipline (or, for that matter, blind obedience to a dictator) is learned; the same principles that apply to any teaching-learning situation apply here.

As with any other teaching-learning situation, you must first be clear about your goals—about the types of behavior you hope to help your pupils achieve. This means thinking through the general objectives discussed in the preceding section in terms of the readiness of your particular boys and girls. Readiness involves as complex a set of factors in learning self-control as it does in learning to read. You will need to appraise your pupils' experience backgrounds and their present levels of competence. First-graders who have never been to school have many routines to learn that are "old stuff" to veterans of the kindergarten. Fourth-graders who have never worked in committees must start slowly. Children who have, because of a series of unfortunate events, been under inconsistent discipline the previous year may have to be taught the ways of behaving that one would normally expect youngsters of their age group to possess. You will also need to give some thought to the capacities of your pupils to learn. First-graders will not be able to see as far-reaching implications of their actions as will older pupils, nor will they arrive as readily at general principles to govern their behavior. Neither will slow learners. You will have to be prepared, in both cases, to teach through many concrete situations and to give much supervision and help. To complicate the problem of readiness still further, you will find in your class a range in experience backgrounds and maturities. Some youngsters will display the self-control and the thoughtfulness typical of pupils several years their senior. The behavior of others will remind you of children much younger. This constellation of backgrounds, present competencies, and abilities to learn must be clearly in your mind as you decide what your next steps should be in helping your pupils to achieve self-discipline.

In developing self-control, as in learning arithmetic, pupils learn what they experience. As with other learnings, precisely what a learner experiences depends on how he interprets the situation in terms of his particular goals. Whether a pupil sees a desired way of behaving as sensible and worth while, or whether he conforms so that he can get on to more interesting activities, depends upon how he sizes things up, not upon what you tell him. He must see for himself that the behavior expected of him "pays off" in helping to achieve a goal. ("We are certainly getting some group products to be proud of since we figured out how to work without interrupting each other." "Neither of the classes next door complained about any noise in the hall, so we may work on our mural out there again today.") It follows also that a pupil must have experiences that help him to recognize that undisciplined ways of behaving do not achieve his goals. His punishments should teach.

As with any other learning, the individual who arrives at general principles to guide his actions is better equipped to meet new situations than the one who has merely acquired routine ways of behaving. You will provide your boys and girls with sufficient experiences to make habitual certain desired ways of behaving, but you will also help them, at their maturity levels, to analyze the situations they face—to develop values and standards to guide their behavior.

The learning curve in achieving self-discipline has its short-term fluctuations and plateaus as does any other learning curve. Good work habits and ability to work effectively with other people are built through repeated practice. This practice needs to be consistent. It takes much longer to develop desired controls if what pupils actually experience is "Maybe this time it doesn't matter" than it does if they experience "We always do it this way." Some beginning teachers tend to give more consistent practice than they realize in behavior which they definitely do *not* desire, at the same time talking vigorously to the group about the goals they *do* want. Jack Jamison spent considerable time with his sixth grade discussing how important it is to give each person a polite hearing in a discussion. However, as a discussion leader, he consistently invited a chorus by asking "Class?" and encouraged pupils to talk out of turn by responding to the loudest voice whether or not a hand was up. Watch Sally Clarkson, too, in her first grade. She says firmly, "Boys and girls, the clock says it's time to clean up now," and then turns to answer Johnny's question. Having satisfied Johnny, she looks around and says again, still pleasantly, "Boys and girls, it's time to clean up." At this point, up come Susie and Jill to show their pictures, neatly maneuvering Sally so that her back is to the group. After a few minutes of discussion with the two girls, Sally surveys her group again and says, in an exasperated tone, "Boys and girls, let's clean up right away. *I mean it!*" What experience is Sally actually giving her group?

You teach for self-discipline, then, as you would teach for any other type of increased competence. You decide where to begin in terms of the readiness, needs, and learning capacities of your group. You make sure that your pupils see the new behavior as purposeful and reasonable. You help them to see, in their terms, the underlying principle upon which they are operating. You provide sufficient practice to guarantee that the new learnings are thoroughly established. And you insure that behaviors once learned are used consistently.

Punishment teaches. We learn from the results of our efforts. Failure teaches as well as success. To some persons punishment refers either to physical pain or to some distasteful and unrelated task imposed because of wrongdoing. In a broader sense, however, one is punished when one's behavior fails to achieve a desired goal. It would be impossible to grow up without running into some snags and meeting some disappointments. Even if a child could be shielded from the results of his errors in judgment, the desirability of doing so is highly questionable. The disciplined person knows that he must accept the consequences of his decisions.

Your problem, as a teacher, will be to decide upon the purposes which punishment should serve and how best to use it to achieve these purposes. Certainly, punishment should deter an individual from his present course of action. If he enjoys what he is doing more than he dislikes the consequences, the punishment is to no avail. ("Go ahead and spank me," said Mary Jane to her mother; "it was worth it.") Further, some teacher-imposed punishments are actually enjoyed by pupils or offer them a way out of a disagreeable situation. David Watson, the first man to teach his pupils in their five years of school, discovered after several futile attempts that asking the boys to stay after school to make up time wasted was not paying off. They liked him so much that the chance to have him alone was too good to miss. Seven-year-old Billy, who was disturbing his group, obeyed his teacher quite happily when she asked him to go back to his seat and read quietly, since reading was his favorite pastime.

Imposed punishment that merely deters is not too useful as a teaching instrument. If children are to learn to appraise their own behavior in terms of its effects upon themselves and others, they must face the consequences of their decisions. Ideally, the consequences of the wrongdoing should indicate why it was wrong and should point the way to the type of behavior that is more acceptable. If Sally Ann dawdles, only to be told to write "I will not waste time" one hundred times, she learns that adults can be disagreeable, but dawdling may be worth it. If her wasting of time causes her to miss the gym class which she loves or results in her losing her turn to feed the goldfish, the consequences point much more directly to the values of wise use of time.

Capitalizing upon the natural consequences of behavior not only helps the pupil to relate cause and effect, but also removes the teacher from the role of a punishing adult and makes him an arbitrator who merely points out that what must be must be. Once you see yourself clearly as playing the latter role, you may find yourself feeling much less conscience-stricken as you help your pupils to realize that certain ways of behaving lead to trouble. "I know you wanted to hear the last of the story, but you took so much time to get your wraps and come back to your seats that we must start for home. The safety guards are expecting us." "Our mothers have all been invited. If John's group was fooling around and is not ready, what can we do but go ahead anyway?" Yes, the other classes go out for drinks, but we tried for three days and we still disturbed the whole second floor. They've asked us please not to go."

All of this presupposes, of course, that the activity seemed interesting and worth while to your pupils in the first place. "How many of you want to go on with this game?" asked Elizabeth Ann McCoy after several efforts to make the directions clear for a far too complex activity—and not a hand went up. "Would you rather stay here with us or go back to your seat?" asked Jane Brown, whose reading activities were well over Sandy's head. "Go to my seat," said Sandy honestly.

It is important that pupils know in advance what the possible consequences of failure to abide by agreements might be. Unless they do, cause-and-effect relationships will not be clear. It is one thing to plan how to save time for a story and then to face the fact that the plans were not followed through. It's another to work ahead without any inkling that time is important, only to have the teacher say, reprovingly, "I'm sorry but we've wasted too much time today to have earned our story." The latter may seem to you, as the teacher, to be a natural consequence, but to most pupils it will be the act of an arbitrary and unfair adult. Too many such seemingly arbitrary decisions can result in a resentful and rebellious group. This does not mean that each day should begin with a recital of impending consequences. Beginning teachers have sometimes found to their regret that such a procedure can start things off in an atmosphere of mistrust and mutual antagonism. There can, however, be positive, cooperative planning that makes goals clear and suggests that you are just as anxious as anyone else to achieve them. "Mr. Johnson says that we may practice in the auditorium if we will not disturb the things backstage. Do you think we can work that out?" "We may go out to play but other classes will be working with their windows open and we mustn't disturb them. Can we plan some quiet games?" It is important, however, for a teacher who foresees the possibility of having to deprive a group of some privilege to warn them. As horseplay begins to appear, for example, it is much fairer for the teacher to forewarn pupils of the consequences ("Now look, if we are just going to waste time, we'd better give up our plan") and carry through his intent, if necessary, than it is to let everybody go on thinking that a little horseplay is all right and then quite suddenly call a whole project off.

Teachers have tried to involve pupils at various points in the punishment process. In at least two ways, the children are invariably involved. First, they must face and think about the consequences of their behavior. Without this analysis of cause-and-effect relationships there can be little growth in the insights that lead to self-control. Second, if they are to learn that one unfortunate result of undisciplined behavior is the damage it does to a cooperative enterprise, there must be times when a whole group suffers because of an error in judgment by one individual, and the individual faces the full force of the resulting group indignation. Allen, in a bright fifth grade, is a good example. Allen was ten years younger than the other children in his family, and he had developed many techniques for charming those about him in order to get his way. In spite of dawdling, clowning, wisecracking, demanding attention, and other behavior which his teacher recognized as undesirable, Allen's fifth-grade friends adored him, made excuses for him, and did his jobs for him. Then came the afternoon when Allen's group moved out to the hall to put the finishing touches on a large backdrop for the second act of a play to be presented in the auditorium the next morning. Allen amused the others with his usual charm while they did the work, until a sixth-grader walked past. He responded to Allen's wisecrack, and Allen jumped up to tussle with him. Over went the full jar of red paint. In the indignant class session that followed, Allen realized for the first time that charm doesn't always solve problems. The play was put on without benefit of backdrop. The entire group was punished for the deficiencies of one of its members. But was this not the lesson which both Allen and the group needed to learn?

Punishing an entire class for one child's misbehavior when the group endeavor is in no way involved is an entirely different matter, however, and can build a strong feeling of injustice. Everybody need not stay after school while Sally cleans her desk, miss a recess period because Peter and James were dawdling, or cancel plans to invite the second grade to see their work because Joanna did not follow directions in completing her picture. There is no justification for making a group miserable merely to use it as a weapon against an individual, nor is there any justification for turning a class into a court to judge and punish wrongdoers. Pupils do not have the mature insights into human be-

Summer Demonstration School, University of Cincinnati,
D. Arthur Bricker, Photographer

Take your pupils in on the plans. Recorded agreements facilitate self-direction.

Summer Demonstration School, University of Cincinnati,
D. Arthur Bricker, Photographer

Make sure that routines are clearly established. A supply table and a helpers' chart reduce confusion.

Summer Demonstration School, University of Cincinnati,
D. Arthur Bricker, Photographer

Provide ample worth-while things to do. Challenging independent activities free the teacher to work with individuals.

havior nor the judgment it takes to appraise most situations. Further, they typically conceive of punishment as an infliction of pain or some other disagreeable consequence. It takes the mature and objective leadership of a teacher to help pupils to evaluate the effects of their acts and learn the disciplines of democracy.

Unwise punishment can teach some negative and undesirable lessons. Pupils can learn that adults can make you do things just because they're bigger. They can develop concepts of persons in authority as punitive and arbitrary. They can grow to hate subjects that are assigned for punishment purposes. They can learn to bargain—balancing the punishment against the satisfactions of disobedience or weighing the risk of being caught against the possibility of getting by. This suggests that among the punishments least likely to lead to positive learnings are spanking, humiliation before the class, assignments of practice activities in skill areas, missing a well-liked activity because of behavior in a situation totally unrelated to it. Punishment teaches. Make sure that it teaches the lessons you want your pupils to learn.

Consistency is essential. One of the most difficult problems faced by many beginning teachers is to learn to be consistent. There are so many things to think about and so many personalities to respond to that agreed-upon procedures are forgotten from time to time. Yet it is very important for pupils to have the security of consistent leadership and the more disturbed the pupil, the more important this security is. Youngsters are taking only their first steps toward self-control. Many of their cues as to what is desirable and what is unacceptable come from the adults around them. They need to be apprised of the limits within which their behavior will be considered acceptable. In each new situation they test just where the boundaries are. Once they have discovered them, they settle down contentedly. If your boundaries are constantly shifting, sometimes very close and sometimes wide open, your pupils will not know where they stand. Consequently (and disastrously, sometimes, for your morale) they will feel compelled each new day to test out all over again just where the limits are. In such a situation a strong feeling of injustice may easily develop. For example, Sarah Belle is reprimanded sharply for behavior that was quite all right for Alice five minutes ago, or even for behavior in which she herself has been engaging for the better part of the morning without the slightest hint that she is out of bounds. If you find yourself met with a rash of "But I was only . . . ," "But Rickie . . . ," "Well make *him* stop . . . ," "You didn't say . . . ," look to the firmness of your boundaries.

In classrooms where there is consistent support, children are expected to follow through on a number of necessary and reasonable agreements. If you and your pupils agree that things are to be out of the way when someone is talking, then everybody abides by this; nobody in the back of the room reads or writes during discussion time. If pencils are to be sharpened and paper dropped in the basket only when it will not disturb anyone, nobody wanders around the room while a child is reporting or while you are giving an explanation. If all agree that it will help in taking turns in discussion to raise hands to be recognized, then voices that call your name (or, what is harder to resist, call out the right answer) are not acknowledged. You will not achieve perfection at once, but you will notice progress much faster if you provide steady help. The teacher who gives up after three or four reminders and just lets things happen for the rest of the day finds that tomorrow he is back where he started. Indeed, he is probably a few steps farther back than when he started, although this may not be apparent until the pupils have had enough experience with his inconsistency to learn how elastic his boundaries are.

A consistent teacher disciplines himself in the behavior he is expecting his group to achieve. Many a teacher carries on a side conversation or checks through a set of attendance cards while a pupil is speaking, without excusing himself. Many times a teacher, who is firm in seeing that children do not interrupt a speaker, will break in himself, without apology. In the classrooms where pupils achieve most rapidly the controls that make for happy human relationships, they must have in you the example of a teacher who practices what he preaches.

A consistent teacher follows through. As an impartial arbitrator, it will often be your job to make sure that the consequences of undisciplined behavior are not avoided. If children fail to earn the time for a story and then hear a chapter anyway because they plead for it, the point of the experience is lost. So are the learnings in a group work situation in which a teacher announces at intervals, "Remember, if our voices are this loud and disturbing we'll have to stop," but never calls a halt. "Don't stop," said one kindergartener to another; "she sounds lots madder than that before she does anything." This implies a closely related point. The skillful teacher does not announce a consequence that cannot be carried out. "You'll stay here till six o'clock if I hear one more desk bang," said panicky Joanna Greene. "We can't," said one of the ringleaders cheerfully, "we've got to be on the bus at 3:45."

If pupils are to be in a secure and consistent atmosphere, the adults with whom they work back each other up. If Mother says "No," Father does not say "Maybe." Whatever difference in philosophy they may have is thrashed out later when the small fry are safely in bed. One of your first steps in getting acquainted with your new school should be to ascertain the playground rules, how pupils come through the halls, what procedures are observed at recess periods and lavatory breaks. It is possible that you will find yourself in a school where you feel that there are more restrictions than are really needed. This is a problem to work out with your colleagues (but not at your first faculty meeting in a new school). For the time being your pupils will be much happier and more secure staying within bounds than they will be if they are scolded by everyone from the principal to the custodian.

It is important to think things through. In your classes in teaching methods you learned to help pupils to think things through, to make sure that they understand *why*. Talking things over is important in building effective self-control. Through discussions you can help pupils to take joint responsibility for setting standards for their own behavior and can provide sound bases for understanding that these standards make sense. They can work with you on the establishment of many of the classroom routines. You can also involve your boys and girls with profit in evaluating their behavior. Some worth-while building of new standards can come from analyzing what happened and suggesting more effective procedures for next time. Furthermore, talking things over can lead to more intelligent understanding of what it means to be a citizen in the school community. Sally McArthur was able to help her fifth-graders to develop a better appreciation of this when they protested bitterly that they were always the ones asked to give up their recess time to keep an eye on younger children going up and down some rather risky stairways. "Let some other class do it," they complained. Sally indicated that she would ask the principal about it. Next day she returned with a list of other all-school responsibilities. Sixth-graders were needed on heavily trafficked streets. The stairways were the next most important safety problem, and fourth-graders were pretty small to handle it. With this information at hand and some more effective plans to take turns, the fifth-graders went contentedly back to their assignment.

Sometimes discussions of desirable behavior degenerate into routine recitals of lists of generalities. Every group work period is held up until pupils list the behavior that makes for a good group; preceding every set of reports, characteristics of a good audience must be listed on the board; before each field trip, the same set of suggestions for courteous behavior is reconstructed. Merely reciting a list of desirable ways to behave does not guarantee that much of this behavior will be put into practice. It is often far more effective to evaluate present behavior, to select one or two specific areas in which growth is needed, and then to work particularly on these.

A sense of timing is important in talking over behavior with a group and making plans for improvement. You will find that the end of a rugged afternoon is not always a strategic time for an extended discussion of the importance of better work habits, although pupils often do stop to evaluate their behavior briefly before a period closes. It is often much better to postpone the detailed discussion about how the work session might be improved until the following day when your pupils prepare to try again. Furthermore, asking pupils to talk in general terms about why good work habits are important (and perhaps adding some strong hints of your own about what will happen if time is wasted) is not nearly so apt to lead to a successful day as a precise and optimistic identification of two or three points at which everybody can try to improve.

Extended discussions are not always necessary in order to help pupils to think about the reasons for disciplined behavior and the standards that should guide their actions. In fact, they are sometimes not nearly so effective as a brief comment that helps to intellectualize the problem. There is a point at which most groups become weary of talking about good behavior and find ways of showing it. Skillful teachers build many insights into the values of disciplined behavior while saying very little. "Of course you'll lose things if you don't put them away." "If you give him a little more room to get his job done, he won't bump you." "It's hard to sit still when it's so hot. Would it help to stand and stretch?" "Take a look before we begin. Have you everything off your desk so that you will be able to give our speakers your full attention?" "It was a good work period, wasn't it? Do you think it helped to keep our voices lower?" If your mind is upon the problem of how to help your pupils to grow in their insights into the value of disciplined behavior, you will find yourself making many such comments before the close of the day.

Common sense sometimes saves the day. Back of the happy, orderly classroom of the competent teacher is a large amount of good humor and common sense. He knows how to size up a situation. He realizes that you cannot expect of ten-year-olds, or even of adolescents, the self-control you would expect of adults. He is able to laugh heartily with the group when something humorous happens and then to say "All right . . . ." and go back to the work at hand. He expects the excited chorus that follows the proposal of a field trip or a party and allows for this exuberant reaction before he tries to get an orderly discussion of plans. He knows that it is human to want to see the fire engines tearing right down the street past the school. He understands, too, that the best of us tosses an eraser once in a while to our friends or jumps over a desk rather than going around by the aisle. The art of sensing when behavior is a surface phenomenon—not really harming anyone and best passed over lightly—and when it is a symptom of a basic lack of self-discipline is extremely important in securing good human relationships in the classroom.

The teacher with common sense realizes that interest and attention spans vary and that many factors outside the classroom, including the weather or the Halloween parade tomorrow, can make a major difference in group solidarity. It is often necessary to give a little more help—to be a little more directive—on days that are exciting. It is helpful also to change pace—switch to another activity, insert a game, or provide a chance to stretch when a tide of restlessness begins to swell. Many a beginning teacher has lost more ground than he has gained by saying to himself as he gritted his teeth and tried to hold his group's wavering attention "There are three more points to make, and I'll make them if it's the last thing I do."

It is important to have the good sense to know when to ease up, even if the behavior normally would not be acceptable. No matter how self-controlled your group, there will inevitably come a time when unusual circumstances cause somebody to become upset. A sensitive teacher realizes when a youngster is under all the pressure he can take and does not aggravate the situation. In Myra Allen's fourth grade, Bill tried to do an arithmetic problem at the board. With all eyes on him he failed and had to let someone else try. As Bill played with his pencil in a disgruntled fashion, Myra said, "Watch now, Bill, we're doing this especially for you," whereupon the group clown mimicked, "Especially for you, Bill," and the usually mild-mannered Bill socked him. Was this a time to add to the frustration by an extended scolding? (And you may well ask whether Myra had not started the whole thing off with her comment.) She recuperated by saying pleasantly but firmly, "Jack, teasing people like that hurts," and to Bill, "But we don't hit people even if we are angry," and went back to the neutral ground of arithmetic. Later, of course, she talked with the youngsters individually, but not until she was sure that some objectivity had been regained.

The teacher with common sense doesn't jockey himself into impossible positions. There is no point to a threat you can't carry out. Neither is there any point to announcing a consequence that is obviously going to be much harder on you than on the culprits. Teachers who are using common sense and good judgment also avoid setting up situations where, to be consistent, they will inevitably have to follow through with punishment whether it is merited or not. Statements such as "If one more person speaks out of turn we'll stop our discussion" or "If I hear one more pencil drop the whole group will stay in" ask for trouble. So does "The next person who loses his paper will write it over ten times." There will inevitably *be* one more voice heard or one more pencil dropped. And the next person to lose his paper will be the neatest child in the room. "We won't go on until I can hear the clock tick for one whole minute" risks a snort from someone who just can't endure the silence. "Do you people really want to take this trip?" dares somebody to say "No"; so does "Would you like to put your library books away now?" Much of the success of helping children grow in self-control depends upon maturity, good judgment, and self-discipline of the adults who give them leadership.

Teachers' personal needs make a difference. Teachers make an important contribution to children's growth in self-discipline by the kinds of persons they are. Often what looks, on the surface, to be an effective procedure is completely invalidated by a tone of voice, manner, or way of expressing suggestions that teaches almost exactly the opposite of what is desired. "I *do* keep consistently reminding them to work cooperatively," said Marion Candido, "but they just quarrel and tattle until I can hardly stand it." Actually a series of threats, scoldings, and other negative statements regarding what would happen if group work did not go well, combined with nagging about situations that couldn't be helped—a book that needed to be borrowed, a voice raised a little with excitement—was irritating this group and providing little, if any, feeling of being accepted. Since they could not quite take out their growing frustration on Marion, they were turning on weaker members as scapegoats.

How is it possible for a teacher who thinks he is working consistently toward giving one type of leadership to his boys and girls (and desires sincerely to achieve this) actually to develop relationships with his pupils that are so entirely different? Teachers bring their own needs, aspirations, and goals and their own present level of self-discipline into classrooms just as truly as do their pupils. They have their own concepts of themselves as competent individuals and their own ideals for themselves as teachers. To build effective relationships with other people you must understand your own aspirations and needs. As you try to understand why your pupils behave as they do in given situations you must learn to look objectively at the motivation for your own behavior.

How important is it to you to be accepted? In some beginners the need for acceptance is so strong that they can hardly force themselves to take a stand in a situation where the group may have to be disappointed or denied. Yet, there will inevitably be situations where, for the sake of the children's growth in self-discipline, rules must be enforced and the consequences of undisciplined behavior be felt. If your own need for acceptance is so strong that you fail to assume your leadership functions, you will certainly fail to help your pupils to grow. Furthermore, you also fail to gain for yourself some of the satisfactions that should be yours as a teacher. Consider, for example, Sally Jones teaching fourth-graders who lacked the control they needed to carry out the cooperative work of putting on a rather elaborate play. After trying to work in bedlam and getting nowhere for three days, Sally finally reluctantly announced that the play would have to be dropped—and then wept most of the night because she had been so mean and was sure the youngsters would never like her again. Next morning, of course, they greeted her at the bus stop as usual because Sally typically had interesting things for them to do. But how long would Sally's successful teaching have continued had her boys and girls discovered that she would allow almost any behavior rather than risk their displeasure? Consider also Jeanine McKay whose group usually responded very well to her leadership until a hot and sticky May day when it seemed that they couldn't do anything pleasant or cooperative for anybody. After the last little tormenter left, Jeanine wailed to her supervisor, "How could they do this to me when I have worked so hard for them?" Every teacher is in Jeanine's position once in a while. But if he reacts to a day when his youngsters have had a difficult time with self-control by feeling that he, personally, has been let down, then he is seeking from his boys and girls satisfaction of a need which should be met through social contacts other than those in the classroom. Have you developed your own circle of friends and sources of affectionate relationships so that you are not dependent upon your pupils to fill your need for acceptance? Are you willing to face their displeasure for the sake of helping them to achieve a learning which is important for their growth?

How important is it for you to be boss? Some beginning teachers conceive of the ideal teacher as one who is always in control, always obeyed, never questioned. Perhaps at times this attitude is a way of covering a deep-down fear that pupils will not respect one's leadership. Sometimes it is contributed to by colleagues' well-meant but misleading advice to "show them who's boss from the start." It may be built partly from memories of "the workout we gave poor Miss Gadby in the eighth grade" and the nightmarish thought, "Suppose it happened to me!" or from respectful memories of Mr. McGraw who "certainly could teach us arithmetic but wouldn't stand for nonsense." Actually, with a lively group—be they kindergarteners or sixth-graders—nobody can be boss all the time, but a person can make many enemies trying. Johanna, who is reading the last page of the story, may not close her book the second she is asked. Twelve-year-old Sue Ellen may be bent on gaining Andy's attention no matter what. The day Penny had a dreadful argument at breakfast with her mother may not be the day when anybody can tell her what to do—especially a teacher who looks and sounds a little like Penny's mother. The fifth-graders who come in, furious because the sixth grade took their kickball during noon play, are not going to "forget it and quietly get out reading books." Such behavior is certainly not a personal affront to the teacher. Can you understand such situations for what they are and give the needed help, or are you tempted to retaliate to show who is in control? In the room where there is lack of understanding, retaliation for small misdemeanors, threats, and constant show of authority, there is always the chance that the children will eventually reach the point where they decide to demonstrate who really is boss. A sufficiently strong teacher can win this battle, but only at the expense of operating as a warden for the rest of the year.

How important is it to you to be smart? For four years of college you have been concentrating on a major of your choice. You have probably been able to make some very respectable grades. How important is it to you that your pupils recognize how much you know? Are you going to be tempted to be sarcastic when Jerry asks a question about something you've just finished explaining? How big a threat to you will John be, with his insatiable reading and his own great need to be accepted as smart which causes him to pounce on your slightest error? Will you be able to let him have the full limelight or will you be tempted to take over and tell the story yourself? What chance will slow-thinking Andy have in your room after you discover that he not only does not grasp what you are trying to explain but would much rather be working on something else? Will there be any temptation to show your boys and girls how little they know by an unusually tricky test or a sweeping allotment of low grades? In studies of pupils' evaluation of best-liked teachers, sympathy, kindliness, patience, fairness, rank high. Sarcasm, having favorites, impatience, are among the most frequently mentioned characteristics of disliked teachers. Children who feel that they are not accepted in the classroom often show through a seemingly "don't care" attitude how they feel about their rejection. For the sake of your pupils' growth as well as your own success as a teacher, you must become the kind of person who can build an accepting and supportive classroom atmosphere.

How important is it for you to be right? It is perhaps partly a reflection of their own schooling that some beginners cling to the concept that teachers should never make mistakes. With all there is to explore in today's world, yours will be a frustrated group and a dull classroom indeed if you hold all discussions to points on which you are sure you have the right answer. If you and your pupils are going to explore new areas together, you must be able to say "Let's look it up" without losing face. Furthermore, you are going to make mistakes on simple things. Have you discovered how peculiar a word can look when it is spelled out on the blackboard? Can you take correction graciously when a little voice says, "You forgot to dot the *i*"? Or will you be tempted to put your would-be-helper in his place with "It's there if you'd just look a little more carefully"? You, as well as your pupils, will at times say or do something extremely funny. Can you enjoy a laugh at yourself? Will you be able to apologize for misunderstanding a child without feeling that you have lost status in his eyes and those of the group? It takes maturity and a strong sense of security to be willing to admit that one is wrong.

Discipline is learned, both by teacher and pupils. If you want your group to grow, you must grow—in self-understanding, in your own ability to meet your needs in satisfying ways, in the maturity of your sources of status and security.

ACHIEVING THE ATMOSPHERE THAT MAKES FOR HAPPY LIVING

Much of the behavior that sends beginning teachers home exhausted, wondering if somebody somewhere does not want to hire a good cook, is forestalled by their more experienced colleagues through a general classroom atmosphere that is conducive to happy living rather than to trouble-making. The number and variety of the activities you provide, the care with which you take your pupils in on the plans, the thoroughness of your own preparation, and your good judgment in handling situations that make difficult demands upon your pupils—each makes its contribution toward orderly and happy working conditions.

Provide ample worth-while things to do. Pupils who do not find in the classroom many things to do that seem reasonable and interesting will discover their own ways of keeping themselves busy. It is as simple as that. This does not mean that you must make all your activities play or dress everything up as a game to hold your pupils' interest and attention. Youngsters will stay at a tough job if they see some point to it, just as you, yourself, will put in long hours of practice to improve your golf score, volunteer to do all the labor if your parents will just allow you to redecorate your room, or devote much of your spare time to a hobby. What *is* important is to make sure that your pupils recognize the purposefulness of what they do. They, like yourself, will find ways of escaping if the job seems utterly stupid.[3]

If you wish to assure that your pupils are happily and gainfully occupied, you must do more than merely plan activities that are purposeful; you must also see to it that there is ample work to do. Experienced teachers typically take several specific steps in order to achieve this. In the first place, they plan for more than they expect to accomplish in a single day. They make sure that there is always something ahead, that the time never comes when they (and their pupils) face ten empty minutes and wonder what to do. Then, they give particular thought to points in their plans where it seems likely that a few children will finish early. They make sure that they have provided extras for these potentially idle hands, and they see to it that the youngsters understand clearly what is to be done next. Experienced teachers are also adept in planning with children the types of activities where there are almost unlimited possibilities for groups and individuals to pursue special

[3] You will find in Chapter 6, and also in Chapters 7, 8, and 9, many suggestions of ways of selecting classroom activities that seem purposeful and worth while to students.

interests if time allows. And, as though all these precautions were not enough, experienced teachers also make sure that their classrooms offer many outlets for individual talents and interests—library books, a writers' bulletin board or a class paper, a shelf of arithmetic games, a science table. If you provide a classroom atmosphere replete with challenges to intellectual curiosity, the temptations to explore illegitimate sources of amusement will be few.

Make sure that there is variety in your day. Beginning teachers often face a difficult task in learning to schedule the day's activities so that their variety and sequence contribute to effective work habits and positive working relationships. Yet this is an important skill to acquire. Many potential behavior problems can be forestalled by astute scheduling.[4]

Some teachers will advise you to plan activities involving "concentration" early in the day and to place later those experiences that will allow for a little more relaxation and moving about. Actually, the research evidence to justify this advice is meager. Any activity that is developed in such a way that it is challenging to pupils can hold their attention just as effectively at the end of the afternoon as in the early morning. In spite of the lack of research evidence, however, you may find that for your pupils one sequence of activities seems to work better than another. Problems of discipline are usually reduced if you follow your "hunches" on this—if only because of your own state of mind. Going from a highly competitive game to a lively discussion, for example, can be disastrous for the self-control of some groups. Sometimes, to take another example, pupils need the help that comes when the teacher takes over leadership of the class as a whole in order to settle down after a period in which they have been moving about in individualized activities. Primary teachers have long realized the value of such all-class sessions in helping pupils to go smoothly through a day. They frequently intersperse brief planning periods or evaluation sessions between meetings of reading groups or independent work periods.

It can be a major contribution to pupils' self-control to provide for changes of pace during the day. It is important to learn to analyze the variety in your schedule in terms of the types of activities in which your pupils are engaged as well as the subjects they are studying. Sometimes a day that looks, on the surface, to be quite varied in its activities actually is monotonous. Look, for example, at the way in which the schedule

[4] How to build an effective daily schedule is discussed in detail in Chapter 6, pages 201-211.

for Marybeth Smith's fourth grade developed: From 1:00 to 1:30 they wrote answers to questions based on their reading. At 1:30 they changed to arithmetic and took a test Marybeth had mimeographed. As they finished they secured paper and wrote a letter to Sally, hospitalized with a broken ankle. At 2:10 everyone took a dictated spelling test. At 2:30 they got out their social studies books and went to work taking notes to answer questions set up the day before, each child working individually. By 3:00, Marybeth was wondering distractedly what had happened to her usually self-controlled and hard-working group. On the surface this looks like a varied schedule. Periods are short; several subject fields are covered. Under the surface what was the afternoon-long activity in which these youngsters engaged? Let it be said to her credit that Marybeth sensed that there had been far too much sitting and writing and the last half-hour was spent singing lustily. It is equally possible for pupils to sit and discuss all afternoon, or to move from one kind of active group work to another until they are overstimulated. A good schedule shifts from writing to talking to moving about as well as from spelling to art to science.

Teachers in whose rooms children work cooperatively and happily also look at the pattern of a week's activities and plan for variety to help hold interest and attention. Reading groups do not do the same thing every day. There is variety in the pattern of arithmetic lessons. Spelling activities are planned so that there is an occasional game. From time to time an excursion, a film, a visit to another class, a party, an assembly program, provides for a major change in the day. It is not possible, nor would it be desirable, to try to ride the crest of a wave of excitement with your boys and girls all the time, but if you want to have a room in which it is more fun to work than it is to engage in extraneous activities, you will provide for high points as well as calm in your day.

Take your pupils in on the plans. Boys and girls can be more intelligently self-directing if they know what the plans are. If your pupils do not have any notion when you are going to say "stop," it is almost impossible for them to manage their independent or small-group activities so that they are ready to proceed to something else. Nor will there be much to do for the child who finishes early except to twiddle his thumbs or annoy others if he hasn't any idea what's coming next. Teachers today help pupils become responsible for their own classroom behavior by involving them in the planning.[5]

[5] For help in how to do this, see Chapter 6, pages 211-219.

Among your most valuable aids in making it possible for your pupils to be self-directing will be written plans—plans they can turn to for guidance as needed. Such devices as minutes of committees, memos regarding reading or arithmetic assignments, lists of "extra" activities to be undertaken when everything else is done, check lists outlining special responsibilities for individuals, all help boys and girls to proceed easily from one activity to the next without aimlessly wandering around the room or standing anxiously at your elbow to ask what they are to do.

It is essential to make the schedule for the day available in writing if you wish to have activities unfold smoothly. Although some youngsters become overanxious if they do not meet the exact deadlines on a schedule, many learn to apportion their time and to take pleasure in being ready for the next step. Certainly you can at least list the sequence of activities for the day and indicate, as work begins, how much time will be given to a single activity. Even with the schedule posted and the time to stop announced, a two- or three-minute warning can be an asset in bringing individual projects or committee activities to a smooth halt. *You* do not willingly stop reading in the middle of a sentence, drop your knitting halfway across the row, or leave that last nail before you finish pounding it in. Your pupils, too, if ordered to stop without warning, will have a strong compulsion to keep going just long enough to finish the task. Much nagging can be avoided if they are given a minute or two to bring the on-going activity to a close.

Careful pre-planning on your part is essential. Many beginning teachers do not realize how many details must be thought through if the activities for the day are to go well. Pauses while you hunt for materials, times when pupils must wait while you put work on the board, points at which everyone tries to ask questions at once because directions were not clear—all these lead to unnecessary confusion. Furthermore, such occurrences are likely to have you sounding baffled and uncertain, which in itself can lead to trouble.

If you want to avoid confusion and long waits during which your boys and girls find other things to occupy themselves, an essential part of your preparation should be to get as many of your teaching aids as possible ready before school begins. It is a great help to put work on the blackboard ahead of time, to check on the number of books available to determine whether or not you will have to ask pupils to shift their desks in order to work together, to mark in your text any pages to which you will want your youngsters to turn for reference, to make sure that the picture or map to which you intend to refer actually makes the point you vaguely remembered that it did. Even a simple set of spelling or arithmetic exercises can be a trap if you have not read them carefully.

It is equally important to think through the details of a complicated procedure step by step. You can tax youngsters' self-control to the limit (and beyond) by passing out entrancing visual aids long before they are to be studied or by having notebooks and pencils out on desks well ahead of the time when you want materials copied from the blackboard. Analyze, for example, the step-by-step procedure employed by Deborah Stuart as she tried to teach her science class how to make a simple compass. Before she gave a word of explanation Deborah put a saucer with water, a cork, and a needle on each desk and distributed seven or eight magnets around the room. Then, having provided all these play-things, she tried to give a theoretical blackboard explanation of compasses. Imagine, too, the day John Jacobson gave each child in his class a milkweed pod and then tried to lead a discussion. Teachers working with craft materials also need to plan with special care, as Lois Anderson discovered when she laid out several skeins of wool, not wound into balls, and invited her class to help themselves to enough for hair for their puppets whenever they were ready. Even as seemingly uncomplicated an activity as a spell-down can end in bedlam and mutual recrimination if you have not thought through the rules carefully and decided exactly how to explain them to your class.

It goes without saying that the better informed a teacher is, the surer he is of his goals, and the more familiar he is with the material he is trying to teach, the more his voice and manner reflect his feelings of security. Pupils respect and work with the teacher who knows his subject. Thorough preparation does more, then, than merely help you avoid awkward pauses and embarrassing moments. The more secure you, yourself, feel in what you are doing, the more easily you will be accorded leadership status in the room.

Make sure that routines are clearly established. Positive classroom routines can be of great help to orderly living. Definite places to store things prevent a scramble involving the whole class in a search for the missing stapler. Pupils can be put in charge of passing paper or gathering in books so that there is not a mob attack on the cupboard. A routine way of handing in papers saves confusion; so does a systematic way of getting wraps. Raising your voice to shout for order over the hum of group work tends to add to the noise; using a chord or a tuneful bell as a signal for attention cuts through the confusion. There can be agreements regarding when to sharpen pencils, how many pupils should be at the library table at once, whether to come to the teacher for help or to wait until he comes to your desk, how many are to be excused to go to the lavatory at one time, and how permission to leave is to be secured. The more policies that can be clearly established before the occasion arises when they are needed, the less you will find yourself having to supervise, reprimand, or scold.

Be prepared to give extra help at trouble spots. Some parts of the day will inevitably be more difficult for youngsters to handle than others. A skillful teacher knows what situations are most likely to cause trouble for his group and is there to give extra help. Any mass movement can lead to confusion—coming in, getting ready for recess, clean-up time, getting books put away after one activity and out for another, coming to reading circle. These are times when five or six youngsters who love you will take advantage of the lull to dash up to tell you something. After four years of wondering if you and your pupils will really get along, this is heady stuff and many a beginner has let his room degenerate into chaos while he held court. An experienced teacher stays on the job. He turns his admirers back with a smile and then when the transition is completed finds some way to meet their individual needs for attention.

It is important to identify aspects of the total school program that may cause a group to become overstimulated. Some youngsters will come back from art class or gym bursting with enthusiasm. If you are the art, music, or physical education teacher you may have to calm down a similar outburst of enthusiasm before you can begin your lesson. Occasionally, in a system where youngsters are working with many teachers, there will be differences in the quality or type of leadership. This may be reflected in children's behavior as they move from one classroom to another. The activities you choose and the calmness of your manner can do much to re-establish normal controls if your pupils have had an unduly exciting or disturbing experience elsewhere in the school.

You should realize, also, that on occasions you will be the target for aggression that really is not meant for you at all. Pupils in a fourth grade were all ready to give their play when the principal sent an apologetic message that he needed the auditorium for a meeting of the safety patrol. Even though immediate plans were made to give the play the next day, Jack Howes was the victim of some black looks and exasperated tones of voice really meant for his principal. A first grade was all set to go hunting for nuts and berries when it rained. Since Thelma James had to be the one to say "No," she was the center of not-too-well-concealed muttering and banging of books for the next few minutes. These are not times to add to the frustration by scolding or by another deprivation; better endure a little letting off of steam and then go to work.

Most teachers have a "bag of tricks" for use at times when everyone is edgy and out of sorts—not as bribes or distractions, but as means of providing a brief change of pace and of focus. Such devices can also help to fill in profitably those three or four minutes of waiting that occur once in a while when a special teacher is a little late or the call to lunch somewhat delayed. An interesting book to read aloud is a great help. Some teachers who are poetry lovers have used spare moments to read, or to let children read, favorite poems. Games that are quiet but give a chance to move about are useful. Some teachers have adapted television quiz techniques to off-the-cuff social studies, science, or spelling reviews. Even a chance to stretch or to get a drink can be helpful. Your ability to sense the points at which such devices are needed reflects the quality of your insight into the needs of boys and girls.

Give some thought to the physical environment in which your pupils are working. The physical setup of your room can contribute to peace and quiet. Youngsters who are in a room that is too hot and stuffy or who are working under inadequate light get restless and edgy in spite of themselves. Often the children can take care of such details, but only if an adult helps them to become aware of what's needed. Because they are preoccupied with many other things, beginning teachers sometimes forget these obvious physical factors that could be employed to their advantage.

Some relatively simple rearranging of furniture can be useful. Chairs for a reading group, for example, should not be located next to the table of arithmetic games where children may be conversing quietly. Books or other materials needed frequently can be secured with much less confusion if they are not placed in a corner where even two or three youngsters must shove each other to get at them. Many teachers like the informality of small groups of desks in squares or circles. However, not all children can be given this freedom in the early fall, and some classes will be so large that such an arrangement makes it difficult for anybody to move around easily.

Many problems can be solved through slight shifts in the seating of children. Some good friends are excellent moral support for each other side by side; others may not yet have developed the needed self-control. Jane Greene turned chaos into order when she shifted the arrangement of her reading group from a long oval in which she sat at a distant end to a circle. Sometimes it will help if you seat the youngsters with the least self-control near the spot where you most frequently work so that you can make full use of a smile or a raised eyebrow. Placing the quiet, shy pupils near you where you will not tend to overlook them and putting those who are most likely to be waving hands wildly on the fringes of the group is another seating shift well worth trying.

As a beginner you may have been advised never to turn your back on a group. This, of course, is not a hard and fast rule but it does make sense not to seat yourself in a reading group with your back to the class or allow a few youngsters to engage you in a conversation while your back is toward the pupils you should be supervising at clean-up time. Eventually you will learn the fine art of writing on the blackboard while you half turn to keep the lesson moving. It helps also if you take a minute or two to survey the whole group to make sure everyone understands the assignment and has the materials he needs before you become engrossed with an individual. These are simple precautions, but they are useful in sensing confusion before things get out of hand.

Uncluttered desks are an aid to attention during reports or discussions. It is much simpler to have books returned, pencils put away, unfinished pictures stored, than it is to leave them out and keep reminding pupils not to handle them. Many teachers of younger children have worked out ways of checking balls, yo-yo's, marbles, and money until noon or recess. In primary grades where children often bring cherished toys, teachers sometimes place these beloved playthings on a sharing table for all to see and then have them taken home at noon.

Your voice, manner, and dress are part of the classroom environment. They can make a contribution to calm and orderly living. Many beginners have discovered that pupils' voices tend to get louder when the teacher raises his voice or becomes excited. The trick of lowering one's voice and slowing down as things get exciting is well worth learning. Men, as well as women, need to learn to dress for children. A rainy day merits something bright; a hot day a cool, fresh look. Even the legibility of your handwriting can contribute to smooth sailing or raise a storm of questions about words and helpful comments about how we make *r*'s in our room. Make your personal contribution to the classroom atmosphere as positive and as dynamic as you are able.

HELPING THE PUPIL WITH A SPECIAL PROBLEM

For your own feelings of security and adequacy as a teacher as well as for the sake of your pupils, you should realize that there will be some children who bring emotional needs and tensions too deep to be satisfied by normal classroom techniques or even by the undivided attention of a skillful, mature, and outgoing teacher. Some authorities estimate that these youngsters make up about 10 per cent of the school population.[6] In other words, your class will not be unusual if three pupils with very troublesome symptoms appear in a group of thirty to thirty-five. Some of these youngsters will have concerned teachers since kindergarten days. It is most unlikely that your best efforts will work miracles. You ought not to consider yourself a failure if signs of progress are infinitesimal or feel guilty about asking for expert assistance in working with such children. After all, you cannot be expected to be an expert in cases where others have not had any great degree of success. Many beginning teachers have endured unnecessary heartaches wondering why they seemingly failed with a youngster because they did not realize the severity of the problem with which they were trying to deal.

If you truly love teaching you will define your role as giving what help you can to the disturbed youngsters in your room. You need to face these problems with a sense of their complexity, however, and with some insights into the probable limits of the type of assistance you can give and the resources you can tap.

Make every effort to understand. Behavior is caused. You have heard this many times. Actually, this concept is crucial in working with a severely disturbed child. You have lost your chance to be of much help once you have pigeonholed a pupil as "lazy," "careless," "disinterested," "just plain ornery," or classified him by any other term that describes a symptom vaguely. No matter how incomprehensible a pupil's behavior may seem to you, something is causing it. One step which every teacher can take in trying to be of help to the pupil who presents a severe adjustment problem is to make a genuine effort to get to know him.

A conscientious teacher seeks to understand every child in his room,

[6] Katherine D'Evelyn, *Meeting Children's Emotional Needs,* p. 39. Englewood Cliffs, N.J.: Prentice-Hall, 1957.

of course. The youngsters in your class will not be in two distinct groups—the well-adjusted children and those with problems. Every pupil at times may face a serious adjustment problem. The better you know each individual, the better able you will be to give help. The severely disturbed child often is trying to adjust to an unusual number of difficult obstacles. Frequently he is struggling with a complex combination of problems which makes it difficult for others to understand his behavior and, therefore, much harder for them to help him. Often he has developed limited ways of satisfying his needs and consequently moves vigorously to defend himself if he seems about to be prevented from using the few techniques he has. (Having few avenues through which to secure recognition by his peers other than to answer questions in class discussions, he calls out if it seems as though his waving hand will be overlooked.) Unfortunately, the few techniques the disturbed child has developed for meeting his needs frequently tend to be negative from the teacher's standpoint—he steals to buy the approval of his group or to hurt those who threaten his status; he uses aggression or lying as his main way of securing status with his peers; he accepts scoldings and reprimands as better than no evidence at all that his teacher knows he is around.

All the sources of information about pupils which were suggested in Chapter 4 can be of help when you begin to study the child with a special problem. You should look into his medical record. A visit to his home or a conference with his parents can often be particularly revealing. You will want to go back over his cumulative records—to note the pattern of his school achievement, the evidence regarding his potential learning ability, the schools he has attended. Conferences with other teachers who have worked with him can be helpful. The principal and the members of the nonteaching professional staff may have information to add. You will also want to talk informally and perhaps often with the child himself. In addition you may wish to secure sociometric evidence regarding his status in the group or to use some informal projective devices to try to get at his reactions to conflict situations. No source of evidence should be left untapped when the problem is one of understanding a disturbed child.

Of particular value in studying children with problems are objective, anecdotal records of behavior. Teachers often make the mistake of interpreting too quickly the behavior of a child who worries them. If the causes of the behavior of such children were obvious, someone would have identified them long ago. A technique that has been very useful in taking a more objective look at the causes of a youngster's behavior is to write anecdotes describing exactly what happened, without much interpretation to explain the behavior. When considerable evidence has accumulated, advance not one hypothesis but several; then go back over the anecdotes to see which hypotheses seem more often to be confirmed. Continue this process until the evidence seems clearly to support one or more of your interpretations.[7] On several occasions, for example, Mary Ellen has had a number of candy bars in her desk. Her mother phones to say she is sure that Mary Ellen has taken money from her purse. This is a problem about which such extended anecdotal evidence might be of help. What does Mary Ellen do with the candy?—eat it? give it to the other children? give it to you as the teacher? just look at it? Does any recognizable pattern of events tend to recur before the candy appears?—does she do poorly in class work? get left out of a group? not achieve a desired leadership role? What seem to be her relationships at home?—are there younger children who seem to be favorites? is the mother's attitude one to which a child might react aggressively by stealing? is there by any chance a rigid prohibition against candy? Such questions, and others like them, suggest hypotheses that can be tested as anecdotal records of Mary Ellen's behavior accumulate.

Uncovering the reasons for pupil's behavior is a slow, baffling process. Indeed, without the help of persons who are trained in psychiatric techniques, much of the story may remain untold. Even so, every insight you do acquire will be of help as you try to decide how best to give assistance to a disturbed youngster in the classroom.

Help the disturbed child to discover positive ways of meeting his needs. Basic needs for affection, status in the group, a feeling of belonging, and a sense of achievement are strong motivating forces. Merely telling a pupil his behavior is out of order; using punishment, isolation, or some other device to discourage his present behavior; or trying to shame him into a new course of action will usually not achieve lasting results. One way or another he is going to satisfy his needs. Furthermore, pupils tend to build their concepts of themselves in the light of what the adults around them seem to expect of them. If a series of reactions from teachers and other adults combine to build the concept "You're bad," "You're a disturbance," "You don't cooperate as well as other children," "You're never ready on time," a pupil may well accept this picture of himself and try to live up to it.

[7] This procedure is described more fully in *Helping Teachers Understand Children.* Washington, D.C.: American Council on Education, 1945.

Earlier, the principle that behavior is caused was suggested as one key to understanding disturbed pupils. Equally important is the principle that behavior is learned. This is true of the undesirable behavior of the pupil who concerns you as well as the more desirable behavior you are hoping to help him develop. The motivation is a basic need. As a pupil seeks to satisfy this need he tries out several possible types of behavior. One or more of these help him to achieve his goal (though not always in a manner pleasing to his parents or teacher). As time goes on he tends to repeat the behavior that seems to work. Thus the youngster who has no positive ways of gaining status in a group may discover that if he is sufficiently obnoxious someone will at least notice him, that the candy he steals from the corner grocery helps to bribe his way into the group, or that if he just embellishes a little his adventures en route to school he is the center of an enthralled audience. Without attempting the therapy of which only a psychiatrist would be capable, you can at least try to help pupils to substitute social for antisocial means of meeting needs.

Helping pupils to substitute positive for negative behavior is not always as easy as it sounds. Negative patterns are often very deeply ingrained, and if they are a youngster's only means to need-satisfaction, he may not relinquish them easily. Furthermore, especially with pupils who are using aggressive behavior as a means of being recognized by their peers and their teacher, it is extremely difficult to arrange the situation so that the undesirable behavior does not pay off. How, for example, do you keep the clown, who disrupts the entire lesson by sprawling in the aisle, from getting the laugh he is after? And if he manages to get your full attention, as well as the fascinated attention of the group as they listen to the scolding you give him, how much of a deterrent will the scolding be? To go calmly ahead with the lesson, making as little as possible of such a situation so that few of its potential satisfactions are achieved, is a challenge that tries the soul of the conscientious teacher. Yet this is sometimes what it takes. There is often an added problem if the youngster in question has had such difficulties that his normal progress in school work has been hampered. This removes one important area of satisfaction open to most pupils—that of achievement. Nevertheless, it is usually possible to find some positive behavior that can be rewarded—perhaps praise for remembering to water the plants, a special assignment because of exceptional art ability, or a word of approval for the one helpful comment made during discussion. Some teachers are also very adept in helping a whole class to take pride in how much improvement a pupil has shown in an area such as spelling, arithmetic, or handwriting, even though his performance is still considerably below average.

In discovering positive ways for disturbed youngsters to meet their needs, many teachers find that they have to reappraise their own attitudes toward reward and recognition—attitudes developed from childhood experiences where special favors went only to the "good" children. It may not seem fair to give Willie the chance to run an errand when his behavior has not merited it. Yet if Willie is to be denied all opportunities to learn how it feels to make a positive contribution, how is he to be weaned from his present behavior patterns? This does not mean that the privileges will always go to the disturbed youngsters, but it does suggest that if their behavior *at the moment* merits trust, opportunities for recognition should not be withheld time after time because of past performances.

As a beginner, you may also need to reappraise your own relationships with individual children. Teachers have sometimes been advised never to show much warmth of affection, and, above all, never to do anything that suggests that all children are not being treated exactly alike. Experienced teachers, however, do not hesitate to give the warmth of affection that some pupils need so badly. They know that youngsters need not be treated exactly alike in order to feel equally secure. Walter comes from a broken home. He lives with an elderly and undemonstrative aunt. Every morning he meets Mrs. Trable at her bus stop and walks hand in hand with her to school. In the same room is Jo Ann who comes from a very secure and affectionate home. A smile and an inquiry concerning the health of her pet rabbit more than meet Jo Ann's needs for affection from Mrs. Trable. "How do you feel when Mr. Anderson spends so much time with the other reading group?" asked the supervisor as the little hostess described her own individual reading project and told what the reading group was doing. "Oh! We don't mind," replied Zelma. "They need him to help with hard words and we don't."

Experienced teachers have also explored the possibilities of helping pupils to reveal some of their personal problems through creative activities. It is possible, if one knows a group well and is able to talk about negative behavior without moralizing, to lead some discussions regarding what causes us to behave as we do. "Hot days like this do make you feel like taking it out on somebody," said a teacher to one particularly aggressive group. "What other kinds of things make you angry?" "Everybody has a disappointment once in a while," said another. "What do you do when things don't work out the way you want them to?"

Helping disturbed youngsters to learn to substitute positive for negative behavior is a long, slow process. Even with well-adjusted children, there will be days when you will wonder whether all your efforts to develop increased self-control have been in vain. The child who is disturbed emotionally has even more marked fluctuations in his behavior. Just as you begin to think that a little progress has been made an event—probably completely beyond your control—will cause him to revert to the old, undesirable patterns. You must learn to look for evidence of progress over weeks, not days, and to be satisfied with gains that to you may seem infinitesimal.

Safeguard the welfare of the group. Teachers are sometimes accused of spending too much of their time with the misfits, the slow learners, the youngsters with special problems, while they leave the cooperative, self-controlled, and able children to fend for themselves. It can, of course, be argued that not all children need the same kind of help and that one must know what a teacher is actually contributing to each child as well as how much time he spends with him before one can be sure that some youngsters are being neglected. Nevertheless, the teacher of a disturbed child faces a major problem in deciding how best to safeguard the welfare of the group while still giving help to the individual.

Certainly there will be times when, for the sake of the group, one merely deters the individual, quite frankly admitting that the main lesson to be taught is that certain behavior will not be tolerated under any circumstances. A fight must be stopped. A pupil must not be allowed deliberately to destroy school property. A group must not be subjected to the emotional disturbance of a temper tantrum. Behavior that destroys utterly the teacher's prestige as a group leader must not be permitted. You may be saying to yourself, "A youngster who is *really* worked up will never stop merely because I tell him to." As a matter of fact, if you act firmly and promptly, he usually will. Remember that the child has had a long series of experiences, all confirming the conditioned response that an adult must be obeyed if he really means what he says. Furthermore, elementary teachers, women as well as men, usually have an advantage in size and strength. A firm hand on a youngster's shoulder often exerts the desired calming effect.

There will be times when a pupil is sufficiently disrupting to group work to merit isolating him rather than allowing a situation to continue to the point where no one is accomplishing anything. Often, it is sufficient to take him out of the group he is disrupting and put him at his own desk with quiet work to do. Sometimes a child who is gaining in self-control will voluntarily find a corner where he thinks he can work undisturbed. There may be times when the disturbance is so severe that isolating a pupil by having him leave the room is warranted, but this is questionable as a standard procedure. "He wasn't ill in the first grade," said the mother of a severely retarded reader, "but he *was* a handful, and I expect he spent more time sitting on his little chair outside the door than he did in the room." If a child is excluded from the classroom it is doubtful if he should ever be left unsupervised. Disturbed children have been known to start fights with others in the hall, to break arms jumping down flights of stairs, and to run away from school. Even in the classroom, disturbed children who are isolated from the group can continue to secure the attention they are seeking if placed where the teacher cannot see them readily. This was the case with Eddie who was banished to the cloakroom, the door to which was at Mary Jane Black's elbow as she worked at the blackboard. Hung in the cloakroom on this particular day were the costumes for the class play. For a good ten minutes before Mary Jane solved the problem of the class giggles, Eddie posed briefly in the cloakroom door in one costume after another, ducking back as she looked around.

In many schools the only person to supervise the pupil who is excluded from the classroom is the principal. Sending a pupil to the principal's office is more likely to be helpful if principal and teacher have a clear understanding ahead of time. Ideally, the principal should be serving as an aid to pupil and teacher in solving a problem, not as a last resort to get the teacher out of a difficult spot. A pupil may be sent with an assignment to be completed or even be sent to rest in the nurse's office with the agreement that he will be allowed to return to the room when he feels he can work with the others again. When a principal merely serves as a person who punishes or who lectures a child about good behavior, it is very doubtful whether any lasting changes will be effected.

An exception can be found to every rule when the problem is one of helping the emotionally disturbed child, but in an overwhelming number of cases, corporal punishment of a severely disturbed child (or any child, for that matter) is of questionable value. Often it merely reinforces a series of experiences, all teaching that people who are bigger will use their strength to beat you. Sometimes it represents one of the easiest atonements for the crime. In many school systems there are specific regulations as to how and by whom a child shall be given physical punishment. For their own legal protection, in addition to their genuine concern for the growth of pupils toward emotional maturity, teachers should abide by these regulations.

Oftentimes in classes where teacher and pupils are accustomed to thinking through standards of behavior and analyzing their difficulties, pupils can be surprisingly mature in accepting deviant behavior without becoming unduly disturbed. They can give help and grow in their insights into the motivation of others by so doing. Ralph Anderson's fifth grade rebelled openly as Sammy for the third day deserted his own group and spent his time heckling and disturbing others. "Send him down to sit in the third grade; maybe he'll see how to behave," they said. Ralph pointed out that this would not be fair to the third grade, and Sammy countered belligerently that nobody in his group liked him and that they wouldn't try out his ideas even when he had some. A discussion of what made people feel at home in a group followed, during which Sammy's group was vociferous in asserting that you could like someone without using his ideas. In the end the children suggested that Sammy choose any three people with whom he thought he could get along and pledged themselves to try hard to work with him if they were chosen.

Secure expert help when needed. Many teachers try to handle by themselves problems on which more expert help is needed. Teachers are not trained for and should not expect to offer the therapy of a psychiatrist or the skilled family counseling of a visiting teacher. How much expert help will be available will depend upon the particular school system. In many places there will be psychological services and trained social workers serving as visiting teachers. Often school attendance officers display skill in handling family problems that is a far cry from the methods of the old-time truant officer. In large cities, there are frequently additional resources in child guidance services in connection with hospitals or universities. Such sources of help will often need to be tapped.

Persons with special psychological training are not miracle workers. Even with the background of courses in psychology and mental hygiene some teachers talk as though all will be well if the school psychologist will just "take a look at Mary Jane." The extended case study to determine causes will still have to be made, and the slow rebuilding of behavior patterns will still have to be done. Furthermore, no matter what individual help is given by the psychologist, the teacher is still the one who will have to teach the youngster how to get along with groups.

You need to realize, too, that principals and supervisors today are persons chosen for the depth of their insights into human behavior. No teacher should hesitate to call on these persons for assistance. It shows much less maturity and good judgment to worry yourself into a state where both you and your pupils suffer than it does to recognize a situation that demands the best professional insights available and to mobilize the full resources of school and community to give the needed help. Children and youth are our greatest national resource. No effort should be counted too great if it sends into the world a mature, self-respecting, disciplined citizen.

BOOKS YOU SHOULD KNOW

Ambrose, Edna, and Miel, Alice. *Children's Social Learning.* Washington, D.C.: Association for Supervision and Curriculum Development, N.E.A. 1958. Pp. vii + 120.

Baruch, D. W. *New Ways in Discipline.* New York: McGraw-Hill Book Co., 1952. Pp. 296.

Cummings, Howard H. (Editor). *Improving Human Relations.* Washington, D.C.: National Council for the Social Studies, 1949. Pp. 158.

Cunningham, Ruth, and associates. *Understanding Group Behavior of Boys and Girls.* New York: Bureau of Publications, Teachers College, Columbia University, 1951. Pp. xviii + 446.

D'Evelyn, Katherine E. *Meeting Children's Emotional Needs.* Englewood Cliffs, N.J.: Prentice-Hall, 1957. Pp. x + 176.

Discipline, Bulletin 99, Washington, D.C.: Association for Childhood Education International, 1957. Pp. 36.

Foshay, Arthur W.; Wann, Kenneth D.; and associates, *Children's Social Values: An Action Research Study.* New York: Bureau of Publications, Teachers College, Columbia University, 1956. Pp. xii + 323.

Helping Teachers Understand Children. Prepared by the staff of the Division on Child Development and Teacher Personnel for the Commission on Teacher Education. Washington, D.C.: American Council on Education, 1945. Pp. xv + 468.

Hymes, James L., Jr. *Behavior and Misbehavior.* Englewood Cliffs, N.J.: Prentice-Hall, 1955. Pp. viii + 140.

Miel, Alice, and Brogan, Peggy. *More Than Social Studies.* Englewood Cliffs, N.J.: Prentice-Hall, 1957. Pp. xii + 452.

Redl, Fritz, and Weinman, David. *Controls from Within.* Glencoe, Ill.: The Free Press, 1952. Pp. 332.

Sheviakov, George V., and Redl, Fritz. (New revision by Sybil K. Richardson.) *Discipline for Today's Children and Youth.* Washington, D.C.: Association for Supervision and Curriculum Development, N.E.A. 1956. Pp. iv + 64.

Trager, Helen G., and Yarrow, Marian R. *They Learn What They Live.* New York: Harper & Brothers, 1952. Pp. 392.

Planning For and With Pupils

CHAPTER 6

"Beginners often start to plan by trying to remember lessons they have seen in other classes or read about. Plans work out better if you forget these and start with an analysis of your group and what they need."

"Even with all our college courses, collecting background information needed for a unit takes time. It helps to start several weeks in advance."

"All through college we have been outlining subject matter. When you plan for work with children, you have to spend as much time thinking about *how* to work with them as you do about *what* you are going to teach."

"Learn to think of everything that could possibly happen. Little things like running out of paste or not having the right paper can spoil a whole lesson."

"When my cooperating teacher went over my plans several days ahead of time, I had time to rework them without feeling rushed."

"If you don't understand your supervisor's suggestion, always ask her to explain it. It is very hard to try to carry out an activity with children if you are not sure what it is supposed to accomplish."

As a student in a teacher-education institution twenty-five or thirty years ago, you would have been required to spend many hours in writing detailed and formal lesson plans preparatory to student teaching. Then, in student teaching, you would have followed these plans precisely step by step. Conscientious students carefully preserved them for future use; they were considered to be valuable and essential equipment for the first teaching job (and sometimes were used for years afterwards). This kind of teaching contrasts vividly with the permissive and flexible approach in classrooms today. The shift in emphasis, however, does not make planning any less important. Planning is the foundation of creative teaching.

Today lesson-planning is a very complex process demanding a high level of knowledge and skill. There are several reasons for this. For one thing, we have expanded our objectives to include helping pupils to become proficient in those intellectual skills unique to a particular subject as well as helping them to acquire information. Our objectives also encompass work habits, general problem-solving skills, and skills in working cooperatively with others. Lesson plans today must provide for these types of skills. Furthermore, we see the function of the school as providing for the maximum growth of each individual in the classroom. This means that no lesson plan, however comprehensive, will serve for all classes. As a matter of fact, even the plan you make with a specific group in mind will require modifications as you put it into operation. We have learned, also, that pupils work more intelligently, intensively, and enthusiastically at a task when they understand its purpose. As a result, teachers' plans today include how to involve pupils in the planning, how to adjust so that pupils' insights and suggestions may be taken into account, and how to allow for weaknesses and strengths as pupils work toward a solution to the problem.

Careful planning, therefore, is a phase of teaching which cannot be overestimated. It is the basis of the teacher's sense of security as he faces the challenge of giving effective leadership to his boys and girls. Any teacher will testify to this as he recalls the day he stepped into a class activity unprepared and tried to live by his wits. Teachers today cannot be opportunists in the classroom if there is to be maximum pupil growth for the time expended.

Effective planning calls for the mastery of skill in making several types of plans. The efficient teacher must be able to establish objectives and identify necessary areas of growth for an entire year. He has to be prepared to block out the details of a related series of activities lasting for several weeks. He needs to know how to plan effectively the details of a lesson for a single period and how to schedule a desirable sequence of activities for a school day. In addition to all this, if pupils are to be involved in the planning process, a teacher must know how to go about helping boys and girls to develop effective techniques in planning. These problems are the focus of the sections which follow in this chapter.

PLANNING FOR THE SCHOOL YEAR

All teachers think through tentative objectives for the school year. In theory, these objectives come from the course of study which expresses the philosophy of the school system in terms of goals for each grade. In reality, however, they represent the teacher's decisions regarding the meaning of the objectives stated in the course of study for pupils with the capacities and needs of his particular group. As a student teacher you are not likely to have sole responsibility for projecting objectives for your class for the entire year. You should, however, have a sense of direction. It will be important for you to understand the philosophy of the school system in which you work and to be aware of the factors which have influenced the decisions of your colleagues in establishing their goals for the year. What you learn from your student-teaching experience will be of immeasurable value on your first job when you find yourself faced with the responsibility of making many of these decisions alone.

Turn to your course of study in determining long-range goals. One of your first responsibilities will be to become thoroughly acquainted with those published materials which establish the curricular pattern for your school. Where there has been an active program of curriculum revision, these materials represent the best thinking of committees of teachers regarding the scope of the experiences proposed for children and youth in the school curriculum, the topics about which these experiences might be organized, and the sequence of activities from grade to grade.

Many courses of study give general statements of philosophy. These usually include a discussion of the purposes of schools in American democracy and a consideration of the significance of research in child development and the psychology of learning. It is important to read such statements carefully. They will orient you to the instructional point of view of the school system and will suggest implications for the establishment of specific goals.

The general areas suggested in the course of study as organizing centers for activities will reveal the curriculum design guiding the choice of pupil experiences in your school system. You will undoubtedly find outlined the specific facts and skills to be stressed, but even more important for your purposes in setting long-term goals are the lists of objectives for each area—the concepts and generalizations considered to be of major importance. These concepts and generalizations represent the large understandings toward which you are expected to work. If your class is to end the year with something more than a "quiz-show" accumulation of specific bits of information, you must think carefully about these broader objectives and what they imply in planning learning experiences for your boys and girls.

Even though they know the areas within which they are expected to work and the general objectives to be achieved, many beginners have difficulty in deciding how to obtain a proper balance among activities. All areas are likely to seem equally important and all may suggest more learning experiences than can be managed in a year's time. Some courses of study give help in deciding where the emphasis is to be through charts showing recommended time allotments and daily schedules. Each teacher is expected to adjust such recommendations to the needs of his particular group, but if you are aware of the time allotments proposed you will understand more clearly why your colleagues stress some areas more than others and why they make certain choices among alternative possibilities.

If you examine the course of study for your school system you will discover that it is a gold mine of suggestions of how to teach, lists of available materials, and descriptions of possible activities for pupils. These usually represent a wealth of experience accumulated over years of teaching. Although you will not want to use all of these suggestions, you should not neglect the help they provide. They will aid you in choosing the types of activities likely to be effective with your group. You may also find some useful hints on how to evaluate pupil progress, lists of standards from grade to grade, and analyses of desirable or expected kinds of behavior for your age group. These, too, can be valuable in determining specific objectives for your class.

No matter at what level you teach, you are only one link in an instructional pattern which, ideally, should result in continuity of growth from kindergarten through twelfth grade. Some beginning teachers make the mistake of looking only at that section of the course of study intended for the grade they are teaching. If you are to be effective in working with your group, you must know something of the experiences which they might have had in the preceding years and the experiences they are likely to have in the grades which follow. Before you begin to project your goals for the year, orient yourself broadly to the objectives of the entire school system.

Use pupils' textbooks as guides in determining long-range goals. Sometimes pupils' textbooks play a greater role than we realize in determining goals for the year. Indeed, there are still some school systems where the adopted textbook is virtually the course of study. Fortunately, the practice of planning lessons by dividing the number of pages by the number of days in the school year is rapidly disappearing. Of course, this procedure never did exist where there was a skilled and broadly prepared teacher. In the hands of a competent teacher, textbooks have always served as aids in achieving the aims of the course of study, whether the classroom has been supplied with texts from a single adopted series or with a variety of texts which serve for reference purposes.

Just how closely you will feel that you should stay within the general framework of a textbook will depend on the philosophy of your school, the pupils, the area to be taught, and the breadth and depth of your professional preparation. As a student teacher you will find, too, that your cooperating teacher's way of working may affect your actions. It is not at all unusual, in the same classroom, for textbooks to be followed rather closely in some areas and used very flexibly as resources in others. More and more, however, in every teaching field, teachers, or teachers and pupils working together, rather than authors of textbooks, are the ones to establish precise goals and determine the sequence of classroom activities.

Even though you are not following exactly the sequences of adopted texts, you will find that the textbooks with which your classroom is equipped can provide helpful and concrete clues concerning what may be expected of the age level you are teaching. These books are based on careful analyses of pupil needs and growth patterns. Vocabulary and topics have usually been tested for difficulty, and the general contents of the books represent the accumulated wisdom of experts in their particular fields. Not all texts in a given field are arranged in exactly the same pattern; each, however, does express in concrete form the basic research regarding desirable goals in the area for which the text is developed. If you examine basal readers for first through sixth grades and then go through series of arithmetic, language, or spelling texts, you will acquire many insights regarding the general nature of growth in these skill areas, the topics typically considered to be relatively simple and those thought to be more difficult, and the possible sequence in which related skills might be developed. Sets of social studies, health, or science texts will provide similar insights as to the kinds of experiences likely to be appropriate to pupils of the age level of your group. Use the textbooks supplied for your pupils' use, then, as another means of orienting yourself as you project goals for the year.

Draw upon your professional background in determining long-term goals. A long time ago a very wise man said, "What is honored in a country will be cultivated there." More recently a sensitive and experienced teacher related this bit of wisdom to the modern classroom by saying, "What is honored by the teacher will be cultivated in the classroom." As a beginning teacher, you might ponder the significance of this in relation to your teaching. In effect, it means that what you have learned during your preparation to be a teacher determines what you will teach. Books, lectures, class discussions, individual conferences, and practical experiences have given you a sense of direction. Each and every course you have taken has provided something that will be of value in determining goals.

As a beginner, you must now make a conscious effort to relate what you have learned to the problem of deciding what kinds of growth seem desirable for your class. Draw upon your theoretical background as you study the objectives for your grade level outlined in the course of study and suggested by the contents of your pupils' textbooks. You will discover that these proposals follow very closely what was discussed in your methods courses as desirable sequences of growth. You will find, also, as you listen to your pupils read, watch them calculate, and examine their written work that what they do bears a close relationship to what you previously learned about the development of skills. Their concepts, the ways they reason, and their interests will mirror what your professional courses suggested you would find. Once you have realized that the practical and the theoretical can be combined, you will discover that you are planning both short-term and long-range goals for your class with a much greater sense of professional security.

Adjust goals and expectations to the particular class. The general goals outlined in the course of study or suggested by the contents of a textbook must always be modified in terms of the capacities and needs of individuals. Regardless of the research on individual differences, there are lay people, and some teachers, too, who believe that we should be able to manage our schools so that each and every individual in the class can start at exactly the same point. The truth of the matter is that regardless of the system of grouping, promotion, acceleration, or retention there is no known method or technique which will guarantee that every pupil knows exactly what the course of study says he should; nor is there any way to be certain that he is ready for precisely what the course of study says he should now be studying.

Careful grouping and thoughtful promotion can reduce to some degree the variation within a group, but even so, differences in abilities and achievement will still exist. Consider the examples which follow. Betty, Art, and Joanna are each nine years old.

Summer Demonstration School, University of **Cincinnati,**
D. Arthur Bricker, Photographer

Consider carefully how to involve pupils in unit planning. Chart holders and bristol board expand bulletin board facilities for posting plans.

Involve pupils in planning their daily schedule. Work proceeds more smoothly when everyone knows what to expect.

D. Arthur Bricker, Photographer
Public Schools, St. Bernard, Ohio,

Public Schools, Cincinnati, Ohio,
Gilbert H. Corlett, Photographer

Help pupils to develop effective techniques of cooperative problem-solving. Committee responsibilities build group-process skills.

Betty, IQ 110, is a prodigious reader of sixth-grade books. She has been tremendously interested in history since her family took her touring through the eastern states. She loves to write stories and has grown up in an environment where correct English is spoken; however, her spelling tends to be phonetic and she hates to take time to look up words. She puts time on arithmetic assignments if she has to.

Art, IQ 135, comes from a lower-class background and still uses many of the typical speech patterns. He is excellent in games, but very poorly coordinated when it comes to handwriting. He devours science materials and has a large collection of comic books about space travel, but he can't be bothered with fiction or poetry.

Joanna, IQ 90, is a most conscientious worker. She takes endless pains with everything she does and shines particularly where she has a routine job to do. She rarely misspells a word, does extremely well with arithmetic computation, and produces careful factual notes in social studies.

Pupils such as these are not unusual in a group. You will probably have thirty or more with equally diverse characteristics and interests. Providing opportunities for the maximum development of each demands individualized objectives. It means capitalizing upon the strengths of each youngster as well as working constructively upon his weaknesses.

Projecting goals for the year for your class involves, then, a combination of what you can learn about the general objectives of the school system in which you work; what is suggested by the focus of your pupils' texts; what your own professional background tells you is desirable; and what you can discover about the readiness, needs, and potentialities of the individuals of your group. Above everything, it calls for insights into the needs of the boys and girls now in front of you. "They said if I'd only plan carefully everything would go smoothly," lamented a beginning teacher. "I spend hours planning but it doesn't seem to make any difference." "You do plan," said her principal, "but you're planning for the wrong children. You're still thinking about your class last year."

PLANNING A UNIT OF WORK

In most elementary school classrooms today, at least some of the pupils' experiences are centered in units of work. Over the years the term "unit of work" has been interpreted in a variety of ways. At one time it ordinarily meant a related series of activities developed around a central topic. These were often extensive in nature with considerable reading, some art and music, possibly committee work for small groups, and finally a culminating activity in the form of a play, an exhibit, or some other fairly elaborate means of integrating and summarizing the work. Sometimes a comprehensive unit encompassed most of the children's activities for the day. Art, music, games, recreational reading, arithmetic, and language arts—every aspect of the day's program was related to the topic at hand.

Today, the concept of a unit is being redefined. It is more often thought of as *a way of working with pupils* in which they share in planning and carrying out the activity. This is the interpretation used in this book. The essence of a unit activity, according to this definition, is *a problem-solving approach to learning* in which teacher and pupils are jointly involved. Together they explore a problem of mutual concern and propose subproblems. They then plan cooperatively a way of working that will provide the required information or enable them to take other steps needed to solve the subproblems they have identified. Next, they carry out their plans, checking on progress from time to time and revising the plans if need be. Eventually they share the results of their work and evaluate to determine if their problem has been solved. Often they plan follow-up activities in order to make use of what they have learned. What makes the series of activities a unit is the underlying plan that holds them together and gives the enterprise unity for the learners. Whether the total job is simple or complex; involves small groups, individualized work, or the class as a whole; utilizes art and music or calls mainly for reading to locate information; ends in an elaborate play or in a simple class discussion—all depend on the original problem and the plans made to solve it.

In the sense in which a unit has just been defined, any subject or skill area can be approached through unit activities. A fifth grade is carrying out a unit when the youngsters decide a Halloween party would be fun; set up committees; make plans for refreshments, games, and a program; and bring the party through to a successful conclusion. It is likewise a unit of work when fourth-graders evaluate their handwriting; decide that more practice is in order, lay plans with their teacher for individualized practice and group demonstrations, think through how to collect "before and after" samples, and finally evaluate their progress and plan for follow-up work. First-graders are engaged in unit activity when they plan to turn the class playhouse into a grocery store; think through what alterations will be needed, what personnel to use, and how to get make-believe items to sell; accomplish their plans; and eventually open their store for business. The six children in a second-grade reading group who decide to read a favorite story to the class, make plans for practice, and two days later read their story are also carrying out a unit—in this case a very short and uncomplicated one.

All such unified activities require careful pre-planning on the part of the teacher. Sometimes one gains the impression that teaching in the modern school is easy—that it is nothing but opening a discussion with a class and following wherever the pupils choose to go. Actually, it takes careful preparation to be the type of group leader who can guide cooperative enterprises so that they result in maximum growth. To plan effectively for a unit, a teacher needs to work at three levels. First, he makes out a preliminary block plan that explores the possibilities of the unit. Second, he plans how and at what points pupils should be involved—he thinks through his job as a group chairman. Third, he revises his block plan and expands it into day-by-day plans as the unit develops.

Develop a preliminary block plan in preparation for work with pupils. The plan that you block out in advance of planning with your pupils should help you to become thoroughly familiar with the possibilities of the unit and the learnings that might result.[1] Preliminary planning should provide you with a depth of background and a feeling of security in your own sense of direction that will allow you to capitalize on the proposals coming from your group. Your block plan, then, should not be a detailed outline of where you are going to "lead" your group and exactly how your planning with them is to work out. It is, rather, a broad exploration or mapping out of the territory so that you will feel comfortable in moving in the direction that seems likely to be most fruitful as you analyze the strengths and weaknesses, suggestions, interests, and backgrounds revealed in your initial planning sessions with the class.

Exactly how you write your block plan, the order in which you outline specific topics, and the amount of detail you include depend upon how much you need in black and white for your own security. It might be helpful to you to know that although it is possible to clutter your thinking with too much detail, most beginners fail to think through carefully enough the specific items that make the difference between

[1] The discussions in Chapters 7, 8, and 9, pages 222-226, 292-295, and 341-346, provide more detailed help in deciding just what might be your objectives for your particular class.

smooth traveling and bogging down. It is safer to err on the side of too much detail until you are sure of yourself. During your student-teaching experience you also face the problem of providing the amount of detail that will make it easy for your cooperating teacher (and perhaps your college supervisor) to evaluate your plan with you. It may be that either of these two persons will have specific suggestions regarding a style that will facilitate this process. In any event, you will have to develop a block plan for yourself not once, but several times before you will find the pattern which works most effectively for you.

The first section in most block plans is a statement of *teacher purposes*. These can be stated on several levels, from the broad objectives of democracy that underlie all teaching to detailed objectives for the unit. Although it will be helpful for you to keep the general objectives of American education in mind, the purposes that will guide your teaching most directly are those that relate to the specific unit. You will not necessarily need a long list, but you should have thought through the basic generalizations and ways of thinking and behaving to which the unit should contribute. In most units there will be related learnings that you hope to develop—techniques for collecting information, discussion skills, work habits, skills in creative expression, information about related topics. These objectives need to be considered carefully. You should also think about your aims for individuals —are there youngsters who should be given special opportunities to use their talents? pupils who need leadership experiences? some who require help with particular skills? If you want your teaching to result in actual changes in the ways in which your pupils behave, you would be well advised to state your goals in terms of the behavior you hope will result, not merely as a list of facts to be mastered. Thus, with major concepts and generalizations, related learnings, and individual needs in mind, Mary Ellen Johnson developed her list of objectives for a fourth-grade study of transportation as follows:

Major Objectives

To be able to select means of transportation suitable for a variety of purposes.

To practice safety measures on bicycles, busses, and other means of transportation used regularly.

To be able to interpret in general terms newspaper articles about faster and more efficient modes of travel.

To be able to interpret in general terms newspaper articles about long-range missiles, needs for international understanding in a shrinking world.

To show respect for the work of persons whose occupations are related to transportation.

To be able to explain the abundance or shortage of produce in local markets in terms of modern advances in refrigeration and speed of transportation.

To be able to identify the purposes of the types of barges and boats on our river.

Related Learnings

To become more independent in locating material.

To learn to take very simple notes.

To learn to work cooperatively without wasting so much time.

To learn how to find major seaports on a map.

To learn to estimate mileage from a map.

Purposes for Individuals

To help John to explore his interest in airplanes.

To provide some group reading experiences for Betty's group where there can be more help in phonetic analysis.

To stimulate Barnie's interest in maps.

To give Joe some group status by sharing his collection of planes.

This list provides Mary Ellen with her sense of direction. No matter what specific turns her class planning sessions take, her list of objectives will help her to see how to make the most of these opportunities. If her unit had as its central focus activities leading to the improvement of fundamental skills (managing a classroom store, developing an oral reading presentation to share with another group, carrying out a plan to improve handwriting), Mary Ellen's major objectives would have related to the skills and understandings she hoped to develop in these areas, and her lists of related learnings would have indicated other values she saw accruing to individuals or to the class as a whole—evaluation techniques, work habits, skills in cooperative problem-solving, special interests. Had the group problem centered in the exercise of creative expression (developing a dramatization, decorating the classroom for Christmas, writing a class magazine), her major objectives would have indicated the growth in creative expression and the corresponding skills which she hoped would result, and her list of related learnings would have indicated such items as work habits she thought would be needed, cooperative techniques she aimed to develop, background information she felt her group would need, and individual talents she hoped to encourage.

It is also important to consider possible *pupil purposes*. If the unit is to be meaningful to your class, your boys and girls must recognize that the problem about which their work centers is worth while. Pupil purposes will clarify as you and your group begin to explore the problem, but you will have to be prepared to lead the opening discussions which establish a sense of purpose and direction. Your list of pupil purposes should help you in doing this effectively. In some cases the unit will develop around questions your pupils have raised, and the list of pupil purposes will emerge readily as you think about the implications of these questions. At other times your task will be that of helping your pupils to recognize the values of a topic suggested in the course of study. Here, your skill in sensing how the assigned topic touches the lives of your boys and girls can contribute much to a meaningful start. Ask yourself: What reasons for studying this area, developing these new skills, or embarking upon this new avenue of creative expression seem most likely to make the activity meaningful to my pupils? To which of their problems or experiences might I refer in trying to make this study purposeful to them? What is its point of contact with their lives? As she thought about her boys and girls, Mary Ellen projected the following as possible pupil purposes:

To compare interesting experiences with various means of transportation.

To find out more about the types of vehicles on the highway seen from our windows.

To be able to trace trips taken over the summer on our map.

To learn about safety on bicycles.

To follow up interests in recent news reports about rockets.

As a third part of the block plan, many teachers prepare a logical outline of the detailed *information to be taught* or *skills to be learned*. Such an outline is, of course, not followed step by step in teaching. It is meant to put at your fingertips, in the form you can use conveniently, the details you hope to cover with your group. This aspect of a block plan can make an important contribution to your feelings of security as your pupils begin to ask questions and collect information. Even though you made an *A* in World Geography six months ago, you will be surprised to realize how fast the curve of forgetting has operated in your own case. A second-grader's assured but fantastic statements about how to feed pets can leave you breathless if you haven't done some checking. Furthermore, an alert group will pose questions your college professors never dreamed of. Did you spend time in History 200 finding out what was used to fill the chinks in log cabins? Or figure out in Physiology 109 why the "blue" blood in our veins flows red when we cut ourselves? You cannot expect to be prepared with all the answers if you encourage pupils, even first-graders, to think for themselves. However, you can use your college texts and reference books to arm yourself with as much background as possible. You will also be well advised to read carefully your pupils' reference books. If you cannot keep the exact contents of each book in mind, it will be of great help if you at least have a general idea of where to direct your pupils for help. Mary Ellen's plan for her transportation unit included information such as the following, outlined in detail:

A list of types of transportation important to be studied and their major purposes.

A list of the major cities served by the airlines in the local airport.

A list of the persons whose inventions have made major changes in transportation and a brief report on their contributions.

An outline of the history of transportation on the local river.

An outline of interesting facts about the local railroad terminal.

A list of the types of trucks likely to be seen on the thoroughfare passing the school.

A list of the persons involved in various capacities in the airlines, the railways, the bus lines.

Some typical lengths of trips to key cities in other parts of the world.

An outline of major facts reported in current articles regarding projected plans for space travel.

A list of the local traffic regulations for pedestrians and bicyclists.

With this much factual information collected, Mary Ellen was prepared as well as she could be for the questions her pupils seemed most likely to ask. Had she been considering how to help a second-grade reading group to share a set of favorite stories with the rest of the class, she would still have outlined carefully what she planned to teach. In this case, however, her list would have indicated in detail the oral reading skills and the understandings regarding how to choose an appropriate story that she wanted to stress. If she had been planning to help third-graders to develop a poetry bulletin board, she would have thought carefully regarding the level of appreciation she hoped to develop and the items of capitalization and punctuation she wished to teach.

A block plan should also project *possible pupil activities.* These cannot be included in detail prior to planning sessions with the class, but possibilities can be thought through and at least a tentative sequence of activities proposed. Certainly, you can plan in detail for the experiences that are to initiate the unit. You can also do some thinking about the types of all-class experiences that are almost certain to be needed in order to clarify new concepts or to develop new skills, although you will probably not plan your lessons in detail at this point. It is helpful to consider where, if at all, individual enterprises or work in small groups might serve a purpose. In all probability, you will want to give your pupils opportunities to put their new learnings to use—through pictures, models, reports, dramatizations, stories, dramatic play. Possibilities for these can be listed. In some units, you will also be able to foresee a logical culmination—the program will be put on, the party held, the store opened for business. In others, you will not know, for sure, how the work can best be drawn together until you and your pupils are well into it.

Many beginners find it difficult to prepare a useful list of possible pupil activities, especially if the original problem is complex and admits of a variety of approaches. If the teacher's list of possible activities is too rigidly structured it invalidates pupil-teacher planning, or if pupil-teacher planning is genuine, all the hard work that went into the teacher's plans often seems to be wasted. It may help if you think of your outline of suggested pupil activities as an opportunity to explore many possible ways of working and to think about the advantages and disadvantages of various lines of action in the quiet of your own room. The purpose of this part of your plan is to prepare yourself to give intelligent leadership as your pupils make suggestions —to make you sensitive to the educational possibilities of each of a variety of procedures, to warn you of pitfalls you might not think of in the heat of a lively discussion, and to enable you to add your suggestions to those of your pupils so that the final plans are as fruitful as possible. Often it is helpful to sketch not one, but several possibilities for steps beyond the opening discussion. It is also important to identify any points at which school regulations permit no choice. It may not, for example, be permissible to ask for money from home to finance a school party, even though your pupils happily volunteer fifty cents apiece. Lunchroom schedules may make it impossible for your class to cook a Mexican lunch in the school kitchen. Mary Ellen's outline of possible activities appears below. You will notice that she has alternatives at every point except the first day. Here she has made a decision regarding the topic for the opening discussion. However, even here, she has tried to prepare herself to be flexible by anticipating possible turns the discussion might take. You will note, too, that she has explored some of her proposals far enough to identify possible difficulties.

Introduction—First Day

1. Lead off with a discussion of where they have traveled and on what vehicles.

2. As opening discussion proceeds, watch for interests and questions regarding:
   (a) New developments in modern transportation.
   (b) Role of our city as a transportation center.
   (c) Types of transportation—bus, plane, boat, etc.

3. By end of opening discussion try to have identified problems on which there can be some class reading—perhaps types of transportation most important today, unless a more urgent need appears in opening discussion.

Possible All-Class Activities

(Choose from among these and add to them as more about pupils' experience backgrounds is discovered.)

1. Background reading and pooling of information (see 3 above).

2. Identification of problems for group work leading out of discussion above.

3. Excursions (plan in terms of needs revealed in opening discussions):
   (a) Airport (would need bus—expense?).
   (b) Railway terminal (good setup for classes—need to make date well ahead).
   (c) Produce market (possible to see types of transportation—not too active late in day—harder to get consultant help).

   (d) Police department would send representatives to talk on safety.
   (e) Jimmy's father would tell us about city busses.

4. Movies (see list of teaching aids later in plan).

5. Language experiences:
   (a) Reading—as a class, for group projects.
   (b) Sharing as class and group work proceeds.
   (c) Reporting on excursions—perhaps develop special vocabulary lists.
   (d) Possibilities for individual notebooks as group work proceeds.
   (e) Safety plays.
   (f) Imaginative stories or letters home if trips eventuate?

Possible Centers for Group Work

(One of these, or some combination of them, could provide the organization for group work. Choose with pupils that which seems likely to be most fruitful and satisfying after opening discussions and some background reading. Develop some or all of the specific activities as group planning suggests these would be appropriate.)

1. Types of transportation:
   (a) Organize groups around each type. Read in detail about history of one type and purposes.
   (b) Develop dioramas of early and present-day transportation.
   (c) Do a mural illustrating changes in transportation.
   (d) Do individual workbooks.
   (e) Develop bulletin boards of clippings and pictures—new cars, trains, planes, etc.
   (f) Plan a display—enough toy cars, planes, and trains at home for this?

2. Imaginary trips:
   (a) Organize groups around types of trips (by car, by plane, by train, by boat).
   (b) Calculate costs of trip, prepare prospectives, read timetables, etc.
   (c) Use maps to show trips; identify major seaports, etc.
   (d) Possibly project trips to other countries to be studied this year—use map work heavily to locate these—good new problem for these children.
   (e) Develop plays or panels on safety in travel.

3. Transportation that goes by our school:
   (a) All-class project to identify vehicles on highway, planes overhead.
   (b) Groups might be formed on type of transportation or on purposes—bus, moving vans, delivery trucks, passenger and Air Force planes.
   (c) Trace history of main highways, travel on river.
   (d) Possibly map main routes from city.
   (e) Report on traffic regulations for bicycles, pedestrians, cars.

Possible Culminating Experiences

1. Committee reports followed by discussion.
2. Possible that work of groups could be summarized in mural, series of pictures, dioramas.
3. Possibly use whatever concrete materials come from groups as center for informal sharing.
4. Parents have not been entertained this year. This might be a good unit to share.

As Mary Ellen and her class begin to explore the topic through some group reading, the questions raised and interests revealed will suggest that one proposal for organizing group work seems likely to be more fruitful than the others. Or it may be that something new representing a modification of Mary Ellen's original ideas may develop. As the group work unfolds, some projects will be seen as more appropriate than others. Whatever the final plan, Mary Ellen has done enough careful thinking about possibilities to give her pupils intelligent leadership. As work proceeds, she will expand in detail whichever aspects of her original list of activities seem likely to be most rewarding.

You will notice, also, if you examine the types of activities listed under the possibilities for group work, that Mary Ellen has foreseen a variety of means through which her ultimate objectives could be reached. Types of transportation will need to be identified, no matter what the final group organization is. Something about the effects of modern inventions can come in. Maps can be used. Safety factors can be discussed. Mary Ellen will achieve her purposes, but she has made flexible plans so that she can still capitalize on the interests and problems of greatest concern to her pupils.

The multiplicity of possibilities needed in a block plan will vary, of course, with the problem and with the maturity of the group. Mary Ellen faced a problem that could be approached fruitfully in many ways. She was working with fourth-graders who were capable of considerable self-direction and reasonably skilled in locating information for themselves. She prepared herself, therefore, to capitalize upon the wide variety of needs, interests, concerns, and experience backgrounds likely to be revealed in group discussions. Had she been developing a block plan for a first-grade unit on school helpers, she, herself, might have taken more responsibility for deciding upon the general sequence of activities. If so, her plan would have indicated definitely the way in which the project would unfold, and alternatives would have been listed only for those points where she felt that her pupils had the maturity and background necessary to make an intelligent contribution to decisions regarding how to proceed. Had Mary Ellen been planning to involve an arithmetic group in a series of meaningful and intensive practice activities in order to achieve certain goals in rapid computation, her block plan would have indicated how she intended to lead the opening discussion and probably just what steps for practice and self-evaluation she intended to propose. Pupil-teacher planning, in this case, would have been focused upon understanding the reason for the arithmetic activities and precisely how to go about them.

A block plan can usefully contain a *survey of teaching aids*. Although this is not usually a first section in the written plan, it is often a valuable early step to take, especially if the unit is centered in a content field.[2] Many teachers have discovered that examining with care the teaching aids available is a very practical means of reviewing in detail the educative possibilities of an area to be studied and of identifying likely pupil activities. To prepare her list of teaching aids, Mary Ellen took the following steps:

She checked the course of study for her school system and noted which references were recommended.

She read carefully the appropriate social studies texts and standard children's references in her classroom, making herself a bibliography which she later posted for her pupils to use.

She went through science texts, texts on health and safety, and basal readers to locate other materials for her bibliography.

She procured from the school and public library trade books on transportation appropriate for her grade level.

She checked the audio-visual aids catalog for her school system for appropriate movies, film strips, and slides and made arrangements to preview some of these.

[2] It is difficult to choose a meaningful term to apply to those disciplines—history, geography, physics, chemistry, civics, biology, economics, and so on—under which our knowledge of the physical and social world is organized, just as it is difficult to choose a term to encompass reading, writing, speaking, calculating, listening, and problem-solving. This volume uses traditional terminology in this chapter and in Chapters 7, 8, and 9—*content* or *subject fields, fundamental skills, creative arts*. If you will read carefully the goals stated at the beginning of each of these chapters, you will see that skills, content, and creativity are inextricably intertwined. There is content to arithmetic, there are skills in the scientific method, there are content and skills in music, and creativity or original thinking is inherent in every field of knowledge.

She contacted travel agencies and other possible sources of free or inexpensive material.

She checked the source books of free and inexpensive material in her college library and ordered those she felt might be helpful.

She looked into the resources of the picture files of the school and public libraries and pulled appropriate items from her own collection.

She checked the file of field experiences maintained in the school office and made some contacts of her own after talking with her cooperating teacher and other colleagues.

She rechecked cumulative records to identify parents who might serve as possible resource people.

She did some thinking about the toys in her pupils' homes and the likelihood of developing displays with these, and checked on the cost of such materials with an eye to possible purchases herself.

A beginner is sometimes tempted to short-cut the process of locating teaching aids, especially if there is an experienced teacher at his elbow who has done the job many times. Nevertheless, it is an important aspect of your growth. Although your cooperating teacher may have an enviable collection of such materials from long years of teaching, you need the experience of locating your own. Perhaps more important, you must do such an exploration if you are to be prepared to guide your pupils as they begin to hunt the resources they need to solve particular problems.

It is also helpful to think through possible *means of evaluation,* even though the details will be worked through as your unit develops. What kinds of evidence will indicate that your pupils understand the generalizations you have been trying to develop? What will show that the desired information or skills have been acquired? On what basis might individual projects or committee work be judged? How will you know that changes in behavior have been effected?[3]

With the major aspects of your plan blocked in enough detail to prepare you to give intelligent leadership, you are ready to initiate the unit with your boys and girls. Out of the planning you do together will emerge a proposal for an exact sequence of activities and an indication of the specific points at which you must be prepared to do some direct teaching.

Consider carefully how to involve pupils in unit planning. With their own block plans as background, how do teachers involve pupils

[3] Chapter 11 will give you more help on this problem.

in unit planning? This is a point at which many beginners have difficulty. They make an excellent block plan, indicating purposes, information, activities, and materials, but they fail to think with equal care about how to involve their pupils in the planning process. This is an important skill to acquire. Often a beginning teacher is hesitant to allow his pupils to express their interests, concerns, and suggestions regarding how to approach a problem under consideration lest he find himself on a track he is not prepared to follow. Thinking through alternatives in your block plan will help, of course, but you also need to prepare carefully and in detail for your part as a group leader. To do this, you will have to shift your role from that of a scholar logically outlining facts and resource materials to that of a committee chairman planning how to achieve good working sessions.

An effective chairman comes with an agenda for each of his planning sessions. He will typically ask his group to consider his agenda and add to it, but he has done some preliminary thinking regarding the questions of *what are the problems we face* and *what points must be considered in laying effective plans to solve these problems.* If you were chairing a committee planning a student-faculty tea, for example, you would come to your committee meetings with tentative lists of topics on which committee thinking is needed. For your first committee meeting some of these topics would be questions to aid you and the committee members in clarifying just what your responsibilities are to be, and some would refer to decisions to be made by the close of the meeting if work is to progress satisfactorily. In subsequent sessions you, as chairman, would come prepared with similar agenda lists, each stemming from your evaluation of what was accomplished in the preceding session, what problems are now facing the committee, and what seem to be the needed next steps. Similarly, as chairman of your class you must learn to think about the topics you and your pupils will need to consider in your planning sessions. This does not mean that you make up your mind ahead of time as to exactly what conclusions your group must reach. Just as you can raise with your faculty-tea committee the problem of refreshments without outlining a menu in advance, so you can raise with your pupils key problems related to their work without deciding in advance precisely what the proposed solutions will be. In either situation, you may well prepare yourself to give effective leadership by jotting down a variety of possible procedures so that you are armed with alternatives and are sensitive to barriers and pitfalls. This is one of the purposes that your block plan serves.

As preparation for the planning session that initiates the new study, you should consider precisely *how to introduce the problem to the class.* This initiating activity should be developed in detail in your block plan prior to any planning sessions with your boys and girls. Some beginners feel compelled to plan very elaborate introductions to units (perhaps because of memories of school days when many activities were remote from their lives and needed dressing up to be interesting). If the topic of the proposed unit is far removed from the lives of your pupils, you may need to plan for experiences to build background and interest. There are many ways of doing this. You may set up an exhibit, take your group on an excursion, plan for a motion picture, set up a special bulletin board display, read a story aloud, engage in some exploratory discussion that draws upon pupils' experience backgrounds. Some of the most purposeful units, however, have very simple beginnings. In some cases there will be a present need or an interest to be recalled. ("We've been bringing in interesting leaves, nuts, and cocoons for several weeks. We will have time now in our science period to learn more about them.") Sometimes preceding activities will lead directly into a new unit. Proposals to develop murals, suggestions for new uses for a primary play corner, plans to share reading activities, proposals for creative writing projects, often develop in this way. ("Could we do a play from our story for the other groups?" "Miss Jones, if we turned our playhouse into a make-believe store, we could sell things.") In cases such as these, all you may need to do by way of initiating the new project is to pick up the suggestion and to help your youngsters begin exploring its possibilities. Whatever the type of introduction you judge to be most appropriate, your plans as a group leader should include precisely what you are going to do or say in your first session with the class. Somebody has to call the meeting to order and start things off. This is the teacher's role.

Beginners sometimes operate on another misconception in launching a unit. This is to believe that no matter how carefully the course of study is being followed, pupils must be made to feel that the unit is entirely of their own choosing. "I brought in all the books on Indians I could find," reported Sally Jamison, "and I borrowed several exhibits from the museum. Sure enough, when I asked them what they wanted to study they said 'Indians'!" One could ask whether Sally's youngsters are learning how citizens in a democracy make choices or discovering what it takes to live peacefully under benevolent dictatorship. It is far better to state the fact frankly if the areas for study have been predetermined and then help your class to explore the new topic until they see its possible contributions to their lives. "This year we are expected to learn about the early people who lived in our country," said Jane Anderson. "Of course you all know that the Indians were here when Columbus landed. But how much do you really know about the Indians that lived right around our own city?"

An important step in outlining your agenda for the discussion that initiates a unit is to consider *how much can reasonably be accomplished in this planning period.* Is it your best judgment that an opening session should strike for a clarification of subproblems and some specific suggestions about how to work? Or might it be better to plan for some preliminary exploration of the total problem by the class as a whole before such detailed plans are laid? What do you think you should try to accomplish by the end of your first planning session in order to have a good jumping-off point for the next? If you are embarking on a relatively simple activity in an area where your pupils have considerable background, as, for example, laying plans for a two- or three-day art project to make some winter decorations for your classroom, you would probably expect to have plans clear and work allotted by the end of the first period. If, however, the project seems likely to be an extensive one involving the acquisition of considerable new information, there may be some preliminary explorations needed before final plans are agreed upon. Often, as with an adult committee, the reaction of your group members will help you to decide how far to proceed. As you and they begin to talk, it may become apparent that everyone needs time to read for background, and you will stop when the problem is defined in general terms and some plans are laid to locate the needed information. On another occasion you may discover more sophistication than you expected, and detailed plans will develop very rapidly. To some extent, you will be able to predict the steps your group is capable of taking after you have worked with them long enough to know their general experience background. However, they will surprise you at times; it is wise planning to identify two or three good stopping points in your agenda for the first day.

If anything, a beginner is likely to try to cover too much in his early planning sessions and to ask his group to make decisions for which they do not have the background. This is an especially important warning to bear in mind if you are initiating a project that will require the amassing of considerable new information. Your pupils typically will not be able to think intelligently about the details of a culminating activity in the first or second planning session of an elaborate activity, nor will they be able to project, on the first day that committees are established, exactly how these committees can best present their information. If you try to involve a class in such remote plans, you may find that tangential questions—what to eat if mothers are invited to see a final program, or what costumes to use for a play—have completely supplanted the information-getting problems that must be solved first. You may also find that trying to force group members to plan beyond the limits of their insights leads to wild suggestions or to a frustrated feeling of wasting time. Part of your job as leader is to sense the background of your pupils and the types of problems they can face intelligently at the moment.

Once in a while a group will catch fire in an early planning session and pop with ideas far beyond what you expected and are prepared to evaluate. This happened to Alec Warton who raised a problem with his class regarding how they might bring together all their thinking about the growth of America (with the pros and cons of a wall map, a mural, or a notebook spelled out as possibilities in his block plan). Janet suggested a big map on the floor; Pete added that they could get clay and rocks from the nearby hill to build real mountains; Bill said he could bring a model railroad so they could have real trains—and the deluge had begun. Within five minutes Alec was overwhelmed with suggestions—some of them fantastic—for the most minute details of the proposed map. As chairman, you have an obligation to help your group reach thoughtful decisions and a right to suggest that final plans be delayed until the possibilities of a proposal are completely explored. In Alec's case, he and his pupils listed their suggestions. Then they thought about some of the immediate problems—space in the classroom, permission to leave the school to get clay, obligations to the school custodian, time that could be devoted to such a project. At this point all went home to sleep on the proposal (except Alec who put in some long hours thinking through details). The map eventually was made after some sober second thoughts regarding the least workable suggestions.

Planning is not done all at once. It is a continuing process involving evaluation of progress, determination of new problems, and proposals of next steps. As your plans unfold, you will need to prepare yourself, day after day, to serve as an effective chairman. This means that you will think through, for each new day, the questions of *what new problems should we consider* and *on what new points do we need to make decisions.* Often an extensive unit develops in several stages—a set of preliminary questions and some experiences designed to answer them; a new set of problems arising out of the early explorations and a new class organization to solve these problems; a plan as to how the total job should be organized and shared and the needed steps taken to bring this plan into being.

You will have noticed that the questions suggested for you to think about as chairman of your class are not of the "what can I say so that they will propose making a mural" type. The problem is not—as democratic planning is defined in this volume—to prepare yourself to ask such skillful and subtle questions that the group will come out doing exactly what you want. Rather, you should think about the types of agreements to be reached, the topics to be explored, the questions to be answered. Exact ways of working will develop as you and your class think through such problems. Your security and your safeguard against wild and unworkable suggestions are the multiple possibilities with their pros and cons that you have sketched in roughly as you laid out your block plan. What activities actually emerge may not be exactly any of the procedures you foresaw, but if you have made intelligent use of all your knowledge of the class in your pre-planning, you will be prepared to capitalize to a maximum degree on the purposes most meaningful to your group in achieving the objectives you, yourself, established.

Expand the block plan as work moves forward. The preceding discussion has indicated how your general survey of possibilities in your block plan begins to achieve more direct focus as you and your class plan together. By the time pupils have been involved in clarifying the original problem and deciding on ways of working, one of the procedures proposed in your original plan, or perhaps a combination of several with some good ideas from your class added, will have assumed priority. You will also be better aware of the strengths and weaknesses of your pupils—the points at which they already seem to be well informed or particularly skilled and the points at which new learnings are indicated. In the light of this preliminary exploration, you are now ready to expand the appropriate sections of your block plan into as much precise detail as you need to teach effectively.

Nothing you can do by way of lecture, discussion, or recitation lessons based on a single text can equal the quality of the learning that comes when you involve pupils in unit activities and use all available procedures and materials (often including lectures, discussions, and recitations) to help them grow. Units of work can, however, be wasteful of time, if there is not intelligent leadership and careful pre-planning by the teacher. In general your pupils will get out of an activity not much more than you put into it.

PLANNING FOR A SINGLE PERIOD

Beginning teachers who lay out meticulous unit plans sometimes fail to be as thoughtful when planning the details of a single lesson. Faced with the multitude of activities that go on in a single day, it is easy to say, "I don't need to think about social studies; they'll just be reading for information," or "Thank goodness, spelling is taken care of; we'll do the exercises," or "I'll use a review game in arithmetic; they love that."

If every minute in the day is to pay off with maximum learning, planning for the single lessons that make up the daily schedule has to be more insightful and detailed than "This will keep them quiet for a half hour," or "They'll love that." Furthermore, particularly in the case of inexperienced teachers, unsuspected difficulties can crop up all too frequently when an activity is not carefully thought through, and what looked like an ideal device for holding interest and attention blows up. There is no way around long hours of planning if you want to be an effective teacher.

Develop daily plans in the light of larger block plans. If classroom work is developing smoothly, daily plans will stem from larger block plans. The section just concluded outlined the type of block plan a teacher prepared for a rather complex unit. You will have similar block plans, although they may be somewhat less elaborate, outlining how you intend to reach long-term goals in every teaching area. What you decide to do today—in developing reading skills, working on spelling, teaching new arithmetic concepts as well as in taking the next steps in social studies or science activities—depends on your appraisal of the needs of your class and your long-term objectives. There should be few arbitrary and isolated activities inserted on the spur of the moment merely because you think they will be interesting or because they happen to appear on the next page of a textbook.

If your day-by-day activities are to be effective, then, you must learn to make a continuous evaluation of your class. As you analyze your group's efforts to write, you should be building lists of difficulties in English, deciding which problems should be given priority, and looking ahead to related activities which could make a special contribution. As you think about the way your poorest readers tackled their word-analysis problems today, you should be making some mental notes of experiences that could be useful tomorrow. As you walk from group to group during a work session, you should be alert for difficulties in locating information, inaccurate concepts, problems in human relationships. When you settle down at your desk to make your plans for tomorrow, you will have to think through in detail how best to handle each of these problems. But you should rarely, if ever, once school has begun, be at a loss for worth-while ideas regarding things that need to be done.

This does not mean that your daily plans are always a neat next step in achieving the objectives you set up in September. New needs will become apparent, and new problems will arise. A second grade may be hard at work on riddles related to a study of animals in the zoo when Alice is hospitalized; here is a letter-writing need (and opportunity) worthy of attention. Group plans you thought would proceed smoothly grind to a standstill because of unforeseen difficulties in locating information; here is a need for help on reference skills. The smooth oral reading of your better reading group degenerates when they move away from easy first-grade materials; here is a word-study problem to solve. Teaching is an endless process of evaluating and rethinking plans. Every day should find you assessing the progress you have made and rethinking your objectives.

Think through carefully the details of each individual lesson. Once you have identified the general areas in which your pupils will need help tomorrow, what should you think through as you plan each of your lessons? The amount of detail you actually put on paper will depend on a combination of the nature of the lesson to be taught, your own feelings of security, and, in the case of student teachers, your cooperating teacher's desire to know what you are intending to do. Written in detail or not, there are certain essentials you will need to think through, even for the simplest plan.

A first step is to consider your *goals*. Specifically, what do you hope to accomplish in your work today? What new skills do you aim to develop? What understandings do you hope to clarify? If your purpose is to improve skills already learned, what improvement do you expect? This type of thinking will not allow you to write a plan that merely says "take up," "review," or "cover." You will have to stop to ask yourself *what* and *why*.

A second step is to think through *the function of the teacher* in achieving the goals. You may have read books on general methodology which discuss the relative merits of "the lecture method," "the discussion method," "the activity method." Actually, a skillful teacher uses all these and many more. The problem is not to adopt one method and reject the others. It is to decide what kind of leadership is needed if a particular set of goals is to be achieved. For example, if Sally Jamison's first grade is in need of new information not available in the books they are able to read, Sally's function may be to provide this in story form adjusted to the age of her class. John Anderson's goal is to help his pupils to arrive at a clear understanding of a new spelling rule; his function will probably be to guide an inductive reasoning process. If Sheldon Clarke's goal is to clarify plans for the assembly program, Sheldon must be prepared to serve as a discussion leader. At the point where the plans for the day call for Amy Jones' third-graders to complete their reference reading, Amy will be sponsoring an independent reading program. This may sound obvious, but many a lesson has missed its mark because the teacher tried to guide an inductive reasoning process at points where he should have been imparting information or lectured when his goal should have been to help his pupils to think for themselves.

It is particularly important to survey *teaching aids*. Many a well-planned lesson has failed because the unwary beginner glanced hastily over a set of examples, borrowed a model from an audio-visual aids laboratory without knowing exactly how it worked, or assumed he knew the contents of the chapter he planned to have read by his class. Put yourself in the place of Wanda Hendrix who planned a lesson on using the index in a social studies text, but failed to check to see whether the topics she had chosen were actually indexed. Consider the confusion in Betty Johnson's first grade when she remembered her empty paste jars just as her first-graders completed cutting out their Thanksgiving decorations and began coming for paste. Imagine, also, the bewilderment in Sam Green's fourth grade when the examples he chose for a first lesson on possessives included all the possible exceptions to the simple rule he had just taught. You cannot be too careful in checking, even though the materials you plan to use seem relatively foolproof.

If you want to be sure your words have not fallen upon deaf ears, you will also think through for each lesson how to test out the new learnings. You will need some *means of evaluation*. What questions could help you discover how much your pupils have actually learned? What practice activities could they engage in? Are there exercises that could be worked through at the blackboard? You will not know, for sure, whether you have achieved your goals unless you plan some new focus where pupils actually can put to use what you have taught.

Whether or not you plan it in detail ahead of time, a *summary*, however brief, is important. Many a well-executed lesson is left dangling without the few concluding statements that could serve to bring together what has been learned and to provide a forward look to future use. A summary need not be a tedious review of all that has gone before. Sometimes beginners err in this direction, as did Frances Cameron. After a lesson on how animals live through the winter, which had already resulted in a reasonably good list on the front board, she turned to the side board and asked the pupils to reconstruct the list from memory. Not content with this, she then had one child in each row read the entire list and, to cap the climax, had each youngster copy it for his notebook. On the other hand, Donald Smith left nothing clinched when he stopped a lesson on capital letters almost in mid-sentence as he glanced at the clock and said, "Well, that's about all for today." Sometimes the activity you plan in order to evaluate new learnings will serve as your summary. Often a sentence or two to give a brief forward look will do the trick. "Do you think we can do a better job of indenting our paragraphs tomorrow?" will help. So will "Let's think quickly now—how many new ideas do you have for your notebooks?" or "Then you can finish your reading in one more day?" Beginners need to learn the knack of tying a bow on the package or, if you prefer, putting a lesson to bed and tucking it in.

Plan thoughtfully how to involve pupils in an individual lesson. A skillful teacher thinks about how to involve pupils as he plans his lessons for the day, just as he thinks about how to involve pupils in unit plans. It is not enough to consider what your part in developing the lesson is going to be; you also need to know what part you are going to accord to your pupils and how you are going to do it.

It would seem obvious that the purposes of a lesson should be made clear to learners, but, as a matter of fact, many beginning teachers neglect to plan *how to make the lesson purposeful to pupils.* You may be so clear yourself about what you want to teach, and why, that you completely forget that boys and girls will not necessarily follow your reasoning if it is not shared with them. Pupils need to know why they are being asked to listen to information or to engage in an activity; otherwise, there is no guarantee that they will learn what the teacher feels is important. Consider the following approaches to a lesson on using the index. Martha Stickle had made careful notes on her pupils' difficulties in locating information for a science report and had planned how to capitalize on these:

MARTHA STICKLE

We had such trouble finding things yesterday—I thought we should take time to learn more about how to use an index.

(Nods from pupils.)

What were some of your problems? Do you remember?

(Several examples from pupils—Martha adds a couple and puts the list on the board.)

Now let's open our social studies book to page . . . . [Lesson follows using the books that actually caused the trouble. Pupils' problems are taken up systematically] What about it? Can we remember this now for our next group work?

(Nods.)

In contrast, Eleanor Evans assumed that her pupils would sense her purpose in planning a similar lesson:

ELEANOR EVANS

Open your language books to page . . . . Will someone read the title of the lesson on this page?

(Hands go up; Bob reads "Using an Index.")

What's an index for?

(Pupils answer.)

Now let's read what our book says about using an index. . . . [Lesson follows, using the examples in the language text entirely. Pupils answer as Eleanor poses the questions.] Why do you think we took time for this today, boys and girls?

(Several guesses before someone finally says, doubtfully, "Because we had trouble yesterday?")

If you want to be sure your lesson will be successful, neither too hard nor too easy, your plan needs to include *how to discover what pupils now know*. This is particularly important the day you are trying to develop a new concept, as Darby Jones discovered when he got halfway through a lesson attempting to develop a new spelling rule before he realized that his pupils were vague as to the meanings of *vowel* and *consonant*—terms that had been sprinkled liberally through his explanation. Even something decided yesterday is not always remembered, as Jane Harrison found out when she said to her first-graders, "Now let's plan to start our groups to work," only to learn that few clearly remembered from the preceding day what groups they had joined. A good plan for a single lesson needs to include some questions, examples, or other opportunities for group reaction that will survey key aspects of present status. A good plan also involves some alternative procedures. ("If I find that they don't know the following points, we will start like this; if they seem well informed, we can extend our work to new ideas by considering this.") Obviously, the longer you have worked with a class, the more astute you will be in judging present competencies and sensing new needs from the work they have done the day before. A teacher who has just finished working with a second-grade arithmetic group, for example, has a reasonably accurate tally of which combinations are still causing trouble, and to how many pupils.

Your plans also need to include *how to involve pupils in working actively to arrive at the new concept or generalization.* Although there will be times when you will plan to give an extended explanation to your class, there will be many more when you will want to consider how best to involve them in arriving at a new understanding. We learn what we experience. If we experience listening to the teacher, what we are best prepared to do is to give back the teacher's words. Even if you are holding the floor with a rather extended explanation, you will need to plan how to throw in the questions that will challenge your group to make use of what they have just heard or will lead them to arrive at a new principle. If your aim is inductive reasoning—to help pupils to arrive at a new number concept or to discover a new letter combination as an aid in analyzing words—you will want to have arranged your examples and your questions so that you can lead them step by step from the concrete illustration to the generalization.

Planning to involve pupils in working with a new idea, or arriving at a new generalization, is different from considering how to involve them in a pupil-teacher planning session. In the latter, there is a genuine problem admitting of several possible solutions—we might work in committees, do independent projects, do a little of both; we might share our findings by a panel, a display, a mural; our store might serve a variety of purposes. The teacher, as chairman, plans how to secure the best thinking of everybody, how to help in weighing pros and cons, how to reach a proposal that seems feasible. There are no predetermined answers. In contrast, involving a class in working actively toward a new generalization *does* involve a predetermined answer. Pupils can think actively together about how to divide twelve dozen cookies among thirty-two persons, but the class certainly does not vote on which of several conflicting calculations is correct. Neither is a vote appropriate on which of several routes to America would be most desirable for Columbus, although youngsters may examine a globe to see what the possibilities are before they hear what actually happened. And, although several incorrect or partially correct proposals may be advanced before pupils arrive at the principle for making plural words ending in *y*, they don't reform existing spelling rules.

SCHEDULING THE DAY'S ACTIVITIES

One of the most difficult problems faced by beginning teachers is how to plan the schedule of the day's activities. In some classrooms, the daily schedule may be relatively inflexible. If you are teaching in a single subject area, it may be that your pupils will come to you for periods of forty-five or fifty minutes. The trend in the elementary school, however, is toward self-contained rooms in which decisions regarding the time to be allotted to specific activities and their sequence are left almost entirely to the teacher's judgment. Whatever the particular time allotment under which you are working, there are several types of problems you must be prepared to handle. First, you are going to have to decide how best to allot your time among the various activities that make up your program for the day. Second, you will have to propose a desirable sequence of activities for a typical day. Then, you must develop the knack of planning carefully the details needed to make any one day go smoothly. Last, but by no means of least importance, you must decide how and when to involve your pupils in the scheduling process.

Consider the philosophy of the school system in deciding upon general time allotments. For beginners, deciding how much time to devote to any one activity is often a difficult problem. Every activity seems important, and it is all too easy to stress one area of study day after day at the expense of others or to fail to give the time needed to capitalize on the potentialities of a problem because others seem pressing. Decisions regarding which activities to include in the day and how much time to allot to them are made at several levels, some of which have already been mentioned. The general curriculum design under which you are working is one determining factor. You may be in a school system where you and your cooperating teacher are completely free to use your time according to your best judgment of pupils' needs and capacities. On the other hand, under some curriculum designs there will be general recommendations regarding where the emphasis is to be placed, frequently expressed in terms of a proposed number of minutes per week. Such suggestions represent the priorities established by a given school system.

Even when a course of study gives specific recommendations of the number of minutes a week to be devoted to given subject areas, these are not meant to be adhered to strictly. Certainly, they are not intended to be used as guides to the exact number of minutes to be devoted to an area of study on any particular day. At least three types of considerations influence a teacher's decisions regarding how and when recommended time allotments should be adjusted. First, teachers consider the needs of the pupils in the particular class. For example, youngsters from homes where there has been little experience with standard English usage may well need more than the recommended amount of time focused on language experiences. Again, in some schools pupils will be busily occupied with after-school dancing classes, music lessons, and other opportunities for creative expression. Although this would not mean eliminating all such experiences from the school day, it does suggest that the time allotments to these areas might be less than they would be in situations where these out-of-school experiences are meager. Consider how general priorities should be adjusted, then, in the light of the special strengths, weaknesses, and experience backgrounds of your pupils.

Teachers also appraise the total experiences that make up the day's work. The integration that results from unit teaching tends to blur sharp differentiations in time allotments. Which time allotment is being used, for example, when pupils write reports on the reading they have done regarding Colonial days or perhaps publish a Colonial newspaper? —that assigned to social studies or that given to language arts? Are third-graders learning science or arithmetic when they make simple graphs to record the results from their experiments in growing plants under a variety of circumstances? Is it reading or spelling time when second-graders work on the sounds of words? Art or social studies when they plan a mural to depict community helpers? If you are certain that your pupils are having ample reading experiences in connection with a science activity, you need not be unduly concerned if reading does not appear as a separate activity on your schedule for a few days. If they have just engaged in a discussion period following a trip to the fire house, you need not necessarily plan for other oral language activities. The important question is whether there is balance in your pupils' experiences over the week or month, regardless of the precise label under which an activity appears on your schedule.

Experienced teachers have also discovered that time is likely to be used more effectively if they do not adhere rigidly to a given number of minutes each day for each teaching area. For example, it is almost impossible to plan so that the lesson with each of three primary reading groups calls for exactly twenty-five minutes every day. One group may be at a point where a ten-minute introduction needs to be followed by independent reading of the story. A second may need time to discuss three stories, choose the one preferred, and select a tentative cast for a play. The third may be working on phonetics activities for which a twenty-five-minute period is about right. To take another example, it may be important during the first planning sessions related to a unit of work to stay at the job until certain decisions are clearly understood. There may be a point later in the unit when a much shorter independent work period will suffice. It is not wise use of time to prolong an activity beyond a natural stopping point merely to use up an arbitrary number of minutes. Perhaps an even more serious waste of time comes from ending an activity before a logical stopping place is reached and then spending ten to fifteen minutes the next day building again the interest and sense of purpose needed to complete the activity.

Establish the framework of a daily schedule in the light of typical needs. The trend toward larger time blocks and more flexible use of time does not mean that there is no similarity in a schedule from day to day. Pupils need the security of a certain amount of routine in their day. So do teachers. Typically, a framework that represents a workable schedule for most days is established and adjustments are then made as special problems demand them.

Many teachers set up the framework for their schedules by thinking of the day as divided into four large time blocks, separated in midmorning and midafternoon by a break for a recess period, lunch and rest in some cases for primary children, perhaps an opportunity for a drink and lavatory break for older groups. Sometimes all-school schedules help to determine when these breaks are to come if playground space is limited or halls tend to be noisy. To each of the four large periods specific activities are assigned. Typically, one generous block is set aside for work in fundamental skills. Not infrequently a second period is also assigned to skill areas, particularly with younger groups or with pupils whose skills are in need of further practice. This leaves two, or perhaps three, blocks of time for unit activities related to such areas as social studies, science, or health. Creative activities also need to be included. If these activities are taught by special teachers, they will probably be scheduled on a regular basis. If not, one of the time blocks devoted to unit activities may serve for a variety of creative experiences—writing, music, art, dramatization.

There will also be routines to be included in the general framework of a daily schedule. Typically there will be bookkeeping activities in the early morning—lunch tickets to sell, notes from parents to check, attendance to record. Time for housekeeping will be needed. Often ten or fifteen minutes at the end of the day is set aside for this. Both primary and intermediate teachers may include regular sharing periods as ways of learning more about pupils and useful opportunities for oral language experiences. There may be other special events scheduled regularly —a weekly visit to the library, a club meeting Friday afternoons, and, in some schools in underprivileged areas, time for showers. Planning and evaluation sessions also need to be scheduled. Some teachers take time at the end of the day to evaluate and look toward tomorrow, and then recheck plans briefly in the morning. Others place their planning sessions at the start of the new day.

The framework of a typical schedule, then, might look as follows:

9:00-10:30 First large time block. (The first twenty minutes might be given to routines and planning. Unit activities or individual and group work on skills could follow. This period is long enough to allow for two shorter periods if needed.)

10:30-10:45 Recess break. (In some primary classrooms the first time block might be shortened to allow more time for lunch, games, and rest.)

10:45-11:45 Second large time block. (This would allow for work in a second area. If the first time block is to be devoted to unit activities, this might focus on skills, and vice versa.)

11:45- 1:00 Lunch.

1:00- 2:00 Third large time block. (This would allow for work in a third large area. In some rooms two periods a week of this or the preceding blocks might be devoted to special work in music or art.)

2:00- 2:30 Recess, rhythms, physical education. (In some schools this period might be lengthened three days a week for special work in the gym and shortened on the other two. In some primary groups music might be an important part of this period. The 10:30 period could be lengthened in similar fashion.)

2:30- 3:30 Fourth large time block. (This might be devoted to unit activities or provide time for creative experiences. Housekeeping and planning might occupy the last fifteen minutes.)

Many factors could influence decisions regarding which activities to assign to which periods. Some teachers feel that early placement of a work period on skills allows children to proceed with individual assignments while the details of getting started on a new day are taken care of. Some place unit activities early, and then call smaller groups for help with skills while the others carry out unit plans. When recess breaks are established on a school-wide basis, the size of the time block on either side of the break could influence such decisions. The less mature the group, the more important it may be to divide a large time block into shorter periods. These shorter periods may perhaps provide for an alternation of times for individual or group work and times when the teacher, as leader, can bring the class together and check on progress. Sometimes, as suggested in the discussion on discipline in Chapter 5, the teacher may have rather strong feelings as to which activities are well placed early and which are effective in winding up the day. Even though it is difficult to produce research evidence that any one subject is actually learned better at a given time of day, a teacher's feelings about his particular group are still important to take into account when setting up a schedule.

Schedule the details of a single day in terms of the demands of ongoing activities. Even though the general framework of your schedule is relatively stable, you will still have decisions to make regarding precisely what is to go on in a single day. To survey the needs of the day, think first of how the activities foreseen in your block plans are progressing. Ask yourself: How far along are we? Was anything not covered yesterday that needs to be picked up today? Were assignments given or special reports volunteered and do these need to be worked in? Did yesterday's work reveal special problems for which time should be taken today? How far along are groups? Do they need more time today? This detailed look at how block plans are unfolding will show you the major activities to be included in the day.

It is important, also, to think about the "extras" that need to be worked into your plan. There may be letters to an ill child, thank-you notes to another class, a current events bulletin board to discuss, valentines to be made. Beginners often find that such activities tend to be pushed aside unless definitely scheduled or sometimes even given priority over regular class work. If they are left "until we have time" many weeks may pass before they are given attention.

You will need to learn to plan, too, for special all-school events for which a place must be given in the schedule. As a new teacher, you may find it frustrating to discover that your schedule needs to be changed to include an unforeseen assembly, a movie that was not expected until next Monday, a request for a meeting of all the safety guards. Yet, if your pupils are to be a part of the school community, they must share in such activities. It is important to check school bulletin boards and notices for announcements of such events. However, some will come unannounced in spite of all your vigilance. It can be helpful to glance over your plans for the day and assign priorities so that the adjustments needed for unheralded interruptions can be made with minimum confusion.

After you have made your survey of the regular activities that need to be included in the day, the extras within your classroom, and the all-school demands on time, you are ready to decide whether any major adjustments need to be made in the normal schedule. Note the activities demanding more than the usual amount of time; locate those that could be shortened or even skipped for the day; decide how best to find room for extras. On many days little if any adjustment in the regular schedule will be needed, but occasionally major changes will be important. Skillful teachers try to guide activities so that demands for extra time in the schedule do not all come at once. For example, if an extra-long period is needed for a rehearsal for a play, an effort is made to plan this for a time when a social studies unit calls for independent reading which could, if necessary, be put off for a day or completed at home.

As a last step in establishing your schedule for the day, it is important to evaluate the variety of activities. Are too many activities of the same type scheduled? Will pupils become restless because they are asked to discuss or to write for too many minutes at a stretch? Is there a balance between new activities calling for intensive discussion and planning and continuing activities where a quick check on plans will be sufficient? In terms of the self-control of the particular group, how many activities involving much moving about are placed side by side? Should something quieting or relaxing be inserted? How long will individuals and groups be expected to be self-directing without the teacher's supervision? Even pupils with good work habits, for example, may lose momentum toward the end of a long, independent work period. Out of such detailed appraisals of requirements of on-going activities, special demands, and needs for variety comes your detailed schedule for the day.

Involve pupils in planning their daily schedule. Should pupils have a share in the scheduling process? It is just as important to involve them here as it is to involve them in other phases of planning. For one thing, pupils who know the schedule are better able to meet commitments, to proceed independently, to clean up and be ready for the next activity. Even if you do not involve your boys and girls actively in the scheduling process, you should at least have the day's schedule in evidence so that they will know what is going to happen next. Listen to Gracie Evans, for example. Her relations with her pupils are friendly, but there is no sharing of the schedule.

ROY
Are we going to finish our puppets today?

GRACIE EVANS
We'll see later. Just sit down now.

SUE
When are we going to talk about the puppet play?

GRACIE EVANS
I'll tell you later. Right now get out a clean piece of paper.

ALLEN
Is this for spelling?

GRACIE EVANS
We'll find out just as soon as everyone is ready.

In contrast, Jean Jackson tries to help her pupils think about the activities to come:

JEAN JACKSON
Is everyone in his seat? Let's look at the schedule. We said our most most important job today was to finish our puppets and to start planning our play?

SUE
That's right, Miss Jackson.

JEAN JACKSON
I thought we probably should give our biggest block of time to it, so it's scheduled for 10 o'clock. Then we can work until noon if we have to. Now before that we have our spelling test and the two reading groups that didn't meet yesterday to work in. If you'll get out paper and number it from 1 to 20, we'll do spelling right now.

Occasionally, overanxious classes worry if they do not meet the exact time limits on the schedule. Some teachers avoid this problem by listing a proposed sequence of activities and then suggesting time limits at the beginning of each activity. In some primary classrooms, a toy clock is used to indicate the deadline—"Let's all be ready to clean up when our clock says 10 o'clock." "We'll all have to stop when the hands of the clock look like this."

There are valuable lessons to be learned about wise use of time if pupils are actually involved in helping to set up the schedule for the day. This takes skillful leadership, however, if you are to avoid wasting time by requiring pupils to state the obvious or to guess about decisions they are not equipped to make. There are exceptions to every example, but it is usually a waste of time to reconstruct the entire schedule every day.

RANDY ZUMA
What shall we do first, John?

JOHN
Spelling.

RANDY ZUMA
And what comes next, Diana?

DIANA
Reading groups.

RANDY ZUMA
Yes, and then? Bobby?

BOBBY
Social studies.

This becomes an unnecessary routine if the order is always the same and the pupils are merely reciting a long-established schedule. On the other hand, they can be helped to be much more self-directing in their activities if they share in thinking about changes in the typical routine.

PETE WHITE
Let's look at our schedule. There's an assembly called for 10:45 and this was when we had planned to finish our notebooks.

SALLY
Well, we could maybe study our spelling at home.

KARL
Yes, Mr. White, let's do notebooks first so we'll be sure to get them in.

PETE WHITE
We'd have to shift our arithmetic, also, to do that.

SALLY
Couldn't we work that in this afternoon?

PETE WHITE
Let's take a look at it now and make sure we're all clear. We go at our notebooks first. Right?

Time may also be wasted if pupils are asked to propose time limits when they have no clear understanding of what is to be involved in the activity they are discussing. Such a planning session cannot be much more than an exercise in reading the teacher's face and voice.

MARY SMYTH
How much time should we plan for our reading groups? [Mary has planned exactly what each group was to do but has not revealed these plans.]

ALICIA
An hour. [Alicia loves to read.]

MARY SMYTH
Now let's think—that's a little long, isn't it?

PETER
Twenty minutes? [Doubtfully, Peter is trying to read his teacher's mind.]

MARY SMYTH
That's just a *little* short, isn't it?

JOAN
Forty minutes?

MARY SMYTH
What about that, boys and girls? Does forty minutes sound about right?

Pupils can acquire a definite sense of direction, however, and learn much about wise use of time if they are asked to think through time allotments for activities in which they are directly involved. Sometimes this goes on in a planning and evaluation session and is then translated by the teacher into a schedule.

ZELMA DOE
You are ready to start painting the mural tomorrow?

CHORUS
Yes Ma'am.

ZELMA DOE
Then we'd better think about using most of the time after recess to work. What about the other groups—do you need a long period, too?

ANDY
Our group needs it.

JILL
We *might* get done early, but we've got those birthday cards for Susan if we do.

ZELMA DOE
Then suppose we use all of our work period right up to noon to let your groups work.

Long-term scheduling can also be helpful in moving activities ahead. Evidence of such plans appears in the form of deadlines of various sorts. In many classrooms a special corner of the blackboard or bulletin board is set aside for such plans. Several lists can often be seen:

Notebooks Due—November 6
Committee Report Dates—Sign below if ready.
Paper Drive—December 1

Teachers who find time to work with individuals and small groups lose no opportunity to help their pupils become as self-directing as their maturity warrants.

Apply general principles of good scheduling when working within the limits of a single period. Teachers who work within the limits of a forty-five- or fifty-minute period sometimes feel that pupil-teacher planning is almost impossible in their situations. Time seems all too short without using part of it each day for a planning session, and the varied activities typically associated with units which teachers and pupils have planned together seem almost impossible to achieve.

Actually, much variety can be planned within the limits of a short period. The secret is to view a week or even a longer period as a time block rather than a single day. Pupils and teacher together may spend Monday, for example, exploring a new area and making tentative plans. Tuesday may see the planning continued in more detail or some preliminary survey work done by the class as a whole. For the next several class sessions pupils may work independently or in small groups to carry out the plans. Eventually a day or more is devoted to sharing individual work and reaching solutions to the initial problem or series of problems.

Pupils need to share in considering the plans and the schedule for the best use of a single period, just as they share when a whole day is to be planned. They can help to sharpen specific problems or to identify skills they lack or special techniques they need to learn. They can also help to decide how long they need for individual or group work and when they will be ready to share their work. The planning process is essentially the same. The difference is that teacher and pupils together face the time restrictions and decide how to achieve the wisest use of the period they have together.

TEACHING PUPILS TO PLAN

How to involve pupils in planning has been discussed in each of the three preceding sections. Effective techniques are not achieved overnight. The skills of cooperative problem-solving are highly complex and sophisticated. It is not uncommon for teachers new to the problems of cooperative planning to experiment with a single session and then to give up because the results did not seem to justify the time expenditure. Pupils have to be taught to plan, and in many cases teachers also have to learn how to mobilize efficiently and effectively the total resources of the class.

Identify problems where planning is possible. One important ability a teacher must develop is that of identifying situations in which genuine planning is possible. These are situations which admit of several solutions—situations in which teacher and pupils are free to identify subproblems and to consider several possible steps in solving them. As suggested earlier, all situations in which there is give-and-take in discussion do not involve planning. Opportunities for genuine planning do not exist when pupils are being helped to arrive inductively at an established generalization or when they are trying to reason their way to (or to guess) an item of information. Opportunities for genuine planning do not always exist either, in questions regarding what is to be studied. If the work of the fifth grade is to concentrate on the growth of America in social studies, the pupils should be told this, as they have no real choice. However, they could share in decisions regarding how to start—perhaps with their city, perhaps with the geography of their country, perhaps with the first persons to set foot on it. If this seems to be too mature a decision the teacher may propose the starting point and the pupils share in considering what they need to know and how to go about securing the information. To take another example, "What do you want to learn in arithmetic this year?" is a problem for which the typical pupil lacks the competence to make a sensible reply. "Let's take this review test and see how much each of us has remembered from last year" can lead to some good cooperative evaluation and planning of immediate next steps.

The purpose of cooperative planning is not to reduce all insights to the level of eight- or ten-year-old thinking. It is to make the most of the previous experiences of the pupils, to build a sense of self-direction, and to develop problem-solving skills *at the level at which the group can operate*. It is perhaps fair to say that many teachers underestimate the maturity of their pupils and think for them in areas where they are well able to think for themselves. However, it is also possible to overestimate the capacity of a group and to ask for decisions well beyond their maturity. In addition, beginning teachers need to take their own feelings of competence into account. It is usually better to start slowly and surely than it is to have your planning sessions end in chaos.

When neither teacher nor pupils are experienced in cooperative planning, first attempts may be more satisfying if the problem does not involve an academic aspect of the curriculum. Pupils may plan how to entertain their mothers or how to display their work for Parents' Night. Decorating the classroom, deciding where to put the library table, considering how best to store supplies, and other aspects of making the classroom attractive offer good problems. Others fall in the area of behavior—how to get pencils sharpened so that others are not disturbed, how to avoid traffic jams in the cloakroom. There will also be all-school problems—how to help in the safety drive, how to decorate the bulletin board outside our door, what to contribute to the school paper.[4] Such concerns have vitality for pupils and are well within the competence of even first-graders. Teachers often feel freer to follow the suggestions of the class in such matters because academic progress is not threatened. They are good situations in which to try out group leadership techniques.

Help pupils to develop effective techniques of cooperative problem-solving. If boys and girls are going to learn to plan effectively, they will need to be helped to develop skills in cooperative problem-solving. In planning sessions that involve the entire class, teaching these skills will be largely your responsibility as a discussion leader. There may be some situations in which one of the pupils is capable of leading an all-class discussion—chairing a club meeting, for example—but for the most part, particularly at the elementary school level, the teacher must accept his role as chairman in all-class planning sessions.

You can teach pupils much about taking turns and about respecting and securing the opinions of others by the way in which you operate as class chairman. Sometimes beginners mistake enthusiasm for a good discussion and try to listen to several voices shouting at once. It is not only appropriate but essential to an effective discussion to work out some ways of hearing one person at a time. With most groups, you will also have to call for a good audience once in a while as enthusiastic side discussions spring up or as pupils whose attention span is short begin to find other things to occupy themselves. It is also important to catch the tentative gesture of the shyer pupil and to ask the more aggressive one to yield the floor. All of this help can be given positively and without nagging or scolding if your mind is clearly on your leadership role. Comments such as the following help to teach the behavior wanted without implying criticism:

[4] For a very stimulating discussion of the types of problems through which experienced teachers found opportunity to plan with pupils, see Alice Miel and associates, *Cooperative Procedures in Learning*. New York: Bureau of Publications, Teachers College, Columbia University, 1952.

Just a minute. That was a good idea but some of us were talking and missed it. Wait until everyone is listening and then tell us again, please, Sandra.

Let's see—who hasn't had a chance yet? Susan, what did you want to say?

John, we've heard from you a couple of times; let's get Alec first.

All right, judging from all the voices you think it is a good idea. Now let's try to talk one at a time so that we can get our plans straight.

Peter, you looked as if you wanted to say something.

Nobody's ideas are crazy just because you disagree. Let's list it and then think about it.

The blackboard can be an effective aid in helping pupils to keep to the point. In some discussions it may be important to list all ideas and questions just as they come and organize them later. This might happen, for example, when specific interests related to a new science or social studies unit are first being pooled. Sometimes, however, you can organize as you go, and pupils whose points are off the track can be asked to hold them:

We are still talking about the committees we need, Ron. Suppose we put *ice cream* over next to the refreshment committee and they can think about it when they meet.

That takes us into how we would work, doesn't it, Joan? Let's hold it until we're sure we have all the general questions listed.

A good leader senses when to draw a planning session to a close. As a beginner you may be fearful that someone's feelings will be hurt if every hand is not acknowledged. Actually, an enthusiastic group can go on listing trivia almost endlessly, especially if there is the added social motive of gaining the attention of classmates and teacher. It is important for pupils to learn not to repeat the obvious or to quibble about small details merely to be heard. Asking for any distinctly new ideas can help; so can a time limit:

There are still five hands up. Are you people sure it is really something new?

We must be done in three more minutes. Are there any other important things we've missed?

Sometimes beginners prolong pupil-teacher planning sessions to the point of extracting every last idea out of the pupils, as if a suggestion from the teacher were somehow undemocratic. It is quite possible for a group to overlook some major point that you know has to be considered. There is no reason why you should not add it. In fact, if you do not, the planning session is likely to degenerate into painful fishing for ideas. Contrast the following. Debby McKay feels that all ideas must come from her class:

DEBBY MCKAY
We have a very good list. I wonder if anyone sees anything missing?

RON
Well, we didn't put down to ask the name of the airport.

DEBBY MCKAY
I don't believe we'd need that. Most of us know it, don't we?

RAY
Not to put our heads out of the bus?

DEBBY MCKAY
Now look at our suggestions about how to behave. We said hands and arms. Wouldn't that mean heads too? But there is something else *very important.*

SALLY
Take money to buy cokes?

DEBBY MCKAY
No, now we really aren't thinking.

On the other hand, June Erikson has realized that her pupils' ability to add new ideas is nearly exhausted:

JUNE ERIKSON
We have a very good list. Let's check—we have arranged for the letter to the bus company; we have our questions to ask at the airport; we know how much money. Oh! I see there is one other big thing we all forgot.

RON
Well, we didn't put down to ask the name of the airport.

JUNE ERIKSON
We know that, don't we? But we all forgot to plan for permission notes from our mothers. We need to get them written and set a date to get them back. Let me check now and see if there was anything else on my list.

Sometimes beginners are bothered with the problem of what to do with the vigorous new idea that threatens to upset all of yesterday's plans. Must you yield the floor, in the name of democracy, to any pupil who has changed his mind, even if it means reversing a week's work? On the other hand, must you hold children to a plan that is obviously not working because they agreed to it? In both cases, the sensible answer seems to be "No." Even adults sometimes forget exactly what was discussed the meeting before (or twenty minutes ago, for that matter) and come up with a new proposal counter to agreed-upon plans. The younger the participant, the more likely this is to occur. If you start off on Tuesday by saying "Let's list all the things we planned yesterday," pupils will certainly treat the planning session as wide open and may take off in a new direction. "Here is a copy of yesterday's plans; all we need to do today is to settle. . . ." is much more efficient and far safer. On the other hand, you will from time to time find yourself in a situation where it is quite obvious that what looked good is not working. This calls for an evaluation session and, if necessary, for new plans.

We learn any skill more readily when we understand the techniques we are trying to acquire. In addition to serving as an effective group leader, teachers need to talk through discussion techniques with their pupils. Some of this you will do in the process of serving as a discussion leader. Explanatory comments such as the following help to teach:

> Is there anyone who hasn't been heard from? We don't want to lose any good ideas.
>
> Let's wait, John; you've had a turn.
>
> Shouldn't we hold that until we've finished talking about . . . ?

In addition, it helps to evaluate good or poor planning sessions—to figure out what took so long or to congratulate pupils on how efficient they are becoming.

Most teachers worry about the overly aggressive child who talks too much or about the very shy youngster who seldom volunteers. If these behaviors are symptomatic of deep-seated emotional needs, there is little likelihood that you will be able to wield any magic wand. There are, however, steps you can take to teach such youngsters how to become part of the group. Refusing to acknowledge the shouts of the aggressive child (and then giving him a turn when his hand goes up), asking him to yield to one who has not yet contributed (and not forgetting to call on him eventually), taking the side of the victim firmly but reasonably if the aggressor resorts to belittling to get his way (and then praising him when he uses good judgment), can all help. In other words, teach him, through your role as chairman, which behaviors will help him to achieve his goals and which will not.

Dealing with the very shy youngster is another story. Sometimes you will be able to catch a wiggle or grin that suggests anxiety to get into the discussion. Sometimes even being one of several answering "Yes" or "No" to a proposal helps. Occasionally the problem will be one where the shy youngster can make a special contribution from his background —"Jimmy, your father works there. Could you find out for us?" Sometimes the ice is best broken in a small committee, and the shy youngster then shares in explaining the committee report to the whole class.

Even the seating arrangement in your classroom can make a difference. If everyone is facing you, the chances are increased that the discussion will go from pupil to teacher and back to a new pupil rather than from pupil to pupil. Even with desks in rows, pupils can turn to face each other. In small groups, pupils need to learn to arrange desks into a circle so that someone is not squeezed out. You may need to be at the blackboard for some discussions, but you may find it contributes to the give-and-take of the discussion if you can sit in the circle rather than be isolated at your desk.

Help pupils learn to evaluate proposals. Cooperative problem-solving involves careful evaluation of proposals as well as good working relationships. Beginning teachers, and many experienced teachers who have not involved pupils in planning, are sometimes fearful lest pupils take off on an impossible or utterly fantastic proposal. This will not happen if your pre-planning has been effective. Democracy has been defined at a number of points in this and preceding chapters as involving much more than a majority vote. The problem is to help a class to arrive at a series of purposeful and sensible proposals. To do this, pupils will need to grow in their ability to evaluate suggestions. Often the final plan will be achieved by consensus with no vote required.

Preceding sections have suggested some of the problems pupils may need to be helped to face in evaluating their proposals. School regulations cannot be set aside. There are also realistic time problems—two ambitious units cannot always run side by side; deadlines may exist; other subject areas will have certain claims to priority; of two proposals achieving much the same ends, one may call for a vastly greater time expenditure. In addition, it is appropriate to think through how much new experience the proposal will contribute—"Plays are fun, but we've put on two. What will we really learn for the time it will take?" Sometimes it is helpful to think through limitations before a discussion starts. "Let's see," said Janice Furgeson. "We can have our Mexican lunch if we don't bother the cook or the custodian. What does that mean about the kind of food we should plan?" With boundaries established, overly ambitious proposals can be rejected with little or no argument.

If children are to learn to evaluate their proposals effectively, they have a right to the teacher's best thinking regarding limitations, difficulties, and possible procedures. If your pupils have learned from experience in previous planning sessions that their ideas, too, will be carefully considered, you may make your proposals without fear that your prestige as leader will turn the entire planning session into an effort to read your mind. Every so often, where there is such mutual give and take, your pupils will tell you quite flatly that they do not agree with you. They will brush aside the difficulties you foresee in their proposals and insist in their youthful enthusiasm that they can make them work. If no school rules are being violated, and other objections have been met—at least in the minds of your class—what are you to do? Mary Simonds faced this problem with her fifth grade as her group planned a play for assembly. The children insisted that each committee could write an act and Susan and Jane volunteered to tie them all together over the weekend. Mary pointed out that when she'd tried to do that for them on another play she'd had to work all weekend, even with all she knew about play construction from college. The desire to work in small groups was too strong. The children insisted they could do it and Jane and Susan, struck with the importance of their assignment, were vociferous that they'd written "lots of plays." What was Mary to do?—veto the plan and insist the play be developed by the class as a whole? or let them try it? She chose the latter as the only alternative to unqualified dictatorship. However, as she went from group to group, she made careful notes on how the various scenes were unfolding. Armed with her notes, she went home to think through how to draw the pieces together if need be. When Jane and Susan returned defeated on Monday, Mary had a plan ready that made use of most of the Friday session. It should be added that groups will surprise you oftener than they will disappoint you; the plan that you would have vetoed as impossible sometimes achieves results beyond your most optimistic expectations.

There has never been a time when there was greater need for the schools to develop citizens skilled in working together and efficient in cooperative problem-solving. We have reached a level of scientific advance where any other means of solving international disputes literally can destroy civilization. We have intercommunication systems that make it possible for us to be linked with persons all over the world on common enterprises. Teaching pupils the techniques of cooperative problem-solving is far more than a device to secure maximum motivation. It could be the most crucial learning for which the school is responsible.

BOOKS YOU SHOULD KNOW

Bush, Robert N. *The Teacher-Pupil Relationship.* Englewood Cliffs, N.J.: Prentice-Hall, 1954. Pp. xvii + 252.

Hanna, Lavone A.; Potter, Gladys L.; and Hagaman, Neva. *Unit Teaching in the Elementary School.* New York: Rinehart and Co., 1955. Pp. x + 592.

Lane, Howard, and Beauchamp, Mary. *Human Relations in Teaching.* Englewood Cliffs, N.J.: Prentice-Hall, 1955. Pp. ix + 353.

Miel, Alice, and associates. *Cooperative Procedures in Learning.* New York: Bureau of Publications, Teachers College, Columbia University, 1952. Pp. x + 512.

Miel, Alice, and Brogan, Peggy. *More Than Social Studies.* Englewood Cliffs, N.J.: Prentice-Hall, 1957. Pp. vii + 452.

Wiles, Kimball. *Teaching for Better Schools.* Englewood Cliffs, N.J.: Prentice-Hall, 1952. Pp. xiii + 397.

Helping Learners Understand Their World

CHAPTER 7

Critics of modern educational practice sometimes claim that teachers in today's schools tend to depreciate the importance of information—that we stress teaching a pupil how to think without providing him with a firm foundation of information on which to base his thinking. Perhaps in some classrooms teachers have permitted more construction activities, dramatics, and just plain "busy work" than could be justified in relation to the concepts the pupils were acquiring. It is much more likely, however, that many such criticisms stem from differing opinions of what information will be of most value to citizens of tomorrow.

Deciding what knowledge is of most worth has always been a difficult problem. It is even more so in today's complex world. If we devote the same amount of time to primitive man, the Greeks and Romans, or the early explorers as we formerly did, we must, of necessity, neglect or treat lightly present-day international events or highly significant recent developments in our own land. In fact, many a student has taken courses in both American and world history in grade school, high school, and college without looking much beyond World War II. Equipping pupils with the broad and varied informational background they will need as effective citizens in tomorrow's world does not mean that they must acquire the identical information learned by their parents.

Decisions regarding what knowledge is of most worth are complicated by the speed at which our world is changing. Additions to our cultural heritage are being made at an ever accelerating rate. Advances in all areas of human endeavor are coming so rapidly that what we teach as fact today may have to be modified tomorrow. No one can predict with certainty what new scientific discovery will change our way of life, what new development will start a chain reaction in our interrelated economic and social structure. Television, radio, newspapers, and an ever increasing flood of books and periodicals all make their bids for attention—and evaluation—by an informed citizen. We are called upon, as never before, to appraise the authority (and, in some cases, the good intent) of individuals who may be urging solutions to national or international problems or advising us to change our brand of toothpaste or soap. We must build adequate foundations for making decisions in areas where complex understanding is required, but we must also help pupils to acquire the skills they need to keep pace with their rapidly changing world.

To make our task even more challenging, interrelationships among the various fields of inquiry are more important than ever before. One cannot understand physics without some knowledge of chemistry and mathematics. Sociology, economics, geography, political science—all contribute to the interpretation of historical events. In fact, all areas of knowledge today are significantly interrelated in one way or another. Although we must provide boys and girls with the experiences that develop fundamental understandings within subject fields, we must also help them to become aware of the ways in which many areas of knowledge contribute to the solution of human problems—even those seemingly simple.

Your task, then, in helping pupils to acquire information about their world is much more challenging than merely acquainting them with the facts in a textbook. To meet this responsibility successfully, there are a number of problems you must be prepared to face. In the first place, you must know clearly what your ultimate goals are. Then, you must decide how to deal with the thousand and one opportunities which will help pupils grow in their understanding of their world—which topics to treat lightly, which to explore deeply, how much detail to attempt in those deemed worthy of extensive study. Third, you will have to provide the experiences that guarantee that accurate concepts and generalizations—not verbalizations alone—are the result of pupils' explorations. Fourth, because you want boys and girls to be active in acquiring and using new information, you will have to make decisions regarding how and when to work through individual and small-group projects. Fifth, you must be prepared to help pupils develop the reference skills they will need to locate new information for themselves. And, as if these were not challenges enough, you have the problem of individualizing classroom activities so that youngsters with special interests or talents are given time and encouragement to pursue them. These major problems are the focus of the sections that follow.

WHAT ARE OUR GOALS IN HELPING PUPILS UNDERSTAND THEIR WORLD?

Obviously, the elementary school assumes only a small part of the task of helping individuals acquire understanding of the world—social and scientific—in which they live. Yet it is at this level that basic attitudes toward knowledge are developed. By what we choose to teach, and by the way we teach it, we can do much to determine the ways in which children will approach more advanced learnings. Your earlier professional courses will undoubtedly have dwelt upon goals in fields related to the social and natural sciences. Now, as you face decisions regarding what content to stress, how to make the most effective use of the resource materials and other teaching aids in your classroom, when and how to involve your pupils in acquiring information for themselves, and how to determine your role as leader and resource person, it may help to think again about the goals you are trying to achieve. What kinds of behavior are characteristic of the learner who is growing in his understanding of his world?

The individual who is growing in his understanding of his world has broad and accurate information. A person who makes competent decisions must have facts with which to think. Not only must he have facts, but he must have a healthy respect for accuracy and for thorough information if he is to be certain that he has reached a correct conclusion. The individual who reaches sound conclusions does not act on half-truths, a smattering of evidence, or a good guess. He has acquired the habit of withholding judgment until he has the information he needs.

What do we mean when we say that a person who makes competent decisions must have information—*facts* with which to think? Facts are certainly not words. Rather, they emerge from memories, images, perceptual experiences, and imaginative thinking. Consider what this means for teaching. Back of even the most simple terms are a host of meanings and interpretations derived from past experiences. *Table* (an article of furniture), for example, does not refer only to a particular object in one's home. It denotes a class of objects, not necessarily distinguished by shape, number of legs, height, or even some aspects of function. We have learned to distinguish a table from a desk, a shelf, a tray, a counter, through many experiences that have helped us to develop a concept of *table*. Most of the significant information we must help our pupils to acquire calls for similar depth of understanding —for concept development. There will be, of course, a certain number of arbitrary items of information which have to be memorized—Columbus sighted the new world in 1492; the first settlement in this country was St. Augustine; vessels carrying blood to the heart are veins. Much more frequently, however, our responsibility for helping pupils acquire information—facts—lies in providing for the depth of meaning that results in clear and accurate concepts. We must learn to make sharp distinctions between information parroted back in the words of the textbook or the encyclopedia and information which is understood. We cannot be content or consider ourselves successful if our pupils toss around lightly such words as *democracy, freedom, truth, light-years, space,* or even such relatively concrete terms as *mountain, farm, forest,* or *jungle*. We must maintain eternal vigilance against the verbalization which is sometimes mistaken for understanding.

When you plan to help your pupils to acquire accurate information, then, you are not working primarily for memorization of the details of a textbook. Your task is to provide the experience that insures meanings as precise and accurate as are consistent with your pupils' levels of development and maturity. You must make certain that your pupils have clear understandings about peoples thousands of miles away, about cultures totally dissimilar to their own, about climates and topography in no way resembling the region in which they live, about organisms infinitesimally small and distances vast beyond imagination, and about a host of everyday, near-at-hand situations that may, in spite of their seeming familiarity, be as foreign to the lives of some of your pupils as are the jungles of Africa or the craters on the moon.

The individual who is growing in his understanding of his world uses his information in solving new problems. It is quite possible for an individual to possess accurate information about a topic and yet not be able to apply it to a new situation. He may, for example, talk intelligently about the nutritional values of certain foods yet choose meals that violate the principles of good nutrition. He may report on the rainfall, temperature, and geographic features of a country about which he has been reading and yet not use this information in interpreting current news releases. The individual who has developed effective understandings has his information organized—he has arrived at generalizations which can be applied to new situations.

Most of the problems an individual faces call for generalizations not from a single field, but from many fields. As he interprets the article in the morning paper reporting the latest international tension he draws upon geography, history, economics, political science, sociology, and perhaps psychology, nuclear physics, and chemistry. Even a housewife preparing a family meal uses—consciously or unconsciously—generalizations from the fields of nutrition, child care, chemistry, aesthetics, and perhaps several others. Furthermore, the individual who solves effectively his day-by-day problems actually puts his generalizations to use. As he faces a new situation he consciously seeks to apply his knowledge. He does not operate with watertight compartments—using accurate information in relation to one situation and reacting from emotion in another where virtually the same principles hold.

It is impossible to teach our pupils all the specific details with which they are—or might be—concerned. If we want to prepare them to act intelligently in new situations, we must be concerned with the generalizations at which they are arriving—the broad principles that will enable them to approach with wisdom a host of related situations. Traditionally, courses of study have emphasized subject fields—social studies, sciences, language arts, mathematics. At the secondary school and college levels the areas have been even more specific—geography, chemistry, physics, algebra, history. It is vitally important that pupils have experiences that help them to acquire the basic generalizations of the areas of knowledge that are their cultural heritage. It is equally crucial, however, that they be helped to face many situations that cut across subject fields—that they learn to relate learnings from many areas in the effective solution of their problems of daily living. Perhaps most important of all, if we are to be certain that our pupils actually put their understandings to use, we must provide many new situations in which they are challenged to do so. If they are to learn to use their knowledge in new situations, they must have worked with teachers who have said, many times over, "I think you have some information that will help you to explain why this is so. . . ."

The individual who is growing in his understanding of his world has effective ways of acquiring new information. We cannot hope, even if we add years of college and graduate study to an individual's twelve years in elementary and secondary school, to equip him with all the information he will need in his lifetime. In fact, the world's knowledge is accumulating so rapidly that it has been estimated that it takes longer today to become expert in a single field than it did fifty years ago to become master of our entire cultural heritage. One of the most important contributions schools can make is to teach pupils how to acquire new information.

The person who brings effective understanding to bear upon his problems possesses the basic techniques for acquiring new information. To the extent of his ability, he is competent in his use of the fundamental skills—reading, calculating, speaking, writing, and (crucial in this day of television and radio) observing and listening. But this is not all. He is acquainted with basic reference materials—dictionaries, atlases, encyclopedias, almanacs—and he is efficient in his use of these reference aids, in selecting appropriate topics and subtopics; in reading tables, graphs, and charts; in using alphabetical order, tables of contents, indexes; in locating what he needs in the library. He knows how to interpret what he reads in newspapers and magazines. He is skilled in distinguishing between fact and opinion, propaganda and information. Perhaps most important, he can organize the information he secures in such a manner as to arrive at logical conclusions.

A person who is independent in securing new information knows more than merely how to locate what he needs in the library or encyclopedia. He also understands the ways in which experts in various fields go about solving problems. We are not doing much to develop the scientists of the future, for example, if we teach science as though all the answers came out of textbooks. Nor are we helping youngsters to become future historians if they are never challenged to think why our records of early days are incomplete or why it is that two historians can disagree in their interpretation of the same facts.

Even if we understand the basic techniques used by specialists to solve new problems in their fields, none of us could (or would) go about discovering for ourselves all the information we require. There is too much to know. We must trust the advice of doctors, lawyers, nuclear physicists, economists, statesmen, news commentators. The more limited a person's intellectual ability, the more likely it is that he will need to rely heavily on the guidance of others in buying a home, deciding what insurance to carry, rearing his children. Through the subtle devices of advertisers, all of us are probably subject to much more advice than we realize regarding what to eat, wear, use as medications, or buy from the supermarket. The individual who is skilled in locating the information he needs knows how to get expert help and how to appraise the competence of the authorities to whom he turns.

Teaching pupils how to acquire information, then, is an addition to our responsibility for making certain that they leave our charge equipped with knowledge about their world. We have not done our assigned task completely unless we have helped the youngsters in our classes to acquire, at their levels of maturity, information in such a way that they also learn techniques that will aid them in gaining further information.

The individual who is growing in his understanding of his world seeks to keep on learning. No matter how satisfactorily the young people graduating from our schools can pass examinations, we must question the effectiveness of our teaching if they do not display a lively continuing interest in the affairs of their world. We need citizens who follow current events, read informational material as well as fiction, feel an obligation to be informed regarding issues about which they must express a preference by their vote, are interested in the natural world around them. In short, we hope that the youngsters graduating from our schools will love to learn.

There will be varying levels, of course, at which intellectual curiosity can be expected to operate. It is not likely that the youngster who grasps ideas slowly will develop into an atomic physicist or a research historian no matter how skillful our teaching has been. It is important, however, that he leave school with lasting interests that are personally satisfying and socially worth while. The more able the pupil, the greater is our obligation to help him to probe deeply into one or more areas of special concern and find satisfaction in so doing. In our society each child must be given an opportunity to develop as much breadth and depth in understanding his world as his capacities and aptitudes permit.

If we are to develop deep and enduring love of learning, we must teach those topics assigned to our particular grade levels in such a way that pupils see them as vitally interesting. To stimulate intellectual curiosity, however, is not enough. Pupils need to be helped to see that the subjects they are studying have a vital contribution to make to their daily living. Furthermore, it is not likely that pupils will graduate with a lively interest in events in the world around them if present-day happenings are not part of the classroom. We have a responsibility to help them become acquainted with their present-day world—to bring the events reflected in the daily papers into the classroom. We must also make sure that youngsters occasionally leave the classroom to become acquainted with their community—parks, industries, city government; in fact, all phases of community life which contribute to broadening interests and understanding.

DECIDING HOW TO TREAT TOPICS FOR STUDY

Teachers who accept responsibility for the goals just outlined (and there are few who do not) have assumed a prodigious task. There is certainly no time to waste upon topics which are trivial or upon activities which are entertaining but do not lead to significant and worth-while growth.

You may be working in a school system where the content you are to teach is outlined, grade by grade, for each subject separately—history, geography, civics, health, nature study, and so on—and adopted textbooks are supplied for each area. On the other hand, you may be in a system where the choice of the topics for the year is left entirely to your judgment as you study and work with your own class. More probably, however, you will be teaching under a curriculum design somewhere between these two extremes, with certain general areas for study, themes, or points of emphasis suggested for each grade but with considerable freedom given to the individual teacher to decide, in terms of the capacities, backgrounds, and needs of his pupils, just how the work will be organized, how much time will be devoted to a particular topic, and how much detail will be included.

Whatever the basis in your school system for selecting the general content to be stressed, you will probably be expected to plan units of work centered around the major areas designated for study. You will help your pupils to identify and clarify specific problems related to the topic under consideration. You and they will plan together how to acquire the information they need. You will guide their experiences as they explore the topic and help them to organize and integrate their findings.

Comprehensive units designated by the course of study or selected by you and your pupils through cooperative planning will not be your only means of helping your boys and girls to explore their world. There will be sharing periods during which the children can bring their special interests to school. Current events, quite unrelated to on-going unit activities, will certainly be the focus of attention. The world of nature will be outside your classroom window with falling leaves, clouds, sleet, mist, spring blossoms, and birds to talk about. There will be holidays to celebrate and all-school assemblies to discuss. Youngsters who are exploring the world of books will be wanting to share their discoveries about pioneer life, animal life in other lands, rockets, and space ships. Television programs, commercial and educational, will relate to their interests. All such concerns merit classroom recognition. They cannot be eliminated or ignored even within a rigidly prescribed course of study. Some of them will be the focus of brief discussions. Others may lead to short units—a problem clarified, a simple plan for securing information, a chance to share findings.

If the curriculum design under which you are working makes you responsible for deciding with your pupils which of their many concerns and interests are to be the centers for extended study and which are to be treated lightly, you will face the major challenge of appraising all the possible problems your boys and girls might explore in an effort to determine those which seem to offer the most valuable learnings. Even if your course of study prescribes the general focus of your work, you will still have choices to make, choices that will influence significantly the value of the study for your pupils. What particular aspects of the assigned topic are likely to be the most meaningful centers for extended study for your boys and girls? How deeply should they be encouraged to explore? Which of all the ramifications of the problem should you emphasize? How complete should be the concepts and generalizations toward which you work?

Select centers for extended study in the light of the general maturity of your group. If your course of study prescribes the topics to be emphasized at your grade level, some basic decisions will already have been made for you regarding the centers for extended study appropriate for your group. These decisions will reflect the manner in which the teachers in your school system view the growing body of research that has contributed to our insights into the ways in which youngsters grow in their ability to understand—analyses of the types of questions pupils ask; investigations of the accuracy of the time and space concepts of pupils of different ages; studies to determine growth patterns in grasping such abstract concepts as democracy, justice, and freedom of speech; surveys of the types of day-by-day problems that pupils actually face. Almost certainly, in these days of television we are going to find ourselves reappraising what we thought we knew about children's backgrounds, interests, and readiness for new learnings. If you are in a school system in which there is an active program of curriculum revision, you will undoubtedly discover that your colleagues are engaged in serious study of this problem. Be this as it may, if your course of study prescribes the topics for extended study, the focus of your work for the year has been indicated. Your primary responsibility, then, will be to decide how to approach the proposed topics so that they are purposeful for your pupils—to identify the point of contact where the concerns and experience backgrounds of your boys and girls touch the general area to be studied. You may well, however, before the year is out, embark with your group upon a number of other studies, brief or extensive, centered around topics of particular interest to them.

If the curriculum design under which you are teaching leaves the decision regarding which topics to explore entirely to the teacher to work out with his class, you will need to use all your techniques for studying boys and girls in order to identify problems of potential educative value—problems that are both appropriate for the maturity level of your pupils and of genuine concern to them. At first it may seem to be virtually impossible to identify a problem suitable for study by your entire class. Actually, however, this is no more difficult than treating a topic designated in a course of study so that it is purposeful to thirty or more individuals.

You will discover clues to a wealth of potentially educative centers for extended study as you listen to your pupils' questions and comments, analyze what they talk about in sharing periods, note the objects they bring to school, study the clippings they add to the current events bulletin board, and observe the books they read. As you begin to evaluate these clues, ask yourself such questions as the following: Which of these concerns seem to involve the largest number of my pupils? Which seem likely to result in the most fruitful learning experiences? Which are least likely to duplicate topics explored intensively last year? Which seem most apt to stimulate growth in an area of inexperience or weakness? Which will provide for the best balance in experiences? Which are likely to be the most effective centers for extended study by pupils of this age? After you have made your own thoughtful appraisal of several potential areas for study, you are ready to involve your pupils in some final decisions. What questions do we really want answered? How much do we already know? How many persons are concerned with this particular problem? Is it an area that will help us grow? If we choose to work on this specific problem, what others will we have to set aside, and why?

The topics for study upon which you and your class finally embark may be quite similar to those recommended in courses of study that have been carefully developed in accordance with the best evidence we have regarding the maturity, potential learning ability, and concerns of children. In fact, if you are uncertain about the centers for study that would be appropriate for your class, it might be helpful to glance over a well-planned course of study from another school system or to look back at the lists of illustrative units in your college texts on methods of teaching in the content fields. You will not, of course, be able to "lift" entire units from such resources if you are selecting activities in terms of the concerns and interests of your pupils, for the way they face a problem will have elements all its own. You can, however, find help in such resources as you try to appraise the educative potential of topics of interest to your pupils.

In courses of study where topics for the year are prescribed, care will have been taken to provide for a well-balanced series of experiences. The topics will be logically related to each other, and the sequence from grade to grade will be planned so that each new year adds systematically to the pupils' growing fund of information. If yours is the choice of the areas of study for the year, you have a similar responsibility to plan for balanced growth. You should read the records from the preceding year to discover the areas in which your pupils worked most intensively and the areas that were relatively untouched. You will also want to study your group carefully to identify strengths and weaknesses. Curriculum designs under which teachers are free to work in terms of the particular needs of the group are not proposed merely to make school easier, more interesting, or more like play. Where they have been adopted, it has been because serious educators see them as the most effective way of achieving a comprehensive and challenging education for boys and girls.

Decide on depth of experience in the light of the maturity and background of your pupils. Once a general center for study has been selected, how deeply should it be explored? Almost any problem has college-level implications if you choose to look for them. What you know about the maturity of your group and their intellectual level will influence your decisions regarding your objectives as well as the original choice of an area appropriate for study. You will typically expect younger pupils and slower learners to attain a limited number of concepts and generalizations and to express these in concrete terms. On the other hand, very able pupils may explore a problem to depths far beyond what you would expect of youngsters of their age level and reach generalizations of a high order. Thus, in a study of housing, third-graders of average ability might spend most of their time studying the types of houses in their neighborhood, discovering what adaptations to local climate are typical, becoming acquainted with the types of workmen who cooperate in building a house, and deriving conclusions regarding how boys and girls can help keep their homes and gardens neat and attractive. By contrast, in a third grade composed largely of intellectually able children, the problem might be extended to include a detailed study of the purposes of a variety of types of building materials and to consideration of typical architecture not only in other parts of the nation, but in selected countries around the world.

You will also need to consider the experience backgrounds of your pupils in formulating your objectives. If the majority of your class are youngsters from limited home environments who have had few opportunities to travel and whose playgrounds have been city streets, you will probably want to provide many concrete experiences even though the children are able intellectually. Where home experiences have been stimulating, opportunities for travel frequent, and the community environment rich in parks, museums, and libraries, youngsters are typically ready to proceed more rapidly. For example, it will take much more by way of motion pictures and film strips, exhibits of handicrafts and pictures, to build accurate concepts of life in Mexico for fourth-graders in a midwestern, underprivileged, rural area than it will to develop comparable understandings for youngsters who live near the border and who have visited the country frequently. Indeed, one might question whether all the vicarious experiences that could be provided for the first group will ever bring them to the level of understanding achieved by the latter.

Typically, there will be a wide range in your class, both in maturity and in experience background. Your problem, more often than not, will be to determine what essential learnings you hope to achieve for all pupils and at the same time to decide how to encourage able youngsters to explore more deeply. You should realize, also, that your pupils will not have equal readiness, in terms of experience, for all problems. To some areas they may bring considerable sophistication, whereas in others you may be forced to work at a much simpler level because previous experiences are meager. Only careful study of the capacities and backgrounds of your pupils (backed by the more experienced judgments of your cooperating teacher, colleagues, or supervisor) can determine the level to which you should gear your work and how high you should set your sights.

Decide on breadth of experience in terms of the potential contribution to the total growth of your pupils. Any problem chosen as a center for group study has a dimension of breadth as well as one of depth. As you begin to think about its educative possibilities you will identify many subproblems appropriate to the maturity and background of your class. The broader your own insights into the implications of children's questions and the interrelationships among fields of knowledge, the more such possible avenues of exploration you will uncover. This will be true not only of topics proposed in your course of study, but of questions your pupils raise as a result of community events, television programs, items in daily papers. You will have to decide upon the boundaries of your study—to choose which of all the ramifications, the related areas, the interesting subproblems, your pupils should be encouraged to explore.

Even if you are teaching under a course of study that prescribes the major centers for study, the time allotments under which you are working will probably be flexible. You must still make some decisions regarding the extensiveness of the activities you plan. If you are teaching under a curriculum design where subject fields are not designated specifically, you will be able more readily to develop plans for a single comprehensive unit without feeling that you are neglecting other prescribed subject matter. You will discover, however, that the concerns of youngsters are not always neatly integrated around a single problem. Because a group is interested in housing does not necessarily mean that they should be drawing houses, making scale drawings in arithmetic, playing house at recess, planting window-box gardens, and singing about houses. There will be times when many of your day's activities will center appropriately around a common topic, but there will be others when you will have several parallel, smaller projects under way.

How do you decide whether to expand a topic to many weeks of intensive work or to treat it more lightly? Several considerations may be of help. In the first place, it is important to consider carefully the learnings you think will result. If the extended study seems likely to take your pupils into new areas where their concepts and information are meager, it can be justified. If it tends mainly to repeat and reinforce concepts already well developed, you might be better advised to move on to another problem. In one fourth-grade study of transportation, for example, the youngsters had completed a careful tracing of the history of transportation, using railroads, automobiles, and airplanes for illustrative purposes. At this point several boys, intrigued with reports about atomic-powered submarines, proposed that a similar extensive study be made of boats. This was vetoed as a class project since it seemed likely to duplicate concepts already clear. The youngsters most concerned, however, went on with their study of boats as an independent project.

As a second guide in deciding how extensively to explore a topic with your pupils, ask yourself what subtopics they can recognize as clearly related to the general problem. You, yourself, may relate the question of what kinds of plants thrive in the neighborhood gardens to geographical understandings of plant life the world around, but this does not mean that these larger issues will necessarily represent meaningful problems to your class. If your pupils cannot see the new aspect of the problem as purposeful, their work at this point becomes a blind following of your suggestions. Quite frequently teachers start work on the problems pupils are able to identify in early planning sessions and then add other topics as the youngsters' increased understanding of the general area makes these meaningful. Perhaps, to pursue the illustration just given, work would begin with questions regarding which plants grow in the pupils' gardens, whether they grow in sunshine or in shade, and whether any special preparation for the soil is necessary. Then, as questions regarding the differences in plant needs for soil, light and shade, and rainfall begin to be raised, plans might be laid to learn about vegetation in parts of the country where there are contrasting climates.

Even though your pupils evidence a strong interest in a special aspect of the problem, you will be well advised to appraise the potential learnings inherent in their proposal in the light of other ways in which you might be using your time. This is a third point to consider in deciding how comprehensive to make a unit. One of the poorest guides you can use in deciding how intensively to explore a problem is to adopt a laissez-faire attitude and say, "As long as the pupils raise issues and are interested, we shall explore them." There is no end to the questions an alert group can ask, or to the side ventures they can suggest. All too easily you can stray far afield from your original problem, as happened to one group which started out to discover how best to ventilate their classroom to avoid drafts and progressed along a series of tangents (each slightly related to the preceding one) until they ended with plans for a parallel study to find out why a water pistol which had been left out all night would not work. Youngsters' questions and expressed interests can be valuable guides to areas in which further study can be worth while, but they must be helped to appraise them thoughtfully. What other problems will have to be passed over or treated lightly to make exploration of this one possible? What time may need to be taken from reading periods, art sessions, or other subject areas to make this intensive study? Is such a choice justified? There are, after all, only a limited number of minutes in the school day. They must be expended wisely.

You will make your decisions regarding the extensiveness of your study, then, in the light of the meaning the problem has for your pupils, their readiness for extended investigation (in terms of their maturity and experience background), the types of learnings likely to result, and the learnings in other areas that might have to be sacrificed if the unit under consideration were expanded. Before the year is out, you and your pupils will probably engage in units of varying degrees of comprehensiveness organized in many ways. Some will be very brief—perhaps a specific science interest that is satisfied in a week, or a short project at Christmas to learn about some of the traditional customs around the world. Other concerns will be a recurring focus of attention throughout the year. Many science problems are like this. Interest in the seasons, for example, could lead to study in the fall of how animals prepare for winter, form the basis later in the year for study of how people protect themselves against winter weather, and develop in the spring into problems related to returning birds or to gardening. Similarly, the plants in your room could be the subject of several short studies—as some begin to suffer from lack of water or sunlight, as new plants are added, as aphids are discovered. There will be times when a single comprehensive problem will occupy most of the periods in your schedule assigned to unit activities and will draw upon many subject fields. There will be other times when your class will work with equal profit on less extensive problems and there will be several projects moving ahead at once—a dramatization of a basal-reader story being developed in one time block; a study of the fruits and vegetables that keep us healthy as the focus for a second time block; and an investigation of the hardships encountered by the Pilgrims as a center of activity for a third.

What happens to the side issues, the questions asked by the alert pupil, the avenues that could lead to fruitful learning if time permitted? Do you just exclude these from your plans? By no means. If you wish to foster a spirit of curiosity and a lively interest in today's world, youngsters' questions, no matter how far from the topic under discussion, merit consideration. Some side issues will, of course, represent only transitory interests, and what was the center of a heated argument today may not be given a second thought tomorrow. In some instances, too, side issues will represent problems which your pupils, at their present levels of maturity, cannot explore very far. A brief discussion or a quick answer will be sufficient. First-grader's interests in a space satellite, for example, would probably be handled in this way. Other topics will be well worthy of extended study. You can provide for this in your plans in several ways. Some of these problems may be set aside for later all-class study. A discussion on how to carry sharp instruments, for example, might lead to more extensive work in safety. Other side issues may become the special concern of certain individuals. Teachers often maintain lists of *Questions We'd Like to Look Into* and encourage volunteers to take on these problems and to report when they are ready. All such arrangements call for careful pupil-teacher planning. It is a fine art to maintain youngsters' curiosities about the many fascinating aspects of their world at a high pitch and at the same time to channel their efforts so that a thorough job is done on a specific problem, but it can be accomplished if teacher and pupils together think about ways and means.

Plan for new experiences to enrich concepts and generalizations. From the vantage point of your college education, you may find yourself feeling that you are doing a superficial teaching job if you stop short of covering all the aspects of a problem appropriate for the general maturity of your pupils, even though you recognize the practical necessity of calling a halt. Yet each extra day expended on one topic means a day less on something else.

You may feel more content to see a project draw to a close without including every experience you recognize as potentially valuable if you realize that concepts and generalizations grow slowly through repeated experiences. The primary child's understanding that plants need many things in order to live is built from a variety of concrete experiences—planting his own garden, helping to care for the classroom window boxes, watching his father take up bulbs for the winter, seeing the cut flowers on the teacher's desk wither, watching the leaves change color in the autumn. It is impossible for you to build this full understanding in a single block of experiences or even in a single year. Often it is far better to proceed to another problem and to count on repeated experiences throughout the year (and through the years following) to contribute to your pupils' growing understanding. The crucial learnings you are trying to develop are those your pupils will need again and again at more and more sophisticated levels of understanding. These you should be building through many types of experiences provided in relation to a wide variety of problems. Opportunities to develop the understanding that the right to vote is inalienable in a democracy, for example, can come through classroom problems, student-council activities, a local election, a national election, a report of the election procedures in a dictatorship, a study of the causes of the American Revolution, a discussion of the powers of England's queen. Not all your eggs are in one basket. You can proceed to other topics, safe in the knowledge that you will have many opportunities before the year is out to stress the same concepts and generalizations. You may likewise be reassured that your approach from a new angle will add dimensions to your pupils' understanding which would not have been possible had you tried to do the entire job through study of a single problem.

PROVIDING THE EXPERIENCES THAT HELP PUPILS GROW IN UNDERSTANDING THEIR WORLD

When you have determined a topic for study and made tentative decisions regarding objectives, appropriate information to be covered, and related problems to be explored, you will have much of your block plan made.[1] To complete your own pre-planning you will need to think through possible pupil activities and to locate needed teaching aids. When you have done this you are ready to embark upon the study with your pupils. The activities that will develop from your joint planning sessions will be simple or complex, extend over several weeks or conclude in a few days depending upon the decisions you have made regarding the educative possibilities of the problem for your boys and girls—decisions resulting from your consideration of the guide lines suggested in the preceding section.

Your ultimate goals should underlie all your plans for pupil activities. Your aim is to help your boys and girls achieve clear and accurate understandings, but it is more than this. You want to develop citizens who can solve problems for themselves—citizens who know how to secure the information they need; who can relate this information to the problem they face; who can apply their understandings intelligently in new situations; who are alert to new ideas and seek to go on learning. To achieve these goals, you must give your pupils experiences in clarifying and solving problems for themselves; you cannot do it for them. They must be helped to be independent in locating information, and they must be encouraged to demonstrate ability to use this information intelligently in order to answer their own questions or to share

[1] See Chapter 6, pages 179-189, for details on how to develop effective block plans.

with others the information they have found. They have to be placed in situations in which they are challenged by their friends as well as by their teacher if their findings are inaccurate or incomplete. These are implications for your teaching that you must bear in mind even if you and your class are following rather closely the sequence of a single textbook. The type of active participation which results when pupils are involved in problem-solving activities seems to furnish our best opportunity to produce citizens who can put to use in new situations what they have learned, who are capable of identifying new problems, and who know how to go about locating the help which they need to solve them.

Whether or not the goals just indicated will actually be achieved depends to a large extent on the quality of your leadership. There is a vast difference between solving problems *with* children and turning a problem over *to* children to solve for themselves. Under unskilled guidance much time can be wasted, many hours frittered away in committee wrangling, and much unnecessary effort put into inaccurate models or notebooks full of materials that are largely copied from available texts. As you guide your pupils' activities there will be times when you will be playing an authority role—telling, demonstrating, explaining. At other times you will be leading discussions. At still others you will be serving as a resource person as your pupils read, search, and discover for themselves. The skill with which you play your varying roles will be a determining factor in the quality of your pupils' growth.

The types of questions which you should consider as you plan the day-by-day lessons through which you help your pupils arrive at new understandings were suggested in Chapter 6. They could be summarized in a general guide for your lesson plans as follows:

What are my goals? What new concepts, generalizations, information, do I hope to teach? What behavior on the part of my pupils will indicate that the new learnings have actually been acquired?

How can I give my pupils a sense of purpose? What is my starting point with them? What problems have they been facing in the course of their activities that makes this new learning appropriate? What interests lead to this new experience? What is my point of contact with their lives?

What steps do I need to take to help my pupils achieve this new understanding? Are there firsthand experiences upon which I should be drawing? What questions should I be prepared to ask in order to make most effective use of these? Should I be supplying new information through lecture or printed matter? What should be the sequence of my comments? What questions should I intersperse to make sure my pupils have understood?

What experience in using the new understanding should I provide? In what ways will I help my pupils work actively with the new understanding? Are there questions to which they should try to apply it through discussion? What notes or summaries should they write? Are there forms of creative expression in which it might be put to use?

How shall I evaluate their progress? What behaviors will tell me that understandings are clear? What types of questions should my pupils be able to answer? To what problems should they be able to apply the new learnings? What will I look for today as evidence that my goals have been achieved? What will be my evidence that the new understandings continue to be used effectively in the days to come?

Whether you are discussing a block of work from a textbook, showing a film to your class, or serving as a resource person, these are the types of questions to which you should give attention as you make your plans for the day. The details of your lesson will depend, of course, on the stage in the project which your pupils have reached and the specific help they need next in order to develop more accurate understandings. What are some of the principles you should have in mind as you consider precisely what this help should be?

Accurate understandings develop when purposes are clear. Pupils observe, listen, and read more intelligently and accurately if they have a definite purpose for so doing—if they have a series of specific questions in mind. It is difficult, however, to ask intelligent questions if one has had little previous experience in the area under consideration. Some of the problems on which you and your pupils embark will stem from out-of-school experiences about which they are quite well informed. Others will be problems about which they know very little. If the latter is the case, you will have some experience background to build before you and your pupils are ready to identify specific questions as a guide to their reading and study.

The procedures you use to provide all-class experiences, if these are needed as background for identifying detailed questions for study, will vary with the problem and the opportunities at hand. In launching a science investigation of how buildings are heated and insulated, Jack Parson sent his pupils home to ask about their own houses. Out of the reports, comparisons, and challenges of vague statements came a list of specific problems. In a second-grade study of community helpers, Carol Jones set up committees to stand in shifts at the window noting the delivery trucks that stopped at the houses across the way. From their reports came the beginning of a list of helpers for further study. Alec

McGhee showed a movie on Switzerland twice to his fourth-graders—the first time to help them to identify general interests and the second time to allow them to ask specific questions. Then they broke into "buzz groups" to pool their questions, which were eventually consolidated into a master list. Alice Robinson's study of how plants and animals adjust to cold weather started with a *Signs of Fall* science table. In beginning a unit on playground safety, Susan Peterson's youngsters made a tentative list of practices which they thought were unsafe and then turned to their texts to expand their list. Miranda Simpson also used her text for background, giving her youngsters a "guided tour" through the West by means of the pictures in the book and then compiling a list of topics which the children thought they would like to investigate further. Introductory all-class experiences such as these make a contribution to the success of the total study, over and beyond the background they provide for the development of thoughtful lists of questions. They also contribute to general interest in the area to be studied and to a sense of commitment to the final group plans.

When you feel that your pupils have sufficient background to raise intelligent questions, you face a second important task—that of helping them to identify specific problems as focal points for further activities. It is often desirable to record pupils' questions and suggestions exactly as they are phrased, at least while you are first compiling this list. The essence of a child's question is easily lost if you fit it too readily into a formal outline. "Why do they skate so much in Holland?" asked Mamie, probably with *Hans Brinker* in mind. "That's a good question," said Connie Whelan; "let's call our topic *Recreation,* shall we?" And *Recreation* went upon the blackboard. When the discussion was over, Connie's list was neat and abstract, *Recreation, Transportation, Government, Occupations,* and so on. If you will stop to think about the full implications of the skating question you will recognize the value of recording problems in the terms in which your pupils view them. How many interesting opportunities (suggested by that provocative word *why*) are going to be lost as the children try to locate information about recreation in Holland? It is important to remember, also, that reading and taking notes about a topic as vague as recreation in Holland are much more difficult and much less challenging than reading to find the answers to seven or eight specific questions. One might ask, too, whether Mamie is going to feel involved and push as deeply into the recreation topic as she might have done if she were working on her own question about skating.

Are detailed questions never to be classified under larger headings? Certainly they are, but this is a step which it is often better to take after the specifics are listed rather than to make it part of the initial process. You can give your pupils some effective experiences in outlining if you will let them help you to decide how their questions can best be grouped, and the resulting organization can often provide an approach to the problem which is much more challenging than the one you had in mind. Sometimes, too, the specific questions can become the basis for individual and small-group investigations. "Let's see," said Donald Kellum, "Bill, you and Pete asked most of the questions about wiring electrical gadgets. Would you two like to head up that committee?"

When the classification job is completed, it is a good idea to make a permanent record both of the major and of the specific topics to be studied. This serves as a point of reference as work proceeds. Primary teachers often transfer such lists to large sheets of oak tag or chart paper and hang them where they can be referred to easily. This technique is also useful at the intermediate grades. Alicia Arthur used cardboard and printed each set of questions on a different sheet. Pupils working on a specific topic frequently picked up their master list and propped it up near them. It is also possible to mimeograph the list for each youngster or to have each pupil copy it for his notebook. Sometimes a class secretary or a secretary for each committee keeps the record. Your list of specific questions represents a statement of pupil purposes for the study that is underway. Through whatever recording device you choose, you should make sure that you and your pupils have these purposes readily at hand as work proceeds.

Accurate understandings develop from concrete experiences. Many a beginning teacher has been discouraged and frustrated when he has discovered that there is meager reference material on a topic or that the books available are too difficult for many of his pupils to grasp. Actually, if you want your pupils to understand the topic under consideration you will not always put top priority on securing information from books. Understanding grows from experience. Even for older children, whose sophisticated verbalization would lead one to believe that a concept is clearly established, firsthand experience is usually very important. Judith Simpson's sixth-graders sounded as though they were aware of the fact that Canadians are much like Americans, though none of her class had actually traveled to Canada. Just to be sure, she invited a Canadian friend to visit. The questions and comments were revealing.

"You talk just like we do; did you learn that when you came here?" "Was that suit really bought in Canada? It looks just like my mother's." "What do you do to keep your houses warm in the winter?" The classroom environment which contributes to pupils' accurate understanding of their world is rich and stimulating in its concrete experiences.

The possibilities for providing pupils with concrete experiences are almost unlimited. Exactly what you will use and how many such experiences you will provide will depend upon the maturity and backgrounds of your pupils. Where experience background is limited, it is often important to take an excursion. Sally Jones' second-graders lived in tenement houses in the heart of a big city. The only milk they saw came in cartons from the delicatessen. Pigeons and sparrows were the birds they knew best. The park nearby had a few trees and some families had window boxes. A few children had cats for pets. Rats and mice were most familiar animals. How much reality can Sally give to a study of how farmers help us unless she packs her youngsters into a bus and takes them to see? For older groups, visits to see how a newspaper is published, how soap is made, how milk is bottled, what goes on in a market, may be appropriate. You may find that the teachers in your school have maintained a file of such excursion possibilities. If this is so you should consult it as you begin to make your block plan.

You do not always need to go out of the school to help your pupils gain firsthand acquaintance with the world around them. Realia—a terrarium, an aquarium, objects that float, leaves, nuts, models, shells, rocks, fossils, jewelry, costumes, handwork, museum exhibits—a host of such concrete materials can be brought into the classroom. You should explore the possibilities of borrowing such materials from the audio-visual aids exchange in your school system or your local museum. Resources may also be available on your college campus. The science department may be willing to loan special models. There may be a local historical collection in your college library. Furthermore, you need not always be the one to supply visual aids. Once your pupils are aware of the need, they can search attics for spinning wheels or old lamps, keep a watchful eye open for specimens as they walk to school, share hobbies, or bring toys that are authentic reproductions. Whenever realia are not too delicate, it is important to allow your pupils to handle them—to learn through their fingers as well as their eyes. Often your exhibit table will be one of the most fruitful sources of new learnings.

People can also come to your room. A father may bring slides of a recent trip. A grandfather who is a retired railroad engineer may tell of his experiences. A local naturalist may bring his collection of birds' eggs or nests. A violinist may help a science group to develop concepts of the relation of vibration to pitch. A mother may bring her collection of pioneer dolls. A grandmother may tell about her childhood in Germany. The school nurse may work with your class on health concepts. The school engineer may help a group of boys explore the intricacies of modern heating plants. Student teachers may have special campus resources which they can tap. Exchange students are often delighted to share information about their country. Friends with special talents or interests can be enlisted. Do not neglect to bring these resources to your class.

Pictures—movies, film strips, slides, photographs—should have an important place in your classroom. They are, however, one step removed from the real-life objects, and precautions are often needed if false concepts are not to result. Size relations can be particularly difficult if the pupil has no firsthand experience upon which to draw. First-grade Allan's concept of a cow was based on his experiences with workbooks where cows, chickens, and cats were reproduced in pictures the same size. Since Allan knew cats, imagine his dismay when he first saw the cow he had hoped to pick up and pet. Even with the help of television, five-year-old Janie was not prepared for a real horse. She had wanted one for Christmas, she confided to her teacher after a trip to a farm, but she believed she'd ask for a puppy instead. Experience with the actual object is undoubtedly the best safeguard. Failing this, it can be helpful to select pictures in which there are at least familiar points of reference. Youngsters who were arguing about the height of redwood trees, for example, were helped when they discovered that the tiny figure standing at the foot of the tree was a full-grown lumberjack.

With the advent of television a new source of concrete experience has been offered to teachers. It may be that your school system is involved in producing educational programs. If so, these may be an important supplement to the work in the classroom. On-the-spot programs can take your pupils into the museum, the factory, or the city council chamber. Demonstrations and exhibits can be transmitted to your room without necessity for elaborate preparation on your part. Television can aid in reducing the environmental poverty of the lower groups and enrich the more adequate backgrounds of the economically favored. Travelogs, special presentations, and broadcasts of special events offer a rich choice in making your class work broader and deeper in developing understanding. Television is, however, only one of the many means which the creative teacher employs in making the experiences of his class more concrete. Its value will depend on your insight and perceptivity.

Maps, graphs, time lines, charts, are a second step from reality, but they have their place, particularly in the classrooms of older pupils. Here, again, you must be responsible for providing a frame of reference so that the symbols or spatial relationships become clear. Jack Williamson started his class work on maps by devising a plan for reorganizing the furniture in the classroom. Then the pupils mapped the streets in their neighborhood and located their own homes. Both of these activities provided experience with drawing details to scale. The next step was to go to the top of the highest building downtown to see how the bend in the river looked from there. Later they worked on more distant spatial relationships. How many pupils had been to the state capital? How long did it take on the train? How many had gone all the way to Chicago? How long did it take? How far does it seem to be on the map? It is doubtful if any of us, no matter how sophisticated our concepts of space relationships may be, really grasps what it means to say that the sun is 93,000,000 miles away or that the stars are light-years distant from us. Robert Allen's group gained some sense of the immensity of space when they discovered that if they made their model of the earth one inch across, the corridor wall from end to end was not long enough to let them use the same scale to place the sun in accurate proportion.

Even verbal comparisons can enrich the meaning of the words of the reference text. "That happened when your grandmother was a little girl." "As tall as our school." "About as long as our classroom." "Just the color of Mary's dress." For this reason, textbooks, stories, and even children's dictionaries are frequently more meaningful if they are rich in detail rather than reduced to the barest essentials. In helping youngsters become acquainted with ways of living in other lands or with life in pioneer days in this country, for example, you will find that your library can supply fiction with authentic settings that will furnish some of these important details. With classes whose reading abilities are limited, teachers often find it profitable to read one or two such books aloud.

A caution may be in order with regard to the use of pupils' work as a means of providing concrete experience. Providing opportunities for boys and girls to test out their understandings by putting them to use is an important aspect of the total process of developing accurate concepts and generalizations. Therefore, before the study is completed you may well have your youngsters build a model volcano, lay out a southern plantation, or put on a pioneer play. These are valuable means of discovering what your pupils have learned; they are, however, of doubtful help in building concepts. It is a far cry from a papier-mâché tiger in a classroom exhibit to the living animal in the zoo, and mother's old skirt and earrings, however fascinating to wear, do not help to build a very realistic picture of a Mexican market place.

You will use concrete aids in a variety of ways and at many points in the development of an extensive study. Some will be the focus of a specific lesson for your whole class as you identify a need for a particular type of information and supply it through an excursion, a movie, or a visit from a resource person. Others—your bulletin boards, displays, models, and picture collections—may remain in your room for the length of the study and be turned to again and again by the entire class, by small groups, or by individuals as special problems arise. Sometimes you will use an excursion or a movie to build experience background and will plan for it early in the sequence of activities. At other times your youngsters will read for background first, and the concrete experiences will serve to enrich their reading. In other words, the concrete aid should be planned for the time when pupils can recognize it as pertinent to the problem at hand. It is highly desirable, therefore, to use special teaching aids with your own class rather than to try to coordinate your efforts with those of other teachers. This may not always be possible. Transportation for a single class can sometimes become prohibitive in price. In such cases, two teachers often plan so that the same excursion serves the needs of both classes. You may discover, also, that in spite of best intentions audio-visual aids departments cannot always get materials to you exactly when you want them. You may even be assigned to a school where it is the custom for all classes at a given grade level to see whatever movies arrive. You will have to adjust to such situations as you find them, and the thoroughness with which you and your class have thought through your total plans and clarified your purposes will do much to help you make such experiences profitable. There will be times, however, when you would be well advised to forego a film rather than to use it inappropriately. In the last analysis, only you can decide how best to use the concrete aids available as you probe the backgrounds of your group and consider the points at which such teaching aids can make their appropriate contributions.

Accurate understandings grow through varied and repeated experiences. More than one kind of firsthand experience will usually be necessary if accurate concepts and generalizations are to be built. You will employ a variety of such aids to learning before you and your group complete an extensive study. Thus, in developing with her fourth grade a unit on *How We Travel Today,* Lorraine Susa prepared a bulletin board on which were pictured major kinds of transportation. Then, when she discovered how few of her pupils had been either to the airport or to the railroad terminal, she arranged for trips to both places. Later, one of the fathers who drove a large trailer truck brought it to school for the youngsters to see and answered questions. The children began to bring in model toys from home, and with their trips to provide firsthand experiences in size relationships, they learned many details from the small models. Meanwhile, committees preparing reports on specific forms of transportation searched magazines at home for pictures. Lorraine was also able to find a helpful motion picture that filled in some needed background on ocean liners, and another about fishing boats. A fifth-grader who had recently come from England told about his ocean trip, and a sixth-grader described a long plane flight.

A similar variety of experiences was in evidence when Blanche Thomas and her first-graders embarked on a unit to learn more about weather conditions. She and her class planned for a daily weather bulletin. Blanche brought some inexpensive thermometers so that more than one person at a time could take the outside temperature. When the first snow began to fall, the youngsters carefully collected snowflakes and then watched them melt when brought indoors. They watched the puddles on the window sill dry in the sun and then tried evaporating water in a pan on their hot plate. They noticed the water condensing on their classroom windows on a cold day and tried to achieve the same effect with a tea kettle and cold objects. Out of these simple experiments and observations, the pupils began to make generalizations about the effect of heat and cold on various forms of moisture, and how these affected weather conditions.

Not all the problems that you and your pupils explore will lend themselves to, or require, such varied concrete experiences. There will be studies for which your youngsters will bring ample experience background and there will be problems much less extensive in their ramifications. You must be the one to judge the amount of firsthand experience needed as you appraise the present level of your pupils' understandings and consider the additional learnings you hope they will achieve.

Accurate understandings develop as pupils think for themselves. You cannot *tell* your pupils the concepts and generalizations you expect them to derive from their experiences and, by the magic of your voice, assure that these understandings will actually be attained. In coming to know the world around us, as in grasping a basic principle of grammar, spelling, or arithmetic, each of us must "see for himself." Understanding comes as we work actively with a new idea. As you plan for the experiences you hope to use to develop more accurate concepts, you must consider how to stimulate your pupils to think.

Seeing a movie or working in a classroom with attractive bulletin boards does not necessarily lead to more accurate concepts unless pupils are helped to react thoughtfully to what they have seen. To get the most out of an excursion, a film, or a visit from a resource person, your boys and girls will need to know precisely what they are looking for. This means that they should have rather specific questions in mind. There is a marked difference between the information derived when there is merely a blanket assignment to "see what you can learn" and the information secured when purposes are clear. Think about the following introduction to a film, for example:

THOMAS DAVIES

Boys and girls, we have a very interesting movie on snakes. Suppose you watch to see just how much you can learn. When we're finished I'm going to ask you some questions to see how sharp your eyes are.

Some of Thomas' pupils were able to answer his questions, but many had been intrigued by aspects of the film which Thomas did not consider to be particularly important.

In contrast, June Thompson used the list of questions which had been the focus of considerable previous group activity:

JUNE THOMPSON

Boys and girls, do you remember how many questions on snakes we still had not answered? Will you pull out our chart so we can see it, John?

JOHN

I think we've found a book that will help on some of these, but we still don't know much about how they live.

JUNE THOMPSON

We have a film that will help you. I had a look at it last night and it will give you some very good pictures of different kinds of snakes. It will also help you with your question about what they eat. I don't think it does much to answer what they do in the winter but you may get a few clues. Suppose you watch it with those questions in mind. Then let's talk a little to find out what we still don't understand. Then we can go back to look at the film again if we wish.

June, obviously, had taken time to preview her film. This is important if your pupils are to have appropriate questions to guide their observing or listening. In like fashion, it is helpful to pay a visit yourself before you take your pupils on an excursion or to contact ahead of time the resource person invited to your room. Without such background, you will have much more difficulty preparing your pupils for the coming experience.

Classroom displays can be set up in ways that stimulate thoughtful observing. In one room questions are posted beside pictures on a bulletin board. "Notice the roofs of the houses. What does that tell you?" "Do you see the man beside the pyramid? How tall would the pyramid be?" "These people are dressed for a festival. Can you find another picture that shows how they would dress on ordinary days?" In another room a chart is posted near the window box to record the growth of some seeds that have been planted. Near a bar magnet suspended from a small scaffold in a third room are some questions: "Which ends repel? Which ends attract? Use the other magnet to find out." Often pupils can be encouraged to observe thoughtfully by being assigned responsibility for organizing classroom materials—to label an exhibit, to group and classify a collection, to decide on a logical scheme for displaying pictures and for captioning them.

The class discussions which you lead must be pointed with equal care toward helping pupils to think for themselves. Building concepts is often a long, slow process. You may easily become impatient with the amount of time it takes for immature learners to arrive at conclusions which seem perfectly obvious to you. It is a great temptation to phrase the new idea for your class and then to assume that because you have said it they understand it. Listen to John Johnson as he tries to help his fourth-graders gain some understanding of the adjustments made by animal life to winter weather:

JOHN JOHNSON

Now, what do animals do when the winter comes?

BILL
Well, the birds fly south or somewhere.

JOHN JOHNSON
That's right. We call that *migrating,* don't we? And some of them go all the way to South America. What about the animals?

SANDY
They all sleep.

JILL
And frogs and fish are all frozen in the ponds.

JOHN JOHNSON
Well, that's not quite right. Actually all the animals don't sleep. But those that do . . . [Here follows a brief lecture on hibernation—changes in body temperature, blood pressure and so on.] Now let's think about the animals and birds we usually see in the winter. How do they take care of themselves in cold weather?

You may well be asking, "What's wrong with John's procedure?" There are certainly times when the teacher, rather than a reference book or a film, will serve as the resource to provide new information for a class. Certainly, too, in dealing with a concept such as hibernation, one would not try to elicit technical information from pupils by a combination of questioning and guessing. But what precautions did John take to make certain that his brief discourse had been understood before he went on to the new aspect of his problem? How sure can he be that Jill's misconception about frogs and fish has really been cleared up?

Even when you are leading a discussion in an area where your pupils have considerable reading background, it is important to challenge them to think about what they are saying. It is all too easy to accept an answer phrased in the words of the text without making sure that your pupils have drawn the correct conclusions. Listen to Margie Simon's pupils discussing their reading about a southern plantation:

MARGIE SIMON
All right, what did you learn about plantations?

JOHN
They had very large houses with porches called verandas.

MARGIE SIMON
That's right. And what else?

BILLY
They were several miles apart.

MARGIE SIMON
That's good, Billy. Now, what other buildings were there?

SUE
There were smoke houses.

MARGIE SIMON
Yes. What else?

ANDY
A laundry.

CATHY
A bakery.

MOLLY
A mill.

RICKY
They had everything on a plantation.

MARGIE SIMON
That's right, Ricky. Now what buildings do we still need to mention?

Margie's pupils can name the correct buildings likely to be found on a plantation, but do they know what this array implies about plantation life? Should Ricky's conclusion, "They had everything on a plantation," have been passed over so lightly? In contrast, Joanne Parker was trying to help her pupils use what they had read to arrive at some basic generalizations:

JOANNE PARKER
All right, what did you learn about plantations?

JOHN
They had very large houses with porches called verandas.

JOANNE PARKER
Let's think about that. Larger than our houses today?

JOHN
Larger than most any around here. Look at all the windows in this picture.

JOANNE PARKER
Did you stop to think why they were so big?

SUE
Well, maybe more people lived in them.

JOANNE PARKER
Why might there have been more people?

ALLEN
Well, the book I read . . . .

It is a fine art to ask the type of question that will stimulate pupils to think. Often it helps to ask: "Why?" "What did you read that makes you reach your conclusion?" "What does this suggest to you about. . .?" Frequently, you will make use of the purposes with which your pupils started to work. ("We wanted to see why they say milk is so important for boys and girls. What did you discover?") Often it helps to involve several youngsters in answering a question rather than to encourage the recitation type of answering which was just illustrated in Margie Simon's discussion about plantations. ("That's one good reason for setting up safety rules for the playground. Have you another suggestion?") Sometimes you will want to send your pupils back to their reference books for more help. ("How could we check on that, for sure?") In planning to lead discussions, you would do well to take time to think about your objectives, to decide how the material to be discussed might contribute to these objectives, and then to plan specifically the types of questions most likely to help your pupils to arrive at logical conclusions. In the give-and-take of discussion, the chances are that you will not use your questions exactly as you phrased them, but the experience of thinking them through will still be helpful.

As you help your pupils discuss what they have been reading, seeing, or hearing, it is very important to listen for hints that concepts might be inaccurate. Youngsters often use words glibly even when they do not know exactly what they mean. In fact, one of the most important values of a discussion technique in teaching is to enable you to find out where ideas are not clear. One fifth-grader astonished her teacher, after what seemed to be an intelligent comment regarding the desire of the Pilgrims to worship in their own way by asking, "But what I don't understand is what kind of idols did the other people in England worship?"Susanne Ames thought she had the concept of pioneer travel clear until one of her pupils asked, "Yes, but how could they get those big wagons through the valleys? They never could go through the valley back of our house." A word mispronounced, the exact words of the book given back in a report, a word misused should cue you to ask more questions. "Explain that." "What would that really look like." "What do you think he would be doing?"

Lessons in which you serve as the discussion leader will not be the only activities through which you will help your pupils to think for themselves. You will also want to provide opportunities through which they, at their levels of maturity, can make use of scientific methods to arrive at their own solutions. Even first-graders can be given experience with the scientific method, as were June Allyne's pupils who wanted to know why their paints dried out more readily when left uncovered. From this problem came a series of experiments with evaporation. Julia Simpson's fifth-graders learned something of the methods of historical research as they embarked on a study of the history of their city. With their teacher's help they learned what information would be contained in archives. Through interviewing older citizens they became aware of the possibility of inaccuracies in firsthand reports. On a trip to the museum they discovered how archaeologists were exploring the Indian cultures in their county. Arnold Swanson's sixth-graders became concerned about the amount of food being left on trays in the school cafeteria and with the cooperation of the school administration planned a simple survey to collect the evidence to show exactly how much waste there was.

Actually, in a study of any magnitude, you will use a variety of techniques to help your pupils to arrive at more accurate understandings. There will be points at which you will encourage them to read widely for information, times when you will guide their study of an audio-visual aid, and points at which you will help them to plan a series of research activities in order to arrive at the answers to their questions for themselves. Whatever your procedure, it is important that you make sure that conditions for effective learning exist—a clear purpose; a challenge to read, listen, or observe carefully; an opportunity to discuss thoughtfully what has just been read, seen, or heard.

Accurate understandings develop as new ideas are put to use. If you want to be sure that your efforts to help your pupils develop accurate understandings have been effective, you will provide opportunities for the new information to be put to use. In a sense, you are doing this every time you ask the type of challenging question that requires a pupil to apply his knowledge accurately in order to arrive at a correct answer. Some of the experiences through which you help pupils grow in their understanding will not involve much more than thoughtful discussions of this sort. In more elaborate projects, however, you will want to provide other types of opportunities to apply what has been learned.

Among the activities that serve most frequently to help pupils put to use what they are learning are those calling for reports or summaries of what is being read, heard, or observed. Older boys or girls will probably do considerable independent reading and note-taking in preparation for sharing what they have discovered with a small committee or with the class as a whole. In the primary grades the records are often in the form of experience charts which teacher and children plan together to summarize an excursion, a movie, some reading, or a discussion with a special resource person. When easy reading matter is limited, these records often serve a dual purpose of helping pupils organize and draw conclusions from their experiences and of providing them with material for later reading experiences. You must be careful, however, to assure that the note-taking or summarizing process actually requires your boys and girls to apply their new information, not merely to give back the words in the book or the words they have just heard.

As the process of obtaining information moves forward, there are many other types of recording devices that will require your pupils to think carefully in order to organize what they have learned. These could involve labeling and classifying exhibits; making classified vocabulary lists; developing a picture dictionary; building a time line; adding new models to a science exhibit; classifying pictures for a bulletin board display; developing maps, charts, and graphs; making notebooks; writing creative stories related to the topic under discussion; doing a series of pictures to illustrate key aspects of the study; planning committee reports or panel discussions. Such activities often run parallel to the experiences of gathering information. As special terminology is identified, it may be included in a class word list or dictionary. New items may be added to a classroom exhibit. A time line may be built gradually, each new date being added as it is discussed in class. In thinking through the schedule for the day, you will want to make special allowance for such activities. They are not likely to contribute very much to pupil growth if they are pushed aside as spare-time projects.

Frequently, the investigation of a problem closes with a series of rather simple sharing or discussion periods where the pupils are helped to tie together whatever loose threads still remain. There may be times, however, when it seems desirable to plan an elaborate culminating activity to summarize all that has been accomplished and to share it with parents or other classes. Illustrative of such culminating activities would be: developing a mural; setting up an exhibit of the work accomplished during the unit; making dioramas; producing a play; publishing a class newspaper or magazine; developing a series of panel discussions; planning a program in which each special committee shares its findings in its own way; setting up a classroom store, post office, farm, circus, or zoo as a culmination of primary learning experiences. Typically, the decision to undertake such an activity is made by you and your pupils rather late in the development of your plans. You, however, may well have given some thought to the desirability of a rather elaborate conclusion to the study and have included some possibilities in your original block plan.

Elaborate culminating activities call for expenditure of much time and effort. Before you embark on one, you should give some careful thought to its educative potentialities for your pupils. At one time there was a tendency to evaluate a unit as "excellent" if the room was filled with handwork, pictures, and displays, and the unit closed with a play or some other ambitious activity. With increased concern regarding problem-solving as the heart of a unit activity has come the realization that it is not always necessary to engage in art, music, or dramatics in order to have effective learning. Although some youngsters may profit from opportunities to show what they have learned through the medium of art, music, or drama, it may be equally appropriate for others to have experience with oral reports, round-table discussions, or the preparation of accurate maps and graphs as culminating activities. You will need to make your decision in terms of the nature of the original problem, the potential educative value of the activity for your pupils, and the other classroom experiences competing for pupils' time.

If you decide upon a culminating activity involving dramatization, art, creative writing, or music, you should do so because you see values for your pupils in the experiences with creative expression that such an activity will provide. In a sense, you and your pupils will engage in two closely related blocks of work—the first consisting of the information-getting activities required to solve the original problem and the second consisting of the experiences in creative expression developed to share the new learnings with others. You will need to plan as carefully for your dramatic production, your mural, or your exhibit as you did for the study of the original problem. The end product can be very simple or it can challenge the most able learners in the school. Models may be fairly rough or may be done to the most exacting scale. A mural may consist of some background scenery and several large figures or it may be developed with intricate symbolic detail. A dramatic presentation may be very simple or it may be a three-act production in blank verse for a speech choir. A science display can be as elaborate as pupils' abilities will allow. Creative writing can result in a one-paragraph story or in a class magazine or newspaper many pages in length. The more able your group, the higher your standards for their summarizing activities should be. This does not mean that able and competent children should never be allowed to draw a series of information-getting activities to a close without an elaborate culmination. If you do decide upon special culminating activities, you should, however, make sure that the learnings that result justify the pupil time that is expended.

Since a culminating activity has the dual purpose of contributing to effective creative expression and, at the same time, adding to the depth of pupils' understandings, it is important that you do not lose sight of the concepts and generalizations you hoped to develop. Sometimes beginning teachers who are meticulously accurate in discussions fail to hold pupils to the same standards in the creative activities which conclude the study. Certainly, we do not want pictures copied from books, reports which are largely in the words of the reference text, or science demonstrations which merely follow the instructions in the textbook. One can be creative, however, and still be authentic. Buildings in a model city can be to scale. The conversation in a play can be planned so that accurate information is conveyed to the audience. Even first-graders operating a make-believe store can think carefully about how clerks behave and what one's responsibilities are as a customer.

Throughout the year, your problem-solving activities with pupils will undoubtedly vary widely in the complexity of the work pattern and the elaborateness of the activity that brings them to a close. One unit may conclude with a play to which parents are invited. A second may lead to an extensive science display. A third may end with a series of rather simple committee reports. Whatever your decision, it should be based on your best judgment regarding the experiences that will result in maximum growth for your class, not upon any preconceived notion of what makes for "well-rounded" learning experience.

Accurate understandings develop when varied experiences are clearly related to an underlying problem. What is the total pattern of the resulting activities when the principles that have just been discussed are put into service? If you are like most beginners, you will feel more secure in handling the brief explorations stemming from the day-by-day interests and concerns which your pupils bring to class than you will in developing a comprehensive unit—a series of related activities extending from two weeks to a month or more. How do such projects look when they are all put together? If teachers are planning with their pupils, the answer will not be the same for any two classes, even if precisely the same topic is the center of study. No one else can provide a model that will serve your purposes exactly. Nevertheless, a look at three teachers and their pupils in action may help in clarifying your thinking.

There need not always be a wide variety of reading materials at hand in order to develop effective learning experiences. Primary teachers are frequently very adept at making use of firsthand experiences and developing their own reading materials as activities progress. Sharon Wilson's study of pets with her first-graders demonstrates how this can be accomplished:

Among the topics suggested for the first grade in the course of study in Sharon Wilson's school system was a study of pets. Many incidents during the year—the children's stories about pets told during sharing periods, dogs following their owners to school, some teasing of a stray kitten—might have provided the starting point for this study. There was ample evidence that many of the children had pets, that they took some responsibility for them, and that there were understandings still to be built regarding how to care for pets. In initiating the unit Sharon prepared an attractive bulletin board upon which she placed pictures of country and city pets—birds, dogs, kittens, ducks, fish, turtles, ponies, white mice, calves, lambs. The opening discussion, with the bulletin board as the focus, gave the children an opportunity to tell about their pets. What kinds of pets did they have? Were their pets little or big? How did they take care of their pets? Which children had lived on a farm? What kinds of pets did farm children have? Would the class like to tell and learn more about caring for pets?

Sharon's opening discussion with her boys and girls told her that they had considerable experience background upon which to draw in laying detailed plans for the study. Nevertheless, she provided for a few more exploratory experiences. There was another discussion about the children's pets (after they had gone home to ask their parents some questions) and some more conversation about the types of pets appropriate for town homes and for farms. Out of these general discussions came specific questions: How do we play with pets? How do we train pets? How do we keep pets healthy and happy? What do we do if pets get sick?

Since the reading abilities of her pupils varied from pre-primer to second-grade level, Sharon was not able to count on all the children being able to do extensive background reading about pets. Consequently, she planned a variety of all-class experiences to develop basic understandings. The children viewed and discussed several motion pictures. With a list of special questions in mind, they visited a nearby pet store to find out how the animals were fed and cared for. John's father, who raised dogs as a hobby, came to talk to the group. Sandy's mother arrived on another day bearing in a box Peanuts, the cat, and four small kittens. She stayed to discuss how to treat baby animals. This experience led to several later discussions on how animals protect and care for their own young. In order to make sure that new understandings would be put to use, Sharon herself acquired some guppies for the class aquarium. The children listened carefully to the directions regarding how to care for these classroom pets and helped to dictate a set of directions to guide those responsible for them. Bonnie was given a turtle and brought to class the instructions for its care. Sharon also continued to read stories and informational material to the group and put out on the library table a variety of books for her better readers and some easy picture stories for those whose reading skill was most limited. *Pets are helpful to people as well as being good companions; pets need many of the same things people do if they are to be well and happy; we care for our pets just as our parents care for us* were the basic generalizations toward which Sharon was working.

During the discussions following the class experiences, individual interests in specific pets began to be voiced. Sharon had delayed making plans for group work until she was sure that she had identified a legitimate function for these groups. The interests in special pets indicated a reasonable focus for the work of committees and a means of helping the children to apply what they had been learning to a specific problem. Accordingly, she asked the youngsters to list the pets in which they were most interested. Dogs, cats, fish, birds, and turtles comprised the list. A sheet was posted for each pet with blank spaces numbered from one through six. Each child signed to study the pet in which he was most interested, and with a little trading to keep happy those who were the last to sign, the organization for committee work was established.

Sharon devoted the period after the morning recess break regularly to the activities connected with this unit. What went on during this period depended upon the point which the project had reached. In the early stages, the larger part of the period was used to build background—to hear stories, to see films, to listen to visitors—and then to discuss and summarize in an experience record what had been learned. This was often followed by an opportunity for individuals to draw pictures or to write stories to illustrate what they had learned and for groups to examine library materials on their special topics. In the later stages of the project, a short discussion period was devoted to hearing and summarizing what each committee had learned about its special assignment and then a longer work session allowed the committees to proceed with several types of projects.

In order to help her youngsters summarize what they had been learning, Sharon developed a variety of experience records with them. These she wrote as the children dictated. The class kept a diary in which was recorded a sentence each day telling how the study was progressing. After excursions, motion pictures, and classroom visitors, the children summarized the special information they had learned. Then, as the focus of class discussion turned to the pets that were the special interest of small groups, they prepared a summary of what they had learned about caring for each pet. In developing the latter records the youngsters on the committee, together with others who had similar pets at home, served as resource people. All these experience charts served as the basis for group and individual reading experiences as the boys and girls illustrated the various records or turned to them for information they needed.

The work of the small groups was focused mainly on summarizing activities that helped the children to demonstrate what they had learned about the particular pet in which they were interested. Each group developed a small mural depicting the pet with which it was concerned. The children made models of their special pets out of wallpaper paste. They painted pictures to be attached to the experience records on their topic. They developed stories about their pets. The children also turned to the library table for information, however. Better readers found many books they could handle and those with more limited ability were helped to develop a basic reference technique as they learned to "read" pictures carefully. When their pet was the focus of group discussion the youngsters were prepared to contribute the results of their research.

There were a number of experiences in creative expression in addition to the activities undertaken by the special committees. These permeated many aspects of the day's schedule. The children learned a number of songs about pets. On several occasions they developed creative rhythmic activities—walking, running, and jumping like their favorite pets. They decorated their bulletin boards with a number of individual pictures. They wrote stories (or, in the case of the youngsters with the most limited writing ability, dictated them to Sharon) and they developed some original songs. In addition, as the opportunity presented itself during the day, Sharon read poems and stories about pets.

A number of skills were developed in the course of this project. Dictating the experience records and other class discussions provided for a number of experiences in oral expression. The experience records, together with the stories Sharon was able to locate in the children's basal readers and a variety of library books, were the bases for many group and individual reading activities. As the children began to write their own stories, Sharon developed with them a number of vocabulary lists to aid in spelling. They also took some time to discuss how to space their stories so that there were even margins and how to write titles properly. There was some handwriting practice as difficulties with various letters were revealed. As the groups developed their murals and made plans for a final program many techniques of cooperative problem-solving were learned.

Parents were invited to the culminating activity of this unit. The plan was mainly to share the experience records that had been developed in the course of the project, to tell about the murals and the other creative efforts, and to sing some of the songs the children had learned. Representatives from each group were chosen to read the experience records. Others told about the work displayed around the room. In addition, the youngsters developed a brief dramatization in which a family went to a pet store to buy a pet, the proprietor discussed how to care for each type of pet, and the pets (children from the various groups) came out to be admired. Writing invitations to parents, drawing a picture as a surprise for each one, and the experiences of greeting the visitors and speaking before an audience, added to the educative values of this concluding activity.

Units do not always develop in a neat pattern of class, small-group, and individual activities within a definite time block. Sometimes the study stretches over a rather lengthy period of time with a complex combination of group and individual work. Such was the case when Audrey Sheldon's third-graders undertook a study of birds that extended over the better part of two full months in the spring.

No special initiating activities were needed to interest Audrey Sheldon's third-graders in a study of birds. Their school was in a suburban community and they had watched nonmigrating birds, rabbits, and squirrels all winter, talked about why some birds stayed and some went south, and helped to feed their winter visitors during bitter weather. In the spring, as the migrating birds began to reappear, Audrey helped the youngsters set up a calendar upon which returning birds could be listed. Soon bird books from home and some paper-backed ones purchased in local stores began to be brought to school. After a couple of days of argument about the identification of birds that could not be clearly seen, John brought his father's field glasses to school. From these firsthand experiences and meaningful questions plans to learn more about birds were developed.

The structure of this study did not emerge in the first few planning sessions. One problem led to another, and Audrey helped her boys and girls to frame new questions and make new plans as new interests developed. First, concerns centered around how to tell birds apart. Soon, the youngsters learned how to study the pictures in the simpler bird books that now loaded the library table and became able to name most of the birds frequently seen from their windows. Then attention turned to the family life of birds—types of nests, numbers of eggs and their color, why the female was less brightly colored than the male, how long it took for the eggs to be hatched, how they were kept warm, how the young were fed, and what responsibility each parent bird took in the process. A nest of robins in a nearby tree that could be watched from an upstairs window gave impetus to this aspect of the study and led to a class record of the birds' activities. Later, interest developed in the types of food various birds ate, as heated discussions arose regarding the helpfulness or harmfulness of various birds to gardeners. Interspersed with work on the preceding topics were a number of discussions on conservation. These stressed the youngsters' responsibility to leave nests and eggs undisturbed, how to build proper bird houses, and ways of protecting song birds from cats. Migration was discussed briefly by the entire group when the first birds returned. Then this topic, together with questions regarding newspaper reports about vanishing species and sundry other specific items of interest, became the special projects of individuals. *Living creatures have many of the same needs; man has a responsibility to conserve natural resources; there are many personal satisfactions to be derived from interests in the natural environment* were among the generalizations Audrey was trying to stress.

All in all, the study of birds extended for almost two months, but Audrey did not devote a full period to it every day. At the points when a new set of questions had been raised, she provided generous blocks of time for class discussions, study of appropriate visual aids, and individual reports. Then there were stretches of several days when individuals pursued special interests, and the period allotted for group work was devoted to social studies and other subject areas. Time was often taken in sharing periods to hear briefly from individuals when someone discovered a new bird or located a nest. At some points other science interests ran parallel. At others, full attention was devoted to birds.

Audrey made use of a wide variety of teaching aids. Perhaps most important were the birds themselves, flashing by the window or perching long enough on the bird bath or telephone wires to be identified. The robins' nest provided another valuable series of firsthand experiences. The youngsters also took two bird walks to the nearby park, and the biology department in the city high school loaned specimens of common birds. Bird books were invaluable for pictures, and two of the boys developed a large-scale diagram of a bird upon which they marked the parts of the body most frequently referred to in the bird books. Disturbing occupied nests was strictly forbidden, but Audrey had stored typical nests of several species collected over the winter and Mr. Jackson, teaching science to the upper grades, had a collection of eggs. The audio-visual aids department was able to loan records of bird calls. There were chapters to be read in the children's science texts, a number of single copies of books about birds written on the children's level, and much the youngsters could understand in the bird books after a little help in finding the page upon which their special bird was discussed.

Audrey used a number of devices to help the children summarize their findings. Each pupil kept his own notebook in which he filed his special reports, the pictures he drew, his own bird list, his copies of some of the class charts, and his creative writing. As a group the children developed charts to help in identifying birds—by color, by their bills, by the food they ate, by the type of nest, as harmful or helpful. They also developed a large mural in which trees and houses were impressionistic but the birds accurate as to shape, color, and size. Each child drew and cut out one or more of his favorite birds to be pasted on this mural. The class record of the robin family provided another type of accurate summary. In addition, several vocabulary lists were developed as the boys and girls began to acquire technical terminology.

There was no clear-cut pattern for group work in this unit, but there were many group and individual enterprises. Groups formed and re-formed as the study took new turns. Youngsters made short reports as they located information to answer one question and then contributed again as they investigated new problems. Bobby, for example, became an expert on robins. Early in the study he used pictures to show how they could be identified and how the young birds differed from their parents. Later he reported on how they built their nests. Then he teamed up with James and Randy to help keep the special record of the robins' nest. When the mural was planned, he was one of a group of six to paint the garden. This informal mixture of all-class discussion, independent work, and short-term groups was characteristic of the entire unit.

Many of the children's creative activities reflected their interest in birds. Their feathered friends were the chief characters in many stories. They developed several original songs and a number of poems. (Audrey fostered this interest by reading poetry to them.) Using paper sacks and colored paper, they developed some bird mobiles which they hung from wires stretched across the room. They also drew and cut out birds and bird houses to decorate the classroom windows. As interest in bird families grew there were a number of spontaneous dramatizations.

There were many new skills developed before the unit was completed. Locating information about particular birds challenged the better readers to acquire some mature reference skills. The technical terminology in the the bird books led to considerable vocabulary development and some advanced word-analysis skills. In order to interpret the information in the bird books effectively, the children had to develop some accurate concepts of size. These they put to use as they made plans so that birds in their mural were in proper scale. Writing reports, stories, and poems gave opportunities for Audrey to work with individuals and with the class as a whole to build more effective communication skills.

No single culminating activity marked the conclusion of this unit. As interests in birds began to be satisfied and questions to be answered, other science concerns began to assume prominence. The children proceeded to these with no particular change of pace. From time to time special reports on birds continued to be made. Allen told about a nest of warblers. Bobby described his first sight of a hummingbird. Joanna reported her discouragement when sparrows drove the wrens away from her bird house and was advised to make her doorway smaller. Bill rescued a nestful of robins deserted after their mother was killed and made daily reports on their progress. In fact, for some of these youngsters, one could envision this third-grade study stretching into a lifelong interest in birds.

Older pupils can be expected to acquire more of the information they need through wide reading. This does not diminish, however, the need for concrete experience as background. Charles Artley used a wealth of useful resources as he undertook with his fifth-graders a study of their state:

America was designated in the course of study as the center for fifth-grade work, but the special focus of the unit was suggested when a booklet prepared by an eleven-year-old girl from Munich depicting life in her part of Germany arrived via the Junior Red Cross. "Could we make one?" was the theme of the opening discussion, after the children had examined the booklet. It was readily apparent that such a project was quite possible, but suggestions were meager when questions were raised regarding what might be included.

All-class activities to build experience background consisted of examining a variety of reference materials that Charles had collected. There were some state calendars with pictures of points of interest, several official booklets from local historical societies, some highway maps listing points of interest for tourists, an official history of the state. Children soon began to add other materials to this collection and after two periods of looking and discussing they were ready to suggest specific topics to include in their booklet.

The topics finally selected as the children discussed what to include in the booklet became the focal points of these pupils' study of their state. Each proposal was evaluated in terms of its probable interest to a child in another country, but also in terms of how much it would contribute to the children's broader acquaintance with their state. Topics of purely local interest were set aside in favor of others that were less familiar. The resulting list contained considerable detail: population, area, important cities, important buildings; industries, transportation, products, climate; history, education, government, famous people; terrain, wild life, natural resources, important rivers; famous landmarks, parks and scenic places, state symbols. This was a project in which it seemed desirable to establish working groups at once, since there was an obvious need to apportion the list of topics. Accordingly, the topics were grouped (as indicated by the punctuation in the preceding list) and five committees were set up. Each child indicated his first, second, and third choices of committees and of people with whom he would prefer to work. On the basis of these preferences Charles developed the list of committee assignments, and after some last-minute changes where people felt very unhappy about their placement, groups were ready to go to work. The activities through which the project developed were a combination of all-class experiences at points where Charles felt that his leadership was important in building new understandings, group research on the special topics in preparation for writing the articles for the proposed book, and individual activities at points where youngsters became interested in side issues not included in the committee plans.

To build background in the light of which the individual reading would be more meaningful, Charles planned some group lessons focused on the history of the state. Several films helped to give a picture of the early settlements, and the standard reference texts with which the classroom was equipped provided more detail. A visit to the local historical society and to the site of the fort that was the origin of their city helped to make the story of early days more real. A time line was developed across the front blackboard in order to relate state history more readily to national events. After their study of historical backgrounds the class as a whole proceeded to learn more about the geography of the state, the natural resources, and the industries. At this point considerable work with maps was done—to locate the state in relation to other countries of similar latitude; to place it accurately in the United States; and, finally, to examine state maps intensively in order to locate major cities, rivers, lakes, and important landmarks. All sorts of maps were used—highway maps, political maps, maps showing the distribution of population and natural resources. Pictures, films, and the pamphlets now arriving from chambers of commerce in other cities helped to provide the needed detail. *Many types of people contribute to human progress; we can understand our present world better if we know something of its history; people adapt their ways of living to the environments in which they find themselves; people change their environments in order to achieve better ways of living; there are many personal satisfactions to be derived from pursuing interests in the natural environment* were among the basic generalizations toward which Charles was working.

Group work paralleled the all-class experiences, and toward the end of the unit the children were able to add considerable detail to the class discussions from their independent reading. As the committees began work, Charles led some all-class discussions of the responsibilities of a committee chairman and the characteristics of a good group member. Chairmen were elected at the first committee meeting and reported from time to time on the progress of the group. Since each committee was responsible for several specific topics, one of the early committee meetings was used to assign these. Children, individually or in pairs, undertook these special responsibilities. Actually, then, although five committees were at work, there was much individual reading and reporting within the framework of the committee organization. As youngsters located information on their special topics they shared this with other groups. Often, in all-class discussion periods, members of one committee reported upon resources they felt would be helpful to the work of another. As the time came to organize the information for inclusion in the booklet, the committee members worked closely together again to decide how all the material that had been gathered could best be organized and presented. At the close of the unit they also planned panel discussions to share their work with the other groups.

There were a number of creative activities as the youngsters tried to put their new understandings to use. The bulletin board, which at first had pictures supplied by Charles, soon began to blossom with children's work—some reproductions of famous landmarks, drawn free-hand by the children but made as accurately as possible, and some creative pictures of state beauty spots. Because pottery was one of the state products, Charles helped the youngsters to make and fire some of their own. In their reading activities, they delved into stories and legends. These experiences led eventually to creative writing of imaginative tales about the early settlements in their state. They listened to records of Johnny Appleseed and wrote some of their own poems. Some of these creative experiences were reflected in the work of the groups, where factual reports began to be supplemented by imaginative tales, poems, and pictures. Toward the conclusion of the unit the children were asked to assume responsibility for part of a school assembly program. They chose to develop this as a pageant showing how famous people in the state had contributed to state and national progress.

Many new skills were needed before this unit was concluded. It was particularly rich in its experiences in locating up-to-date information. The youngsters wrote to chambers of commerce and to state and local historical societies for pamphlets. They watched the daily papers for current events and they discovered that grandparents and other senior residents could help to fill in historical detail. Because their reference texts did not present material neatly organized around the special topics upon which individuals and small groups were at work, the children had many valuable experiences in learning how to locate special topics in an index. Note-taking and summarizing skills were polished as the reading progressed and reports were written. There were experiences with arithmetic, too. The study of maps contributed to the youngsters' techniques in reading legends and working with scales. The bulletins from chambers of commerce provided tables and graphs regarding local industries which the children learned to interpret. Later, as they compiled their group reports, they used some graphic forms of their own. When reproductions of famous dwellings were made, care was taken to keep these in proper scale. Reproducing state maps offered other valuable experiences with accurate dimensions.

This unit was particularly rich in the variety of reference aids that finally accumulated. The bulletin board displayed a large state map; the state seal; and the state flag, bird, and flower. Quite a display of postcards was collected. Pictures of presidents born in the state were located, as were pictures of their homes. Calendars provided photographs of scenic spots, as did some of the materials from tourist bureaus and chambers of commerce. One corner of the bulletin board was saved for newspaper clippings of state events of importance. Homes and attics yielded a variety of articles from pioneer days. The local museum sent a display of Indian artifacts.

Able children had ample opportunity to explore. There was no limit to the comprehensiveness of their final reports other than the deadline for completing the work. As the project progressed, individuals volunteered to report on a number of additional topics of special interest. Toward the conclusion of the unit, several children cooperated in developing quiz games regarding special items of information—marking the counties correctly on a blank map, matching lists of counties with county seats, identifying famous people and landmarks from a series of clues.

The unit was completed when the reports, pictures, graphs, and maps were bound in booklet form. There was no elaborate culminating activity, but time was allowed each group to display and to tell about its special contribution. Since the work had involved much individual study of special problems, these final reports were arranged so that each youngster could tell of his special part in the project.

The three units that have just been described do not provide patterns which could be followed exactly by other teachers. In fact, they were effective as learning experiences because they were developed in terms of the way particular groups of pupils faced their problems. Their chief contribution to your work will lie in the insights they provide regarding the types of experiences that might be profitable as children are helped to explore an extensive problem and the varied ways of working that might be utilized. You, with your boys and girls, must develop the plans that will best meet your needs.

GUIDING SMALL-GROUP ACTIVITIES

In exploring with your boys and girls a problem of any magnitude, you will undoubtedly make provision for individuals and small groups to undertake some independent research and summarizing activities. If these experiences are to make their most effective contribution to the growth of your pupils, you will need to have a clear understanding of the purposes that they can best serve and of your role as a teacher in guiding them.

Why provide for work in groups? Could you not cover more subject matter and do it more thoroughly if you guided all the activities yourself? Part of the answer lies in the fact that to grow in the ways of democracy one must live them. Youngsters are not likely to graduate from our schools prepared to assume leadership functions in our society or to operate effectively in cooperative relationships if their only experiences are with a benevolent dictatorship. There are, however, many opportunities during the school day to provide experiences in democratic living—parties to plan, the classroom to decorate, all-school service responsibilities to assume, housekeeping chores in the classroom to organize. We should be ill advised, indeed, to sacrifice learning in the content fields solely for the sake of teaching the skills of democratic living. Group work is justified as an approach to building understandings only if it contributes to effective learning.

What values should you hope to achieve through a classroom organization that provides opportunities for pupils to work individually or in small groups? There are several, provided, of course, that you are able to guide small-group activity effectively. Obviously, it is important for pupils to learn how to solve problems for themselves. Your goals in helping your boys and girls to understand their world encompass more than helping them to acquire information. You also have the responsibility of planning the experiences through which they acquire information so that they learn to use a scientific approach to the solution of problems. When small groups or individuals engage in independent problem-solving activities they have an opportunity to develop some of these important techniques.

Group work should enable you to individualize your teaching. It is very difficult, even in a class period of better than a half-hour, to sense the confusions and the problems of individuals when you are in front of the entire class trying to think what you can say or do next to keep your discussion moving. However, even five minutes spent listening to a small group at work can be informative regarding individual strengths, weaknesses, and problems. Once groups have been organized and have developed a plan of work, it is likely that they will be self-directing for the next several days. This means that you are free to give help as needed—to aid one youngster in locating information, to work on the reading problems of another, to proofread a report with a third.

Small-group activities also make it possible for you to provide more effectively for individual talents, needs, and interests. When you direct the activities of the class as one large group, you must, of necessity, hold everyone to the same subject matter. When, however, you work within a small-group organization, it is possible for special groups or individuals to investigate aspects of the total problem of particular concern to them and to explore these subproblems as deeply as their maturity and capacities will allow.

Whether the potential benefits of small-group and individual activities will be realized depends, of course, on your skill as a teacher and leader. You must be able to decide when group work is appropriate and what kind of group organization will best achieve your objectives. You need, also, to learn to use your time wisely in giving help while groups are at work. In addition, you must become skilled in helping your pupils learn how to work together effectively. Guiding this type of classroom organization calls for a high level of professional competence.

The aspects of the problem to be allotted to small groups and individuals should be carefully chosen. If pupils' experiences in small-group or individual activities are to be effective, your first step should be to consider which aspects of the problem can best be handled in this manner. There is no single pattern appropriate for all situations. Each problem will call for a different way of working. Certain general principles, however, can be suggested to guide your thinking.

Typically, small-group or individual work is not the most effective means through which to develop the concepts and generalizations you consider to be basic learnings for your total class. It is difficult, even for able sixth-graders, to present the type of report and lead the discussion needed to guarantee that their friends will grasp new and essential understandings. This calls for adult leadership. Usually, then, you will retain for yourself much of the responsibility of guiding the reading, providing the visual aids, and leading the discussions designed to develop understandings essential for everyone.

Is there a legitimate place for individual or small-group work in the information-getting process? Unquestionably there is. If you are to help your pupils learn how to locate information and solve problems for themselves, you must give them practice. Furthermore, if you wish to stimulate deep and lasting interests you must provide opportunities to explore areas of special concern. Special aspects of the total problem provide effective centers for such experiences. With younger pupils, these may involve doing rather than reading. For example, in Darlene Smith's second grade the youngsters became much interested in what plants need for proper growth. After some general discussion in order to pool existing information and to raise problems, the children developed a list of theories they wanted to test. Do plants need sunlight? Do they need water? Does the temperature make a difference? At this point small groups were formed, each to decide with Darlene's help how one of these theories could be tested and eventually to report its findings to the entire class. The more mature the children and the better their reading skills, the more possibilities there are for small-group and individual activities involving extended reference work. Thus, after Ben Arnold's fifth-graders had done some all-class discussion and map study by way of orientation to the westward movement, groups undertook to locate detailed information regarding each of the major trails to the West. These findings were reported orally and then summarized in notebooks for other groups to read.

You may be saying, "Yes, but while the children in a small group may be becoming thoroughly informed about one aspect of the problem, think what they are missing by not becoming equally well acquainted with all the other aspects." You must remember, however, that there are practical limitations to the total amount of time that can be devoted to any one project. You may be able to allow a week for five small groups each to explore one special topic intensively, but you could rarely multiply this time expenditure by five in order to provide for equally detailed work by everyone on all five special topics. When you plan for a combination of all-class and small-group or individual activities in developing new understandings you are, in effect, providing an opportunity for each child to develop a core of essential learnings under your guidance, to become moderately well informed about other aspects of the problem through the reports of his peers, and to become a specialist in an area of his choosing.

Small-group activities need not always be used in the information-getting process. Sometimes the scantiness or difficulty of the available reference material or the limited experience background of your pupils may make it highly desirable for you to work with the class as a whole during most of the activities leading to the development of new understandings. Group work may then be planned at the point where the new learnings are put to use—to develop pictures or models, plan and produce a play, prepare summary reports for a class notebook. If your pupils have had limited experiences in working in small groups, such summarizing activities are often an effective way to begin. Concrete problems such as these are frequently much more easily attacked cooperatively than are problems calling for the location, pooling, and summarizing of information.

The organization for small-group and individual work should develop from the needs of the situation. The number of groups at work and their size will depend upon the way your plans are unfolding and the maturity of the pupils. It may seem to you, at first, that three or four groups are all that you can possibly manage at one time. However, since the quality of the end product depends on how well the members of a committee can work cooperatively, there may be times when more groups, smaller in size, will achieve smoother working relationships. It is possible, also, that some aspects of a problem may best be assumed by a single child, or by a pair. Such dispersed activities can be supervised more readily than you might imagine. If you and your pupils have planned in detail, you may well find that a seemingly complex pattern actually allows you to devote more time to problems of locating or interpreting new information and less to problems of human relationships.

There is no one way of assigning pupils to groups. In general, pupils should share in decisions regarding how they will work, but this does not mean that friends always work together or that everyone is allowed to read about the most popular topic or to volunteer for the most glamorous job while other important aspects of the project are inadequately covered. If you want your boys and girls to grow in their ability to organize their work, you will use an all-class planning session to assign priorities to certain jobs or topics and arrive at some agreements regarding the number of persons needed for specific jobs. This should be done before you ask for pupil preferences. When there has been this kind of all-class planning, it is then quite legitimate to ask for volunteers to take on special aspects of the problem. "We have too many people interested in reading more about hurricanes and cyclones. It's important for us to learn more about weather stations, too. Can we have some people change to this group?" It is also legitimate to ask pupils with special talents to take on particular responsibility. "If you want a mural, we should probably have at least one person who is good in art to help." "The books on this topic are very hard. I wonder if one or two good readers would volunteer to serve on this committee?"

How complicated the total pattern for work becomes will depend upon the problem and the maturity of your pupils. Sometimes the plan may be relatively simple—much of the new information developed under your guidance and some simple group activities used only toward the close of the unit to summarize what has been learned. Sometimes the questions suggested in your planning sessions and the related problems intriguing your class may lead to a much more complex organization. For example, an able youngster might be participating in all-class activities, working with a committee group to locate information on a special problem, serving with another group to develop a special exhibit, building his own notebook to summarize his work, and getting together with two of his pals at home to complete a model that he hasn't had time to finish at school.

Class organization for work is a tool by means of which you and your pupils achieve your objectives. The test of its effectiveness is the learning that results. It may be complicated or simple. You may play a major leadership role or you may serve largely as a resource person. The problem, the maturity of your pupils, and their needs should be your guide rather than any preconceived notions about how a "good" unit should be organized.

Effective group work calls for careful planning. Group work can become ineffective and wasteful of time and effort unless it has been carefully planned. Committees and pupils undertaking individual projects need a clear sense of purpose. They need to visualize how their work fits into the total plan and they need to know precisely what they are expected to accomplish.

Even when goals and small-group purposes have been defined carefully in your opening planning sessions, you would do well to spend a few minutes with each committee during the first work period. Considerable wrangling can sometimes occur before a plan of action is decided upon. If you meet briefly with each committee to hear a report of its plans and to give help when problems of interpersonal relationships have arisen, the group work is usually off to a much smoother start.

You should also make strategic use of brief planning and evaluation sessions as group work proceeds. A committee that starts enthusiastically often bogs down, especially if the job to be done is comprehensive. Even mature youngsters do not always keep their goals clearly in mind, and after a few days of "All right, it's time for our groups," the original interest in the problem may be diluted by last night's television and the school volley ball game. Immature groups can forget overnight what their plans were or even to which committee they belong. It is helpful to take a few minutes at the beginning of each work session to make sure that plans are clear and needed material is at hand. Equally valuable is the policy of asking for brief progress reports at the end of the work session, although some precautions are needed in such evaluation sessions to prevent enthusiastic groups from giving their final reports several times over.

Records are another important aid in group work. Committees need their plans in writing. Lists can be used to check off jobs accomplished. Time schedules can be posted as reminders of deadlines. Lists of "extras" to be done whenever someone has time can be posted and checked off as accomplished. A valuable additional learning that can be derived from a successful unit is increased ability to plan and to budget time. This does not come in a laissez-faire atmosphere where group work is allowed to muddle along day after day without checks on progress or concern for efficiency.

Group work calls for active teacher participation. You do not go back to your desk to correct papers once you are sure that plans are understood and the committees are at work. Here is your opportunity to get better acquainted with individuals, to straighten out misconceptions, to help with needed reference skills, to solve problems of interpersonal relationships, to work on summarizing and reporting skills.

At the beginning of a group work period many teachers spend a few minutes circulating from group to group, pausing only briefly to make sure that no unforeseen difficulties have arisen. The less mature your pupils and the less skilled they are in working together, the more important such a preliminary survey may be. You may stop for a minute to help one group work out a personal relationships problem where two dominant leaders have disagreed, help someone in a second group locate needed materials, listen long enough to the plans in another to satisfy yourself that work will move ahead smoothly.

Once you are sure that everyone is at work, you can give your undivided attention to special problems—one group at a time. Your help can be particularly valuable at the points where your committees are facing the more complex aspects of their work. Initial group planning sessions are usually times when you should stay long enough with each committee to be sure that detailed plans have been worked through. With immature children, the first steps toward locating needed information are often difficult. Groups which have been reading for information frequently need special assistance as they begin to formulate their reports; it is a rare chairman of elementary school age who can help a committee to consolidate and organize extensive reading without some overlapping and confusion in sequence. Youngsters preparing a model or planning a brief dramatization sometimes become so involved in the mechanics of their plan that they forget its educational objectives.

Many teachers use part of their time during group work periods to give help to those pupils who are in need of direct guidance. In some classes the poorest readers may be invited to join a committee which works with the teacher in reading group fashion. Sometimes pupils with limited language skills are given special help in preparing their reports. Occasionally there is a pupil who merits individual attention, either because he is having more than ordinary difficulty with the work or because he has unusual talents and interests. In some primary grades where reference reading skills are limited, assignment to committees may be made on the basis of reading skill so that the teacher may work with each committee in much the same fashion as with a reading group. Giving such special assistance to individuals or small groups may seem, at first glance, likely to result in the neglect of others. This will not be the case if you are careful to identify special problems as you go from group to group. Other pupils in the class, too, will receive your help but in ways and at times that meet their particular needs.

Your active leadership will also be important at the point where committees are sharing their work with the class as a whole. Normally, you will guarantee a polite audience for the report and allow the committee to carry out uninterrupted its plans for reporting. Questions and comments usually follow. At this point you can be very useful. It is not always easy for a pupil chairman to sense the gist of a question or to answer it so that the point is clear. You may be needed to clarify the question and to make sure that the answer from the committee is clearly understood. Sometimes in order to maintain the audience atmosphere you will do a bit of role playing, raising your hand as a pupil would in order to ask the question or contribute the additional piece of information that brings into clearer focus the main points of the report. There may also be times when you should add a few summary statements in order to be sure that the audience has grasped the gist of the report. You can be more helpful in this if, as you go from group to group, you make some notes for yourself regarding the major understandings to which the report is likely to contribute and the clarification that might be needed if the full value of the report is to be realized.

Help needs to be provided in developing group-process techniques. Group work is not going to go smoothly the first time your class attempts it, any more than your pupils' first efforts to share in planning sessions will be smooth. You will have to help your pupils develop techniques of cooperative problem-solving.

You will forestall some difficulties by the skill with which you help your pupils to establish specific purposes. Children who know what their job is and accept it as important are far more likely to work together cooperatively than sets of five or six individuals who are assigned a general topic but feel no personal commitment. This may explain why pupils who seemingly get nowhere with topics assigned to them in a study related to a content field sometimes surprise you by their efficiency and the smoothness of their interpersonal relationships when they work together to plan a class party.

Part of the help you give as you go from group to group may be on problems of how to work cooperatively. John tells you he wants to shift groups because his committee won't listen to his plans. Susan and Jane report that the boys in their group are just being silly. Alice's group seems to have dispersed, each with his own book but with no clear plans. These are symptoms of difficulties with the group process. Sometimes they are also symptoms of deep-seated individual needs. In neither case will it help much for the group members to be told to "settle down and get to work." Such problems need to be talked through, disagreements and difficulties brought into the open, and plans for next steps suggested.

Although some problems of interpersonal relationships will be best settled in the group in which the difficulty arose, others will have implications for the whole class. In almost all the groups there may be misconceptions of the chairman's role; there may be a common tendency to plunge into new work without plans; individuals may be so intrigued with the opportunity to sit and chat that they do not settle down to work; or there may be common problems of how to divide responsibility. These problems can be talked through in a class session. Sometimes the youngsters in groups that are operating smoothly will have helpful suggestions to offer. Such class discussions, however, will not necessarily build better group work techniques unless they are followed up. You, yourself, may go from group to group to see how the suggestions are being put to use and to give assistance where further difficulties are arising. It can also be helpful, at the end of the period, to ask for an evaluation of how well the group work went and to identify special aspects of the cooperative process upon which the group members feel they should continue to work.

Perhaps the two greatest difficulties faced by beginners in guiding

Accurate understandings develop from concrete experiences. Classifying exhibits and displays contributes to clearer concepts.

Public Schools, Cincinnati, Ohio, Marsh, Photographers

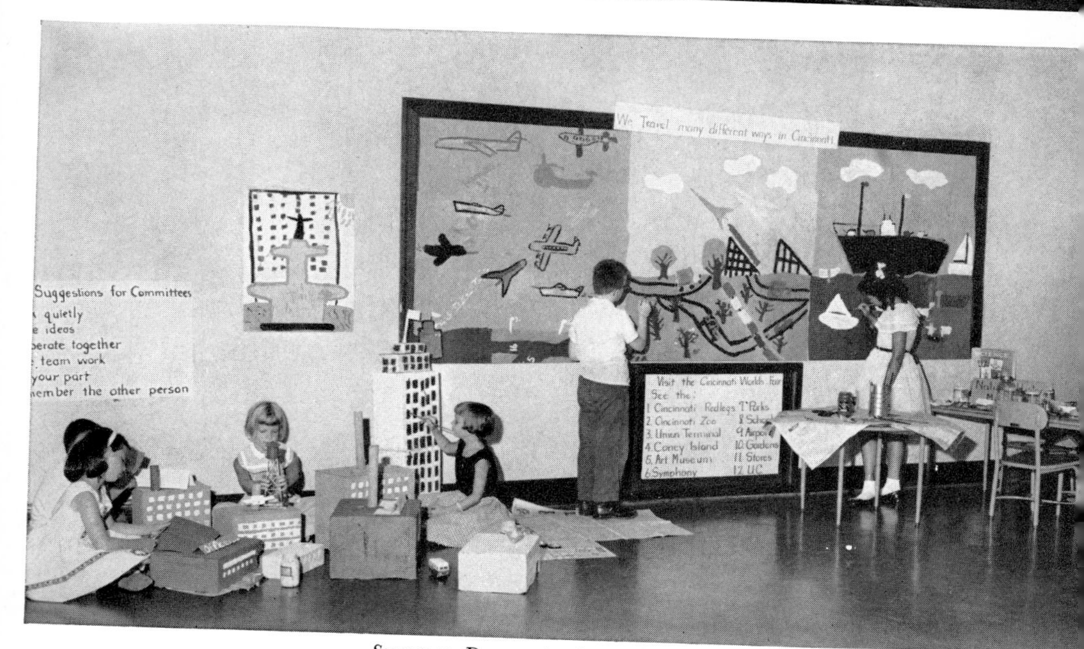

Summer Demonstration School, University of Cincinnati, D. Arthur Bricker, Photographer

Accurate understandings develop as new ideas are put to use. Many forms of creative expression can serve to culminate a unit.

Summer Demonstration School, University of Cincinnati,
D. Arthur Bricker, Photographer

Accurate understandings develop as pupils think for themselves. A bulletin board extends the variety of available references.

the work of groups are impatience with the group process, on the one hand, and failure to work for sufficiently high standards, on the other. Undoubtedly there will be wrangling, days when groups bog down, and individuals whose personal needs cause them to be disrupting influences in the group. These are problems upon which you will work, step by step, for the sake of the growth in democratic skills and in independent work habits which you will ultimately achieve. You should not expect to achieve perfection overnight. We do know, however, that the skills of cooperative problem-solving can be learned. If you find yourself evaluating your group work day after day in such terms as "They just waste time," "They aren't interested," "They don't want to do a thing but fool around," it is time to look at your own teaching techniques.

DEVELOPING NEEDED REFERENCE SKILLS

If pupils are to be able to locate information efficiently and interpret it accurately, they must develop increasing command of reference skills. They must learn to locate needed resources and be able to comprehend the information contained therein. They must become skilled observers and listeners. They will need to take notes and keep records. They will have to make reports—both oral and written. Because any skill is best developed when related to the actual situation in which it is needed, a good share of pupils' work on reference skills should be planned in the light of the demands of unit activities in the content fields.

You will give help on skills in a number of ways and at many points as the study of an extensive problem develops. As your pupils start to locate new materials, to read and take notes, or to prepare reports, you will undoubtedly take a few minutes to talk about skills. "How could we find these topics most rapidly?" "We have our list of questions. How can we use them to save time as we read?" "Our last reports were hard to follow. How did we say we might improve?" Then, as individual or group work proceeds, there will be opportunities to work on special problems. You may spend a few minutes on how to use an index with a youngster who is aimlessly turning pages, listen to plans for a committee report, work on note-taking with a child who is copying materials word by word from his textbook. It will also, at times, be appropriate to devote a full period to a reference problem. The entire class may take time to discuss how to locate information in the encyclopedia, practice note-taking, or draw up criteria for a good report. Activities such as these may be scheduled during the time block set aside for skill development; but the situation that provides the most effective practice is often the one in which your pupils actually need to use the new skill, and the reference texts with which they are struggling are frequently your most valuable teaching aids.

Beginning teachers are sometimes reluctant to use the time set aside for work in the content fields to concentrate on skills. There seems to be so much content to be covered that it is hard to take a period, or even five minutes, to talk about problems of reading, note-taking, or reporting. If you will stop to think, however, you will realize that often all that is needed is a brief comment regarding last week's messy notes or a reminder to reread the characteristics of a good report posted on the bulletin board. Nevertheless, the expenditure of considerable time and effort can be justified if your pupils lack basic reference skills. In fact, if you do not give such help, you may fail to achieve many of your other goals. It is better to concentrate for a week on developing efficient reading skills (or to do some careful planning on your part to adjust your activities to your pupils' present levels of operation) than to face a semester of time wasting and ineffective efforts to locate needed information.

The general teaching principles that will guide you in helping boys and girls develop more effective reference skills are the same as those that characterize the effective teaching of any skill. Your pupils need to be helped to evaluate their present efforts and to identify the points at which a higher level of proficiency is needed. They need to understand clearly the new techniques they are trying to develop. They need, also, opportunities to practice, interspersed with evaluation sessions to assess progress and reveal new needs. With these needs in mind, the following discussion considers some of the related problems which teachers have found most troublesome.

Attention needs to be given to effective reading skills. Learning to read accurately for information begins in first grade. Among the first materials are experience records—plans, news of the day, summaries of trips, special vocabulary lists. Simple picture materials are among the earliest reference books. Titles of books, chapter titles, and tables of contents tend to be the first reference aids. With increased maturity should come greater skill with alphabetical order, guide words, key reference words, cross references. Older pupils will work with books with more complicated formats—chapter headings, paragraph headings, summaries.

There will be an ever increasing technical vocabulary to handle. Each content field has its own special vocabulary. These are the concepts which you will need to make meaningful through a variety of activities; they may also present difficult word-analysis problems. New place names and personal names will complicate the reading problem—*Newfoundland, Ponce de Leon, Popocatepetl.* In the areas of science and mathematics, there will be an increasing number of symbols and equations. In addition to all these special vocabulary demands there will be a host of technical meanings for familiar terms—a *wooded* shore; a *mixed* number; the *mouth* of a river.

Effective reading of reference materials also calls for increasing ability to handle visual aids—pictures, maps, graphs, charts, tables. First-graders will turn mainly to pictures, but even at this level there may be simple graphic devices—weather charts or graphs to show how many mothers have joined the Parent-Teacher Association. Older pupils must become skillful in reading maps, interpreting size relationships accurately on charts or graphs, reading percentages or other numerical information given in tables.

Your pupils must learn to adjust their reading skills flexibly to the particular problem they face. They will need to be able to locate exact information to answer some questions and to pull together several items of information in order to arrive at a conclusion to answer others. As they take on more extensive reading responsibilities, it will become important for them to learn to use a combination of skimming and detailed reading—to locate quickly the appropriate topics and then to read slowly and carefully for specific answers.

From first grade, there are evaluation skills to be learned. With first-graders, this may be a matter of recognizing that a picture of a fire house or a school does not look like the one with which the pupil is acquainted, or of distinguishing between a story about a real horse and one about a horse that talks or flies. Older pupils will face problems of resolving discrepancies in dates or tables, of deciding on the accuracy of reports in the daily papers, of deciding how much to accept of the background of a fictional story.

How do teachers go about helping their pupils to develop more effective reading skills? Perhaps one of your most important steps is to identify the new skills which are likely to be demanded by the plans for the unit and the materials available. Plans to develop such new skills should comprise one section in your total block plan. It is helpful, also, to think about the reading difficulties that were apparent during the preceding unit and to identify opportunities in the present unit for additional practice. With such a survey of needed skills as background, you are ready to plan for specific lessons. Perhaps map work is particularly important. This may be your pupils' first attempt to make extended use of the encyclopedia. The questions they have posed may call for considerable skill with indexes. You may be working with a problem where ability to read the newspaper is important. Such lessons would be planned for the times at which your pupils first need to put the new skill to use. Then, as they start to work, they have a realistic opportunity to practice the new skill and you will be able to evaluate individual progress and to give additional help as needed.

Your alertness to hints of difficulty as class work proceeds can be an important factor in improving reading skills. Ask yourself what the trouble might be when you hear an inaccurate answer, see pupils' notes copied in the words of the text, watch a youngster handling books aimlessly, or hear conflicting reports from pupils who have been reading about the same topic. These are indications that reading skills are not functioning effectively, and from them should come some of your plans to give additional help to individuals, to small groups with a common problem, or perhaps to your class as a whole.

What about the pupils who can't read much of the classroom material? Refining the reference techniques of good readers is not nearly as great a task as this. As you face such problems, it is important to remember that the textbook is not the only teaching aid. Films, pictures, collections, exhibits, excursions, pupils' home experiences, and your own skill as a reporter provide other avenues to building understanding. These should be capitalized upon to make concepts meaningful for all pupils, but they are particularly valuable when reading skills are limited.

Granted that many understandings can be developed without the use of books, you should not merely avoid the reading problem with youngsters who have limited skill. Unless you help, they will go to their next teacher even more handicapped than they are now. Of all the adjustments that might be made, the least effective is to have pupils take turns reading the text aloud. If the material is too difficult for silent comprehension, it is not going to make any more sense if stumbled over orally. True, oral reading provides an opportunity to help with hard words, but this is not an economical way to build new vocabulary. It is far better, if you want poor readers to become acquainted with parts of a very difficult book, to read aloud yourself or to assign this task to one of the youngsters who reads well.

One of the most important positive first steps to take in helping poorer readers is to locate simpler reading matter. In science, for example, the same general topics are likely to appear in books written for several grade levels—living things, weather, energy, the stars. You should not overlook the factual information that can be derived from a simple fictional story with an authentic setting, or the learnings that can come from a series of excellent photographs, even though the accompanying text is difficult. Your local or school librarian can be of major assistance in helping to locate such materials. Many teachers build their own reading materials for retarded readers in the form of experience records. Such group summaries of important information are commonplace in the primary grades, but they can be used with equal effectiveness with older pupils. Some teachers mimeograph simplified versions of materials containing important information. Whenever you place in the hands of the retarded reader something he can grasp, you have at least provided him an opportunity to practice whatever reading skills he possesses.

When the only available reference material is difficult, there are several ways of simplifying the reading problem. One move, helpful even for good readers, is to build special vocabulary lists. These may contain technical words, personal and place names, and words that have special connotations for the unit. Such lists not only provide one more opportunity to develop meaningful concepts, but also help poorer readers to become thoroughly familiar with many of the words likely to be the stumbling blocks when they read. Teachers have found many ways of using such lists so that they make worth-while contributions to unit activities in addition to helping with reading problems. Children may build a class dictionary or make their own picture dictionaries. Lists can serve as summaries of aspects of the unit (*People We Know; Places We've Read About; Kinds of Snakes*). Labels can be attached to an exhibit or a bulletin board display. Pronunciation keys are often included in these lists and sometimes short sentences which use the word in context. Further review of essential vocabulary can be given by using such lists as aids to spelling when reports are being written or as the basis for games or quizzes to check on pronunciation and meanings.

You can simplify the reading problem considerably by the skill with which you help your pupils to clarify their purposes. This is important even for better readers. The youngster who has only a vague notion that he is to locate "something about farms" will have trouble choosing a specific reference book. Then, even when he has found a book that deals with farms, he will still have difficulty deciding which facts are pertinent. If, on the other hand, he is reading specifically to find the most common crops in different parts of the country, to discover what kinds of work a farmer has to do, or to learn what crops are typical of his community, he is more likely to read discriminatingly and to interpret graphs, pictures, and tables intelligently. The more limited a pupil's reading skill, the more carefully you must help him to determine precisely what he is looking for.

Some teachers have organized their classrooms in ways that will free them to help poor readers. In some primary grades, children have tackled social studies and science problems in their regular reading groups. In other classrooms teachers have worked with poor readers as a special group while committees of better readers took on independent research responsibilities. Part of the time spent circulating among working groups can also be devoted to giving brief help on individual reading problems. You are not necessarily neglecting better readers if you use some of your time this way. They need to develop skill in locating material independently and in coordinating information from several sources. If youngsters have clear plans and the resources they need, they can be given valuable opportunities to develop mature reading skills by being allowed to pursue their plans independently. *Equal* opportunity to learn does not necessarily mean the *same* help from the teacher.

Plans should be made to improve observing and listening skills. Observing and listening seem to be so much an inborn means of securing information that teachers do not always analyze the special skills involved. Yet skills there are. Even first-graders can learn to give attention to specific details and to use simple instruments—thermometers, rulers—to aid in making their observations accurate. Older pupils will need to become accurate in identifying the distinguishing characteristics of objects they observe—classifying flowers, rocks, leaves; identifying birds; studying the artifacts in a museum exhibit. Older pupils also must learn to use a variety of aids to accurate observation—scales, rulers, compasses, microscopes, thermometers, rain gauges. They are involved in many studies where accurate records of observation are important

—changes in weight of white rats being fed different diets, rainfall for the month, the growth of plants under differing conditions.

Listening begins with younger pupils through learning to give others a polite audience in sharing periods, to follow the give-and-take of discussions and conversations, to attend carefully to the teacher's directions, announcements, and requests. Older pupils need more sophistication in following the trend of a discussion, in identifying points of disagreement and needs for compromise, in sensing when the comment they are bursting to make will pull the discussion off the track. They must also be able to give intelligent attention to longer and more complex reports and explanations than do their younger brothers and sisters.

Good observers and listeners, like good readers, must learn to be selective. Pupils must be able to keep a specific problem in mind and to identify in the report, explanation, film, or demonstration the precise answers to their questions. They must grow increasingly skillful in recognizing where confusion still exists and further explanations are needed. Good listening or observing involves active participation, not merely passive assimilation.

As do good readers, good observers and listeners evaluate the accuracy of what they are watching or hearing. With first-graders the problem may be to decide whether a picture is authentic or merely an imaginative reproduction, whether the pupil who is reporting an incident on the playground is giving the facts accurately or embroidering from his imagination. The more mature your pupils, the more likely they are to face problems involving propaganda analysis, of distinguishing fact from fiction in a television production, in deciding whether a film has given a well-rounded picture of the lives of people from another land.

Accurate and thoughtful observing and listening is, at least in part, a reflection of the total classroom atmosphere. You must help boys and girls to learn that it is important to give their undivided attention to the speaker or to whatever is being observed. One practical step, particularly with immature groups, is to make sure that potential distractions are removed. Desks can be cleared; children can be seated so that they can see and hear easily; chairs can be placed so that there is elbow room; good friends can, if necessary, be separated. It is equally important to secure an attentive audience before you begin. It is often a temptation to move ahead before everyone is ready, hoping that this will encourage the stragglers whose desks aren't quite clear to hurry.

Actually, such a procedure is far more apt to teach the dawdlers that they can have a few minutes of grace if they want it. It is usually more effective to wait and to teach the child who is reporting to wait until he has the full attention of the group.

It is difficult to observe or to listen attentively and selectively if one does not know quite what one is listening or looking for. Questions raised prior to a film or posted next to a bulletin board display make an important contribution to good observing. Likewise, recalling for the class the original purposes of the committee making a report or referring to the over-all plans for the unit contribute to selective listening. There is an added incentive for careful observing or listening when pupils know that they are to have an opportunity to use what they have just gleaned from their experience—to discuss, to write a short report, to ask questions of the reporters, to decide which of the items of information presented through the observing or listening experience are most important for a class notebook or a group experience record.

Sometimes accurate observing or listening can be given increased importance by making special assignments to small groups. On a trip to the grocery store, one committee may be responsible for noting the types of fruits and vegetables, a second for seeing how the cashier works, a third for discovering which foods are refrigerated. In questioning a foreign visitor, one group may ask about schools, a second about climate and topography, a third about city and rural life. In learning about heating and ventilation, each child may interview his own parents and a committee may talk to the school engineer. Youngsters who assume such responsibilities have a particular reason for paying careful attention, since the entire class is relying on their reports.

Even with the most compelling of motives, accurate observing and listening become difficult if the material being presented is hard to understand or the report is vague and confused. "They were polite to you; now let's be polite to them" will not guarantee a quiet audience for long if the persons reporting are poorly prepared. Neither will a film hold attention if the concepts are too difficult for the group. There comes a point, too, when fatigue sets in. Pupils who listened politely and with careful attention to two committee reports may not be able to take a third in the same day, even though the material is equally well prepared. In planning for observing or listening sessions, you must, therefore, be sure that the quality and the quantity of the presentations are appropriate for the maturity of your pupils.

Pupils can be helped to develop standards for effective listening and observing. In many classrooms youngsters talk over what it means to be a good audience or what characterizes a good listener. Sometimes a committee that has just given a report is asked to comment on the quality of the audience participation. As pupils begin to take more responsibility for small-group discussions, there will be opportunities to analyze the give-and-take of the discussion, to discuss how to resolve disagreements, to take a look at the chairman's job. As with the development of any skill, progress is likely to be more rapid when pupils know exactly what they are attempting to achieve. Inaccurate observing and listening need to be challenged, just as does inaccurate reading. You can suspect that the listening or observing has not been precise when you hear such statements as "That gimmick on the side. . . ," "Well, that funny guy in the movie. . . ," "Oh! Millions, I guess." These are your cues to ask for more definite explanations. You teach pupils to observe and listen carefully through your own attitudes toward accuracy perhaps even more effectively than you do through the special practice you provide.

Help needs to be given with recording and reporting skills. Recording what has been learned and reporting these findings—either in oral or written form—are closely related skills. Children in the early primary grades will engage in few independent note-taking activities. The records that help to summarize various aspects of the units will, for the most part, be written by the teacher at pupils' dictation. Even third- and fourth-graders who are able to read independently for information will ordinarily take only very simple notes. By the fifth and sixth grades, however, pupils should be expected to take accurate notes and to outline and summarize material as their particular reference problems demand.

Reporting starts in the early primary grades through sharing and discussion sessions. Third- and fourth-graders can be expected to make written as well as oral reports, but these are likely to be in simple paragraph form. When committees report, each child will probably talk about his particular aspect of the problem. Older pupils should be experimenting with a greater variety of devices for written reports—notebooks, diaries, class newspapers. They should also become more skilled in coordinating the reports of the various group members into a well-organized presentation—a panel discussion, a series of coordinated talks.

Selectivity and critical evaluation are as important in good recording and reporting as they are in effective reading, listening, and observing. Whether the pupil is locating information or sharing it with others, he must determine precisely what is pertinent for his purposes. Flexibility and versatility are important attributes of good recording and reporting. To be most useful, a pupil's style of note-taking must be adjusted to his needs. Sometimes a brief memo will suffice; sometimes a detailed outline will be required. Likewise, pupils must learn to select their means of reporting in terms of their purposes. A panel may be effective for sharing opinions in a controversial area, but a series of separate presentations may be more appropriate when information is to be shared. Dramatization can give a helpful picture of life in other countries or eras, but this medium is not always effective in conveying detailed information. Adaptations of television or radio quiz shows can place specific facts before an audience, but do not always leave the listener with his information logically organized.

In good reporting, there are also a host of problems related to presenting information in a logical order. The written reports of younger children will frequently be confined to a single paragraph, but even in this it is important to think about logical order. Older pupils will be facing the more complex task of pulling together information into several related paragraphs or of organizing an oral presentation so that the listener is taken logically from topic to topic.

Recording and reporting information are among the most difficult language skills for elementary school pupils to acquire. You would do well to plan for definite lessons at the points where your pupils are facing new or more complex skills in these areas. As part of such lessons it will be important to help them to clarify the purpose of the note-taking or reporting activity and to develop standards. Sometimes it can be useful to provide practice for the class as a whole before groups or individuals try to use the new technique on their special projects. Everyone may take notes on a film, for example, or make an outline of the same pages of a social studies text or of a factual story in a basal reader. Pupils may then discuss the kinds of notes or outlines they have made and identify strengths and weaknesses in their work. A second trial session may follow. Then, with clearer insights into effective ways of working, individuals may move ahead on their special projects.

It is very important, in developing better recording and reporting skills, to individualize your assistance. The problem is essentially one of helping pupils to develop effective means of communication. No matter how carefully you develop standards with your class as a whole, there will be countless individual problems as each youngster carries out his special project. Asking one pupil why he selected the point he did in making his notes, helping another to identify vague sentences as he reads his report aloud to you, and checking on the outline prepared by a third—such individualized help represents a wise investment of your time and effort.

Pupils can also assist each other in developing better reporting skills. This is often better done, however, while the report is being prepared than as part of the final reporting session. Reports to the class as a whole should be primarily for sharing new information and the audience should be listening to learn, not to analyze the way in which the speaker has organized his material or to appraise his use of English (although you, as his teacher, will be noting these things). Although you may, at the close of a discussion, ask the listeners to identify what made the report effective or to suggest improvements, you will want to direct most of the discussion to what has been learned. On the other hand, in the committee sessions devoted to preparing the final report it is quite appropriate to focus attention on the aspects of the job. In the interest of an effective final presentation each person can expect to be critical and, in his turn, to be frankly criticized. This is a process in which the teacher can share with good effect, challenging inaccurate statements, asking the group to consider problems of overlapping information, discussing how best to use accompanying visual aids, or even questioning the organization of the presentation.

Perhaps one of the problems of greatest concern to teachers is the tendency of some youngsters to copy directly the words of the book. This can be symptomatic of a number of difficulties, and you will need to study your own situation to discover just what the problem really is. It is important to appraise the purposes for which your pupils are reading. Vague topics phrased in much the same way as the headings of the text are more likely to lead to wholesale copying than are specific questions. You would do well, also, to examine the difficulty of the material. Even college students are tempted occasionally to use the exact words of the text when they are not quite sure what these words mean. Often, too, copying occurs when pupils with limited skill in written expression undertake a report too elaborate for their capabilities. If this is the case, you might, for the moment, revert to the primary teacher's system of developing experience records. Your youngsters may read the material, discuss it, and then suggest important points which you record for them on the blackboard. The resulting cooperative effort can be copied later for each pupil's notebook, or placed on oak tag as part of a class report. Sometimes pupils with limited skills can take a first step toward writing reports of their own by reading for the answer to a question and then closing their books and writing what they have learned in one clear sentence. It can be helpful, also, to allow pupils with limited language skills to summarize what they have learned in a picture, diorama, or mural, and then to write a short paragraph explaining their work.

Your own standards will influence your pupils' standards in note-taking and reporting. If you stress original wording, even though the report is brief, your pupils are more likely to value original wording. If you challenge inaccuracies and encourage pupils whose facts are vague to go back to their books to check, they will begin to challenge each other. Respect for accurate informaton, logical thinking, and clear reporting must be taught.

STIMULATING INDIVIDUAL INTERESTS

In helping pupils understand their world, teachers have a responsibility greater than merely making certain that a common core of basic understandings is acquired by all. We must provide the opportunities for satisfying and challenging experiences that will produce the teachers, scientists, physicians, historians, economists, of tomorrow. The elementary school is not too soon to begin to build toward deep and lasting interests.

Much is being written today about the need for top-flight persons in every field of endeavor. Much is also being written about the type of schooling they need. Sometimes such articles seem to be recommending a greater *quantity* of work—more dates and facts in history, more hours of work in science. Sometimes, too, school systems in other countries are praised for *placing early* in the school program specific courses labeled physics, chemistry, or biology. If we are to help youngsters of high potential to develop the zeal for knowledge that will eventually take them into college and to positions where creative thinking is needed, we must make more discriminating judgments than these regarding the school experiences they need.

One thing an able learner can do efficiently without particularly extending himself is to memorize the dates and facts in textbooks. But is the acquisition of a greater quantity of factual information, vital though facts may be to sound scholarship, our only goal for able pupils? What other attributes are characteristic of the persons on the forefront in any field of endeavor?—ability to think creatively about a problem, to analyze a complex situation, and to propose an original solution? ability to proceed independently? depth and breadth of interest in a chosen field? a critical and analytical approach to new information? Foundations for these attitudes and skills as well as foundations for sound scholarship are laid in the elementary school.

If we are to help able pupils to develop an independent and creative approach to new information, we must make the most of classroom opportunities to explore fields of knowledge extensively and independently. Many possibilities have been described in the preceding sections. It will not be amiss to take a second look as you appraise your efforts to challenge able pupils.

Capitalize upon possibilities for individual and small-group activities. Unit activities offer many occasions for encouraging individual pupils to pursue special interests. Although you will plan carefully to assure a core of basic learnings for everyone, there will be, even in the briefest and least complex unit, some individualized work. In many units, the most extensive opportunities to encourage individual exploration come at the point where small groups assume responsibility for various aspects of the problem. Sometimes able pupils can appropriately undertake some of these special projects alone. However, many important learnings can come from working with others. Able pupils can secure valuable experiences in leadership as well as learn much about clarifying a problem through the group discussions leading to detailed work plans. As group members proceed to locate needed information there is, of course, no limit to the amount of reading an able pupil may do except that set by the reference materials available. When it comes to planning a committee report or developing a play or a mural, he can have valuable experience in organizing and summarizing information. This is not to imply that less able pupils merely wait to be told what to do. They share, also, to the extent of their abilities. One of the important by-products of group experiences which involve youngsters of differing capacities is increased awareness that everyone has a contribution to make.

Many all-class activities planned to enrich concepts can also serve to stimulate individual interests. A bulletin board containing current news releases bearing on the topic under discussion can be a stimulation to an able pupil to turn to recent newspapers and magazines for help.

A classroom exhibit offers another opportunity for each individual to contribute as much as his insights allow. A class magazine or notebook offers many opportunities for special articles. Often a mural or a large-scale diorama can be planned so that individuals may continue to add details as they uncover new information. Such projects can grow as pupils' understandings develop. Youngsters can contribute from many levels of insight and breadths of reading background.

Related problems, side issues, and good suggestions that cannot be incorporated into the plans for a unit may often be the centers of special research by youngsters who have time to spare. Challenging questions may call for special reports. There may be a series of science experiments to try at home or a set of problems upon which the help of parents or community members can be sought. Models or dioramas may at times serve as extra projects. Youngsters may volunteer to write a play as a spare-time activity. Several may report on a television program related to the unit. The teacher may bring in a set of library books concerning an interesting side issue. In classrooms where able youngsters are challenged to work to full capacity, there are always more interesting things to be done than time will allow.

Does the pupil who engages in more extensive activities feel imposed upon? Not if pupil-teacher planning has been genuine and he is convinced of the importance of the project. Many of the most worthwhile activities connected with a unit of work may be classified as "open-ended." Undertaken by a pupil who grasps new ideas slowly, they result in simple products which demonstrate minimum understanding. In the hands of the more able child, they have almost unlimited possibilities. The able learner is not being given "extra" assignments through such projects. He is being involved in educative activities of high interest value and encouraged to explore to his heart's content.

Hold standards of scholarship as high as pupils' capacities will permit. How do you assure that the able pupil has a thorough foundation, that he does not merely flit from one topic of special interest to another? If you have planned your units so that you are the one to guide the study of a core of common learnings, you will have guaranteed for every pupil at least minimum essentials for the problem under consideration. Individual and group activities are, then, in the nature of enriching experiences which allow each pupil to progress as far beyond the learnings considered basic for the entire group as his capabilities permit.

You will take steps, however, to assure that projects undertaken by individuals and small groups are carefully thought through. This is done through the planning sessions which outline the contributions the special projects are expected to make, through planning sessions with committees or individuals, and through reporting periods where special projects are shared and discussed. Here are your opportunities to pose new questions, to point out important aspects of the problem of which pupils have not been aware, to encourage wider reading when able youngsters show a tendency to be satisfied with few details.

Perhaps your most important opportunity to challenge pupils comes as you meet with small groups and individuals while independent work is proceeding. This is your chance to direct an able youngster to a more difficult reference, to ask him to defend a vague statement in his report, to suggest applications to modern living which he has not identified, to encourage him to try a more complicated graphic device for reporting his information. Slower learners will receive your individualized attention, too, but it will be more often in the form of assistance in reading difficult material, in clarifying basic concepts, and in making an understandable report of what has been learned.

You are not contributing to shallow and haphazard scholarship when you encourage the pupil who should be developing wide interests and independence in solving problems to undertake a project of his own. As a matter of fact, since he absorbs information readily, he is much more likely to have acquired a deeper fund of knowledge by the end of the unit than if you had guided his every step through a series of recitation lessons over the textbook. As is true in developing reference skills, *equal* help to pupils of many levels of ability does not mean the *same* help. The more able your pupils, the more they merit your encouragement as they delve deeply into independent pursuits.

Capitalize upon opportunities for growth offered through the entire school day. Your efforts to stimulate individual interests will extend far beyond the blocks of time scheduled for unit activities. Every part of the school day can contribute. Every aspect of the classroom environment—the library corner, the exhibit table, bulletin boards, the science work bench—has a part to play.

Sharing periods have a regular place in most primary schedules. They can also be of value in the intermediate grades. Children can be encouraged to tell about hobbies, to describe week-end trips or visits to museums, to bring pictures or souvenirs received from other parts of the country, to watch for fossils or unusual leaves in the park. Objects of special interest can be placed on a sharing table or in a classroom museum and individuals encouraged to volunteer for special reports when more information is needed.

If children are to understand today's world, special emphasis must be given to interesting them in current happenings. Some teachers maintain bulletin boards to which pupils contribute items of individual or group interest. Occasionally a period may be set aside to discuss topics of unusual interest. Where pupils publish a school newspaper, it is possible to report local or national events. It is important not only to read about current events, but where possible to have firsthand contact with them. Teachers may take time from work designated by the course of study to allow older pupils to follow a local or national election. Younger groups may profitably observe the equipment needed to build the annex to their school or to pave the street. Time may be scheduled for a visit to the scene of some important local event; interesting speakers may come to the school, or children may be encouraged to attend travelogs by prominent persons.

Television, both commercial and educational, is opening new vistas. Some programs will fit well into your on-going activities, but others will merit special attention. If you want your pupils to develop alert curiosity about their world, it is worth the expenditure of the necessary time to follow an event of national significance or to profit from an exceptional science program or travelog. For your class as a whole, such experiences may contribute only to one or two lively discussions, but for an able pupil they may open the doors to independent exploration, especially if you provide appropriate books to read.

You can accomplish much through a recreational reading program. Even for first-graders there is a substantial amount of informational material. In the intermediate grades there is a wealth of biographies, science materials, stories of other lands, and historical tales with authentic detail. Periods when youngsters are sharing their independent reading provide many opportunities to encourage ventures into new areas. Such encouragement need not be for able pupils alone. With the help of your local librarian, you should also be able to bring to class a wide variety of simple, well-illustrated, factual materials for your less able readers.

Many teachers plan the week's schedule so that there is time for individuals to pursue special projects. Others open the classroom doors early in order to help pupils with their special interests. In such independent or "free" work periods a youngster with strong science interests may ask for help in classifying his collection of rocks. Another may need guidance in securing some background about countries represented in his stamp collection. Several pupils may be pursuing special reading interests. Some may write, paint, or draw. Some may work with the special materials on the science table. If you really want to encourage individual interests, you must make sure that your schedule allows time for independent activities.

Back of most youngsters with vital interests and hobbies stand teachers or other adults who share their enthusiasms. Your success in stimulating broad interests in your pupils will depend as much, if not more, on your *attitude* toward knowledge as it will on your scholarship. The teachers who made the most vital contributions to your interests and enthusiasms were those who themselves had deep interests and lively curiosity. So it will be with your pupils. The kind of person you are will determine in large measure the attitudes toward knowledge that you will teach.

BOOKS YOU SHOULD KNOW

Blough, Glenn O., and Campbell, Marjorie H. *Making and Using Classroom Science Materials in the Elementary School.* New York: Dryden Press, 1954. Pp. vi + 229.

Blough, Glenn O., and Huggett, Albert J. *Elementary School Science and How to Teach It.* New York: The Dryden Press, 1951. Pp. xi + 532.

Burnett, R. Will. *Teaching Science in the Elementary School.* New York: Rinehart and Co., 1953. Pp. xv + 541.

Craig, Gerald S. *Science for the Elementary-School Teacher.* New Edition. Boston: Ginn and Co., 1958. Pp. x + 894.

Dale, Edgar. *Audio-Visual Methods in Teaching.* Revised Edition. New York: The Dryden Press, 1954. Pp. 534.

Education for the Gifted. Part II, The Fifty-seventh Yearbook of the National Society for the Study of Education. Chicago: The University of Chicago Press, 1958. Pp. xi + 420.

Grout, Ruth E. *Health Teaching in Schools.* Third Edition. Philadelphia: W.B. Saunders Co., 1958. Pp. vii + 359.

Irwin, Leslie W.; Humphrey, James H.; and Johnson, Warren R. *Methods and Materials in School Health Education.* St. Louis: The C.V. Mosby Co., 1956. Pp. 367.

Learning and the Teacher. 1959 Yearbook of the Association for Supervision and Curriculum Development, N.E.A. Washington, D.C.: The Association, 1959. Pp. x + 222.

Michaelis, John U. *Social Studies for Children in a Democracy.* Second Edition. Englewood Cliffs, N.J.: Prentice-Hall, 1956. Pp. xvi + 523.

Miel, Alice, and Brogan, Peggy. *More Than Social Studies.* Englewood Cliffs, N.J.: Prentice-Hall, 1957. Pp. xii + 452.

Moffatt, Maurice P., and Howell, Hazel W. *Elementary Social Studies Instruction.* New York: Longmans, Green and Co., 1952. Pp. ix + 486.

Olsen, Edward G. (Editor). *School and Community*. Second Edition. Englewood Cliffs, N.J.: Prentice-Hall, 1954. Pp. ix + 534.

Preston, Ralph C. *Teaching Social Studies in the Elementary Schools.* Revised Edition. New York: Rinehart and Co., 1958. Pp. xviii + 382.

Russell, David H. *Children's Thinking.* Boston: Ginn and Co., 1956. Pp. xii + 449.

Smith, Helen Norman, and Wolverton, Mary E. *Health Education in the Elementary School.* New York: The Ronald Press Co., 1959. Pp. 325.

Smith, Marion F. *Teaching the Slow Learning Child.* New York: Harper & Brothers, 1954. Pp. 175.

The Education of Exceptional Children. Part II, The Forty-ninth Yearbook of the National Society for the Study of Education. Chicago: The University of Chicago Press, 1950. Pp. xiii + 350.

Wesley, Edgar B., and Adams, Mary A. *Teaching Social Studies in Elementary Schools.* Revised Edition. Boston: D.C. Heath and Co., 1952. Pp. xiii + 466.

Wittich, Walter A., and Schuller, Charles F. *Audio-Visual Materials: Their Nature and Use.* New York: Harper & Brothers, 1953. Pp. 564.

Witty, Paul (Editor). *The Gifted Child.* The American Association for Gifted Children. Boston: D.C. Heath and Co., 1951. Pp. xii + 338.

Developing Fundamental Skills

CHAPTER 8

The high school graduate's skill (or lack of skill) in reading, writing, spelling, and calculating is frequently used to evaluate the effectiveness of modern educational methods. Actually, evidence from available research (in contrast to the impression sometimes gained by the man on the street) indicates that in developing these skills we are doing as well as, and in most cases better than, we were doing twenty-five years ago. We must remember, however, that youngsters who in a former day would have left school at the age of fourteen with an eighth-grade certificate are now staying with us until they are eighteen and that some whose lack of skill would not have been apparent had they become day laborers or gone into domestic service are applying for clerical or secretarial jobs where their shortcomings are immediately obvious.

Few teachers are willing to rest on their laurels even though research indicates that we are losing no ground in spite of the increased proportions and complexity of our task. Fewer still are content to point to the increasing numbers in our schools as an obstacle to more effective teaching of skills. At no time in our history has there been greater need for individuals who can read critically and intelligently, communicate accurately, interpret correctly the bombardments of radio and television, use the skills of critical thinking and cooperative problem-solving, calculate, and display those physical skills which are important to good health and recreation. As in every other area of growth for which schools are responsible, we are being asked to take on a bigger job than ever before and to do it better.

Helping pupils to develop effective skills will pose a number of major problems for you. As in helping learners to understand this world, you must see clearly your ultimate goals. You must also know how to adjust your program of skill development in the light of the needs of the thirty or more individuals in your room—to decide where to begin and what sequence of experiences to provide. You will be helping your pupils to acquire increased proficiency, and you must plan this help in such a way that they understand the principles underlying the new techniques they are learning. Then, you must be able to provide the practice that will assure a polished performance. Finally, you must be able to individualize your work so that youngsters with varying capacities and needs are given the help they require for maximum progress. These problems are the focus of the sections that follow.

WHAT IS A SKILLED PERFORMANCE?

Effective teaching starts with goals. It is easy to say, in general terms, that we want citizens who can read, write, calculate, and spell, but the teacher who is truly effective in developing skills must be much more precise in his aims. This is not the place to summarize detailed objectives in each of the areas included in what we commonly call the skills. You will undoubtedly have at hand textbooks in which you can review such specifics. However, the problem of establishing goals which was thoroughly discussed in last year's methods course will assume new depth of meaning to you now as you face the full responsibility for planning the activities of a group of boys and girls. A second look, therefore, at the key aspects of a skilled performance to guide you in appraising your plans will be worth while. What kinds of behavior characterize a skilled performer?

A skilled performer is efficient. The word "skilled" implies proficiency. The skilled performer does more than merely arrive at the right answer, construct the desired object, or hit the ball to the right place. He does all these efficiently—wasting little motion and achieving maximum results. If he is reading, he can locate the information he needs with a minimum of effort; he makes use of the guide words in the dictionary and the alphabetical order of the encyclopedia. In arithmetic he is accurate in his number combinations; he has a systematic approach to a column of figures. Regardless of the task, the skilled performer wastes few motions. A gradual reduction of random and inept procedures is evidence of increasing skill.

As a teacher of the skills, you will be more concerned with the way your pupils are working than with the end results of their efforts. No better illustration of this can be found than teaching in the field of physical education. Although the final score in the game is important to the coach, his teaching is constantly focused on techniques. Teachers of the so-called "academic" skills likewise need to be conscious of their coaching roles. You will not help your class to develop the spelling skills they need if, for example, you praise the results of the Friday test but are not concerned with whether the words are learned through letter-by-letter memorization or by the combined use of syllables, sound, and configuration. Correct answers in arithmetic (within limits) can be arrived at by counting on one's fingers, but this technique is certainly not an illustration of a skilled performance.

All this points up the fact that those who teach reading, writing, or problem-solving skills must be thoroughly familiar with the details of a skilled performance in these areas. In textbooks on teaching reading, language, or spelling you may have been frustrated (or even bored) by theoretical analyses of skills. "Why bother with all that theory," is a common cry. "Give us something that we can use." Nevertheless, if you are to be effective as a teacher, you will need to draw constantly on your understanding of the essentials of the skill you are teaching. The effectiveness of every decision you make will depend upon your analysis of your pupils' present performances.

A skilled performer is flexible. A skillful athlete adjusts to new situations. The more complex the game, the more likely the success of his performance will depend upon how well he meets one new situation after another. So it is with reading, arithmetic, and language. Telling *horse* from *house* requires a word-analysis approach different from telling *automobile* from *automatic,* and neither single letters nor syllables will help in deciding which pronunciation of *read* is correct. For the latter, one must be skilled in using the context of a sentence as an aid to pronunciation. If a person is effective in arithmetic, he can do a quick estimate as well as solve the problem with pencil and paper. A stranger is not greeted with the same informality used to greet a classmate, nor is a sports article for the school newspaper written in the same style as would be used for an editorial. Stereotyped behavior is *not* characteristic of a skilled performer; it *is* characteristic of the unskilled or the insecure beginner.

As a teacher you must be conscious of the types of adjustments that represent a skilled performance in a wide variety of situations. More important, you will need to provide situations that call for flexibility. Particularly vital will be the opportunities you can create to help your pupils learn to adjust their skills to the demands of on-going classroom activities. Just as the coach plans practice in a scrimmage situation, so you will need to plan for activities that require pupils to meet new situations. Routine practice exercises, all planned and performed in much the same way and without provision for flexibility and variety, will not do the job.

A skilled performer knows what he is about. A championship tennis player knows his most effective strokes as well as those he is trying to improve. He does not need to wait for his coach to tell him when he has turned in a good performance; he knows how to go about directing his own practice. Furthermore, a championship tennis player understands the principles upon which he is operating. He knows the relationship between the angle of his racket and the bounce of the ball. He works consciously to achieve the stance that will give the best placement and velocity to his serve. So it should be with any skill. An important aspect of growth in learning to read is increased sensitivity to what makes for a skillful reader. A good speller understands the purpose of the techniques he uses to study words. A skilled mathematician does not work mechanically; he has insights into the basic structure of the number system and he draws upon these in solving new problems.

In the classroom it is not uncommon to see uneven attention given to underlying principles. In spelling and English usage, for example, one frequently observes heavy emphasis on rules, not always, however, focused so that learners can see how using the rules leads to a more skillful performance. On the other hand, in some areas general principles are neglected. Both beginning and experienced teachers in college arithmetic classes have sometimes been startled to discover that there is logic to the number system. In spelling, some individuals apparently go through life without discovering the seemingly obvious principle that there is a relationship between the order of the sounds one hears and the way a word is spelled.

Effective teaching of skills focuses on developing two types of understanding. First, the learner needs to become aware of his own performance—to evaluate his own strengths and weaknesses and to take an intelligent share in planning his own practice. He should be able to recognize his successes and failures, whether or not his teacher is at hand to help him evaluate. Second, the learner needs to grow in his understanding of the basic principles governing the skill he is learning. Although he may, for example, still practice for efficiency, he should be aware of the spelling rule that applies to a group of derivatives or have the knowledge of place values that is the key to the number system. Obviously, too, he needs to be helped to learn such basic principles through activities that encourage him to put them to use.

A skilled performer takes pleasure in his skill. If the pupil grows into an adult whose chief source of information is television and radio, it is apparent that we have not been very successful in teaching him to read. Nor is our teaching of arithmetic successful if a student who made reasonably good grades panics in college when asked to calculate an IQ or to work out a percentage. How effective is a physical education program if, after graduation, a student never again participates in a sport? Can we say that our instruction was good if the college student approaches a term paper requiring reference work by asking his instructor "Do I have to use footnotes?"

Favorable attitudes are an important goal in effective teaching of skills. Pupils need to enjoy what they are doing, to feel successful with it, and to want to participate in it. This is not a matter of making school easy, letting down standards, or sugar-coating. It is hard, cold, practical realization of the fact that one does not voluntarily devote a large proportion of time to something which he does not feel is satisfying and worth while. It is possible to force a college student to read by requiring English for graduation from college, but there are no regulations to make him read additional books at home. If we would have him read voluntarily, we must be sure that he finds some values in it. We do not lower standards by this procedure; actually, we raise them. Those who become interested in a subject tend to seek still more challenging experiences in that subject. The professional pianist reaches heights of skill far beyond the amateur, and the amateur who loves music extends his skills beyond the novice who hated his piano lessons in childhood and will have nothing more to do with music. Proficiency, adaptability, understanding, and interest—these are the goals you are seeking in helping your pupils to grow in their command of those areas usually classified as "the skills."

DECIDING WHERE TO BEGIN

You will provide for growth in the fundamental skills at a number of points in your daily schedule. Undoubtedly, you will guide a developmental program—a planned series of activities designed to build increased skill in a systematic fashion. This does not necessarily mean, however, that you will be following adopted textbooks page by page. One of the most challenging problems you will face is that of providing the sequence of activities that will contribute to the maximum growth of your boys and girls. There will also be demands for new techniques stemming from the activities in units centered in the content fields—language skills needed to write business letters in order to secure special information; measuring skills required to draw a map to scale; reference techniques needed so that the encyclopedia can be used more efficiently. In addition, before the year is over, you will probably embark with your pupils upon a number of extensive unit activities in which the major learnings will fall within a skill area—publishing a class magazine, managing a class store, developing an extended recreational reading program. And, if you are making your full contribution to skill development, you will be encouraging individuals with special interests or capacities to venture on their own—to explore the structure of the number system, to embark upon extensive recreational reading, to delve into the history of word origins, to write poetry.

How do you make decisions regarding what activities to provide for a program as varied and complex as that which has just been outlined? A basic principle underlying all effective teaching is to begin where the learner is. You have heard this many times, but you will never understand its true significance until you begin to plan your teaching in the basic skill subjects—reading, spelling, oral and written communication, and arithmetic. The range in competence is likely to be from one or two grades below your pupils' actual grade placement to several grades above. Even in first grade where you might expect that everybody would start even, there will be some youngsters who remind you of kindergarteners and others who are more like second-graders. Similar variation will be found in physical coordination, in strength, in ability to carry a tune, or in any other trait you care to mention.

If you are not to waste time emphasizing the obvious for your able pupils or teaching over the heads of those at the other end of the scale, you will have to be very astute in identifying individual needs. Neither your course of study nor the textbooks designed for your grade level can tell you exactly where to begin. The progress of your class will depend largely upon the quality of your professional insights—your sensitivity to children's needs and your knowledge of the fundamental techniques in teaching skills. How do you decide where to begin?

Assess the range of abilities in your class. A first step to be taken by every teacher in the early fall is to ascertain the range of abilities in his class. Many of the techniques suggested in Chapter 4 will be helpful to you in this. If scores on standardized tests are available for your class, study them. Such scores must, of course, be interpreted with caution in the case of an individual pupil; they are nevertheless helpful in giving you a general idea of what to expect of your class. Where does the median, or middle score, fall? If your pupils are, for the most part, at or beyond their grade expectancy, you must be prepared to provide activities focused toward a higher level of skill than that usually recommended for youngsters of your grade. If, on the other hand, the class average tends to fall generally below grade expectancy, you will need to build from a more basic level than that usually considered appropriate for your grade. Even more important than median scores is the range of abilities in your class. Is your group relatively homogeneous? If so, it will not be necessary to plan for as many levels as you otherwise might. Individual strengths and weaknesses, however, will still make it impossible to plan exactly the same lessons for all. Do you have youngsters who are distinctly below the class level or who are noticeably above? When this is the case, successful teaching means that you must provide the kinds of special help required by these students.

In some schools, teachers file at the end of the year rather complete records of the work in which their classes have been engaged. These may be included in the individual cumulative record folders, or they may be in the form of a supplementary report on the class as a whole. Such records may consist of lists of children's library reading, samples of written work, and lists of the books used most frequently as basal texts. If such records do exist, it is important to examine them. A long summer, however, will have provided opportunities both to forget and to grow. No teacher expects to begin at the exact point where his predecessor left off, and no one who is realistic expects that every pupil will maintain at top efficiency the skills he learned a year ago.

No matter how detailed the records from last year, a survey of present status will be necessary to supplement them. In the early fall most teachers plan challenging activities that will help to reveal pupils' levels of competence. They do not rush to establish reading groups or arithmetic sections immediately. A short autobiography or a report on summer vacation, for example, can show language needs. Sharing periods and planning sessions can be studied for skill in oral communication. A discussion of library reading over the summer can tell you something about reading interests and levels; so will pupils' reactions to the classroom library. As a beginner, you may find it more difficult to identify individual strengths and weaknesses in the confusion of a class discussion than to analyze a set of papers in the quiet of your own room.

The former can be done, however, if you select a single technique and a specific time to watch for it rather than trying to analyze all of the clues in the on-going classroom situation.

You will also find it helpful to use informal classroom tests. A rough estimate of reading level, for example, can be secured in a few oral reading sessions using stories selected from near the beginning and near the end of several books from a series of basal readers. As a rule of thumb, materials which you decide to use for instructional purposes in reading should not contain more than approximately one unfamiliar word in twenty, excluding place names and personal names.

In assessing spelling competence, tests can be developed from the words usually taught in the preceding and succeeding years or, in the school systems where the teacher is free to work with the spelling needs of individual pupils, from master lists indicating the general difficulty levels of common words. Words that are missed by 40 to 50 per cent of the class are good starting points. To plan spelling activities around words difficult for only 5 per cent of the class tends to waste the time of too many pupils on words they already know. On the other hand, to base a spelling program upon words missed by 95 per cent of the class is to set one's sights too high and to risk discouragement, failure, and expenditure of time and effort on words not likely to be crucial in the pupils' writing vocabularies. You would also, of course, study your pupils' written work and make some lists for yourself of the words they are misspelling most frequently in their day-to-day activities.

In arithmetic, your textbooks will offer a variety of review tests on which pupils can try themselves out. Some texts on the teaching of arithmetic contain graded sets of examples which may be helpful. Although one must be careful not to be overly reliant upon workbooks and prepared sets of work exercises, an alert and discerning teacher may find these valuable in determining the proficiency level not only of individual pupils, but of the entire class. The careful teacher will not, of course, neglect opportunities to study individual work at the blackboard or individual seat work. A most effective method of determining individual difficulties in arithmetic is to watch the way the pupil works an example. Sometimes a well-directed question or two, or asking the pupil to "work the examples out loud" will show exactly where he is having difficulty.

Careful observation and listening will be especially effective in determining your pupils' levels of performance in language usage. Written exercises, sufficiently short for the maturity level of the pupils, may be analyzed to determine errors in punctuation and capitalization. Often these can be effectively used in conjunction with activities to appraise spelling competence in actual use. Deciding which errors to correct first may pose a difficult problem. Language is an area in which environmental influences—the home, the community, the peer group—do more to determine usage than does previous teaching. Too often we tend to appraise our pupils by our own college standards rather than by the more realistic expectations for their grade and are overwhelmed by the magnitude of the task we seem to face. In planning your program, priorities should be established on a combined basis of difficulty, need in child life, and need in adult life. Punctuation at the end of a sentence and capitals for the beginning of a sentence, in personal names, and in the name of the community and the school would be stressed early. They are not difficult to teach, and they represent a crucial need both in school and in adult life. How to punctuate a bibliography would come later; it certainly represents a higher level of difficulty, and it is not a need of primary children. To use another example, you will eventually want a pupil to sense the error both in *ain't I* and in *it is me*. In deciding which error to correct first, it is important for you to recognize that *ain't I* will mark him as illiterate in the adult world, whereas there are circumstances under which *it is me* might be considered acceptable (if one judges acceptability by the appearance of an expression in the speech of those recognized as masters of the language). The explanation of why *it is me* is incorrect is also more difficult to put across to a young child. You pace your teaching in the area of language usage, then, to your pupils' needs and capacities for understanding.

The procedures just discussed are equally applicable in the field of physical education. If you will plan early in the fall for games, stunts, and rhythmic activities representative of the level of physical coordination expected of children of the age you are teaching, you will readily identify those youngsters whose achievement is unusual for their age, those whose performance is about what you expected, and those for whom an adjusted program seems indicated. As with any other skill, you will draw upon all that you have learned about typical sequences of development in deciding upon the quality of performance to expect.

The general suggestions just given require many qualifications. There will always be classes where individuals will surprise you by the speed with which they accelerate or by the discouraging plateaus they hit. Appraising pupil performance and deciding where to begin is certainly not easy. Careful, patient searching, examination of records, analyses of tests, study of written work, attention to individuals, and sensitivity to the classroom situation—these used appropriately and with increasing discrimination are the keys to a successful beginning in teaching skills.

Pinpoint specific problems. To make your teaching fully effective, you will need to know individual strengths and weaknesses as well as the general levels at which your pupils are working. Susan and Sally may both have grade scores of 4.0 on a standardized reading test. Susan, however, may have rushed through the work, trying forty items and missing about half of them. Sally may have worked carefully but correctly through twenty and been stopped at this point because time was called. John may misspell seven words in a group of twenty, but every miss may be an excellent phonetic equivalent. Joanna's seven misspelled words may reveal letters so tangled that all semblance to the original word is lost. Analysis of Barbie's arithmetic test may reveal accurate combinations, but no understanding of the process of carrying. Ben, on the other hand, may show an understanding of carrying, but be inaccurate in his combinations. Joe may manage the hard words in his second-grade reader by a shrewd combination of context clues and initial sounds. Anna Beth may have a consistent phonetic approach, but be so dependent on the method that she seldom uses the context to check on the reasonableness of the word. In each of these cases teaching will have to be adjusted to the specific strengths or deficiencies of the individual.

How do teachers become well enough acquainted with pupils to make such fine distinctions? Certainly it is not done all at once at the beginning of the school year. Discovering exactly which techniques a pupil is using well or which he is using poorly calls for continuous analysis. This is true whether you are helping a pupil to become more skilled in reading or arithmetic or helping him to develop into a better swimmer, dancer, or ball player.

Part of the secret of identifying individual needs lies in a classroom organization that allows the teacher to work with individual pupils or with small groups. No matter how skillfully you phrase your questions and stimulate participation, you will find it almost impossible to discover exactly what is troubling each individual youngster as long as you are handling all thirty-five as a single group. Experienced teachers use many techniques to free themselves to work with individuals. These range from planning independent projects with pupils to taking a few minutes to walk down the aisles observing individuals at work. Finding time to give individual help is a crucial problem in the teaching of skills.

Teachers who are skillful in identifying individual needs and difficulties have learned to focus their attention on how a pupil works, not merely on whether he arrives at the correct answers. An inexperienced teacher is often tempted to say, "I can't understand how he ever got an answer like that," and then perhaps adds, "He just doesn't think," or some other general statement that dismisses any further investigation regarding the child's way of working. Conversely, the teacher who is expert in diagnosing individual difficulties says, "I wonder why he made that mistake," and then proceeds to find out. Often this means encouraging a pupil to talk about how he went at the task. As you listen to experienced teachers at work, you will hear many comments that suggest this diagnostic process in action. "How many had trouble with that one?" "You read right over the answer, John. I wonder why?" "Work that problem aloud, Janice, and let's see if we can find where you had trouble."

Survey needs arising from classroom activities. "Begin where the learner is" means more than appraising his particular strengths and weaknesses and the general level of his performance. It also means starting with those problems which he actually faces. If you want your teaching of skills to achieve maximum efficiency, the sequence of experiences and the stress given to each technique will not be determined by the adopted text or by the course of study. It will come from your best judgment regarding the problems confronting your class and the help which the pupils should be given in the light of their present level of competence.

Today's emphasis on making maximum use of the classroom setting rests on sound psychological bases. Problems often arise in the on-going classroom situation which cannot be anticipated in a program of skill development that is rigidly bound to the sequential order of a text or workbook. For example, a social studies unit calls for writing the word *pioneers,* but the word is placed late in the spelling text. A fifth grade has become intrigued with the idea of writing conversation in stories. The first unit in the language text is on the oral aspects of storytelling and reporting, but the use of quotation marks is three units beyond. Some second-graders need to make simple measurements to redecorate their library corner, but *telling time* comes first in the course of study. It does not seem reasonable to teachers faced with such situations to deny pupils help when they need it. All this is simply a realization of the fact that learners operate in terms of the purposes they recognize. Telling them that when they get to high school they will be glad they learned a technique, or even that they can expect to use it three months hence, is not nearly as effective as demonstrating that it can be used right now.

Perhaps an equally important reason for teaching skills when they are actually needed stems from what we know about transfer of learning. Over and over again, studies have indicated the value of practice in situations similar to those in which the skill is to be used. A spelling test on Friday over an assigned list of fifteen words is not the same as spelling correctly all the words in a letter; nor is underlining the subjects and predicates in a mimeographed page of sentences the same as using complete sentences correctly in the story. Dramatizing make-believe introductions when no entertaining is foreseen does not have the sharpness that comes from planning how one's mother should be introduced at tomorrow's party or how the welcoming committee should greet guests. The successful coach may work on specific techniques, but he also provides scrimmage situations. In a similar manner the successful coach of classroom skills makes sure there is sufficient practice in real-life settings. When pupils are being helped to develop skills they actually need in order to be effective in an on-going classroom activity, the natural practice opportunity is readily at hand.

There is still another reason for working in terms of the day-by-day needs of your class. This originates from recognition of the fact that whatever we fail to use repeatedly we tend to forget. The basketball player who works with a construction gang all summer may come back in top physical condition, but his ball handling will not be as proficient as it was at the peak of the preceding season. The same principle applies for all the aspects of reading, spelling, writing, and speaking in which we want pupils to become proficient. There are not enough hours in the school day to maintain all skills at high competence if we rely on drill alone. Whenever we can focus our teaching on a technique which the pupil actually needs all day long, at home after school, and in the summer, we multiply many times over the possibility for life itself to provide the practice that keeps his competence high.

Look at your classroom activities, then, in deciding where to begin. What words do your pupils require for their particular writing problems? What explorations of their social or scientific worlds are they making and what reading vocabulary do these call for?—special words about firemen? policemen? neighborhood stores? pets? What are they trying to write and what difficulties are they meeting?—sentence structure? punctuation? choice of words? What number needs are they facing?—collecting money? measuring? interpreting large numbers? calculating? What reference reading or note-taking skills do they require?—dictionary skills? ability to locate information? outlining? What difficulties are they having in communicating orally with others? —limited vocabulary? tangled sentences? grammatical problems? Here are the points at which your pupils need help, the problems they are actually facing in which they will put their new skills to use day after day.

Use pupil needs, not the textbook, to determine sequence. Even experienced teachers are sometimes doubtful of their ability to develop high proficiency in skills if they work from classroom needs alone. Although they see the merit of beginning at the level at which pupils are operating, they often wonder if it is not safer to follow, from that point, the logically organized plan of the adopted text. Will the normal course of classroom activities actually require those competencies pupils will need in adult life? Won't there occasionally arise classroom situations that will demand skills well beyond those the pupils are capable of learning at their present level of maturity? Won't there be gaps in pupils' learning?—points at which they will miss a step in a necessary sequence of experiences? new problems to which they will come completely unprepared because they have faced no previous demands for competence? These questions disturb the veteran as well as the neophyte in teaching.

Planning a program in terms of those activities that pupils see as purposeful certainly demands much more of a teacher than merely following an adopted text or course of study, but the result will not be sketchy and inadequate if you understand and practice basic principles for effective teaching in skill development. Will the normal course of classroom activities actually require those competencies pupils will need in later life? It will if you make sure that your pupils are working in a stimulating classroom atmosphere. There must be many things to read—books, bulletin boards, class plans, directions, letters. There should be motivation for communication—class newspapers and magazines, writers' corners, bulletin boards, reports to be written, letters and get-well cards to be sent, sharing periods, planning sessions, discussions, conversations with teachers and friends. It is essential that there be opportunities to calculate—purchases to be made, party favors to be measured and counted, lunch money to be recorded, science projects to be graphed. Every skill needed in adult life can be identified in simpler forms in such classroom settings. In fact, a stimulating classroom atmosphere will demand so many competencies that your most crucial problem will often be to set up priorities for where to begin. Even more mature groups will not necessarily recognize the importance of better techniques, however, unless they can be helped to see where their present performance is inadequate. This means that teachers must develop a keen sense of what is needed for an efficient performance in each new situation. If, in your own case, you were taught arithmetic, grammar, and punctuation largely as intellectual gymnastics unrelated to daily use, you will now have to face the challenge of discovering the practical values of these areas. If you do not sense their applications to daily living, you are not likely to demand of your pupils the level of competence they should be displaying in their day-by-day classroom activities.

But, if you work from the needs of the group rather than from the sequence of the textbook, won't you be teaching over your pupils' heads at times? Not if you recognize that your instruction can be focused at many levels. At some points you will be building readiness; at others, you will introduce a new technique with the knowledge that it is not likely to be used frequently enough to warrant much stress; and at still others, you will take time to do the job thoroughly. First-graders, for example, may watch as you look up a topic in the encyclopedia and learn to appreciate such books as sources of information, or they may copy a correctly spelled letter to mother and build readiness for later spelling activities thereby. Second-graders, needing to know how many cupcakes will be required for a party if each is to receive half a cake, may stand together in two's and be counted. Fourth-graders, writing the only business letter they will need for months, may pattern their letter after the form in their language texts without stopping to become sufficiently skilled to reproduce it from memory. Fifth-graders may experiment with more precise choice of adjectives in their creative stories without learning to identify all types of adjectives. Such preliminary experiences not only build more mature attitudes toward the importance of correct form, but they also lay valuable foundations for later intensive work.

Granted that the classroom environment will supply ample opportunities for a higher level of skill development, isn't it likely that there will be gaps in pupils' learning if the sequential order of a text-

Summer Demonstration School, University of Cincinnati,
D. Arthur Bricker, Photographer

Understanding grows from experience. Concrete aids contribute to accurate number concepts.

Public Schools, St. Bernard, Ohio,
D. Arthur Bricker, Photographer

The skilled performer is increasingly efficient. Singing games develop coordination and a sense of rhythm.

Public Schools, Hamilton County, Ohio,
Audrey B. Norris, Photographer

Plans for practice should encompass the entire day. New words are reviewed through experiences in creative writing.

Summer Demonstration School, University of Cincinnati,
D. Arthur Bricker, Photographer

Choose activities that facilitate self-direction. Special interest reports encourage independent reading.

book is not followed? This depends on whether a teacher understands the principles governing the sequence of development in the various skill areas well enough to deviate intelligently from basal texts. Actually, the order of topics in any textbook is to some extent arbitrary. You will perhaps see this most clearly if you examine several books intended for the same grade level. In language texts, for example, there is no basic reason for placing storytelling before letter writing except the author's professional judgment as to which will typically be needed first. In basal readers the authors will have used a variety of word lists as a guide to their choice of vocabulary, but there is no one key set of words with which all learners should begin. As soon as primary youngsters develop the knack of analyzing new words for themselves, the doors to the world of books swing open rapidly. Similarly in arithmetic, there is no hard and fast rule that demands that telling time should be placed before or after beginning to count; youngsters can start to multiply by adding; percentage, as related to dollars and cents, has been taught both as an approach to fractions and as the next step after fractions. In spelling, words are assigned to grade levels on the basis of information regarding the difficulty of the word, its importance in adult writing, and the point at which it will probably be most needed by children. (*Santa Claus* is not an easy word to spell, for example, but it is needed in first and second grades.) Moreover, no two authors of spelling texts have ever arrived at exactly the same choice of words for each grade. You need not, then, be seriously worried if you use your texts as resources and at times reverse the order of their topics, as long as you, yourself, are aware of the breadth of competence you want your pupils to acquire eventually.

But what about gaps, in the sense of failing to provide the step-by-step development needed for real competence? Won't pupils lack the background to solve new problems? After all, textbook writers do use some type of spiral plan, for a lesson-by-lesson teaching procedure, so that the pupil is required to perform a skill with progressively increasing competence. Letter writing, in more complex forms, may be spaced throughout a language text, or work on fractions may be started simply in an early section of an arithmetic text and then returned to at more difficult levels. Working from pupil needs does not imply that we fail to recognize that such step-by-step progression to higher levels of skill is important. Not all learners, however, acquire new skills by taking practice in doses of exactly the same size. One pupil could arrive at a high level of competence through a series of lessons evenly spaced over several months; a second might reach the same point through lessons concentrated in two or three intensive blocks of work. In one study in arithmetic,[1] all formal practice was delayed for some pupils until the sixth grade. Then under intensive instruction they achieved in one year, as measured by standardized tests, the level expected of pupils of the same age for whom arithmetic had been a regular part of a school day. This is the same principle that prompts a mathematics faculty to offer to mature college students a year of algebra which is the equivalent of two or more years of high school work. Of course, this is not an argument for postponing all learning until the pupil is mature enough to grasp it in the shortest possible time span. Such evidence does suggest, however, that you can safely adapt textbook sequences to the particular needs of individuals in your class. In some instances this may mean taking a more mature group into an advanced series of problems which have been placed several lessons later in the texts. In the case of immature youngsters, it may mean providing additional work to supplement the practice exercises in a text.

Such evidence suggests, also, that there will be times when you can well afford to wait until classroom activities demand a new level of competence, secure in the knowledge that the increased maturity of your group will help them take a larger jump with ease. For example, in a school where both primary and intermediate grades are amply equipped with encyclopedias and other standard reference texts, primary pupils might develop considerable proficiency with these materials through repeated experiences, each contributing to slightly increased competence. On the other hand, in a school where only the intermediate grades are equipped with such teaching aids, fourth-graders could learn of the same techniques in a concentrated series of lessons. It is this same recognition of the greater ease and speed with which more mature learners can acquire skills that offers teachers a ray of hope if they find in their rooms pupils of average intelligence who are severely retarded in one or more of the fundamental skills. Given intensive remedial instruction, such youngsters have the mature intellectual ability needed to catch up (provided they have not built up such strong feelings of failure and frustration that they cannot bring themselves to try).

Developing the sequence of activities in the skills areas in terms of

[1] L.P. Benezet, "The Story of an Experiment," *The Journal of the National Education Association*, XXIV (November, December, 1935), pp. 241-44, 301-303; XXV (January, 1936), pp. 7-8.

the actual needs of a class does suggest that there will be details left for high school teachers and even college professors to polish. You have undoubtedly learned in college fine points about listing footnotes and bibliographies that you did not master in high school. In all probability you also improved your library reference techniques and your ability to do an intelligent job of skimming. However, you did not come to college completely unprepared for these tasks. Your high school teachers helped you to develop as much expertness as your high school work demanded. As a matter of fact, even if your high school teachers had tried to develop all the skill your college professors seemed likely to demand, the chances are that, short of intensive drill month after month, you would have forgotten at least part of whatever you had not been using regularly. This is also true at the elementary school level. Teachers are sometimes accused of neglecting certain techniques. The truth often is that lack of use caused them to lose sharpness before the time when high school teachers demanded them.

DEVELOPING NEEDED INSIGHTS

The development of higher levels of proficiency in skills is really a combination of helping pupils to see the need for more expertness; building insight into the principles that govern the more effective way of operating; and then providing sufficient practice over days, weeks, perhaps months, to develop the smoothness and proficiency of a truly skilled performance. If your program of skill development is planned in the light of pupil needs revealed through on-going classroom activities—as suggested in the preceding section—you should have little difficulty in helping your boys and girls to see the value of more expertness. Whether they achieve successfully a higher level of performance depends upon your skill as a teacher. You must develop your lessons so that your boys and girls acquire insight into the new skill and you must plan for practice activities that will make maximum contributions to their proficiency. The present section considers some of the principles that should guide your teaching in developing pupils' insights into more expert ways of working. The section that follows takes a look at the problem of providing for effective practice.

The points to think about in planning a lesson to help pupils develop higher levels of understanding were discussed in detail in Chapter 6. Those suggestions could be summarized in a framework for a lesson plan that looks as follows:

What are my goals? What new techniques am I trying to develop? What behaviors do I expect of my pupils at the end of this work?

How can I give my pupils a sense of purpose? What is my starting point with them. Are there classroom problems to be recalled? Are there analyses of previous lessons to think about? What earlier plans should they be helped to remember?

What steps do I need to take to help my pupils understand the new technique? Are there questions I should ask to uncover what they now know? Are there illustrations I shall need to use? What questions will help them to arrive at the new principle? What explanations should I be prepared to give? What activities should we do together so that I will know that my point has been put across?

What practice shall I provide? In what types of activities should I have them engage today in order to make sure that the new understandings and techniques are put to use? How am I going to guarantee continued use of the new technique so that competence is maintained?

How shall I evaluate their progress? What behaviors will tell me that they have acquired the new technique? What evidence of this do I wish to collect today? What evidence from other classroom activities will tell me that the new technique is actually being put to use?

These are the types of questions you must ask in preparing yourself to help your boys and girls to gain insight into a new way of working. What are some of the principles of effective teaching that you should have in mind as you develop the details of your lessons?

Insight comes gradually. Methods in the teaching of the fundamental skills—reading, spelling, English usage, arithmetic—have an interesting history. If you have ever examined textbooks of the early 1900's, you will recall many evidences of the "mental discipline" theory of transfer. Even for young pupils, lists of long and difficult spelling words were common; arithmetic problems made use of very large numbers; much time was given to grammatical principles, the diagramming of sentences, and lists of punctuation and spelling rules.

Early psychological studies exploring the validity of the mental discipline concept demonstrated that a pupil could be letter perfect in grammatical rules and yet not use them effectively in daily life. Likewise, youngsters who could reduce 396/480 to its lowest terms were not automatically proficient with halves, quarters, and thirds. As a result of these studies, there was increased interest in discovering exactly which techniques would be most useful in daily life, with the object of focusing drill directly upon them. Studies were made, for example, of the relative difficulty of addition combinations in arithmetic. Teachers were urged to provide for more repetition of those items known to be most troublesome. In spelling and grammar, memorization of rules with the objective of being able to give the rule or identify correctly the parts of speech in a sentence was de-emphasized.

You may hear occasional comments that suggest misunderstanding of the shift in emphasis. "Schools don't care about grammar any more." "Arithmetic is much easier today." Such statements do not reflect the true situation. The purpose of the research was to discover ways of emphasizing correct form in grammar that would actually result in better speech, and of teaching arithmetic, reading, and spelling so that pupils would handle competently problems they face in adult life.

Almost as quickly as there appeared studies questioning the effectiveness of an approach to skill development based on the principles of mental discipline, there came others that suggested new procedures whereby rules and grammatical principles could be made more effective in daily living. Whereas memorizing a rule and applying it to a series of exercises isolated from day-by-day living did not guarantee its use in daily life, concentrating on how it could be used to solve everyday problems rendered it very valuable, indeed, to learners. Grammatical concepts can be of great value, for example, if a person learns how to apply them in proofreading his papers and correcting his own speech. Then, with a number of studies, influenced in part by the Gestalt psychologists, came more emphasis on helping a pupil to see relationships in such a way that he would be able to guide his own activities independently. A pupil who has memorized arithmetic combinations is helpless to do anything except guess if he forgets 7×8; whereas one who understands the relationship between multiplication and addition may add together seven 8's, or solve the problem from some other angle. Hence today the tendency is to de-emphasize the flash-card type of drill as a basic technique in developing a new skill and to work first toward understanding. Here, too, you may hear comments reflecting a misconception of this shift in emphasis—"They don't believe in drill any more," "Children today are expected to learn without really working at it." Again, this is not the case. What we are trying to do is to develop the kind of understanding that makes a person able to handle a new situation competently and to use practice at the point in the learning process where it is most likely to be effective.

Concurrently with the research investigating the importance of helping a pupil to understand why he should proceed as he does and of providing ample practice in situations similar to those with which he will be dealing in real life, there were also studies which showed that growth in understanding is a gradual process. The very young child, for example, does not deal well with complex abstractions. For him the study of grammar may have its beginnings with "People say it this way" or "Tell us what John *did*—what you've said doesn't tell a whole story." Likewise, understanding of the rules of capitalization and punctuation may start with "We begin people's names with capital letters because their names are important," or "We put a period here to show that this idea is finished," or "This is a new idea, so we'll show it by using a capital letter." In word analysis, the beginning may be "In the word *comes* I can see *come*"; in arithmetic, it may be "See in how many ways I can make my beads say four."

The result of our investigations of the way concepts and generalizations grow, of the importance of developing understandings that can be and are used, and of the value of putting these understandings to work in many real-life situations has been to place the complicated abstract formulation of a rule late in the learning process. The more technical aspects of grammar, the difficult punctuation rules, the complex spelling rules are, therefore, customarily taught as a climax to the pupil's growing mastery of a field, not as the first step. In grammar, for example, we have recognized that grasping the fascinating logic of our language is a task that takes considerable intellectual maturity. If we try to do the entire job in the elementary school, all but the brightest youngsters (and some of them, too) are discouraged and baffled, even though they may, after long hours of drill, memorize abstract definitions of the various parts of speech and learn to pick out the most obvious examples. Place the same challenge in the ninth or tenth grade with a teacher who does not consider the task of teaching grammar to be an imposition, and children with reasonable intellectual ability take to it with considerable zeal. This does not mean, of course, that grammar is completely neglected earlier. Teachers begin to work for correct speech as soon as youngsters walk in the kindergarten door. As writing begins, they talk about good sentences. When pupils gain additional skill in written expression they experiment with more precise adjectives and adverbs and learn the names for these aids to more picturesque writing.

Similarly, in teaching reading we do not start with the structure of the phonetic system. Word analysis is begun only after pupils have acquired a familiar stock of words which can be used for the purpose of comparison in understanding how one can identify familiar sounds. The complexities of rules for syllabication, the formation of plurals, and the addition of prefixes and suffixes will come later in the gradual process of building understandings about the structure of words.

There are close parallels in other skill areas. In learning to swim, youngsters are encouraged to float and paddle first—to get the general "feel" of what it is like to be in the water—before they begin to work on precise arm and leg movements. They become acquainted with general demands of the game before they get down to the detail of rules or the precise techniques of handling the ball. In music, time-honored exercises and scales have been replaced as the first experiences for beginners by little tunes. Reading notes comes later, after there are some familiar songs to use as points of reference.

In helping pupils to develop a new technique in reading, perfect a complex arithmetic process, or learn a new rule of punctuation or capitalization, your first step, then, will be to develop as much understanding as is necessary in accordance with the new problem and the maturity of your group. At some points your explanation will be very simple. At others, you will be working toward a rather thorough development of abstract principles. If you try to develop the abstraction too soon, you are likely to have your pupils memorizing and reciting principles they do not understand. If, however, you fail to seize legitimate opportunities to develop more basic understandings, your class will go on to the next grade lacking the background they should have. The teacher who presents all the new words before the story and never says to a child "You can figure that one out" is handicapping his growth toward independence in word analysis. So is the one who fails to help third- and fourth-graders begin to develop acquaintance with the more common grammatical terms.

Understanding grows from experience. If a first step in developing a new or more efficient way of working is to help pupils understand the new process, how do teachers go about it? One of the most important educational principles is that understanding grows from a wealth of concrete experiences. It is easy enough, for example, to drill until a first-grader (or even a four- or a three-year-old) will say "four" when you say "two plus two." If, however, he is to understand what he is saying, he will need many experiences with real objects in real situations such as "We need four chairs. How many each should John and

Billy bring?" Or "There are four people in our group, and our lunch plate has two cookies. How many more do we need?"

Among the most marked shifts in teaching in every skill area is a vastly increased emphasis in the early grades on building concrete background. In reading, we work toward a vocabulary of thoroughly familiar words with which pupils can begin to make comparisons and derive sounds. Spelling is postponed until the pupil has a supply of words he can read, and the first spelling activities provide the experience of copying familiar words correctly. Work with numbers involves many types of concrete objects, ranging from actual classroom equipment to semi-abstract number representations. Sharing and discussion periods, where pupils can use clear sentences to communicate, precede written expression. Concepts develop from concrete experience as truly in the areas of language and number as in the fields of social studies, science, and health.

If you have watched primary teachers at work, you will have observed many illustrations of how to provide meaningful concrete experience. "If we have ten pieces of paper and five people, how many go to each person? It's like putting ten pieces into five piles, isn't it?" "Sometimes the way a word starts will help you. Does anyone know this much of it?" "Was that all you wanted our story to say about the fireman, Ellen? Then what mark do we use to show you are finished?" "Let's look at these two letters and see if we can remember how to write them so that people can tell which is which."

Concrete experience is no less important in the upper grades. In arithmetic, for example, carrying and borrowing become much more meaningful if they are done first with bundles of toothpicks and a little later with an abacus. Fractions are better understood when circles or other geometric figures are actually cut apart. Tables of measurement make more sense if pint and quart measures can be handled. Similar illustrations may be found in the area of language arts. Youngsters who have had experience in using adjectives to make their stories more colorful and descriptive are developing meanings for the concept *adjective* which makes its function as a part of speech more useful in later explorations of the grammatical structure of our language. The function of a prefix is developed more readily if pupils are thinking of a group of words they know, such as *untie, unwashed, uninteresting.* It is easier to list the characteristics of good oral reading if pupils have had satisfying experiences with good oral performances. And, to round out the examples, it is easier to talk about precisely what is needed for improved skill in a game after a pupil has had sufficient experience to know where his present techniques are inadequate.

Your starting point, then, in making a new technique meaningful to your class is to think about the concrete experiences that might serve for illustrative purposes. Have your pupils already had many experiences closely related to the step you wish to help them to take? If so, you may need only to locate two or three good illustrations in a textbook, or refer to several previous class experiences closely related to what you want to teach. "We've been discovering many ways to sound out words for ourselves. The words in this story will help you to find a new way. Let's look at the words I've written here." "You have noticed the paragraphs in the stories in your reader. How do you think they decide when to start a new paragraph?" On other occasions you may need to plan for extensive experiences with concrete materials —as you might to clarify the process of borrowing in subtraction, or to build understanding of fractions.

There are exceptions to every rule, but generally the illustrations you choose as a basis for your new lesson should focus as clearly as possible on exactly what you want to teach—no more and no less. Usually, too, it is safer to teach one step at a time. For example, learning where the punctuation marks go in a simple quotation (John said, "I can do it.") is quite sufficient for most classes for one lesson, and the explanation that the quotation marks go around exactly what John said is enough. Woe betide the ambitious beginner who tries to work on simple quotes, divided quotes, and indirect quotes all in the first lesson! There is, however, another side to this. If you are sure that your class has had experience with differing forms, you had better be prepared to show the reasons for the differences. The plural of *lady* is *ladies,* but the plural of *monkey* is *monkeys.* If this is common knowledge in your class, you will be wise to use both types of examples in deriving the rule. By the same reasoning, one might well work on *their* and *there* in the same spelling lesson, but decide not to go out of one's way to discuss *pear* and *pare* during the lesson when *pair* is the focus of attention. Similarly, in teaching games, a simplified version is often used first and only the essential rules of the game stressed until pupils begin to develop a "feel" for what they are doing. Refinements are then added as the youngsters' increased competence demonstrates that they are ready for these.

Understanding comes through active participation. Another inescapable psychological principle is that to understand, each of us has to "see for himself." From your own experience, you will realize that if your background has been unusually rich and you are on the verge of discovering a new principle for yourself, someone else can phrase it for you. All too often, however, telling the learner the answer enables him to say the correct words but not necessarily to know what he's doing. Because this is true, much of your teaching of new punctuation and grammatical rules, arithmetic principles, or new ways of analyzing words will have to be of an inductive nature—starting with concrete experiences and asking the questions that stimulate your pupils to work their own ways through to a new discovery.

It is realization of the importance of helping pupils to arrive at their own conclusions that prompts a first-grade teacher to list a series of familiar words beginning with the same sound and then say to her pupils "Can you hear how they start? Now can you find the letters that make that sound?" rather than putting the single letter on the board and saying "Today we're going to learn the sound this letter makes." In arithmetic this principle causes a first-grade teacher to encourage youngsters to derive number combinations with concrete objects.

Beginning teachers sometimes grow impatient with the inductive process. Why not merely tell pupils the answer and save time? This is what Sally Archer tried to do with the *y* to *i* rule in spelling:

SALLY ARCHER

Boys and girls, today we're going to learn a new spelling rule. I've written it here where we can all see it. Who'd like to read it for us?

(Jimmy reads, "When the word ends in *y* preceded by a consonant, we form the plural by changing the *y* to *i* and adding *es;* but when the word ends in *y* preceded by a vowel, we form the plural by adding *s*.")

How many know what a consonant is?

(Several vague answers are to the effect that it is not a vowel, so Sally takes time to get vowels and consonants straight.)

Now let's look at our rule again. When the word ends in *y* preceded by a consonant, what do we do? Read it for us, Jerry.

(Jerry reads.)

And when it ends in *y* preceded by a vowel? Who'd like to read that one?

(Alice reads.)

Now let's try it out. I've written some words up here. [Sally's list contains *lady, baby, key, donkey,* and others.] Who'd like to do *lady*? Make it into more than one. What would it be, Bruce?

(Bruce says "Ladies.")

And how would you spell it?

(Bruce does so correctly—this is a word he's used many times before.)

Why did you make it *ies,* Bruce?

(Bruce says "Because it's more than one lady.")

Yes, but what did our rule say?"

(Bruce looks confused. Betty volunteers, "You change the *y* to *i* and add *es*.")

That's right, but *when*?

(Peter chimes in, "When it's more than one.")

You can complete this lesson for yourself, in all probability drawing on at least one harassing experience of your own. Contrast this approach with Diane Smith's lesson:

DIANE SMITH

Boys and girls, we've been learning to spell a number of words that have interesting things happen when we make them plural. What do I mean by *plural*?

(Several answers assure her that the term is clear.)

I thought you would like to look at some of these and see if you can figure out a rule that would help you when you meet new ones like them. Let's look at the list here on the board. [Her list has familiar words such as *lady, baby,* in one column; *key, donkey, boy,* and others are in a second.] Let's spell the plurals of these.

(Various children do so correctly because the words have been learned previously.)

What happens to all the words over here?

(Someone volunteers that the *y* has been changed to *i*.)

But what about these?

(Several people say "Just *s*.")

Now why?

(From this point on the pupils analyze the lists until the two parts of the rule are roughly stated.)

Now let's try it out on some words we've not spelled before. [Diane's next list contains words familiar from reading but well beyond the spelling vocabulary of her group. Here they must use the rule to be right.]

"But," you say, "some procedures just can't be explained; they have to be memorized." This is certainly true. How to punctuate business and friendly letters would be a good example. So would the placement of the punctuation with reference to the quotation marks in a direct quotation. There are also some obscure spelling rules to which there are more exceptions than words that follow the rule, and other rules which, although they work consistently, apply to only a handful of words. It is important for you to realize that there are many times when you and your pupils will look at some examples, figure out from your concrete experience with them what the right procedure is without trying to discover a logical explanation and then practice the new process consistently until its use is assured.

On the other hand, the chances are very good that our present-day understanding of how to make learnings meaningful for pupils was not always acted upon at the time when you were taught some of your basic language and number concepts. Some of the procedures that you memorized blindly may well have logical explanations that would be helpful to your pupils. Consider, for example, the problem of division by fractions. How do you divide 8 by ½? "That's easy," you say; "invert the fraction and multiply." But why? "Well it's the rule; you can't explain it exactly." Now let's go back a little to a spot where you are more sure of yourself and see. What do you want to know when you divide 8 by 2? How many two's, or pairs, in 8? What about 9 by 3? How many sets of three in 9? What about 8 by 1? How many one's in 8? All right, now what are you asking when you divide 8 by ½? How many halves in 8? Could you draw a picture of it? The shortcut is to invert and multiply. Do you see why, now? Obviously, more illustrations would be needed for youngsters, but this represents an example of the kind of understanding you yourself must have if your pupils are to be helped to develop insights.

Take an example from the field of language—that baffling problem of possessives. When is it *'s* and when *s'*? You can probably give the rule. "Use *'s* when the word is singular and *s'* when it is plural except in the case of plurals that do not end in *s*. In these cases use *'s*." Is there a *why* that could help you? Let's look at some examples:

The boy's coat	The woman's coat
The boys' coats	The women's coats

Forget about the *s* for a minute. Where does the apostrophe go each time? After the full word that tells the owner—*boy* or *boys, woman* or *women*. All of them end in *'s* except *boys'* where the *s* after the apostrophe is omitted. Can you guess why it has been lost? Probably because the double *s* was awkward to say and was finally dropped from our speech and writing.

In all probability, you will need to study the history of numbers and language before you develop the sureness of understanding that helps you to phrase such explanations clearly for your class. This is particularly important for teachers in the upper grades where more complex understandings are needed. Even at the primary levels, however, there will be many times when the quality of the pupils' learning will depend on your insights into the nature of the process you are teaching.

MAKING PRACTICE PAY OFF

Your efforts to help your pupils to understand the principles on which they are operating have as their ultimate goal the independent use of these principles in meeting new situations. Knowing the sounds of letters is not of much value unless a pupil can use them in working out new words for himself. There is not much point in exploring the relationships among addition, subtraction, division, and multiplication facts if this doesn't help to solve new problems. "I didn't know what 34 ten's was," reported second-grade Jimmy who was figuring out how much money would be collected if everyone brought a dime, "but I knew that there were ten dimes in a dollar. So I had three dollars, and 4 ten's was forty cents."

Your lesson plans, in order to develop proficiency in skills, must include ample opportunities to try out newly learned techniques. Practice can be planned on at least three levels. First, teachers typically allow time for some cooperative activities following the development of a new technique in order to make sure that everyone understands. They punctuate a few sample sentences at the board, try out the new sound in some unfamiliar words, work out three or four arithmetic problems together with the pupils. Second, teachers often conclude a lesson with some individual work. This may be in the form of examples prepared by the teacher or found in a textbook or it may be a classroom problem in which the new technique is needed—pupils use their new knowledge about punctuating letters by writing a thank-you note or put to use in a social studies unit a lesson on note-taking or outlining. Such an independent work session provides time to satisfy yourself that individuals really can use what they've learned. Third, practice activities concluding the lesson that develops a new principle are frequently followed with additional practice for several more days, or in some cases for several weeks, until the new way of working is thoroughly established.

You will most certainly have discovered, if you have made a careful survey of the needs of your class, that you have no time to waste. Every minute of practice must pay off. You will have to provide, before the year is out, for every aspect of the skill appropriate to the maturity of your class. You will have to think about the needs of those youngsters in your room who are the most able as well as those who are having the greatest difficulty. And you are going to have to employ teaching methods that guarantee maximum learning from the practice experiences you provide.

Practice activities need to be selected with maximum growth in mind. A common weakness of beginners in planning for special practice is to adopt three or four types of activities that pupils seem to enjoy (and with which the teachers themselves feel at home) and then to use these routinely. Every reading group ends with a set of factual questions (or, perhaps even more limited, with pupils reading the entire story aloud in turn). Spelling lessons routinely require everyone to do all the practice activities provided by the textbook author (or end with an assignment to write each word five times). A system of completion or multiple-choice sentences is used over and over again for practice with each new item of English usage. The arithmetic exercises provided in a textbook or workbook are always worked completely and then reworked by being placed on the blackboard.

Obviously, no such routine pattern of activities is going to accomplish efficiently the goals you seek. It does not provide for the varied and flexible ability to use new techniques that your pupils will need as they try to adjust to many classroom situations. You must learn to plan for variety in your practice sessions. Effective practice contributes to many facets of the skill and requires pupils to apply general principles in many types of situations. In planning for reading activities, for example, some stories lend themselves well to reading for factual information, but some should be read mainly for the gist of the plot; some should be enjoyed for their humor, and some analyzed for the author's effective choice of words. Some lists of spelling words will make a contribution to children's understanding of how to use plurals; some may provide excellent help in listening for syllables; and some will contain more than the usual supply of words with double letters. An efficient teacher appraises such possibilities in the light of the strengths and weaknesses of his pupils. If you find yourself asking in general terms for suggestions for "seat work" or "busy work" or saying to yourself as you plan "I don't have to think about the arithmetic for tomorrow; we will just take up . . . ," it is time to re-evaluate the effectiveness of your skills program. What you plan should do more than merely keep your pupils busy and in their seats. This is the reason why your plans for every lesson must start with goals—with the needs of your pupils and the types of behavior you wish them to acquire.

Another error frequently made by beginning teachers, and equally conducive to wasting time, is that of attempting to use indiscriminately all the suggestions provided by the author or authors of whatever textbooks are adopted for your grade. Teachers' manuals will, in many cases, almost put the words of a lesson into your mouth. There will be suggested activities in the youngsters' texts, still others in your teachers' manual, and in some schools you will find your room equipped with workbooks replete with all sorts of supplementary devices. These are a treasure chest of suggestions that will be of great assistance in providing the variety your pupils need. If, however, you use all such suggestions without discrimination, you are going to waste pupils' time. You will undoubtedly be duplicating for some pupils practice already amply supplied by on-going classroom activities. And, although such a procedure might seem to provide well-rounded experiences for all, you may not be giving enough help to the pupil who is having unusual difficulty. Equally important, your attempts to follow conscientiously all the suggestions in texts and workbooks are likely to leave very little time to devote to solving problems arising from class activities if, indeed, you get to such problems at all.

Effective choice of practice activities cannot be made on the basis of "It keeps them busy," "It can't do them any harm," or even "They enjoy it." As suggested earlier in this chapter, you, not the textbook author, must be the one to decide what choice of activities will make for the most effective growth for the individuals in your class. Your planning should include thoughtful evaluation of the special needs of your class and of the activities you might use. You may have some youngsters who spell phonetically but miss the nonphonetic elements. Which of their new words could be used to stress the need for a careful look? Carrying is still uncertain for another group. Which selection of problems will provide the needed practice? When asked to punctuate sentences which the teacher writes at the board, most in the class do very well, but they are woefully careless in their written work. What new activity would put them on their own so that proofreading could be stressed?

Pupils need to become self-directing in their practice. The most carefully chosen practice opportunities lose much of their value if pupils are not aware of the purpose. Effective teachers of physical skills often put teachers of the traditional "three R's" to shame by the care with which they help learners to see the specific purposes of the practice. Listen to someone helping a tennis or basketball player, and you will hear reasons for his suggestions. "You are placing your foot so that you can't get a good sweep with your arm. Try turning a little." "It takes more of an angle than that. See how your ball bounces." In learning to read, to communicate, and to calculate, pupils need the same sense of knowing what they are working for. They must recognize their own strengths and weaknesses; they need to know why the new techniques are important; and they must see how the practice in which they are engaged will help them achieve these new skills.

There are many points at which you should involve pupils in identifying their needs and thinking about the purpose of the new practice activities. In the first place, any assignment you make should be introduced so that its purpose and the reason why it is important are made clear. You will recognize in this statement a reflection of earlier discussions on lesson plans: *What are my goals? How can I make this activity purposeful to my pupils?* Julia Simpson starts a fourth-grade lesson on the use of capitals in place names by saying "As I read your papers I noticed that many of you are still forgetting to use capital letters when you write the names of cities. Look to see if you have a large red *C* in the margin anywhere on your paper." Jackie Anson starts an oral reading session of her second grade with "We wanted to read this story aloud because we thought it was exciting, didn't we? Do you think you can make it sound exciting?" Andy McKay begins a handwriting lesson with "Some of you objected because your spelling words were marked incorrect when I couldn't tell *a*'s from *o*'s. Let's learn to make them properly today so that won't happen again." Such comments are often heard in rooms where problems are clear and the focus of the practice is sharp.

The most efficient ball player does more than accept the coach's evaluation of his work. He learns to appraise his own performance and to make some of his own plans for improvement. You will want to use many opportunities in the classroom to involve your pupils in appraising their own strengths and weaknesses. Typically, they should be working with you in evaluating their written work. Many a beginning teacher spends night after night correcting papers when he should be investing some of this time in making himself a more stimulating person. You are the individual in your class least in need of practice in proofreading and checking arithmetic problems. Of course, you will want to take an unhurried look at your pupils' performances from time to time, but for the most part your teaching will be more effective if you and your pupils together correct their work and identify needs for more practice. Pupils may grade their own pre-tests in spelling and then list, in their individual spelling notebooks, the words needing special practice. They may evaluate their own handwriting and enter in a writing notebook the letters on which they need to practice. An arithmetic group may analyze a trial test to see what types of errors each person made. Members of a reading group may listen to a recording of their efforts and note individual needs for progress. In all such situations you, as the teacher, are helping your pupils to set higher standards and to become more aware of their needs.

Evaluation sessions such as those just mentioned assume more importance in pupils' eyes if there are ways for them to keep records of their needs and their progress. Like yourself, a youngster will work harder to improve if he has concrete evidence that persons he respects think his efforts are important. Such records of progress might include an individual spelling list, a dictionary of hard words from reading activities, a proofreading sheet to use as a reminder before written work is handed in, a check list of oral reading errors, a series of arithmetic progress charts on which pupils who have mastered a given table or operation may sign their names. Sometimes pupils and teachers build cumulative files of typical performances—a handwriting folder in which sample papers are filed, a creative writing folder in which representative stories and poems are stored, a social studies or science notebook in which samples of work are kept. Such records of work need to be used, of course, if they are to be aids to self-evaluation. Pupils may take time to compare present efforts with those of some months back. Techniques which have been mastered can be checked off and new problems added. Pupil and teacher together may study the evidence and decide where further work is necessary.

In classrooms where pupils are helping to evaluate their own progress you will hear many group discussions of desirable standards. The results of such discussions are often posted—*Ways to Study a Hard Word, A Good Listener, When We Read Aloud, Points to Check Before a Story Is Finished.* Once such standards are established, you can use the lists both as reminders and as bases of evaluation. "About what would you want to compliment Jack, particularly?" "How do you think our last oral reading sounded—are there things we should work on?" "I found a dozen articles lacking periods at the end of sentences. What does that say about our proofreading?"

Classroom atmospheres where pupils sense their needs and plan ways to work on them are frank and aboveboard. Pupils talk freely of their difficulties and comment with generous enthusiasm when someone begins to do better. You may worry sometimes about seeming to criticize a pupil. After all, he is doing his best and the work is hard for him. Shouldn't he be encouraged? It may well be that with some youngsters you should tread softly; certainly all deserve generous praise when they improve. However, the typical child is aware of his deficiencies. He notices the fact that his spelling paper has ten mistakes whereas his neighbor's has only two or the fact that others seem to be going right ahead with calculations that baffle him. Far from being discouraged, he may take heart if a teacher whose judgment he respects points out frankly that he needs help and then begins to give it in a matter of fact way. His courage rises still more if he sees himself beginning to improve. You may recall the thrill of bettering your golf score by a point or two, even though you were still in the "duffer" class. So it may be with Jimmy who makes five errors in spelling instead of eight. Sometimes we talk as if being first is the only motive which will stimulate an all-out effort on the part of a pupil. Actually, the satisfaction of "beating" oneself—of feeling increased mastery of a situation—is a very powerful motive indeed.

Practice sessions need to be teaching sessions. It follows from what has been said that some very important learning hinges upon the way teachers work with practice activities. The times when you and your pupils are checking a series of practice exercises provide valuable opportunities to help pupils identify errors and see where more practice is indicated. Your practice sessions should be teaching sessions.

Sometimes, under the time pressure of all the help pupils seem to need, beginning teachers fail to do much more than make sure that everyone has heard the correct answer. This is not enough. Pupils should be involved actively in identifying where they were wrong and, even more important, in arriving at the correct answer for themselves. Thus, you will hear skillful teachers using comments and questions to reveal ineffective ways of working and to stress better ones. "What helped you to figure out that word?" "If you hadn't remembered four times five, how could you have worked it out?" "What made you decide that a question mark was needed?" "Why do you suppose they asked us to underline the double letters in these words?"

The teaching that goes on as teacher and pupils together work through a series of practice activities is not necessarily a process of stopping for an extended lesson. Contrast the procedures of Sarah Brown and Grace Jamison in checking a pre-test in spelling. Sarah is mainly concerned that her pupils hear the word spelled correctly:

SARAH BROWN

The next word is *Indians.* Will you write it for us, Barnie?

(Barnie writes *Indains.)*

How many agree?

(Very few hands go up.)

What should it be, Janie?

(Janie comes to the board and writes *Indians.*)

That's right, Janie. Barnie, you need to spend more time on your spelling. Our next word is . . . .

Grace, on the other hand, takes a little time to be sure that the cause of the error is cleared away:

GRACE JAMISON

The next word is *Indians.* Will you write it for us, Barnie?

(Barnie writes *Indains.*)

How many spelled it like that?

(Seven hands go up.)

What should it be, Janie?

(Janie writes it correctly.)

That's right. What did you people who missed it forget to do?

(Barnie says "Remember it's *i a.*")

Yes, that's the part to remember, but something could have helped you when you studied it. Say it for us, Barnie.

(Barnie says the word.)

Can you hear which letter comes first?

(Pupils nod.)

How many who missed it really listened to the sounds in the word when they studied?

(A couple of hands go up tentatively.)

This is a hard one. Let's all say it. Can you hear which sound comes first?

(Nods.)

Suppose you write it a few times if you missed it. Say it quietly to yourself as you do, and be sure to listen to the sounds.

Not every word would necessarily merit this much attention, but when several youngsters seem to have a common problem, it may not take much longer than it did Grace to give the needed extra stress to a technique that pupils should be using more consistently. You may notice, also, that Grace's procedure of asking "How many spelled it like that?" encouraged pupils to acknowledge their error.

Obviously, teachers must know the essentials of a skilled performance in every area they teach. If Grace Jamison had not been aware of the fact that one of the essential techniques in spelling is to translate sounds heard into letter equivalents, she might not have put her stress where she did. With other words you might have heard her asking questions emphasizing other spelling techniques, ascertaining whether the pupils were alert to nonphonetic elements, or sensitive to the fact that a rule they had just learned was applicable.

One of the dilemmas often confronting beginners is posed by the one or two youngsters in a small group who don't "catch on." Should all those who have the right answer wait while Belinda struggles with a new concept? Probably not. This is an unjustifiable expenditure of pupil time. However, it is possible, after Belinda has had her chance to try, to involve the others in helping her. Thus they test out their ability to explain the new procedure. Then, when the others are gainfully occupied, the teacher is free to spend some time with Belinda.

Often beginning teachers rely heavily on team games as sources of practice. Perhaps this is partially because of a well-meant effort to make learning more enjoyable and challenging for pupils. Probably, also, a game seems to be a clear-cut and definite type of activity to plan. Some precautions are in order, however, if games are going to be used. One of the least desirable features of a spelling bee or an arithmetic baseball game is that they do not allow for much teaching if an error is made. This problem can be partially solved if the pupil who makes the mistake looks up or works out the correct answer in his own notebook and checks it with the teacher at the end of the game. Equally undesirable is the feature of eliminating from the team the child who made the error, with the result that those who most need the help actually get the least practice. There is the fact, too, that games typically require pupils to take turns, one at a time. Thus, in a ten-minute spelling period, Billy may be active in spelling only two words. This objection can be met, in part, if those whose turn has not come work the problem at their seats and assist in checking the answers of their team mates. A safe conclusion might be that team games have motivating value once in a while and occasionally serve as a challenging demonstration of competence when a new technique is well polished, but that the majority of practice sessions should allow for maximum participation—by both pupils and teacher.

Games which in reality are practice devices with which pupils work independently or in small groups—word bingo, spelling crossword puzzles, number games—provide more opportunity for individual pupils to practice. They have, however, some of the same disadvantages as do team games in that they do not usually resemble very closely the situations in which pupils will actually put the skills to use. Nor do they always give the teacher much opportunity to help the youngsters analyze their errors. Like team games, they should be used judiciously.

Plans for practice should encompass the entire day. If you are to help your pupils to achieve maximum growth, you will need to interpret the term "practice" very broadly. It should include day-by-day opportunities to use the new skills as well as the special activities you plan. As a matter of fact, the richer your total program, the more you will find yourself using on-going classroom activities as realistic sources of practice instead of setting up special exercises. Why work with imaginary headings for letters, for example, when there are real letters to be written? Why do an exercise on types of sentences when a group is faced with the practical job of writing interesting reports so that the editors of the school paper will accept them? Why work on an assigned handwriting lesson when there is a note to mother to be written carefully?

The proportion of the needed practice to be provided by on-going classroom activities depends, to some extent, upon the maturity of the pupils. At the primary level where the foundations for reading, spelling, handwriting, and arithmetic are being laid, the practice activities centering in these areas may be developed in a more carefully organized and sequential program than that for older pupils, when a major goal is to teach them to use their skills flexibly in a variety of daily problems. However, this general statement needs qualification. Some primary teachers have been able to work out remarkably successful reading programs on a completely individualized basis, each child progressing at his own pace through simple books of his own choosing. Even more frequently primary teachers have been able to plan so that work in spelling, handwriting, and communication grows directly from the day-by-day activities of their classes. It is probably safe to say that on-going classroom activities do not always offer equally rich sources of practice for the sequential development of arithmetic skills as they do for skills in the language fields. However, here again skillful teachers have found ways of providing a remarkable amount of experience in the course of the typical day.

Using the entire day as a source of practice does not mean stopping everything for a fifteen- or twenty-minute lesson on reading, spelling, language, or arithmetic whenever a new need appears. Much of the help you give during the on-going activities of the day will be quite brief. Often it will be merely a reminder. As second-graders start to copy a group note to go home to mother, their teacher reminds them of the letters they have been practicing specially in handwriting and they look to be sure that their sentences have capitals and periods. A fifth-grader stumbles over a place name in social studies, and his teacher suggests that he use the glossary to help with the pronunciation. Fourth-graders have difficulty in spelling some terms in a science report. Their teacher adds these to a list labeled *Science Spelling Aids* and then reminds them to be sure to check their spelling against the list. Third-graders build a bulletin board list of the rules about capital letters they have discovered in their reading and are reminded to refer to these before they start to write their stories. Sixth-graders make a large outline map by projecting the one in their text and then use simplified principles of ratio and proportion to get surface features in proper scale. After he reads a social studies report, Billy is complimented on the way he put into practice skills in oral reading which have been previously talked through. The difference between guaranteeing that a skill will be put to use and not having it practiced beyond the boundaries of the skills period is often a matter of a word or two from the teacher.

In trying to make sure that skills will carry over, some beginning teachers never start an activity without a complete review of everything the pupils have learned. This can become a ritual that pupils perform without very much thought. Often it is more emphatic to point to the one or two skills needing the most stress. Contrast the following lessons. Susan Cromwell is unwilling to let her group begin until the complete set of rules to guide their written work has been formulated:

SUSAN CROMWELL

Then you think it would be fun to write some Christmas stories for a special booklet to take home?

(Enthusiastic nods.)

All right, but before we start let's think what we said about a good story. John?

(John says "We must indent our paragraphs.")

"That's right. [There is a pause while Susan writes the reminder on the board.] And what else, Alice?

("Remember to start each sentence with a capital" is Alice's response.)

Yes, that's very important. [Another pause while Susan writes.] Sadie? . . .

[This process goes on until a half-dozen items are listed.]

Jon Apby, on the other hand, is attempting to make functional those rules most pertinent to the task at hand:

JON APBY

Then you think it would be fun to write some Christmas stories for a special booklet to take home?

(Enthusiastic nods.)

While you're trying to get your story ideas down, you're not going to want to worry too much about proofreading, but for the last three days we have been working on one thing you might want to remember. Yes, John?

(John says "Indent our paragraphs?")

Yes. It will be easier to follow your story if you think about your paragraphs a little. Then, when you're ready to put it in final form, you have your list of points to check in proofreading, do you not?

(Several voices say "Yes, sir.")

Then let's get started, and I'll be around if you run into problems. . . .

Jon is not letting his pupils forget the importance of correct punctuation and spelling. However, in his proofreading check sheet, he has a much less time-consuming means of reminding his class about technical standards than that provided by Susan's reconstruction of the list. It is important to notice also that whereas Susan has fenced in creativity by her stress on correct usage, Jon has made the writing a two-step process, with the first job that of getting the story down on paper.

There will be times, of course, when it is quite proper to plan for more intensive instruction in the skills needed in relation to on-going classroom activities. Today, time limits are not so tightly drawn that periods assigned to social studies, science, or health cannot be spent on the skills needed for successful work in these areas. Often your practice materials will be the very books being used to locate information or an actual problem to be faced. A social studies project demands a large map drawn to scale; time from the social studies period may well be spent on the arithmetic involved. Children in a science group need bar graphs to record the growth of their plants; this may call for a science period stressing arithmetic. One social studies class spends a day practicing use of indexes and tables of contents; a second class takes time to analyze the skills of note-taking; a third considers the language skills involved in having a good discussion. In one primary room, the children building a train learn to measure; the first-graders in another develop a special vocabulary list of words learned on their trip to the fire house. Integration of activities does not mean that special focus on specific probems related to skills is lost in the activities of a larger unit. It does mean that your block plan for developing unit activities should include a list of the specific skills that might be given attention and that your day-by-day plans, as the unit unfolds, should allow time as needed to develop whatever proficiencies will help the unit activities move forward smoothly.[2]

Additional practice should be provided through extended unit activities which focus on skills. In addition to specific practice activities and all the practice that daily classroom experiences can offer, many teachers plan from time to time to develop with their pupils extensive unit activities in which the major learnings fall within a so-called "skill" area. Such units may be relatively independent of other ongoing classroom activities. Often they call for a large measure of creative activity.

In the field of language, a sixth grade may publish the school paper. Writing a variety of articles, proofreading, editing, making announcements to other classes, interviewing of school visitors, may all be involved. Publishing a class magazine can lead to a similar series of related language experiences. In a primary grade, it may be a storytellers' club that meets once a week, or a writers' bulletin board, or a class storybook, or individual booklets in which the best of the year's work is collected as a gift for mother. Oral language experiences also may develop into extended units. Sometimes a unit in a content field culminates in a play. At this point, the major learnings shift from social studies or science content to the many language skills involved in such a production. In another class, pupils may summarize their learnings in their own choral-speaking production. A primary group may plan a series of oral reports, supplemented by pictures, in order to share with parents a unit on housing.

In arithmetic, a primary class may plan a classroom store (sometimes

[2] Reread Chapter 7, pages 273-284, for a discussion of the development of the reference skills important in the development of units in the content fields.

selling make-believe articles for play money). Besides the social and consumer education learnings in such situations, there is also a major contribution to number concepts and skill in computation. A fifth grade may sponsor a sale of seeds and use graphs to plot the profits. A sixth grade may undertake a school survey in answer to a Parent-Teacher Association request and report the results in a variety of graphs and tables. Fourth-graders may decide to make curtains for their room, with all the measuring and the calculating of expenses that this entails.

In reading, an able group could embark upon an exploration of American folk tales to be reported to the class. A first-grade group may plan how to dramatize a favorite story to share with those in the class who have not read it. Fourth-graders may develop a program to demonstrate to their mothers how they learn to read. A group of third-graders may plan a special bulletin board depicting scenes from favorite stories. One class may develop a program for an upper-grade assembly centering around their experiences in choral speaking; a second may dramatize three of their best-liked stories; a third may sponsor a book fair in order to interest others in the library.

Units of the type just suggested may last for varying lengths of time. Some, such as a play or a special assembly program, will typically be given attention for a few weeks and then concluded. Projects such as a school newspaper, a writers' bulletin board, a class magazine, or a club established for the purpose of sharing library books may provide a fruitful source of experience for the entire year. Such activities pose many realistic needs for more effective skills and provide for generous amounts of practice. You will want to capitalize upon such opportunities when the occasion permits.

MEETING INDIVIDUAL NEEDS

All that has been said in the preceding sections about making new learnings meaningful and providing effective practice has to be multiplied many times over—for all the skills you wish to teach and for pupils of varying ability in each skill area. If your reaction is typical of that of most conscientious teachers, you have long been doubting your ability to provide the help for the wide range of needs which you have been discovering. How can one teacher spread himself so thin? Although skills are important, so are many other learnings. Where is the time to do it all? What about the gifted child—won't he be neglected? And how can anyone find the extra time needed by the youngster who is retarded? A very natural reaction of many beginners (and of many experienced teachers also) is to wonder whether administrative procedures could not simplify the problem. Should there not be some way to put in one room pupils with the same needs so that all could do the exercises in the same textbook?

If you will think back over what you learned in educational psychology, you will realize that many difficulties beset us when we try to fit the complexities of human nature into a few neat pigeonholes. In the first place, if you want to have a stimulating classroom in which pupils are actually putting their skills to work, there is no way that you can guide their activities to conform to the sequence of problems outlined in a textbook, no matter how astute a textbook author's insights into children's needs may be. Any program responsive to the problems being faced by a particular group must be planned by their teacher.

Although it is easy to talk about "slow" or "fast" learners, it is a rare pupil who is equally retarded or equally able in all areas. Take forty fifth-graders, all of whose IQ's are exactly 100 on a standardized intelligence test. The range in reading skills is likely to be several years. The same may be true of arithmetic, but those who are skilled readers will not necessarily be equally able in mathematics. Sort out forty, all of whom read at exactly fifth-grade level according to standardized tests. Their IQ's typically will vary from the high 80's to 120 or better. One might say "Choose from the entire school and send the fifth-grade readers to one teacher, the fourth-grade readers to another; then do the same thing all over again for arithmetic." But how long will Mary Jane (IQ 80, age thirteen), Peter (IQ 135, age eight), and John (IQ 100, age eleven) continue to read at fifth-grade level? And what happens to the opportunities for integrated activities during the remainder of the day?

Yes, but couldn't pupils who are not up to grade be held back so that one would not have to adjust to any below grade level? It is all very well to point out that a pupil two years retarded in reading will not get along in fifth grade without special help. But is this any guarantee that he will fit neatly into the third grade with no trouble to his classmates, his teacher, or himself? There is still a difficult placement problem to solve.

Attitudes of both pupils and parents also need to be considered. In a school where there are just enough pupils for two groups, is it wise to have thirty youngsters labeling themselves as superior and another thirty calling themselves second-rate on the basis of a standardized test? If you recall the margin of error in any standardized test you will shudder to think how many youngsters in such a situation will be building a false self-concept. You should shudder, too, to think of the home tensions and anxieties that could result and of what the outcomes might be in the case of a pupil already discouraged and partially defeated.

Certainly, thoughtful promotion, retention, and grouping policies based on all that is known about each child can produce better placement for pupils and reduce to some extent the anxieties of teachers. However, a range of abilities will still be yours to face. Nobody claims that the job is easy, but it must be attempted if individuals are to be given the best possible opportunities to grow. How do skillful teachers make the best use of their time?

Use flexible methods of grouping. One of the characteristics of classrooms where teachers make wise use of their time is flexibility of grouping within the class. Sometimes an array of standardized test scores covering several grades suggests to the beginner that there must be an infinite number of groups in each skill area. You see yourself trying to provide for fifth-, sixth-, seventh-, eighth-, ninth-, and perhaps tenth-grade readers all in the sixth grade and for an equal number of groups for each of the other skills. Any such proposal, however, is a misinterpretation of the test scores.[3] There is not such a marked difference between a sixth- and a seventh-grade book, for example, as to render the former useless to a youngster with a seventh-grade score on a reading test. If he reads well, his needs lie in the direction of better reference techniques, deeper appreciation for literature, and more flexible speed. Such skills can be developed with many types of materials, some conceivably graded as low as fourth grade. You will, then, not need as many working groups in reading as your test scores would indicate, and this is equally true of other skill areas.

Earlier, it was pointed out that you needed to learn to look behind the general level of a pupil's performance to see his specific difficulties. This suggests that the demands for specialized help will multiply. Actually, however, there are ways of grouping youngsters with similar problems if you plan your grouping flexibly. For example, ten to a dozen third-graders may be having unusual difficulty with phonetic elements, both in reading and spelling. These youngsters could meet

[3] Read Chapters 4 and 11, pages 118-120 and 444-448, for help on interpreting test scores.

twice a week to work on word-study problems. Similarly, there might be a group of pupils who are still uncertain about their multiplication tables, or a handful needing special help with spelling, while the others are engaged in relatively independent study. There will be times, also, when an entire class will face the same problem—first steps with a dictionary, the first business letter of the year, first attempts to take notes. You do not have to work with small groups if it is apparent that everyone needs much the same help.

It is possible, too, to individualize your assistance without meeting separately with groups operating at different levels. For example, all could work on spelling for a half-hour period set aside for this purpose, but each pupil could be studying his own list of errors. All could be reading so that they may share the plot of a story with the class, yet each youngster could be working with a library book at his own level. There might be a practice period in handwriting, with each pupil working to correct his own errors. Such sessions presuppose, of course, that you have been planning with your groups so that they know their own needs and realize the purpose of the practice activities in which they are engaged.

Capitalize on the capacities of your group. Half the battle of meeting individual needs is won when you realize that not all pupils require the same kind of help. Typically, the more able the learner, the more he is in need of challenging experiences in which he can proceed independently. Even in first grade, the able child needs the satisfaction of finishing his own library book or of writing a story all by himself. In the upper elementary grades we are aiming toward library techniques that will allow the reader to get extensive information for himself, toward enjoyment of the two-hundred-page library book, toward the series of articles written for the school paper. Such activities require a teacher's guidance if a pupil is to grow through engaging in them, but this need not be in the nature of day-by-day supervision. Often a planning session with your more able groups may be followed by two or three days of independent work, during which you need be available only briefly to check on progress and help with problems. Then, as your more skilled groups become ready to summarize or share their work, more generous help may again be needed from you. You are not neglecting able pupils when you encourage them to work on their own provided you plan their activities as a challenge to their maturing powers, not as a way of keeping them occupied while you work with less able pupils. In contrast, pupils who are in need of remedial help may benefit from short but regular periods under your close guidance. Even these youngsters, however, will profit from simplified activities at which they can work independently. A second-grade reader in fourth grade needs the fun of enjoying an easy library book just as much as (and perhaps more than) does his able classmate who loves to read.

Times when pupils are engaged in independent activities offer you an opportunity to give some special help. Sometimes you will be calling together a small group in need of instruction, but you should use some of this time for working with individuals. It may be a matter of encouraging one youngster to use the dictionary in spelling a word. You may take time to read aloud a report with another so that through listening he may understand why his sentence structure is poor. You may sense that another is completely confused with an arithmetic process and ask him to work it aloud for you.

In meeting individual needs, then, you do not face a problem of allotting your time and attention on an absolutely even basis—fifteen minutes per pupil, no more, no less. Your problem is to sense where you are needed, capitalizing whenever possible upon opportunities to free yourself to work with small groups and individuals as your pupils take on more challenging and complicated independent jobs.

Make sure your pupils know the plans. In the classrooms where pupils are able to proceed independently and teachers are free to work with individuals, everybody knows what he is to do. At a number of points in this and other chapters there have been suggestions regarding ways of involving pupils in planning. One useful procedure is to post and discuss briefly the schedule for the day so that all may know what is ahead of them. The most effective schedules often give proposed activities in considerable detail. Work for special groups in reading and arithmetic; jobs to be completed in social studies, science, or health; "extras," such as get-well cards, stories due for the school paper, library reports—all are listed. Some teachers even post a second list of "Things we'd like to do if everything else is done."

If pupils have shared in analyzing their errors and understand the purpose of special practice activities for those having particular difficulty, this also helps individuals to proceed on their own. In one room there may be an arithmetic practice sheet—"If you missed question 1 on our check test, practice examples 3, 7, and 10 on page 35. If you missed question 2, practice. . . ." In another, children may be working as spelling partners to dictate individual lists of hard words. In a third, the youngsters having the greatest difficulty with word analysis may be completing some sets of phonetic exercises.

Unit activities offer opportunities for long-range planning which enable teacher and pupils to proceed independently for several days. Such activities also allow for work at several levels of difficulty. Articles for a school paper or stories for a class magazine offer challenges both for the youngster who writes a single paragraph and for the budding novelist who produces a hair-raising serial for the benefit of the class. In another room, it may be an arithmetic problems book to which one may contribute an original problem if all his other work is completed. In still another it may be a library club. The better informed your pupils are regarding the work that is ahead and the more keenly they feel that this work is worth while, the better your guarantee that effective learning experiences can be geared to a variety of needs and capacities.

Choose activities that facilitate self-direction. Your choice of activities, as well as the way in which you plan with your pupils, can do much to facilitate their ability to work independently and thus to free you to give help to individuals. It is a major help, for example, to choose practice activities in which the directions are simple and easy to follow. Sometimes the trick of doing one or two examples with your pupils before they work alone can avoid much confusion and many unnecessary questions.

It is important to make sure that materials used for independent work actually *can* be handled independently. In reading, this means providing books with vocabulary loads a pupil should reasonably be expected to handle without your constant attention, or planning independent activities that call for the rereading of a familiar story. Teachers may also help youngsters to be more independent in their writing activities by posting words which are likely to present spelling problems —lists of social studies or science words, lists of words about Halloween or Christmas. Pupils can also develop and use their own spelling dictionaries.

For youngsters needing extended remedial help, teachers have often found it valuable to select a special series of workbooks or texts and workbooks in which activities are challenging and directions simple. They then plan an independent program with the individual or small group needing the special help and check regularly on progress. For such remedial programs, it is particularly important to choose materials which are easy enough to allow the pupils to proceed with confidence.

With able pupils the problem often is to capitalize upon the children's own sense of direction and to provide them with the materials they need to pursue their interests. Even in the early primary grades, these youngsters frequently have all the necessary skills to undertake ambitious independent projects. If you have been adept in using on-going classroom activities as a source of practice for your boys and girls, you will probably have under way many projects which will challenge your able learners.

Employ flexible scheduling. The preceding suggestions imply that teachers who meet individual needs most effectively work within a flexible schedule. You cannot provide for the type of independent, individualized work that has just been described if your plans call for an arbitrary number of minutes with every group every day. Sometimes you will actually waste time by holding a group for the last five minutes when a block of work clearly has been completed. On the other hand, by stopping five minutes short of finishing the job merely because the clock says your period is up, you may have to build all the momentum again tomorrow.

Teachers who find time for individuals try to stagger demands for their assistance. For example, rather than starting three reading groups on three new stories during the same morning, or developing new arithmetic processes with two groups, they plan so that new work for one group parallels continuing work for another. In reading, group one discusses a new story, and then reads silently; group two has completed reading a story and comes to talk about it; group three is planning to read a story aloud to the class and needs the whole period to practice. In arithmetic, group one listens to a short explanation of some practice activities and goes to work; group two then works with the teacher to master a new process. If you are systematic in choosing practice activities that facilitate independent work on the part of your pupils, you will not find it difficult to plan so that you can focus your attention where it is most needed, secure in the knowledge that others in your class are not wasting their time.

Capitalize on the opportunities for growth offered by the entire school day. Teachers who gain time to work with individuals make skillful use of the experiences of the entire school day. They do not attempt to plan a separate and independent program in each skill area and then duplicate these efforts during the rest of the day. If, for example, there have been an unusual number of requests to report during sharing period, these together with other regular class activities may provide ample opportunity for oral expression. A separate language period need not then be scheduled. Likewise, if an upper grade is facing the task of locating materials for a new social studies unit, this may provide sufficient practice on new skills for the day. Your total skills program is an integrated program. You identify problems arising during the day on which you should give help during your skills periods. You feel free to use social studies or science time for help on skills if a problem related closely to progress in these areas arises. From the time that you save by making effective use of all your opportunities to teach come the extra minutes you spend with individuals.

This chapter has completed the circle, and ends where it began. The insights of a skillful teacher are at the heart of an effective program for skill development. If you do not want to waste the time of some individuals and to fail to give the appropriate help to others, you must identify the special needs of your class, see where regular classroom activities are already providing ample practice and where supplementing is needed, and decide what explanations and experiences will best develop the learnings important to the maximum progress of your class.

BOOKS YOU SHOULD KNOW

Brueckner, Leo J., and Bond, Guy L. *The Diagnosis and Treatment of Learning Difficulties.* New York: Appleton-Century-Crofts, 1955. Pp. ix + 424.

Brueckner, Leo J., and Grossnickle, Foster E. *Making Arithmetic Meaningful.* Philadelphia: The John C. Winston Co., 1953. Pp. v + 570.

Bucher, C.A., and Reade, E.M. *Physical Education in the Modern Elementary School.* New York: The Macmillan Co., 1958. Pp. 437.

Burton, William H. (Collaborators: Baker, Clara B., and Kemp, Grace K.) *Reading in Child Development.* Indianapolis: The Bobbs-Merrill Co., 1956. Pp. xvi + 608.

Dawson, Mildred A., and Zollinger, Marian. *Guiding Language Learning.* Yonkers-on-Hudson, N.Y.: World Book Co., 1957. Pp. 534.

Education for the Gifted. Part II, The Fifty-seventh Yearbook of the National Society for the Study of Education. Chicago: The University of Chicago Press, 1958. Pp. xi + 420.

Evans, Ruth; Bacon, Thelma I.; Bacon, Mary E.; and Stapleton, Joie L. *Physical Education for Elementary Schools.* New York: McGraw-Hill Book Co., 1958. Pp. xi + 317.

Fitzgerald, James A. *The Teaching of Spelling.* Milwaukee: Bruce Publishing Co., 1951. Pp. xiii + 233.

Freeman, Frank N. *Teaching Handwriting.* What Research Says to the Teacher, No. 4. Washington D.C.: National Education Association, 1954. Pp. 33.

Gates, Arthur I. *Teaching Reading.* What Research Says to the Teacher, No. 1, Washington, D.C.: National Education Association, 1953. Pp. 33.

Herrick, Virgil E., and Jacobs, Leland B. *Children and the Language Arts.* Englewood Cliffs, N.J.: Prentice-Hall, 1955. Pp. xiv + 524.

Hildreth, Gertrude H. *Teaching Reading.* New York: Henry Holt and Co., 1958. Pp. vii + 612.

Hildreth, Gertrude H. *Teaching Spelling.* New York: Henry Holt and Co., 1955. Pp. 346.

Horn, Ernest. *Teaching Spelling.* What Research Says to the Teacher, No. 3. Washington, D.C.: National Education Association, 1954. Pp. 32.

Language Arts for Today's Children. Prepared by the Commission on the English Curriculum of the National Council of Teachers of English. New York: Appleton-Century-Crofts, 1954. Pp. xvi + 431.

Latchaw, Marjorie. *A Pocket Guide of Games and Rhythms for the Elementary School.* Englewood Cliffs, N.J.: Prentice-Hall, 1956. Pp. iv + 316.

Marks, John L.; Purdy, C. Richard; and Kinney, Lucien B. *Teaching Arithmetic for Understanding.* New York: McGraw-Hill Book Co., 1958. Pp. xiv + 429.

McKim, Margaret G. *Guiding Growth in Reading.* New York: The Macmillan Co., 1955. Pp. xx + 528.

Miller, Arthur G., and Whitcomb, Virginia. *Physical Education in the Elementary School Curriculum.* Englewood Cliffs, N.J.: Prentice-Hall, 1957. Pp. xii + 331.

Morton, Robert L. *Teaching Arithmetic.* What Research Says to the Teacher, No. 2. Washington, D.C.: National Education Association, 1953. Pp. 33.

Morton, Robert L. *Teaching Children Arithmetic.* Morristown, N.J.: Silver-Burdett Co., 1953. Pp. xvii + 566.

Shane, Harold G. *Research Helps in Teaching the Language Arts.* Washington, D.C.: Association for Supervision and Curriculum Development, N.E.A., 1955. Pp. vii + 80.

Smith, Marion F. *Teaching the Slow Learning Child.* New York: Harper & Brothers, 1954. Pp. 175.

Spitzer, Herbert F. *The Teaching of Arithmetic.* Second Edition. Boston: Houghton Mifflin Co., 1954. Pp. 416.

Strickland, Ruth G. *The Language Arts in the Elementary School.* Second Edition. Boston: D.C. Heath and Co., 1957. Pp. xiv + 464.

The Three R's in the Elementary School. Association for Supervision and Curriculum Development, N.E.A. Washington, D.C.: The Association, 1952. Pp. ix + 152.

Witty, Paul (Editor). *The Gifted Child.* The American Association for Gifted Children. Boston: D.C. Heath and Co., 1951. Pp. xii + 338.

Guiding Growth in Creative Expression

CHAPTER 9

Whether we, as a nation or as a world, move forward to higher levels of civilization, stagnate, or eventually destroy ourselves depends upon the quality of our original thinking. Creativity is important not only in scientific endeavors, but perhaps even more in social living and international relations—in fact, in all aspects of human activity. We are living in a world where creative action is needed as never before.

There are personal as well as societal needs for the development of powers of creative expression. As the productive capacity of our industrial society increases, it appears certain that more and more time will be available for leisure and the cultivation of individual talents and interests. It is not enough for the citizen to have free time to participate in meaningless or worthless leisure-time activities. Leisure activities must be personally satisfying and significant or boredom and frustration will be the chief outcomes. Merely to keep busy is not sufficient; the human mind, regardless of level of ability, must be stimulated with activities which make life meaningful and worth while.

A candid evaluation of our efforts to date in freeing the creative potential of our pupils suggests that we have not been particularly successful. Even with better-equipped schools, more adequately prepared teachers, richer curricula, more boys and girls in school for longer periods of time, thousands of youngsters still leave our classrooms without having had challenging experiences in approaching creatively problems related to the natural or social sciences. Many graduate with little or no interest in or understanding of how to live more wisely or more completely. Instead of cultivating music creatively or appreciatively they avoid it or remain satisfied with the current and popular. Art and its various forms are considered to be only for the artistically gifted. Literature with all its diversity is supposed to be for the few. The so-called "useful arts"—home decoration, sewing, cabinet making, cooking—are valued not for what they give to the worth-whileness of living, but for the financial rewards for one's proficiency and skill.

As a matter of fact, we, as teachers, have not always understood that creative effort is essential to all pupils and that all pupils regardless of ability have the capacity to work creatively in some area. It is probably not an exaggeration to say that many teachers believe that creativity is limited to a very few individuals and that most pupils have little or no potential for creative development. It may not even be too far-fetched to assert that many teachers consider themselves to be limited in their own capacities for creative expression. These attitudes and beliefs are, of course, at wide variance with the facts regarding creativity.

Even a little thought about the realities of living would suggest that creative expression is an integral part of all aspects of human activity. Often, when we use the term "creativity," we tend to think of art, music, writing, dance; but this is far too limited a viewpoint. A housewife is creative when she rearranges the furniture to suit her family's needs or experiments with a new combination of spices when she cooks. The carpenter is creative when he constructs a set of shelves to convert a small storeroom into a library. There is creative thinking when members of a school faculty devise a system for a midmorning coffee break or plan how to adjust the school program to meet the special health problems of a group of underprivileged children. If we are to be truly creative teachers, and at the same time teachers who help children to be creative, our first task is to recognize the creative possibilities in all aspects of our living—fine arts, literature, mathematics, science, social studies, industrial arts, technical vocations, sports.

Creativity is not only inherent in all aspects of human activity, but it is present in all levels of intelligence and at all maturity levels. It is not limited to a few gifted persons, to the economically favored or to the socially elite. The three-year old is creative when he devises a game with kitchen pots and pans. The first-grader is creative when he draws his own valentine for his mother. There is creative expression in the way third-graders decorate a winter bulletin board. The fifth-grader who plans his own diorama to demonstrate ancient and modern means of transportation is creative; so is his friend who works out the plot for an original play. The adolescent girl who makes over an out-of-date dress is creating, as is the boy who rebuilds his "hot rod." If an important function of the school is to make life more fruitful and worth while, teachers must find the creative potential of each pupil, whatever his level of ability, and develop it to the fullest in all aspects of school activity.

This does not mean that "creativity" is about to become a new subject in the course of study or that the creative side of living and learning will be emphasized to the neglect of other worth-while purposes. Creative expression is not a separate entity; it is an aspect of everything we do. Children and youth learn as a whole; there is also wholeness to what they learn. Skills, concepts and generalizations, and a deep and abiding interest and appreciation that causes the learner to seek new experiences for his own personal satisfaction were listed as goals in the two preceding chapters. In those chapters the stress was on the first two aspects of the total teaching process—developing concepts and generalizations and developing skills. In the present chapter the focus is on the third side of the triangle—developing the quality of original thinking that leads to seeking new experiences and arriving at new answers. Although this chapter will perhaps be of particular help to beginning teachers facing problems in relation to the arts, music, dance, and writing, it has implications for other aspects of the school curriculum, just as each of the two preceding chapters had implications for the development of lasting interests and creative expression.

In guiding your pupils' growth in creative expression, as in guiding their growth in any other aspect of development, you must know precisely what your goals are. Then, as in the case of building understandings or developing fundamental skills, you need to decide which of the many potentially educative experiences through which you might work are most likely to lead to maximum growth. As you and your pupils embark upon selected activities you will face the particularly challenging problem of deciding how to guide their work so that you foster truly creative expression. You must also be able to help your boys and girls to develop personal insights and standards without, in the process of so doing, blocking their freedom of self-expression. Finally, as in developing skills and understandings, you must be able to plan your classroom activities so that there is maximum opportunity for growth provided for youngsters with many types and degrees of talent.

WHAT ARE OUR GOALS IN HELPING PUPILS GROW IN CREATIVITY?

In general, teachers in the elementary schools have a reasonably clear sense of goals in developing fundamental skills. To a lesser extent, perhaps, they have definite ideas about what types of growth are essential if their pupils are to grow in understanding the world in which they live. In the area of creative expression, however, we are sometimes less certain. Creativity is personal and individual. Its characteristics sometimes seem to defy classification. Yet without a sense of direction, teaching is likely to miss its mark. What should your over-all goals be as you try to help your pupils to grow in creativity, be they six or twelve, talented or seemingly lacking capacity for creative expression, engaged in activities related to the so-called creative arts or tackling a problem related to the natural or social sciences? What types of behavior are characteristic of the creative person?

The creative person continually reinterprets experience. If you look for synonyms for creativity, you will discover such terms as *original, fresh, new, inventive, unique.* The essence of creativity is originality. The creative person sees things in new lights and puts ideas together in new ways. The creative scientist puts facts together to arrive at a new theory; so does the historian who proposes a new interpretation of historical data. A composer combines notes into harmonies not heard before; an artist develops unique color combinations on his canvas; a dress designer originates a new treatment of sleeves, waistlines, or hems. The creative person does not dwell in a tightly structured world. He sees unlimited possibilities for new interpretations and fresh approaches to his problems. Creativity involves a constant reinterpretation of experiences.

One important responsibility for teachers, in encouraging pupils to approach their problems creatively, is to develop a classroom in which originality is welcomed. This is not a simple matter. With thirty or more youngsters in your room and specific objectives outlined by the course of study, it is not always easy to give children the freedom they need to work out their own solutions to problems. Certainly, it is difficult to extend this freedom to all aspects of the day—to provide for a creative approach to areas such as social studies, science, and mathematics as well as to literature, music, and art. You will face problems, too, in adjusting your leadership to the maturity of your group and in helping your pupils to develop a healthy respect for accurate facts and logical reasoning while, at the same time, encouraging independence and creativity in their thinking. Yet, the energy and initiative with which pupils of any age will tackle a problem when they are given freedom to think are a constant source of astonishment and delight to their teachers. You have a responsibility to offer them this freedom.

The creative person gives honest expression of the world as he views it. The product that is truly creative is an honest expression of the way in which the creator sees and feels his world. The artist shares his emotional and intellectual insights through his paintings; the musician does it through his manner of combining tones and rhythms. What the creative person is trying to say is not always immediately obvious to the observer or listener. Feelings, mood, and an outlook on the world of nature can be expressed through art without the painting of identifiable objects. Musical notes are not always arranged in singable tunes. Each person speaks for himself. He expresses what is meaningful to him, and he chooses his own medium for expression. The creative product is unique because its creator is unique.

It is all too easy to discourage a pupil who gives honest expression to his feelings about the world and his relation to it. In former days, many art programs in the schools called for reproducing or copying—every youngster working on the same assignment, painting the same flower, or coloring pages from the same stencil. This is a far cry from encouraging pupils to express their feelings about their world in their own ways. Even in classrooms where teachers realize that the end product is not the most important part of the creative process, original expression is sometimes unconsciously discouraged. A thoughtless comment or an invidious comparison—these deterrents are easily detected by perceptive pupils. It is often far safer to retreat to the conventional than to risk exposing one's soul a second time. Tolerance, open-mindedness, and respect for the unique worth of each individual are the keys to the nurture of originality.

As a teacher, yours will be the responsibility for developing a permissive and supporting classroom atmosphere that encourages originality and honesty of expression. Encouraging the pupil to express what he sees and feels may yield unusual and even bizarre end products from your adult point of view, yet the experience may be of incalculable value to the child himself. If you want to foster creativity, you will not condemn unconventionality in the creative arts. Rather, you will urge each pupil, regardless of intellectual level or talent, to make his contribution in his own way and through his chosen medium. Individuality, freedom to grow, opportunity to develop new ways of self-expression, ought to be the right of every pupil.

The creative person is progressively more proficient. Creative expression demands skill. The composer not only envisions a new composition, but he has the technical competence to translate what he feels into notes that can be played by an orchestra. The skilled writer has exceptional command of the language. The choreographer brings depth of experience with the dance to his ballet. Children and youth need to be helped to develop the techniques that will facilitate their efforts in creative expression.

Techniques grow with maturity. We would not expect the same standards of the first-grader as we would of the fifth- or sixth-grader. Neither would we expect the same levels of accomplishment of the slower pupil as we do from the more talented. What we do expect is that the pupil show consistent growth in his ability to work with materials, facts, and ideas. With increased skill comes more effective creative expression. Teachers have a responsibility to help boys and girls acquire the techniques that will make it possible for them to express themselves in more satisfying ways.

Providing the help and encouragement that allows pupils to express themselves in their own ways, while still guaranteeing growth in the skills that are the means to more effective self-expression, poses a very difficult problem for teachers. It is easy, on the one hand, to be so fearful of stifling a pupil's originality that one never calls his attention to technique, even though his lack of skill seriously interferes with the effectiveness of his expression. On the other hand, technique can be stressed to the point where the pupil's full attention is upon this aspect of expression, and originality is smothered. Ability to produce finished, polished products comes as an end result of a long learning process. The teacher who develops creativity in the pupil meets the child where he is and by patient encouragement—even faith—brings him to higher and higher levels of attainment. No pupil can be creative without skill, but no pupil is without potential skill. Proficiency comes with maturity and—this is our responsibility—with careful teaching.

The creative person is sensitive to his environment. Creativity and appreciation go hand in hand. The artist who stirs us with the quality of his creative expression does so because of his unique perception of the world around him. The poet, by his sensitivity, opens our eyes to details of everyday living to which we may have previously been blind. This is not to say that each creative artist sees or feels the same elements in his environment. Depth and quality of insight depend on profoundness of intellectual perception, intensity of emotional response, and experiential background. Sensitivity is an attribute of the individual personality.

Pupils need to be helped to grow in sensitive awareness of their environment. Although it is often said that the creative individual "pictures in the mind's eye," one may sometimes doubt this as one watches the struggling youngster twist and wiggle, sees his distorted facial expressions and exasperated actions, his talking to himself, his new starts, his new directions, his polishing and repolishing, and his occasional dissatisfaction at the final result. The greater his need to express himself because of his depth of insight, the greater the struggle may be.

An important aspect of your responsibility in helping your pupils to develop sensitive awareness of their world is to provide a rich classroom atmosphere for them to explore. Books, objects to handle, pets, plants, pictures, musical equipment, poems to hear and to read, songs to sing—all these and many more can contribute to the richness of a pupil's insights into his world. You must do more, however, than merely provide for a stimulating classroom environment. You must be sensitive, yourself, to the wonders of the world around you and willing to share your insights with your boys and girls. Actually, the simplest object or the grayest day has beauty if seen through the eyes of a perceptive individual. Creative activity sometimes has most unexpected beginnings. It is more certain to occur when sensitive teachers utilize the full resources of the classroom environment to stimulate the child to creative action.

The creative person feels deep personal satisfaction in his work. Perhaps the best test of the skill with which a teacher has been able to encourage creative expression is the degree to which a pupil continues to seek new experiences. Does he go on writing poetry after he leaves school? Keep puttering with his scientific interests? Join a choir or a glee club? Become a do-it-yourself homemaker? Keep reading popular books on mathematics? Borrow books regularly from the local library? Pursue deep and lasting hobbies? Regardless of the richness of the experiences we hope we have provided, our programs must be rated low if deep and abiding interests are not developed. We need to send into the world persons who find in creative activities lasting sources of personal satisfaction.

If we are to help our pupils find in their creative experiences sources of personal satisfaction, we must plan schedules that will allow time to explore, to pursue special interests, or to complete individual projects. Books, art and writing materials, musical instruments, science equipment, all will be used advantageously for creative experimentation. This means that you must develop a permissive atmosphere where individuals feel free and have the time for the depth of exploration needed to attain personal satisfactions from the process.

DECIDING WHERE TO BEGIN

You will provide opportunities for creative expression in your daily schedule in a number of ways. Units of work in areas related to the social or natural sciences will demand creative expression as part of the total experience. These may be activities lasting for a day, or they may involve much more elaborate plans—units within units, so to speak—such as a play or program to close a unit on Our City. There will also be units, some extensive, some short, stemming directly from interests in art, music, dramatics. Typical of such activities might be a class newspaper, a play, a proposal to develop a program of Christmas carols to share with primary children, a plan to refurnish the classroom play corner, plans to decorate the classroom for Halloween, a puppet show. In addition, and perhaps most important, if you are really stimulating your pupils to creative expression there will be a stream of individual enterprises, some going on during periods you set aside for independent activities, some squeezed in during other aspects of the day as youngsters find time to finish a poem, write a story, paint another picture, get together to compose a tune for a song. With adjustments because of the nature of the schedule, this variety of activities is also typical of the classroom of the creative teacher of art or music—some activities planned with the children to solve a problem arising through other classroom activities, some group projects originating in the special classrooms, and some opportunities for individual exploration.

The problem of deciding exactly what experiences should be provided for any particular class—where to begin, what types of activities to plan, what standards to hold—is even more difficult when planning how to encourage pupils in creative expression than it is when mapping out an effective skills program or deciding how extensive a unit of work in science or social studies should be. Individual differences and the general maturity level of the pupils must be taken into account in every aspect of the school program, but in the area of creative expression each pupil's special interests, talents, needs, and modes of expression must be honored as unique. The problem is complicated enough for the teacher of a self-contained classroom who can draw upon the resources of the total school day. For the specialist in music or art, to whom pupils come for a single period, perhaps only twice a week, providing an effective program becomes even more difficult. How do you plan the type of program that will meet effectively the needs of a particular group of boys and girls and capitalize on their talents?

Start with talents where you find them. How do you decide where to begin in helping your pupils to grow in creative expression? As with planning any other aspect of your program, your first step will be to survey the capacities and needs of your pupils. As a student teacher, you will have the benefit of the insights of your cooperating teacher, but when you have your own classroom, you will start out with thirty or more wiggling, eager strangers—each with his own purposes, talents, and insights. The chances are that the cumulative records will reveal less to you about your pupils' abilities in creative expression than they will about their skills in reading or arithmetic, although their previous teacher may have filed some descriptive notes. Whereas objective test records will probably be available to help you survey your pupils' present command of fundamental skills, there are few such instruments to help you in studying individual interests and potential talents. You will have to rely mainly upon your own powers of observation, your sensitivity to pupils' needs, and just plain common sense and good judgment.[1]

The exploratory activities with which most teachers begin in the early fall can be just as useful in uncovering special talents and interests as they are in revealing reading needs or language deficiencies. Children may be given opportunities to write or tell about themselves and their families and perhaps to report on summer vacations. Plans may be made to decorate the classroom. Time may be taken to explore the classroom library. A sharing period may be included in the schedule and perhaps a sharing table or a corner museum established. It will not be long before individual characteristics begin to stand out. Mary and Alicia volunteer to help set up an autumn bulletin board. First-grade Susan gravitates to the easel. Russell seems to express grace and rhythm in every movement. Frank's attempt to draw his home for a get-acquainted bulletin board indicates a very limited sense of perspective, but he shows definite organizational qualities when it comes to figuring out how best to use space in the library corner. Carl reports with obvious enthusiasm on the historical fiction he has been reading. Five-year-old Sammy displays a fine sense of climax as he holds the kindergarten spellbound with his story of how his lost puppy was found.

[1] This is an area where the techniques outlined in Chapter 4 for observing pupils and gathering information about them as they work can be of particular value.

Harry's sparkling eyes and appreciative comments as he shows the class his insect collection reveal strong science interests and a deepening awareness of the beauties of nature. There will be others, too, with characteristics which are obviously personal and original. Whether you are working with kindergarteners or sixth-graders, you will soon begin to identify something unique about each pupil if you observe your boys and girls wisely. These are the talents you will plan to foster as you begin to think about the types of experiences to provide.

In addition to studying their pupils during the course of the regular program, most teachers also plan for special activities in which their observations can be focused more directly on the range of creative potential in particular areas. There may be a storytelling session where groups of five or six meet with the teacher to share special experiences. There are many opportunities for art in the opening days of school—pictures may be needed to decorate a bulletin board; a trip to the park may eventuate in a series of pictures showing what interested each child the most; pupils may draw themselves engaged in their favorite activities for a get-acquainted session. Because music is a cherished experience for most youngsters, it is appropriate to stop to sing, to discuss favorite songs, to discover which pupils play musical instruments, to participate in some creative rhythms while listening to a favorite record. Sharing sessions can be focused on favorite books, favorite television programs, hobbies. Such planned get-acquainted sessions are as appropriate in the rooms of the specialists in music and art as they are in the regular classroom; they can reveal much about individuals.

Many classrooms can be arranged so that there are centers for special activities—an art corner, a library table, a music corner, a workbench, a science interest center. Teachers who are anxious to encourage creative expression frequently plan the schedule of activities in the early part of the school year so that there is time for individual exploration. Sometimes the last period in the afternoon is scheduled for independent work two or three times a week. Typically teacher and children plan together for such periods, after which youngsters proceed with their plans individually or in small groups. Such independent activity periods provide time for you to talk with a child building a model at the science table, listen to the group reading stories, give some advice to the young authors about to cast a play, read a poem being polished for the school paper. As you give such help, you can note which pupils gravitate to which kinds of activities, what levels of performance they demonstrate, what special interests are revealed. Similar periods for independent exploration are appropriate in special art or music classrooms and just as fruitful in what they will reveal about individual strengths and weaknesses, talents, needs, and interests.

Appraise the opportunities for creative expression inherent in regular classroom activities. Identifying the creative potentials in your pupils and the level of technical competence at which they are now operating is a first step in considering the types of experiences they need. To decide upon your exact starting points, you will need to look at the opportunities inherent in your regular classroom activities. If creative expression is to become for your pupils a way of thinking and working—an essential aspect of daily living—it must be part and parcel of the day's activities. In the classrooms of sensitive teachers there are so many opportunities for creative expression that the problem is usually one of deciding which to choose in building a program for boys and girls.

A careful survey of your room will reveal many opportunities for art expression. Pictures will be needed to make your classroom more attractive. Bulletin boards can be brightened by colorful borders. Children's stories can be attractively displayed. Your library or play corner may merit redecoration. Murals may be needed to summarize unit activities. Get-well cards may be sent to a child who is hospitalized. The list is almost endless, and from such needs to put art to use in daily living will come some of your plans for special experiences with art media.

Classroom opportunities for music and rhythmic experiences are no less abundant. There will be occasions for singing just for the fun of singing and needs for activity that can be well met through experiences with rhythms. There will be songs for special occasions, such as Thanksgiving, Christmas, Halloween, and songs needed to enrich the work of unit activities—songs about postmen, trains, firemen. Older children may want to explore the forms of music expression in other countries. Records may be in demand for background music for a rest period, for interim music between the acts of a play, for marching on and off stage in an auditorium session. When there are musical instruments available for exploration, there will be demands for help in using them, for planning the accompaniment to an original song, for including a rhythm band as part of the entertainment when parents come to visit.

Points at which creative writing is needed are equally numerous. There may be a school paper to which to contribute, or a class magazine or newspaper. Unit activities call for a variety of reports, stories, poems. Special days offer opportunities for stories and poems—Valentine stories, Christmas tales. Trips and excursions may need to be recorded so that others may share the experience. Music experiences may lead to the writing of original songs. You will be able to extend this list manyfold from your own previous experiences with classrooms.

In the typical classroom program, experiences in creative dramatics are no less in demand. Youngsters may share their reading experiences through dramatization or pantomime. A group in social studies may present its findings in dramatic form. A primary play corner may be the source of one informal bit of play making after another. A problem in playground relations may seem to be best handled through role playing. An assembly program may provide an opportunity for tableaux, choral speaking, or a play. These are situations arising not once but many times during the school year.

Special teachers of art and music can utilize these same sources of help in thinking through the experiences they wish to provide for boys and girls. If the organization of your school permits you to go to the classroom to work with both the regular homeroom teacher and the children, you can expect to draw upon the homeroom teacher's insights in determining how your contribution can be most effective. If the children come to you, you may want to confer with the homeroom teacher so that he can help the youngsters plan how best to present their classroom problems on which your help will be needed. There will also be demands from the school community for help with assemblies, special exhibits for the display cases in the hall, scenery for a play, and events such as Christmas, Valentine's Day, Thanksgiving. In addition to all these sources of purposeful experiences, you will undoubtedly wish to allow classroom time for exploration—singing, listening, experimenting with musical instruments or art media—and will plan part of your program, as would the teacher of a self-contained class, around the special needs and interests that result. Certainly, whether programs in the creative arts are planned as part of a regular class day or developed by specialists, there is no excuse for a rigidly organized, preconceived sequence of experiences bearing no relationship to the purposes and special needs of the children. Nor is there any excuse for situations in which specialists and homeroom teachers fail to plan together so that the special skills and insights of each are used effectively in the interest of a rich and stimulating program for boys and girls. Such programs are exactly the opposite of what we mean when we talk about encouraging creativity.

Plan for special help on skills as needs arise. Granted that experiences in creative expression must be closely related to pupils' problems of daily living if they are to have meaning, should there not also be some attention given to a carefully planned sequential series of experiences? If these are not provided in an orderly fashion, how will necessary skills be taught and contacts with a wide variety of media be assured? If classroom needs and children's concerns are the focal points from which programs in the creative arts develop, will not the experiences of many classes be one-sided and meager? Certainly, you will want to plan your pupils' activities so as to give practice in specific techniques and to introduce new media. Just as it is possible to start from pupil needs in reading, spelling, or arithmetic and still provide for orderly and sequential skill development, so is it possible in art or music.[2] Furthermore, in the creative arts there are fewer sequences of learnings essential to the development of effective skill than there are in areas such as reading or arithmetic. Certainly, too, it would be extremely difficult to foster creative expression as a part of pupils' daily living if a preconceived sequence of activities prescribed by a textbook or course of study had to be followed systematically. You must be prepared to assure a rich and well-rounded program, while working in terms of day-by-day classroom opportunities.

The teacher of the so-called fundamental skills makes sure that there will be opportunities to develop all the basic techniques important to an effective reader, speller, or mathematician by providing a rich and stimulating classroom atmosphere in which these many types of problems will arise. In like fashion, if you want to work from your pupils' needs to develop a well-rounded program in the creative arts, you must make sure that there is a rich and stimulating classroom atmosphere. Youngsters will not, out of the blue, make requests for a rhythm band, ask to learn how to use a new art medium, or beg to be taught to write poetry unless they are working in a setting that provides encouragement to undertake such activities. In an atmosphere rich in opportunities to be creative, however, you need have few anxieties that there will not, over the year, arise genuine needs to learn to use all the techniques and media with which you hope to help your pupils to become acquainted.

As with the development of the fundamental skills, then, your own professional judgment, rather than an outline in the course of study or the sequence of activities proposed in a music or a language arts text, should be your guide when it comes to deciding the point at which

[2] Reread the discussion in Chapter 8, pages 303-307. Many of the same principles are applicable here.

help with specific techniques is needed and what that help should be. From your own experience you know that water colors and fine brushes are rarely an effective medium for beginners, that tools with sharp edges must be reserved for hands that can use them safely, that beginners are unlikely to gain much from a lesson on perspective, that reading notes in music calls for considerable intellectual maturity, that limited handwriting and spelling skills suggest oral rather that written experiences in storytelling in the first grade. This professional background, combined with your study of the needs of individuals, will be your guide in deciding when a new medium should be introduced or when practice with an advanced technique should be provided. You, not the author-specialist in art or music education a thousand miles away, must be the one to make the final decisions regarding how best to release the creative potential of your boys and girls.

GUIDING THE EXPERIENCES THAT FOSTER CREATIVE EXPRESSION

Once you have identified the concerns, needs, and interests that are initial starting points in providing experiences in creative expression, how do you guide these experiences so that pupils will be truly creative—original, honest in expressing what they feel, increasingly in command of the techniques they need to give effective expression to what they are thinking? Such results have not always come from activities centered in the creative arts. If you will appraise your own background frankly, you will be indeed fortunate if you do not identify at least one series of experiences in art, music, creative writing, or dramatics in which your efforts were anything but creative, as defined by the goals suggested in this chapter.

In fostering growth in creative expression, perhaps even more than in helping your pupils to grow in understanding their world or in improving their proficiency with fundamental skills, much will depend upon the sensitivity with which you guide the efforts of individual children. Even so, you will also be laying plans for specific lessons. Some of these will serve to demonstrate or to give practice with a new technique (introducing for the first time how to use clay or papier-mâché or demonstrating how to play a flutophone). Others will build insights and standards (analyzing the literary qualities of a selection or discovering the unique characteristics of folk music or folk tales). In planning such specific lessons you will need to consider questions similar to those important in planning a single lesson in any other area:

What are my goals? What is the new technique or insight that I hope to develop? What changes in behavior do I expect of my pupils as a result of this experience?

How can I give my pupils a sense of purpose? What is my starting point with them? What aspect of their work caused this new problem to arise? How can I help them to see the value of the new experience? What is my point of contact with their lives and activities?

What steps do I need to take to help my pupils understand the new techniques or develop appreciation of the new form of expression? Should I give a demonstration? If so, what steps should my demonstration follow? Are there special explanations needed? How should I involve my pupils in thinking? Do I want them handling materials while I demonstrate? If so, what precautionary instructions will be needed? Do I need to examine models with them? If so, what questions could I ask to help develop more sensitive appreciation? What precautions shall I take to assure that truly creative expression on the part of my pupils results from this experience?

What opportunities to use the new skill or insight shall I provide? Do I plan to have pupils put this new technique or understanding to use in their own projects or should there be some common practice? If I have them practice with a common assignment, how can I encourage them to deviate from this pattern when they start on their own? What alternatives should I be prepared to suggest in order to stimulate their thinking?

How shall I evaluate progress? What types of behavior will tell me that I have achieved my goals? Through what activities should I secure my evidence? What should I look for in the future as continued evidence that learning has been effective?

Developing pupils' creative potential does not call for any less careful planning or for steps in planning any different from those which distinguish all good teaching. The difference lies in the goal and, consequently, in the way you think through and carry out your plans. In teaching a lesson on fractions, for example, you are helping your pupils to derive an established rule, although you may encourage original thinking in order to arrive at it. In helping pupils to grow in understanding their world, there are accurate concepts to be developed, although, again, a skillful teacher encourages originality and independent enterprise in the explorations that lead to the development of the new concept. In helping pupils to become more skilled in creative expression, too, there will be times when you will want to help your pupils to arrive at established concepts or principles—to understand the specific meaning of a half note, the reason for not overloading a paint brush, or the importance of planning for a climax in a story. For the most part, however, the goals you seek will be individual and unique and will lead to an outcome which is original and different. Your guidance must provide the understanding, support, and encouragement that makes it possible for your pupils to be different, to develop their own means of self-expression. What basic principles should you have in mind as you go about it?

Creative expression is fostered by a rich classroom environment. The creative pupil is sensitive to his social setting; he takes his cues from his surroundings. A classroom furnished with only the conventional equipment is barren, bleak, cold, and forbidding. Few of us need further description. We have all had experience with such school environments. On the other hand, we know how attractive an appropriately equipped classroom can be. Take a look, for example, at the classrooms of some creative teachers:

Miss Hale taught middle-grades science. Her own background in science was not extensive, but she was a most enthusiastic and ingenious teacher. Her room was a veritable museum. Where these scientific materials came from was really no mystery. Her pupils scoured the woods and countryside. The time they spent in this activity was the joy of Miss Hale and—at times—the despair of some of the other teachers. Their exhibits, arrangements, and posters overflowed the room into the halls and into the homerooms. Some of the pupils developed a lifelong interest in science. One of them is now the curator in a nationally known zoological garden.

Miss Hayden in the fourth-grade room loved books, poetry, and writing. She brought her own books, procured more from school funds, borrowed from pupils, the parents, and the library. One book corner is ordinarily sufficient for a classroom, but Miss Hayden's room had books on the reading table, books in bookcases and, better still, books on the children's desks. They were used not only for classwork, but for ideas and information in dramatics, the room newspaper, speech work, and written compositions. The walls, except for necessary blackboards, were covered with bulletin boards. There the children placed book jackets, photographs, posters, and original illustrations. Much of the art work and some of the music could be traced to ideas from the books. Many of the posters and illustrations were of original design. Compositions selected by the pupils were reserved for one special bulletin board.

Miss McCarthy's first-grade room offered a rich variety of possibilities for her beginners. Near the door was a bulletin board upon which there was an attractive arrangement of pictures, changed with the seasons. Across the front of the room under the blackboard was a clothesline on which children's pictures could be hung. On the shelves under the windows were plants, an aquarium, a terrarium, and a collection of nuts, leaves, rocks, and other interesting objects brought in by the children. In the back of the room was a play corner with dolls, a toy stove, furniture, some doll dishes, and other possibilities for dramatic play. In center rear was a library table, flanked by low bookshelves and graced with a plant. Next came an easel and a workbench. Hung from another easel were the children's stories about their latest excursion. Chairs and tables were arranged so that space at the front and the back of the room gave elbow room for large pieces of work, such as a mural.

Mr. White taught music. It seemed to the teachers that he was a genius in scrounging music and musical instruments. Over a period of time he accumulated a variety of horns, trumpets, banjos, xylophones, flutophones, with which his pupils could experiment. In one corner of his room stood a table with instruments the children had made, some with the cooperation of the science teacher—a wooden xylophone, glasses filled with water, a variety of percussion devices for rhythm activities. On another table were musical toys the children had brought from home—a set of bells, a small xylophone. His room also boasted a record player and a tape recorder. On one bulletin board were likely to be pictures of famous composers or articles about current musical events. A bookshelf was stocked with stories of the lives of composers, children's stories on operas, books about musical instruments.

Mr. Anderson taught art. His workshop was the despair of the custodian and the delight of his pupils. A number of large cardboard cartons housed various and sundry discard materials. Pupils had easy access to scraps of wire, broken screens, boxes, egg cartons, plastic materials, metal, bottle caps, beads, gift wrapping, bits of cloth, coat hangers, and other items too numerous to mention. The bulletin boards were filled to overflowing. Wires and clotheslines were stretched across the room for drying purposes and on these hung original and colorful child art forms. Still more stood on tops of cabinets and on window sills. On the teacher's desk stood a vase with spring blossoms brought by the children. On a table near the sink stood several battered dish pans. Pupils mixed wheat paste with water at this place and proceeded to construct three-dimensional papier-mâché animals and figures. An old fernery served as a paint distribution center. In it stood many jars of paint and many empty jars as well as smaller ointment jars. Numerous brushes of various sizes were also located here, as well as some old discarded toothbrushes. A carefully prepared chart with removable tabs hung behind the teacher's desk. These tabs listed pupils' names and their respective responsibilities as monitors in the art room.

The foregoing illustrations appear so perfect that the beginner may be discouraged. These teachers, nevertheless, are real persons who did the things described. You would not want to imitate them, but what they accomplished shows how rich a classroom environment can be under the guidance of a teacher who knows what he wants to achieve for his pupils.

Many of the simple steps taken by teachers to make classrooms more attractive places in which to work also contribute to pupils' insights into the beauties of their world. Miss Manon calls her youngsters together with musical chimes rather than tapping a pencil on her desk. Miss Johnson and her children cultivate a variety of plants "just to look at." Mrs. McWhite's youngsters take great pride in their orderly library corner with its bright covers for the chair backs. In Mrs. Swanson's kindergarten is a rocking chair about which pupils group for story hours. Mr. Stevens' boys and girls have decorated their bulletin board with original fraction charts. Mrs. Allen's youngsters have their own bulletin board of pictures and cartoons with captions attached. Mr. Archer's children, tired of pulling shades and a dark room on sunny days, made themselves muslin drapes which pulled across the full side wall of windows. On a rainy day, Miss Whitney could be counted on to wear a bright dress. Teachers who bring beauty, order, and originality into the simplest aspects of living are themselves creative, imaginative, and sensitive persons.

In the classrooms of creative teachers, a stimulating environment is not bounded by the walls of the room. In a city school, some third-graders took great delight in their traffic light, flashing red, amber, and green so cheerfully just outside their window on rainy days. In another city school, youngsters stopped periodically to watch their view—across the apartments in the valley and up to the homes and church spires on the distant hilltops. They watched the rains approaching; the fog lifting; the sun making the distant houses sparkle; the colors in the early morning, high noon, and in late afternoon; the skyline. In a residential district first-graders loved their tree, as it turned to bronze and gold, stood as a stark silhouette in winter, was changed to fairyland with ice and snow, and blossomed again in the spring. In another classroom, youngsters grew to love the clouds. In still another, they stopped occasionally to listen for interesting sounds. Outside the classroom windows there is a world of stimulation to creative expression for teachers and pupils who are sensitive to it.

Furnishing a classroom with stimulating, useful materials is not an easy task. As a student teacher you will undoubtedly profit by all that your cooperating teacher has collected, but when you walk into your first classroom on the job, you may find that the previous teacher has taken most of his accumulation with him. How well you can do will depend upon your ingenuity, patience, and resourcefulness. You would be wise to make note of the many commonplace, everyday materials your cooperating teacher manages to put to use. You would also be wise to start your own picture collection and to build the habit of thinking about possible resource materials by supplying as many extras as you can in your student-teaching assignment. On your first full-time job, the principal can be of help; other teachers will make contributions; and the school custodian may be an unsuspected source of assistance. Above all, however, you will have to help yourself.

Creative expression blossoms under a sensitive and perceptive teacher. Classroom atmospheres can be rich and stimulating in rooms that seem relatively unattractive. Conversely, rooms that strike the visitor at first glance as being unusually rich and stimulating can, on further acquaintance, turn out to be restrictive and unfertile. The youngsters in the preceding illustrations would not have grown to love their traffic signal, their view, or their tree had there not been teachers sensitive to the beauties in the outdoor environment, natural or man-made. Nor would there have been delight in classroom furnishings, neatness and order, plants in the window, had teachers not been sensitive to the aesthetic satisfactions in everyday living. The most essential element in a stimulating classroom environment is a sensitive and perceptive teacher.

Sensitive and perceptive teachers find deep personal satisfactions in the various creative arts which they share generously with their pupils, not as old-time "appreciation lessons" but just for the joy of sharing something beautiful. Student teachers often make a major contribution at this point. Sally Peterson brings her poetry notebook and reads to the children when time permits. Sam Johnson, the solo cornetist in the college band, brings his instrument and plays for the children. Anne Wilson has a trained voice; although most of her teaching of music is devoted to helping the children to express themselves, she does not hesitate once in a while to sing for them. Andrew MacIntosh on occasion delights his art class by drawing cartoons for them. Max Larsen shares his college training in speech and dramatics by reading aloud to his sixth-graders stories a little too difficult for them to read for themselves. Roberta White holds her kindergarteners spellbound with her stories, illustrating them with line drawings as she goes along. Rachel Adams plays favorites from her record collection during her first-graders' rest periods. Pupils do not create in a vacuum, nor do they build standards of appreciation without contact with creative expression of high quality. Teachers who themselves have deep and perceptive insights contribute much by sharing these.

Even more important, sensitive and perceptive teachers recognize latent abilities in pupils and take measures to insure that these are released and developed. The few talented and gifted pupils whom you have in your classroom may create with little or no help from you, but the remainder need stimulation and encouragement. Many potentially creative children are not self-starters. They need to be pushed, usually gently but sometimes with vigor. Here the astute teacher has an important role. Discovering vital interests and special abilities is a real test of the teacher's perceptivity. Creativity seems to follow no given paths. It manifests itself by vague and almost imperceptible signals rather than by words or by doing. The perceptive and sensitive teacher, then, is a good reader of signals. If you can sense the cues, you can take the necessary action. No one can teach creativity, but the discerning and understanding teacher can help to free the creative urge that seeks to express itself.

Sally McNamara was an expert in this respect. Tom Winters wrote the usual stereotyped compositions. Sally, however, noticed an occasional flare for using the right word in the right place. Knowing Tom, she decided not to force him to write, but she did make sure that he had an opportunity to attempt ways of expressing himself. Tom worked on the room newspaper. Sally saw to it that his feature articles were praised by the group and by other teachers. Even the principal sometimes commended him. Tom was not the only pupil who was unobtrusively encouraged. Patty expressed an interest in writing a play for the history class. Henry had some ability with ceramic material. John showed some talent in music. In fact, there was no pupil in her class in whom Sally did not discern some special ability. How she did it was her secret. If you asked her, she probably couldn't explain it, but sensitivity to individuals was at the heart of it.

Mildred Walker also managed to free the potential of individuals. One year her medium was a unit on the poetry of Robert Louis Stevenson which culminated for her fourth-graders in a program and tea for parents. Some of Stevenson's poems were set to music; others were read. Explanatory notes for the assembly program were written, invitations to the parents were sent, arrangements for greeting assembly guests and parents were worked out in detail. An attractive tea table was set, and napkins were decorated. There was something for each pupil and each group to do. Even John, who couldn't handle verbal materials very well, had a creative contribution to make—he was the stage manager.

Perceptive teachers are able to sense what a pupil is trying to express in his creative effort and to give the help that makes it possible for the budding artist, poet, musician, or writer to say things in his own way. Consider, for example, the approaches of two beginners whose fifth-graders decided it would be fun to paint the clump of pine trees sparkling with snow, visible from the classroom window. Rowena Sands is more concerned about the end product than she is about her pupils' growing ability to express themselves:

ROWENA SANDS
That's good, Sammy, but put a little more snow down here, don't you think?

SAMMY
Okay, I guess so.

BETTY
Miss Sands, I can't make mine look like a pine tree.

ROWENA SANDS
Give me your brush for a minute. There! Make your strokes a little firmer. Do you see?

BETTY
Yes ma'am. Won't you finish that one for me, Miss Sands? Then I can do the others.

In contrast, John Birk is concerned about helping his pupils to achieve their own insights and modes of expression:

JOHN BIRK
How are you getting along, Sammy?

SAMMY
Okay, I guess. Do I have enough snow?

JOHN BIRK
That depends on how the trees look to you. Do you feel it should be heavy snow?

SAMMY

I think so. The branches are almost falling down. Say! Maybe that's what mine needs. They're pretty straight.

JOHN BIRK

Why don't you stand back from yours a little and see what you think?

BETTY

Mr. Birk, I can't make mine look like a pine tree.

JOHN BIRK

Come back here with me where you can see them easily. What is it that let's you know they're pine trees?

BETTY

Well, the dark green; but mine still don't look right.

JOHN BIRK

Let's keep on studying them. What does their shape remind you of?

Children will not give honest expression to their own perceptions in situations where teachers' standards obviously have to be met. The sensitive teacher does not withhold his help from a pupil in difficulty, but he gives it in ways that aid the pupil in his own perception and expression.

In the classrooms of sensitive teachers, there is generous acceptance of original thinking whenever it occurs. These are not situations where children are encouraged to be original during art and music time and to work by the book in reading, spelling, social studies, and science. There will be unit activities in these areas, encouragement for groups and individuals to propose new ways of working, generous appreciation of an original idea. Listen to such teachers as they go about the day's work. "Billy used a grown-up word to describe what is happening to our windows. He said the water *evaporates.* That would be a good one for us all to know." "John and Jerry have a very interesting proposal to keep our bookshelves more tidy; tell us about it, boys." "James thinks he has another way of proving that plants need sunlight. That's good thinking, James. Do you want someone to help you with it?" "Sandra thinks this would be a very good story to make into a play. What do you want to do about it?" "Rose has just thought up another way of showing halves and quarters. Some of the rest of you might like to work out something different, too." Originality and creativity are aspects of every classroom activity under teachers such as these.

There is much talk in educational circles about the creative teacher. Often such talk refers to the teacher who does the unusual and startling in teaching procedure. No teacher needs to do the unexpected to be a creative teacher. All that is necessary is that he become progressively more skillful in recognizing inherent creative abilities in his pupils. Sharing experiences and achievements with them, providing opportunities for personal development, encouraging and showing appreciation for individual accomplishments—these are the characteristics of the sensitive creative teacher.

Creative expression develops most readily in a permissive atmosphere. The classrooms described in the preceding pages have permissive atmospheres. This is a term that has come to have many meanings in educational circles. To some, it implies situations in which children do exactly as they please. Certainly, a permissive, democratic atmosphere is not one in which children decide everything. It is, however, a situation in which there is pupil-teacher planning—a situation in which pupils, in degrees appropriate to their maturity, share in determining the rules under which they will live as a classroom group, the activities in which they will engage, the problems they wish to solve, and the ways in which they plan to attack them. No one pupil takes over the room, nor do you abdicate your role as leader. Your function is to secure the maximum pupil participation consistent with the situation.

In terms of fostering creative expression, developing a permissive atmosphere has several specific implications. In the first place, it means that you will involve pupils in planning their activities. If you are to encourage youngsters to think for themselves, they must share in planning the scenery for a play, in deciding how to decorate their classroom for Christmas, in considering how to use folk songs and dances in a report on life in other lands, in making new wallpaper for the playhouse, or in deciding what particular project they are going to undertake during an independent work period.

In a permissive atmosphere, one feels free to be oneself and to express what one sees in one's own way. Rowena Sands, whose guidance of the fifth-graders painting the pine trees was described earlier, couldn't provide such permissiveness. In the end, her pupils' paintings came out as she wanted them, touched up in spots with her own hand. To permit pupils to make choices which you know in the light of your experience and more sophisticated judgment are not going to yield the best results requires self-restraint. Often it is a calculated risk—a risk in which you cross your fingers and hope for the best. Regardless of the strain on your nerves, pupils who develop creatively must have freedom to plan, to carry out their plans, to err, to accept their errors as learning experiences, and to go on to more productive effort. Above all, they must feel secure in being themselves.

It is quite possible that your ability to give help without imposing your own standards is related to your personality and to your conception of yourself as a teacher. Jonathan Jones played all the leading roles in the college plays. Everyone expected Jonathan's pupils to do exceptionally well in dramatics. Their final productions were a credit to Jonathan's dramatic insights, but certainly not to his skill in developing creativity, as each child moved and spoke exactly as he had been told. Sara Watson had found deep personal satisfactions in caring for little children all her life. She was an older sister and a much-sought baby sitter. When she started to teach, she could not resist appeals for help. She drew a picture here, supplied a word there, fixed up a rhyme for a struggling poet, took home a confused act in a play and polished it. All these services offered deep personal satisfactions to Sara and allowed her to play the role of the helpful mother to her group, but what was happening to her pupils' ability to create for themselves? It will be difficult for you to provide the permissive atmosphere in which your pupils can grow if it is important to your self-esteem or to your need for affection to keep them dependent upon you. You must find ways of satisfying your own personal needs that do not interfere with your pupils' maximum growth.

Permissiveness also means freedom to choose the medium in which one feels most at ease in expressing oneself. Sometimes in our zeal to give each pupil contact with each medium we run the risk of reducing all to the same level of mediocrity. Some will write, some will sing, some dance, some paint. Although you will hope to expand your pupils' acquaintance with many media, you will also want to encourage those with particular bents. Sally Johnson achieved this in the summary of a health unit on Foods We Need. One small group had developed a play around family meals. Several other youngsters made posters advertising the foods they had studied. Under the leadership of a pupil talented in music, three girls wrote a song with a chorus, set it to music, and developed a little dance to go with it. A group of boys made large papier-mâché models. Several youngsters wrote original poems or stories. One group demonstrated a table setting, complete with napkins, centerpiece, and place cards. Here was creativity, yet each pupil expressed what he felt in his own way.

If you are responsible strictly for experiences in art, crafts, or music, your freedom in permitting each pupil to work with his own medium may be restricted to some degree, but you can still do much if you plan for individual and small-group activities rather than teaching your class as a whole. Miss Ray's art room presents a challenging example to beginners. A casual visitor might well report that there was "little order in that room." Yet even a few minutes' observation revealed an organized busyness which was characteristic of all of Miss Ray's classes. The working rules had been decided early in the year. After a few weeks everyone knew exactly what to do at the beginning and end of each class period. In between, the pupils worked individually and cooperatively on a variety of projects, some connected with the assigned unit, some representing special, individual requests. Most of her pupils were not particularly gifted in art media, yet at system-wide exhibits, the work of her pupils was always the subject of favorable comment. In class, the pupils proceeded at their own rate, sometimes working alone, sometimes conferring with others. She moved about giving help when asked, making suggestions here and there and encouraging and advising the unsure and the hesitant. There was often trial and error, starting and restarting, mistakes, and compliments when the results were good or exceeded the creator's own expectations. No one remembers whether great artists were developed in Miss Ray's art classes, but confidence and willingness to try were outstanding characteristics of most of the pupils. Stage scenery for school assemblies and dramatic productions were designed and completed. Decorations for school events and parties were no problem. Enthusiasm and ingenuity in most cases had to be controlled rather than encouraged.

Teachers are individuals. Each one works in his own way and each is in his own way unique. Not every teacher can attain the same results, but every teacher can be a developer of creative expression if only he will give pupils a chance. Permissiveness is a key, a way of achieving creative results. How permissive the classroom should be is to be decided by each teacher, working cooperatively with his pupils.

Creative expression is stimulated in an accepting and responsive group atmosphere. Pupils themselves are part of the classroom environment, and a very important part. Creativity is a personal matter, but there is joy in sharing with others and a wealth of stimulation from working with one's friends on cooperative projects. Teachers who are skillful in releasing the creative potential of boys and girls find many ways in which pupils can encourage and stimulate each other.

One of the characteristics of classrooms in which there is a wealth of creative expression is a multitude of ways of sharing creative efforts. Sally Thompson sets up a writers' bulletin board in her classroom; here children's stories and poems are posted. In Janice Arthur's room, each child has his own notebook in which he is collecting the best of his writing as an Easter gift for his parents. In Susan Smythe's first grade, she and her cooperating teacher serve as secretaries for the youngsters; the stories are mimeographed and stapled with blank pages so that the young authors can illustrate their own works. In Ron Jones' fifth grade the boys and girls are "publishing" a class newspaper by pasting creative stories, articles, poems, and pictures on large sheets of brown paper. Simone Clarke's third-graders have "storytelling parties" where well-prepared readers may share their favorite books with others. Every three or four weeks Barbara Ronson's reading groups find a story or poem particularly suitable for sharing with the remainder of the class. The hall bulletin board outside Rhonda Flick's fourth grade is typically filled with samples from the latest class project. As their study of animals in the zoo develops, Joan Anderson's pupils write riddles in rhyme and post them for others to share. Claire Clarke's second-graders cooperate in composing and illustrating a class record of their study of community helpers. The list is endless.

Sharing is no less in evidence in art and music rooms. Pupils' work may be posted on bulletin boards. A group may take responsibility for the display cases in the halls of the school. Another class may volunteer to decorate the school lunchroom. A third may plan special decorations for a Parent-Teacher Association meeting. One music class works toward a program of carols to sing around the Christmas tree; a second decides to tape some carols and poems to send to the first-graders as a Christmas gift; a third works toward a class program. Everyone plans musical or art contributions for a Thanksgiving program. A fourth-grade rhythm band volunteers to play for the primary assembly. These are a far cry from the art exhibits, music festivals, and cantatas of other days when long hours went into highly polished performances for adult approval and only those with the greatest talent were recognized. Everybody shares; and although talent is given recognition, everybody's best efforts receive credit.

Skillful teachers also use group creative efforts as means of stimulating individuals. An exploratory experience is often needed to establish the mood. Listen to Ella Jenks, whose cooperating teacher assigned her the responsibility of developing a group poem for the school Thanksgiving assembly:

ELLA JENKS
Boys and girls, each class has been asked to contribute an original poem for the Thanksgiving program. Let's explore a bit, shall we? What do you think of when you think of Thanksgiving? [Ella jots ideas on board as pupils name them.]

TOMMY
Turkey dinner.

ALEC
Holidays.

BETTY
Thankfulness.

ELAINE
Church.

JANE
The Pilgrims and their first Thanksgiving.

ART
Snow.

BILLY
My grandmother. We all go there for Thanksgiving.

ELLA JENKS
Thanksgiving means many kinds of things, doesn't it?

(Nods.)

Are there any you think we might especially want in our poem?

BETTY
We should have thankfulness, because that's what our assembly is about.

JOHN
We could work in lots of things we're thankful for.

ELAINE
Start "We thank Thee, God."

ELLA JENKS

Could you finish your line, Elaine?

ELAINE

We thank Thee, God, for friends and parents.

JOHN

That's too long.

ELLA JENKS

Let's just play with possibilities now until we get what we like. Would anyone else like to try a first line?

(Through this combination of exploring and testing several first lines that "strike a fire" are identified. By this time several youngsters are beginning to play with other lines and the group disbands to try out their ideas overnight. The next day and the days following are days of experimenting and polishing until a poem which satisifies the group is ready.)

A responsive group in a permissive atmosphere will also stimulate one another to engage in many day-by-day creative efforts that are often equally rewarding in releasing individual potential. In one class an imaginative pupil advances the idea that invitations to the class play might be written in verse. Taking up this suggestion, a second pupil proposes that the invitations would be more attractive if they are also illustrated in color. Sam Jones' fourth-graders are having a party for their mothers; they have been working on a unit on Colonial times and one group proposes that place mats and napkins might be decorated with various Colonial themes. The second grade decides to have a pet show as a culmination of their unit; one committee suggests that posters advertising the event be placed in the halls. A sixth-grade science class uses a colored design on a large sheet of wrapping paper to represent the location of the North Star in relation to the Big Dipper; another group from the same class develops somewhat the same idea after having fortuitously seen the Northern Lights a few nights before.

Each of us likes to do something which is different and to get some recognition for it. A carving in soap, a painting representing one's own idea of how some historical personage looked, some work done in the home shop—these and similar individual projects represent attempts to secure personal recognition. They also represent an opportunity for you to encourage and stimulate to further production.

Creative expression can be facilitated through effective skill development. Where do skills come in? Shouldn't music classes be learning to read notes? art groups be learning about perspective? writers be learning to spell and punctuate? Certainly skills are important. At one time they were considered so basic to creative expression that elementary school children were given little or no freedom to create. Punctuation and capitalization rules and spelling were the focus of language programs; in the art classes all pupils drew or constructed the same object, working for polished techniques with pencils and brushes; music groups spent long hours with music notation. Only after such techniques were thoroughly mastered, it was held, would it be possible for pupils to be creative.

Today, the sequence of our teaching is reversed. Children are given the opportunity to explore media first, to develop interests, to discover means of self-expression. Then, as needs become apparent, techniques are polished. This does not mean, of course, that a trio of eager first-graders would be turned loose with poster paint and brushes with no instruction whatsoever, a fourth-grade class handed the paste and paper for papier-mâché puppet heads without supervision, or some fifth-graders allowed to play games with a jar of clay. It does mean that instruction is paced to pupils' insights and to the problems they are encountering. A youngster can be working on his own creative effort and learning better techniques at one and the same time.

Watch Glen Johnson helping his fourth-graders with puppets. These are required for a play and this group has not handled puppets before. Therefore, they need to work with something simple. Glen suggests a hand puppet and shows a model (carefully putting it away later so that it will not be copied). With agreement on the type of puppet, Glen proceeds to demonstrate how a head can be made. Everyone listens carefully while Glen explains the basic principles of stripping papier-mâché over a light bulb. He talks in general terms about features, but he holds off on the details, knowing that the explanation will have to be given over again when the heads are further along. Then his class starts to work. Glen goes from table to table, helping with specific problems as they arise. When the time comes to fold the top layers into features, all stop to watch again. Glen demonstrates several possibilities—ways of making noses large or small, of filling in cheeks, and adding chins. Then he carefully removes his samples and goes back to giving help as individual problems arise. Step by step the puppets are developed. Techniques are polished as problems arise. Nobody is trying to duplicate a model. Individuals are creating as they are developing skill.

In music, the start is with songs by rote, rhythms for fun to accompany favorite airs, and songs and rhythms developed creatively as individual and group enterprises. Then comes the time when somebody wants to save a creative rhythm or a tune so that it can be danced or sung again. Here is an opportunity to introduce the meaning of notes. A child brings a toy instrument from home with a little book of tunes to be played by referring to numbers or colors. Here is another opportunity to relate experience to reading notes. Somebody else is taking piano lessons. Soon many in the group are ready for the satisfactions of learning to read notes.

Writing skills are developed in somewhat similar fashion. In the primary grades children's first creative efforts are likely to be oral and to be transcribed by the teacher. A little later they may copy the results of a group effort, with due attention to capitals, letter formation, and periods. As they begin to write for themselves, new problems of spelling, capitalization, and punctuation arise. These are handled as they come up, sometimes with the class as a whole (as when everybody wants to try to put conversation in his story) and sometimes with smaller groups or individuals (as when talented Billy decides to write a play and needs help in putting down his dialogue). Skills are not neglected, but the need for them in the creative activity determines their sequence.

Although they accept in theory the general proposition that skill development should be in response to a need, many teachers are concerned with what this means in practice. If a child becomes unduly aware of the techniques he should be using, his preoccupation may get in the way of his creative response. On the other hand, if one does not make him conscious of technique, the end product may be far inferior to what he is capable of producing. For example, must one ignore spelling completely in the name of creativity in writing? Creativity is a personal affair, true, but in many cases the end product is also a means of communicating one's feelings to others. Eventually, for the satisfaction of both producer and consumer, the end product needs to attain a level of effectiveness commensurate with the maturity and ability of its creator.

You will discover many ways of giving help with techniques through means that do not block creativity. For one thing, you will use your professional judgment in helping youngsters to plan a job that is reasonably within their present level of skill. You will use simpler rhythm instruments with younger pupils, choose paint brushes large enough to be comfortable in little hands, use paper properly lined for beginning handwriting. You will also discover ways of helping young-

Creative expression develops most readily in a permissive atmosphere. Suggestions to young artists help to make independent work satisfying.

Summer Demonstration School,
University of Cincinnati,
D. Arthur Bricker, Photographer

Public Schools, Cincinnati, Ohio,
Gilbert H. Corlett, Photographer

Creative expression is fostered in a rich classroom environment. Opportunities to experiment are important in musical expression.

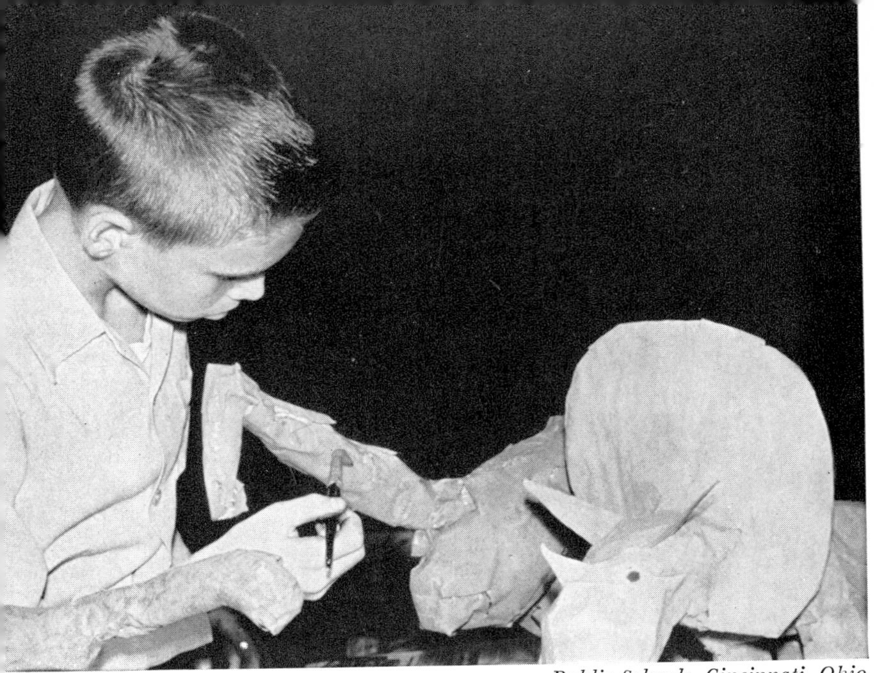

Public Schools, Cincinnati, Ohio,
Gilbert H. Corlett, Photographer

Make a special effort to identify pupils with unusual talent. Papier-mâché is a satisfying medium for young sculptors.

Public Schools, Cincinnati, Ohio,
Marsden H. Gribbell, Photographer

Creative expression is stimulated in a responsive group atmosphere. Novel illustrations for original stories hold an appreciative audience.

sters polish their efforts after they have focused their full creative energies on deciding exactly what they want to express. A song can be enjoyed for its tunefulness and rhythm, and then the articulation of word endings can be practiced so that those in the back of the room can hear clearly. Lists of words posted in the classroom can aid with spelling problems; so can teachers if they make themselves available with a pad and pencil to write the words youngsters need. Pupils can first write what they feel and then proofread against a list of class reminders before the final product is copied carefully for the bulletin board. Such two-step performances safeguard the creative response and still provide for a satisfying end product in which development of skill is an essential concomitant. There is a thrill to expressing exactly what one sees and feels, but part of this thrill lies in possessing the skills one needs to achieve a product that is completely satisfying. If you want to free your pupils to express themselves creatively, you must provide them with the tools they need to convert their visions into concrete realities.

DEVELOPING PERSONAL INSIGHTS AND STANDARDS

Pupils will not grow in their insights, their sensitivity to the world around them, and the depth of their appreciation unless they are working with teachers who are concerned with these aspects of growth. Freeing pupils to express themselves in their own ways is half the job in developing creativity; helping them to develop deeper insights and build higher standards is the other. Actually, freeing pupils' creative potential and helping them to develop higher standards of personal appreciation are aspects of the same whole. It is very difficult to do one well without also doing the other. Your role in helping pupils to grow in personal understandings, achieve higher standards, and develop deeper values is an extremely important one in the total process of stimulating creative expression.

Whether or not there ever will be a universally accepted set of values in matters aesthetic is a matter of some disagreement. Many persons point to the uniqueness of creative expression as evidence that no absolute set of standards can ever be developed. Certainly you, as a beginning teacher, will probably feel that your own level of appreciation is not what you would like it to be in any area. You can, however, offer your group something priceless, namely, your own personal set of growing, developing values. On these you will base your work in helping your pupils to develop more sensitive insights and higher standards.

As you extend your own contacts with the richness of our cultural heritage and deepen your own insights, you will become better and better able to help your pupils grow.

Values and standards are generalizations. They are attained through many experiences; they gain depth and richness as pupils become more mature. Your problem is not to equip your pupils with sets of rules by which they may judge their own creative products and those of others to be good or bad, right or wrong, but to help them develop insights into the many elements that contribute to the result that the artist himself and others recognize as satisfying. How do you go about it?

Standards grow slowly. One of the most difficult problems faced by many beginners is that of recognizing the level of appreciation of which their pupils are capable. A typical first-grader does not see things in perspective. What is most important to him is likely to be drawn largest in his picture. Suns and moons are endowed, by the kindergartener, with personality and smile benignly. The fourth grader will not hold the standards for a dramatic performance that you will hold. The poem that is deeply satisfying to you will not necessarily have the same appeal to a sixth-grader. You must start with pupils where they are. If you want to help your youngsters develop deeper insights, you will bring to bear all that you have learned about the typical art forms of pupils of the age group you are teaching, their capacity for musical and rhythmic expression and appreciation, their typical language forms. You will need to learn to see the world through your pupils' eyes.

There is a fine line between sensitive encouragement that helps a pupil to recognize and preserve the outstanding elements in his work and adult direction that results in a product, which, however polished and admirable, does not represent the child's own values. How can you decide how much help you are to give? One guide line runs through all the sections that follow: *Work in ways that help your pupils to set their own standards and identify their own strengths and weaknesses.* If you can resist the temptation to tell your pupils how to think and what to do next or the temptation to pick up a pencil or paint brush and finish the job for them, you have established one of the strongest safeguards against imposing an adult standard that does not have meaning for them. Likewise, you will need to learn to accept a pupil's feeling that he is satisfied with his product. You may help him take an objective look at his work and encourage him to think whether it conveys the meaning he intended, but when he feels that it expresses exactly what he wanted to express, the job, for him, is done. Perhaps to you the product will seem limited from an aesthetic standpoint, but if it is his honest work, and a satisfying experience to him, this represents his level of insight for the moment. If you have a classroom environment rich in stimulations to creative expression, the time will come when he will see new possibilities and set his sights higher. You will not, however, change his sense of proportion in his paintings by advising that he put a fence he does not want around his horse, or increase his sensitivity to good poetry by attaching two more lines to a poem that he feels is already complete. This does not say that pupils should be denied the guidance that will help them to take pride in their work. Their standards, however, will grow as effective teaching helps them to achieve the goals they are capable of envisioning at their present levels of maturity, not through having them take pride in a product in which the finishing touches have been added by somebody else.

Your problem will be complicated, of course, because not all your pupils will react in the same way. Each youngster will have his own unique perceptions. Jane may be very sensitive to color combinations; Jack may have little feeling for them. Arthur, from babyhood, may have responded actively and with appreciation to rhythm; Allen may seem quite satisfied with his off-beat skipping. Susannah may have a genuine love of beautiful words; George may seem much more entranced with a model of a steam engine. Only as you become acquainted with your pupils will you be able to sense what new experiences might be provided and what next steps individuals are able to take.

Standards are attained through active participation. As with concepts and generalizations in other fields of knowledge, the learner must reach higher orders of insights in the fields of art, drama, or music through his own efforts. To make sure that a pupil understands a new spelling rule, you help him to formulate it out of many specific experiences. You develop insights into principles governing the addition of fractions by actually working with concrete materials. In similar fashion, to guarantee that a pupil is arriving at conclusions regarding more effective use of colors in his pictures or more graphic choice of vocabulary in his writing, you must help him to come to these conclusions after many firsthand experiences.

Some of your most effective assistance in building high standards is likely to be given as you work with individuals. Here is your opportunity to concentrate on the particular problem of expression faced by a single pupil. As you help him to analyze what he is trying to do and to consider how best to achieve his goals, you are contributing to his insights into more effective forms of expression. If you observe skillful teachers as they work with individuals, you will identify many comments that suggest that pupils are being helped to develop higher standards for themselves. Listen to Mildred Winders as Sandy comes for help with his picture:

SANDY
Is this all right, Miss Winders?

MILDRED WINDERS
It's your picture, Sandy. How could you decide if it's what you want?

SANDY
Well, they have to see it while I talk. I guess I should see if it shows up.

MILDRED WINDERS
Shall I hold it while you stand back? How does it look?

SANDY
My man doesn't show hardly at all, and his head's sort of lost against the pink house.

MILDRED WINDERS
What do you think would help?

SANDY
I guess he has to be darker—and maybe I need to put a hat on him. . . .

Follow Sara Random as she gives help with some stories. "Read it to me, John. . . . Is that what you wanted to say?" "What kind of man do you want people to think he was, Betsy? Can you think of some words you could use to describe him?" These youngsters are not being told what to say or to draw but they are being helped to act upon generalizations basic to effective expression: careful choice of words can help in conveying meaning to an audience; it can be helpful to stand off and view one's product as another person might see it.

Pupils can also be given significant help in building higher standards through cooperative evaluation of their efforts. It has been said that teachers are educational gardeners who provide the learning conditions under which boys and girls can grow—in skill, in understanding, in creativity. This is only partly true. Pupils need the encouragement and approval of the teacher, but they also need encouragement and approval of each other. Recognition of accomplishment by one's peers is frequently of greater significance than commendation from someone who has not assisted in the execution of the project. All this means, of course, that the development of group feeling and group evaluation is extremely important for the progressive growth of insights and values.

If group evaluation is to lead to higher standards, there must be thoughtful identification of good points and sympathetic discussion of those that are not so good. All too often, evaluation sessions are limited to comments such as "I liked it," "It was good," "We could hear him," "He stood straight," "I liked the colors." These are not specific enough to be of much help in developing deeper insights and higher standards. The key questions often are: "Why is it good?" and "What makes this way of doing it particularly appropriate?" For example, listen to John Barnes analyzing some creative dramatics with his pupils. The first attempt to dramatize Act I of a play has just been concluded:

JOHN BARNES
Well, what do you think?

ALICE
It was good.

BILL
They did fine.

SANDY
It worked out all right as a first act.

JOHN BARNES
If you think you want to keep this idea as a first act, let's look at it a little more carefully. What do you like particularly about it? Are there parts of it we want to be sure to save?

HELEN
I liked the way Andy started off by sneaking in.

JOHN BARNES
Can you figure out what he did that made it so good?

ART
Well, you sort of felt somebody was right after him.

HELEN
He kept looking around, and he tiptoed.

JOHN BARNES
Was that what you hoped they'd feel, Andy?

ANDY
Yes, I pretended all the shadows were like people.

Group evaluation of the work of individuals can also be pointed toward specific elements. For example, Mary Alice Smith's group, somewhat limited in ability, talked about Thanksgiving poems. After some time had been taken to develop background, each pupil wrote his own short poem. As each one read his original poem, the others listened. Listen to what took place as Mary Alice and her class worked together to achieve more mature standards:

MARY ALICE SMITH
We enjoyed that, John. Did you notice what a quiet audience you had? What did you like especially, boys and girls?

BOB
The way he started, "I am thankful all the year. . . ."

MARY ALICE SMITH
That's an important idea, isn't it? Do you think he should leave that line the way it is?

(Nods.)

What else did you think was especially good?

MARGIE
I thought it was interesting to start all those lines with "for," but they didn't rhyme.

MARY ALICE SMITH
Poems don't always need to rhyme. Did those lines suggest important ideas to you?

(Nods.)

JIM
All but the one about pumpkins. That sounded like Halloween.

MARY ALICE SMITH
Was anyone else confused about that line?

(Nods.)

What were you thinking of, John?

JOHN
Well, pumpkins are ripe in the fall. You bring in all the garden things then.

MARY ALICE SMITH
You wanted that line to suggest harvest time?

JOHN
Yes.

MARY ALICE SMITH
That seems to be the line that they want you to polish a little, John. What about the way the poem ended?

JOHN
I couldn't think how to finish it.

ROSE
Maybe he could say, "I am thankful."

ART
Begin it like it started?

MARY ALICE SMITH
Does that give you the help you wanted, John?

You will have noted another essential characteristic of the type of cooperative evaluation that has just been described. The help given was positive. This is a very important consideration. Unless you are careful such a session may easily degenerate into a free-for-all in which some pupils may take over the class. "He didn't say it right." "Oh, that doesn't rhyme." "He doesn't read it the way it ought to be read."

There is still another important characteristic of these evaluation sessions. They are helping to develop higher standards, but these standards are attained by the pupils themselves. They are not situations in which the teacher takes over, identifies all the errors himself, and "directs" the group to a more polished performance. Contrast, for example, the following approaches as two sixth-grade groups begin to polish a choral-speaking production. Barbara Jamison had strong interests in the field of speech and was anxious to have her pupils demonstrate that she knew how to direct a good performance:

BARBARA JAMISON
That was good, but it was very sing-songy. Listen to me [Barbara reads the poem with considerable expression.] Now let's try it again.

(The pupils read through the poem.)

That's better, but it's still pretty sing-songy. And John, your line doesn't sound as if you are happy. Try to sound excited, like this. . . . [Barbara demonstrates.] Try it, John.

(John mimics Barbara as nearly as he can.)

Now let's try it once more. Listen to me read it first.

(Through the process of imitating Barbara's style, a reasonably polished performance is finally achieved.)

In contrast, Judy Simpson wanted to make sure that her pupils were growing in their own ability to identify the characteristics of a polished performance:

JUDY SIMPSON
How did you like it?

ALEC
Pretty good.

PETER
It sounded choppy to me.

JOAN
Yes, sing-songy, sort of.

JUDY SIMPSON
I thought so, too. Can you figure out why?

JOAN
Well, we don't say it so people can tell which words belong together.

JUDY SIMPSON
Would you like to try the first verse for us, Joan? See if you can show us what you mean.

(Joan does a fair job.)

Would someone else like to try?

(Several volunteers achieve slightly different versions.)

Are these better?

PETER

Yes, Jane's especially. I liked the way she kept right on past the end of the line.

JANE

Miss Simpson, if a chorus said the first lines and somebody else did the last ones, that might help.

JOHN

Yes, maybe have just one person with the last two lines?

JUDY SIMPSON

That's an idea I hadn't thought of. Do you want to try it that way?

(Approving murmurs from several pupils. Work now proceeds in a combination of analyzing and testing until the presentation is polished to the satisfaction of the group.)

Both classes will undoubtedly achieve a good performance, but Barbara's youngsters are not drawing their own conclusions regarding what will make it so. Judy's class, on the other hand, is beginning to think actively about the elements that go into effective expression through choral speech.

There is much satisfaction in achieving an effective piece of work. Your pupils, individually or as a group, have a right to your help in thinking about better ways of expressing themselves. Your responsibility is to see that they achieve the reality of higher standards they accept as well as the outer trappings of a polished performance. Help them to do work of which they can be proud, but help them to grow as they do it.

Models can be helpful. How and when to use models in developing insights can be a troublesome problem. At one time they were considered to be very important in helping pupils to develop depth of insight and higher standards of appreciation. Classes examined reproductions of paintings by great masters, analyzed paragraphs from the classics, and at times imitated the model in their own work. The results were anything but creative, and genuine growth in standards was questionable.

Because models have sometimes been misused, some authorities argue that they never should be part of a program focused on developing creativity. Such an extreme position is open to question. The fact that some teachers have used models unwisely to set external standards does not mean that you need do so. If pupils are to grow in their own ability to judge effective writing, painting, music, there may well be times when they should have opportunity to analyze the techniques used by someone else to achieve a similar goal.

There are several principles you should take into account in deciding whether and when you and your pupils should analyze a model. One is the fact that interpreting and evaluating creative efforts representing external standards—models—are skills which develop rather late in the elementary school years. Younger pupils will enjoy a beautiful picture, listen appreciatively to a good record, and be charmed by a well-told story, but they are not ready to analyze the techniques the artist, composer, or author used to achieve his goals. To attempt such an analysis too early may stifle creativity and freedom of growth. After pupils have had sufficient experience with their own efforts to recognize some of their problems they are better able to approach the work of others.

When pupils are ready to look at the work of others in the light of their own problems, it is often safer to begin in situations unrelated to any specific creative problem. Older pupils may analyze a well-written story in a basal reader in order to see the structure of the author's plot or to identify the ways in which his choice of adjectives or adverbs make the story more graphic. "They say a picture is worth a thousand words," said one perceptive fifth-grader after analyzing a particularly graphic story, "but if you use words like these you can paint pictures." Classes may analyze their reading to collect lists of "quotation helpers"—words that could replace *said* to make a story more interesting—or to build lists of synonyms. Groups in art may consider how a painter achieves perspective or study a series of posters to see how effectively one can use color, lettering, or space. Music groups may analyze a particularly effective use of rhythm or harmony. Such experiences can lend much to the depth of pupils' insights and their discoveries can be recalled to them when next they start on an enterprise of their own.

When you and your pupils turn to a model for help on a specific problem, it is important that they first have enough experience to know where their difficulties lie. What you will want to do is to help them examine someone else's work in order to discover principles to guide their own next steps. Merely placing the model before your group as a sample copy may produce an excellent imitation, but this is not what you want. Follow Sara Jeffers as she tried to introduce a lesson to help her pupils make more effective choices of words:

SARA JEFFERS

Today we are going to think about using more interesting words when we write. You know, the people who do this very well are newspaper writers. I'd like to read you some sample headlines. Listen carefully to these: "SCHOOLS CLOSE," "BLIZZARD HITS," "FIRE LOSS 200,000." Did they make you want to read the articles, John?

(John says "Yes," and several others nod.)

Now, I'd like to see you write some good headlines. Pretend you're a reporter. Then write a paragraph to match your headline.

(Sara gets: "BIG STORM," "SCHOOL OPEN," "FIRE HITS," and others.)

In contrast, Jane Adamson's pupils had both a clear purpose for achieving more graphic writing and opportunity to think for themselves about their problem before they began to do any examining of other people's work. Furthermore, although the task they faced called for application of the principles they discovered through their analysis of their models, it was not possible for them to imitate:

JANE ADAMSON

We are going to write our reports on our school survey today so that Mrs. Johnson can have them for the Parent-Teacher Association bulletin. Did you do some thinking about how to write an article so that people would want to read it?

JOHN

Well, for one thing it needs an interesting title. I know *I* look at titles.

JULIE

And pictures. If it's an interesting picture, I read it.

JANE ADAMSON

Mrs. Johnson says there will not be space for pictures, but we can certainly work on interesting titles. Did you look at some of the headlines in the papers? How many brought some in?

(Several hands go up.)

Shall we listen to them? Mary, will you read yours?

MARY

BLIZZARD HITS.

JANE ADAMSON

Why did that one make you want to read the article, Mary?

MARY

Well, we just had the blizzard, so I wanted to know more about it.

JANE ADAMSON

Does that suggest something to think about in writing a good title?

JOHN

Make it short?

JANE ADAMSON

That's true of Mary's headline, isn't it? Look at the ones you brought in. Are most of them quite short?

(Nods.)

All right, let's put down "make it short." Now what about the word "blizzard"? Why not say "storm"?

(Using pupils' comments on samples secured, Jane goes on to analyze headlines and topic sentences. Then the pupils try appropriate titles and lead sentences for their own articles.)

Use models, then, but do not use them to destroy the urge to be original, to express oneself in one's own way. Help your pupils to grow in their insights into an effective production by looking at it analytically with them, but free them to utilize the principles they have discovered to achieve their own goals in their own unique fashions.

Standards develop from a rich experience background. We respond with warmth to those things which are familiar. Persons who love good music have heard it frequently, often from early childhood. Perceptive readers have backgrounds of satisfying experiences with good books. All that you do to bring into the classroom environment the richness of our cultural heritage in art, music, literature, contributes to your pupils' insights and to their discrimination in the books they select, the pictures they hang on their walls, the music they choose to hear. Their standards grow from their experiences. This, however, is not a matter of inserting into your schedule specific appreciation lessons; it is a question of planning your entire day—long periods and five-minute waits—so that your boys and girls are surrounded with some of the best of the creative expression that their world has to offer.

If you want your pupils' interests and appreciations to widen and deepen, you will see to it that there is variety in their cultural fare. Both popular music and classical numbers have a contribution to make. Factual materials can be as fascinating as fiction. The media through which an artist may express himself are almost limitless. Selecting carefully with the maturity level of your pupils in mind, you should be deepening their insights and extending their horizons by the breadth of the experiences you provide.

The contributions of talented pupils should form part of the rich classroom atmosphere you are trying to build. John can draw well; Henry has a gift for graphic writing; Jane designs posters and Harry knows how to use colors to make the posters attractive; Willie reads poetry aloud beautifully; Allan is handy with tools; Gus can handle numbers well. Each has something he can do perhaps better than anyone else—and he is valued for the contribution he can make to the richness of the classroom environment. A group in which members stimulate each other is one in which each person knows what the others can do best.

In many communities, there will be opportunities to extend your pupils' cultural contacts beyond the school. There may be children's symphony or theater. Sometimes there are opportunities to see fine motion pictures at reduced rates. Visits to local museums can be richly rewarding. Television and radio certainly have much to offer of an aesthetic nature. Your responsibility is to be alert to such opportunities and to help in making them available to your pupils.

All this suggests that you, yourself, must be working actively to deepen your own insights and widen your acquaintance with a variety of forms of expression. Attending a concert, visiting an art museum, reading widely—these are as much a part of your professional activities as are attending faculty meetings or grading papers. One of your most important obligations to your pupils is to make sure that you do not let the pressure of your multitudinous responsibilities prevent you from engaging in the activities that will make you a more vital person.

MEETING THE NEEDS OF THE TALENTED PUPIL

Much is being written today concerning the problem of providing for the needs of the talented pupil. In all probability, our increased awareness of individual differences is resulting in learning experiences better adapted to a wide range of abilities and aptitudes than was the case thirty years ago. This is no reason for complacency, however. Children and youth are our greatest national resource. Equality of opportunity in a democracy does not mean the same opportunity for all. Conscientious teachers are ever alert to the need of nurturing the gifts of the talented pupil.

A classroom and school organization that takes into account the capacities of every learner is automatically geared to meeting the needs of the talented child. In a sense, this entire chapter has been centered around the problem of caring for individual differences. The ways in which you achieve this offer the basic avenues through which you will give encouragement to the talented child. You study each individual in order to identify his concerns and potential creative abilities. Your teaching methods, both for encouraging pupils to express themselves creatively and for helping them to develop personal standards and insights, are those that foster originality, individuality, and personal development. The scheduling of pupils' activities is designed to allow for individualization. There is time for individual and small-group projects. When all-class activities of a unit nature are undertaken, there are opportunities for individuals to contribute at the point and through the medium in which they feel most at home. This is a classroom setting designed to help each pupil to achieve his maximum potential, whether he be classified by the outside world as limited in ability or as talented.

In such a classroom setting, in so far as time and human strength will allow, you will be attempting to give the talented pupil freedom, stimulation, and guidance. What more can any teacher do? In one sense, the story has been told. However, there are special possibilities within such a program of which you should become aware if you, in your first position, are to bend all your resources toward nurturing the pupil with a special gift.

Make a special effort to identify pupils with unusual talent. A first step to take is to attempt to identify those pupils whose talents are exceptional. This is not an easy task. You will have to use your own good judgment, and you will have to be particularly astute in distinguishing between potential creative talent and a polished technical performance. The youngster you are seeking may not be the one who turns out the excellent reproduction of the picture in the textbook or the one whose written work is a model of correctness. You are looking for the child with originality, inventiveness, the power to transform the everyday world by the depth of his insights. If you are a regular homeroom teacher, yourself not unduly gifted, you may well ask specialists in music, art, dramatics, or literature for help in validating your conclusions. Frequently it will take many years of patient encouragement and sympathetic understanding before you will know how good your "hunch" was. There are no simple devices for identifying our talented pupils, yet if their gifts are to be nurtured by the school, someone must feel an obligation to be alert in identifying them.

Develop special talents through your regular classroom activities. Your classroom schedule should allow for work periods during which pupils may be encouraged to pursue intensively a variety of individual interests. Youngsters with exceptional talent should be urged to use such opportunities to pursue their special bents. Sometimes we talk about "well-rounded development," as if each person must achieve approximately the same level of proficiency in everything. Certainly, a strong case could be made for encouraging all pupils to explore to some extent in all areas. (Can we know whether we like a food if we have not tasted it?) All persons, however, do not feel equally at home in every media. Each of us has a right to the satisfaction of top-flight achievement in an area of expression perculiarly his own. You should have a program, then, to encourage pupils to explore in areas representing their particular talent.

There will also be ways of encouraging individuals to use their special talents in group projects. The talented youngster in art may be the one to serve as chairman for the committee producing the mural or for the group which has volunteered a special display for the exhibit cases in art. Skilled musicians may supply the music between the acts of a play or be responsible for an original song and dance to be sung around an imaginary pioneer campfire. Gifted dramatists may work out an original play; the youngster with writing talent may serve as the editor of the class newspaper or be one of the persons holding the class spellbound by their continued stories. In the typical unit activity, there are many places in which individuals can find need for their unique contributions.

Your help, as talented pupils go about their work, should be geared to their level of insight. More proficient techniques should accompany deeper insights and more original ideas. This is another point at which an individualized program can be used to advantage. As you work with your pupils one at a time, or in groups of two or three, you will have your chance to help the child with a flair for writing to analyze the elements of plot, climax, and suspense that go into a good story. Your guidance of the talented artist may take him much more deeply than his friends into principles of perspective or uses of color. You may help the musical youngster to learn how to transcribe his original melody. This is a problem basically no different from the one you face as you think about challenging the best readers in your room or stimulating the pupils with deep interests in science. To help individuals develop to the full extent of their ability, you must provide the leadership and encouragement that take them a step further than where they are now—be they "at grade," "below grade," or several notches "above grade."

Obviously a wealth of stimulation in your classroom environment makes a major contribution to the talented child. He needs opportunities to investigate new media in his chosen field. Particularly he may need the opportunity to work with materials not usually considered appropriate for youngsters of his maturity. This is where the art or music room, equipped with many resources to explore, can often make an unusual contribution. However, you can do much through the materials and equipment you supply and the freedom you provide to explore.

Bring the specialized assistance of school and community to bear. The talented pupil deserves stimulating contacts with others who are gifted in his field. If you are the art or music specialist in your building, you may be the person with special talent and training to whom pupils turn for help. If you are in a self-contained room, the chances are that you will have talent in areas important to some pupils but not to others. In this case you have the responsibility of referring your pupils for more expert help.

The problem of how best to plan a schedule to make available the help of the specialist to pupils who need it most is a challenge to an entire school faculty. You may find yourself involved in one of a number of plans. In some schools, pupils will come as class groups on a regular schedule. In others, specialists come to homerooms to work both with the pupils and their teacher. Where there are no specialists as members of the school faculty, teachers with strengths in specific areas often help each other—by consultation over lunch, by open noonhour periods when pupils with special problems can come for help, by trading classes at points where youngsters clearly need expert advice. In some schools interest groups, early morning sessions, or systems of free periods are being used to route talented pupils, often of several ages, to the persons best able to help them. Whatever the system in your particular school, you will have the responsibility of deciding when the problem faced by an able youngster demands more competence than yours and seeing to it that he gets more expert help. Conversely, if you are the specialist, yours will be the responsibility of making yourself available to assist with the problems these pupils face.

In many communities, avenues for special help for gifted pupils extend beyond school doors. There may be classes in the local art museum, opportunities to submit original compositions to the children's symphony, a community orchestra, a church choir. Part of your responsibility to the talented child should be to know when such resources exist and to set in motion whatever machinery is needed to make them available to him. Perhaps you are asking why parents should not be the ones responsible for their children's out-of-school creative experiences. You may well have heard persons expressing serious concern about the seeming anxiousness of the school to take on responsibilities formerly considered to be those of home and community. This, schools could never do, even if educational leaders were disposed to think that they should. Yet, educators have inescapable leadership responsibilities. At times these may be to provide services not usually considered part of the school program; at times to guide children and youth to the community agency already effectively organized to give help; and at times to mobilize the community to meet a special need. Nurturing the unique contribution of each child and youth is a responsibility of all aspects of our society—home, school, church, youth movements, other community agencies.

BOOKS YOU SHOULD KNOW

Andrews, Gladys. *Creative Rhythmic Movement for Children.* Englewood Cliffs, N.J.: Prentice-Hall, 1954. Pp. viii + 198.

Applegate, Mauree. *Helping Children Write.* Evanston, Ill.: Row, Peterson, 1954. Pp. vii + 173.

Burrows, Alvina T., and others. *They All Want to Write.* Englewood Cliffs, N.J.: Prentice-Hall, 1952. Pp. xvi + 240.

D'Amico, Victor. *Creative Teaching in Art.* Revised Edition. Scranton, Pa.: International Textbook Co., 1953. Pp. xi + 257.

Durland, Frances C. *Creative Dramatics for Children.* Yellow Springs, Ohio: The Antioch Press, 1952. Pp. 181.

Education for the Gifted. Part II, The Fifty-seventh Yearbook of the National Society for the Study of Education. Chicago: The University of Chicago Press, 1958. Pp. xi + 420.

Gaitskell, Charles D. *Children and Their Art.* New York: Harcourt, Brace and Co., 1958. Pp. 446.

Ghiselin, Brewster (Editor). *The Creative Process: A Symposium.* Berkeley: University of California Press, 1952. Pp. 251. (Mentor Book, MD 132.)

Kerber, Adolf B., and Jett, Thomas F., Jr. *The Teaching of Creative Poetry.* Indianapolis: The Waldemar Press, 1956. Pp. iii + 128.

Lowenfeld, Viktor. *Creative and Mental Growth.* Third Edition. New York: The Macmillan Co., 1957. Pp. 541.

Mursell, James L. *Developmental Teaching.* New York: McGraw-Hill Book Co., 1949. Pp. vii + 374.

Myers, Louise K. *Teaching Children Music in the Elementary School.* Second Edition. Englewood Cliffs, N.J.: Prentice-Hall, 1956. Pp. ix + 374.

Nye, Robert E., and Nye, Vernice T. *Music in the Elementary School.* Englewood Cliffs, N.J.: Prentice-Hall, 1957. Pp. 290.

Russell, David H. *Children's Thinking.* Boston: Ginn and Co., 1956. Pp. xii + 449.

Smith, Marion F. *Teaching the Slow Learning Child.* New York: Harper & Brothers, 1954. Pp. 175.

Making the Most of the Total School Setting

CHAPTER 10

Miss Jackson's first-graders have just hung up their wraps. About half the children are in their seats at work with library books, numbers and reading activities, and a variety of art materials. The others are busy about classroom chores—watering plants, measuring food for the goldfish, recording the weather and temperature for the classroom news bulletin, straightening the play corner, checking books in the classroom library. At her desk, with the help of two youngsters, Miss Jackson is collecting money for lunch checks. Messengers will be needed to take this to the office. Attendance also must be checked—a child at each table tells who is missing—and the report sent to the office. A trip to the park is planned for two days hence and permission notes from parents are being collected. Today is Sally's birthday. Just before school opened Sally's mother appeared with cupcakes. These will be a pleasant supplement to midmorning juice, but arrangements to serve them will have to be made. Valentine's Day is a week off, but Miss Jackson has already begun to plan for it. At 9:15 two sixth-graders ask permission to remind the children that all contributions to the school paper must be in by the end of the week. . . .

Upstairs, Mr. Swanson's sixth-graders are equally busy. Not all the children are in the classroom as yet. Safety guards, primary helpers, and office helpers will come in as they complete their responsibilities. Those in the room are engaged in a variety of ways—watering plants, changing the water in the aquarium, checking in library books which had been borrowed overnight. Money for lunch checks must be collected and attendance reported. Pairs of youngsters will do this under Mr. Swanson's supervision. This is the day for a special assembly featuring a troupe of professional puppeteers. Time must be scheduled for this. Plans on the blackboard indicate that preparations for a Valentine party are already under way. Mr. Swanson's class is responsible for the school paper. At 9:10 reporters leave to remind other classes of the deadline when news is due. Later in the morning an editorial planning session will be needed. An announcement from the physical education instructor reminds the class of a volleyball game immediately after school. The student-council representatives ask ten minutes to report on yesterday's meeting. . . .

Life in a present-day elementary school classroom is far from the smooth progression of carefully planned lessons often envisioned by the uninitiated. The inevitable interruptions for special assemblies, programs, and parties; the service responsibilities that take pupils out of their classrooms; the inter-age choirs, teams, and student-council groups that involve just enough children to make it difficult to proceed with a group project; and the seemingly endless number of bookkeeping, recording, and housekeeping chores in the classroom are sometimes regarded by the beginning teacher as undesirable barriers to achieving effectively the major purposes of the school. Yet in these experiences reside some of the most vital opportunities for boys and girls to learn in a genuine community setting what it means to meet the obligations of citizenship. And in assemblies, choirs, teams, school papers, interest groups, lie also some important means of stimulating and broadening pupil interests and of developing skills in communication, creative expression, and physical dexterity.

Experienced teachers will tell you, however, that careful planning is essential if the educational potentialities of the total school community are to be used to maximum advantage. There can come a saturation point beyond which the contribution of one more assembly, one more invitation to visit another class, or one more special event is negative, regardless of its intrinsic worth. There is the possibility, too, that children's talents will be exploited through the long hours of additional rehearsal needed to perfect a program far beyond the point where the practice experiences are truly educative. Service responsibilities, likewise, can result in unjustifiable use of pupil time if youngsters are called away from their classrooms for long periods merely to serve as messengers, to run errands, or to answer telephones in routine situations which could be handled as well or better through efficient administrative use of bulletins, secretarial help, or the custodial force.

How best to coordinate the total school program of assemblies, interest groups, and service groups; what types of experiences should be provided; and how extensively pupils should be involved are problems which demand the best thinking of the entire school faculty. Decisions regarding these problems will differ with such factors as the size of the school, the curriculum design, the richness or poverty of pupils' out-of-school experiences, the need to build feelings of allegiance to the school, the availability of secretarial and other help, the faculty strength and talent available to sponsor special activities, and the areas in which regular classroom experiences seem most in need of supplementation.

Whatever the over-all plan to capitalize upon the educative opportunities of the school community, its contribution to the growth of boys and girls will depend largely upon the effectiveness with which each classroom teacher works with his particular group. There are at least three major types of skills which you, as a beginning teacher, must acquire. First, you must be able to identify the potential learnings in the special activities in which your pupils engage. As with any other aspect of your teaching, the quality of your leadership will depend upon your sense of goals. Second, you must learn to coordinate effectively the special responsibilities and activities in which your pupils engage with your regular day-by-day classroom experiences. Third, you must be able to give effective leadership when your pupils embark on an extensive project or when you are asked to sponsor a special activity with an inter-age group—to help your pupils derive maximum benefit from such experiences as planning a class party; to make truly worth while the activities of the safety patrol, a school club, a choir, an intramural athletic program.

WHAT ARE OUR GOALS IN HELPING PUPILS GROW AS MEMBERS OF THE SCHOOL COMMUNITY?

In what types of enterprises are your pupils likely to be involved as members of the school community? The list of specific activities which teachers have found to be of educative value for their pupils is endless. In general, however, the experiences through which school faculties have sought to enrich the learnings of the boys and girls under their care may be classified as follows:

Service responsibilities: Responsibilities within the classroom for plants, pets, library books, passing papers, housekeeping; school-wide responsibilities such as safety guards, primary helpers, lunchroom helpers, office helpers, managers of lost and found departments, supervisors of lunch hour games; community service projects to clean up school grounds, improve the appearance of the school by planting flowers, be of service to local merchants or clubs.

Assembly and program experiences: Responsibilities as participants in school assemblies, programs for parents, classroom programs to which parents or other classes are invited; opportunities as an audience to enjoy movies, speakers, special musical events, special dramatic performances, brought to the school by the faculty or board of education.

Student government experiences: Classroom opportunities as officers in a classroom club; responsibilities as officers or delegates in a student council.

Publication experiences: Classroom responsibilities for a room publication; responsibilities as publishers or contributors to a school paper or magazine.

Social experiences: Responsibilities in the classroom for parties, entertaining parents, celebrating birthdays or special holidays, making guests feel at home; school-wide responsibilities as guides to visitors, ushers at assemblies, hosts and hostesses for an open house.

Special interest experiences: Opportunities to participate in classroom clubs and hobby groups; school-wide experiences that cut across grade-level lines in school choruses, after-school clubs, interest groups.

Physical education experiences: Opportunities to participate in classroom physical education programs and activities during recess breaks; school-wide experiences in teams, dance or other interest groups, noon games.

Because primary children are taking their first steps in learning to live and work within the complex school setting, they will engage mainly in activities within their own classrooms. Their first responsibilities will be related to maintaining an effective environment for group living—caring for plants, keeping the play corner tidy, being responsible for the library corner, helping to clean up at the end of the day. There may be special assemblies geared to the interest level of younger children, but for the most part programs will be in the classroom setting. The contacts of younger children with school service programs are likely to be as followers—cooperating with safety guards, working with the sixth-graders who help on the playground. If there is a student council in the school, the primary classes may send representatives, but the extent of their participation is likely to be confined to a simple report to their classmates. They will make contributions to the school paper, but these are usually developed under the supervision of their teacher, perhaps as a group experience. Basically, the social orientation of primary youngsters is still toward their teacher and toward other adults. They need to work in uncomplicated situations where adult leadership can be provided.

Older pupils can assume responsibility for wider aspects of classroom living; they are reaching the point in their social development where they can profit from broader school responsibilities. Their classroom plans for parties, entertainment of parents and other classes, and clubs will be more elaborate than those of younger pupils. With help, they can operate responsibly in positions involving the supervision of younger children—as members of the safety patrol, primary helpers, lunchroom helpers, leaders of lunchroom games. Although student councils are more commonly found in secondary schools, there are some types of all-school problems to which youngsters in the intermediate grades can make a contribution through a student-council organization. Intermediate-graders are better able to listen effectively in a large school assembly and to work cooperatively on all-school projects. They can profit in many ways from experiences that take them beyond the walls of their classroom.

Obviously, many kinds of learnings can result from the types of activities that have just been listed. Your task will be to decide how the projects undertaken by your boys and girls can best contribute to their growth—to analyze their present competencies and inadequacies and to consider which of the many potential learnings to stress. What are the opportunities for growth of which you should be particularly aware?

Be alert to opportunities to develop improved insights and skills in human relations. One of the most important learnings that can come from the experience of assuming duties as a member of the classroom or the school community is the basic understanding that the welfare of all the members of a community depends upon the degree to which each person carries out his particular responsibilities. Whether the task be an individual one, such as adjusting the window shades, or a responsibility as a member of a committee, the failure of a pupil to meet his obligations can have a direct effect upon the welfare of the group. Bobby blithely promises to bring a box to be decorated for Valentine's Day and forgets. Sandy and Jim fail to report on the morning that they are in charge of the Lost and Found Department and the complaints of dissatisfied customers are relayed to the rest of the class. Janice and her committee waste time and the third-grade classroom is the only one with an undecorated Christmas window. Tommy and Ben scuffle and the plate of crackers for midmorning lunch ends in the wastepaper basket. Sandra loses the notebook containing the student-council minutes. The effect upon group morale of such failures to meet obligations tends to be transmitted to the delinquent quickly and often with telling force. Likewise, of course, the contribution to group welfare of a job well done is readily apparent to all. Here are some excellent occasions to help your pupils think through the importance of meeting obligations, of not making promises that cannot be fulfilled. There are important opportunities, also, to discuss whether persons who have failed the group should be given another chance and what the obligations of responsible citizens are in helping to rehabilitate delinquents.

In the cooperative projects which your pupils undertake lie many opportunities to learn how to work together. Barbara wants to cut out small Christmas trees for the holiday bulletin board; Joan wants bells. How do committees resolve such conflicts? In her position as chairman of the game committee for the party, Joanna bosses everyone, and the members of the committee rebel and threaten to resign. What can be learned from this about the duties of the chairman? And is resigning the most effective way to remedy the situation? Sandy retires from the committee in tears when blunt John says, "That's crazy!"; Russ strikes John for a similar comment. How does one express disagreement without hurting people's feelings? Should one become upset when another person disagrees? And what are the obligations of the group in listening politely to the suggestions of each individual?

In the intermediate grades, particularly, school clubs, classroom clubs, and student-council activities are valuable means of expanding pupils' skills in cooperative problem-solving and of teaching some of the simpler aspects of parliamentary procedure. Primary youngsters will not typically do much more than to select a committee chairman or a master of ceremonies for a program. Older groups, however, can benefit from projects where they elect a president, a secretary, and perhaps a treasurer; learn how to make, second, and vote upon motions; and learn how to utilize the services of standing committees. These are early but important steps in becoming acquainted with some of the formalities through which members of a democratic group govern themselves.

Service responsibilities and situations in which other persons are being entertained provide many occasions for your boys and girls to learn about the needs and feelings of others. How should the class hospitality committee help a new child to feel at home? What social amenities would be appropriate if there is an adult visitor? How should an audience behave in order to be most courteous and helpful to those on the stage? What type of assembly program should sixth-graders plan if primary children are to be among the invited guests? What should be done to express appreciation to those who have planned and presented a special program? What types of games should primary playground leaders be prepared to direct? These and similar questions will allow you to help your pupils to think about the courtesies due to others and the ways in which the needs and interests of persons older or younger differ from their own.

In schools where children are given responsibilities as safety guards, playground leaders, lunchroom helpers, supervisors of primary games, those in authority roles must learn appropriate ways of behaving and those who are followers must understand their obligations to the persons responsible for their welfare. What does the leader do if a primary child insists on disturbing a game? How does a safety guard speak to a child who is jaywalking? What is the responsibility of the youngster whose cooperation is requested? The disciplines of democracy are learned slowly. In the realities of life within the school community are some of the most important opportunities for boys and girls to learn what it means to live in a society in which the citizens themselves have responsibilities for enforcing the laws.

Identify opportunities to develop effective work habits. Classroom and all-school responsibilities offer many ways to help pupils develop efficient methods of working. Even in serving as a paper-passer or waterer-of-plants in the first grade, a youngster must learn to think through step by step just what his responsibilities are and then proceed to carry them out efficiently. The activities undertaken by older pupils —managing a club program, planning a class party, publishing a school paper—frequently call for complex plans. Goals have to be clearly stated, the responsibilities of committees outlined in detail, the sequence of activities leading to the conclusion of the project thought through, and deadlines set. Groups and individuals must carry out their parts of the project as planned.

There will be many problems through which you can help pupils learn to make efficient use of personnel. They will face decisions regarding how many persons are required to carry out specific housekeeping duties or to form an efficient working committee. Within committees there will be problems of how to organize the work so that the best use is made of the time and energies of each individual. There will also be many occasions to consider how one decides on the best person for the job. What qualifications are needed in a club secretary? a master of ceremonies? a student-council president? Does one vote for one's friend if he is not the best man for the office? On what bases does one select a committee? Pupils can also be given some valuable experiences in taking turns. Are there situations in which the less able pupil may be given a chance to take on leadership responsibilities? Must the most talented actress always have the starring role in the play? Solving such problems is an important step in learning how to help each individual to make his most effective contribution to a cooperative enterprise.

The realities of classroom and school service responsibilities offer some important lessons, also, in promptness and wise use of time. Persons serving as safety guards, playground helpers, or office helpers must not be late. If those with housekeeping tasks dawdle at the end of the day, no one will be ready to start home on time. There is no point in submitting an article to the school paper after the deadline is past. If invitations have gone home, the program must go on, even if the scenery is not completed. There will be additional lessons in using time wisely as you and your pupils decide how to adjust for emergency situations —the unscheduled assembly, the unexpected invitation to visit another class, the request from the office secretary to have the copy for the school paper in her hands a day earlier than was expected. In a world of ready mixes and vacuum cleaners in which there no longer exist many of the home chores that formerly served to help boys and girls to plan carefully and carry out obligations promptly, it becomes increasingly important that teachers make wise use of school activities to teach such lessons.

Look for opportunities to supplement experiences in regular curriculum areas. Club experiences, assemblies, classroom programs, interest groups, school papers, offer many opportunities to enrich regular classroom experiences. The most apparent, perhaps, will be the occasions for supplementing pupils' experiences in creative expression. These will range from the carefully rehearsed performances of the school choir, or the presentation of an auditorium play, to the decorations, informal storytelling, dramatization, and singing in a classroom Christmas party.

You will also identify readily opportunities to foster growth in oral and written expression. You may think first of announcements, reports, and other activities that help pupils to develop poise before groups; however, these are but a small part of the total possible language experiences. Entertaining calls for invitations, and being entertained calls for thank-you notes. Committee planning sessions require a high level of discussion techniques; club and student-council meetings demand the more formal procedures of parliamentary order. Reporters for the school paper must be able to make announcements to other classes and to conduct interviews; those writing for the paper have a wide variety of forms of written expression from which to choose. Groups responsible for an all-school service project may need to explain to children of different ages just what their plans are. Youngsters who serve as guides or as classroom hosts and hostesses must be able to introduce themselves to visitors, to welcome guests graciously, and to give clear explanations of their class work. The list is almost endless. It includes many of your most realistic opportunities to help boys and girls to appreciate the importance of clear communication.

There are also needs for effective use of numbers. Considerable measurement can be involved in putting borders around bulletin boards or planning other special classroom decorations. Youngsters who help to collect money for lunch checks must be able to add correctly and to make change. The financial computations needed to procure the refreshments for a class party can be complicated. Playground leaders must be able to keep accurate scores in games. Special service projects often involve arithmetic—the lunchroom helpers may develop graphs to show the amount of food wasted; the safety guards plan posters showing the amount of traffic on the streets near the school; the reporters for the school paper decide to publish a series of surveys in graphic form.

You will discover many opportunities to expand pupils' understanding of their world. Preparing to take part in an assembly can be a stimulating learning experience. Each class, at its own level, may discuss the meaning and origin of Thanksgiving as a prelude to a Thanksgiving assembly. Fifth-graders may read about Christmas customs around the world. First-graders may discuss signs of spring in preparing for their part in a primary assembly. Assemblies featuring special speakers, movies, and programs prepared by other classes can spark new interests, especially if you allow discussion time and provide follow-up reading. Classroom clubs, school clubs, and interest groups not only provide outlets for pupils with special interests and talents, but also focus upon topics closely related to classroom work. Groups with special service responsibilities can often be helped to consider the wider implications of their tasks—lunchroom helpers may study wise choice of food, members of the safety patrol explore local traffic regulations, the editors of the school paper engage in an extended study of modern means of communication. Within your classroom, responsibilities for plants, lights, ventilation, the aquarium, the class pet, a current events bulletin board, are all potential centers for wider study. Through these special school activities you help your boys and girls to maintain alert interest in the world around them. Some of your pupils' most fruitful unit activities may stem from such experiences.

Identify opportunities to help individuals develop feelings of group status and self-respect. The law-abiding citizen feels that he is a respected member of his community. He fulfills the obligations of citizenship faithfully; he knows that he is accepted as a person who can make a worth-while contribution to group welfare; and he takes pride in his community. The behavior of the delinquent suggests few such feelings of acceptance. He makes little positive contribution to his community, disregards its laws, and is destructive of property. Service responsibilities to the class and the school represent one means of helping boys and girls to feel that they are respected and needed by those with whom they live and work.

Opportunities to be of service in the school, and their concomitant contributions to feelings of security, status, and self-respect, tend to come most frequently to those who need them least. The reason is obvious. Positions of responsibility are given to responsible people. Representatives to the student council or the safety patrol tend to be those persons deemed most worthy. Yet the pupil who feels rejected by his classmates, his teacher, and the school administration, and who shows his feelings through antisocial acts, is often the one who most needs positive proof that he has a worth-while contribution to make to his fellows. This does not mean that you will deny to pupils who have demonstrated leadership capacities and a sense of responsibility the opportunity to be of service to their school. Nor will you allow to continue to serve in a position of trust a pupil who has consistently betrayed the confidence of the group. It does suggest, however, that it is important to rotate classroom and school responsibilities so that every youngster has a chance to participate, regardless of his record. To deny the child who has demonstrated antisocial tendencies or the one who is not working up to capacity the right to share in such activities "until he earns it" may be to deny him the most important stimulation to improvement.

You may quite possibly find yourself in a neighborhood where there has been very little in pupils' home and community backgrounds to build pride in the school or interest in its curriculum. If this is the case, you may find the school faculty sponsoring a carefully planned series of classroom and school service projects designed to develop a sense of loyalty to the school and pride in its buildings and grounds. Youngsters may wear badges designating them as school helpers or members of the student council. Assemblies may feature the contributions of special groups. Classes may be given responsibility for the display cases and bulletin boards in the halls. It may seem to you that such a program is distracting unduly from what you consider to be the regular work of the classroom. If you are teaching in the upper grades you may be discouraged to find your day shortened at both ends so that school helpers can be at their posts. In some schools service responsibilities may be overdone; but before you pass judgment, study your pupils and talk over the problem with your colleagues, your principal, or your cooperating teacher. Even a seemingly routine activity which you classify as a waste of time may be paying off in a sense of pride and self-respect that sends a youngster back to your classroom more eager to learn and better able to get along with his classmates and with you.

COORDINATING SPECIAL ACTIVITIES EFFECTIVELY IN THE DAILY SCHEDULE

Most beginning teachers worry more about setting up a classroom schedule in which regular learning experiences and special activities are coordinated effectively than they do about guiding a special project. Helping pupils to prepare a program to entertain another class or publish a school paper is very similar to developing any other unit of work. But how do you keep regular classroom activities moving ahead and still find time for housekeeping chores and, in the case of older groups, for pupil responsibilities in school-wide projects? How do you adjust regularly scheduled activities effectively to allow for assemblies or other special events, particularly if the latter occur with little or no warning? What types of activities will provide profitable learning experiences for those youngsters who remain in the classroom while others are involved in a school-wide project? Solving these problems involves a combination of effective scheduling, careful planning with your pupils, and skill in making use of short-term and individualized learning experiences.

Provide for special activities in setting up the daily schedule. Thoughtful scheduling can do much to reduce your sense of confusion and frustration in coping with the varied activities that make up your pupils' day. It is helpful to designate a definite time allotment for any activities that you know will recur routinely.[1] If your pupils, as a class, have undertaken a school-wide responsibility in which problems tend to occur on a day-by-day basis, as might those connected with supervising lunchroom games, you may also find it helpful to set a specific time to discuss these difficulties. For example, they might be given consideration immediately after the plans for the day are laid, or be made the first point of discussion after lunch. Likewise, if the student council meets

[1] See Chapter 6, pages 203-207, for a discussion of the general framework of a daily schedule.

Monday morning, the first period each Monday afternoon might be set aside for the report from your representative or, if your pupils have a classroom club, a definite afternoon may be designated for meetings.

It will probably be necessary to experiment with your total schedule in order to discover which regular classroom activities best follow a period scheduled for special responsibilities. Some teachers, both at the primary and intermediate levels, schedule for the first large time block an independent work period in which children engage in reading, number, and language experiences. Such a plan allows those who do not have special responsibilities to proceed with regular classroom activities and the teacher to start work with individuals or small groups. In other classrooms a period for independent reading may start the day. In situations where some pupils must report to assigned posts prior to noon and the close of school, independent work or recreational reading programs may be planned to coincide with these periods. You may be saying, "Yes, but doesn't this mean that some pupils will *never* have a chance for individual help or independent reading?" This would be true if independent activities were scheduled only at such times, but in a well-planned week, this will not be the case.

If your class has undertaken a major project that involves considerable planning and effort—as would a school paper, a class party, a program, the sponsorship of a series of noon movies—this will need to be provided for on the same basis as would any other extensive project. You will survey other on-going activities, decide which time block can best be used for the special project, and allow, on any given day, as much time as seems desirable to enable your pupils to take the appropriate next steps in carrying out their plans. Typically, such extended special projects are not merely added to an already full schedule. Rather, they replace other activities that make a similar contribution to pupils' total growth. For example, while Sam Martin's sixth grade prepared the first edition of the *North Star* all his planned language experiences centered around this project. During the time when Jane Wilson's fourth-graders were carefully nurturing the seedlings they hoped to transplant to the garden plot in front of the school, they engaged in few other science activities. When Willa Swanson's first-graders decided to cook their lunch at school, this project absorbed the time usually set aside for health activities as well as a sizable part of the regular arithmetic period. Jack Jones' program to which parents were invited was a direct outgrowth of a social studies unit; he inserted it in the time block allotted to social studies and then devoted the periods normally set aside for art and music experiences to produce scenery and prepare some songs and dances.

Assemblies, invitations to visit other classes, and similar special events will call for special adjustments of your schedule. In deciding how best to allow for such experiences think about the amount of time that will probably be required to make the experience worth while. Typically, if your pupils are to be an intelligent audience they should be given some background for what they are to hear or to see. Then, follow-up discussion is usually desirable. If the focus of the special program seems remote from your children's on-going interests and problems, you may decide that brief follow-up activities are sufficient. On other occasions it may be desirable to spend considerable time in order to utilize the special program as motivation for a classroom project. Once you have decided approximately how much time to devote to the special experience, you are ready to think through adjustments in your regular schedule. Consider the status of on-going projects. Which ones are moving well and could be set aside for the day without endangering the end result? Which are going slowly, or have reached a crucial point where it is important that plans not be disrupted? Which activities could be completed at home? Consider, too, the pattern of activities over the week. Have you, by chance, postponed work in a skill area two or three times already? Are there other projects that have been pushed aside day after day "until we have time"? These may be the activities you would not slight again.

Even with all your diligence in reading notices and your principal's best efforts to keep you informed, there will be days when the first indication that you and your class are due in the auditorium at 10:30 will come at 8:45 as you check the bulletin board before going to your room. You will adjust more effectively to such emergencies if, as you plan for tomorrow's activities, you regularly assign priorities, using the questions suggested in the preceding paragraph as your guide. This is a worthwhile precaution, even though the incidence of external interruptions in your school is limited. Internal interruptions—problems of many sorts arising as plans for the day unfold—will often call for similar readjustments in your schedule.

Involve pupils in planning for effective use of time. The boys and girls who sail serenely through a complicated day, adjusting easily to emergency changes in plans are usually those who have been involved in planning for wise use of time. One of the first steps taken by most teachers in September is to acquaint pupils with the general framework of the schedule and to talk about their responsibilities in timing their work so as to fit smoothly into the school-wide schedule for recess breaks, physical education activities, lunch periods, library visits. How best to manage housekeeping and other needed service responsibilities in the classroom is also discussed early in the school year. This is the point, too, at which most teachers take time to talk about the types of activities in which pupils who do not have housekeeping jobs should be engaged and how they can facilitate the work of those with special responsibilities. If some pupils are members of the safety patrol or involved in other school-wide service projects, they are helped to understand the importance of returning to the classroom promptly and quietly. The efficiency with which your program operates for the year will depend to a large extent upon how carefully you establish routines in the early fall.

The more experienced pupils become in helping to plan their daily schedule, the more likely they are to be able to proceed intelligently and efficiently on the days when the schedule has to be adjusted to allow for a special event or activity. Your responsibility, in helping your pupils to consider how best to adjust the schedule for a special event, will be to raise with them the same problems regarding how best to establish priorities that you, yourself, have considered in thinking through a tentative schedule for the day. How far along are we in our various classroom activities? Which can best be set aside to make room for this special event? Which must be given attention today?

It goes without saying that the classroom records you have been using to keep plans clear can be a valuable aid in coordinating regular and special activities. Schedules of special events can be posted; regular schedules can indicate clean-up time and other special work periods. Lists of committees with special responsibilities can be helpful; among these are the helpers' charts so prevalent in primary classrooms. Plans for a special project can be recorded in the same manner as are plans for any other unit of work. In short, every step you and your pupils can take together to set up effective working conditions will be helpful in aiding them in working smoothly in a complex classroom setting.

Make effective use of short-term and individualized learning experiences. In spite of all your efforts to maintain a schedule where everyone has a job to do, there will be occasions when some of your pupils are busily engaged in a special project while you are wondering what to do with the rest. This will not happen often in the primary grades where pupils' activities are confined mainly to the four walls of their

Public Schools, Cincinnati, Ohio,
Marsh, Photographers

Make the most of day-by-day problems stemming from classroom routines. Responsibility for lunch tickets fosters arithmetic skills.

Public Schools, Cincinnati, Ohio,
Gilbert H. Corlett, Photographer

Be alert to opportunities to develop improved insights and skills in human relations. Noontime hosts and hostesses learn much in playing with primary children.

Public Schools, Cincinnati, Ohio
Gilbert H. Corlett, Photographer

Look for opportunities to supplement experiences in regular classroom areas. Preparing for a school assembly calls for skills in creative expression.

Develop extensive service projects so that many learnings result. Appropriate posters demand communication skills.

Public Schools, Cincinnati, Ohio,
Marsh, Photographers

classrooms, but it is not an uncommon occurrence at the intermediate level. The members of the student council may leave for an hour-long meeting; the safety patrol may be needed for a special assembly; or, what is even more devastating, the members of the choir may be needed for a series of rehearsals, or a half-dozen youngsters may have key parts in a play being planned for a Parent-Teacher Association meeting. Keeping pupils without special responsibilities occupied for ten or fifteen minutes in the morning is relatively simple, but what do you do with them for an hour or more? To proceed to new work is wasteful of time and effort, yet it is manifestly unfair to allow part of your group to fritter away time because others are being given special experiences elsewhere in the school.

Actually, the times when only part of your class is present provide some important opportunities to give individualized help. Practically every activity you have devised to adjust your program to individual strengths and weaknesses may be put to use here. If your pupils have been using check sheets in arithmetic, personal lists of spelling errors, special practice books in handwriting, or work-type activities in reading, this is your time to check on progress.

Periods when only part of your class is present can also be used to encourage individual interests. If you have been providing time in your regular schedule for projects related to pupils' hobbies, talents, and interests, those remaining in the room may go on with these. The lists of questions which you and your pupils may have compiled in relation to their unit activities can be used to encourage individual research. If you have been developing a class notebook or bulletin board to encourage creative writing, some youngsters may proceed with their special writing plans. Others may have recreational reading to pursue. The smaller group and the general informality of such situations can provide you with some valuable opportunities to talk to individuals about these special concerns.

Sometimes it is important to plan so that the boys and girls remaining in the classroom are given things to do that will contribute to feelings of importance and status. It can be discouraging to the pupil who cannot sing or who is not talented enough to have a key acting part to be left in the classroom while others are having an exciting time in the auditorium. In most school systems teachers have recognized this as one of the disadvantages of an ambitious auditorium program at the elementary school level and have substituted instead simpler productions and programs in which all pupils have a part. Nevertheless, there will be times when long hours of rehearsal are justified and you may be left in charge of the pupils not participating. If so, you will want to provide a type of activity that is especially exciting and satisfying. Sometimes there are aspects of the production in which your group can be involved—making props, painting scenery, making costumes. Sometimes, if a holiday is near, they can be the ones to decorate the room. In one situation the student teacher helped the pupils who remained to plan a Christmas party, complete with a play of their own as a surprise for the assembly group. In another, the youngsters used their time to develop some effective choral-speaking productions. In such situations you may also be grateful for a stock of educational games—variations of spelling bees, arithmetic relays, adaptations of television quiz programs—which enliven the period but still make a contribution to pupil growth.

Learning in your classroom goes on even though part of your group is absent. When not all of your class are present avoid those activities in which all pupils need to have a common learning experience, and capitalize upon those which provide for special interests and individual help. And, at times, add some new and challenging short-term projects to meet the special demands of the situation.

GUIDING SPECIAL ACTIVITIES TO ASSURE MAXIMUM GROWTH

At one time assemblies, club and interest groups, recreation programs, service groups, student councils, school papers, were thought of as aspects of the school program quite distinct from regular classroom activities. They were classified as "extracurricular" projects and sponsored by designated members of the school faculty. Today, the vital contribution of such activities to the meaningful development of concepts, understandings, and skills is more clearly recognized and the distinction between in-class and extra-class activities is rapidly vanishing. In your school there may be a special-interest program, a safety patrol or other service group, a student council, or a school paper operating on a school-wide basis, but more and more of the activities once called "extras" are now planned as an integral part of the regular classroom program.[2] Service activities, too, are often made the responsi-

[2] Chapters 7, 8, and 9 contain a number of examples of teachers and pupils publishing school papers, planning parties, and preparing programs to entertain parents or other classes.

bility of a single class working with their teacher. One class may supply lunchroom helpers; a second, manage the Lost and Found Department; a third, act as helpers for primary children; a fourth, sponsor indoor games on a rainy day. In guiding the special activities in which your pupils are engaged as members of the school community, you will typically, then, be able to utilize all you know about the needs, talents, and interests of your particular class; you will be free to decide upon the most appropriate adjustment of your schedule to allow for the special activity; and you will be in a position to achieve maximum integration with regular classroom experiences.

Whether you are working with your own boys and girls or sponsoring a group established on a school-wide basis, you should come to the activity as carefully prepared as you would for any other aspect of your teaching. You will do your own pre-planning just as thoughtfully as you would in laying out a block plan for any other project of comparable size and complexity, and you will plan with your pupils in just as much detail. Special activities do, however, pose some additional problems about which you should be thinking. Some, such as class parties and programs, call for intensive effort for a block of time lasting from several days to several weeks, much as do unit activities in science, health, or social studies. With these, your problem, as it is with any unit of work, will be to decide how ambitious such projects should be. Not all activities, however, can be wrapped up as neatly as this. Housekeeping routines go on all year in a relatively unvaried fashion. Yet, to be justified, these must be managed so that they continue to contribute to pupil growth. Clubs, interest groups, physical education and recreation activities, also run all year; but these pose the special problem of how to develop a challenging program from week to week. Activities such as publishing a school paper, serving on a safety patrol, or acting as a member of a student council are other types of year-long responsibilities —responsibilities that make fluctuating demands upon pupils' time. These pose still other problems if they are to continue to yield educational benefits to the end of the year. How do you plan so as to make the best use of such varied types of activities?

Make the most of day-by-day problems stemming from classroom routines. Helping with housekeeping responsibilities, collecting money for lunch checks and helping to check attendance, serving as classroom hosts and hostesses or as librarians, represent relatively routine aspects of the school day. How much teaching you will do in relation to such activities depends partly upon the maturity of your group and partly upon the special needs to which you think the activities could contribute.

Certainly, some of the most important learnings that should come from engaging in classroom service responsibilities lie in the area of habits and attitudes—neatness and orderliness, precision and accuracy in keeping records, promptness and faithfulness in meeting obligations, thoughtfulness and courtesy toward visitors. In the early fall this means identifying with your boys and girls the classroom jobs for which they can take responsibility, discussing why these jobs are important to happy and comfortable living in the classroom, and planning how they can be done most efficiently. You must do more, however, than post a helpers' chart or a list of room committees. Your boys and girls will need supervision if they are to carry out their responsibilities efficiently and faithfully; they will also need to be involved in evaluation sessions where jobs well done can be recognized and problems talked through. There is, after all, not much incentive to continue to clear the floor of every scrap of waste paper or to straighten the library books carefully day after day if nobody ever comments on what a good job has been done and how much help it has been.

If you are teaching in a situation where it is apparent from your pupils' behavior that homes are also stressing neatness, promptness, and conscientiousness in meeting obligations, you may well decide to keep classroom service responsibilities to a minimum. If, on the other hand, the classroom seems to be the most effective situation through which to teach boys and girls the importance of an orderly and attractive environment, you may deem it desirable to give them extensive experiences in good housekeeping. Older groups, particularly, can take responsibility for changing the borders of the bulletin board, for working out more efficient ways of storing books and paper, and for supervising the work of committees charged with special clean-up responsibilities.

Frequently, classroom service responsibilities call for skills or knowledge unrelated to problems of good housekeeping. For example, at the point where pupils seem mature enough to help in collecting money, the teacher might well take time with the entire class to practice making change and adding sums of money. For pupils who have had few social responsibilities at home, the problem of how to take care of a classroom visitor—how to introduce oneself, what to say to him—can take considerable discussion and perhaps even some practice with the teacher playing the role of the visitor. Likewise, responsibilities for plants or animals in the room can lead to several days of investigation regarding exactly what care is needed. You are justified in devoting additional time to such related learnings. In fact, if you do not do so your pupils will not derive full benefits from the classroom service responsibilities they undertake.

Plan activities scheduled on a regular basis so that the program makes a consistent contribution to growth. Activities that are scheduled on a daily, biweekly, or weekly basis require a carefully developed program if they are to make their most effective contribution to pupil growth. The recreation and physical education activities in your school will most certainly be scheduled regularly in this way. In the primary grades these activities are likely to be the responsibility of the regular classroom teacher, but at the intermediate level they may be the special responsibility of a teacher of physical education. Even here, however, the classroom teacher is often expected to supplement this program with supervised play.

Your course of study will be particularly helpful in outlining specifically the activities that might be included in an effective physical education program. Before the year is out, you will want to make sure that your pupils, through activities appropriate to their maturity, have varied opportunities for physical development. The program should include rhythmic and dance activities as well as games and activities designed to develop motor coordination and skills. There will need to be opportunities to develop skill with balls, bats, jump ropes, and other equipment. Older pupils, particularly, need experiences to develop skills in team games. However, you will also want to help your youngsters to grow in competence with individual games such as hopscotch and shuffleboard. In supervised play pupils should be free to choose the activity they prefer, but your supervision can be very important in assuring that playground space and equipment are shared, in acting as an umpire, and in helping younger pupils to organize singing and other simple group activities.

In some schools, special club or interest programs are also scheduled on a regular basis. These are more likely to involve intermediate-grade than primary pupils. Some of these programs are planned so that for one afternoon a week pupils leave their regular classrooms to go to an interest group of their choice, each teacher sponsoring a group in which he is able to make a unique contribution through his particular talents, background, or interest. In situations where community recreation facilities are limited, there may be an after-school program featuring team games, dramatics groups, art and music activities, science clubs, crafts groups. In other schools the plan may be less ambitious. Art, music, and science classrooms may be opened early in the morning or at noon for pupils with special interests, or one or two teachers with special talents may volunteer to work with after-school groups—a science club, a group learning Indian dancing, a volleyball or baseball league. Some teachers also sponsor classroom clubs. Those, too, usually meet on a regular weekly or biweekly basis. Typically the club has a special focus for its activities, and pupils work under the teacher's guidance planning the programs and chairing the meetings.

You are likely to find in your course of study discussions of the typical science, language, number, art, music, and social science interests of boys and girls. These will offer you suggestions of possible centers of activity for a dramatics, writers', or science club. It is important to recognize, however, that when clubs and special-interest programs are sponsored by a school faculty or by an individual teacher, they are usually designed to encourage the talents and special interests of pupils through enriching and supplementing the regular classroom program. In deciding precisely what the focus of the activities of a special group is to be, you should keep this objective in mind. When a club or interest program is planned on a school-wide basis, several faculty meetings may be devoted to identifying the areas in which regular classroom activities can best be supplemented. In your own classroom, a club can sometimes be given responsibility for certain aspects of your regular program. In Joan Craig's fourth grade, for example, The Bookworms met once a week to review library books and share recreational reading. In Marvin Smith's sixth grade current events were the focus of the club meetings. Peggy Raleigh's science club pursued an interest in bird-watching far beyond what the regular time allotment for science activities would allow.

Once your club or interest group is launched and some special projects are identified as centers for activity, your guidance will be very similar to that which you would give to any similar learning experience. Normally, over the year you and your group will undertake a series of projects. Some of these will be highly individualized; others will involve the coordinated efforts of the total group. Whatever the project, it will be particularly important for you to make sure that individuals with special interests and talents are given the encouragement and stimulation that a club or interest program is designed to provide. If you are making the most effective use of all the potential learnings in the special program, you will also plan to help your pupils to assume more initiative in chairing their meetings and in planning their programs than they normally would take in other aspects of their classroom activities. Your help, however, will be required at many points both in planning and in carrying out the plans.

Develop extensive service projects so that many learnings result. Activities such as publishing a school or classroom paper, sponsoring noon-hour movies or games for rainy days, and serving on student councils and safety patrols pose still another type of problem to the teachers who are supervising them. Such projects represent year-long obligations. Yet the expenditure of time is necessarily much greater than it is for housekeeping responsibilities in the classroom. A teacher is not justified in undertaking such an extensive project with his group unless he is sure that it will continue to be a rich source of learnings throughout the year.

Actually, the problem of planning so that an extensive project such as a school paper continues to yield new learnings is not as difficult as it sounds. Because such projects are complex, new problems will continually arise. Your class will not be content with the first paper they publish nor will they feel that the first day of sponsoring noon movies has gone as smoothly as they desire. The comment you are most likely to hear is, "Let's do it again." Furthermore, because the more mature pupils tend to undertake such projects, they are apt to see many ramifications of their original plans. Some of the proposals not feasible at first may well be developed later. Then, too, most of these extended projects will require a complicated committee organization. If this is so, you can provide for many new learnings by the simple process of having pupils exchange jobs.

The sequence of experiences in which Mike McGhee's sixth-graders were engaged during the course of the year in publishing their school paper is a good example of how many educative experiences such a project can provide:

Publishing the first issue involved planning what types of articles should be included, setting up editorial committees for each major section of the paper, and electing an editor-in-chief, two assistants, and a corps of reporters to contact other rooms. The next step was to do some writing of news and articles. Eventually editorial groups took over, with the inevitable problems of deciding the policy for accepting some articles and rejecting others. Once the articles had been selected decisions had to be made regarding the format of the paper and instructions given to the school secretary who was to do the typing.

When the first edition came out, class evaluation indicated a number of points where improvement was needed. The same editorial groups and reporters were anxious to try again. When the time came to publish the third edition plans were made to change jobs, with resulting new learnings for everyone.

Once the major learnings related to the mechanics of editorial work had been achieved, the children were helped to explore other types of problems. In sequence during the year came more specific attempts to write short stories and poems, a study of the editorials of the local papers, and eventually a study of advertising and propaganda techniques. Needless to say, these special studies and the deadlines for the publication of the paper were spaced over several months so that other types of language activities could be interspersed.

Jane Johnson used her fifth-grade responsibilities for a lost and found department as an equally fruitful source of new learnings:

The first discussions were mainly about procedure. Where would articles be stored? How would a record of inquiries be kept? How would those whose possessions were found be notified? How long and when would the department be open? How would other classes be apprised of the plans? Planning a schedule of responsibilities, fixing storage shelves, designing simple inquiry and notification slips for mimeographing, writing announcements for other classes, and choosing those persons best fitted to talk to other groups were the next steps. Details of smooth operation were the focus of considerable discussion for several days after the department was opened.

For several weeks the department was operated routinely while other class work moved forward. Before the year was out, however, Jane's youngsters had embarked on these related projects: they wrote letters to each class reminding them again of their regulations; they conducted an advertising campaign when they discovered that articles were not promptly claimed; they planned brief skits on the importance of putting names on possessions and asked permission to present these in each class; they became appalled by the expense to parents of replacing unclaimed articles, visited a local store to check on prices, and wrote a series of reports for the school paper presenting their findings; they planned a program for the Parent-Teacher Association telling about their activities and urging cooperation in labeling articles.

These special activities, like the projects related to Mike's school newspaper, were scheduled so that other types of activities could be interspersed. There were periods when the department took little more time than that needed to keep it open for fifteen minutes in the morning and at noon, and there were periods of from several days to a week when it absorbed much of the time normally given to written language experiences. Such decisions depended in part upon the urgency of the problems related to managing the department and in part upon the value of the related learnings.

It is equally important to think about varied learnings for those boys and girls who serve as members of a student council. The activities of the council in the school where Sara Jones did her student teaching are illustrative of the types of services that an elementary school council can perform:

The council met once a week for a half-hour. There were two representatives from each room from the second through the sixth grade. A president, vice-president, and secretary were elected from among the council representatives. A representative of the safety patrol and one from the school paper met with the council once a month in order to coordinate the efforts of these three school-wide services. Time was allowed at each council meeting for representatives to report problems or questions raised by the members of their classes, and council discussions were regularly reported back to class.

The first meetings in the early fall were devoted to clarifying the duties of council members, to learning the essentials of parliamentary procedures, and to deciding on an appropriate style and color for buttons to be worn by school helpers when on duty. Next, attention was turned to problems of how the council could help to interpret school regulations—reasons for playground regulations, procedures in the lunchroom, safety rules for balls and bicycles.

Once responsibilities for helping to orient pupils to school regulations had been met, the council was ready for special projects. The school was asked to participate in fire prevention week and a committee from the council visited the nearby fire house and reported what they had learned. Later, when parts of the school were being painted, they discussed and then reported to their classes ways of facilitating the work of the painters. After Christmas they sponsored a clean-up campaign, both indoors and on the school grounds. In the spring when a flowering crab tree was donated to the school, the council took responsibility for organizing the tree-planting ceremony, soliciting original poems from their classes, and welcoming guests. As a final project they helped to sponsor a hobby show. Much time was expended in discussing in council and then in classes the characteristics of a good hobby. For several weeks prior to the show, examples of good hobbies were displayed. Then, when the day came, council members arranged the display and guided the classes that came to visit. The year closed with an evaluation of council activities and recommendations for next year's group.

Similar variety in experiences might well characterize the activities of the members of the safety patrol, the group sponsoring a series of noon movies, or the children acting as helpers in the primary grades. Not all projects will be as elaborate, of course, as those that have just been reported. Mike and Jane were using the realistic problems of the school paper and the Lost and Found Department to make a rich contribution to their pupils' language experiences. Had other classroom projects seemed likely to make equally worth-while contributions to growth in language skills, the paper might have been published less frequently, or the extra projects undertaken by the members of the Lost and Found Department might have been curtailed. As a teacher you have the ultimate responsibility of making sure that all of your pupils' activities—regular classroom work or special projects—are coordinated to contribute to a well-balanced program.

Decide on the elaborateness of programs and other special projects in terms of their potential contribution to pupil growth. Over the year you and your boys and girls will undoubtedly be involved in a number of classroom programs, assembly programs, and class parties. Some of these will be culminating activities for units; some will be celebrations of special days; some will be just for fun. In some cases parents or other classes will be your guests; in others, the only audience will be the members of your own class. Some of these undertakings will be simple; others will be quite elaborate. Some will take place in the school auditorium, but many will be in your regular classroom setting.

Perhaps one of the most troublesome problems facing beginning teachers is to decide how elaborate such special activities should be. A classroom party, for example, can be a simple matter of passing juice and crackers and singing a few songs, or it can be the vehicle for extensive social learnings with committees to plan refreshments, provide decorations, plan a program, greet guests, and even report on correct manners. Likewise, a program can be built mainly around a very simple plan for sharing group and individual work, or it can be expanded into a production that calls for many weeks of rehearsal.

There is a danger, particularly when parents or another class have been invited as guests, that an activity may be planned which is far too elaborate for the actual contribution it makes to pupil growth. There is also a danger that standards of performance will be set so high that they cannot be achieved without many more rehearsals than the activity merits or far too much behind-the-scenes management by the teacher. It is only natural to feel that your reputation as a teacher is at stake when you have invited guests. It is a temptation to write the announcer's part for him so that he will give a smoother introduction, to rework the children's lines in the play or their reports so that they are a little more polished, to have some extra rehearsals so that the production will run more smoothly, or to ask your pupils to put in long hours coloring complicated decorations on napkins or place mats. To do this may seem to reflect to your credit, but it is not likely to increase the learning necessary to real growth.

Certainly, it is important for your boys and girls to have the satisfaction of doing a job of which they can be proud when their parents or friends are invited to visit. For that matter, it is important for them to find satisfaction in work well done when they, themselves, are the only audience. However, there is little justification, educationally, for attempting to raise the quality of their performance to a point that can only be reached by speaking words written by adults, following adult direction faithfully, or spending hour after hour in rehearsal merely to achieve a slightly more polished performance. Nor is there always justification for embarking upon an elaborate project, even though it is within your pupils' capabilities, if by so doing other more important learning experiences are neglected.

In deciding how elaborate to make a program or a party, you should ask yourself three questions. First, what new learnings will this activity afford for my boys and girls? Second, how important to their total growth are the learnings in other activities that may have to be curtailed or set aside to make room for this one? Third, how complicated an activity and what standards of performance are appropriate for the maturity and capacities of my youngsters? Sally Smith and Marilyn McAdams were both considering Christmas parties for their third grades. Sally's youngsters had attended many such social events at home; their poise was excellent, their manners good. Sally chose to have a very simple party. Marilyn's group had had few experiences with parties at home; their lunchroom manners were poor; their experiences in entertaining guests were limited. Marilyn spent much more time helping the children to plan their party, discussing manners, and planning how the refreshments could be attractively served. Jane Wilson's fifth-graders had had few experiences with dramatization all year; they were able youngsters, quite capable of planning a three-act play; the study of the Pilgrims which they had just completed lent itself readily to a summary through dramatization. Jane devoted her language experiences for the next three weeks to the production of a play. Donald

Raleigh's fifth-graders had produced a short play as part of a Christmas assembly; they were in the midst of a very fruitful science project that demanded considerable extra time; in the course of their social studies unit they had developed some interesting Then-and-Now dioramas which they were most anxious to have admired. Donald helped them to plan to tell the fourth grade about this work through some simple reports that required practically no extra preparation.

You are not giving a poor impression of your pupils' work to parents and other guests by allowing them to see a rather simple program with the imperfections that are certain to be present when spontaneity has been encouraged and rehearsal time kept within reasonable bounds. In fact, it is most important for parents to see their children's work as it actually develops in the regular school setting if they are to understand the purposes of the school and the nature of its program. It is at least in part because teachers have recognized this fact that many of the activities in which parents are entertained are centered in classroom programs rather than in elaborate auditorium productions. In their normal classroom environment youngsters can be more relaxed; they can take time after a program to explain how they worked and what they think they learned.

Even auditorium programs can be effective without making unduly heavy demands upon pupil time. A carol service at Christmas may be developed by having each room sing a favorite carol. In a Thanksgiving assembly, each class can be responsible for one short contribution—a song, a poem, or a story. A primary assembly can be worked out effectively by allowing each class to share one interesting activity, using as props some of the pictures they have drawn or the experience records they have written. Even when the pupils of a single class have responsibility for an auditorium session, an excellent and very interesting picture of their work can often be given by making use of what has actually gone on from day to day. Such was the case when Janice Osborne's fifth-graders decided to invite their parents and the other upper-grade children to the culmination of their study of the western states. For background they used four large pictures representing aspects of western life that had been done as committees summarized their research. On tables at each side of the stage they placed dioramas done by other committees. On another table across the back they displayed all the materials they had collected for a western exhibit. For the program each committee told in its own words what its picture or diorama represented. Two youngsters explained how the exhibit was developed.

Several read original stories and poems. Two read excerpts from committee reports and showed how the complete report had been compiled. As a climax they dramatized an old-time spelling bee. Then the guests were invited to view the work more closely and the members of the class stood by to answer questions. The complete production took only one rehearsal, but it provided the youngsters with some excellent experience in deciding what would give the best picture of their work, in putting the program together in an effective sequence, and in speaking before an audience.

Your basic responsibility as a teacher is to plan and to guide the experiences of your boys and girls so that maximum growth results. This is your obligation, whether the activity be related to a special event or part of your regular program. If you have made your choices with the welfare of your pupils in mind, those with whom your activities are shared will recognize the soundness of your judgment. They, like you, are interested in helping boys and girls to grow.

BOOKS YOU SHOULD KNOW

Ambrose, Edna, and Miel, Alice. *Children's Social Learning.* Washington, D.C.: Association for Supervision and Curriculum Development, N.E.A. 1958. Pp. vii + 120.

Creating a Good Environment for Learning. 1954 Yearbook of the Association for Supervision and Curriculum Development, N.E.A. Washington, D.C.: The Association, 1954. Pp. ix + 307.

Kyte, George C. *The Elementary School Teacher at Work.* New York: The Dryden Press, 1957. Pp. xii + 530.

Lane, Howard, and Beauchamp, Mary. *Human Relations in Teaching.* Englewood Cliffs, N.J.: Prentice-Hall, 1955. Pp. ix + 353.

Miel, Alice, and Brogan, Peggy. *More Than Social Studies.* Englewood Cliffs, N.J.: Prentice-Hall, 1957. Pp. xii + 452.

Otto, Henry J. *Social Education in Elementary Schools.* New York: Rinehart and Co., 1956. Pp. xii + 493.

Evaluating and Reporting Pupil Progress

CHAPTER 11

Harold Simpson had been responsible for his class for only a week when his cooperating teacher asked him to stay for a conference so that they could evaluate the progress his pupils were making. "How can I tell so soon?" asked Harold. "We're not far enough along for any tests yet. I wasn't planning for any evaluation for about two more weeks."

Sue James reported to her supervisor, "I'm so discouraged I don't know what to do. I thought my children were really learning something and then I gave them a test. You should have seen their scores. Not a single mark over 70!"

Andrea Petrov wailed in despair to a group of student-teacher friends, "Dr. Anderson will never think I'm doing a very good job. *Your* classes do such beautiful art work and write so easily. Mine couldn't do that if they spent two years in every grade."

Rachelle Burns exclaimed to her colleagues at lunch, "I am so discouraged. I just got back the reports of our standardized reading tests and my class has the lowest average of all the fourth grades in our school system. And I'd been working on reading so hard!"

In discussing his lesson plans with his cooperating teacher John Walton said, "I don't see why you go to so much bother to decide what language skills to teach next. They're all there in the textbook. Why don't we just start at the beginning and teach them one after the other?"

Alexander McNulty faithfully took home and graded every piece of written work from his pupils. These he handed back with admonitions regarding the need to do better work. His pupils recopied most papers, but they were given very little opportunity to discuss their errors.

Each of the persons just named is operating on a limited conception of the meaning of evaluation and its purposes. Harold and Sue see evaluation as a periodic testing process and Sue has not realized that there might be imperfections in her test rather than in her pupils' learning. Andrea and Rachelle are appraising the progress of their classes in terms of arbitrary standards—in Andrea's case, the work of other groups whose abilities and backgrounds may be very dissimilar and in Rachelle's, the norms of a standardized test. John and Alexander are perhaps making the most serious error (at least in so far as effective teaching is concerned)—neither is aware of the relation of evaluation to his own day-by-day lesson planning or to the growth of his pupils.

Evaluation may be defined as the process of determining the extent to which values or goals have been attained. It is an integral aspect of teaching. Experienced teachers will tell you that the evaluation of the progress of boys and girls (and by implication the evaluation of their own teaching) is a difficult process. So is the interpretation of this evaluation to parents and others. You have a number of important skills to acquire—skills which could scarcely have been perfected in college classes in psychology and measurement, helpful though these courses may have been. You must learn how to use evaluation procedures with maximum effectiveness in your day-by-day teaching-learning experiences. You must be able to determine appropriate standards against which to appraise the progress of your pupils. You will have to develop skill in collecting the concrete evidence you need and in using tests—standardized and teacher-made—appropriately. It will be important to teach your pupils to evaluate their own growth. Last, but certainly of major consequence, you must develop skill in reporting pupil progress—in keeping parents informed, in building the cumulative records needed by the teacher to whom your pupils go next, and in helping pupils themselves to gain insight into their strengths, weaknesses, progress, and needs.

USING EVALUATION IN DAILY WORK

What part does evaluation play in your daily work? It is easy to say that evaluation is an integral aspect of teaching, but such a statement is too general to be of much help. Exactly what does this mean in practice?

Your experiences with college and high school examination periods may have led you to believe that evaluation is an intermittent business—we teach for a while and then stop to let our pupils demonstrate what they have learned (or what they have been able to "cram" the night before). It is quite possible that you have had one or more experiences where there was a stretch of several weeks, if not months, before your teacher seemed to make any effort to appraise your progress.

It may be, too, that the main purpose of such periodic appraisals seemed to be to rate you as an *A, B,* or *C* student rather than to help you to improve. If these have been your experiences with evaluation, you may need to rethink rather carefully the role it should play in the teaching-learning process.

True, you and your pupils will stop periodically to take stock—to demonstrate speed and accuracy with a process in arithmetic, to take a spelling test, to appraise the effectiveness of a mural just completed, to see how many facts can be recalled from a social studies or science unit, to analyze behavior on a recent excursion, to think back over the afternoon when parents were invited to a school play. However, such periodic evaluation sessions are only a small part of the total evaluation program. Basically the purpose of evaluation is to promote growth, not merely to demonstrate at the end of a series of activities that growth has taken place. It should aid teachers and learners in identifying strengths and weaknesses and in laying plans for next steps. Eventually, in most school systems, a series of appraisals will be translated into letter grades or other means of informing interested persons of a pupil's progress, but the rating of pupils is not the primary purpose of evaluation. What are its functions in the classroom?

Evaluation provides the basis for pupil growth. Whether or not you are conscious of it, the day-by-day plans that guide your teaching activities are based on evaluation. The purpose of instruction is to produce certain changes in pupils. When you (or, more often, you and your pupils) make a decision regarding what changes are desirable, you are engaged in evaluation—you have appraised present status and made some judgments regarding the growth you wish to achieve.

Evaluation procedures are involved whenever teacher and pupils establish objectives, whether these be for a single lesson or for a series of activities extending over several weeks. Fourth-graders discuss a set of oral reports and develop a list of standards. First-graders talk through their difficulties on the playground and suggest some "ground rules" for future play periods. Sixth-graders pause after the first rehearsal of a play to list points where improvement is needed. In a fourth grade the children keep individual lists of spelling difficulties. John plans with his teacher for some special practice in word analysis. Helen takes a speed test to appraise her competence with arithmetic combinations. Sessions such as these help pupils to establish clear goals, make them aware of the value of new learnings, and give them the sense of direction they need to proceed independently with agreed-upon plans.

Back of such joint evaluation sessions, of course, lie the teacher's careful appraisals of strengths and weaknesses and his best judgments regarding next steps. As you listen to youngsters read you should be making evaluative decisions regarding what skills to stress. When you examine a set of papers you will be looking at handwriting, sentence structure, punctuation. As you lead a group discussion you will be thinking about the quality of participation, noting that some youngsters must be drawn out and that others need help in accepting and respecting the contributions of their classmates. As your pupils engage in independent activity you will be appraising their work habits. When they speak you should be thinking about language patterns. As a discussion regarding a science interest proceeds you will note vague concepts, errors in thinking, and needs for more experience background. From such appraisals come goals—long-term goals for several months, goals for a unit of work, goals for the lessons of a single day.

You do not stop using evaluation procedures once you and your pupils have established goals for a new activity. You are evaluating when you pose, at the beginning of an activity, questions that help you to identify your pupils' present levels of understanding and competence. As a lesson proceeds you provide activities or ask questions to help in determining how well pupils are grasping what is being explained. These activities and questions provide on-the-spot evaluations. Many times your lesson will close with activities in which your pupils put their new learnings to use—after you talk about the form of a thank-you note, you write one; after you analyze how some bothersome capital letters are written, you practice; after you talk about how to make oral reading more interesting, you take turns reading a paragraph or two. From your appraisal of the quality of learning revealed in such practice sessions come decisions regarding the need for further teaching and more experience. The procedures are usually informal. Indeed, decisions regarding further experience sometimes hinge on rather subtle clues. However, it is this kind of continuous appraisal that makes your teaching effective.

The pupils, as well as the teacher, engage in informal evaluation as lessons move forward. Listen to some teachers at work and notice how automatically they include their pupils in the appraisal process. "All right, John has shown us how to work the second problem. Now look at your papers. How many are having trouble?" "You are looking puzzled. How many still don't quite see why it is warmer in summer than in winter?" "Could we hear from your groups? Is anybody having difficulty locating material?" "Robbie, you did much better in working out hard words for yourself today, didn't you?" "How many misspelled that word? Look to see which letters caused you trouble."

You also utilize evaluation procedures in making decisions regarding classroom organization. When you bring together a half-dozen youngsters for special help in word study it is because you have evidence that they have similar problems. You base your decisions regarding the nature of the schedule for the day on your appraisal of the pupils' work habits, their typical attention spans, their maturity or immaturity in adjusting to change. Whether your plan for a unit of work calls for extensive small-group work or for many activities in which you work with the class as a whole depends upon evaluation of such factors as reading skill, ability to work cooperatively, needs for common experience background. Your thinking regarding the types of activities most likely to be appropriate for small groups is guided by similar evidence. Pupils often share in such evaluative decisions. They think with you regarding which activities to put first on the schedule, how many people will be needed for a specific job, when a project demands youngsters with special talent.

When you are doing effective teaching, then, evaluation is an integral part of the process, not only for you but for the pupils as well. You bring to each planning session your appraisal of the strengths and weaknesses of your group. In these sessions you and your pupils look at their work together, appraise strengths and weaknesses, identify new needs, and make plans to meet these needs. As the plans unfold, continuing evaluation points to new problems. Not only your plans for specific lessons but your schedule and your classroom organization as well grow from your appraisal of competencies and needs.

Evaluation is the means for helping pupils to become self-directing. The mature individual takes responsibility for his own decisions. He is able to appraise his own strengths and weaknesses realistically. He can analyze a problem for himself, propose next steps, and carry them out. He is able to make sound judgments and wise choices as he faces the multitude of alternatives which life presents. Such mature problem-solving abilities do not develop without opportunity.

In terms of their maturity you teach your pupils through planning and evaluation sessions to look critically and thoughtfully at their difficulties and at the things they do well. You help them to analyze activities that went smoothly and activities that went poorly, to look dispassionately at their errors in judgment as well as at the times when they planned successfully. As you and they propose next steps you stop to think about the reasonableness and probable effectiveness of the proposals. They learn with you how to appraise alternatives and when to withhold judgment until more evidence is secured. Such experiences make a fundamental contribution to two of the most important abilities needed by citizens in a democracy—self-direction and self-evaluation.

Evaluation provides the data needed to assure continuity of growth. You do not teach for today alone. Your contribution to the growth of boys and girls is only one in a series stretching from nursery school or kindergarten to high school or college. Even for the year that your pupils are with you, you are not the only person responsible for their growth. Parents, scout leaders, playground supervisors, librarians, Sunday school teachers, and other school personnel are making their contributions, too. You do not use evaluation procedures, then, only to serve yourself and your class. You must provide data upon which others can base their plans for working with your boys and girls, both for this year and for the years to come.

Sometimes beginning teachers seem to assume that there are two types of evaluation programs, one relatively independent of the other—a continuous program which is a guide to pupil-teacher planning from day to day and a periodic program which serves as the basis for letter grades to be sent to parents and entered in cumulative records. Actually, whether the problem is day-by-day planning or developing cumulative records and reports to parents, an effective evaluation program is *both* continuous and periodic. Many of the devices that you use to help your pupils collect continuous evidence of their progress—the folders of typical work, the special spelling notebooks, the check lists of difficulties in English usage, the collections of stories or pictures, the social studies or science notebooks—provide important data when it comes to preparing reports and cumulative records. The times when you and your pupils stop to take stock—to take a quiz, to complete a series of check sheets in arithmetic, to appraise a culminating activity in social studies—also contribute both to planning from day to day and to the accumulating evidence that is summarized in records and reports for parents and other teachers. You must learn to use all appropriate evidence, whatever your purposes for evaluation.

Providing for continuity of growth is a two-way process. When you are planning an effective program for your boys and girls, it is just as important for you to know about their home and community experiences as it is to collect evidence about their progress in school. You will want to put to effective use all the techniques you have developed for working with parents and for getting acquainted with your pupils' community setting. You will also want to make strategic use of cumulative records. Mary Jane's health record shows a history of minor illnesses; this may give you a valuable clue in appraising her uneven progress in learning to read. Randy's mother reports that in spite of all their efforts he is finding it hard to share his parents' affection with his new sister; here is help for you in studying Randy's difficulties with his friends at school. The librarian tells you that Gordon has shown an insatiable interest in historical fiction; this is important in planning for your social studies unit. Victor and his father are plunging into a study of geology; here is talent and interest in science of which you need to be aware. The more effectively you can tap such sources of information, the better you will be able to assure that school, home, and community make a continuous and consistent contribution to the growth of boys and girls.

Evaluation procedures help the teacher to look at his own effectiveness. "Start where your pupils are." "Meet the needs of your group." "Work in terms of individual strengths and weaknesses." This is a precarious philosophy if teachers do not have some bench marks from which to appraise their efforts. It is all too easy to fall into a pattern of accepting from a group of boys and girls a level of achievement that does not match their capabilities, especially if one is convinced through a series of mediocre performances that they are rather slow. Yet the fault may lie in the teaching. Beginning teachers who say "They aren't interested" or "I've tried everything and they still can't learn" are often revealing more about their own competence than they are about their pupils' progress and capabilities. It is possible, also, for a teacher to hold standards that are far too high and to make himself and his pupils miserable (to say nothing of losing his chance to develop many learnings appropriate to their maturity levels) by trying to drive them to attainments of which they are not capable. If you are truly interested in developing high professional competence you will learn to use evaluation procedures to appraise your own success as a teacher as well as to help you study the progress of your boys and girls.

In a sense, each time you evaluate your pupils you are evaluating yourself. You note the confusion of the group working at the mural and wonder how clear your directions were. You ask some questions about factual information discussed yesterday and realize to your dismay that the points you thought you had explained clearly are still vague. You see that your better readers have fallen into the habit of looking to you helplessly when they meet a hard word and realize that you have been guilty of responding too quickly to pleas for help instead of encouraging them to try new words for themselves. As you walk down the aisles you note with satisfaction how much Bobby's handwriting has improved. You listen to shy little Roberta making her first report to the class and pat yourself on the back for a job well done. Through your reassurance, Harold's interest in science begins to blossom and the class looks forward to his explanations and demonstrations of new projects. You are repeatedly asked by the boys and girls to play some more of the records from your own collection and you realize that your encouragement of listening to good music has been effective.

If you have learned to be objective in appraising your successes and failures you will pick up countless clues during the day to the quality of your performance. You will want, however, to make specific efforts to look at your work from objective vantage points. Since all teachers have a responsibility to evaluate their own efforts continuously and to appraise the general effectiveness of the total educational program, you will undoubtedly find a number of provisions in operation in your school system for assisting you and your colleagues in these tasks. There may well be a program of standardized tests. These can be helpful if you employ due precautions in interpreting them. Some of your colleagues may be involved in research programs to test out in action in their classrooms the merits of new materials or of new ways of working. Others may be serving on curriculum or textbook committees. Their discussions of promising professional practices can be of help to you in looking at the quality of your classroom work. Speakers, teachers' institutes, and workshops can be very helpful in bringing the perspective of national thinking to the local situation. You should not neglect the professional library with which your school is undoubtedly equipped; here is another valuable aid to viewing your work in perspective. Your colleagues make full use of all such avenues to professional improvement as they evaluate their work in the classroom.

Perhaps most important, you must learn to capitalize upon the supervisory help provided. The principal, the supervisors in your school system, and, in the case of student teachers, the cooperating teacher and the college supervisor are there to help you. They view the process of evaluating you in the same way as you view it in evaluating your pupils—as an opportunity to help you become increasingly self-directing in your activities and increasingly mature and wise in your choices. Ratings and letter grades are for them, as they are for you in working with your pupils, a necessary aspect of their work but not the most important aspect. If you are to continue to develop in your professional competence you need to display, at your level of maturity, the same capabilities for self-evaluation you expect from your pupils.

ESTABLISHING STANDARDS

Evaluation comes from the root word *value*. To *evaluate* means to judge the worth of a performance or product. You do not evaluate when you say that Barnie can read a third-grade book. This is a fact—a measure that describes Barnie's present status in reading. You do evaluate, however, when you go on to say "This is very good for a first-grader" or "This is not nearly as good a job as a fourth-grader of Barnie's ability should be able to do" or "Considering Barnie's IQ, I am very pleased with this performance." Likewise, you are not evaluating when you say that Diane had eight questions correct out of ten on a short quiz. Raw scores on quizzes are measures. You begin to evaluate when you say "Considering how simple those questions were and how much time we spent on them, this is disappointing" or "This is very good work; those questions were meant to challenge the best thinkers in my class" or "This is by far Diane's best performance." On the basis of your evaluative judgments, not your measurements, you plan next steps. You decide that more help is needed in some areas or that the level of achievement in others is quite satisfactory in the light of a pupil's total growth.

To evaluate you must have standards—expectations against which you can examine the total program you have planned. Setting standards is a major problem not only for beginners, but for experienced teachers. In fact, from your reading of educational literature you know that the question of determining desirable standards for American schools is a constant challenge to our ablest professional leaders.

This is not the place to solve the philosophical problem of what shall be the ultimate goals of American education, nor will any other single volume do so. However, to evaluate the progress of your pupils with some feeling of security you must be able to combine, on a practical level, your best insights from three major areas: what you understand to be the over-all objectives of education in general and of your school system in particular; what you understand these objectives to mean for pupils of the maturity levels of those whom you are teaching; and what you believe to be appropriate adjustments of your general standards in the light of the strengths and weaknesses of individuals. This should have a familiar ring. Every decision you make regarding how and what to teach has this threefold foundation. This section will help you to focus your thinking on the implications for evaluating pupil growth.

Standards need to be related to basic educational objectives. Effective evaluation of pupil growth must be concerned with the pupil's total progress toward desired educational objectives, not with his achievement in a single area. If you listen to your colleagues as they discuss the experiences they are planning for their boys and girls, you will identify many questions that relate to the balance within the total program. "They read exceptionally well but their written English is very poor. I've been wondering how much extra time I'd be justified in giving to it. After all, it will be important when they reach high school." "We seem to take time away from academic work almost every day to think through the difficulties they get into on the playground. I wonder if I should?" "They would spend all day on their science activities, but should I allow able children to be this one-sided in their interests?" "When they read as poorly as mine do, I wonder if it's right to spend much time on subjects such as art and music?" These are problems of appraising pupils' total growth and deciding on appropriate balance in their activities. You will face similar decisions every day as you think through your schedule; determine how much time to allot to several problems, each of which seems equally pressing; or decide how best to find time for the unscheduled assembly or the request from the principal's office for cooperation on a special project. You make these decisions on the basis of your insights into broad educational goals and your judgment regarding which of these goals should be given priority.

If you will reread the statements outlining goals for various aspects of your teaching[1] you will perhaps be impressed anew with the realization of how exceedingly broad our educational objectives are. As you begin to consider how effective your program has been for your boys and girls, you will be looking for growth in specific skills and broader

[1] See Chapter 5, pages 130-139; Chapter 7, pages 222-226; Chapter 8, pages 292-295; Chapter 9, pages 341-346, and Chapter 10, pages 389-397.

grasp of items of information, but you will also be looking for growth in problem-solving skills, for ability to use skills or knowledge effectively in a variety of new situations, for positive attitudes toward learning, for deep and abiding interests. In evaluation of pupil progress, you must learn to ask yourself how effectively each of these types of growth is being achieved.

Standards need to be established in terms of the general maturity of the pupils you teach. Before you can evaluate the progress of your pupils you will need to translate your broad educational objectives into appropriate goals for your age group. Skill in discussion techniques, for example, means something very different for first-graders from what it does for high school youth. What you judge to be good sentence structure for a nine-year-old will certainly not be the standard you will hold for him when he is twelve. One of the most difficult problems faced by beginning teachers is the determination of appropriate expectations. If you set your sights too low, you will waste the potentialities of your class. On the other hand, holding standards that are too high can lead to a frustrating and discouraging year, both for you and for the pupils.

What aids do you have in translating general objectives into appropriate goals for your pupils? Perhaps most important, your previous college courses and professional texts have helped you to develop sensitivity to typical levels of pupil growth.[2] Your student-teaching experience and your first few years on the job should provide you with an important opportunity to bring to life this professional background by relating it to the actual classroom behavior of boys and girls.

Your general professional background is not always of sufficient help when you face such concrete problems as deciding whether to demand better punctuation skills of your pupils, whether to rate a series of committee reports as adequate, how to evaluate the mural your first-graders have finished so proudly, or how much depth of understanding to expect as your third-graders embark on a study of weather. There are specific aids useful in building a more concrete frame of reference against which to appraise your pupils' work. Examine the course of study for your school system. This summarizes the best insights of experienced teachers regarding the expectations to hold for pupils of different ages. Look, also, at the textbooks published for the grade you are teaching and at their accompanying manuals.

[2] The sections in Chapters 7, 8, and 9 which are focused on the general problems of deciding where to begin and what to emphasize summarize briefly the gist of this professional background. See pages 227-236, 295-307, and 346-352.

These, too, suggest expectations based on a combination of the judgment of experts in the field, the insights of teachers, and the research evidence regarding pupil growth. Examine, also, whatever scores on standardized tests are available. They will give you some idea of your pupils' abilities and attainments in the light of local or national norms. The beginner who does not make use of resources such as these in learning how to appraise the present status and needs of his pupils is by-passing valuable assistance.

Your colleagues, supervisor, and, in the case of student teachers, your cooperating teacher will be other very real sources of help as you strive to develop appropriate standards for your grade. Here are persons whose insights into typical pupil performances reflect many years of firsthand experience. You should be matching the goals and the standards you have set for your pupils against theirs and, at points where you disagree, asking for conferences so that you may benefit from the thinking that was back of their decisions.

Your own experiences with boys and girls will also help you to refine your standards. If, prior to student teaching, you have had the opportunity to work with other age groups, you will already have begun to develop some sensitivity regarding the quality of work to expect from pupils of differing ages, maturities, capacities, and experience backgrounds. As you analyze the success of your lessons during your student-teaching experience and your first years in your own classroom, your insights will deepen. How good a first-draft report can your youngsters write, for example, after careful preliminary discussion? How well can they give the gist of a story that they have just read silently? How skilled are they in locating information for themselves? Out of countless such observations your sense of general expectations for the age group with which you are working will grow. Do not make the mistake, however, of failing to relate your pupils' performances to the quality of your own teaching. Many a beginner has put the blame on the wrong shoulders when he has said, "They just can't get it."

Standards need to be adjusted to the potential ability and experience background of pupils. Your general standards for your grade will need further interpretation when you evaluate the progress of individuals. You might state, in terms of what you know about grade-level expectancies, that third-grade Susannah, IQ 85, is doing high second-grade work in arithmetic, but you probably would not evaluate this as a poor job for Susannah. Nor would you rate as excellent the work of Peter, IQ 140, in the same grade if he could barely handle a fourth-grade reading book, even if this were the top performance in the class. For Candy, sketching the plans for a mural in proper perspective may require only a few minutes. Brian, the same age, may be doing remarkably well if he manages to produce a likeness even remotely resembling what he had envisioned.

What guides can you use in deciding how to adjust general grade-level expectations to individuals? Probably the measure most readily at hand will be a pupil's mental age. This is frequently recommended as a basis for appraising pupil achievement, especially in relation to skills in such areas as reading and arithmetic and the intellectual adeptness with which a pupil arrives at concepts and generalizations in the subject fields. Although a child's mental age is probably a better indication of his general level of intellectual achievement than his chronological age, it must be used with caution. All too often teachers forget that there can be considerable variation from one intelligence test to the next. They tend to forget, also, that a pupil with a specific academic weakness, such as limited reading skill, often does poorly on a group intelligence test. It is a false concept, too, to assume that a pupil's achievement can never rise above the level indicated by his mental age or, conversely, that a youngster with a high IQ will automatically bring to his school work all the sophistication that his mental age might suggest. With these precautions in mind and a determination to seek confirmation of your "hunches" through careful observation of each child in action, you will probably set more appropriate standards if you think of ten-year-old Harry, IQ 70, as operating more as a seven- or eight-year-old and of Bonnie, IQ 140 and also ten, as potentially able to read, calculate, and reason like a thirteen- or fourteen-year-old. There will be, however, many practical situations in which Harry's ten years of living will help him to operate more intelligently than the typical seven-year-old and many problems appropriate for thirteen- and fourteen-year-olds for which Bonnie lacks adolescent sophistication and experience background.

It is important to consider the experience backgrounds of your pupils as well as their intelligence test scores in determining expectations for their work. If the English usage that Russell has heard at home all his life has been illiterate or colloquial, he may be doing very well indeed if he has eliminated all but an occasional *ain't* from his speech. For Ronnie, whose parents are both college graduates, this may represent no particular achievement. Would you not, also, adjust your standards for the child who is ill and is just now catching up? Many teachers would give lavish praise and encouragement for the ability and drive of such a youngster, even though his achievement is temporarily below what one would expect from a pupil of his ability. Furthermore, you will appraise in somewhat different terms the progress of youngsters who have no books at home and whose intellectual stimulation must come almost entirely from the school than you will the progress of pupils who have had every advantage of travel, week-end excursions to museums and nearby points of interest, rich home resources in reference materials, and parents ready to lend a willing hand with home projects. This may sound like an argument for holding lower ultimate standards for those youngsters who are able but who are handicapped by the homes and communities from which they come. It is not meant to be such. Certainly the responsibility of the school is to help each youngster to make maximum use of his potential ability regardless of the home and community setting. We are not, however, likely to achieve this objective for all pupils unless we are able to appraise their present status, start where they are, and hold for them goals that are challenging but realistic.

Have you thought about the importance of special abilities and how your standards may need to be adjusted in the light of them? The more carefully you have studied individuals, the more aware you will have become of variation in their talents. Talent in art and music is not always closely related to intellectual ability. Of three able pupils, John may have deep interests in science, Allen be devouring books on archaeology and history, and Darnelle writing poetry. In trying to decide whether and when to provide challenging new experiences, you will face some searching questions in evaluating the present status of pupils similar to these. Should John and Allen be dissuaded from their scientific or historical interests in order to up-grade their love of poetry or should Darnelle be encouraged to exchange her books for test tubes? There may be times when you will evaluate a pupil's performance in one area as satisfactory, even though his achievement does not measure up to the level indicated by his mental age, and will help him to devote his free time to developing a strong interest or talent in another field. For example, you might rate fifth-grade Joan's ability to handle fifth- and sixth-grade books as quite satisfactory, in spite of her 130 IQ, and foster instead her exceptional musical talent. Or if Sam is scientifically inclined, you would not necessarily curtail his science experiences because his achievement in music and art is not exceptional. Satisfactory growth does not necessarily mean even growth in all areas.

As you were reading the foregoing paragraphs you were perhaps voicing the dilemma that concerns all conscientious teachers—what is to go on report cards? Certainly one would not be satisfied to see an able learner fritter away his time and one cannot ask more of the slower youngster than that he extend himself to the utmost. Certainly, too, the accomplishments of a youngster from an improverished environmental background may be exceptional when compared with those of the pupil from a privileged home, even though the report he makes or the notebook he prepares may be less outstanding. But who gets the *A*, who the *B*, and who the *C*? This is a problem so complicated that an entire section later in this chapter is devoted to it. At the moment, the point at issue is how you arrive at your decisions regarding whether to evaluate the progress of individuals as satisfactory, exceptional, or unsatisfactory—decisions which guide your planning in providing new experiences for them. These judgments you make in the light of the factors that have been discussed.

COLLECTING EVIDENCE FROM CLASSROOM ACTIVITIES

Even if you had made no definite effort to collect concrete evidence, you probably could describe the performances of most pupils in your class. "Patty is one of my best thinkers, but she is very careless in her written work." "These are my poorest readers; I am using third-grade books with them." "Bill's coordination is very poor. You should see his handwriting." "Carl is one of our most creative artists." "This group does a marvelous job of collecting information independently." Such comments come from informal record-collecting processes. The more sensitive a teacher's insights are as he works with his pupils from day to day, the more accurate such offhand evaluative statements are likely to be.

A "halo" effect, however, often accompanies informal approaches to appraisal and evaluations based on general impressions. Without concrete evidence at hand it is very easy to let Randy's cooperative manner obscure the lack of depth in his thinking or Vaughn's excellent oral reading color your appraisal of his comprehension. Remember, too, that you are not the only person involved in the evaluative process. Your pupils need objective evidence if they are to grow in their ability to evaluate themselves. Eventually, also, you are going to have to summarize and interpret your evidence for parents and for other teachers. For these purposes as well as for your own sense of security you need more than educated guesses about pupil progress. To be sure of your evaluations, make the data-collecting job a systematic one.

The techniques you will employ to collect evidence regarding progress and needs are similar to those suggested in Chapter 4.[3] You will face several new problems, however, when you use these data-gathering devices for evaluation purposes. You will have to determine the types of evidence appropriate for evaluating growth toward a variety of goals, the amount of evidence needed, the means of making this evidence as accurate as possible, and the ways of using the data-collecting process as an educative activity for your pupils. Basically these same problems exist whether you are using on-going classroom activities and work products as the source of data or employing standardized or teacher-made tests. The present section is focused on problems of collecting evidence from classroom activities. The section that follows is devoted to using tests.

Objectives determine the specific kinds of evidence collected. Evaluation has been defined as the process of determining the extent to which goals or objectives are being attained. The evidence you will need to collect, then, depends on the objectives with which you are concerned. Objectives, however, can be stated at different levels of generality. The broader the objective, the more difficult and complicated the evaluation process becomes. For example, what would you accept as evidence that fourth-graders are developing effective work habits? that sixth-graders are coming to understand their cultural heritage? that third-graders are growing in their ability to write creatively? or that first-graders are learning to read? Before you can feel secure in evaluating your pupils' progress toward goals such as these you must devise ways of defining more precisely the evidence you need.

An important step before beginning to collect evidence is to translate general objectives into specific goals. Beginning teachers who fail to do this often evaluate on the basis of evidence that is not clearly related to their objectives. If you are concerned with your pupils' growing ability to spell correctly in their day-by-day writing, for example, your evaluation cannot be entirely based on the results of Friday tests. You do not have evidence regarding a pupil's ability to write creatively if your data concern only the correctness of his usage, spelling, and pronunciation. Nor do you know enough about the effectiveness of his command of English grammar if your record book shows only the results of multiple-choice exercises in which he is asked merely to identify

[3] See pages 105-116.

the correct form. A mural that would rate high from an artistic viewpoint or a well-acted play does not necessarily reveal how clearly your pupils have grasped underlying geographic, historical, or social concepts. Accurate oral reading does not always signify comprehension. If you will take time to specify precisely the goals you are seeking you will see more clearly what kinds of evidence you need.

A procedure that is helpful in defining goals precisely is to state them in terms of pupil behavior. What kinds of behavior, for example, would signify that fourth-graders are developing effective work habits? Are the following behavioral descriptions applicable to this goal? What others would you add?

Gets the materials he needs without wasting time.

Can state what aspect of the over-all plans he has completed and what his job is for today.

Keeps a list of the books he has read and sources he has gone to for information.

Has his notebook organized so that he can locate needed material readily.

Keeps up to date with his record of new words or other assignments agreed upon as individual projects.

What might be some of the specific behaviors listed by a first-grade teacher concerned with pupils' reading skill?

Comments intelligently on what he has just read.

Voice and phrasing indicate comprehension of the story when he reads aloud.

Recognizes without difficulty most of the words appearing frequently in his reading matter.

Is beginning to attack new words for himself.

Uses the context to check on the appropriateness of the new word he has just figured out.

Comments spontaneously on letter combinations and similarities among words.

Seeks opportunities to read.

What behaviors might demonstrate command of social studies concepts and content in a sixth-grade mural or play?

Pupils are accurate in their portrayal of the life of the times.

They can document their points and justify the selection they made for their production.

Time and space relationships are accurately portrayed.

The information conveyed to the audience is sufficient to build a clear picture of the area under consideration.

Pupils can draw analogies with their present-day living.

These lists are incomplete. You could add other points and quite probably, in the light of your objectives for your particular group, delete some of those suggested. Your ultimate lists should be your own, built in terms of the specific goals you have been trying to attain. You will find that the time you invest in translating these goals into descriptions of behavior is well spent. Behavioral goals are meaningful. They indicate types of concrete evidence that can be observed or collected.

The device of translating goals into specific behavior is just as useful in evaluating a single piece of work as it is in appraising pupil growth within a subject area. Suppose, for example, your fourth-graders have each written an imaginary diary as members of Columbus' crew. How do you evaluate these for growth in social studies concepts and skills? A list somewhat similar to that suggested for the sixth-grade mural might be your starting point. Once you have identified a half-dozen or more elements that will tell you whether facts and concepts have been clearly grasped, you are ready to establish a tentative scale. In the light of your master list, what would you consider to be an excellent grasp of background content? What lacks would cause you to rate it strong but not a first-class job? What represents the minimum performance you would consider acceptable? What types of errors, gaps, or deficiencies would cause you to consider the job to be poor? What represents adequate performance in such language skills as handwriting, sentence structure, punctuation, spelling? With your tentative scale defined as clearly as possible, you are ready to start reading papers. If the assignment is a new venture both for you and your pupils, you might check your scale by reading selected papers—two or three from youngsters known from other types of evidence to have a clear grasp of the area; some from those whose work is usually satisfactory but not, on an absolute scale, outstanding; and a couple from those for whom the learning has been a major struggle. Such sampling often suggests new points to add to the original scale. Sometimes it indicates factors operating against the original standards. Sufficient time may not have been allowed for as thorough a job as was hoped for. Preliminary plans may not have been clear and certain types of evidence included in your original list may not appear on anybody's paper.

In evaluating pupils' work in terms of behavioral goals, you still face the general problem of appraising performance in terms of individual capacities. Your list of specific behaviors will suggest the types of evidence which you will seek. Evaluating the evidence in terms of the capabilities of a particular child and translating your evaluation into terms the pupil and his parents will understand are, of course, equally important aspects of the total process.

Evaluation should be based on many types of evidence. Growth can be revealed in many ways. Limiting yourself to one type of evidence may lead to biased and inaccurate evaluation. The reason for this becomes readily apparent once you begin to translate general objectives into behavioral goals. Sarah may do very well on a Friday spelling test but hand in written work during the week containing misspelling of these same words; furthermore, she may never take time to check an unfamiliar word in the dictionary. Jimmy gives back the facts from his history text on a completion test, but he fails to use them when applicable; he also accepts without question anything he finds in print. Roxanna speaks fluently, but she cannot put her words on paper. Arthur takes out two or three library books each week, but he can't tell you what they were about. John talks intelligently about scientific aspects of the solar system in one breath and reports as truth what he has seen in a science fiction movie on television in the next. Such contradictory evidence is important if your evaluations of pupil growth are to be accurate.

The teachers whose evaluations are the most insightful tap a wide variety of sources for their evidence. Pupils' written work will certainly be an important source of data, particularly in the case of older children, but you should also be studying evidence revealed in discussions, comments, and other oral performances where you can see how your pupils use their learnings in informal settings. Furthermore, your plans for written work should be laid so as to yield data on progress toward a variety of goals—ability to recall facts accurately, to solve problems using these facts, to apply concepts to present-day situations, to apply generalizations to new situations. Often it is important to gather evidence at times other than those designated in your schedule for work in a specific area. Not all reading skills will be put to use during reading time. Command of spelling and punctuation skills is revealed in all written work. Oral communication permeates the entire day. Ability to use effectively concepts and generalizations regarding the social and scientific world may be revealed in a discussion regarding a clipping on the bulletin board or a recent event of national or international significance. Attitudes and interests are often expressed freely in informal circumstances—during play periods, periods for independent reading, in the lunchroom, before school begins. You will need to learn how to use efficiently all such day-by-day opportunities for collecting information.

You may well protest that a teacher cannot evaluate growth in all areas all of the time. This is quite true. You will need to employ everything you have learned about how to observe if you are to be successful. The accuracy with which you define your goals will make a major difference in the ease with which you collect your data. Then, although you will wish to have ample evidence for each pupil, this does not necessarily mean trying to collect all types of evidence at once or recording every scrap of available evidence. You can make plans for a systematic sampling of behavior. Your experiences in observing pupils should have helped you to identify aspects of your day's work during which it is particularly appropriate to collect certain types of evidence. These experiences should also have taught you the knack of concentrating on those individuals for whom you need more data. Robby may be so outspoken during discussions that you have no trouble at all in assessing the quality of his thinking; Sandy is quiet. You may concentrate your attention on Sandy, then, during today's discussion. If you are systematic in using the evidence you have collected from past performances as a basis for your plans, you will soon discover that you have developed the habit of making a mental note to look more carefully at pupils for whom your data are limited—to check on your impression that Ruth really wasn't sure of the facts on which she reported so glibly yesterday or that Allan is still in need of help with the principles of long division.

Evaluation procedures should result in concrete evidence. For your own security as well as for the purpose of evaluating progress with the pupils you will need definite evidence. It takes careful planning to collect the information you will require and still have time for all the other responsibilities which a teacher must assume in the classroom.

The teachers who build the most comprehensive records have found ways of making much of the data-collecting process an integral aspect of their teaching. They have learned to use effectively the rich and varied sources of evidence residing in on-going classroom activities so that they do a minimum of stopping to collect special data merely for evaluation purposes. They have also learned how to file such data systematically so that a contribution is made both to the regular classroom procedure and to a comprehensive picture of pupil growth. Pupils are typically involved in this process. For example, each youngster may keep his own spelling record by pasting pre-tests and final tests in a notebook (or by keeping a special notebook for testing purposes) and by developing in another section of his notebook his own personal list of "demons" as revealed in other written work. Here is concrete evidence which teacher and pupil can examine together and which can be shared with parents. Yet it has demanded no extra time. Some such record is vital if pupils are to be helped to take responsibility for their own growth in learning to spell.

The possibilities for classroom records that help pupils to appraise their own growth and yet yield the evidence needed for reporting to parents and building cumulative records are almost endless. Among those you will find in common use are:

Handwriting folders in which sample papers collected at intervals are filed.

Personal check lists of English errors kept in the child's notebook.

Notebooks or folders in which a pupil's creative writing is dated and filed.

Inventory tests on computations in arithmetic, filed in a pupil's arithmetic file at the end of a block of work on each new computation skill.

Lists of library books, briefly annotated.

Logs or diaries in which a pupil records his own contribution to a unit of work and his comments on the day's activities.

Notebooks in which are collected all of a pupil's work for a particular unit—bibliographies, reports, quizzes, creative writing, pictures.

You will probably also be using certain record-keeping devices for your class as a whole as an aid to on-going activities. These can be filed and analyzed for information regarding individuals:

Lists of committees can give you a picture of the specific aspects of projects on which each child has worked over the past few weeks.

Class magazines or newspapers will provide samples of individual work and can be studied for the number and variety of contributions from each child.

Check lists can be maintained to show what activities were chosen by individuals during independent work periods.

Helpers' charts can be analyzed to see what room responsibilities have been assumed by individuals.

Names of individuals who shared in the experience can be added to murals or experience records. These can be studied later if data are needed on the types of activities in which a pupil has shared.

Teachers can keep flow charts, recording the contributions and questions of class members during group discussions.

Pupils' preferences for working partners on class activities can be studied for sociometric data.

Lists of questions recorded at the beginning of a unit or lists of plans filed by committees can be consulted if details are needed regarding a pupil's experiences in connection with a unit.

The experience charts developed in relation to a primary unit will provide a record of the nature and sequence of class activities.

Lists of standards established through class discussion—for audience behavior, for oral reading, for proofreading papers—provide evidence of group objectives.

Teacher's plans can reveal objectives for groups and for individuals, special types of practice provided for individuals, special experiences provided for the class as a whole.

You will undoubtedly keep certain types of evidence in your own daily record book. This should contain more than a series of numbers or grades which you average to determine *A*'s and *B*'s for the periodic reporting period. You will want to record ratings for special papers and assignments and results of quizzes, but you should also be writing comments—notes regarding special strengths or weaknesses, lists of specific errors. You may for your own guidance enter ages, IQ's, and recent achievement test scores. It is often helpful to provide space for attendance records. For some classes, a place in the record book to check off assignments completed on time may be useful. Sometimes it is also valuable to provide a space where you can check participation in special activities so that you can see at a glance the names of your safety guards and room helpers. Some teachers have found it useful to set up double pages for each major area for study and to allow five or six lines for each individual so that comments can be entered. There is no best pattern for planning a record book. Just how you set yours up depends upon the use you intend to make of it.

Because the space for notes in record books is limited, many teachers maintain a folder for each pupil. Samples of work are filed in such folders and periodically evaluated. Pupils can be given some important experiences in self-evaluation if they share in deciding which materials are representative of their work and in analyzing their own growth, as indicated by the accumulation of work in the folder. Such collections of typical work can be much more meaningful to parents than scores on tests or letter grades. For example, if you want to convince a parent that Franklin has improved in his work habits, it is helpful to have two of his assignments before you—one completed early in the year and one collected just prior to the conference. These can be compared as to accuracy, completeness, neatness, and other standards considered to be important.

To the samples of pupils' work you may want to add anecdotes of significant behavior. Some teachers keep a pencil and pad available for the purpose of making brief notes regarding pupils' attitudes, reactions, and behavior. These notes are then dated and included in the children's folders, or, if the children have access to their folders for evaluation purposes, filed in some other way for the teacher's use.

USING CLASSROOM AND STANDARDIZED TESTS[4]

You will undoubtedly make use of classroom and standardized tests in the evaluation process. In many school systems there will be two types of testing programs: a program of teacher-made tests used by a particular teacher at points appropriate for his class and a program of standardized tests. The latter is often set up on a system-wide basis, but in many schools teachers are free to request additional standardized tests as the need for them arises. Whether you are working with the scores on standardized tests or using those from your own tests, you have certain skills to acquire. You need to be able to design or select tests which will give you the information you need. You must learn to interpret accurately the scores your pupils make. It will be important

[4] There are many technical problems involved in constructing and interpreting tests. It will be helpful, as you study this section, to have at hand one of the comprehensive texts on evaluation and measurement listed in the bibliography of this chapter.

to know when and how to supplement tests with other data and to have some criteria for interpreting discrepancies between a pupil's test score and his daily classroom performance. In addition, you must be able to use tests effectively to help pupils grow; data-collecting which does not make a contribution to pupil growth is always subject to question.

The form of the test should be planned with objectives in mind. The information yielded by classroom tests differs from that secured from samples of pupils' day-by-day classroom work in several ways. In the first place, the pupils know that they are being tested, whereas they are not always aware of appraisals made on a day-to-day basis. Then, too, a test calls for responses to the same items from everyone; it provides a sample of work by which you can compare pupil with pupil and gives you a chance to appraise the grasp of certain common facts, generalizations, or skills for every member in your class. Some of the concrete materials you collect from day to day are likewise similar for all pupils, but your day-by-day evidence is usually less uniform. A test is given at a specified time and place; it represents a periodic stock-taking for which pupils can prepare. In contrast, day-by-day data-collecting tends to be a continuous process done under a variety of circumstances. You will make use of classroom tests, then, at the points where you wish to give your entire class a systematic review of certain specific concepts, facts, or skills. Teachers of the intermediate grades, whose pupils possess the language skills necessary to acquit themselves effectively on a test, will use this means of evaluation more frequently than those teaching primary children. Even at the intermediate level, however, these instruments are only one of many types of evidence used to evaluate pupil progress. The more ample and varied your total accumulation of data, the less you may feel the need of tests.

If tests are to be of value, they must be designed to reveal the information you want. For example, if you are interested in a pupil's command of facts and specific information, you will not include items in your test that call for an expression of opinion. If your major concern is with his reading comprehension of the general plot of a story, you will not have him answer questions stressing specific details, nor will you restrict him by setting a time limit. When you are trying to ascertain whether he can comprehend the relationships in an arithmetic problem and estimate a reasonable answer, you will not make the computation unusually difficult.

Test items can be classified under two main heads: *selection* items and *supply* items. Selection items include true-false, multiple-choice, and matching types. Here the pupil is asked to *select* from the two or more alternative answers for the item. Supply items include completion, short-answer essay, and essay types. Here the pupil *supplies* the correct answer from his own background. From your own experience with high school and college tests you undoubtedly know the general characteristics of these two basic types of test items. You are also probably aware of some of their strengths and weaknesses as well as the pitfalls to be avoided in constructing them. Nevertheless, a closer look is appropriate now that you are about to construct some of your own.

Selection items—true-false, multiple choice, and matching—are often used to measure a pupil's recognition of facts. However, such items, if properly constructed, can be used also to measure a pupil's concepts and his ability to apply basic principles. For example, the following item asks for a fact:

_____Lean meat is rich in (1) protein; (2) carbohydrates; (3) fats.

It could be rephrased to get at a generalization by either of the following:

_____Why do we need lean meat in our diets? (1) It contains elements important in building muscles and bones. (2) It gives quick energy. (3) It gives fuel for our bodies.

_____John wants to make the baseball team, but his coach says he is too thin and tired. Which of the following should John be sure to eat every day? (1) lean meat; (2) spinach; (3) honey and other sweets.

Although true-false, multiple-choice, and matching items have been grouped under the general category of selection items, there are special situations for which each is appropriate. True-false items are the easiest to construct. A test made up of true-false items is particularly useful when you want a quick estimate of your pupils' grasp of a number of specific pieces of information. Such items are not as suitable if you wish to determine whether a pupil can apply a generalization to a new situation. They offer, of course, the greatest opportunity for the pupil to gain points by shrewd guesses. A penalty for guessing can be imposed by using the formula R − W (items right minus items wrong) in scoring the test but many teachers regard such mathematical refinements as inappropriate. Multiple-choice items are more difficult to construct but are preferred over true-false items by many teachers. Since the pupil must choose among at least three, or at times four or five, possible answers, the chances of his gaining points by correct guesses are considerably less than they are on a true-false test. Perhaps more important, multiple-choice items can be phrased so that the pupil is called upon to apply a principle correctly or to distinguish among fine shades of meaning. As a result, clearer differentiations are often made among pupils at the extremes of the achievement scale. Matching items are similar to multiple-choice items in that the pupil must distinguish among several possible answers. They are particularly useful, however, when you wish to ascertain whether your boys and girls have developed clear and accurate differentiations among a group of related facts. For example, can they identify clearly the major contributions of each of five or six famous explorers? Do they know the major industries in each of five or six key cities? Can they distinguish clearly among a series of terms in geography—cape, peninsula, isthmus, bay, gulf, delta?

Certain precautions are needed when preparing a test using any type of selection item. First, it is very important to go back to your original objectives and to list the facts, generalizations, or skills which you want to measure. Think also about whether any of these learnings are more important than any others in your original objectives. If so, they might merit two or three test questions instead of one. Decide, too, upon the test form that seems most likely to reveal the learnings about which you are concerned. It may be that your pupils are mature enough for you to use several types of items, or, to avoid confusion, you may choose the one type that seems most likely to yield the kind of evidence you need. Give some thought, also, to the time you allow for the test. This will help you to decide how many questions to include.

With your general pattern for the test determined, you are ready to write specific items to get at the information you desire. Typically you will not use sentences direct from your text. What you want to measure, after all, is your pupils' ability to identify correct answers, not merely to give back the words of the book. It is important to use simple vocabulary and clear, short sentences. You will want to be careful not to build into test items cues to correct answers—*no, all,* and *every* usually denote a false item on a true-false test; the answer on a multiple-choice test must fit grammatically with the main question or stem; an unduly long and carefully qualified answer is usually right; an obviously ridiculous choice in a multiple-choice item can be ruled out and this simplifies the choice. Be sure also to read your test carefully for ambiguous wording and to make certain that the answer to one question does not hinge on a pupil's ability to answer correctly a preceding question.

As a final step, make sure that the directions are clear and that the method for indicating the correct answer is as uncomplicated as you can make it. For example, eighteen items on a matching question will confuse the reader by their sheer number. Far better, break this into three questions of six items each. It is often easier for a young child to circle *yes* or *no* than it is to write *true* or *false*. If you start out with the choices in multiple-choice items labeled *a, b, c,* do not change halfway through to choices numbered 1, 2, 3. It is often a good plan to provide one or two sample items which you and your pupils may work together. Younger pupils, particularly, may need help with difficult words. Sometimes it is wise to read the entire test with them to forestall reading problems. If pupils must work from the blackboard you will need to explain clearly how much is to be copied and how correct answers are to be indicated on their papers. What you are seeking is accurate evidence of your pupils' knowledge; it is important to make sure that scores are not invalidated by vague directions or reading difficulties.

Supply items—completion, short-answer essay, and essay items—require the pupil to recall what he has learned without the aid of alternatives from which to choose. They can be particularly valuable in demanding original thinking and the ability to organize ideas in written form. Typically, they are more effective when used with pupils who have reasonable proficiency in written expression.

Completion questions give pupils the least freedom to organize their own thinking. Because these items can be scored with a key prepared ahead of time, they are often classified with selection items under the general (and misleading) nomenclature of "objective" tests. Several precautions are needed if completion questions are to be effective. It is important, for one thing, that the context indicate clearly the type of answer to be supplied. It is important, also, for the required answer to be a needed item of information, not a logical deduction or a word appropriate for the context. (What do you learn about a child's information, for example, if you ask him to supply an appropriate word in the following: "Chicago is the ____ of many transcontinental railroads.") Sometimes so many words are omitted that the pupil is at a loss regarding the meaning of the item. ("——, ——, and —— are important to midwestern ____.") And, although it does not always obscure the meaning, it is usually of more help to the reader to supply the first part of the sentence and to place the blank for the answer near the end. ("The incandescent bulb was invented by ____," is somewhat easier for the reader than "____ invented the incandescent bulb.")

Essay questions, whether requiring a short answer or a discussion of several pages, need to be phrased in sufficiently general terms to give the pupil freedom to organize his answers, but at the same time be specific enough to indicate what type of answer is required. "Discuss the Indians who lived around Western City" is vague and could lead to any one of a variety of answers. "How did the Indians who lived around Western City make a living?" is more definite. "Compare the homes, agriculture, and customs of the Indians who lived around Western City with those who lived in New Mexico" is a form that requires the writer to bring together related learnings. "Why did the Indians who lived around Western City grow crops instead of hunting?" calls for sensitivity to cause-and-effect relationships. "Pretend you are one of the Indians who lived around Western City and write the story of a typical day" or "Which would you rather be, one of the Indians who lived around Western City or an Apache? Why?"—both call for an imaginative application of facts to a new problem. Some of these forms of questions obviously require a higher level of reasoning than others. Recalling ("Name three persons who explored the West and tell one important thing each one did") and describing ("Tell what the Conestoga wagon looked like") are easier than comparing ("Compare the early settlements in New England with those in Virginia") or explaining ("Why were so many of the early Western settlements located on rivers?").

Teachers who enjoy the challenge of test construction have developed intriguing variations of typical forms. Situational items are among the most promising. They not only add interest to the test, but they approach more closely the ultimate objective of most teaching: Can the pupil apply what he has learned intelligently in a new situation? Situational items are adaptable either as selection items or as essay questions. Suppose, for example, that Susan Jones has just finished a safety unit which has devoted considerable time to what to do in case of fire. Susan might pose for her pupils a question such as the following:

> Mary Jane is left alone at home with her two-year-old brother. While she answers the telephone, he turns on the gas stove and the kitchen curtain catches fire.

(Write *good* before everything it would be good for Mary Jane to do; and write *bad* before everything she should not do.)

_____Take her baby brother out of the house.
_____Phone the fire department.
_____Run to the store where her mother is and ask her what to do.
_____Throw salt at the curtains.
_____Pull down the curtains and carry them outside.

The question form here is true-false. However, if Susan is interested in making sure that her pupils can identify an appropriate sequence of procedures, she might ask the following. Here the pupil is given the items from which to select, but he must supply the sequence from his own background.

(Before the first thing Mary Jane should do write the number 1; before the second thing she should do write the number 2; and so on.)

_____Take her baby brother out of the house.
_____Run to the store where her mother is shopping and tell her mother.
_____Call the fire department.
_____Go to the neighbor for help.

If Susan wants to know whether her pupils can apply what they have learned without any reminders, she might secure essay-type answers by asking: "Tell exactly what Mary Jane should do. What do you think she should do first, what second, and so on?" Or, if Susan wanted to be sure specific principles were clear, she might turn either of the sets of items above into short-answer essay tests by leaving three or four lines after each statement and asking her pupils to explain why they marked it as they did.

You are using a situational test (in a modified matching form) if you give your pupils a mimeographed map with certain land formations clearly numbered and ask them to place the correct number next to each of the geographic terms on a list. This can be turned into a supply item if you provide no vocabulary list and merely ask each pupil to enter on his map the correct term for each land formation marked. Science teachers have experimented with new forms of matching tests by posting on bulletin boards sets of numbered pictures illustrating new science terms and asking pupils to place next to each item on a list of terms the number of the picture which best illustrates it. If you want to employ classroom tests effectively to measure progress toward a variety of behavioral goals, you will experiment with the forms of your tests until you discover those that serve your specific purposes particularly well.

You will not use standardized tests as frequently in your evaluation procedures as you will classroom tests. In fact, in many school systems standardized tests are only given once a year, often in the fall as an additional guide to planning the year's work rather than in the spring when the teacher can do nothing about the scores other than wonder how he could have been more helpful to Sammy or Annie Lou. Whenever you do turn to standardized tests for help in evaluating the growth of individuals, it is important to remember that they, too, are useful only in so far as they are appropriate for your objectives. Because standardized tests are commercially produced, accompanied by printed norms and scoring keys, and often bear the names of persons recognized as authorities in the field, it is a temptation to feel that here, at last, is an accurate measure of a pupil's skill. Yet it is quite possible that the test used in your school system is designed to measure objectives different in significant aspects from those for which you have been striving. For example, many teachers of third- and fourth-graders put a much higher premium on reading comprehension and accurate identification of new words than they do on speed. Yet there are standardized tests for reading achievement for these grade levels with relatively short time limits. Some recent standardized tests measure spelling achievement by the pupil's ability to select the correct spelling of a word from a set that contains three or four misspellings. This is not exactly the same skill that is required to spell a word correctly from dictation. Because scoring by key is considered to be desirable, most tests of English usage merely require the child to select the correct form. This is a far cry from using the correct form habitually in speaking. Obviously the likelihood of inappropriate blocks of test items is increased in any of the content fields where there are innumerable possible variations in the choice of content to be stressed. It is very important, then, to examine the standardized tests being used in your system. You would not discard them merely because you find items that you have not taught specifically. Standardized tests are, after all, designed to challenge your most able pupil. You do have a right, however, to decide whether the test as a whole stresses objectives you consider to be appropriate for your pupils. In the last analysis *you,* not your test—standardized or teacher-made—evaluate your pupils' progress. To be of help in evaluation your tests must give the evidence you are seeking regarding your pupils' growth toward specific objectives.

Raw scores on tests must be translated into meaningful information. Many beginning teachers carry into their classroom one of two misconceptions regarding how to interpret the scores on tests. One is to assume that a percentage of the total score—a 70, an 80, a 95—means the same for all tests and that it is always evaluated as indicative of a certain level of work. ("I'm so disappointed with my pupils; not a mark over 70 in the bunch"; "Mine did so well. Just think! Half the class had 90's.") The other misconception is the assumption that test scores (and by implication, abilities) always arrange themselves on a bell-shaped curve from which one can neatly chop off set percentages of *A*'s, *B*'s, *C*'s, *D*'s, and *F*'s. Both of these assumptions regarding the interpretation of test scores are false.

The number of items correct on a test is a measure which is not nearly as stable as many of our other measures. If we put a pupil upon a scale and he weighs sixty pounds, other scales will show about the same weight—give or take a pound or two. Such consistency does not exist with tests. Some are easy; some are difficult. Slight changes in wording can influence a score by several points. So can a strategically placed review. It will be necessary for you to learn how to translate the scores on each test into meaningful information.

As a matter of fact, the totals you arrive at when you score a teacher-made test are based on your subjective judgment. You may assign two points apiece to each of fifty selection items. Or you may decide that ten of these represent crucial concepts and merit four points each, that ten more merit three points each, and that the remaining thirty should be given a point apiece. Both of these systems add to one-hundred points for your test, but it is most unlikely that they will yield identical scores for any one individual. Your subjective judgment also enters into the scoring of essay tests. In some cases you may give four points apiece for each of twenty-five items of information and end up with a total score of one-hundred for the test and no headaches for yourself in grading it. However, you do not usually choose an essay form if you merely wish to evaluate a pupil's grasp of specific items of information. More often you will be trying to appraise reasoning ability, power to apply generalizations in new situations, ability to sense cause-and-effect relationships, ability to organize information. To hold your standards constant in evaluating such factors from one pupil's paper to the next you will probably establish a scale similar to that suggested earlier for the reading of children's reports and stories.[5] However, whether you

[5] Reread pages 431-432 in this chapter.

end up with an *excellent, good, fair, poor* rating system, or work out a scheme of securing numerical scores, it has been *your* decision. Nothing in your test, in and of itself, automatically tells you what scores to assign.

How, then, do you go about interpreting your pupils' scores on one of your tests? First, consider what your expectations are. In spelling, after a week of study, it may be that you will expect the majority of your class to have 90 per cent or more of the words on the list correct. This might also be the case on a final speed test over arithmetic combinations, or on a quick review over science vocabulary that has been thoroughly stressed. If you have planned your test to reveal how many of your group have mastered a task thoroughly, then thorough mastery is the satisfactory (or average) performance. Less than thorough mastery represents a disappointing (or poor) job. Translated into per cent correct, this might mean that 100 per cent would be called excellent, 95 per cent good, and 90 per cent or less fair or poor. On the other hand, there will be times when your expectations are not couched in terms of perfection. You may give, for example, an essay question in social studies in which you fully expect, and hope, to discover a wide range of insight or background. Your expectation for acceptable work may be phrased in terms of a given amount of accurate factual data discussed in such a way as to show major interrelations. ("I hope that they will at least be clear on the following facts . . . and that they can point to at least three of the following implications. . . .") Whatever the numerical scores you assign, papers that achieve this standard are your acceptable or average papers. Those youngsters showing information and insight beyond your expectations earn your exceptional ratings and those who dismay you with how little they have grasped represent the other end of your scale. If you plan carefully, you can devise a point system so that those papers you deem to be of outstanding but not exceptional quality fall in the 80's; those you deem to be excellent, in the 90's; and those poor, in the 60's; however, if your numerical scale were to run from 1 to 25 instead of from 0 to 100 you would still be able to identify the scores that represent average, poor, or excellent papers by examining the quality of the job that was actually done in the light of the standards you have set. In many cases, it may be much simpler and more accurate to enter verbal ratings or letter symbols in your record book and forget about numerical scores.

Another aid in interpreting raw scores on tests, helpful particularly when you have less effective means of establishing your own scale of excellence than you have with essay questions, is to study carefully the distribution of scores by making a tally of the number right. (The examples which follow are from tests scored on a basis of 100, but the principle would be the same, were the highest possible score 10, 17, or 25.) Rarely at any grade level do pupils who are interested in school work come to a test completely unprepared or treat a test lightly. If, therefore, the top score is 60 per cent and the average 45, this rarely means that everyone has failed the test. It surely does not mean this if you have confirming evidence from other sources that your pupils' grasp of the area is good. In all probability something in the wording or format of your test or in the directions you used caused everyone trouble. Roberta Peterson discovered this when she gave her pupils a final review test over possessives. Not a child had more than 60 per cent of the questions correct. A careful glance at Roberta's test showed why. It was very long, and since she had set a time limit, few had finished. The task was complex; pupils were to take the form they were given, write its plural and then write a sentence using the plural possessive. But this was not all! Ingenious Roberta had included every well-known rule for forming plurals, and, not satisfied with this, she had changed directions in the middle of the test so that, for the last half, the pupils had to start with the plural form, give the singular, and then use the possessive! On this test 60 per cent correct was excellent, indeed. Conversely, of course, a distribution of near-perfect scores in an area where perfection was not your expectation may not mean that your pupils learned much more than you thought they did. It may be that your test contained far too many easy questions.

Examining the pattern of your pupils' performances when you interpret their test scores is, in effect, using the distribution curve as an aid in grading. This does not mean that you are compelled to give *A*'s to a percentage of those youngsters with top scores or to fail a set proportion of those at the bottom. After you have thought about your expectations and taken a careful look at the format of the test, it may be that you will decide that nobody has done an outstanding job. Conversely, there will be times when your conclusion will be that most of your class has, indeed, done an excellent piece of work. You may also, in terms of school-wide or city-wide standards, find yourself saying, "For this group of slower pupils I am well satisfied, but I know that this would not be a top performance for the typical youngster of this age."

Many problems of how to interpret the raw scores on tests fade away if you do not think of them as the basis for numerical or letter grades on a report card. For the purpose of planning for future work, you have the information you need when you note that five youngsters are still vague with regard to certain terminology, that your whole class would seem to merit more review on the cause-and-effect relationships in an historical sequence, or that a dozen should give more time to two-digit subtraction. Facing the strings of 70's, 80's, and 90's in your grade book is another story. Averaging numbers, each of which actually has a different meaning when translated into evidence of progress, is a questionable business. Sometimes it leads to final evaluations that are downright unfair. What happens to the final grade of a youngster who, after a 50 on a first test suddenly "catches on" and does exceptional work? Or to the grade of the top pupil in your class whose test scores show a line of 70's because you have given a series of difficult tests? It is often much wiser to enter in your record book not only your pupil's scores, but the distribution on the test and your comments regarding how you interpreted your distribution. Then, when you face the task of translating a youngster's test scores along with other evidences of his work into a report to his parents, look at the general trend of his work. Has it been, typically, outstanding? about average? at a level that has worried you? When you use these classifications, are you thinking in terms of the class as a whole? the pupil's own capacity? expectations based on your consideration of city-wide standards? After you have answered such questions, you are ready to translate your evaluation of each pupil into whatever letter or numerical code is used by your school system to convey the information about a child's progress to his parents.

Scores on standardized tests have to be interpreted with equal care. The fact that the norms for these tests have been developed from the scores of thousands of youngsters tends to lend them an aura of accuracy that can be misleading. You will need to be as careful in determining the meaning of a grade score of 3.2 or 5.6 on a standardized test of reading or arithmetic as you will in interpreting an 85 or 90 on a test of your own. A variety of statistical procedures can be used in setting up the norms for a standardized test. You will want to know, for example, whether the norms for the test you are using were developed from the scores of pupils at age for grade (all retarded pupils eliminated) or whether the scores of all the pupils in each grade were used. It is also important to look at the number of test items on which the norms are based. If, for example, a subtest contains only ten items and the grade norms for this subtest extend from 3.5 to 7.0, it is quite possible for a pupil to raise or lower his grade score by a year on a single fortunate or unlucky guess. Sometimes scores at the extremes of the norms have to be interpreted differently from those in the middle. If a test is designed for grades four through six, a grade score of 3.0 may not mean third-grade ability; it could signify such a poor performance that a pupil could do correctly only one or two items. Likewise, a score of 10.0 may simply mean that the pupil has a near-perfect score and needs to take a more advanced test to demonstrate his full ability. These factors in the statistical make-up of the test can be determined only by examining the test manual and studying the tables of norms. It also goes without saying that you should not be unduly disturbed if there appear to be discrepancies in a pupil's performance on norms from two tests published by different companies.

Even when you are satisfied that you know the statistical factors for which to allow in studying your pupils' scores on standardized tests, you still must look at individual performances thoughtfully. A year's retardation in reading for a third-grader typically signifies more serious difficulty with classroom materials than a year's retardation for a sixth-grader. A low score could result from slow, careful work if time is called before the pupil has been able to demonstrate his capacity to handle difficult items. A low score could also signify merely that one aspect of the skills covered by the test has not been one of your major objectives for the class. You must add to all these warnings the reminder that a grade score of 3.0 for a fifth-grader does not necessarily mean that he reasons exactly the same as a youngster in grade three. It tells you that on this particular job his score was similar to that made by an average third-grader. By the same token, a grade score of 9.0 does not mean ninth-grade maturity in all areas. If you will employ such precautions intelligently as you study pupils' scores on standardized tests, these instruments can be of real service to you in appraising present status and projecting next steps.

Scores on tests need to be supported by other evidence. A test—be it commercially produced or one of your own—is simply another sample of a pupil's work. It is collected at a given point of time and subject to all the influences—distractions, weather, tensions, illness—that cause performance on any single job to fluctuate. Sometimes, because it is possible to total points on a test and to enter a score in a grade book, we are lulled into feeling that these instruments have provided us with an accurate and trustworthy picture of our pupils' work.

Even the terminology we use tends to give a false sense of security.

We sometimes classify tests as objective and subjective—objective tests being those for which an answer key can be supplied so that any number of independent graders will arrive at the same totals, and subjective tests being those on which the grader must use his judgment. It is an easy (and false) step from such a definition to assume that the *objective* test is an accurate measure and the *subjective* an inaccurate measure. You do not necessarily secure an accurate measure of a pupil's ability because you can score his tests with an answer key. *You* were subjective in constructing your questions—they represent your idea of what he should have learned and your phrasing of this learning. The pupil also was subjective in reading the questions—he interpreted them from his background and with his reading skill. Using an objective test merely shifts the possible source of error from one point in the testing process to another. Even in the most rigorously standardized commercial test, you must allow for a margin of error. The tests you construct will not usually approach these in accuracy of wording, careful editing, and freedom from ambiguous items.

You are doing your pupils a grave injustice if you do not seek in their daily work a wide variety of confirming evidence. In fact, primary teachers will use few if any instruments that can be dignified by the title of teacher-made tests. Even in the intermediate grades, these materials represent only a small amount of the data used for evaluation purposes. If several other independent pieces of evidence indicate satisfactory command of a skill, concept, or generalization you can, with clear conscience, discount a less satisfying demonstration of competence on a single test paper.

It is also important to look within your test to identify factors influencing the test score other than a pupil's competence in the area covered by the test. Was reading skill involved?—slow and deliberate reading? careless errors? Did a single weakness influence the performance on several related items?—inaccurate computation give the impression of confused understanding of the processes of long division? confusion among two or three terms result in a series of misstatements on a science quiz? extreme disability in written English result in an incoherent answer to a social studies question although a series of selection items indicated the facts were actually clear? Both in planning what help to provide next and in deciding what to include in reports to parents or on cumulative records, it is important to be accurate in your insights regarding what a pupil's difficulties actually are.

When you are studying a score from a standardized test in appraising a pupil's present status, you need to be equally careful both to seek confirming evidence in his everyday work and to study the pattern of his work on the test for evidence of related difficulties. This does not mean that you immediately cast a test score aside as inaccurate if it does not happen to agree with your impression of a child's work. Some teachers who are conscious of all the factors that need to be considered in interpreting scores on standardized tests are tempted to do this. It may be that the test will help to correct a negative impression on your part. Ronnie may be so generally disturbing, for example, and so hard to settle down to work that you miss completely the fact that his very able mind is absorbing information like a sponge. His high scores on standardized tests of reading and arithmetic may provide the stimulus you need to reappraise your evaluation. You may have checked off Penny as a dawdler—basing your evidence on a series of incomplete pieces of work. Penny's perfect but painfully slow work on a reading test may throw an entirely new light on the situation. A skilled diagnostician, be he a teacher or a physician, does not disregard clues until he has taken a careful look at the total pattern, no matter how inconsequential or unrelated these clues may seem to be.

Pupils should grow through the testing process. The ultimate purpose of a test, as of any other piece of work done by a pupil, is to help him grow. If you score your tests, enter totals in the grade book, and forget about them, you are failing to capitalize upon their most significant contribution. These are pieces of evidence regarding what your pupils have learned, where they are confused, and where more teaching is in order. You should study them, as you would any other samples of pupils' work, for guidance regarding the follow-up experiences that seem to be needed. Under some circumstances you will find it helpful to make a thorough analysis of the test; in other cases, your general impression will be sufficient.

You will not have used your test effectively in helping pupils to grow if you do not let them share in analyzing the evidence it reveals. Time should be taken to go over the test question by question not only to help boys and girls identify the correct answers, but to determine what caused the original confusion. Pupils can also be helped to grow in their skill in self-evaluation if they share in decisions regarding when a test seems desirable and what evidence it should reveal. For example, Sam Larsen and his youngsters discussed the progress they had made with multiplication combinations and decided that each child should aim for a perfect score on a speed test patterned after one in their text.

Gail McMaster and her fifth-graders talked over their growing list of science vocabulary and decided that a test would be a good way to discover which terms they really understood. After considerable experience in proofreading their own stories, Betty Barton's youngsters agreed to proofread a common paragraph to demonstrate their present performance level. After they had amassed a bewildering amount of information regarding national elections, David Anson's group decided that a test over major facts would be a help in making sure that their thinking was straight. In each of these cases (and in many more examples you could give from your experiences with youngsters) the pupils analyzed the completed tests with great interest in order to determine where group and individual strengths and weaknesses lay.

The purposes of a standardized test can likewise be explained to pupils and the results shared. You will want to use some caution in making actual grade scores public. Even with all your professional knowledge you are sometimes tempted to interpret such scores unwisely. Your pupils, or for that matter their parents, have none of your training. However, test results can be turned into words. "Your paper showed that you do as well as most people in fifth-grade multiplication and subtraction, John. But it shows that you have some trouble in reading problems. That's just what we said yesterday when we looked at your paper, isn't it?"

A test is of little value, then, if the results are not used in some way to help the pupil. They should give him a better understanding of himself—his needs, interests, strengths, and weaknesses. They should provide him with a more realistic picture of his abilities, educational progress, and possible vocational choices. Perhaps most important, they should help you to plan more effectively for the learning experiences he needs.

HELPING PUPILS DEVELOP SKILL IN SELF-EVALUATION

Boys and girls do not develop skills in self-evaluation without help. Teachers build these skills by involving their pupils in situation after situation where evaluation is needed. Evaluative experiences can be more worth while for pupils, however, if teachers are conscious of the procedures they are using. What are the characteristics of the classrooms in which pupils are helped most effectively to develop their own powers of self-evaluation?

Pupils are helped to see evaluation as an aid to growth. The basic characteristic of a classroom in which pupils are learning to appraise effectively their own strengths and weaknesses is its accepting atmosphere. Children are respected for what they are, not for the degree to which they can approach straight *A*'s on a report card. Strengths are acknowledged frankly and praised generously. Weaknesses are faced with equal frankness and plans laid to overcome them.

These are classrooms in which the stress is on improvement—on doing a better job today than you did yesterday, on achieving progressively higher standards whatever your present level of operation may be. They are not situations in which all pupils, regardless of ability, are encouraged to compete for the *A* or the 100 per cent. Each child is helped to measure his achievement in terms of his own goals. The less able youngster is not defeated time after time by having his best efforts rejected. Neither is the talented child allowed to accept as a good job a piece of work far below his capacity merely because it is the top achievement in his room.

In such classrooms generous praise is given to the pupils who are able to identify their own needs. "How many had a perfect paper?" is not heard nearly as often as "Look at your papers—do you see the questions with which you need more help?" This does not mean that the stress is always on failures—on points where work does not measure up. Successes are emphasized with equal frequency. "All right, where do you think we've really polished it so that it's the job we want?" asked Rhonda Cummins. After this list was completed, she added "Now, what are the points on which we need to improve?" "Check your handwriting against our master charts," said Peggy Jones. "Mark *OK* beside each letter you think you formed acceptably. Now, put a check beside each one you feel you should practice, and when I come around, be ready to tell me where you think you need to improve."

Such classrooms are also optimistic. The stress is on the future, not on the past. Strengths and weaknesses are analyzed as a basis for next steps. Difficulties are faced, but pupils see clearly that something can be done about them. "I read too fast out loud," said Janet, "and I read right over the hard words. But Mother is helping me at home and so are all the kids in the reading group." "We're trying to make it like a real bus," explained first-grade William. "First we had all the seats together but now we are fixing it so people can walk down the middle. And when we looked at the school bus we saw that our door had to be over on this side."

These are the kinds of situations in which pupils give generous praise and frank help to one another. They are accustomed to talking about difficulties as well as good points, feel responsible for their fellows' progress, and become involved in it. "I just think we should tell Janet," interrupted a fifth-grader, "how much her special work in speech is helping. I could understand every word she said." "Let Billy show Dr. Swanson how we do it," chorused some third-graders. "He's our best one in arithmetic."

You will meet persons who doubt if such frank acceptance of successes and failures and such enthusiastic plans for progress actually can be achieved. "Competition is the key to making them work," one often hears. "If they don't have grades to work for, they'll just loaf." Such a statement has little psychological support. Satisfying intellectual curiosity, mastering challenging situations, respecting oneself, achieving status in the group through one's contributions—these are basic psychological needs providing strong incentives to achieve high standards. True, a child can learn to satisfy his need for status in a group by beating the other fellow to a higher grade. (At least, those who are the most able intellectually can do so.) He can also learn to set his level of aspiration and to build his self-concept entirely in relation to the values and standards of his peer group (as indicated by the comparative ratings his teacher puts on his papers). However, these are not the only ways of satisfying such basic needs; one can ask whether they are, indeed, acceptable ways.

You will hear other reasons for advocating a classroom atmosphere that is highly competitive. "After all," people say, "a pupil is going into a competitive world where he must face the fact that there are situations in which others can do better work than he. As an adult he will find out, too, that anything less than a first-class performance is not acceptable." However, it can be questioned whether the world into which a pupil is going is as competitive as it is often said to be. Basically, in his interrelated industrial society, in his community clubs and church groups, and in his family life, an adult's success or failure depends upon his ability to work effectively with others as well as upon the high standards he holds for himself.

Objective self-appraisal and a feeling of genuine concern for others does not develop when pious phrases about putting forth one's best efforts are mouthed in an atmosphere in which ultimate evaluations are made by the teacher in terms of an arbitrary achievement scale. "Let's not worry right now about grades," said June Ellis when her fifth-graders asked her to define precisely what would be considered as an *A* notebook and how individual contributions to the group project would be assessed. "After all, what really matters is how much you learn and what you can share with others. Grades aren't the important thing." "I don't know about the rest of the kids," said outspoken Andy, "but grades are *most definitely* the important thing for me. When it's all done *you're* going to put a grade on it and *my mother* won't let me watch television for a week if I don't get an *A*."

Goals must be clear. In the classrooms that have been described, pupils are helped to establish clear goals, whether the problem before the group is to plan a month's related experiences or to decide how to untangle the traffic jam in the cloakroom. For example, think back over the sequence of activities that characterizes a unit of work. Pupils and teacher outline specific questions or problems with which they begin work. As they become more familiar with the area, new goals are added. Each group lists its own specific goals. And through this entire process teachers help to develop high standards of workmanship—challenging inaccurate statements, sending youngsters back to their textbooks to check, talking about how to take effective notes, encouraging more accurate observations.

Similar procedures characterize the development of fundamental skills. Pupils and teacher talk about the technique they wish to develop —the letter that is needed, the clear handwriting required in a note to be taken home, the accurate knowledge of arithmetic essential if one is to serve as a collector of lunch money. The new process is explained and then practice begins. As the new technique is put to use additional problems are identified and new goals are set.

This is also the pattern in encouraging pupils to develop skills in creative self-expression. The basic decision involves a goal—what do you want to communicate through your picture, your story, your song? As pupils begin to work toward their major goal teachers help them to become aware of specific objectives. They evaluate the developing product together, set new goals, and decide how to achieve them.

Interpersonal relationships and skills in cooperative problem-solving are built in the same way. Billy's group is at six's and seven's—the planning session has resulted in nothing but wrangling. The problem is analyzed and grievances are aired—Billy is not letting anyone else make any suggestions, and Sam and Sarah are not helping the situation by playing with chalk and not listening. Better ways of working are thought out—both for the chairman and for the committee members.

Tomorrow the committee tries again, reports progress and, more likely than not, new problems.

In many classrooms there will be evidence of standard-setting processes posted on bulletin boards, under such headings as *A Good Audience, Responsibilities of a Chairman, A Good Report, Proofreader's Guide, Helps for Hard Words, Rules for Our Library*. Such lists, however, indicate only a small part of the total experiences in setting goals. The process is a continuous round of appraisal, planning, and work toward new goals and higher standards.

Pupils need to be involved actively in the appraisal process. If your pupils are to learn to appraise their own strengths and weaknesses, they need to have many experiences in applying standards. They should be involved actively at every step of the appraisal process. Questions are not listed at the beginning of a unit and forgotten. Lists of standards are not posted and then neglected.

Pupils in the classrooms that were described earlier in this chapter are actively involved in collecting the concrete evidence needed for appraisal purposes. They maintain their own cumulative folders of spelling papers or arithmetic work sheets. They help to decide which of their creative stories to add to their notebooks. They plan to make tape recordings of their oral reading. They and their teachers talk over the need for a test and decide what aspects of their work it should cover.

Teachers also involve pupils in the appraisal process by looking at the evidence with them. Although every teacher takes home papers or notebooks once in a while, one of the important characteristics of the rooms in which pupils are developing effective appraisal skills is the number of times that teacher and pupils appraise work together. There may be group discussions when everyone examines his own paper and reports on his difficulties, or individual sessions when a teacher works for a few minutes with each child in turn. There are, also, sessions where everyone helps to identify the strengths and needs for improvement in a group product and sessions where individual enterprises—reports, stories, poems, pictures—are offered for group criticism and approval.

Children are helped in these classrooms to become self-directing through situation after situation in which they relate their appraisals of present status to future plans. "A check sheet is posted over here. If you will note the number of the questions you missed, I've listed four or five exercises in your textbook that will give you practice." "When everyone has started, I'd like to meet with the people who wanted special help with their spelling." "Your groups were all having trouble locating information. Let's take some time today to learn more about it."

Helping pupils to develop powers of self-evaluation and self-direction is not reserved for a specific time block in the schedule. It is part and parcel of everything you do. Basically, the way that you involve boys and girls in the evaluation process is an expression of what you believe about the nature and purposes of education.

REPORTING PUPIL PROGRESS

Appraising pupil progress as a basis for planning day-by-day classroom experiences is one major aspect of your evaluation program. Communicating these appraisals to parents, to teachers to whom the pupils will go next, and to pupils themselves is a second—and an equally important—task.

If you are to carry out your reporting responsibilities effectively, there are a number of skills you must develop. You will have to learn to use whatever reporting system is in operation in your school. You must also become skilled in developing a variety of contacts with parents in addition to the formal report that goes home. Making contributions to your pupils' cumulative records will be still another aspect of your reporting responsibilities. Helping pupils understand the recording and reporting system is also involved. And, if you are concerned with the over-all problem of building more sensitive public understanding of educational objectives and methods, you will make certain that your communication with parents and others contributes to this long-range goal.

When is an *A* an *A*? At a number of points on preceding pages you have read statements such as the following: "How you *appraise* or *evaluate* your evidence of the growth of a particular pupil is one problem; how you *communicate* this appraisal to his parents is another." School personnel have developed many ways of communicating with parents. Some use a system of letters, parent-teacher conferences, or a combination of these. More frequently a system of letter grades, ratings, or percentages is in use.

The philosophy of the school system often determines the method of communication adopted. If the acquisition of factual information and fundamental skills is valued above all other areas of growth, numerical grades (99, 98, 97, . . .) are likely to be employed. It is probably a reflection of the broader aims of most elementary schools that numerical grades have been gradually abandoned in favor of letter grades. A five-letter scale (*A, B, C, D, F*) is currently the one in widespread use, but some school systems have experimented with other possibilities. (A three-letter scale is one—*S*, meaning *satisfactory; I*, meaning *improving but not at a satisfactory level yet;* and *U*, meaning *unsatisfactory*.) You will also find some situations in which teachers of the primary grades use a three-letter scale and those in the upper grades a five-letter one. On some report cards double columns are used, one for a rating in terms of absolute standards and a second for a rating in terms of effort. Developing a truly effective communication instrument is a task of major proportions. If you could tour the country, you would discover in many school systems teachers (or, better still, parents and teachers) attempting to develop new and better ways of reporting to meet their particular needs.

Your responsibility will, of necessity, be to learn to use whatever communciation system is in operation in your school and to use it so that the information you convey through your designation of letters, ratings, or percentages is similar to that conveyed by other teachers. However, there are many problems connected with the assignment of grades of which you should be aware, even though for the sake of clear communication you abide carefully by the conventions established in the school where you are teaching.

What should be the basis upon which letter grades are assigned? Who is to receive the *A*, for example?—George, IQ 135, who is getting by with work several years below his capacity although it still rates high when placed on a scale along with that of his classmates? or Cindy, IQ 85, who is exceeding all expectations but whose work does not measure up in comparison with that of her peers except in handwriting? (Assume, for the sake of discussion, that these IQ's and the corresponding mental ages are accurate.) Who gets the *D*?—George, who is achieving far below his own capacity? or Cindy, who is doing remarkably well for hers? One cannot convey both types of appraisal for either youngster in a single letter grade.

Because of your orientation to high school and college rating systems where the grade typically derives from a scale based on quality of performance, you may say "There's no argument; George does better work than Cindy." But do you actually want to convey to George's parents the impression that he is an excellent student when he is doing what, for George, is a slipshod job? And do you want Cindy's parents to be disappointed and urge her to do better when she has already extended herself to the limit? On the other hand, it will be equally confusing to both sets of parents if George receives low ratings for work known to be good for his grade level or Cindy *A*'s for work so low that at the end of the year the decision is to have her repeat the grade.

The attitudes of George and Cindy have to be kept in mind, too. If you want George to face his capabilities realistically, should you tell him by an *A* that standards that barely keep him ahead of his peers are quite acceptable? Certainly you are not helping Cindy if by your grades you encourage her to develop unrealistic aspirations for college and a professional career. But does this mean that she must be told over and over again, year after year, that the teachers whose judgments she respects value her best efforts as third-rate? (You may be pointing out that she *is* good in handwriting, but this, like an *A* in conduct, is cold comfort in a competitive, grade-centered situation.)

You may generalize from these two youngsters to the problem faced by the teacher assigned the lowest of four fourth grades in a school where grouping is based on IQ's. Granted that the class will not be as homogeneous in other areas as their IQ's would indicate; nevertheless in comparison with the top group the work of many will look inferior. Are there to be few *A*'s or *B*'s given all year, no matter how enthusiastically these youngsters apply themselves?

One other complication can be added. Report cards seldom allow for ratings on all the facets of a subject. George *does* have a better-than-average grasp of social studies content, but he is careless in his use of reference materials; relies far too often on logical reasoning rather than research; secures perfect test papers when he can give facts, but has little interest in applying these to local community problems. What letter grade should be assigned to this constellation of abilities? Cindy pronounces words beautifully, but her inability to see relationships results in expressionless oral reading and low comprehension. Which of these skills should her letter grade in reading describe? "Average them in both cases," you say. But how are George's or Cindy's parents to know how the average was attained?

If, by now, you are shaking your head and muttering "There's no solution," you are expressing the sentiments of many teachers. A letter grade cannot possibly communicate evaluations as complicated as those just indicated. Letters home, of course, could do so:

George is a very pleasant and cooperative boy. His attendance has been perfect and he has never been tardy. His work has been of real concern to me, however. In comparison with the work of his classmates, George hands in papers and notebooks that are among the best in the class. For George, however, this is unsatisfactory work. He has excellent reasoning ability, but he tends to rely on this to make a good case in an argument without checking his sources. In our last science unit he was one of the few children who failed to bring from home some news clippings related to his project. George does do an excellent job in arithmetic computation and his spelling is superior. Could we confer some time about ways to challenge his truly fine potentiality?

Cindy has been a joy to have in our class this year. As you know, when she came to us she was finding school work a real struggle. She is still not doing the work that would be considered average for a youngster her age, but her progress has been remarkable. She is working with a third-grade reader and will probably not be ready for a fourth-grade text for some time yet. But have you noticed how many library books she has taken home to read? They are simple, but she is finding great satisfaction in them. Cindy's handwriting is excellent and she is much in demand when special letters have to be mailed. She is still working to perfect her multiplication facts. You might wish to hear these and her spelling at home. If you could drop by the school at your convenience I should be happy to show you how you could help.

It is because letters like these do tell the story that some schools are substituting them for *A*'s and *B*'s on report cards.

Because your colleagues will also have been struggling with George-Cindy rating problems, you may find any one of a number of ingenious compromises in effect. In some school systems an *Effort* column is used to convey to parents the information about the degree to which their child has applied himself. Sometimes there are agreements about how to use the letter grades at either end of the scale. George may be given *B*'s, but he does not earn an *A* unless he works up to capacity. Cindy may be given *C*'s (and perhaps a rare *B*) but she does not receive a *D* as long as she is working hard. Occasionally you will find an agreement regarding the way low grades are to be used to warn parents if it seems likely that a youngster will not be promoted. Sometimes the grade is based on a scale of excellence but a brief note is appended to explain extenuating circumstances. Sometimes the grade represents an appraisal in relation to capacity and a code or note is appended to explain this. (Cindy's reading grade might be indicated as A_3 meaning *Excellent progress for Cindy but she is reading a third-grade book.*) Whatever the special conventions in your school, you will need to follow them conscientiously for the sake of clear communication. You cannot say, as Humpty Dumpty said to Alice, "When *I* use a word, it means just what I choose it to mean—neither more nor less."

Report cards need to be supplemented with other types of parent contacts. No conscientious teacher considers that his responsibility in sharing with parents his evaluation of a pupil's work is ended when the report card goes home; nor does he feel that he has secured the help he needs in working with a child if he receives no communication from a home other than a signature. The more frequent the contacts between home and school, the more effective the guidance of the pupil is likely to be.

School systems have devised (often in cooperation with committees of parents) a variety of ways of supplementing the letter grades on a report card. Notes to parents are among the most widely used supplementary devices. Sometimes these are added in a space provided on the report card. Sometimes pupils write, under the teacher's guidance, a special supplementary letter. Often teachers find time to write brief notes about outstanding work or problems in the interim between reporting periods. Sometimes a comprehensive letter replaces the formal letter-grade report. Letters to the home have to be carefully written. Vague statements often leave parents longing for the seeming security of letter grades. Allen Anderson's first attempt, although reassuring in a general way to the child's parents, did not provide them with much definite information.

> Sally is getting along much better than she did before Christmas. Her reading is improving. So is her arithmetic, but she still needs help in spelling. She does very nice work in art and music. Her social relationships with the other children are improving. She is definitely on her way to a good year.

With his principal's help, Allen rewrote his letter:

> Sally has seemed much happier in class since Christmas. She is now working in a fourth-grade reader and with the special help in phonetics she can now handle most words of less than three syllables. She has mastered all her fundamental combinations in arithmetic, which is quite satisfactory for fourth-grade work. She still has trouble using a phonetic approach to spelling. We are practicing with her by dictating phonetically accurate words. In our last social studies unit Sally took responsibility for the mural. The members of her group accepted her leadership and worked with her

very well. She has also been playing the piano for groups to sing at recess. She seems to be on her way to a good year.

In some school systems parents are invited to visit following a reporting period for the purpose of exchanging ideas about pupils' progress. A teacher prepares carefully for such conferences. He will probably assemble samples of the pupil's work (perhaps asking the pupil to help him choose). These will include work for which praise can honestly be given as well as work indicating problem areas. He may also go back to the child's cumulative record to check on personal data. If he is giving the pupil special help that could be supplemented at home, he will have typical teaching materials at hand. If the parent is to visit the class prior to the conference, the schedule may be adjusted so that the youngster may be seen in action. Even the place in the room where parent and teacher confer merits consideration. Some teachers, for example, feel that conferences do not get off to a good start if they remain seated behind their desks. Careful thought also has to be given, of course, to what to say to the parent. It is important to be honest without being unduly discouraging or alarming. It is also important to talk about the problems with which the parent is concerned. A parent who wants to know how well his child can read does not appreciate being told how cooperative the youngster is or being vaguely reassured that "he will read when he is ready." This is a point at which the actual samples of the child's work can be of major assistance.

Many teachers also make it a practice to invite groups of parents to the classroom to share special experiences with children. These can be effective means of conveying information about pupil progress if they are planned so that children can tell about and show the varied products that developed from typical classroom activities. Often teachers help parents to gain insight into present-day teaching procedures by asking youngsters to tell how they worked. "How did we use reference books in this unit?" "Would the editorial committee tell how they used their proofreading check sheets?" It can also be of value in helping parents to see how traditional goals are being achieved through modern methods to ask pupils to tell what they have learned. "Would someone tell about the spelling words that we needed for this project?" "We had to do considerable arithmetic before we completed this work. Who would like to tell about it?" Teachers have sometimes helped pupils to summarize such learnings on charts for parents to read. (*Kinds of Writing We Did; Arithmetic We Used; Reading Skills We Needed.*)

Such an open-door policy of sharing with parents, as a group, work that can be praised not only provides an important means of interpreting the total classroom program, but often paves the way for individual parent conferences.

Contributions must be made to cumulative records. How your collections of concrete evidence will be used to contribute to pupils' cumulative records will depend upon the type of record maintained in your particular school system. Many teachers go over a pupil's folder with him periodically. The accumulated work samples are appraised and one or two typical of present status selected to be left in the folder. Progress is summarized on a master sheet and perhaps decisions made regarding what to report to parents. These master sheets may be filed at the end of the year in the child's permanent folder. In some schools, typical samples of the pupil's work are filed along with standardized test booklets in the cumulative record to remain for at least a year as a guide to his next teacher. You will need to ascertain the type of cumulative record in use in your school system and to lay plans to assure that the needed evidence is available. Whatever the form maintained as a permanent record, you will still have the responsibility of collecting for the year records as extensive as you need for the purposes of guiding the growth of your boys and girls.

Pupils need to be helped to understand reports of their progress. If you have involved your pupils in the types of planning and evaluation sessions that have been described in this volume, they will know a great deal about their own progress. They will need, however, special help in interpreting the ratings on their report cards if a system of letter grades is in use. If notes are being written to their parents in lieu of a more formal grading system, pupils should be aware of the tenor of these notes—perhaps even write a supplementary letter of their own or help to draft part of what the teacher writes. This is not only important if pupils are to have a share in the full evaluation process, but it is a major aid in reporting to parents. Youngsters who have shared in evaluating their progress are often our most effective supporters and interpreters at home.

Teachers use a number of devices to assure that pupils understand the basis upon which the letter grades on their report cards have been assigned. They often find time to sit down with each pupil at reporting period, go over his notebooks or the folder containing samples of his work, and talk with him about how to communicate the joint appraisal of his work to his parents.

MISS SAMPSON

John, you're really improving in your spelling. Look at that graph!

JOHN

I'm still getting four or five words wrong, though. I can't seem to remember all those extra letters you can't hear.

MISS SAMPSON

Yes. We're going to have to give you a grade so that your father and mother will know that there's more work to do. I suppose it had better be a *C*, but let's put down an *A* for effort, and I'll write a note so that they'll know how well you're doing. Have you shown them your notebook recently?

Other teachers talk briefly with each child as he is given his report card. Sometimes it is helpful to have all-class discussion of the grading system. Where there has been frank consideration of strengths and weaknesses all along, comments on report cards can be made openly without serious risk of invidious comparisons and hurt feelings. "Peter, your mother will be very pleased to see that your reading is improving. He's really come along very well, hasn't he, boys and girls?" "Penny, you can be very proud of that *effort* grade. You really helped us finish our project succesfully." "Allen, we need to let your parents know that you just don't take time to proofread things carefully. I tried to show it in your language grade."

Reporting systems should contribute to broader understanding of the total educational program. When a teacher sends a report card home, talks with a parent in a conference, or invites a group of parents to visit the classroom, he is doing more than reporting on Jane's or Jimmy's progress. He is also interpreting the objectives of the school system and the reasons back of the teaching procedures he is using, the experiences he is providing for boys and girls, the adjustments he is making to individual differences.

Evaluation procedures, such as those discussed in this chapter, can make a major contribution in interpreting the over-all school program. Perhaps most important, the children themselves are aware of the objectives of the school. They have been helped to identify educational goals and they understand the steps being taken to assist them in achieving these goals. As a result, they can be effective ambassadors when questions related to school procedures are raised at home.

In the type of data collected for evaluation purposes lies another important means of interpreting the school to the home. Teachers have more evidence at hand than letter grades. It is possible to show a parent the type of work that the child is actually doing, to point specifically to evidence of progress or difficulties. Furthermore, if varied data have been collected, the evidence is at hand to demonstrate the breadth of educational goals and the importance of making sure that pupils can apply what they have learned to a variety of situations.

Letters home, conferences, and school visits promote closer relationships between home and school. Parents are welcome in the school for a variety of purposes. They have many opportunities to see, firsthand, the work that goes on in present-day classrooms. They are involved by the school in a number of activities that help to interpret modern methods—parent-teacher study groups, special speakers, special bulletins interpreting aspects of the program, grade-level meetings, visiting days, open houses.

Interpreting educational objectives and teaching principles is an even broader responsibility, however, than reporting effectively the progress of individual children and cooperating in activities that allow parents and teachers to work together. You interpret the school to parents and other interested persons through everything you do or say—through your professional interpretation of the work of your colleagues, supervisors, and college instructors; through the answers you give to questions about your teaching procedures; through the way you teach; and through the kind of person you are.

BOOKS YOU SHOULD KNOW

Bradfield, James M., and Moredock, H. Stewart. *Measurement and Evaluation in Education.* New York: The Macmillan Co., 1957. Pp. xiv + 509.

Buros, Oscar K. (Editor). *The Fourth Mental Measurements Yearbook.* Highland Park, N.J.: The Gryphon Press, 1953. Pp. xxiv + 1163.

Cronbach, Lee J. *Essentials of Psychological Testing.* New York: Harper & Brothers, 1949. Pp. xiii +475.

D'Evelyn, Katherine E. *Individual Parent-Teacher Conferences.* New York: Bureau of Publications, Teachers College, Columbia University, 1945. Pp. 99.

Lindquist, E.F. (Editor). *Educational Measurement.* Washington, D.C.: American Council on Education, 1951. Pp. xx + 820.

Ross, C.C., and Stanley, Julian C. *Measurement in Today's Schools.* Third Edition. Englewood Cliffs, N.J.: Prentice-Hall, 1954. Pp. xviii + 485.

Rothney, John W.M. *Evaluating and Reporting Pupil Progress.* What Research Says to the Teacher, No. 7. Washington, D.C.: National Education Association, 1955. Pp. 33.

Stout, Irving W., and Langdon, Grace. *Parent-Teacher Relationships.* What Research Says to the Teacher, No. 16. Washington, D.C.: National Education Association, 1958. Pp. 31.

Strang, Ruth. *Every Teacher's Records.* Revised Edition. New York: Bureau of Publications, Teachers College, Columbia University, 1942. Pp. 48.

Strang, Ruth. *Reporting to Parents.* New York: Bureau of Publications, Teachers College, Columbia University, 1947. Pp. 105.

Thomas, R. Murray. *Judging Student Progress.* New York: Longmans, Green and Co., 1954. Pp. vii + 421.

Thorndike, Robert L., and Hagen, Elizabeth. *Measurement and Evaluation in Psychology and Education.* New York: John Wiley and Sons, 1955. Pp. viii + 575.

Traxler, Arthur E., and others. *Introduction to Testing and the Use of Test Results in Public Schools.* New York: Harper & Brothers, 1953. Pp. 113.

Wrightstone, J. Wayne; Justman, Joseph; and Robbins, Irving. *Evaluation in Modern Education.* New York: American Book Co., 1956. Pp. xi + 481.

Wrinkle, William L. *Improving Marking and Reporting Practices.* New York: Rinehart and Co., 1947. Pp. 120.

Being a Good Classroom Administrator

CHAPTER 12

An effective teacher is a good classroom administrator. He handles the many aspects of classroom management in ways that provide maximum freedom for himself and his pupils to pursue their plans. Where there are opportunities for his boys and girls to grow through participating in the details of classroom management, he sees that they are involved.

Only a person who has spent considerable time in a classroom has a clear conception of how extensive the administrative responsibilities of a teacher can be. There are problems of providing for effective working conditions in the classroom—storing materials; using cupboards, bookshelves, and bulletin boards efficiently; arranging furniture. There are reports and records to be filed promptly in order to facilitate the over-all administration of the school. There are special problems at the opening of the year—securing supplies, filing enrollment records, helping a new group of boys and girls to get off to a good start. And, as the year winds to a close, there is the matter of planning a worth-while program while taking care of all the details connected with storing books and filing final reports.

Each teacher must work out the details of his own classroom management in the light of the administrative policy of his school. It is possible, however, to identify the types of problems which every teacher must be prepared to handle and to suggest procedures which experienced teachers have found helpful. This chapter is meant primarily for beginners, facing alone for the first time the intricacies of classroom administration. It should suggest to student teachers policies and procedures about which to inquire carefully while there are experienced persons at hand to give advice.

BEGINNING THE SCHOOL YEAR

The time you devote to planning and to caring for administrative details before school opens will pay large dividends once the year is actually under way. In all probability the persons with administrative responsibilities in your school system will have made plans to help you get off to a good start. Before school opens there may be a teachers' institute during which special sessions are devoted to the problems of the new teacher. Your principal may call a staff meeting to discuss administrative details peculiar to your building. He will probably have prepared class lists, perhaps have mimeographed a special bulletin of instructions and taken other steps to facilitate the opening day. He may have designated his assistant principal or experienced teachers to give help on specific types of problems. Certainly, he will see that the building is open several days before school begins so that you may arrange your classroom, consult with him, meet other teachers, and learn something about school policies and the general layout of the building.[1]

In addition to the over-all problems of becoming familiar with the policies and organization of a new building, you will face several that are peculiar to the opening of school. You will want to make sure that your classroom is properly equipped. You will need to know precisely the procedures for enrolling pupils and for checking class lists on the first day. Then, for your own security in getting off to a smooth start with your pupils, you should plan carefully the classroom experiences for the first few days and the ways in which you intend to proceed in establishing work habits and behavior patterns.

Secure needed supplies and equipment. You will not, of course, know how well your classroom is equipped until you walk into it in the fall. Experienced teachers accumulate materials year after year. The result is a rich classroom environment that is a mixture of personal and school property. You can expect to be starting in a classroom that is much more sparsely equipped than were those in which you have seen experienced teachers at work. You may find that the textbooks which are part of the regular classroom equipment have been stored in your room and that supplies ordered the previous spring have been delivered, but it could be the policy in your building to store everything in a central supply room. In this case, you will be responsible

[1] Reread Chapter 3 for suggestions regarding the types of information you should seek.

for filing the proper requisitions to secure the supplies and equipment you need.

Unless your school system is one in which pupils purchase their textbooks, it will be your job to insure that the correct number of the appropriate texts are in your room. Your class list, supplied by the principal, will tell you how many pupils to expect. If materials have been stored in your room, your predecessor may have left an inventory or at least have filed one in the principal's office. You, in your turn, will be accountable for the equipment at the end of the year. One of your first steps should be to check this inventory. If one is not available, make your own so that you will know exactly what books and materials you have at hand. In addition, you will need to know what the policy is with regard to requisitioning additional books or giving back a surplus. If all textbooks have been stored in a central book room, your responsibility will be to ascertain which sets should be in your classroom and how you can secure additional sets when you need them. It would be wise to inquire, also, whether you are expected to obtain exactly the number needed for the pupils on your class list and to requisition new books as you gain new pupils or whether you are to keep a small surplus on hand.

There are definite advantages to "giving out books" the first day. You will need to know which books are to be placed in a pupil's hands for his personal use throughout the year and which remain on your bookshelves. You should ascertain, also, what the procedures are in assigning books to children and what accounting system is in use. In addition, there will be a school policy with regard to the parents' responsibility if a child loses or destroys a book and, in some cases, a policy with regard to whether or not books are to be taken home. All this information should be in your possession before school begins.

If your school system does not issue free textbooks, you may find yourself working under a plan in which each pupil pays a specified rental for each book. If this is the case, there will be, no doubt, a school-wide procedure for accounting for the rentals and keeping records of the books issued. This, ordinarily, is not a scheme which you can master while handling the thousand and one details which will confront you on the first day of school. Become thoroughly familiar with it ahead of time and plan carefully the activities that will keep your pupils gainfully occupied while you are involved in the bookkeeping process. It is possible, though less likely, that in your system pupils will be required to purchase their own texts. If so, you will need to know the recommended list and where to secure samples to show your class. Inquire, also, about policy regarding those youngsters who cannot afford to purchase books.

Although you may not want to use supplementary or reference books immediately, you should be thinking about the ones you will need and ascertaining the sources of such additional materials. There may be certain standard reference aids, such as dictionaries and encyclopedias, with which your classroom is equipped. In some schools, however, such materials are located in a central place from which they can be borrowed, or are rotated among teachers of the same grade or among grades at a given level—certain books available for primary youngsters, others for those in the intermediate grades. You are almost certain, if yours is to be a rich program, to need books in addition to those standard references available in your school. Here your principal or, in a large school system, your supervisor can be of help. There may be a central source from which special books may be secured or a system for securing a loan collection from the library. Do not hesitate to ask for help in locating such materials.

Securing supplies is another problem facing you before school opens. In some schools the principal requisitions supplies on the basis of the number of pupils in each room and a specified allowance for each pupil. In others, the teacher makes the requisition from the catalog listing what is available in a central warehouse. This may have been done for your classroom the preceding spring so that your supplies will be delivered to your room or be ready to be picked up. It is possible, however, that you will be responsible for requisitioning what you need from a school supply room, or even for making out your own requisition from a catalog of materials available in a central warehouse. In some schools you may be expected to order a year's supply and to store your materials in your room, or to use a specified shelf in a central storage room. In others, it may be the custom to replenish supplies from the school supply room as the year goes along. It is possible, too, that procedures will differ with different types of material. Paper, pens, ink, paper clips, glue, and other such expendables may be ordered in quantity and stored in your room. On the other hand, expensive art supplies or materials for science demonstrations may be secured in small quantities as needed from a special source. Ascertain what the procedures are in your building and precisely what requisition forms are to be used.

Until you think it through for yourself, you will have little idea of the variety of materials needed to equip your room and only the vaguest notions about amounts. Your principal will expect to help you with this, of course, but you may feel more secure if you know what you are about. In some school systems lists will have been developed indicating standard equipment for a primary or an intermediate classroom. The following, taken from a bulletin[2] containing detailed listings of needed materials and supplies, will illustrate the types of items you should be thinking about for your stationery and art equipment. You should, of course, not expect the policy on supplies in your building to follow such lists exactly.

SUGGESTED EQUIPMENT AND SUPPLIES FOR PRIMARY GROUP OF 25 CHILDREN

Art Equipment and Supplies

- 1 doz. Brushes, paint, 1″ camel's hair or bristle, 12″ handle
- 1½ doz. Brushes, paint, ¾″ camel's hair or bristle, 12″ handle
- 1 doz. Brushes, paste
- 1 box Chalk, assorted colors, 1 gross to box
- 1 box Chalk, poster
- 250 lbs. Clay, dry or mixed
- 25 Clay Boards, 12″ × 15″
- 23 doz. Crayons, 4 doz. each, red, blue, green, 3 doz. yellow, 2 doz. each orange, black, brown, violet; include some oil base and water color crayons
- 2 Easels, double, or Table for tray of paint jars and container for brushes; or
- 12–25 Easels, individual, small, or oilcloth covered boards
- 10 boxes Laundry Starch (for making finger paint)
- 6 yds. Oilcloth
- 1 Pail, galvanized with cover, for clay
- 47 lbs. Paint, cold water, 6 lbs. each, red, green, blue, yellow; 4 lbs. each, white, turquoise, black; 3 lbs. each, orange, brown, flesh
- 6 pts. Paint, finger, 1 each, red, yellow, green, blue, brown, black
- 1 pkg. Paper, bogus, 18″ × 24″, 500 shts. to pkg.
- 2 pkg. Paper, construction, 12″ × 18″, 100 shts. to pkg., assorted colors
- 8 pkg. Paper, finger painting, 16″ × 22″, 100 shts. to pkg.
- 4 pkg. Paper, manila, 12″ × 15″, 500 shts. to pkg.
- 2 pkg. Paper, manila, 18″ × 36″
- 2 pkg. Paper, poster, 18″ × 24″, 500 shts. to pkg., assorted colors
- 7 reams Paper, unprinted news, 18″ × 24″, 32 lbs. to ream

[2] Reprinted by permission of the Association for Childhood Education International, 1200 15th St., N.W., Washington 5, D.C. from *Equipment and Supplies*. General Service Bulletin No. 39, pp. 10-11, 13 and 13-14, 16. This bulletin, which indicates sources of many types of tested materials, can be an invaluable aid.

Art Equipment and Supplies

1 roll Paper, wrapping, 24″ wide, brown
1 roll Paper, wrapping, 36″ wide
2 qts. Paste
25 Scissors, some blunt and some sharp points
2 boxes Soap Flakes (for making own finger paint)
2 boxes Tissues, paper, for paint rags, 500 to pkg.
Wheat Paste Powder (for making finger paint and papier mâché)

Stationery Equipment and Supplies

1 box Adhesive Mending Tape
1 box Carbon Paper
2 boxes Chalk, yellow, dustless
1 Chart Liner
2 boxes Clips
1½ doz. Erasers, chalkboard
3 doz. Erasers, pencil
4 boxes Fasteners, 100 to box; 2 boxes 1″, 2 boxes ¾″
2 bottles Ink, India, black
2 boxes Labels, gummed
1 roll Masking Tape
Paper, chart, large ruled for reading experiences
1 box Paper, master copy for duplicator
5 reams Paper, typing
10 reams Paper, writing, 9″ × 12″, 1″ rulings
5 reams Paper, writing, 9″ × 12″, without rulings
10 reams Paper, writing, 8″ × 10½″, 5 reams with ½″ rulings, 5 reams with ⅜″ rulings
1 Papercutter
1 Pen, felt, marking, with ink
1 Pencil Sharpener
1 gross Pencils, (beginners to be used in grades one and two)
6 Pens, lettering assorted
1 box Pins
1 Punch, eyelet, and eyelets
3 boxes Reinforcements
2 boxes Rubber Bands
12 Rulers, 12″ with ¼″, ½″, 1″ markings
3 rolls Scotch Tape, large
1 Stapler
4 boxes Staples
2 balls String
2 boxes Suspension Rings
1 ream Tagboard, manila
8 boxes Thumbtacks
1 Typewriter, primer type
Typewriter Ribbons
Access to Duplicator

SUGGESTED EQUIPMENT AND SUPPLIES FOR INTERMEDIATE GROUP OF 30 CHILDREN

Art Equipment and Supplies

1 qt. Alcohol
1 doz. Brushes, round wash, large
1 doz. Brushes, flat, ½″ or ¾″
3 boxes Chalk, colored
2 boxes Charcoal
100 lbs. Clay, with oil base
12 lbs. Clay, pottery
6 boxes Crayons, hard pressed, various colors
12 Drawing Boards, 20″ ×

Art Equipment and Supplies

26″, preferably of wood (substitute, wall board)
4 Easels, double with tray for paint jars
Glazes
1 Hot Plate, electric
1 Iron, electric
15 Jars, glass with lids, pt. and ½ pt., for paint, or 15 cans, baby food size
1 Kiln, electric
36 Mat Boards, gray or white, 22″ × 28″, for mounting
5 yds. Oilcloth
Pails, galvanized with cover, for clay
11 qts. Paint, poster, 1 qt. each color, red, yellow, ultramarine blue, turquoise, green, orange, magenta, violet, black, white, brown; or
11 lbs. Paint, cold water, 1 lb. each color, as above
12 boxes Paint, water color, same colors as above
6 jars Paint, finger, 8 oz. each, 1 each, red, yellow, green, blue, brown, black
1 Pan, flat
1 ream Paper, bogus, 18″ × 24″
1 ream Paper, bogus, 22″ × 28″
1 roll Paper, brown, for murals
1 ream Paper, construction, colored, 12″ × 18″
1 ream Paper, construction, colored, 18″ × 24″
1 ream Paper, drawing, white, 12″ × 18″
1 ream Paper, drawing, white, 18″ × 24″
2 reams Paper, finger paint
2 reams Paper, manila, 18″ × 24″
2 reams Paper, unprinted news
2 qts. Paste
6 lbs. Patching Plaster, or Plaster of Paris
30 Scissors
2 Spatter Guns, or tooth brush and screen wire
4 Trays for paint jars

Stationery Equipment and Supplies

3 boxes Chalk, dustless
2 Charts, 1 each manuscript and penmanship
12 boxes Clips, bulldog
1 Compass
3 doz. Erasers, 1 doz. each, chalkboard, pencil, ink
1 qt. Ink, writing
3 bottles Ink, India
2 Mat Knives
1 Mimeograph
10 reams Paper, ruled
5 reams Paper, unruled
1 Paper Cutter
3 doz. Pencils
1 Pencil Sharpener
2 boxes Pens
2 boxes Pins
2 Pointers
1 Printing Press
30 Rulers
1 Stapler and Staples
12 boxes Thumbtacks
Yardsticks
Access to Duplicator

You will need to ascertain your responsibility in accounting for supplies and equipment. Typically, you will be expected to teach pupils to use materials economically. You will not be able to order unlimited amounts, although, in an emergency, someone will certainly try to be of help. You may need to account at the end of the year for expensive items such as scissors, and you will certainly be responsible for keeping any permanent equipment in your room in good condition and for reporting needs for repairs promptly.

Every school will have its policies with regard to asking pupils to purchase supplies. Even in schools where many materials are made available, there is likely to be some equipment which the pupil is expected to purchase. You will probably want to give your pupils this list the first day of school, and, in some situations, you may be responsible for listing the items requested by the special teachers as well. Find out what your list should contain and whether there is a school policy with regard to recommending a special brand or type of equipment. In some schools, for example, there will be a policy with regard to the type of pen a pupil may use. Find out, too, whether you may ask a pupil to purchase an item with which your classroom is already equipped. For example, many teachers feel that children need the experience of being responsible for their own rulers or for their own supply of paper. However, in some situations where these are available in the classroom, it is not permissible to ask pupils to purchase their own. In addition, check on policy with regard to the elaborateness of the equipment you may recommend. May you ask each pupil to have a loose-leaf notebook? a pencil box? a box of paints?

There is likely to be a school policy with regard to collecting money from pupils for materials which are purchased by the school. In some situations funds are collected for paper, which the school then distributes. Funds for children's weekly magazines may also be collected. Workbooks present a special problem about which you should inquire. In some school systems, teachers are free to ask pupils to purchase as many such materials as they feel will facilitate their work. In others, the specific workbooks will have to be approved by persons with supervisory responsibilities and it will not be permissible to supplement these with similar materials from other series, even if parents are willing to purchase them. In some schools, workbooks will be supplied from school funds, but not considered expendable, and you will have to devise a system for their use which does not involve writing in them. If pupils are expected to purchase their own workbooks, you will also need to know who does the ordering. Obviously, too, in the case of any materials for which you are responsible for collecting funds, you will want to have a simple but efficient accounting system worked out ahead of time.

In the few days before school begins you will also have an opportunity to discover how one goes about securing additional furniture for a classroom or storing surplus equipment. Do you report your problem to your principal, who then issues the request to the school custodian? Is there a school secretary who handles such requests? Or do you go directly to the custodian? It is much easier for all concerned if you can go through the correct channels from the beginning.

Ascertain your administrative responsibilities for the opening day. Policies with regard to routing pupils to their new teachers, enrolling youngsters who have not attended the school before, and reporting attendance on the first day vary from school to school. You will be off to a much smoother start if you are quite clear as to the procedures in your building. If your principal has mimeographed a special list of instructions, read it with great care. In the confusion of the first day, principals can become justifiably irritated if teachers take up time to ask about procedures that are clearly outlined. On the other hand, do not fail to ask if something does not sound logical. It is far better to be doubly sure you know what you are doing than to discover that an error on your part has created confusion for other people.

You will need to know what the procedures are with regard to enrolling new pupils. Kindergarteners, and first-graders in schools where there is no kindergarten, are sometimes enrolled the spring before. Even so, there will be new children in the fall and teachers at these levels may find that they are to devote the first day to enrolling pupils and meeting parents. Beyond first grade, in schools of any size, there is likely to be a system whereby a new pupil reports to the principal's office and receives a special slip assigning him to your class. You may, however, be responsible for obtaining from him certain information needed by the office. Be sure you know what you must do the first day other than to add his name to your roll.

There are many patterns for routing pupils to their new teachers. In some schools, pupils will have reported to their new classrooms on the last day of school. In others, partly to spare the feelings of those who are not promoted, the number of the new room is placed on the report card. Still another pattern is to have the pupils report to the room in which they worked the year before, thence to be routed to their new rooms. Be sure you know what to expect and what your part in the process is to be. Whatever the general procedure, you will be responsible for checking to be sure that the pupils in front of you are actually those whose names are on your class list. You may also be expected to try to get some information regarding the youngsters on your list who fail to report.

Even with the best planning, there will be some emergencies the first day. In a school with two or three classes at the same grade level, somebody will forget the room to which he is assigned. A youngster who withdrew from the school in January may be back in the district and may come to your room along with his pals, assuming that this is where he belongs. A parent may by-pass the principal's office and appear at your classroom door with a report card from another city indicating that the child has been promoted to your grade. Find out ahead of time what your procedure is to be in such cases. In some large schools there will be one or more teachers on each floor with a master list to help route lost children. In large schools it is probable, also, that you will be under strict orders not to accept a new child without a notice from the office.

In most schools, there will be special attendance reports required by the office promptly on the first day. It may be important for your principal to be able to follow up immediately if a family has moved from the school district. In a large school system, he may be responsible for filing a preliminary attendance report before the end of the day. Make sure you know precisely what information is needed from you and when it is due. You will probably also be responsible for bringing office cards up to date with regard to changes in addresses or in family status—parents may remarry, children may be placed with relatives. Teachers in some schools collect additional personal data—information regarding whether the mother is working, whom to contact if a child is ill, whether the child walks to school or rides the bus, what families nearby might be phoned in case of emergency. You may not be required to complete all such forms on the first day, but find out when the information is needed and schedule time to secure it.

Plan pupil activities carefully for the first day. Although you should properly be concerned with enrollment procedures and other administrative details for the first day, your most thoughtful effort should be focused upon planning the activities for your boys and girls. You may be facing a short day which closes at noon or you may be expected to teach until regular dismissal time. Short day or long, think through carefully what you plan to do. You will want to build, from the beginning, the attitudes you desire toward school, toward other children, and toward yourself as a teacher.

You can do some valuable preparation ahead of time if you will study your class list and cumulative records. Become familiar with names and identify items of information that will help you in associating names and faces quickly. There are few things more helpful in building classroom rapport than being able to say "Donna" rather than "you, in the blue dress."

Preparation ahead of time should include some thinking about how to make your classroom attractive. It is a worth-while experience for pupils to share in the decoration of their classroom, but for this first day plan your own. Flowers on your desk, a bright bulletin board, a welcome sign on the blackboard, books out on the library table, all help to build an hospitable atmosphere. You will save confusion by writing any needed lists and directions on the blackboard before your pupils arrive. Anticipate, also, any materials you will need and make sure that they are in your room. The middle of the first morning is no time to send a messenger for special art supplies.

Your schedule for the first day should provide, as far as time permits, a sequence of activities similar to that of any regular day. You will want to build from the beginning the ways of working and the routines that you hope to maintain for the year. There should be a balance between discussion and individual work which the pupils do quietly at their desks. Songs, stories, games, or other activities of a recreational nature should be included. You will want to discover the school policy with regard to opening exercises and to start with whatever is customary. If it is the practice in your school for the class as a whole to take a lavatory break, you would schedule this at its regular time. Certainly, special care will be taken to help beginners to locate the bathroom facilities and to acquaint them with the procedure in asking to be excused. Your day's activities will, of course, have to be fitted around the routines of beginning a new year—registration procedures, announcements regarding supplies to be purchased, explanations to older pupils of the schedules upon which they go to special teachers of music and art, procedures for giving out textbooks. Think through these extras, decide which ones must be taken care of immediately and which can be placed later in the day, and merge them as smoothly as you can with your plans for pupil activities. Give particular thought to the points at which you are going to be occupied with checking records or registering one child at a time and make sure that there are ample interesting individual activities to keep your pupils at work.

Specifically, what types of activities are appropriate for the first day? This will depend somewhat upon the age of your group. Undoubtedly you will want to spend some time getting acquainted. Many teachers find it helpful to have the youngsters prepare large name signs for their desks or to write name tags which can be pinned to the clothing of primary pupils. If you are teaching kindergarteners and first-graders, you may wish to call them to a circle in the front of the room and to encourage each one to tell a little about himself. Older pupils, too, may profitably be involved in a sharing period where they can talk about themselves. Get-acquainted activities may be extended to advantage to include some written work. Your first thought may be to ask for an account of what went on over vacation, but this time-worn topic is not the only one you can use. Pupils may draw pictures or write about their families, their pets, the things they like to do best. Older groups may do short autobiographies. It is even possible to use get-acquainted activities as the basis of a short unit. Pupils may prepare a special bulletin board containing snapshots and stories about themselves and their families, publish a get-acquainted news bulletin, or draw to scale a map of their community and mark their homes on it.

Do not neglect the possibilities in helping pupils to get acquainted with their new classroom. You may wish to examine the library collection with them, to talk about uses for a display table, or to discuss ways in which bulletin boards can be put to use. For beginners, get-acquainted activities often include a trip through the school to identify offices, lavatories, playrooms, the lunchroom, and other facilities of special interest.

You will want to plan some activities for your first day that can definitely be identified as "school work." For first-graders, these may include listening to a story, learning a song, drawing a picture, learning to play a new game. It may also be revealing to spend a discussion period investigating kindergarteners' and first-graders' readiness for school. Who can write his name? Who can count to ten? Who knows a poem? Older pupils may be given an inventory test in arithmetic, take a spelling test, do some oral reading from materials graded as to difficulty.

The first week or so with beginners will probably be centered largely in establishing routines, learning to handle classroom equipment, exploring the various interest centers in the room, and engaging in a variety of sharing and other language experiences that are planned on a day-to-day basis. With older groups, activities related to a short unit of work may well be launched within the first few days. Often, it is even possible to talk about this the day school begins. In a school where there is considerable intervisitation among classes, youngsters often come to their new room quite sophisticated regarding the work of their grade and well able to contribute to a discussion on how to get started. Sometimes it is useful to plan a short introductory unit that will enable you to become better acquainted with the abilities of your group. A unit centered on transportation or on learning to read maps can help to launch a year's study of other countries for fourth-graders. A study of the local community or the state or a unit on national parks can serve as a good beginning for a study of the United States. It is possible, also, to do a little prearranging of your environment in order to lead into a short unit—some objects in a science corner, a bulletin board about pets, a series of pictures indicating signs of fall. Do not neglect, either, the possibilities in your pupils' worlds. A new addition to the school may be in the process of construction, a rocket or space satellite be in the headlines. These are often leads to exciting classroom ventures in the early fall.[3]

Lay sound foundations for effective classroom living. As you make your plans for the first day and for the first few weeks, think carefully about the ways of working, the standards of discussion, the attitudes toward other people, and the routines that you hope to develop. It is far easier to help your pupils practice desirable ways of behaving from the beginning than it is to try to re-establish a good working atmosphere after several days of confusion and disorder.

Your pupils will be looking to you for leadership. There are many ways of assuring them from the start that you intend to assume this responsibility. As you think about your first day, plan carefully for every routine from the moment the pupils arrive. Decide whether you prefer to assign them to seats or to have them choose where they prefer to sit and be on hand at the door to greet them pleasantly and to direct them. Give some thought to the possibility of a rainy day, and work out a simple plan for getting in and out of the cloakroom with wraps. If there are lockers for pupils' possessions, decide whether or not you want to assign these the first day and, if you do, what plan you intend to use. Be definite and specific about your directions and your first

[3] For other suggestions regarding helpful ways of getting started, reread the appropriate sections in Chapters 7, 8 and 9.

assignments. Do not hesitate to ask firmly (but pleasantly) for the behavior you consider appropriate.

As you and your pupils undertake each new activity there will be opportunities to discuss desirable procedures. All youngsters except beginners will know from previous years what constitutes appropriate classroom behavior and can make suggestions. As a group clusters around the pencil sharpener, work out a way of taking turns. Before you go down the hall, talk about the importance of not disturbing other classes. If papers are to be passed in, be ready to suggest a system for doing this. When beginners first come to a circle in the front of the room, talk about how to get there without pushing or shoving. You can save yourself much lecturing and nagging if you will foresee such opportunities to develop desirable procedures, plan for them ahead of time, and capitalize upon them as they occur.

You can establish many standards of desirable classroom behavior by the positiveness of your leadership. "Just a minute, please. It's hard to hear you all at once. Let's take turns." "It is very important that you all fill this in correctly. I'll wait until everybody has his pencil and is watching." "Let's not get drinks while someone is talking. We'll have a work period in a few minutes when you can move around." "In school there are times when it's very important for everybody to listen. Are you all comfortable and ready for our story now?" Your pupils will be trying to discover where the boundaries are in this new situation. You and they, both, will feel more secure if you establish the limits definitely, but pleasantly, from the start.

Obviously, you will spare no pains to plan interesting activities for your first days and to make sure that you have an ample supply. No beginner, and for that matter no experienced teacher who wishes to get off to a good start, can neglect his planning. It is far better to discover that what you planned for a day will take a week to complete than it is to have bored and noisy children seeking something to amuse themselves.

Above all, keep your sense of perspective. It is only natural to be apprehensive regarding your ability to start your pupils on the road to self-discipline. Yet every experienced teacher will tell you that perfection is not achieved overnight. Your youngsters will continue to test you out until they are sure where you stand and how firmly your feet are planted. Furthermore, it takes time to learn ways of behaving just as it takes time to learn to read. Helping boys and girls to grow toward self-discipline is one of the most complex teaching responsibilities you face. Accept it for the challenge that it is.

MANAGING RECORDS AND REPORTS

Every teacher must assume a certain number of clerical responsibilities. Few aspects of your work will be more of a burden to you than the management of records and reports if you do not learn to handle them efficiently and expeditiously. How complicated your record-keeping responsibilities will be depends upon the policies in your school and in the larger school system.[4] Certainly, you will be responsible for attendance records. You will also be expected to maintain comprehensive and accurate records of pupil progress—to develop a class book, to keep cumulative records up to date, and to be responsible for reports to parents. In addition, there will be a variety of requisition forms, special referral blanks, lists for the Parent-Teacher Association, accounts of moneys collected, all of which you will be expected to submit promptly.

It is impossible to give you precise instructions regarding the records and reports you may have to handle. Although the general procedure is quite similar from one school system to another, details differ from system to system and even from building to building within a system. Your principal, or someone designated by him, will be your most valuable source of help in handling the details of the reports and records required in your building. One of your first steps in a new school should be to collect a full set of the forms you will be asked to use and to read them and any accompanying directions carefully. Confusing though some of these forms may seem to be, there is usually a reason for each item of information requested and for each step you are asked to take.

Keep attendance records carefully. In most states, attendance records are the basis of state financial aid. The attendance reports of all the teachers in your building will be consolidated into your principal's report to some central authority. At the end of the school year a consolidated yearly report will typically be made to the State Department of Education. State funds are probably apportioned to your school system on the basis of average daily membership (pupils enrolled) or average daily attendance (pupils present). Ordinarily these two statistics

[4] Chapter 3, pages 65-71, suggests the policies about which you should inquire on coming into a new building.

are not the only basis for state aid, but one or the other is necessary in most states. It is important, therefore, for you to keep your attendance records carefully from the first day of school.

The basic recording device that you will use for your day-by-day attendance records is the class register. This is filed permanently at the end of the year. It becomes legal evidence and may be referred to, years later, for information regarding one of your pupils or his family. It is very important that you follow exactly the instructions given for entering pupils' names and other pertinent data and for indicating attendance. You will probably be asked to enter your pupils' names in ink. Certainly, you will be expected to write neatly. There may also be regulations with regard to alphabetizing names and to grouping pupils by sex. It can even be important to enter a name on each line rather than to skip lines. These are all matters about which you should inquire if your instructions do not seem to cover them.

In a large school system, there is usually an interval of a week or so allowed between the opening day and the point at which the school enrollment is considered to be fixed. You may, therefore, not be issued your register at once, or you may be asked not to enter your pupils' names until a given date. Since special procedures are needed to remove a pupil's name once it is entered on a register, it is important that you follow such instructions implicitly, even though you are anxious to get your record-keeping under way. Be careful, also, to check on the personal data you are asked to enter. Do not assume that a mother's last name will be the same as that of the child or that a child will report his birthday accurately. Go back to the school enrollment cards or to your duplicates of them and check.

Many beginning teachers say that the monthly report (which summarizes attendance for the month) is the most confusing aspect of reporting attendance. Actually, completing this report is well within your competence, but it will require careful following of directions, accuracy, and some simple arithmetic. Start in plenty of time; read the directions carefully; and, if you are not absolutely certain that you are correct, work out a trial form and ask your principal, or someone designated by him, to check it with you. Turning to a sympathetic colleague next door for help on a monthly report is a risky business. You may select the one person for whom the intricacies of this particular form are destined forever to remain a mystery.

School personnel have legal responsibilities in seeing to it that the youngsters on their registers actually come to school. There will probably be a policy in your building regarding how many days a child may be absent before someone takes steps to determine the cause of the absence. Often the teacher is the one responsible for the preliminary phone call or home visit to determine what is wrong. After a certain point, a case of illegal absence will usually be referred to an attendance officer. You will need to know exactly what your responsibilities are in this regard and to follow through promptly.

Devise a workable plan for maintaining up-to-date records of pupil progress. Procedures in recording and reporting pupil progress have already been discussed in considerable detail.[5] You will not be the only person who may need to use the data you are collecting. You may be called upon at any time to confer with a parent or to provide information needed by your principal, your supervisor, or the school psychologist. The more extensive the information you attempt to collect, the better organized your recording and filing system must be.

Some general suggestions for setting up a class book were given in Chapter 11. In some schools, you will be asked to follow a specific procedure so that the entries in your grade book are made in the same code as those of other teachers. Often, however, you will be left to devise your own recording system. If you develop your own code, it would be wise to explain it on one of the inside covers of your book. Without this explanation someone who has to turn to your records during your absence will be able to make very little of the strings of zero's; plus and minus signs; *A*'s, *B*'s, and *C*'s; 1's, 2's, and 3's; 90's, 80's, and 70's (and in some grade books all of these, each serving its own purposes).

It is important, also, to decide how many samples of your pupils' work you will need to examine for the purposes of your records and then to plan your own schedule so that you have time to check the work you collect and to enter the ratings promptly. You will not achieve the continuous evaluation you desire if you allow the stacks of papers which contain the evidence to pile up on your desk. The teacher who has the most efficient organization for collecting evidence for evaluation purposes does not do the whole job himself. He involves the pupils in record-collecting and lets them help him by dictating entries for his book.

Several types of pupil folders or notebooks were described in Chapter 11 as possible aids in collecting data for evaluation purposes. These can result in an unwieldly conglomeration of bits of work unless you have a well-organized plan both for collecting this evidence and for evaluat-

[5] See Chapter 11, pp. 444-448 and 456-464.

ing it periodically and entering summary data in your record book, or on summary sheets filed in the folder for this purpose. Perhaps you will set up a rotation system where you work with one set of folders each week. Or you may plan an individual work period during which you can take a few minutes with each pupil to review his work in a given area. Whatever your procedure, you will do well not to allow the pressure of other activities to cause you to set this task aside week after week. It is far wiser to collect a limited amount of evidence for appraisal purposes, and actually to use it, than to swamp yourself with more data than you can handle.

Problems of promotion and nonpromotion are studied seriously in most schools. You may find that it is the policy in your building to begin to collect special evidence and to consult with parents as early as January. In the case of some youngsters whose promotion is in question, a psychological examination may be needed, and this is not always easily scheduled on an emergency basis. One important aspect of your responsibility in maintaining records of pupil progress is that of identifying early those youngsters whose promotion is in question. You will want to consult promptly with your principal with regard to these problems. Often it will be wise to collect additional data and perhaps to make some anecdotal records. It is not fair to the child or to his parents to raise the question of nonpromotion late in the year without warning.

What data you will be responsible for adding to the cumulative record, and when these data are to be added, will depend upon the comprehensiveness of the record system in your school. Normally, teachers are expected to keep these records up to date. This means that the scores on a standardized test are added as soon as possible. It can be important, also, to make sure that personal data are accurate. Stepparents or new guardians, new babies in the home, new addresses, changes in the employment of either parent, are among the items that you might be expected to keep current.

For the year that a child is in your room, you are the one with special responsibility for seeing to it that the information needed to help him is at hand. Make sure that you know of any special data you will be expected to supply. Make sure, also, that your records are systematic, clear, and legible so that others can use them if need be.

Be prompt and accurate in submitting reports requested to the office. In spite of your principal's best effort to routinize office procedures so that teachers are free to get on with the business of teaching, there will be a variety of administrative details which each classroom teacher must handle either because he has special access to the facts or because it is more efficient to delegate the task than it is to ask an overworked school secretary to do the job for everyone. There may be special requisition forms to be made out, reports to be filed when a child is referred to the school nurse or when there is an accident on the playground, referral forms to be completed if psychological services are required, lists to be prepared for the Parent-Teacher Association, money to be collected for a variety of purposes.

If you want to establish your reputation as a responsible staff member, you will take at least three steps with regard to such administrative details. First, you will read carefully all bulletins and notices from the principal's office and make whatever other moves seem necessary to acquaint yourself with your responsibilities. Second, you will make special note of deadlines and plan whatever adjustments are necessary either in your own work schedule or in that of your pupils in order to submit your reports promptly. Third, you will follow directions carefully and fill in any information requested completely and accurately. Remember that you are part of a larger school organization. The extra minute you spend to make your report accurate, or the minor adjustment you make to submit it promptly, can result in a major saving of time and effort on the part of the person who must do the final record-keeping. Be sure, therefore, that you meet your obligations faithfully.

PROVIDING EFFECTIVE WORKING CONDITIONS IN THE CLASSROOM

When a visitor first steps into a classroom, he is likely to judge the learning environment by the wealth of stimulating teaching aids—the contents of the bulletin boards, the displays, the plants, the tables of number games or science materials. Less spectacular, but equally important to effective learning, is the arrangement of the room itself—the adjustments for physical needs, the availability of supplies and equipment, the arrangement of desks, the neatness and orderliness of the room.

Boys and girls can participate with profit in developing efficient and attractive working conditions in their classroom. There are many valuable health lessons to be learned by being responsible for effective lighting, temperature, and ventilation. There are worth-while work habits to be developed from experiences in arranging furniture. And there are aesthetic satisfactions in helping to provide for an attractive and orderly place in which to work.

Make sure that physical needs are met. Experienced teachers make a number of adjustments in order to provide a healthful environment in which pupils can work. Beginning teachers must become consciously aware of this need. In many modern schools temperature and ventilation are controlled through a central heating system, but often classroom adjustments are required. Good lighting is important. Train yourself to become aware of times when the lights should be turned on or shades adjusted for bright sunlight. Discover, also, which parts of your blackboard can be seen easily under any circumstances and which call for adjustments of the shades at special times of the day. Become sensitive, too, to the conditions under which individual children are working. Although you may arrange your desks in squares or circles for discussion purposes, you should not allow a pupil to write for an extended period of time either facing a strong light or with his work in too deep a shadow. In some schools you will also need to be sensitive to noise and perhaps to plan your schedule so as to avoid holding discussions while other classes are playing under your windows. In classrooms where there is much small-group activity, it is also desirable to make sure that pupils who move from their regular desks work in seats appropriate to their size.

You will, of course, pay particular attention to youngsters with physical handicaps. Make sure that they are placed so that they are in the best possible location to see or to hear. Become aware of the forgetful child whose glasses are likely to remain in his pocket if someone does not remind hm. Adjust your position and the tone of your voice, if necessary, for the sake of the youngster with a hearing loss.

You must also think through your classroom adjustments for meeting physiological needs. With younger pupils, there probably will be a break for toileting. With older pupils, you will need to establish regulations regarding permission to leave the room and the number of pupils who may be out at once. These, of course, are arrangements you would set up on the first day of school. Some plan will also be needed regarding getting drinks. Experienced teachers are sensitive to the ways in which needs for rest and physical activity manifest themselves, and plan their schedules so that there is a balance between quiet work and physical activity appropriate to the maturity of their pupils. Such adjustments are not only important for health purposes, but they also can make a major contribution to the smoothness of lessons.

Many of the adjustments to meet physical needs are arrangements for which even primary boys and girls can take considerable responsibility if the problem is talked over with them. Committees or individual pupils can take responsibility for lights, for blinds, for closing doors if it is noisy. Each child can be made personally responsible for moving to a position where he can see or for turning his desk so that he does not face the light directly as he writes. However, they will tend to become engrossed in other activities and forget. It is your job to remind them.

See to it that books and supplies are easily accessible. Work is facilitated in a situation where books and supplies are easily accessible. The more independent your pupils can be in getting books, paper, and other equipment for themselves, the more smoothly work will proceed while you are occupied with small groups or individuals. As you plan how to use your cupboard and bookcase space, give some thought to the frequency with which books and materials will be used and to the numbers of children who may wish to get to them at once. If for example, you foresee groups of eight or ten children needing to get at sets of science or social studies materials, these might best be placed in a bookcase or on a table approachable from two directions rather than in a corner cupboard that might prove to be a cul-de-sac. On the other hand, the single adult dictionary that would be used only occasionally could well be in a less accessible spot.

When storage space is limited, many teachers have avoided confusion by putting children in charge of passing and collecting books, passing paper, handing out and collecting scissors and special equipment. Often a child is designated for each row or table. Sometimes a committee serves for a whole week. Sometimes a pupil is chosen as each new need arises. The latter system, however, does not give either you or your pupils as much freedom to proceed about your work without worrying about the problem of securing equipment as does either of the first two.

Experienced teachers have developed a number of ingenious ways for keeping books and supplies in order. A board with a hook for each pair of scissors allows you to check at a glance to be sure all have been returned. Cardboard file boxes make good paper containers. Small plastic trays are convenient holders for paper clips, thumbtacks, pins, and other small articles. Flat open boxes labeled *spelling, arithmetic, language,* can serve as receptacles for written work. Glass jars are useful for extra pencils. A little ingenuity on your part with paint or wallpaper and paste can make these utilitarian items an attractive addition to your room. It helps, also, if the pupil responsible for the particular equipment sees that everything is returned and in order before he leaves for the day.

Although it is important to make your pupils as independent as possible in getting the materials they need, it is just as important to reserve some storage space for yourself and to make this strictly off limits. A file in your room will help to meet this need, but you will also want cupboard space in which you can store special supplies and equipment, keep pupils' papers, and place other materials of your own, safe in the knowledge that they will not be disturbed. You are a member of the classroom, too, and you should give as careful thought to your own working conditions as you do to those of your pupils.

Plan for the functional use of space. The typical classroom today has much of the atmosphere of a workshop. Children work at movable desks or tables which are grouped in a variety of ways. Around the room are centers for special interests—a science table, a library corner, a display shelf, an easel, a circle of chairs for a reading group, perhaps a piano. You will have to plan so that your boys and girls will be able to move easily about the room and will have the space they need to pursue many types of activities.

Just how you organize your desks or tables will depend upon the size of your classroom, the number of pupils, and the type of curriculum design under which you are working. The most important characteristic of movable furniture is that it *is* movable. If you have a large class and are planning in the early fall to have a number of all-class activities which you will lead, it may be most convenient to have your pupils in orderly rows. Later, as they undertake more independent work you and they may develop more flexible seating arrangements. A little planning will make it possible for your youngsters to move their desks quickly and quietly in order to arrange circles for committee work or to clear a large working space for a mural or a stage. Set up your regular arrangement in terms of the type of activity in which your pupils will be most frequently engaged, and then adjust as new needs for the use of space arise.

The location of special activity centers also deserves some thought. This will be determined partially by the amount of space available in various parts of your room. However, where you do have a choice, consider carefully the nature of the special activity. In primary grades, for example, it is often an advantage to have the circle for reading activities near a blackboard. Normally, you would not place either your reading circle or your library table near a play corner or some other center where children would need to be talking in low voices. You should also give some thought to the line of traffic to the pencil sharpener, the paper cupboard, and other sources of frequently used supplies.

No matter what the need and how attractive the classroom arrangement that might result, your pupils should never, under any circumstances, be allowed to move furniture so that doorways are blocked. In case of fire, the safety of your group may depend upon how quickly you can evacuate your room. You would never want to risk panic because a youngster stumbles over a chair or because three or four find themselves blocked in a corner.

Bulletin board space needs to be thoughtfully apportioned also. It is often helpful to designate parts of your board for different aspects of your program—a writers' corner, a current events section, a display center for visual aids, a place for children's pictures or murals. It may be convenient to save part of the board near the door for current notices and announcements which might need to be referred to when pupils leave in the afternoon. If there is to be a board at which several pupils may be working at once to develop a special display, it would save confusion to choose one to which they have easy access. Save, for yourself, however, at least one portion of your bulletin board. You can bring much beauty to your classroom by posting attractive seasonal pictures, displaying an unusual piece of brocade, or featuring a fine reproduction of a masterpiece. Keep one spot in your room for such purposes.

Catalog supplementary teaching aids. Many a valuable picture is never used because it is buried at the bottom of a box in somebody's closet. It will be a rare occasion when you feel that you have all the teaching aids you need. You can, however, be certain that you have located everything available if you will take the time to catalog and file it systematically.[6]

An annotated card file is one practical device for maintaining an up-to-date record of the children's books which make special contributions

[6] The suggestions for filing described in this section are adapted from Margaret G. McKim, *Guiding Growth in Reading,* pp. 186-189. New York: The Macmillan Company, 1955. Permission to quote granted. The original suggestions for filing pictures and articles from which the system outlined here was developed are found in Mildred English and Florence B. Stratemeyer, "Selection and Organization of Materials of Instruction," *Materials of Instruction,* pp. 129-148. Eighth Yearbook of the Department of Supervisors and Directors of Instruction of the National Education Association. New York: Teachers College, Columbia University, 1935.

to particular topics. Some teachers list in such files only materials not at hand in the classroom. Others classify classroom books as well and even stories in basal reader series and chapters in supplementary reference books, so that they may locate quickly all the available references on a given topic. It is also possible to expand such a file to include annotations regarding films, filmstrips, and other visual or auditory aids. If notes relating to these are placed on cards of different colors, they can be readily identified.

If your file is to be efficient, you will need to develop a standard form for recording pertinent data about each type of teaching aid for which you are making annotations and to discipline yourself to follow this form consistently. Typically, such a file will be more useful if the entries are classified according to the topic or topics upon which they bear rather than filed alphabetically by title, or, in the case of books, by author. This topical classification should be placed in the upper left-hand corner of your card. The larger the number of cards within each topical classification, the more important it will be to arrange them systematically. Subtopics within the general category may be used for this or the cards under each topic may be filed alphabetically by title or by author. Whatever your preference, this information should be placed in the left-hand corner directly under the topical classification. Below would be entered the remaining bibliographical information so that the full reference is at hand if needed: author, title, publisher, date of publication, total number of pages, special pages or chapters bearing upon the particular topic. If you are entering information about a book located in the public library, record the library call number. If the book is available in the school, you may wish to work out a code to indicate its location—classroom library, school library, storage room, another classroom. Similar data regarding location may be important for films, film-strips, or records. Frequently a teaching aid will be useful for more than one topic. If so, the full bibliographical data can be listed once, and cross-reference cards placed under other appropriate topics.

The type of annotation made regarding the item you are entering in your file will depend upon its potential contribution to pupil growth. If you are listing fiction, valuable for recreational reading only, you will need a brief note regarding the particular appeal of the book to boys and girls. If it is a book or other teaching aid useful for informational purposes, indicate the nature of its special contribution. Often, in annotating informational reading matter, it is wise to appraise the educational possibilities in the illustrations. Your estimate of the reading difficulty of such material can be helpful when it comes to deciding which pupils should be encouraged to refer to it. If the file is for your use alone, you might devise abbreviations to save time in making such entries. Some teachers, however, write their annotations so that pupils, too, can turn to the file for assistance in locating special references. When this is the case, the comments are carefully phrased for younger readers.

Pictures, clippings, maps, pamphlets, and other such teaching aids in repeated use can easily be misplaced. If they are to be readily available, they need to be classified and filed in convenient containers—folders, envelopes, boxes. Both you and your pupils will be able to use these special teaching aids more freely if you work out a call-number code to be entered on each piece of material so that it can be re-filed easily. A system of call numbers will also obviate the problem of rearranging folders in a file drawer in order to maintain alphabetical order as new topics are added. The folder for each new topic can be placed at the end of your file, regardless of the letter of the alphabet with which the topic begins, and assigned the next available call number. A simple system which will allow you to use both topics and subtopics in your file is to assign numerals to major topics—animals, transportation, weather, and so on—and letters of the alphabet to subtopics. The topics you choose—both the major topics and the subtopics—need to be inclusive enough in scope to encompass a reasonable body of material, but sufficiently limited to assure that an unwieldy variety of items does not collect in any one folder. Exactly which topics you use will depend partly upon what you are teaching and partly upon your own preferences. A portion of a file of folders set up as just described might look as follows:

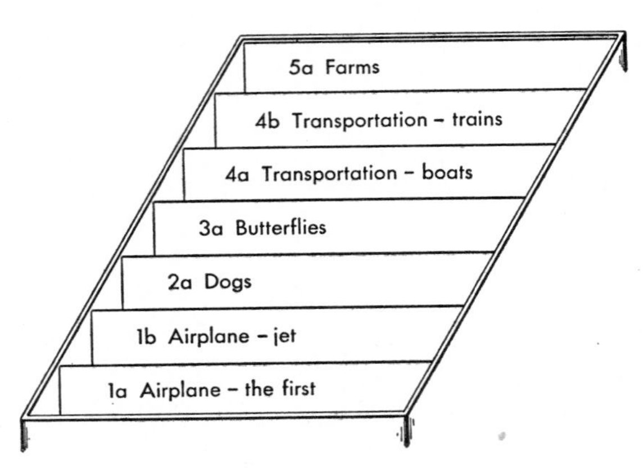

Since the folders are not in alphabetical order in the file itself, an alphabetized list of topics needs to be available for ready reference. Such a list can be posted near the file, or cards of a special color be added to an annotated card file such as the one discussed earlier. The alphabetical list for the portion of the file just illustrated would read as follows:

TOPIC	CODE NUMBER
Airplane	
The first	1a
Jet	1b
Animals	
Dogs	2a
Boats	4a
Butterflies	3a
Dogs	2a
Farms	5a
Trains	4b
Transportation	
Airplanes (see airplane)	
Boats	4a
Trains	4b

Pictures, clippings, and other items on single sheets of paper will become ragged with repeated use. So will paper-backed pamphlets. It is a wise policy to mount single items on heavy paper or on cardboard. Material that must be folded to be filed will wear less rapidly if it and its mounting are cut at the fold and hinged. Covers can be stapled on pamphlets. Older boys and girls can help with this and often can share with profit in the task of classifying materials and entering call numbers. If you take pains with your filing and classification, your boys and girls, as well as yourself, will be able to make extensive use of your materials file with little loss or destruction of its contents.

Make your room an attractive place in which to live. In any classroom in which people are busy, a certain amount of confusion will reign. This, however, should not discourage you from maintaining an attractive environment or from helping your boys and girls to achieve standards of neatness and orderliness conducive to effective work.

Give some thought to the little things that make a classroom colorful—borders and attractive captions for bulletin boards, children's work attractively displayed, flowers or unusual paperweights on your desk, a bright runner on your library table, colorful labels indicating where materials are to be stored, neat printing and a bit of decoration on helpers' charts or other class records. The list is endless and even the drabbest room can come to life if you and your boys and girls put your minds to it.

"Variety," says the old adage, "is the spice of life." A classroom that was bright and gay in the fall loses its glamour if the same borders remain on bulletin boards, pictures once put up are never taken down, and special signs and notices remain posted long after they have served their purposes. Learn to make changes in your room. Put a new bit of beauty on your special bulletin board. Change the style of your birthday chart once a month. Develop seasonal borders for your bulletin boards. Change the decorations on your writers' corner bulletin board from oak leaves to snowflakes as winter comes along.

Many of your problems of maintaining an interesting and attractive room will be solved if you make appropriate use of materials contributing to the development of your regular program. Children's pictures can be posted. Bulletin boards can be developed to show customs or scenery in other lands. Creative writing can be displayed. A trip to the park can lead to some mobiles made from autumn leaves, branches, berries, and nuts, to hang from wires strung across the room. In a classroom where there is an interesting and challenging program, there is little excuse for empty walls and dull bulletin boards.

In part, the attractiveness of a room comes from its neatness and cleanliness. Things will not be orderly and spotless at all times, of course, but it is important to help your pupils learn to be good housekeepers. Your own desk, at least, should be in reasonable order, and pupils' desks and lockers should be tidied at regular intervals. The plants in your room should be well cared for. If you have established committees responsible for books, paper, the library table, the shades, and the blackboards, it will not take long to have things in order at noon and again when it is time to leave.

One of the situations your boys and girls will face over and over again in life is that of maintaining attractive and orderly living and working quarters. The experiences you provide for them in school will be reflected in their behavior at home and eventually in offices where they will work and in homes of their own. Do not count it a waste of time to teach them to find pleasure in a neat and attractive room.

ENDING THE SCHOOL YEAR

Because school years and college semesters rarely coincide, first-year teachers who amass during their student-teaching experience considerable information about how school begins sometimes have very little idea of what must be done to wind things up in June. Yet this part of the year, too, poses problems of classroom administration. There will be a variety of final reports due (upon the completion of which the receipt of your final salary check may depend). Your books and equipment will have to be stored for the summer. And, in the midst of hot weather and impending vacations, you will be responsible for maintaining a satisfying program for your boys and girls.

Start early to complete needed reports. It is a helpful step to ascertain early what final reports will be due and to schedule your time so that you can complete these without a last-minute rush. In many school systems, teachers are given help on this. Requests for final reports of various sorts may start to arrive early in the spring, and deadlines may be staggered so that everything does not pile up in June. Be sure you inquire, however, if no such plan seems to be in operation in your building.

Certainly, there will be final reports to make on pupil progress. You will have a last set of report cards to complete and cumulative records to bring up to date. In some schools there will also be forms to file summarizing specific aspects of the program—lists of the books used by each pupil in the instructional reading program, final progress sheets in arithmetic. If such special reports are required, you will undoubtedly have had them at hand from early in the year and should be able to complete them well ahead of the last-minute rush.

You will probably be asked to complete some special reports regarding supplies and equipment. You may be the one to requisition your own supplies for the coming year. In some school systems you will also be allotted a specified sum which you may use to order supplementary books for your classroom collection. The chances are that you will be asked to file an inventory of the books and, perhaps, of the equipment in your room. Texts in the possession of pupils will have to be recalled and action taken with regard to fines or assessments if books have been damaged, lost, or destroyed. You may also be responsible for filing a list of needed repairs that should be taken care of over the summer. If you are thinking about such responsibilities ahead of time, it is far easier to prepare them when the request arrives.

All the warnings previously issued regarding promptness and accuracy in submitting reports pertain to those required at the end of the year. You may not be easy to locate over the summer. Do not leave the person responsible for administrative decisions wondering what one of your cryptic notes means or force him to spend long extra hours redoing a requisition because you did not enter prices or catalog numbers correctly. Whether or not it is required, it is a wise procedure to keep a duplicate of your inventory and of any requests for repairs or orders of supplies. It is often easier to check in the fall if your own list is at hand than it is to try to locate the copy you filed with your principal.

Store equipment and supplies carefully. The steps you take to store your equipment and supplies will depend upon the policy of your school system. In some situations all texts are returned to a central book room and surplus supplies to the school supply room. In others, sets of supplementary books are returned but the standard texts with which the classroom is equipped are stored in the room—in cupboards, bookshelves, and sometimes in pupils' desks—as are surplus stationery and special equipment such as scissors, rulers, pens. Whatever the system, it will be important to make sure that equipment is carefully protected from dust and neatly stored.

It is particularly important that you make sure that all borrowed materials are returned to their proper source. Gather in your last set of library books. Inquire whether sets of texts supplied to you by your supervisor from a central collection are to be returned or whether they are to remain in your room. If you have been sharing dictionaries or encyclopedias with another class discover where these materials are to be stored during the summer and make sure that your copies are returned. Inquire, also, about the disposition of maps, globes, or other visual aids which you have secured from a central source. Above all, make doubly sure that books, pictures, pamphlets, and other materials that are the personal possessions of your colleagues are returned to them.

Plan carefully for pupils' closing activities. Policy with regard to your classroom program for the last days of school will differ from situation to situation. In some schools, teachers are expected to maintain a regular program to the end of the year and then to return for a day or so to store books and complete the business of closing the classroom for the summer. In other situations, the process of checking in textbooks, making inventories, and storing materials is begun while school is still in session and the teacher is expected to plan for activities that will be educationally profitable without requiring the use of all classroom resources.

Even though it is the policy in your school to maintain a regular program to the end of the year, you will be wise to plan so that the culminating activities of an elaborate unit come a week or more before the closing day. It is a major job to dismantle exhibits and bulletin boards, return library books, evaluate notebooks, decide how to dispose of dioramas and other creative work. Last-minute chores in closing the room will be greatly facilitated if work dear to the children has been taken safely home, pictures you want to save are filed, and the only items remaining on your bulletin boards are decorations that can be dropped into the wastebasket.

There are a number of short-term activities which will be profitable learning experiences without adding major clean-up problems to the regular housekeeping chores of finishing the year. You may wish to engage in some summarizing activities to appraise pupil competence in fundamental skills. Final review tests could be given in areas such as reading and spelling or, to make the closing of the year more exciting, spell-downs and arithmetic games might be planned. There are possibilities in the area of creative expression. Reading groups may prepare little programs to share their favorite stories. Plans may be laid for one final party for which youngsters can prepare a variety of stories, poems, dramatizations. Children may decorate the bulletin board with pictures of summer scenes or write stories and poems about summer fun. There can be some profitable short units looking toward summer activities—a unit on safety at play, recreational reading activities focused on summer use of the library, a survey of summer recreation possibilities. It is also possible to involve your pupils in preparing collections of their work to be taken home. If you have been collecting samples of creative writing, of art work, of handwriting, for appraisal purposes you may select one or two for the cumulative record and let the youngsters staple the others into a booklet with an attractive cover. Thus desks are cleared and a final appraisal of work is made in the same process.

You will want to inquire particularly about school policies for the final day. It may be the tradition to have a last class party at this time or to plan for a special all-school assembly to wind up the year. Oftentimes such special events can be a pleasant and profitable focus for your activities for the last few days.

Ascertain, also, what the policy is on giving out report cards. In some schools pupils go to their new teachers for part of the last morning. If this is the plan, you must be prepared with some get-acquainted activities for the boys and girls who come to you. Whether or not pupils go to their new rooms, you may have to be prepared to offer comfort to the one or two who must face the prospect of spending a second year in the same grade. Even though decisions regarding nonpromotion will almost certainly have been talked through with a child's parents, you will need to discover whose responsibility it is to talk with the child and when this should be done.

Just as you plan carefully in September so that positive attitudes toward school are built from the first, so you plan carefully in May or June to make sure that these same positive attitudes continue to the end. You will want to make the closing of the year as interesting and challenging as the beginning.

BOOKS YOU SHOULD KNOW

Chamberlain, Leo M., and Kindred, Leslie W. *The Teacher and School Organization*. Third Edition. Englewood Cliffs, N.J.: Prentice-Hall, 1958. Pp. xxii + 550.

Equipment and Supplies. General Service Bulletin No. 39. Washington, D.C.: Association for Childhood Education International, 1957. Pp. 92.

Organizing the Elementary School for Living and Learning. 1947 Yearbook of the Association for Supervision and Curriculum Development, N.E.A. Washington, D.C.: The Association, 1947. Pp. 211.

Otto, Henry J. *Elementary-School Organization and Administration*. Third Edition. New York: Appleton-Century-Crofts, 1954. Pp. xvii + 719.

Space, Arrangement, Beauty in School. Bulletin No. 102. Washington, D.C.: Association for Childhood Education International, 1958. Pp. 52.

Staff Relations in School Administration. Thirty-third Yearbook of the American Association of School Administrators, National Education Association Washington, D.C.: The Association, 1955. Pp. 242.

Yauch, Wilbur A. *Helping Teachers Understand Principals*. New York: Appleton-Century-Crofts, 1957. Pp. xii + 98.

Growing As a Teacher

PART IV

Finding the Right Teaching Position

CHAPTER 13

After four years in college preparing to be a teacher, your most important concern, except, of course, that of obtaining your degree, will be to find the teaching position in which you can be happy and successful. Securing the right teaching position is not ordinarily a matter of chance or good luck. Once you begin to consider this important step seriously you will find the task more complicated than you had thought it to be. One does not go blithely to a superintendent of schools and ask for a job. There are professional channels to be followed and ground rules to be observed.

In some colleges, there is a definite program designed to inform prospective teachers concerning professional opportunities. If this has been the case in your institution, careful guidance and pertinent information will have been given to you from the time you first entered the teacher-education program. As a freshman you may have been told, for example, about trends in job opportunities—that positions were more likely to be available in some teaching areas than in others. At that time, or perhaps later, you may have been advised that your background of experience and your personal characteristics might better suit you for success in one teaching field than in another. Undoubtedly, your cooperating teacher, your college supervisor, and perhaps the principal in the school in which you do your student teaching will also counsel with you regarding the type of position for which you seem best fitted. All this is evidence that those who have worked closely with you in your preparation for teaching are interested in your future success in the teaching profession.

During the time that you are engaged in student teaching you will undoubtedly begin to work actively toward securing the type of position in which your own self-appraisal and the advice of others have led you to believe you will be successful. In many colleges, those who are responsible for teacher placement will be ready to help you at this point. This is not to say that you cannot secure a teaching position entirely by your own efforts. It has been done. You will, however, by working with the placement director and your faculty advisor, stand a better chance of securing the kind of position in which you can be successful and happy.

This chapter contains specific suggestions regarding how to go about securing the position you want—how to make effective use of your college placement services; how to make application to superintendents of schools and how to decide whether the positions they have available are right for you; and what professional amenities to observe in making applications and signing contracts.

MAKING EFFECTIVE USE OF YOUR COLLEGE PLACEMENT FACILITIES

In most colleges, the persons who work most actively in helping students to secure teaching positions are those charged with the responsibility for teacher placement. The exact name of the office will vary from college to college. The more common titles are *Bureau of Placement, Bureau of Recommendations, or Office of Teacher Placement.* The title of the office is really not important to you. What is important is the kind of services, information, and advice available through the persons in the office. Ordinarily the director of the placement office maintains close relationships with school officials within the college area and knows something about teaching opportunities at a greater distance. Usually he will have a definite procedure for bringing together personal information, college records, and written statements regarding your performance as a college student, as a student teacher, and as a person. He will also be able to advise you about certification, not only in your own state but in other states as well. During your senior year, and especially in your final quarter or semester, he or his assistants will be at your service to answer your questions and to advise you regarding what steps to take in securing a teaching position. You should not be hesitant about asking questions or seeking advice. It is not only to your best interest, but also to the best interest of the college that you be placed in the position most likely to guarantee that you will become a successful teacher.

Find out about teaching opportunities. One of your first steps will probably be to consult with someone in your college placement office about the teaching positions available. Regardless of all the publicity about the shortage of teachers, there are some localities in which there is actually an oversupply at some grade levels or in some subject areas or special fields. Fortunately, as a person preparing to be a teacher in the elementary school, this is less likely to be the case for you than for some of your friends whose teaching interests are at other levels. It appears that there will be a need for you in almost any part of the country for the next several years.

Because of the shortage of teachers at the elementary level, your placement director will probably know of many available positions. He will have direct acquaintance with the needs of local school officials. Numerous inquiries will also have come to his office from school districts in neighboring parts of the state and from superintendents at a greater distance. In the course of a placement season he will receive notices of vacancies from the far corners of the United States and sometimes from overseas. He will also know when representatives of school systems plan to visit your campus for the purpose of interviewing prospective teachers. The methods by which this information is made available will vary. Sometimes notices of vacancies are posted on a bulletin board for general inspection. Sometimes you will be informed personally if the vacancy seems particularly suited to your preparation and personal characteristics. This, of course, is one reason why you should register with the placement office and talk to the placement director rather early in your last semester.

Although the teacher placement office is likely to be the best source of information about teaching vacancies, there are other possibilities about which you should know. Among these are your own acquaintance with school officials in your home community and leads given by friends or relatives. Such sources of information are, of course, legitimate, but you should be careful in exploiting them. Usually it is best to consult your placement director before you proceed very far in applying for a teaching position located through such sources. Oftentimes, he will have information about these situations which you do not possess. He may, for example, know of conditions within the school system which would make it inadvisable for you to make application. He may also know enough about the specific position to be dubious regarding its suitability for you. In any event, he will have some worthwhile suggestions regarding steps to take in making application which will be helpful if you are genuinely interested in the vacancy.

Prepare credentials carefully. When you talk to a school official, he will ask about your *credentials.* This may be a new term to you. It refers to a copy of the registration forms you complete for your placement office together with copies of the statements secured from the persons you have listed as references. Placement officers routinely ask graduating students to prepare sets of registration papers—usually in quadruplicate. These forms will ask for such information as your present as well as your permanent address and telephone number. You will also be asked for certain personal data—age, height, weight, marital status, educational background, and work experience. In addition, there will be professional data requested. You will be asked to indicate the kind of certificate you now have or will have after graduation. Other kinds of professional information may include the kind of teaching position you would like to obtain and the grade level or special subjects or areas in which you feel best qualified. You may also be required to indicate special abilities or activities in which you have participated. Do not neglect these. Sometimes they mean the difference between obtaining a position before graduation and waiting until later in the summer. Some registration forms also provide space for the listing of courses, credits, and grades. If you are not asked for this information, you will certainly be required to submit copies of your college transcript.

By this time, and certainly by the time you have completed the registration forms, you will be asking "Why all this bother?" The answer to this question is simple. All the bother enables the placement director to have at hand several copies of your credentials for his own use and for the use of prospective employers. In these days of rapid communication, the telephone is used more and more frequently in teacher placement. Often a superintendent will describe the teaching position over the phone and ask for a certain kind of teacher. If the placement director does not know you well he will study your credentials and perhaps read them to the superintendent. If the school superintendent comes to the campus he will usually have studied your credentials before he interviews you. On the other hand, if you are being interviewed at the office of the superintendent, your credentials will often have preceded you. Whatever the specific practice, your credentials will certainly be studied by your prospective employer before you are offered a contract.

You can now understand why credentials or, as they are sometimes called, "confidential folders" are so important. Incidentally, the term "confidential folder" is perhaps even more appropriate than "credentials." Your credentials are confidential and are never submitted to or inspected by anyone other than persons interested in you as a prospective teacher. Since the registration forms that you have filled in as part of your credentials often provide your employer's first impression of you, you must be very careful in completing these forms. Be sure that the information is accurate and complete. If a statement regarding your reasons for wanting to teach is requested, write it thoughtfully. Do not make a poor impression by careless writing or sloppy typing.

Use care in listing persons who know about you and your work. Registration forms typically contain a section in which you must list names of persons who can write a statement about you. These statements are an important part of your credentials. You should do some careful thinking about the individuals you list. It is usually best to give the names of persons who have knowledge of you in different kinds of situations. You will certainly give as references your faculty advisor, your cooperating teacher, and perhaps the principal of the school in which you were placed for student teaching. You will also want to list one or more professors who know your competence in academic fields. Sometimes, too, you may want to give names of persons for whom you have worked and perhaps the names of your physician and your minister, priest, or rabbi.

Persons named by you and from whom your placement office secures statements are known as *references*. It is courteous to request permission from these persons before you list their names on the registration form. Requesting permission serves a double purpose; it establishes your reputation as a considerate, courteous individual and at the same time it identifies you in the mind of the reference. It may surprise you, but some people cannot associate names with individuals. They may have forgotten who you are or they may remember you vaguely as "the quiet little girl in the front seat."

Ordinarily the placement office will send the reference form direct to the person you have named as a reference, but sometimes you may be asked to deliver the form yourself. In any case, do not expect to see what has been written about you. The statement is a highly confidential and professional document; it tells such points about you as scholarship, adaptability, judgment, leadership, personal appearance, health and vitality, social qualities, loyalty, attitude toward work, and probable teaching success. Your references would not write frankly were they not sure that their statements would be treated as confidential.

Although you will never see the statements written about you, it may help you in deciding which persons to give as references to read some that have been written about other student teachers.[1] Here are some samples: one set—those of Ellen Wilson—concerning an excellent prospect; and the other—those of Ronald Hill—concerning a person about whom the faculty supervisor and the cooperating teacher both have some reservations. Read what her faculty supervisor has to say regarding Ellen Wilson:

Ellen Wilson was under my supervision for her student teaching. She is a very able young woman intellectually, an excellent teacher, and a joy to supervise. I believe she will develop into an outstanding member of the profession.

For student teaching Miss Wilson was placed with an able fifth grade. There were enough pupils with learning difficulties and with problems of behavior, however, to test out her teaching skill. Miss Wilson took over complete responsibility for her pupils from approximately mid-October until the end of her student-teaching assignment in January. In addition to unit activities in social studies, she did considerable work with creative writing and choral speaking. She developed much group interest in recreational reading. She plans meticulously, and she has both the intellectual ability to challenge able children and the ingenuity to make work interesting to those who are slower.

Miss Wilson has a long history of work with children as a camp counselor and as a recreation leader. She plays the piano and is interested in the arts. I would have no hesitation in placing Miss Wilson in any type of teaching situation, although she perhaps has an unusual contribution to make to able children.

Ellen's cooperating teacher likewise writes of her performance in somewhat different phrasing:

Miss Wilson has been a student teacher of unusual ability. She has been very faithful, adaptable, and eager to profit from constructive criticism. Her appearance and manner reflect appropriateness and warmth of personality. Her classroom attitude is notable for its wholesomeness. She has sympathy for children and an understanding of their problems and stages of development unusual in a student. She is able to plan and direct children with their best interests in mind. She should be an asset to any school system.

Now read the statements for Ronald Hill who has had some difficulties in adjusting to teaching. His faculty advisor says:

For his student teaching, Mr. Hill was placed with a fifth grade in which there was a wide range of abilities. He was responsible for two social studies

[1] Names and other identifying details in these statements have been changed.

units, and developed a class paper and a rather elaborate plan to encourage a recreational reading program. Mr. Hill tended to be somewhat "academic" in his teaching and at first allowed for very little pupil-teacher planning in his procedures. Over the semester, however, he made considerable growth in his ability to involve pupils in planning and to work through problems of interpersonal relationships with them.

Mr. Hill's contribution to his pupils will probably come through the thoroughness with which he covers the topics suggested in the course of study and the standards of behavior he will hold for pupils. He is not likely to be exceptionally ingenious in the variety of activities he will provide.

His cooperating teacher reports some different aspects of Ronald's work.

Mr. Hill is a mild-mannered person with a soft, quiet approach to his class. He seldom raises his voice to reprove a child and yet he is able to maintain order and respect. He is willing and ready to cooperate with his supervisors and to ask how he might improve his techniques and procedures. He might develop more imagination and creative ability but even lacking those qualities to some degree would not be a deterrent to a successful teaching career.

At all times he has been neat in appearance, well groomed and tastefully dressed. His ready smile encourages children to confide in him and love him. He does need some correction in pronunciation of words for he still carries a dialect which creeps out occasionally, but this can be corrected easily. Mr. Hill appears to be fairly well read and has a good background of academic work which helps him to illustrate his work. He has wide traveling experience by virtue of his years in the military service.

His classroom leadership is sound; a bit guarded, perhaps because he is not a person who plunges into a project without taking time to consider and to examine the consequences carefully. This shows up in his teaching for he waits thoughtfully before he attempts a new piece of work. I do think that Mr. Hill will make a good teacher for he does have patience, kindness, and an even temper. He is, above all, industrious and reliable.

You can see from these statements just how thorough a written evaluation of your work is likely to be if you give as references persons who have worked closely with you in a variety of capacities. You may perhaps be saying, "Yes, but the better they know me, the more of my weaknesses they will know." Frank statements thoughtfully prepared, such as those for Ronald Hill, can be most helpful, however, to an employing officer. Ronald stands a much better chance of being placed in a position suited to him with these comments on file than he would had there been vague and mildly flattering statements telling nothing. Not all evaluations, of course, are written as carefully as those you just read. However, a series of statements written by persons who know you well and in different situations does serve to give the placement director and the employing officer a rather good picture of what you can do and the type of position in which you should be placed.

Submit a good photograph. Nowadays you are not likely to obtain a teaching position without a personal interview with the employing school official. Even so, there will probably need to be a photograph submitted with each set of credentials. Your placement officer will tell you how many prints you should file. The photograph requested by your placement bureau will probably be approximately 2 × 3 inches in size. To avoid delay in registering with the placement bureau, you ought to secure these some months in advance of the time when you will be actively seeking a teaching position. When you submit your photograph, write your name and the date it was taken on the back of each print. A nameless photograph usually—and sometimes quickly—finds its way into the wastebasket.

Your photograph should be appropriate and in good taste. Furthermore, you should look like yourself. Snapshots are ordinarily not acceptable. If you have a photograph that is not of the proper size, your placement bureau can probably supply you with the name of a photographer who specializes in making reproductions. The cost of these is nominal—usually not more than two or three dollars per dozen. Here again, however, it is better to have a new photograph taken than it is to use one which is inappropriate. A few dollars well spent may pay large dividends. Oftentimes obscure and intangible impressions make the difference between getting the position you want and having to accept one not quite as desirable.

Ascertain when a commercial teachers' agency can help you. In these days when positions for elementary school teachers are relatively plentiful, your own college placement bureau will, under ordinary circumstances, provide all the help you will need in securing the teaching position you want. There are, however, certain instances where you may require additional assistance. One of these might be when you are looking for a teaching position which is outside of the usual placement territory of your own college bureau. In such cases it might be helpful to avail yourself of the services of a commercial teachers' agency. This is a private business which serves somewhat the same purpose as your own college placement bureau, but which charges a fee for its services. The fee is usually a percentage of your first year's salary in the teaching position obtained.

Commercial teachers' agencies have different names and different titles, but their purpose is always the same—to secure a teaching position for you for which a fee is charged. If you decide to use the services of one of these firms, you would do well to inquire about its status. Be sure, also, that you are aware of the conditions of the contract you will have to sign. Read it carefully and be sure you understand it. You will be wise to talk to your placement director before you register with a commercial teachers' agency. He will know the names and addresses of responsible firms and will be able to give you sound advice regarding the circumstances under which you should use them.

Apply for the proper teaching certificate. One of your most important responsibilities if you plan to teach in the public schools is to make application for your teaching certificate. In some teacher-education institutions you may be furnished with the proper certificate without application, but more often you will have to secure the appropriate forms, complete them as directed, and return them to the college certifying officer. Some time before graduation, information will probably be sent to you regarding exactly what procedure to follow. Do not neglect this advice or fail to inquire if you do not receive official notice. Some beginning teachers have been delinquent in this, only to discover later that their first month's pay check is being held up pending evidence that they possess a valid certificate.

As you pursue the teacher-education program in your college the chances are that you will be meeting the requirements for the appropriate teaching certificate concurrently with preparing for your degree. A college degree, however, does not *necessarily* mean that you will have met certification requirements. You, yourself, should make certain that you will not be caught short when you are ready to apply for a teaching position. Study the college bulletin carefully. Both degree and certification requirements may be outlined there. If not, there may be supplementary information, mimeographed or printed, which will tell you what you want to know. If you still cannot find the right answers, ask your advisor or the certifying officer designated by the college authorities.

In most states, certification for teaching is a prerogative of the state department of education. Your college probably follows the requirements set forth in the directives of this department. There may, however, be some variation. Although the state sets minimum standards, the college has the authority to exceed these standards. In some states, too, a college which has been approved as a teacher-education institution has been delegated the authority to recommend its graduates for certification. If so, you, as a graduate, cannot secure a certificate without the recommendation of the college authorities. This is often the reason why you must apply for a certificate through the certifying officer of the college.

You have, no doubt, already learned that each state has slightly different requirements for certification. If you plan to teach in a state other than the one in which your college is situated, you will be wise to inquire long before your last semester of work about its certification requirements. There may be, for example, such state requirements as knowledge of the state constitution, a course in state history, a special course in education, or a background of specific academic courses. Meeting these requirements is, of course, your responsibility. Your college officials can, however, advise and help you.

IDENTIFYING AND APPLYING FOR THE TEACHING POSITION IN WHICH YOU CAN BE SUCCESSFUL

Registering with your placement office is only a first step in securing a teaching position. You still have ahead of you the exciting (and sometimes tedious) process of identifying positions which are right for you, filing applications for them, and being interviewed. In this process your college authorities can be of major help. They know you; they also know superintendents and school systems. Professional placement officers do not see their responsibility as securing just any position for an applicant. They want you to be located in a situation where you can make a truly professional contribution to the education of boys and girls.

Decide for yourself what type of position will be right for you. As you approach the time when you are actively to enter the teaching profession, you will be the recipient of much gratuitous and unsolicited advice concerning the kind of position you should accept. There will be some, for example, who will tell you that there is more status in teaching in a large city. Others will say that there is less status if you work with slow-learning or underprivileged boys and girls. Listen to such kinds of advice politely, but then make up your own mind. You are the person (with the professional advice of your college supervisor and your placement director) best equipped to decide what position will be best for you.

By the time you have completed your teacher-education program, you should have had wide experience with children of varying ages, intellectual levels, and socioeconomic backgrounds. You also should have had occasion to observe the ways in which schools are organized and how teachers and administrators work together for the benefit of boys and girls. You may have had some opportunity to work in a city school, a suburban school, and a school in a rural area. All such experiences will help you to reach some general decisions regarding the type of community and school in which you are interested.

To proceed intelligently in locating a teaching position in which you will be successful, you should be working from more than a general impression of the type of situation you prefer. You should have done some careful evaluation of your own strengths and weaknesses. Persons who will make an outstanding contribution in one situation will not always be equally successful in another. If you have some skill in working with underprivileged children, you should consider carefully a position where you will have an opportunity to help them. If, on the other hand, you are somewhat short of patience with children who do not handle verbal materials easily, you should look for a position where you can work with pupils more able academically. Likewise, you may have found that you are happier in a small community than in a large city. If this is so, perhaps you ought to seek a position in a suburban school or one in a rural or semirural area. There will be many other such factors to consider. It is not a sign of incompetence on your part to indicate frankly to your placement officer or to an employing official the types of situations in which you feel least comfortable. Nor is it a sign of egotism to be equally frank regarding the circumstances under which you feel that you can do your best work. Employing officials are just as anxious as you are to see that you secure a position in which you will be successful.

Write business-like letters of inquiry or of application if these are necessary. When you have clarified your own thinking regarding the type of position you want and its location, you are ready to consult with your placement director regarding specific openings in your chosen location and how to go about applying for them. If the position is near your college, it is often appropriate to make a telephone call or perhaps to have the placement director make it for you. If the superintendent is interested in your qualifications, arrangements for an interview may be set up then and there.

Most placement officers have access to a national directory of school systems and superintendents. If the director of your placement bureau has no information about the school system in which you are interested, he will know the person to contact to secure the information you want. He may write a letter for you, but he is quite likely to suggest that you, yourself, write a *letter of inquiry* to the superintendent. This letter should state that you are interested in a position at your selected grade level, but it should also indicate that you are qualified to teach at certain grade levels. It is usually best to enclose a self-addressed stamped envelope. An example of a letter of inquiry is given here, but you would, of course, make necessary modifications to fit your own background of experience and training.

1200 Maine Street
Colerain, Ohio
May 2, 1959

Mr. J.M. Smart
Superintendent of Schools
American City, Pennsylvania

Dear Mr. Smart:

I shall graduate in June from Colerain College with the degree of Bachelor of Science in Education with special preparation for the kindergarten and primary grades. I am also qualified to teach any one of the intermediate grades, although I prefer the first grade.

Because I expect to live in American City next year I am interested in securing a teaching position in your school system. If you have a teaching vacancy in one of the grades for which I am qualified, I shall appreciate your consideration. My credentials are available at the Placement Bureau of Colerain College. I can arrange an interview at your convenience. A Friday or a Saturday, however, would pose a somewhat easier travel problem for me.

Sincerely yours,

(Miss) Mary Smith

On the other hand, let us suppose that you or the placement director know positively that there is vacant the kind of position you want. Your course of action is then to write a *letter of application*. Again you would modify the sample letter below to suit your situation.

1200 Maine Street
Colerain, Ohio
May 2, 1959

Mr. J.M. Smart
Superintendent of Schools
American City, Pennsylvania

Dear Mr. Smart:

Dr. Frank Jones, Director of the Placement Bureau at Colerain College, has told me that you have a teaching vacancy in one of your first grades. I shall graduate from Colerain College in June with a Bachelor of Science degree in Education. I have a major in kindergarten and primary education, but I prefer to teach first grade. I am definitely interested in your first-grade position because I expect to live in American City next year.

My credentials are on file at the Placement Bureau at Colerain College. Dr. Jones will be glad to send them at your request. If you are interested in my qualifications, I should like an application form so that I may complete it and return it to your office. I can arrange for an interview at your convenience. A Friday or a Saturday, however, would present a somewhat easier travel problem for me.

Sincerely yours,

(Miss) Mary Smith

The form of your letter of inquiry or of application is often just as important as its contents. It should meet the standards of any good business letter. It should be written neatly without erasures or ink blots. Good quality paper must be used—preferably white business paper and envelope. It is better to have the letter expertly typed; but if you must write in longhand, write legibly, using blue or black ink. Limit your letter to one page if possible; if not, write on only one side of the paper. Your phrasing should be clear, concise, and direct. Be sure that the spelling and punctuation are correct. Proofread the letter or have someone else do it for you. Above all, don't forget to sign your name. This will be the first impression of you secured by your prospective employer. Do not allow carelessness on your part to make it negative.

Complete application blanks carefully and in detail. Even though you write a letter of application and have your credentials forwarded, most school systems will require you to complete an application form that has been developed specifically for the use of the employing officer in that system. These forms vary in size and content from one school system to another. In some large city systems there may be a four-page folder with sections for personal history, educational history, position for which application is being made, teaching experience, nonteaching experience, military service record, professional references, character references, certificates held, physical condition, and extracurricular activities. Most application forms, however, are not so comprehensive. They will more often consist of a single page with sections for personal history, educational history, and references.

When you complete an application form, you should be as careful as you are when you write a letter of inquiry or of application or fill in your registration blanks for your placement office. Write neatly or use a typewriter, check spelling, and above all read the application carefully and answer the questions honestly. If the form requires the submission of a photograph, be sure to attach it securely. Cellophane tape or a staple will serve the purpose. Do not use glue or a paper clip. A photograph separated from the application form is useless.

Some school systems may require supplementary information and documents with your application. One of the documents which you are likely to be asked to supply is an official college transcript. Employing officers want to know what grades you have attained and the pattern of courses which you have taken. Of course, if you are applying for a position before your last semester or quarter has ended, your transcript will be incomplete, but this is not a serious matter. The official will be able to judge your work from the record available.

Another document which may be required is a birth certificate. Retirement may seem in the far distant future, but you will join a retirement scheme when you accept employment, and proof of your age is likely to be needed. Different states have different offices for the registry of births and you will have to ascertain where to apply. Even if you are not required to submit a birth certificate in order to obtain employment, there is certain to be a time in your life when you will need one. You should know how to go about securing it.

The third document which you will need is the appropriate teaching certificate. You are not, however, eligible for this until you have completed your program of teacher education. It is probable, therefore, that you will have to attach a statement to your application to the effect that you do not yet possess the appropriate certificate but that upon graduation you will be eligible for it. The exact name of the certificate is important. Find out from your placement director or college advisor what the correct title of your certificate will be.

If you have been in the military service, the employing official will want to examine your discharge papers or your certificate of service.

In many school systems you will be given credit on the salary schedule for military service and your papers will be used to substantiate what your length of service has been. Although your military papers will usually be returned to you, it is wise to supply photostatic copies rather than the original documents.

Completing the necessary application blanks and supplying the required papers may seem to you to be a lot of trouble, but remember that a decision regarding whether or not to call you for an interview is likely to be made on the basis of your application. Remember, too, that offers of positions as well as appointments for interviews are sometimes delayed if the necessary papers have not been received. You cannot be too careful if you really want a teaching position in the school system where you are applying.

Respond thoughtfully in your interview with an employing official. It is unusual for a school superintendent or employing official to offer an individual a teaching position without a personal interview. From your own point of view, it is unwise to accept a position before you have visited a school and community and have had an opportunity to ask questions. For your prospective employer, the interview serves as a means of judging your personal appearance, voice, interest, and adaptability and of securing your reaction to possible teaching assignments, local conditions, and school regulations. An interview, however, is not a one-sided affair conducted only for the benefit of the employing official. It enables you to gain information about the demands of the position for which you are applying, the community, living conditions, salary, opportunities for advancement, and local teaching regulations. You will not, of course, appear at a board of education office and expect to be interviewed without an appointment. Make your appointment ahead of time and then be sure to be *on time,* or preferably a few minutes early.

Naturally you will want to appear at your best at the interview. The initial impression you make on your prospective employer is conditioned by many factors. Among the most important are your attitude, your apparent interest, your use of the English language, your posture and carriage, and the appropriateness of your dress and grooming. Some of these are factors well within your control but others are not. A false front, assumed merely to impress, can be identified rather easily. The employing officer will be attempting to discover what kind of person you really are and how well you will fit into his school system. If he is going to decide that you are not the person suited for the vacancy he has in mind, it is far better that he do so in the interview rather than discover it after you have been on the job for three months.

Some specific hints as to how you may make a good impression will not be amiss. Probably of most importance is good grooming and appropriate dress. One would not, of course, dress as if attending a formal college function, nor, on the other hand, should the informal dress sometimes seen on college campuses be worn. Young men in sport shirts and unpressed trousers and young women in slacks have been known to appear for interviews with consequent disastrous results to their job aspirations and repercussions in the college placement office. It does one no harm to prepare for the interview by having one's hair neatly combed, or in the case of a young woman to use lipstick and make-up in appropriate moderation.

Your poise, the ease with which you converse with a stranger, and your general manner contribute to a good impression. It is not unusual to be nervous and ill at ease prior to the opening of an interview. Remember, however, that most employing officials will try to conduct the interview in a friendly, informal manner. You, too, can be friendly and informal as long as you are serious when the discussion demands it. You will create the best impression if you are as natural and as frank as possible. In general, the employing officer will be the one to direct the course of the interview. Allow him to speak as freely as he desires without interrupting unnecessarily. At the same time, be prepared to pick up the conversation rather than have an embarrassing pause occur. You will probably have questions to ask about the school or community and points you would like to make about your own qualifications or interests. Do not hesitate to insert these as the occasion permits. Be a good listener, too. Watch for indications that the interviewer wants to bring the interview to a close. If you are sensitive to the general atmosphere of the interview situation, you will not attempt to carry the interview beyond that point.

What should you be prepared to talk about? There is no way of telling, for sure. Employing officers have many ways of getting to know people. Frequently they are as much interested in your frankness, your sincerity, and your poise as they are in the exact answers to their questions. In general you should be prepared to discuss such professional topics as your educational philosophy and perhaps some recent books on education, especially those in your own teaching field. You could be asked about some of the topics of the day, such as television programs, current movies, popular novels, sports, and national and international affairs. It is quite likely that you will be asked about your professional aspirations. You cannot possibly prepare yourself, a few days before an interview, to talk intelligently on current affairs about which you have not been reading consistently, but you *can* be prepared to talk definitely about your professional plans and the ways in which you expect to improve yourself professionally. Certainly you should not hesitate to ask questions—after all, the interview is for your benefit as well as for the benefit of the employing official.

Listen now as Sarah Yancey, personnel director in a large city school system, carries on an interview with Ellen Wilson who has applied for a position in the intermediate grades.

SARAH YANCEY

Miss Wilson, we know quite a lot about you from your letter of application, the application form, your credentials from your college placement office, and your college transcript. What we want to do today is to get better acquainted with each other and give you an opportunity to find out something about what we have to offer you. Let's begin by asking what grade you would really like to teach and why?

ELLEN WILSON

Well, I think I like the fifth grade best of all. Although I have had some experience with second grade and sixth grade, I did my student teaching with fifth-graders and I think I really did my best work there. I like ten-year-olds very much. I found it much harder to work with primary children.

SARAH YANCEY

Your faculty advisor says you worked with some rather able fifth-graders. How do you think you might get along with slow-learning children?

ELLEN WILSON

Oh, I think I could work with them, too. I was with slower groups last year. You have to be a little more patient and, of course, you don't expect nearly as much. But I don't really think you teach differently.

SARAH YANCEY

You know, of course, Miss Wilson, that this is a large city and we have elementary schools in communities representing many different socio-economic levels. In what kind of school do you think you would like to work?

ELLEN WILSON

Well, I don't think it would matter much as long as they were not primary children. Of course, if I had my choice I would like to teach pupils like the ones I had in student teaching. That was a higher economic level. I wouldn't hesitate to try a class in an underprivileged district, though.

SARAH YANCEY

Of course, we have many assignments to make. I couldn't tell you just now where you will be placed. You have been very helpful, though, in indicating your feelings about it. We would want to assign you where you would be happy and make your best contribution to boys and girls. Let's change the direction of questioning a little. Have you done much work with children outside of your work in college?

ELLEN WILSON

Yes, I've been a camp counselor and a playground leader. Then I have worked with the church school and for one of my college classes I worked with underprivileged children in a settlement house.

SARAH YANCEY

That's fine. Have you belonged to any organizations in college?

ELLEN WILSON

Yes, I was a member of the Elementary Education Club and served on the student council. I've always been active in the YWCA, and I have served on several campus committees.

SARAH YANCEY

What kind of reading do you do in your spare time?

ELLEN WILSON

Well, since this is my last semester I've been pretty busy and haven't had much time for anything but school work. I really haven't read any novels this year. I do try to look at news magazines, but I must confess I don't have time for much more than the front page of the newspaper. I try to listen to the news on the radio, though, and I find time for some of the music programs on television.

SARAH YANCEY

Where would you say the greatest public concern about education is today?

ELLEN WILSON

From what I've heard and a little reading, perhaps programs for gifted children and perhaps science in the schools, or maybe both of these together. It seems to me, though, that people need to visit schools more. I thought the teachers worked very hard at it where I did my student teaching.

SARAH YANCEY

Have you read any recent accounts of European schools?

ELLEN WILSON

I might just as well confess that I haven't. I did hear one television panel.

SARAH YANCEY

Miss Wilson, so far I have been asking all the questions. Perhaps you have some you would like to ask.

ELLEN WILSON

Yes, I do. If I come to your school system, what would my salary be?

SARAH YANCEY

Here's our salary schedule. You can see what your beginning salary would be. Of course, you must figure on some deductions such as income tax and teachers' retirement.

ELLEN WILSON

I was wondering, too, how large a class am I likely to have?

SARAH YANCEY

Well, we try to hold our class load to thirty pupils, but we can't always do that. It will depend somewhat on the way the principal organizes his schedule.

ELLEN WILSON

As you know, Miss Yancey, I do not live in your city. What kind of living conditions can I expect to find here?

SARAH YANCEY

We try to help you find a suitable place to live. Mrs. Nelson in our office has a list of places available. Sometimes two or more of our teachers rent an apartment together. Is there anything else I could tell you?

ELLEN WILSON

No, those were the questions which bothered me.

SARAH YANCEY

I think, then, that this covers most of the items we have in mind. I believe you would be happy in our school system and we are pleased with you. However, we always take a little time to think about you after we have seen you, and I know that you will want to think about us. You will hear from us definitely in a few days. When you do receive your contract, be sure to return it promptly.

ELLEN WILSON

I shall. Thank you very much, Miss Yancey. I've enjoyed meeting you.

You will notice that Miss Yancey and Ellen Wilson covered many of the matters with which you, as an applicant, would be concerned.

From the report of the interview you can surmise the easy, informal way in which it was conducted. Miss Yancey took the leadership, but, at the same time, Ellen had an opportunity to express herself and to ask questions. Do not expect, however, that all interviews are conducted exactly in this way. The structure of the interview and the questions asked will vary from situation to situation. Some interviews will be cozy and informal, others stiff and formal, and there will be those in between. After a few experiences, you will be able to "spot" the techniques and adjust your approach accordingly.

MAINTAINING PROFESSIONAL ETHICS IN SECURING A POSITION

Determining the professional procedures in applying for and accepting a teaching position is not always easy for the beginner. Until you actually begin to apply for positions, the process may seem to be simple and straightforward—you complete the needed forms, you are interviewed, if you are offered the position, you say "yes" or "no." Actually, however, you are very likely to find yourself facing situations that are complicated and confusing. As a matter of fact, even the veteran teacher is sometimes at a loss regarding the ethical step to take. Many of the problems involving professional ethics about which you may find yourself uncertain will center around whether to apply for more than one position at a time; how much information to give employing officials; how long to delay in signing a contract if one is offered to you; and how and under what circumstances to ask to be released from a contract already signed.

Apply for as many positions as you wish. You may hear comments in professional circles that imply that it is unethical to apply for more than one position at a time. Just what reasoning is back of this is uncertain. Perhaps it stems from a belief that when there is a shortage of teachers it is unfair to arouse false hopes in the minds of four or five employing officials at once. Certainly, in times when teachers were abundant and positions scarce, persons just out of college often applied for many positions before they found employment. The fact that conditions of supply and demand have changed does not make it any less proper for teachers today to apply for several positions at once. It is better to turn down an offer or two than not to secure the type of position you desire because you wait for Superintendent

Smith to make up his mind before you file your application with Superintendent Brown.

The ethics of applying for teaching positions are simple. Apply for as many positions as you wish. Do not panic, however, and "broadcast" applications to school systems which seem unlikely to offer you the kind of position in which you feel you would be successful. Be selective. Investigate carefully, using the most competent advice available to you, and then apply only to those school systems in which it seems likely that you will become a successful teacher. At least until the shortage of elementary teachers has abated considerably, you stand a good chance of eventually locating the type of position you prefer unless factors beyond your control restrict severely the geographic area in which you must be located.

You should make every effort to be courteous and tactful in your relationships with prospective employers, whether or not you are offered a position. Certainly, you should show enthusiastic interest in every position for which you are interviewed, even though the tenor of the interview makes you increasingly dubious as to whether you would accept employment if it were offered to you. It is a thoughtful (and prudent) move to write a letter thanking an employing officer for granting you an interview, even though you are not offered a position. This is a courtesy that will cause you to be remembered favorably and perhaps contacted the next time there is an opening.

You also have a professional obligation to keep everyone who is interested in you—including the director of your placement office—informed of your progress. After you have accepted a position, be prompt in notifying other employers who are still considering your application that you are no longer interested. By so doing you may save busy school officials unnecessary expenditure of time and effort and yourself embarrassment. Little things sometimes make big and lasting impressions. Do not brand yourself in the eyes of placement officials and of employers to whom you might at a later date be applying for another position as someone insensitive to the administrative problems faced by employing officials.

Be honest, open, and aboveboard with school officials. Because you are inexperienced in applying for teaching positions, you may have a tendency to withhold information which, in reality, might be helpful to you in securing an appointment. School officials want the facts from you. They respect straightforward and aboveboard statements. Frankness and honesty will react in your favor. If there is any type of teaching situation in which you doubt your competence, say so. In a school system of any size, your prospective employer may be able to consider another assignment for you. In a small system, it may at least be possible to plan to give you special help at your point of weakness. Certainly, if there are elements in the situation which make your probable success very dubious, it is best to discover them before you accept employment.

Be equally frank if you are asked about other positions for which you have applied. An employing officer often faces a difficult task in filling his vacancies. He has a right to know what his chances of securing you are likely to be. Particularly is it important that you be honest with him regarding your intentions if you definitely prefer another position and would consider what he has to offer only if the other job does not materialize. Furthermore, employing officials within a reasonable geographic radius are likely to match notes on candidates for positions. An attempt to keep several persons "on the string" by concealing your moves often leads only to building in everybody's eyes a reputation for being unprofessional.

Above all, do not be afraid to ask questions. In your desire to secure a position and your inexperience with employing officials, you may be hesitant in asking for information which you must have in order to make an intelligent decision regarding whether or not to accept the position. Questions which deal with school organization, salaries, supervision, promotion policies, pensions and retirement, professional improvement, and housing are among the types that you might ask. The only restriction is that you be courteous, tactful, and cheerful and that your questions be in good taste.

Decide promptly whether or not to accept the position offered to you. Once you have been offered a teaching position, you have a professional obligation to decide promptly whether or not you wish to accept it. This does not mean that you must accept at once if offered a contract at the conclusion of the interview or that you must return it with your signature by the next mail. You should, however, make up your mind within a reasonable time. Sometimes the employing official will specify a time limit, for example, three days or five days. If this is the case, you must be prompt, for the official may want to offer the position to someone else. The fact that the contract was sent to you indicates that you were the first choice. Often there will be a second-choice person waiting to hear. You have no right to be dilatory beyond the time limit.

Occasionally circumstances beyond your control will cause you to want to delay your decision beyond the deadline given you. You may be waiting to hear from another position slightly more to your liking or there may be personal factors which cause you to be doubtful regarding how long you will be in the community. You need not necessarily refuse a situation because you cannot make up your mind within the time limit. First, talk it over with the employing official. If he feels that the deadline must stand, then you have no choice but to make up your mind. He may, however, be able to extend the deadline or to employ you on the understanding that you will be released without prejudice if the factors which you feared might force you to break your contract do materialize. It is quite within the bounds of professional ethics, too, to contact a second employer from whom you have been hoping to hear and ask when you can expect to have his decision. You may raise ethically with an employing officer any problem you face in deciding whether to sign a contract. The only unprofessional move is to conceal information which you know has an important bearing upon how you make up your mind.

After four years in college, living with some very natural doubts regarding whether you will be given an opportunity to practice your profession, there is always a tendency to accept the first position that is offered. This is a tendency which it will be well to resist unless the position is exactly what you want. There are cycles in teacher placement about which you should know. Many superintendents prefer to hire teachers before May 15, and you may be one of those who is employed prior to that date. There is another cycle immediately after graduation. By that time, the school year is ending and superintendents have had a better opportunity to inventory their vacancies for next year. You may be the one to secure a position at this time—between June 15 and July 1. After July 1, superintendents usually take vacations, returning in late July and early August to find additional vacancies. Placement directors know that some of the best positions are available in August. If you have the fortitude to take a chance, you can usually secure just what you want even this late in the summer. This advice is given not to encourage you to wait until August, but to reassure you that you can usually locate exactly the position you want if you weigh each offer carefully, make your decisions within the limits specified, and refuse to be panicked if you do not find just what you desire immediately.

Consider carefully before you ask to be released from a contract. A contract is a document which binds both parties concerned to certain obligations. It cannot be broken without the consent of both parties. It is assumed that when you sign a contract you intend to fulfill your obligations and you have the right to expect the board of education which offers you the contract to do likewise. You should never break a contract without the consent of the board of education and then only for the most compelling and urgent reasons. You do not, for example, ask to be released from one contract simply because you have received an offer of a better teaching position. You might, however, ask to be released because of urgent personal reasons—marriage, removal to a distant community, or personal or family illness.

If you do find it necessary to ask for a release from your contract, discuss the facts frankly and honestly with the appropriate school official. School officials are reasonable people and will release you without prejudice if they are convinced of your sincerity and good intent. They will usually release you, too, if you don't have good reasons, but such action is often to your disadvantage. Sometimes a derogatory memorandum is placed in your file and your placement office notified that the school system considers you an unreliable prospect.

If you are to become a respected member of the teaching profession, you must take care to maintain your professional reputation. This you can do if you are honest, frank, and judicious. Everyone—employers, college officials, supervisors—is as anxious as yourself to see you placed where you will be successful. Fulfill your obligations with meticulous care.

BOOKS YOU SHOULD KNOW

Eye, Glen C., and Lane, Willard R. *The New Teacher Comes to School.* New York: Harper & Brothers, 1956. Pp. xii + 376.

Huggett, Albert J., and Stinnett, T.M. *Professional Problems of Teachers.* New York: The Macmillan Co., 1956. Pp. ix + 468.

Richey, Robert W. *Planning for Teaching.* Second Edition. New York: McGraw-Hill Book Co., 1958. Pp. xv + 550.

Yauch, Wilbur A.; Bartels, Martin H.; and Morris, Emmet. *The Beginning Teacher.* New York: Henry Holt and Co., 1955. Pp. xii + 339.

Planning for Continued Growth

CHAPTER 14

As a teacher in the elementary school you would probably state your primary professional objective as insuring the continued growth of the boys and girls in your classroom. Perhaps you have not thought about it seriously, but you have another obligation—insuring your own continued growth. Your years in college have, no doubt, been profitable and satisfying. If you look back to the days when you were a freshman you can see how much you have grown in knowledge, sophistication, and self-confidence. Without really thinking about it, you have become a competent and self-assured person. This is as it should be, but once you begin teaching you will soon discover that you are far from a finished product. You have chosen a profession demanding breadth and depth of academic background, sensitive understanding of human behavior, and a high level of technical competence in guiding the learning experiences of boys and girls. All this, of course, cannot be mastered in a few years of college work. In fact, it cannot be *completely* mastered in a lifetime.

In recent years serious consideration has been given to the extension of the teacher-education program. Some authorities have argued that a teacher cannot be adequately prepared within the customary four years of undergraduate work. Others, however, have questioned the wisdom of lengthening the period of pre-service preparation. They suggest, instead, that the most effective contribution to a teacher's increased competence is made at the time when he is responsible for his own classroom. More and more school systems, therefore, are sponsoring in-service programs which offer a variety of possibilities to teachers for continued professional and personal growth.

If you are seriously interested in becoming a master teacher, you will plan carefully for your growth in service. There will be supervisory help available to you in evaluating your work and improving your day-to-day skills. There will also be opportunities for you to participate in professional activities—in-service programs sponsored by your school system, professional organizations, and professional and academic work at college. And, if you truly wish to become a more interesting person, you will not neglect the possibilities of travel, work experience, and a planned reading program. Some of the considerations that should be in your thinking as you appraise these avenues to further growth are the focus of the remainder of this chapter.

ACHIEVING GROWTH THROUGH CONTINUOUS EVALUATION

Without question, the teachers who make the most growth on the job are those who engage in continuous self-evaluation. They study objectively the success of their efforts in the classroom as evidenced by the growth of their pupils. They utilize the help of persons in administrative and supervisory positions in analyzing their work in the classroom and their relationships to colleagues and parents. And they stop, periodically, to take a systematic look at their strengths and weaknesses, using lists of teacher competencies and instruments of self-appraisal as guides.

Of all your experiences as a student teacher, none will be more important to your continued professional growth than those of appraising your own strengths and weaknesses—alone or in conference with your cooperating teacher or your college supervisor. It is essential to your continued growth in your own classroom that you maintain the same desire to learn how to do a better job which you exhibited during your student-teaching experience—that you analyze your own work just as critically, that you expect and welcome help just as freely from those in supervisory positions, and that you make just as effective use of rating scales and other devices for periodic self-appraisal.

Capitalize upon your own ability to analyze your classroom performance. Whether or not you grow on the job once you have taken over sole responsibility for a class of your own will depend largely upon how skillful you are in evaluating the success of your efforts from day to day. Certainly those persons who have supervisory responsibilities in your school system will be anxious to be of assistance to you, but most of the decisions regarding what went well or what went badly today and how best to proceed tomorrow will have to be your own.

How do you go about analyzing your pupils' growth to determine where your teaching procedures have been successful? The answer to this question is not easy, but the process is essentially the same in your own classroom as it was when there was a cooperating teacher at your side to help. You will establish standards as a basis for appraising pupil growth—by using the scores of standardized tests, studying the recommendations in the course of study, examining pupils' textbooks, consulting with your supervisors and your colleagues. In the light of these standards you will collect and analyze evidence regarding your pupils' growth—by observing them in a variety of classroom settings, collecting samples of their work, giving classroom tests, listening to what they say in discussions or in answer to your questions. As you study the evidence you will be deciding not only where your pupils have succeeded or failed but also where your own teaching procedures merit further scrutiny.

But how will you know, with no one to help you to analyze the situation, just what has gone wrong at points where you are reasonably sure that your teaching was not successful, or, for that matter, what you did that contributed to a satisfactory day? Few teachers are ever certain that they have judged a situation correctly until they actually try again tomorrow, but the better your grasp of educational principles and the more sensitive your insights into the crucial elements in a complex teaching situation, the better your judgment is likely to be regarding what steps to take next and when to ask your principal or supervisor for expert advice. This is a point at which the many conferences with your cooperating teacher and your college supervisor will pay rich dividends. You will undoubtedly have analyzed with these persons numerous situations similar to those which will concern you in your first full-time teaching position. You will do well to think about the strengths and weaknesses that you were helped to identify during those conferences. Some of your less effective teaching patterns may recur under pressure of the new situation. You are likely to find helpful, also, your memories of previous discussions regarding what may happen to a well-behaved group or to an individual child on a rainy day, before holidays, or at times when there are emotional pressures beyond your control. Many a beginner spends sleepless nights worrying about situations that were not of his causing. You will not grow in professional skills and insights if you blame your pupils or events elsewhere in the school for all your unsatisfactory days, but neither will you grow if you defeat yourself with self-criticism regarding situations which your most skillful colleagues might have handled no better.

In analyzing day-to-day successes and failures you would do well to go back to your professional library, and to the earlier chapters in this volume, to reread the discussions of effective teaching procedures. There is no real gap between "theory and practice." There are only theories misapplied and practices misused. You can do much to help yourself to grow if you conscientiously reappraise and apply all that you have learned about educational procedures to the particular classroom situation you now face.

Make the most of supervisory conferences. Even though you solve many classroom problems for yourself, it is important to remember that you are one of a team working for better learning experiences for boys and girls. Practically all elementary schools today have a principal. One of his tasks—probably his most important task—is to provide instructional leadership and supervisory service. You may be fortunate enough to be teaching in a school system that has several individuals working full time as supervisors. You may find, too, that your school has the policy of assigning an experienced teacher to help the beginner get off to a good start. In some situations there will be, in addition, an in-service program developed jointly by the school system and local teacher-education institution. All of your co-workers will be interested in helping you to succeed in teaching and in seeing that you like your job and grow professionally.

When two or more persons are assigned supervisory responsibilities in a school they usually plan carefully to delimit their spheres of action so that the teachers they are trying to help do not find themselves the recipients of contradictory advice. Even so, it will be important to know just what is the administrative and supervisory hierarchy and to whom you are responsible. If an experienced teacher is assigned as a "buddy," his responsibilities are likely to be strictly advisory in nature. If there is a supervisor working throughout the school system, he will typically serve in a consultative capacity. The principal is usually the one to whom the teachers are directly responsible. If you are confused about the division of responsibilities, your principal will be the best person to clarify personnel relationships for you.

Many beginning teachers falsely assume that it is a sign of weakness to discuss any problems with a principal or a supervisor—that the problems they are having are unique and that they must face them alone. This represents a misunderstanding of the purpose of supervision as it is typically conceived today. Most supervisors and principals are eager to help beginners do a good job. They will not look for perfection from you; in fact, they will expect you to make mistakes as all beginners and even experienced teachers do.

What types of problems should you take to your principal or supervisor? Certainly you should expect assistance in becoming oriented to the organization of your particular school and to school policies and procedures. Much more important to your professional growth, however, you should expect help in evaluating your teaching procedures, your classroom organization, your use of materials, your plans for meeting individual needs, your management of interpersonal relationships in the classroom. You should expect, also, a frank analysis of your personal strengths and weaknesses in so far as these affect your work with boys and girls or your relationships with colleagues. Although the persons responsible for your supervision will not expect you to ask their approval for every minor decision you make, they will be available to give assistance when you need it.

There are certain steps that you should be prepared to take if you want your supervisor or principal to help you. In the first place, you should expect such persons to visit your classroom and you should be willing to let them see the situations which are causing you concern. If you save for a supervisory visit a lesson you know will "go well" or give your pupils a quiet work period while you come back to talk with the visitor, you will not get much help in analyzing your problems. In some school systems it is expected that you will be available for a conference after the supervisory visit. If the arrangements for this conference are your responsibility, you should ask promptly for an appointment before you and your supervisor forget what was observed. If your supervisor (who is much busier than you) asks you to talk through lunch or to stay immediately after school, do your best to rearrange your schedule in order to do so. Just as your cooperating teacher expected you to analyze your own procedures and to raise problems in a conference, so will those who are supervising you on the job. They can be more helpful to a teacher who is able to point specifically to the problems that concern him than they can to the one who says vaguely, "The children seem to be so noisy." Persons supervising you will also welcome evidence that you are objective in your desire to improve and anxious to have them offer suggestions about situations for which you have not specifically asked assistance. If it is apparent that you are discouraged, defensive, and fearful of criticism, those working with you will be cautious in trying to give help. Last, and perhaps most important, the supervisor and the principal will be looking for evidence that you have thought seriously about their suggestions and are attempting to put them to use. In other words, the same attitudes and procedures that made it possible for your cooperating teacher and college supervisor to help you are the ones that will enable you to profit from supervisory relationships in your first teaching position.

Utilize aids to systematic self-appraisal. Your own insights as you evaluate your success in the classroom from day to day and the insights of those who work with you in supervisory relationships will give you much understanding of your own capacities and needs as a teacher. However, it is important, once in a while, to take a broader and more systematic look at yourself—both at your personal development and at your professional competencies.

A helpful approach to systematic self-appraisal is to evaluate yourself in the light of one or more of the many existing statements describing the characteristics of an effective teacher. It is quite likely that you were asked to do this at more than one point in the course of your preparation to become a teacher. As a freshman, you may have been urged to think seriously about the characteristics of a successful teacher as a basis for planning your college program. It is possible that in your institution you were required to complete a self-appraisal form as a part of the process of being admitted to the professional work of the junior and senior years or to the student-teaching program. In all probability those persons who supervise the student teachers in your institution used a special rating sheet upon which you were asked to rate yourself at the end of your student-teaching experience, or which your cooperating teacher or your college supervisor rated with you. All these represent attempts to help you to take an objective look at your own potentialities as a teacher.

The school system that employs you may likewise ask you to engage in systematic self-appraisal. Below are reproduced the specific items upon which each teacher in a large city system[1] is asked to rate himself and which he then discusses with his principal and sometimes with his supervisor as part of a comprehensive appraisal plan too complex to describe in detail here. Beginners are asked to rate themselves each year for the first three years, even though their work is considered satisfactory. Thereafter the self-appraisal is at longer stated intervals. The

[1] From *An Evaluation of Teaching Performance* in use in the Cincinnati Public Schools, Cincinnati, Ohio. Permission to quote granted.

scale that the teachers are asked to use is quite simple. Each item is checked in terms of whether the teacher deems it to be one of his strongest characteristics or one of his weakest characteristics (one on which he would like to improve).

I. PERSONAL QUALITIES AND PERFORMANCE

A. Staff Relationships

1. Promotes friendly intra-school relationships.
2. Adjusts easily to changes in procedure; does not consider his own program all-important.
3. Carries a fair share of out-of-class responsibilities.
4. Accepts criticism or recognition gracefully.
5. Accepts group decisions without necessarily agreeing.
6. Uses discretion and consideration in speaking of his school or colleagues.
7. Cooperates with immediate administrators and supervisors.

B. Community Relationships

8. Works understandingly and cooperatively with parents.
9. Supports and participates in parent-teacher groups.
10. Participates in community activities.
11. Interprets the school's program and policies to the community as occasion permits.

C. Appearance and Manner

12. Dresses appropriately; is well-groomed, and poised.
13. Speaks clearly, using good English in a well-modulated voice.
14. Shows genuine respect, concern, and warmth for others, both child and adult.
15. Attempts to correct personal habits and mannerisms which detract from effective teaching.
16. Is physically able to perform his duties; is not handicapped by too frequent absence or illness.
17. Maintains sound emotional adjustment; is calm and mature in his reactions.

II. TEACHING PERFORMANCE

A. Teaching Techniques

18. Helps each child set appropriate goals for himself.
19. Varies method and content to suit individual differences and goals.
20. Directs interesting, varied, and stimulating classes.

21. Practices principles of democratic leadership with children and adults.
22. Plans each day carefully, but is flexible in utilizing immediate educational opportunities.
23. Helps children develop and strengthen their moral and spiritual qualities.

B. *Classroom Environment*

24. Maintains an attractive and healthful classroom.
25. Has work areas arranged for maximum pupil stimulation and accomplishment.
26. Recognizes each child's emotional and social needs.
27. Has genuine concern for all his children regardless of their cultural, intellectual, or academic status.
28. Is respected by pupils; secures voluntary cooperation; has a minimum of behavior problems.
29. Handles behavior problems individually when possible.

C. *Pupil Growth*

30. Helps children achieve satisfactorily in skill subjects.
31. Helps children evaluate themselves and their growth as a means to further growth.
32. Encourages growth in democratic participation and sharing of responsibilities.
33. Helps students integrate their learning experience into a meaningful pattern.
34. Encourages pupils to make their own judgments according to their various levels of maturity.
35. Helps children acquire good study and work habits.
36. Helps children develop the ability to work profitably in classroom situations.

III. PROFESSIONAL QUALITIES

37. Displays the refinement, character, and objectivity expected of the professional person.
38. Is proud of his profession and attempts to promote respect for it.
39. Accepts personal responsibility for compliance with rules and for attention to administrative requests.
40. Does not abuse privileges.
41. Is continuously growing professionally through study, experimentation, and participation in professional activities.
42. Is critical of and constantly trying to improve his own work.
43. Initiates or participates fully in activities designed to meet the needs of his particular school.
44. Possesses adequate subject matter background.

You will notice that those responsible for teacher personnel in this school system are interested in the personal and professional characteristics of their teachers as well as in their skill in the classroom. You will be interested, too, to learn that the complete appraisal blank from which these items were taken provides a place for the teacher to indicate the professional activities—work on committees and in professional educational organizations—in which he has been engaged. It also asks for extracurricular activities sponsored—athletics, clubs, publications, dramatics. It further provides an opportunity for the teacher to list other activities which he feels have made a contribution to his effectiveness as a teacher—college courses taken, institutes attended; travel, recreation, hobbies, or other activities he deems to have been of value.

It is difficult to rate oneself fairly and objectively on appraisal forms. To feel competent and adequate is a basic human need, and it is all too easy to rationalize—to blame the administrative organization in the school or the children's home and community backgrounds for one's problems, whereas the facts may be that the teacher next door is doing a very capable job under the same working conditions and with children from the same types of homes. It is equally difficult, and equally important, to be objective about one's strengths. Many a teacher who gives superb leadership to children tends to belittle his own efforts and to feel certain that most of his colleagues are doing a better job. Yet the value of self-appraisal is largely lost if you cannot view your own competencies impartially. Actually, experiences from early childhood have combined to make you secure or insecure, able to face your strengths and weaknesses or disposed to hide them from yourself. Your day-by-day experiences of analyzing your successes and failures in student teaching and relating them to your own competence as a teacher will have done far more to help you become objective in your viewpoint than any single attempt to rate yourself on a formal rating sheet.

Regardless of the method by which you appraise yourself, it is vital to your continued growth as a teacher that you be able to recognize your own strengths and weaknesses. In the long pull, you will act in terms of how you view yourself, not in terms of what someone else tells you about your proficiency. Ultimately you, yourself, must take the steps that will make you a better teacher. It will be difficult to do this intelligently unless you have learned to look at yourself objectively.

ACHIEVING GROWTH THROUGH PARTICIPATION IN PROFESSIONAL ACTIVITIES

All teachers have an obligation to keep abreast of new developments in their profession. When you begin to consider the ways in which you might strengthen your professional competence, it will be natural for you to think first of more college work. This, however, is only one of the many avenues to professional growth. In all probability, the school system in which you are employed will provide a number of in-service education activities—opportunities for teachers to come together in a variety of ways, sometimes under the leadership of personnel within the system and sometimes under expert consultant help from other places. There are also professional organizations which you may join. In addition, you will certainly wish to embark upon a program of professional reading.

Choosing among the opportunities for professional growth is sometimes a difficult task for a beginner. There will be some professional activities in which you will be expected to engage—building meetings, supervisory conferences, system-wide meetings to discuss matters of policy and curriculum. Many other activities will, however, be on a voluntary basis. What factors should you consider in deciding which in-service activities to choose, which organizations to join, when and what kind of advanced college program to plan, and what professional reading to do?

Make thoughtful choices among in-service activities. The in-service activities in which you engage will be among your most important steps toward greater professional competence. These are your opportunities to work with your colleagues on problems of mutual concern, to learn more about their educational philosophies, and to benefit from the wealth of their insights into classroom policies and procedures. These are the opportunities, too, that enable you to become truly a part of the school system in which you are employed, contributing your share to the solution of common problems.

The types of in-service activities provided for teachers vary with the educational insights of those in positions of professional leadership, the philosophy of the school system, and, to some extent, its size and financial support. Certainly, there will be faculty meetings in your building. Although these may occasionally serve as a means of making announcements and clarifying administrative details, they will more often be meetings dealing with problems of professional concern to the teachers in the building. It is probable that you will be expected to serve on one or more faculty committees established to study special aspects of the program in your school. You may also have an opportunity to meet with teachers working at the same grade level or teaching in the same subject area.

If you accept a position in a school system in which yours is one of several schools, you may find that system-wide activities are an important part of the organized in-service program. Some of these will be meetings of the entire teaching staff for the purpose of arriving at system-wide understanding of new administrative procedures or of deciding how to implement the proposals of committees which have been considering curriculum changes. There may also be system-wide committees serving a variety of purposes—appraising textbooks, working on a plan for revising the system of reporting to parents, discussing means of stimulating able children or of helping slower learners. Many school systems sponsor workshops and institutes in which teachers are given opportunity to work on specific instructional problems under expert leadership or to hear some authority speak on a topic of common interest. You may find, too, groups of teachers meeting regularly in study groups or participating in research programs planned on a system-wide basis.

How will you decide how many in-service activities to undertake and which to choose? The most important warning to the beginner is not to undertake too much. You should be involved in sufficient activities to feel part of your school system and to become well acquainted with your colleagues, but you will find your first experience in taking full responsibility for a group of boys and girls a busy and exhausting one. You must allow yourself time to do the job properly.

You will, of course, be expected to attend the faculty meetings in your school and to assume your share of responsibility on faculty committees. You will also want (and probably be expected) to participate in any activities designed for the orientation of beginning teachers. Beyond this, you may wish to attend an institute or a workshop focused upon classroom problems that are of particular concern to you. Your principal and your supervisor can be particularly helpful in making such decisions. You should discuss the in-service program with them early in the school year.

Most in-service programs today are based upon the philosophy that desirable change and professional growth are more likely to result if teachers are actively involved in the problem-solving process. There may be a few lectures to attend, but, for the most part, you will find teachers responsible for identifying problems, planning the steps needed to solve them, and taking these steps. When consultants are invited to participate, it is likely to be after the problems upon which expert help is needed have been clearly identified. To get the most out of such activities, you must bring to them all your understanding of the processes of cooperative problem-solving. It will be important for you to come with problems and questions and with an alert interest in the topic being studied. Persons who arrive with blank minds "to see what I can learn" usually leave with minds still blank. You will need to remember, too, that the democratic process is often slow. There are certain to be differences of opinion, varying rates at which new ideas will be grasped, and deep-seated personal needs and prejudices that block objective participation. Adults who display endless patience in helping children to work their way to a successful solution to a problem often fail to exhibit the same skill in working with their colleagues. Yet, the success of a proposed solution often depends upon whether all those participating have understood and accepted it. You will gain much more from meetings where you and your colleagues are working on problems of mutual concern if you learn to analyze the group processes in operation and exert your efforts toward moving the discussion forward. You will also, if you have learned to be objective about your participation in the group, spend considerable time analyzing and evaluating your own effectiveness in situations requiring cooperative problem-solving.

Beginners may need to realize that in most school systems there are administrative policies and school traditions that cannot readily be changed. It is all too easy, sometimes, for the newcomer to say "The way we did it last year was. . . ." or "Why don't we just. . . ?" Yet factors of which you are not aware may make it difficult to implement your suggestion or proposal. In most schools changes are made only after thorough discussion and planning, and then not until there is the understanding and consent of all who will be involved. As a new teacher you must be patient and willing to work through the established channels for decision-making. If you are observant you will discover that there are usually good reasons for the policies and routines which are operating. Your new ideas will be welcome, but you will do well to listen carefully to your colleagues who are more experienced and who have a broader understanding of all the factors involved in the accomplishment of the proposed changes.

Affiliate with professional organizations. Professional organizations represent another important means of promoting professional growth. At the local level, they provide an opportunity to work with your colleagues on professional problems. At the state and national levels, they help to bring you in contact with new developments in the profession and with those persons giving significant professional leadership. Through the research and the publications which they sponsor, these groups contribute to higher professional standards. You should give serious consideration to affiliating with professional organizations on three levels—local, state, and national.

Investigate carefully the programs of local groups. These offer an effective opportunity to participate actively and to work cooperatively with your colleagues. You should affiliate actively with the local teachers' association, if one is in existence. The local organization is, in a sense, a grass-roots group. It is operated by local teachers and works on problems of immediate concern to them. Through it you will have an opportunity to influence the educational plans, standards, and policies in your school system. Because local associations are often affiliated with state and national organizations you will, through the local delegates to larger meetings, help to determine the policies and practices of these groups. As a professional person, you have a responsibility to work with and through groups that stand for the up-grading of the profession. This is the primary objective of your local teachers' association.

In some school systems there will be other local professional groups —branches of state and national organizations—whose objectives and programs are directed toward improving the professional competence of their members. You may find organizations for primary or intermediate teachers, for teachers of slow learners, for teachers concerned with better methods of teaching reading, English, arithmetic, science, social studies. Such groups often supplement the in-service education programs sponsored by the school administration. Whether you join one or more of such groups during your first few years of teaching depends on many factors. In making up your mind, ask yourself the following questions: What contribution does this organization seem likely to make to my professional growth? Will I have the time and energy to participate in its program and contribute to its work? Does its focus represent an area in which I have a special professional or personal interest? Is it a group through which I would have an opportunity to build valuable professional relationships with my colleagues? Does it duplicate or does it supplement help I am already receiving through other in-service activities?

At the state level the state education association, whose membership includes teachers from every part of the state and every branch of the profession, works actively in the interests of teacher welfare and the advancement of education on a state-wide basis. You will want to support its work. Active membership in the state education association has both immediate and long-term benefits. In an immediate sense, you are affiliating with like-minded professional people, and you are demonstrating that you wish to be counted as a member of the profession. You should take pride in belonging. The long-term results of affiliating with a state organization will appear in improved educational opportunities in the state. It is no happenstance that those states that spend the most for educational purposes and have the best state-wide programs of education are also the ones with strong and effective state teachers' associations. State associations have fought for and obtained minimum salary, retirement, and tenure laws for teachers. Improvements in these and other benefits are still needed and the state association, with your support, will continue to work for the elevation of the profession.

Nationally, the National Education Association is an organization that works on a broad scale to foster the improved professional status of teaching. It is a potent educational force in this country. The association has a number of commissions constantly at work investigating ways of improving teaching and conditions for teaching. The investigations of the research division, reported in the *Research Bulletin,* cover practically every aspect of administration and teaching and many topics dealing with teacher welfare. This bulletin will be an indispensable source of information on employment practices, tenure, enrollment trends, teaching procedures. The association is also of help through other publications. The *NEA Journal,* which you will receive regularly with your membership, will help you to stay abreast of educational happenings throughout the nation. The bulletins, pamphlets, periodicals, and yearbooks of affiliated organizations, such as the Department of Classroom Teachers and the Association for Supervision and Curriculum Development, are particularly worth while in their emphasis upon classroom problems and promising practices.

At the national level, also, there are associations representing practically every subject taught in the elementary school today. These are the groups broadly concerned with the improvement of instruction in the elementary school, with better understanding of learners, with curriculum problems, with fostering educational research, with philosophy of education. Some are affiliated with the National Education Association; some are independent. Regardless of what your area of special interest may be, a national group probably exists to offer you service. Many teachers carry membership in at least two such organizations—one concerned with instructional problems in general, and one related to a specific teaching field. If you decide to join one or more of these organizations, your choice may be influenced in part by whether or not there is a local branch in your school system, the meetings of which you can readily attend. Even if no local chapter exists, you will find the periodicals, the yearbooks, and the other publications of any one of these national organizations to be valuable sources of professional information and suggestions.

Plan for further college work. It is a rare graduate who is able to work into his college program all the courses in which he is interested. Now that you have met the requirements for your degree and your certificate you may want to do something about this. The college work that you undertake should, however, be more than merely an accumulation of courses. It should be part of a carefully planned program for professional and personal growth.

It is important as background for planning about more college work to think about what you would like to be doing, as a professional person, ten or fifteen years from now. Perhaps you see yourself still in the classroom. But at what grade levels and with what competencies?—skilled in child guidance? expert in remedial teaching? skilled in working with children who are deaf, blind, slow learners, gifted? Do you see yourself out of the classroom giving other types of professional leadership?—a principal? a supervisor? a psychologist? a visiting teacher? in a teacher-education institution supervising student teachers? Some of these long-term professional objectives will require that you meet higher certification requirements. Some will be difficult to achieve without a doctorate. Some may require that you plan to spend a year or more at a university noted for its leadership in the field of your special interest. As a beginning teacher you probably will feel that for the next few years your major responsibility is to do the very best that you can in your own classroom. You are quite right in this, and many graduate schools will discourage you if you talk about plunging immediately into full-time graduate work without any classroom experience. It is not, however, too soon to think about a program of graduate study to accompany your early years of teaching.

Whatever your professional objectives, you should give some consideration to courses that will expand your understanding of the rapidly changing world in which you live. Scientific discoveries, followed by technological adaptations, have affected the lives of every citizen. The policies of our federal government and its economic and political commitments to other nations have made every American more conscious of international relations than ever before. An expanding economy and an increasing population have introduced many new problems into our economic and social thinking. Evidence from medicine, anthropology, psychology, sociology, is throwing new light upon how children and youth grow, learn, and achieve emotional maturity. New research techniques and new applications of statistical procedures are being developed in many of the social science fields with corresponding new insights. Even if your undergraduate education was strong in all these areas you will soon find your knowledge out of date unless you engage in a planned program of reading, advanced study, or both. Many graduate faculties in institutions that prepare teachers recognize this and urge that a certain amount of the work for an advanced degree be taken in the so-called "academic" areas.

Undoubtedly, you will want to include in your plans for graduate study some additional professional courses—courses that are focused upon the professional problems of educators. It may be that your own self-evaluation has helped you to identify areas in which your teaching skills are not as strong as you would like them to be. It could be, also, that the position which you finally accepted has made unexpected demands upon you. When this is the case, you might wish to plan early in your graduate program to take some work that bears directly upon your immediate teaching problems. It could well be, however, that courses which will help you to integrate your thinking—to examine your philosophy of education and to build perspective from which to view your classroom experiences more thoughtfully—will be among your most valuable aids to solving your problems of day-by-day teaching. Selecting the appropriate courses to improve your effectiveness as a teacher is a matter which you should weigh thoughtfully.

Develop a program of professional reading. In-service activities, professional organizations, more college courses—these are important and professionally rewarding, but they are not the only means of continued growth. One of your most profitable avenues will be further professional reading. Professional periodicals should be part of your reading program, but you should also endeavor to read significant new professional books. You will find it a stimulating and satisfying experience, also, to go back to the educational classics—to read some of the works of the educational leaders who have had a profound influence upon modern educational thinking. If you want to plan a reading program that contributes richly to your professional growth, you will not stop with books in the field of education. Many of our educational insights have been significantly influenced by findings from psychology, anthropology, sociology, philosophy. Much of our educational planning today reflects new developments in science, economics, government, and international relations. The more you bring from other disciplines, the more insightful your understanding of educational problems will be.

Professional books and periodicals, of course, should not be the only kinds of reading you do. Daily newspapers and news magazines will add greatly to your understanding of what is going on in the world in which you live. You will discover, too, that many household and popular magazines contain articles of professional interest that are of sufficient value to justify some expenditure of time. In fact, there is seemingly no limit to your sources of information, knowledge, and understanding.

ACHIEVING GROWTH THROUGH A PROGRAM FOR PERSONAL DEVELOPMENT

Sometimes the teacher who is most deeply dedicated to his profession can by his very devotion render himself less effective than he would otherwise be. It is all too easy to fill after-school hours with planning lessons and grading papers, to give professional organizations priority over other community groups, to form friendships almost exclusively within a circle of professional colleagues. Yet, you owe it to your pupils, as well as to yourself, to make sure that your personal life is stimulating and well balanced. They need the wealth of new ideas that you can bring from participation in nonprofessional activities. They need, also, the security and understanding that comes from the teacher who has many sources of emotional satisfaction in the richness of his personal living.

As you begin your first full-time teaching experience, you should be thinking about your personal growth just as carefully as you think about your professional growth. There should be at least two dimensions to your planning; you should be considering ways of developing your personal interests and talents and you should be thinking of ways to extend your contacts with individuals and with groups beyond the circle of your professional acquaintances and organizations to the wider community in which you are working.

Develop your personal interests and talents. You will be busy during your first years of teaching. You should not, however, allow your preoccupation with school work to cause you to neglect those aspects of personal living which you find most satisfying. If cooking, sewing, and puttering around with housekeeping are relaxing to you, it might well be worth the investment of a little more of your salary to maintain an apartment of your own and to begin to furnish it to your taste. Your classroom and your home will be the two places in which you will spend the greatest proportion of your time. There are certainly many aesthetic satisfactions in making them places in which you will enjoy living.

It is important that you budget your time so as to allow for participation in the recreational activities which afford you satisfaction. For some persons this may mean participating in or watching sports. Others may enjoy music, drama, folk dancing. Still others will have special hobbies—ceramics, woodworking, collecting records. Whatever your special interest, you are likely to find kindred souls if you will let your enthusiasm be known. You should not feel at all guilty about setting aside a set of papers once in a while in order to devote an evening to an activity that is personally satisfying to you. You will come back to your boys and girls with a new zest for living and often with new experiences which you can share.

It may be that the weight of your college courses allowed you very little time to explore the satisfactions that can come through engaging in some form of creative expression—painting, writing, poetry, whittling, modeling, sewing, singing, playing a musical instrument, refinishing furniture. If you find yourself in a community with an active adult-education program, you may wish to participate in some of these activities. Not only will you derive much personal satisfaction, but you will often acquire skills that can readily be shared with your boys and girls in the classroom.

Once you are out of college, you should consider seriously investing some summers and some midyear vacations in travel. Some colleges conduct tours especially designed for teachers during the summer months. So do the National Education Association and some state associations. You can, however, plan some profitable travel experiences on your own if you will do a little preparation. Visiting a battlefield of the War Between the States may not, in and of itself, be very educative, but if you do some reading ahead of time the trip may prove very worth while. Likewise, a visit to the Grand Canyon or to the Painted Desert is certain to be pleasurable and awe-inspiring, but some knowledge of the geological era and of the phenomena that account for these formations can make your trip much more valuable. Needless to say, the typical teacher on vacation is an inveterate collector of souvenirs, postcards, snapshots, and slides to share with his next year's class.

Last, but certainly not of least importance, you should extend your reading program beyond books of professional interest. It has already been suggested that you delve into outstanding contributions from many disciplines. You should also be reading just for the pleasure of reading—learning about the lives of others through biography; traveling through the writing of explorers; exploring through the eyes of top-flight scientists the wonders of the natural world; enjoying the beauty of phrase, the adept choice of words, of the poet and the master of prose; and, if it affords you intellectual stimulation, helping your favorite detective to solve the crime. You may be protesting, "But I never have time." This, however, is likely to be an excuse. Even fifteen minutes to a half-hour of reading each day adds up to many hours of enjoyment before the year is out.

Participate in community activities. Dedicated teachers can be smothered by classroom responsibilities. They can also be smothered by their professional affiliations. Certainly anyone who has a deep and sincere interest in his work will find the company of others with like concerns stimulating. It would be unfortunate, however, not to maintain contacts with persons outside of the teaching profession. Probably no group faces as often as do teachers the challenge of interpreting their work to persons in other fields and of reflecting in their work the changes taking place in the community, the nation, and the world. You will carry out your teaching responsibilities more intelligently if you have wide acquaintance with many different kinds of people and with the problems, values, and trends in your world.

You should not neglect opportunities to affiliate with groups whose membership cuts across professional lines. There are many such in most communities. Your church may sponsor a young adults' club. The local YMCA and YWCA may provide a variety of educational and recreational activities. As with your professional organizations, you will need to consider what contribution each group can make to your personal growth and also whether or not you can afford the time to participate actively in its program. In terms of broadening your own horizons, however, it may be important to maintain at least one such affiliation even if it means cutting down to some extent upon your professional commitments.

Many teachers have found that working at something other than teaching during the summer months has given them much pleasure and afforded a wholesome perspective on teaching as a lifework. You might combine summer work experiences with travel if you accept a camp position or work in a summer resort. However, there is much to be said for seeking local employment, if such is available. Work experience will bring you in contact with people whose lives are very different from your own. This, of itself, can be a valuable learning, especially if it throws light on the backgrounds and aspirations of youngsters whom you have never fully understood. You will return to the inevitable irritations of your own working conditions much more content once you have experienced some of the problems of others.

Equally important as a means of personal development is participation in community affairs. Traditionally this has been an area in which teachers have not been active to any considerable extent. Today, however, teachers are found actively at work in many civic organizations—as members of service clubs, as workers in community campaigns, on boards of directors in adult-education councils or other groups concerned with education. These and other civic services are of value to the community. They are enriching to the individual teacher. And they make an important contribution to the status of the profession.

To be active in the community as well as in the profession will take planning. If there is to be room for extras you will have to learn how to work efficiently and how to budget your time. You will have to learn to make value judgments—to decide what represents a good day's work in your teaching activities and to be willing to call a halt in order to find room for civic, social, or recreational activities. Perhaps most important, you will need to be able to say "no" when the activity in which you are asked to participate seems likely to demand more time and effort than you feel you can spare.

Personal and professional growth are so interrelated that it is hard to tell where one ends and the other begins. The "whole teacher" comes to school just as does the "whole child." The steps you take to develop your personal interests, to enrich your life and enlarge your horizons through new experiences, and to expand your contacts with persons in your community can make a professional contribution to the growth of boys and girls that is often more significant than the new methods which you might learn in a college class or in a teachers' institute.

BOOKS YOU SHOULD KNOW

Books discussing avenues to personal and professional growth:

Bruce, William F., and Holden, A. John, Jr. *The Teacher's Personal Development.* New York: Henry Holt and Co., 1957. Pp. vi + 346.

Corey, Stephen M. *Action Research to Improve School Practices.* New York: Bureau of Publications, Teachers College, Columbia University, 1953. Pp. 161.

Eye, Glen G., and Lane, Willard R. *The New Teacher Comes to School.* New York: Harper & Brothers, 1956. Pp. xii + 376.

Huggett, Albert J., and Stinnett, T.M. *Professional Problems of Teachers.* New York: The Macmillan Co., 1956. Pp. ix + 468.

In-Service Education. Part I, Fifty-sixth Yearbook of the National Society for the Study of Education. Chicago: The University of Chicago Press, 1957. Pp. xiv + 376.

Kearney, Nolan C. *A Teacher's Professional Guide.* Englewood Cliffs, N.J.: Prentice-Hall, 1958. Pp. ix + 358.

Lieberman, Myron. *Education As a Profession.* Englewood Cliffs, N.J.: Prentice-Hall, 1956. Pp. xviii + 540.

MacKenzie, Gordon N.; Corey, Stephen M.; and associates. *Instructional Leadership.* New York: Bureau of Publications, Teachers College, Columbia University, 1954. Pp. xiii + 209.

Prall, Charles E., and Cushman, C. Leslie. *Teacher Education in Service.* Washington, D.C.: American Council on Education, 1944. Pp. xiii + 405.

Vander Werf, Lester S. *How to Evaluate Teachers and Teaching.* New York: Rinehart and Co., 1958. Pp. vi + 58.

Yauch, Wilbur A.; Bartels, Martin H.; and Morris, Emmet. *The Beginning Teacher.* New York: Henry Holt and Co., 1955. Pp. xii + 339.

Organizations and government agencies whose publications will be particularly helpful in your teaching:

Association for Childhood Education International
1200 Fifteenth St., N.W.
Washington 5, D.C.

International Reading Association
5835 Kimbark Avenue
Chicago 37, Illinois

National Council of Teachers of English
211 West Sixty-eighth Street
Chicago, Illinois

National Education Association
1201 Sixteenth St., N.W.
Washington 6, D.C.

The following departments of the National Education Association, all at the above address, publish their own materials.

American Association for Health, Physical Education, and Recreation
Association for Supervision and Curriculum Development

Department of Classroom Teachers
Department of Rural Education
Council for Exceptional Children
Music Educators National Conference
National Art Education Association
National Council for the Social Studies
National Council of Teachers of Mathematics
National Science Teachers Association

National Society for the Study of Education
5835 Kimbark Avenue
Chicago 37, Illinois

U.S. Department of Health, Education, and Welfare, Office of Education, Washington, D.C.

For Cooperating Teachers

PART V

Helping Beginners Grow

CHAPTER 15

"We plan together right from the first. I try to help the student to feel that he is jointly responsible for the classroom. As the year goes on, he takes on more and more responsibility for carrying out the plans."

"I try to draw the student into all discussions with the children so that they will become used to the idea that two of us are there to help them."

"Every Friday afternoon we have an hour's conference when we do most of our mutual planning."

"Our student teachers worked right along with the regular faculty on special programs."

"Our principal takes time to acquaint the students with over-all school policies. We also try to find time for them to work in the office and to visit other classrooms."

"My student and I checked the college rating sheets independently and then conferred about them."

"Three-way conferences with the college supervisor have been very valuable; so have the duplicate copies of notes made by the college supervisor."

"The student's reports on the discussions in the student-teaching seminar were most helpful. I value the new ideas."

Increased participation in teacher education by public school personnel through student-teaching programs is a significant indication that education has "come of age" as a profession. This important development is not merely a matter of necessity where the numbers of prospective teachers have overtaxed the available classrooms in the laboratory and demonstration schools. It is, above all, recognition that all members of a profession have a mutual responsibility for inducting neophytes into that profession. From the standpoint of the teacher-education institution, the establishment of comprehensive student-teaching programs indicates an increased awareness of the value of providing extended contacts with many types of school situations. Working closely with an experienced professional colleague is one of the most significant aspects of the education of the teacher-to-be.

Actually the practical experience known as *student teaching* is part of a continuum which begins with planned contacts with children and schools in the first days of the prospective teacher's college work and extends into the early years of his professional employment. In this continuum those professional teachers who share their classrooms during what is ordinarily the potential teacher's longest and most responsible contact with a group of children have a particularly important part to play. It is in recognition of this role that many prefer the title "cooperating teacher" to that of "supervising teacher" or "critic teacher." The education of teachers today is truly a cooperative enterprise—school officials, classroom teachers, college faculty members, and students, all working hand in hand. No matter how carefully related to the classroom previous college courses have been, there is a high hurdle to be taken when the student teacher attempts to transform professional theory into classroom practice appropriate to the needs of a particular group of pupils. This is the point in the student's growth where the experience of working cooperatively with a skilled classroom teacher becomes invaluable.

Students may be assigned to cooperating teachers in a variety of ways. In laboratory and demonstration schools, working with students is a responsibility which is an accepted part of the job. In some public schools, cooperating teachers are invited to participate in the student-teaching program by the college personnel. In others, the superintendent, the principal, or the supervisor makes the assignment. Ideally, teachers should be consulted before the responsibility for a student is added to the not inconsequential professional obligations which are already their lot—for responsibility it is, regardless of the satisfactions and rewards it brings. Whatever the procedure by which they are selected, conscientious teachers frequently have misgivings regarding their ability to be of help. What kinds of experiences will have to be provided? How much responsibility should the student be asked to take and how rapidly? What type of help will a cooperating teacher be expected to give? What will be the expectations of college personnel?

The purpose of this chapter is to assist cooperating teachers in providing suitable experiences for students, but students themselves and college supervisors may also find it useful. To be effective, the student-teaching program has to be the result of cooperative planning. Experiences of cooperating teachers can be shared. Students usually have worth-while suggestions. College supervisors have the advantage of years of experience in working with successive groups. Each of the key persons involved needs to understand the goals, problems, and methods of the others. An open-minded attitude on the part of each person concerned is the foundation of a functional program of practical experience for the potential teacher.

WHAT KINDS OF EXPERIENCES WILL THE STUDENT TEACHER NEED?

What should be the objectives of the student-teaching program? The kinds of experiences that will be needed by any specific student will be determined by several factors. Among these are the time allotted to the student-teaching program by the college, the nature of the student's previous contacts with children, the ways in which theory has been related to practice in his college classes, the amount of transfer from college courses to the actual classroom situation, and the student's personal traits and attitudes. Just how each of these factors would be weighed depends on the particular student.

There is, among teacher-education institutions, no commonly accepted allotment of time for organized field experience. The plan followed by the individual college will be influenced by such factors as the existing philosophy of education, the availability of teaching centers, the number and kinds of professional programs, and in some cases, the type of daily schedule which can be worked out for the individual student. Some student-teaching programs provide classroom experience lasting for a year, others for a semester or half-semester. Some students are required to live in the community—often at a considerable distance from the college—and to spend full time in the school. Others may do their student teaching for a half-day and attend college classes during the other half. Students may even be assigned for less than a half-day—a period or two—or for two or three half-days a week, or perhaps for one or two full days a week. It is not unusual to find variations in time allotments even within the same college. Such variations make generalizations regarding how best to utilize the student's time in the classroom almost impossible.

The trend today is toward providing extended contacts with children prior to student teaching. Notwithstanding this significant development, students will come with varied background experiences with boys and girls. These may include playground or club work, orientation visits to schools, guided observation in a variety of classrooms, and quite often participation experiences with a single class or group of children for an extended period. On the other hand, there will be some students who have had little or no experience in the classroom. Such diversity will result in very different needs, especially in the early part of the student-teaching experience. Some students will be ready to take over the class after a short period of familiarization; others will require a more gradual initiation to full-fledged responsibility.

One does not learn to teach from the textbook alone. Watching children learn and relating theory to practice are obvious accompaniments of a well-rounded program of teacher education. Nevertheless, college courses will vary widely in the degree to which the work is correlated and integrated with classroom experience. In some colleges, separate methods courses may be taught by three or four different instructors with little parallel classroom experience or even relationship among the courses. In others the work may consist of an integrated "core" program with extensive coordinate classroom activities. In some institutions, this core may be simultaneous with student teaching. Under this plan, the student will be making his first theoretical analyses of teaching procedures at the same time that he is becoming acquainted with his own classroom. Students from such varied backgrounds will come with widely divergent needs for guidance in their first contacts with their student-teaching assignment.

Even in the case of two students with identical college backgrounds, there will be differences in ability to apply what has been learned to the new situation. One of the most challenging problems in teacher education is that of assuring maximum transfer from the college classroom to the student-teaching classroom. In common with other learners, beginning teachers develop concepts gradually; there will be differences in the degree to which they see as applicable what was talked over in the college class last year. Although the trend toward providing classroom contacts which parallel closely the college psychology and methods courses has been of major help in illuminating what might otherwise be purely academic discussions, both student and cooperating teacher must expect that many principles and procedures will have to be worked through again in relation to the student-teaching situation.

To the possibilities of differences in professional competence must be added personal differences in academic accomplishment, in talents, in insights, in ability to adjust to new situations. Perhaps more important, students will bring differing feelings of adequacy in human relations and differing levels of aspiration. For some, any day that seems less than perfection may represent a major threat to self-esteem. Others, from the start, will take in stride the challenges, satisfactions, frustrations, and surprises of learning to work with thirty or more youngsters.

Just as the needs, capacities, and previous experiences of the individuals in a classroom determine the specific goals for the year, so the professional and personal qualifications of each student influence the objectives of his student-teaching program. Ideally, the student-teaching program should be flexible, continuing for as short or as long a period as is needed for the student to achieve a desirable level of competence. Practically, in most cases, the length of the experience will be defined, and the problem will be to start where the student is and to help him proceed as far toward attaining competence in dealing with the professional problems of teaching as his capacities and previous experience will allow.

What are the major professional problems with which beginning teachers (and, for that matter, all teachers) must be able to cope? Student teachers, as well as cooperating teachers, would do well to think about the goals suggested in the remainder of this section. Awareness of the types of competence they will be expected to acquire can help students to make the most of the classroom responsibilities they are asked to assume.

It is important that students have experience in developing effective human relationships in the classroom. Among the problems that cause beginning teachers to consider leaving the profession, discipline ranks high. The student teacher must have ample opportunity to learn how to establish himself as the democratic leader of his group. He needs security in his ability to help pupils develop increasing self-control. He must acquire as automatic a goodly number of those common-sense procedures by which experienced teachers achieve a classroom atmosphere conducive to happy living and smooth working relationships.

Establishing good work habits and a democratic classroom atmosphere is only part of the problem of developing effective human relationships. Every teacher is likely to have in his class one or more individuals whose inner tensions make it difficult for them to adjust to the patterns of behavior expected of the group. It is essential that the student teacher have experience in helping to guide these pupils, in being responsible for studying them and deciding what to do in group situations in which such youngsters find it difficult to operate. He needs to see how parent conferences may be used to help such children and to become familiar with the services of the professional workers who can assist him. In short, in so far as he is able, the student teacher needs to take responsibility for every aspect of the problem of developing effective human relationships in his group.

Experience in guiding the learning activities in the classroom is needed. Responsibility for the growth of a group of boys and girls means guiding their learning—in the development of skills, in the acquisition of information and the formation of concepts and generalizations, in creative expression. If he is to feel secure in his decisions in his first full-time position, the beginner should have had experience in planning independently for each step of the teaching process—evaluating the needs and present level of competence of his group, deciding what new goals are appropriate, deciding how he will achieve these goals, locating his resource materials, and executing and evaluating his plan. He needs to feel secure in planning activities as simple as an effective spelling lesson and as complicated as an extensive and highly organized unit of work.

Sometimes a beginner who can formulate effectively the plans for a single lesson meets his Waterloo when it comes to scheduling the activities for the day or managing the experiences of groups and individuals working at many levels of competence. Although the student teacher will undoubtedly assume responsibility gradually, before his assignment has ended he needs to have learned what it is like to take full charge of scheduling and guiding the activities of his class—for deciding how his time as the teacher is to be spent, for worrying about the half-dozen children who finish early and stand at his elbow asking what to do next, for deciding whether to wait for the youngster who invariably finishes last, for making sure that all the groups working on special projects have their plans clearly in mind. In other words, he must become aware of just how much planning has to go into an effective day.

Not all learning activities are confined to the regular classroom schedule. The beginning teacher will have to decide how best to help his pupils profit from attending an all-school concert, from cooperating in a school service project, from abiding by school regulations in the lunchroom. Then there are Halloween, Thanksgiving, Christmas, Valentine's Day, birthday celebrations, special assemblies. Some pupils may be on the student council, the safety patrol, an office helpers' list.

All these extra activities must be worked into the school day. The prospective teacher needs to know how to do this. He must be able to plan for a regular program, but his life in the first classroom of his own is likely to be miserable indeed if he does not know how to adjust his carefully laid plans to the exigencies of unforeseen events.

Experience in evaluation and reporting to parents is essential. Taking full responsibility for deciding what shall go into a day involves evaluation—identifying pupils' strengths and weaknesses and deciding upon appropriate next steps. This calls for sensitivity in studying children while they are at work as well as ability to evaluate written work and skill in using a variety of teacher-made and standardized instruments for measurement. Perhaps most important, it calls for ability to set standards—to judge what can appropriately be expected of individuals, to decide what new levels of achievement to hold.

Every teacher must also be able to translate what he knows about individuals into symbols or words that will convey accurate meaning to the child, his parents, and the next teacher who works with him. How to conduct a conference with a parent, what precautions to take in writing a letter home, what to say in a home visit and how to invite oneself to a home, how to interpret the school program to parents during a school open house or a class program—these are all problems a first-year teacher must face. Such problems are handled with security only after there has been firsthand experience.

Proficiency in handling housekeeping and clerical responsibilities must be acquired. Many a first-year teacher is overwhelmed by the multitude of minor details that must be taken care of in the course of a normal day. Moneys have to be collected, attendance reports kept, supplies ordered, visual aids secured, special requests from the office met. It is all too easy for cooperating teachers to continue to share these responsibilities on the basis that two pairs of hands can get chores done faster than one. This is not, however, a favor to the student. Beginners need to become thoroughly familiar with the types of records that may be expected of them. They must also be helped to realize their obligation to carry out their own clerical responsibilities promptly and accurately. Perhaps most important, they must learn, through ample firsthand experience, how to manage the classroom program so that work proceeds smoothly while administrative responsibilities are being met.

The student teacher needs to participate as a member of the faculty. Some of the beginning teacher's anxieties relate to fitting into a new school. The student-teaching experience should provide activities that prepare for operating as an effective faculty member. The new teacher must understand the principal's role and the responsibilities of teachers to him. He needs to be aware of the interrelated functions of the school nurse, the custodian, the lunchroom personnel, and other persons who also have some responsibility for the welfare of boys and girls. Lunchroom supervision, hall duties, special assignments—these are obligations which are part of the teacher's work. Some knowledge of them is essential. Perhaps equally important, the beginner needs the "feel" of the interpersonal relationships characteristic of a closely knit school faculty—the ways committees operate, the problems that are discussed around the luncheon table, the social events, the joking and easy informality that make for group morale. These are important experiences if the student is to be a contributing faculty member next year.

Skill in self-evaluation must be developed. The ultimate objective of the student-teaching program, then, is to provide the student with the varied and wide experiences which will permit him to operate as nearly like a full-time faculty member as his assignment and his capacities will allow. The student-teaching experience will not have made its full contribution, however, unless the student has learned to evaluate his own competence and to plan for his own further growth. He needs opportunities to look objectively at his strengths and to identify those areas in which he feels least sure of himself. Where the student teaching program makes its maximum contribution, the student shares actively in planning for his own growth experiences. Only the student, with the help of his cooperating teacher and college supervisor, can determine the combination and proportion of activities which will insure optimum growth.

HELPING STUDENT TEACHERS FEEL AT HOME

How to help the student teacher to feel that he is accepted in the classroom is a first and very practical concern of many cooperating teachers. Much depends upon the feelings of security developed when the first contacts are made. In some situations the student teacher will be responsible for meeting the cooperating teacher before he reports to the school. This makes a preliminary conference possible, perhaps at the school where the student can see the classroom and become acquainted with some of the teaching aids. Sometimes the student-teaching assignment will begin with the first day of school. This frequently alleviates some of the tensions of beginning, since all are concerned with becoming acquainted—pupils, cooperating teacher, and student. There will be other situations in which the student comes after school has begun, and there is very little opportunity for any preliminary contacts. In such cases care must be wisely exercised to insure that the student becomes a part of the group as rapidly and as easily as possible. Whatever the plan governing the beginning of the student-teaching assignment, cooperating teachers will face problems of how to help the beginning teacher to feel secure and easy in his relations with themselves; how to assist him in becoming established as a teacher in the eyes of the pupils; and what steps will help him feel at home in the school faculty and the community.

The beginner needs to feel secure in his relations with his cooperating teacher. It is safe to say that most beginners approach the student-teaching experience with two major concerns, both within the area of human relations: how they will get along with their cooperating teachers and how they will be accepted by their pupils. It is important both for cooperating teacher and for student to realize that the cooperative relations they desire will not usually emerge full-blown the first day they meet. Adjustments by both persons are likely to be needed before easy working relationships are achieved.

In the first few days many little things can contribute to a student's feelings of security in his relationships with his cooperating teacher. Students report with satisfaction comments such as, "I am always so glad to have someone to share the responsibility for these children"; "I enjoy very much working with you people from the college"; "There are so many things we can do for these youngsters when there are two of us"; "We've been looking forward to you; the children were quite disappointed when we had no one last semester." On the other hand, too frank a sharing of concerns during the first few days can arouse anxieties. "I wondered if I should have a student when this group is so slow, but Mr. Jackson talked me into it." "I'm afraid you'll find me dreadfully old-fashioned; I've been away from college for a long time"; "I must confess I was a little concerned when I heard you were coming; Miss Simonds worried so much about her student last year." Phrasing expectations in overly glowing terms in an effort to help a student to feel secure can also cause tensions. "I'm counting on you to show me all the latest methods, you know"; "I'm glad to see that you play the piano; we'll expect some wonderful experiences in music this year."

Students comment with appreciation on many specific steps taken to help them feel at home. Knowing whether to hang one's coat with the children's or in the teacher's closet, where to sit, whether to put one's books on the teacher's desk, whether to borrow the teacher's copies of textbooks or to take some from the shelves for children, whether classroom books may be taken home—these may represent more crucial problems when one is anxious to be accepted than they would appear on the surface. Knowing whether to move about the room while the children are working or to sit still and whether to answer the questions of children who come to one for help, raise other dilemmas where specific indications of what to do can be very reassuring. There can also be uncertain moments during recess or lunch breaks. Should one "tag along" or seem to have one's own plans made? Is the teacher's room for the use of students, too? Although students typically will have been advised in college pre-planning sessions not to hesitate to ask when they are uncertain, it can sometimes be quite a struggle to decide whether to raise a question that might make one appear hopelessly naïve and uninformed. The first steps of becoming acquainted can be made much easier if cooperating teachers will be particularly aware of the values of being outgoing and definite in their advice.

It is a major contribution to a beginner's feelings of acceptance to realize from the start that he is going to have a share in planning for the well-being of the class. On the other hand, there needs to be reassurance that he is not going to be left without support. "She asked me what kind of news I thought they should have on their first bulletin board," reported Arnold Stevenson. "How could I know?" Most cooperating teachers develop ways of thinking their plans aloud during the first few weeks so that students become involved in the process without having to make the full decision themselves. "We probably should try to have a fairly good idea of how well they read by the end of the week." "Have you seen teachers make a tally of language errors from a set of papers like these? I think we would find it revealing." "Perhaps we should take time tomorrow to reorganize their seating. Did you notice how badly that group in the corner fell apart?"

The typical beginner often comes apprehensive about how rapidly he may be asked to take on responsibilities and sometimes fearful lest he not be capable of carrying out his first assignments. Cooperating teachers can ease the tension considerably by indicating some of the procedures they have found most helpful in working with students. It is reassuring to hear from the lips of the person with whom one is to work closely that there will be time for cooperative planning, that one may start with an activity in which one feels secure, or that one is to be inducted into responsibility gradually.

Perhaps no procedure demonstrates more clearly that one has a place in a new classroom than being given a job to do, even though it may take only a few minutes. On the first day of school this may involve helping children to fill in registration forms, preparing name tags to paste on desks, going with two children to deliver materials to the office, helping individuals with spelling as the youngsters write a short autobiography or a description of their summer activities for their new teacher. If school has already begun, pupils may be invited to go to the student for help in a specific area, a committee may be asked to seek his advice in setting up a bulletin board, the student may be involved by telling something about his college or sharing experiences from his special background.

In giving the student teacher his first taste of responsibility, it is advisable to be specific. Even though the activity seems likely to be one in which he has been engaged before, this is a new situation and there can be understandable anxiety about doing things just right. Advice on how to proceed can often be directed toward the children as well so that there is no seeming coaching from the side lines. "Let's all look at the sample here to see just how these cards are to be filled in; then I shall check this half of the room and Mr. Dick will do the other." "Miss Grayson will serve as our resource person in spelling today. Let's see, Miss Grayson, won't it be easier if you come to them when their hands are up rather than having everyone come back to you? And would someone like to tell Miss Grayson how we're trying to use spelling to help us learn to use the dictionary?" "We're lucky Mr. Anson came today. This is just when we needed somebody new to look at our mural. Mr. Anson, the mural committee has the list of things we said a good mural should accomplish. Would you like to help them discuss one point at a time?"

The beginner needs to feel accepted by the class. How shall the student teacher be introduced to the pupils? It is safe to say that regardless of the exact phrasing used older pupils, particularly, will recognize that he is from the college and that he is there to learn more about teaching. Sometimes their devotion to him and concern for his success are touching. "What did you think of your student?" asked one alert fifth-grader of the college supervisor. "Don't you think he deserves an *A*?" "Don't worry, Mr. Jackson," said one group that normally delighted in seeing how precarious they could make the situation, "when your supervisor's here we won't let you down." "We like Miss Sharp," said a second-grader. "Can't you fix it so she can stay with us all year?"

Even though the pupils are often aware of the student teacher's status, it is helpful to introduce him as a teacher rather than as a student. ("Mr. King is going to work with us this semester. Next year he'll have a class of his own. We should accomplish a lot with two teachers to help.") A number of steps can be taken to demonstrate from the start that the student is, indeed, another teacher. Drawing him into the discussions helps. His advice can be asked in areas where he is known to have competence. Involving him in activities where he can be of service to children, such as those indicated in the preceding section, does much to establish him with the group. When this is done, it is important to see that pupils actually do turn to him for help in whatever areas he has assumed responsibility. ("Mr. Smith is helping you with that; suppose you ask him.") It is also helpful to plan early activities which place the student teacher in front of the class as a whole in situations that are not too likely to tempt the venturesome to try to discover how much latitude he will allow. Depending on the particular situation, experiences with the total group such as the following may be considered: taking attendance, reading a story, sharing a special experience, dictating a list of spelling words, escorting the class down the hall to the library, walking out with the lines at noon.

A student teacher can establish himself more rapidly with a group if he knows names. He will probably have been advised to make his own seating charts. Procedures that will aid him in matching names and faces can be helpful. Children can be encouraged to introduce themselves as the student works with a small committee. In the early fall, games to help children learn one another's names can involve both cooperating teacher and student. Seeing that each child writes his name clearly on his written work enables the newcomer to spot the names as he moves around the room giving help. Even the rather routine secretarial activities of preparing attendance books, taking roll, and checking registration cards may be of value.

Individuals begin to stand out more clearly when one knows a little of their backgrounds. Students will probably come prepared to study pupils intensively when the occasion offers. In the first few weeks, projects for the children such as writing a short autobiography or developing a bulletin board of pictures and descriptions of homes and families can be particularly useful in helping the student to feel that he is beginning to know pupils as individuals. It can also be of value to have access to cumulative records, although these are often best looked at first in conference situations where the cooperating teacher's insights can temper the student's judgment. In addition, many cooperating teachers use a good share of the early conference periods to discuss with students the needs of individuals.

It is important to be sure that the student is acquainted early with specific classroom regulations—agreements regarding when pencils are to be sharpened, how people are to be excused to leave the room, when one may get a drink. When the student knows of these specific agreements, he is better prepared to forestall ingenious attempts to play one adult against another. Beginners need to be advised specifically with regard to their responsibility for the behavior of individuals when a cooperating teacher is at work with the class. Everyone is to have books away, but Johnny has a comic book on his knee; Billy has been taking delicious tugs at Janie's braids with one eye on the newcomer in the back of the room; people are supposed to be paying attention to the planning session, but Caroline is addressing explanatory comments under her breath to the intriguing new source of adult attention; the cooperating teacher is called into the hall and everyone begins to get silly—what is the newcomer supposed to do? Unless there are unusual circumstances, most cooperating teachers expect the student to make the appropriate move as a teacher in such situations, but without specific reassurance he may be uncertain whether this will be acceptable. Isn't it a little presumptuous for a student to motion to a child to put a book away after the cooperating teacher has already asked for this? Won't this give the impression that one thinks the cooperating teacher does not know what is going on?

Ultimately, of course, the student teacher must establish himself with the class on the strength of his own leadership. Often it is helpful to leave him with the class for short periods of time—to walk in a little late, leaving him to get people in their seats and ready to work; to run an errand while he is teaching; to send him ahead to the library with the children. Well-meant efforts to control the situation from the side lines often contribute to the student's feelings of insecurity and inadequacy and sometimes convince the class that here is someone with little or no authority in his own right. Establishing effective interpersonal relationships is a year-long proposition, however, not a feat accomplished in the first few days. Basically, it calls for growth on the part of the student in many aspects of human understanding, good teaching, and common-sense organizational ability.

The beginner needs to feel at home in the school. A student teacher needs to feel a part of the school as a whole as well as a member of the classroom to which he is assigned. Principals have developed a number of devices that help in this. In many schools the student's name is entered on the regular faculty roster. If teachers sign in the time of their arrival, so does he. If there is a handbook for new faculty, the student is supplied with one. In some schools, principals find time for an early conference with the student teachers in which background information about the school and community is given and school policies are outlined. Sometimes folios of the various forms used in the school system—absence records, order blanks for visual aids, attendance forms—are provided. Students have also been invited to attend faculty meetings. In some situations, it has proved helpful to take the student out of his assigned classroom long enough to enable him to get the "feel" of the school by visiting in other rooms, observing in the offices of the nurse and other special personnel, and perhaps spending a half-day working in the principal's office.

Cooperating teachers can also make definite efforts to help students become acquainted with other teachers. Inviting the student to stay at the school for lunch, if his is a half-day assignment, is a gracious gesture. Normally, the typical intervisitation that goes on before school begins and during breaks offers other opportunities for the student to meet individual faculty members. In some situations students have been included in faculty social affairs. Students have also reported appreciatively opportunities to work with their cooperating teachers on special faculty projects—sharing responsibility for part of a Christmas program, helping with the faculty planning for a Halloween entertainment.

Problems sometimes arise as to how far to involve a student when faculty members face problems of a semiconfidential nature that need to be talked through. If the student feels welcome in the lunchroom and in the teachers' lounge, he is almost certain, before the year is out, to be present when vigorous disagreement with a request from the office is being expressed, concern is being voiced regarding the difficulties of the new teacher down the hall, or information is being shared about problems in the home of some child. There will also be times when another teacher drops by the classroom to discuss a problem that cannot be aired in the hall or the lounge. Such situations can prove awkward for all concerned, and there is no easy formula for handling them. One general guide might be that the give-and-take of normal faculty disagreements can provide important preparation for participating as a regular faculty member next year, provided there is an opportunity for the student teacher to discuss these professionally afterwards. A second guide probably should be that it is important to explain to the student frankly why certain types of information cannot be shared with him and to give him advice regarding what his behavior should be when situations arise that seem to have confidential aspects. Should he go on working with his bulletin board or stop to be sociable when the principal walks in? If he doesn't come over to chat will he be thought shy or distant? It is helpful to be told specifically that it is quite in order to greet the visitor and then go on with one's work. It is reassuring, also, to be invited specifically to join a conversation when this is appropriate. Before entering upon student teaching, students probably will have engaged in discussions regarding professional behavior in a school. Here again, however, the aid of the cooperating teacher is needed in making the transition to the specific situation.

The student teacher needs to be accepted by parents and community. Over the semester, it is important for the student teacher to come to feel that he is acquainted with the community and accepted by the parents. In some situations, cooperating teachers will face the problem of explaining the importance of the student-teaching program to parents and of gaining the acceptance of the student as a person who is to have at least partial responsibility for their children.

There are many ways of helping the student to feel that he is coming to know parents. Attending Parent-Teacher Association meetings and being present at an open house when parents are visiting the classroom are among the most obvious. Many cooperating teachers also arrange to take the student with them on a certain number of home visits. Sometimes the student can make the home contact alone—walking home with a child who is ill, taking books to a youngster who is going to be out for several days. Often there are opportunities for a parent and a student teacher to work together—taking a special committee to the museum, planning a Christmas treat for the class. Cooperating teachers have also found ways of involving students in parent conferences—perhaps the student has been the one to observe evidence of decided growth on the part of the pupil. In the area of parent contacts, students will feel more secure if there are opportunities prior to the parent's arrival to discuss policy, with a conference time afterwards to analyze what occurred.

What can be done to interpret the student-teaching program to parents? Probably nothing is more useful than concrete evidence that pupils are benefiting from the presence of another teacher (unless, perhaps, it is the successful job done by a first-year teacher who has graduated from the same program). The way in which the student teacher is introduced to the pupils (and is talked about at home) can contribute to his acceptance. So can his first classroom responsibilities if they are successful and interesting to the pupils. It is usually possible, also, as parents visit to point to a project that has been the student's special responsibility. In most elementary schools it is customary to plan at least one class project to which parents are invited. This provides another opportunity to point out the share the student has had in the development of the project. Often, the student's presence makes it possible either for student or cooperating teacher to give time to a group in need of special help. Parents whose youngsters have been the recipients of this attention tend to value the student-teaching program. In addition, it can be very reassuring to parents to be told the ways in which the student and the cooperating teacher are working together—the planning sessions, the conferences, the cooperative teaching, that insure a rich program for pupils. Faculty supervisors can frequently help in giving such explanations. College resources may also be tapped to enrich other aspects of the school program and parents apprised of this. The school which opens its doors to student teachers is assuming a major professional obligation. The success of this cooperative undertaking must be judged by the degree to which the lives of youngsters are enriched here and now as well as by the later success of the student.

HELPING BEGINNERS MOVE INTO FULL RESPONSIBILITY

It would be most unusual if cooperating teachers did not have some misgivings when they face the responsibility of guiding the student teacher through the full range of the professional experiences necessary for a successful first year on the job. An invitation to become a cooperating teacher typically signifies a reputation for devotion to children and exceptional skill in meeting their needs. Naturally there is some trepidation when it comes to trusting the well-being and progress of the pupils to the inexpert hands of a beginner. Nevertheless, the welfare of many future groups of pupils depends on the thoroughness and effectiveness of the student-teaching experience.

Pupils need not suffer, however, if the student teacher's induction into full-time responsibility is skillfully executed. He needs to be helped to take on increased responsibility at the pace at which he can handle it successfully. If student teaching is a gradual induction process, the beginner typically brings to each new responsibility a zeal, a desire to provide challenging activities, and a genuine fondness for children that more than counterbalance any lack of adeptness in teaching techniques. What procedures on the part of the cooperating teachers will contribute to successful progress toward full-time teaching?

Early experiences should build security. For what types of activities should a student teacher first take responsibility? There are probably as many answers to this question as there are student-teaching situations. A combination of factors may influence the decision in any one room—the student's own feelings of confidence, his competence, the needs of the pupils and the projects in which they are engaged, the way in which the cooperating teacher feels most secure in delegating responsibility.

Ideally, the student himself should express a preference regarding the activities with which he would like to begin. However, some may be reluctant to make suggestions lest they interfere with the cooperating teacher's plans. Others may view every possibility with trepidation, and some will not recognize the hazards involved in their proposals. In the beginning, the cooperating teacher often must be the one to assign specific responsibilities. These early experiences should be selected with two objectives in mind: to give the student the security that comes from success and to develop the children's ready acceptance of him as a leader because of the quality of his contribution.

Whether or not a student's first major responsibility should be with a small group or with the class as a whole depends on the particular student and on the situations that present themselves in his class. Although it is helpful to the student in establishing himself with the group to have some early responsibilities that put him before the class as a whole—taking attendance, escorting the group to the gym, reading a story—an all-class contact more extensive than those just mentioned can be threatening to some students unless it is preceded by considerable experience with small groups. Others, however, may welcome the opportunity to work with the whole class in the same spirit in which one dives into ice-cold water rather than wading in.

Often a student's special talent makes a good starting point. Janet McCardy reads aloud very well and takes over a primary story-and-rest period as her first major responsibility. Janice Watson is a talented musician and starts by teaching her first grade some songs. John Abernathy is a veteran whose overseas experiences make it appropriate for him to supervise the sixth-grade group in preparing a map of Europe. Anna Mae Simpson is at home in art and creative dramatics and takes over the group preparing a puppet show. Sally Zelinka has spent several years as a playground leader and feels competent to take her third-grade class out for games.

Frequently, the responsibilities assigned to the student teacher to help him become acquainted with pupils lead directly into his first definite teaching assignment. Kathleen Anderson has been helping with individual spelling problems; now she takes the responsibility for directing the study of a set of words. Jonathan Maxwell has been helping a small group to arrange a current events bulletin board; now he works with them to develop their reports to the class. Belinda O'Neill starts by helping a group to appraise their mural and then goes on to guide the work of these youngsters as they plan to add more details. It is not usually a matter of being an observer one day and a teacher the next. The process is gradual, and the difference between the independent responsibility taken on today and that assumed tomorrow can often scarcely be noticed.

Cooperative teaching can provide a smooth transition to increased responsibility. From a student teacher's first venture, the steps which lead to full responsibility for the class may be large or small, rapid or slow, depending on the student, the class, and the cooperating teacher's feeling of security. Cooperative teaching is often helpful in assuring a successful transition to full-time teaching. Both persons work actively with increasing responsibility for leadership being assumed by the student.

In classrooms where pupils are involved democratically in planning and evaluating their activities, it is easy to include the student in planning sessions even while the cooperating teacher is assuming major leadership functions:

COOPERATING TEACHER

Mr. Cardy and I thought about your projects last night; it seemed to us that one good work session would finish them. What do you think?

JOHN

Our group isn't that far along. We've got an awful lot to do.

ALEC CARDY
John, you were absent yesterday. We're farther ahead than you think.

COOPERATING TEACHER
Then you think John's group can wind their work up today, Mr. Cardy?

ALEC CARDY
I think so. What do you say, Belinda?

Soon the student will be sufficiently involved in aspects of the program so that it is a simple matter to turn over to him more responsibility for leadership of the planning session:

COOPERATING TEACHER
Mr. Cardy, the big thing today is to get the play under way, isn't it?

ALEC CARDY
That's right. Boys and girls, let's check yesterday's plans here and see what's most important.

JANIE
We still don't know whether we want costumes and what scenery we want.

ALEC CARDY
Shall we put that down to settle today, then?

Often student teachers take on, as their first independent teaching responsibility, the direction of the work of an arithmetic, a reading, or a spelling group. This is a situation that lends itself readily to cooperative teaching. While the student works with a group in one corner of the room, the cooperating teacher works with a second group in another. Under such circumstances, it can be a valuable experience to the student to be responsible for seeing to it that both groups report to their teachers with the equipment they need and for keeping an eye on those at their seats. Because transitions are awkward for beginners, it can be a valuable experience, too, for the student to call the groups back at the end of the period and to supervise them as they put books away and get ready for the activity to follow. If the student merely works with his small group and leaves the cooperating teacher to supervise gathering in papers and getting out materials for the next lesson, he is failing to develop skills that can make a major contribution to the smooth running of his class next year:

SANDY MIX
It's time to meet with our reading groups now. Are your papers all away?

Let's look up here, then, so that we'll know what we're doing. Billy's group were going to finish their pictures about the story—is that right?

(Several voices from Billy's group say "Yes, Ma'am.")

Will you get out your pictures right now, please? Now, Miss Sampson wants her people in the back of the room. Do they need anything, Miss Sampson?

MISS SAMPSON

Yes; bring a pencil. We're going to try ourselves out on our new words today.

SANDY MIX

All right. And I want my people to come up here. John, will you get the books for us? Now, before my group begins, is there anyone in Billy's group having any difficulty getting started with your picture? Suppose you finish ahead of us, what might you do next?

Cooperative teaching can also provide a smooth induction into full responsibility for developing an elaborate unit of work in the content fields. In the first unit, the cooperating teacher may take major responsibility for planning with the pupils with the student assisting in clarifying problems and deciding on ways of working. Once plans are laid, both student and cooperating teacher give help. Sometimes each may take specific responsibility for guiding the work of two or three subcommittees; sometimes both circulate, giving help wherever it is needed. Responsibility for all-class activities may be shared. The student may set up a series of demonstrations or work with visual aids in areas where his competence is strongest; the cooperating teacher may take over for others. At the end of the unit, a short culminating activity might be developed under the leadership of the student. Later, the student takes over the complete responsibility for planning, setting up work procedures, and deciding on visual aids and the cooperating teacher serves merely as a resource person as specific committees go to work.

Establishing an atmosphere of cooperative teaching from the beginning has advantages over and above the support it offers to the student as he makes the transition to full-time classroom responsibility. It makes it possible for the cooperating teacher to continue to give special help to individuals without seeming to encroach on the student's area of leadership. There is always a talented child who could be stimulated to venture into new fields if time for individual conferences only permitted, a bright youngster whose zeal for science should be encouraged by a special reading program, a pupil whose difficulties in reading or spelling could be cleared up if only there were time for individual help. Although the student teacher should cope with this range in ability without help before his assignment ends, it would be a tragic misuse of the talents of the two teachers in the room if such youngsters did not receive extra help while it is available.

Cooperative teaching also makes it possible for the cooperating teacher to resume the leadership of an activity for a week or so without seeming to the children to be showing any lack of faith in the student teacher. This can be highly desirable when the student has reached a point where he recognizes his own inadequacies and feels the need to observe an experienced teacher's techniques. It is sometimes also desirable for the cooperating teacher to take over an activity in which a student has shown proficiency in order to allow him more time for planning and locating the materials related to a new project. By the end of the student-teaching assignment, of course, the student needs to know from firsthand experience what adjustments in one's personal life it will take to assume full responsibility for planning every aspect of the program. His progress toward successful full-time responsibility may be more rapid, however, if he is afforded temporary relief at points where he must solve a new teaching problem of major proportions.

Increased responsibility should be accompanied by careful planning. As the student begins to take on increased responsibility, the experience ought to offer more than merely an opportunity to experiment with his own ideas about how to teach. There should be joint planning sessions which will enable him to grow through thinking through classroom problems under the guidance of an experienced teacher. These sessions should help to forestall at least some types of difficulties so that the plan the student actually puts into effect results in a richer experience for youngsters (and a more satisfying one for himself) than would have come from his initial inexperienced suggestions. It is true that we learn from experience, but the intellectual consideration of a problem can be a type of learning experience.

In spite of considerable emphasis in college classes, students do not always realize the detail that must go into an effective lesson plan. A common error is to make a plan which gives an outline of facts to be presented but which does not show how the pupils are to be involved —what problems they will be asked to solve, what practice materials they might need, and what help they might be given as the lesson proceeds. As any experienced teacher knows, such vague notes in the name of lesson-planning as "take up spelling," "read next story," or "group work" can lead to disaster. Cooperating teachers should not hesitate to request, and students should expect to supply in writing, plans sufficiently detailed for the security of both parties. These should include both unit plans and plans for the day. In contrast to earlier times in teacher education, the student may not have been required in college to use any set pattern for writing his plans, the assumption being that they are an instrument for his personal use and that the form that might be helpful to one person could be relatively ineffective for another. The cooperating teacher should expect, therefore, to give the student some assistance in developing the type of plan appropriate to the needs of the particular situation. It is often helpful, also, for the student to examine the cooperating teacher's written plans. It is always reassuring to know that experienced teachers actually put into practice what they recommend for others.

Learning to select activities appropriate for a particular class can be a major hurdle for some beginners. It is often helpful if the first planning sessions are cooperative, with teacher and student jointly evaluating the strengths and weaknesses of the children and projecting next steps. What will unscramble the confusion of this social studies committee?—what factors seem to be causing the trouble? are there individual conflicts to take into account? do they lack important skills? with what aspects of their work should they be given special help the next time they meet? What types of reading experiences do these able children need? —what skills seem well mastered? in what areas have they had limited opportunities? Should we be discouraged that yesterday's lesson on capitals seems not to be reflected at all in today's stories? —what follow-up is needed? how many times must a point be repeated before everyone gets it? How should the performance of this class in writing letters be evaluated?—from a college point of view it seems inadequate, but is it appropriate for third grade? Planning sessions such as these, in which the student is encouraged to share his insights and to propose next steps, can make a major contribution to the security with which he begins to plan on his own.

As the student begins to assume more responsibility for independent planning it can be particularly helpful to him to have ample time to formulate his plans. This is not possible for all aspects of the program, but there are many points at which generous time for preparation can be allowed. It may be that the units of work in science, social studies, and health are outlined in the course of study. If so, the student can be allowed to select well in advance those for which he will assume major responsibility. This will enable him to explore resources fully, to make his block or unit plan in careful detail and to review the subject matter involved. The plan can then be evaluated by the cooperating teacher and discussed with the student while there is still opportunity to make changes.

What does the cooperating teacher do if a student teacher's plans do not develop as his own would? If the plan seems likely to work out successfully, the student should certainly be congratulated on thinking for himself and encouraged to try his wings. If there seems to be an obvious weakness, the problem can be discussed with the student and alternative procedures worked out. Two cautions are in order here. First, the student needs to understand why the alternative procedure is suggested and precisely what problem it is likely to forestall. Second, because it is difficult to use another's idea effectively if it is only half understood, he needs time to think through the new proposal in detail and to incorporate it into his plans. The temptation to suggest that a student change completely his plans for the day, if it is now 8:45 and the youngsters are walking in the door, should be resisted unless he is known to be exceptionally secure and versatile. However fraught with pitfalls, a plan which is the student's own and clearly understood by him has a better chance of success than one suggested by the cooperating teacher whose purposes and reasoning have not been comprehended.

Even though student teachers typically regard student teaching as a learning experience and expect to be given help, there will be some who experience difficulty in accepting suggestions. There will be the occasional student who is so unsure of his own ability that the slightest attempt to raise questions regarding his plans is taken as evidence that he has already failed. Faced with this situation, the cooperating teacher is probably well advised to give praise and encouragement until the student has developed a greater sense of security. There are other students (probably also insecure if one could get below the surface) who find it very difficult to accept the possibility that their proposed course of action might not work. In the face of such resistance, a cooperating teacher may have to grit his teeth and endure failures until the student reaches the point where he can be more objective about advice. Let it be said in defense of this procedure that it is extremely difficult to have so bad a single day that the pieces cannot be picked up tomorrow. Cooperating teachers, too, on their own worst days, have cause to be grateful for the resiliency of youngsters.

Help from the side lines can be made constructive. How does the cooperating teacher occupy himself while the student teacher is in charge of the group? Dare he interrupt if an error is made? Should he try to pass a note to the student or signal with raised eyebrows that something is amiss? Suppose the lesson is dragging far too slowly—can anything be done to speed it up? How far does he allow a disciplinary situation to build up before he steps in?

The answers to questions such as these depend on the complex constellation of factors in the immediate situation. The student's sense of security is a major consideration. With some student teachers, a word or a gesture from the cooperating teacher indicating that something is awry may result in panic. If this seems likely, the only defensible procedure is to take up the problem in conference later, counting on some effective reteaching by the student to rectify the error. Other students think readily on their feet and welcome the help, preferring to be "tipped off" to a point they are missing rather than to have a lesson less effective than it would otherwise be. Where there are sound relationships between student and cooperating teacher, it is to be hoped that students will feel free to say how they feel regarding interruptions. If the question is talked through, an understanding can be reached so that both the student and cooperating teacher know how to proceed when the emergency does arise.

The general classroom atmosphere can also make a difference in the ease with which a cooperating teacher can enter into the lesson. If the situation has been one where children, student teacher, and cooperating teacher have been used to cooperative planning, each feeling free to contribute his best thinking, it will not seem unusual to the children to hear the cooperating teacher offer a suggestion. At another point, it may be the student who is contributing from the side lines. The following interchanges may illustrate. Linda Nash's cooperating teacher refers to class plans in order to give help:

LINDA NASH

Look at the picture on the next page. How do you think the Pilgrims did their washing?

BOBBIE

They're right on the ocean. They must have used sea water.

SALLY
But if they did, why couldn't they wash their clothes on board ship?

LINDA NASH
Let's read what it says about the picture and see if it helps.

ANDY
It doesn't say what water they used. But you can't get soap suds from salt water.

COOPERATING TEACHER
Miss Nash, that's a good question for these people to add to their list, isn't it? I think you'll find some of the other books will tell you.

LINDA NASH
All right, let's put it down so we won't forget it. Thank you for helping us, Mrs. Crosby.

College personnel, too, are sometimes brought into an informal discussion, as was Janie Williams' supervisor.

BOBBIE
But we've got to turn him loose or he'll starve. [Bobbie is speaking of a snake brought to the third-grade classroom in the late fall.]

SUSAN
No, he won't. He'll just sleep and if he sleeps outside he'll freeze to death, won't he, Miss Williams?

JANIE WILLIAMS
I don't know for sure, Susan. Miss McDermit, can you help us?

COOPERATING TEACHER
I know Mr. Johnson has kept some snakes in the science laboratory, but we'd better talk to him to make sure what they need. What do you think, Dr. Rose?

COLLEGE SUPERVISOR
I think you folks had better talk to Mr. Johnson. Will you tell me what you found out when I come back next time?

JANIE WILLIAMS
We'll remember, won't we, boys and girls?

The student's relationships with the children also need to be considered in deciding whether to interrupt a lesson. If the leadership has been weak and the lessons dull, one would not add from the side lines another piece of evidence confirming the pupils' feelings. Sometimes, help from the cooperating teacher at the point where the student's relationships with the group are precarious can pull the class entirely away. Many a cooperating teacher has added a comment from the back of the room in a well-meant effort to help, only to find the entire group facing him while the student stood in the front, alone and foresaken. On the other hand, a secure student is often able to establish an "everybody makes mistakes" atmosphere where the pupils themselves help to correct him. "I *think* you've spelled that wrong," says John. "Will you look it up to be sure, John?" replies Sarah Gayner; and, as John makes the correction, "Thank you, John; I'm so glad you caught that before we all wrote it down."

A certain amount of role playing has its advantages in making corrections or additions smoothly at crucial points. The cooperating teacher signals for the floor as would any other pupil, and asks a question or adds a point. "Miss Smith, we're still confused back here. Are we to draw the design for our covers on notebook paper first so that you can see it before we use the colored paper?" "Miss Johnson, several people near me don't seem sure what they're to do until their reading group meets." "Mr. Adamson, I saw that geyser last summer. I wonder if you'd like the boys and girls to hear a little more about it."

Probably the most difficult type of situation in which to work from the side lines in such a way as to give genuine support to the student is in the area of interpersonal relationships—discipline in its broadest connotations. This is an aspect of teaching where it is virtually impossible to enter actively into the situation in order to strengthen the student's hand without, in the long run, weakening it. In the end, he must be the one to demonstrate to the group where his boundaries lie and how firm they are. Although the cooperating teacher can undoubtedly maintain any degree of control he wishes from the back of the room, this typically does not establish the student as a group leader.

In a situation involving classroom control it is possible, by a role-playing approach, to alert the student to potential confusion which he has been too engrossed to notice. "We could hear better back here, Mr. Ronson, if the bulletin board committee would use softer voices." "Miss Black, I believe these people used up all their story time because they forgot our plan about putting books away." "Excuse me, Mr. Keller, but three people have been back to ask me what to do next. Would you mind taking a minute to straighten them out?" It is possible, also, to give very firm support aloud to whatever the student teacher has requested. "Not now. Miss Black is waiting for you to put your books away." "Miss Clarkson said only two people at the easel, John. You'll have to wait until she has room for you." "If Mr. Edwards thinks you were too noisy to work in the hall, that's all there is to it. We warned you, remember?" Even though the student's decision reveals his inexperience, it is usually more helpful to group morale to support him and talk it out later than it is to contradict him. Divided discipline is as ineffective at school as at home. Where the student has not realized a school rule exists, it is often still possible to correct the situation without seeming to override him. "I'm sorry, Mr. Garson; I completely forgot to tell you that the traffic is so heavy here we must let these people cross the streets before the safety guards go home. But if you feel they were wasting time, I think we should cut short our story time tomorrow to finish this work."

There are times in the life of any teacher when he must ask other authorities to help with a child presenting unusual behavior problems. For the student teacher, the cooperating teacher may be the one to lend the weight of established authority to the student's newer voice in the case of the youngster who is having difficulty in working cooperatively with others. Typically, it is wise to map out procedures ahead of time. What type of appeal, for example, should be made in the presence of the child? What support should the student expect and the cooperating teacher be ready to give? What follow-up of the cooperating teacher's action should the student plan?

SANDRA POLLY

I'm sorry, Miss Cresky, but Billy can't seem to leave other people alone. Could he sit here by you and read?

MISS CRESKY

Certainly he can. You've had a bad day, haven't you, Billy? Do you want him back, Miss Polly, if he feels he can work with you?

SANDRA POLLY

Yes. Billy is a very nice painter, and I'm sure the committee will be glad to have him when he's ready to help.

Beyond question, the typical student will need time to make his own mistakes and to establish his own leadership. It would be unwise (and, for that matter, impossible) to guide and supervise his work so carefully that nothing ever goes wrong. Over and above on-the-spot assistance through skillful cooperative planning and teaching, it is important to provide conference time to analyze situations with the student in detail, pointing out as clearly as possible the elements that contributed both positively and negatively to the goals he desired. This important means of helping students to grow is discussed in the next section.

The foregoing presupposes, of course, that college advisory systems prior to student teaching have guided those not suited for the profession into areas more appropriate to their capacities. Where there is no solution that seems to contribute to both the growth of the student teacher and the well-being of the pupils, the youngsters, of course, must come first—and the college supervisor be consulted.

Observation can be a valuable aid to learning. What is the place of observation in the student-teaching experience? Certainly, the full resources of the classroom have not been utilized unless opportunities are afforded to observe an experienced teacher at work. However, the points in the student-teaching sequence at which observation is provided and the specific purposes of the student make a difference in the effectiveness of the experience.

At times, cooperating teachers have placed the entire observation period early—students watch for two or three weeks, perhaps, before they take any active leadership responsibility with the children. This plan has not always been satisfactory, even when a student teacher brings to the experience considerable know-how from classroom contacts the preceding year. The day tends to grow very long, and there seems to come a point of diminishing returns when the subtler aspects of what is going on are lost partly because the student has not had enough close contacts with the youngsters to sense when their needs are being skillfully met and partly because he is not always able to appreciate how effectively another person is avoiding pitfalls until he has tried to handle a situation himself. Students undoubtedly need some opportunities to observe in the early weeks of getting acquainted with a new class and a new cooperating teacher. These observation periods can be profitably interspersed, however, with the types of short-term responsibilities discussed previously as desirable ways to help the student to establish himself with the children.

The focus of the student's first observations should be on problems of getting acquainted. There are names to learn; procedures to acquire for passing papers, collecting books, getting wraps; and countless other activities where some sensible and fairly automatic rules and regulations are needed if thirty or more individuals are to live together peacefully and effectively. Beginners also need the reassurance of having seen the general techniques used by their cooperating teachers in planning with children, handling a reading group, or helping a social studies committee. Students will frequently come armed with general lists drawn up in college classes suggesting what to observe, but it is most helpful in these beginning weeks for cooperating teachers to point out specific aspects of the program or specific ways of working with individuals where it is deemed advisable for the student to follow similar procedures.

Observation can be extended with profit well beyond the beginning days. In situations where there is cooperative teaching some opportunities to observe are achieved in the natural course of events. Often it can be helpful if the cooperating teacher resumes a specific responsibility after the student has had an opportunity to experiment with it. It is reassuring to the student to know that such requests are expected and will not be taken as evidence of his inadequacy. Gladys Robinson feels that her planning sessions have been dragging and asks her cooperating teacher to take over for a few days so that she can try to analyze what makes the difference. Suzanne Jones asks for time to observe her cooperating teacher at work with a reading group in order to see how she handles problems of word analysis. John Arthur panics at the thought of helping his pupils to write Thanksgiving poems and his cooperating teacher volunteers to demonstrate for him.

Some students and cooperating teachers have reported that it is worth while to plan for an increased amount of observation as the student-teaching period comes to a close. In addition to giving the student a last objective look at expert teaching, this procedure may help to return the class smoothly to the leadership of the cooperating teacher. If the student-teaching program closes before the school year is out, this transition should be thought through cooperatively for the sake of the children.

Observation can also be used to help both student and cooperating teacher to gain better understanding of individuals. While the cooperating teacher leads the discussion, the student makes a tally of the flow of comments. While the cooperating teacher gives help to social studies groups, the student collects anecdotes on the activities of Jerome as he interrupts group after group. Sometimes the situation is reversed, the student teacher taking over the leadership responsibility while the cooperating teacher carries out the study of individuals. Such experiences can add much, both to the student's insights into the needs of individuals and to his data-collecting skills.

In some situations, observation has also been used effectively to enrich the student's total experience in the school. He may follow his group to the gym or to the music class to see how they are handled by another teacher, or if he is responsible for the physical education or music programs himself, he may follow the class in which he has the greatest concern back to their regular teacher. If he is on a half-day assignment, he may profit from returning to observe the program for the full day. It may be that the class next door presents behavior problems totally different from those of his group. Mrs. Sanderson down the hall may be experimenting with a tape recorder, or Mr. Bandy in the sixth grade be trying out an individualized reading program. Such visitation can add much to a student's insights, particularly if it is planned late enough in his experience to insure that he brings considerable depth of understanding.

Obviously, any observation is more valuable when its purpose is clear and there is guidance regarding the particular points to note. The problems which suggest the need for observation should be identified ahead of time in conference and some foci for observation thought through. Then the observation should be discussed dispassionately after the student has an opportunity to do some thinking about what he has seen.

MAKING THE MOST OF CONFERENCES

Opportunities to talk things through are essential if the student teacher is to derive maximum benefit from his classroom experiences. Undoubtedly there will be much informal consultation during the regular school day—a few minutes before school opens, a quick reaction at noon, a suggestion offered or question answered during a recess. Such short conferences are essential where people are cooperatively responsible for the well-being of thirty or more youngsters. However, these brief contacts do not provide the time required to help a student think through all the complex problems that confront him. He needs to be helped to grow in his ability to analyze classroom problems, in his insights into broad educational objectives, and in his ability to evaluate his own strengths and weaknesses and to understand himself.

The ways in which student teachers and cooperating teachers have managed to find time for conferences are many. Ideally, administrators should realize that accepting responsibility for a student teacher calls for an additional expenditure of time and should release the cooperating teacher from other duties shared by the school faculty to allow for conferences. This, however, is not always done. On the contrary, in some schools the presence of a student teacher is taken to mean that the cooperating teacher will be free for extra assignments. Nevertheless, conference time is important. Sometimes the weekly schedule provides an open period when the class is working with another teacher. Occasionally the student and cooperating teacher agree to use a lunch hour for this purpose, or set aside an afternoon once a week. Whatever the plan, it can be helpful to both people in working out other aspects of their busy schedules if the arrangement is definite and the length of the conference agreed upon. It can be discouraging to a conscientious student to plan time after time for a conference only to find that his cooperating teacher has been called to another meeting. In view of the cooperating teacher's heavy professional obligations, it should, in most cases, be the student teacher who takes the major responsibility for adjusting his schedule to provide for the most convenient conference time. There may, however, be certain college obligations which cannot be set aside. The student should be urged to make these known so that he is not placed in the position of being criticized for failing in his responsibilities in one situation because of his efforts to be cooperative in another.

Conferences can have many points of focus. Conferences can serve many purposes. Undoubtedly, most will focus on teaching problems. Some will be devoted to cooperative planning; others to thinking through alternatives to the proposals in the student's plans as he begins to take on more independent responsibility for the day's activities. It is also important to use conference time to help the student analyze his performance—to note places that went well and activities that were ragged; to figure out why it was that a plan that looked excellent did not work out as foreseen.

Conferences can profitably be used for purposes other than the demands of the particular classroom. Some sessions may well be devoted to helping the student understand general school policies. Some of the details of the school organization and specific regulations ought to be explained relatively early. Later, it may be helpful to discuss such problems as the method of reporting to parents, steps to take in helping the severely disturbed child, means of securing visual aids and other equipment, the teacher's responsibilities on professional committees, the local system of reporting attendance and keeping other types of records. Granted that such topics also receive attention in college classes, there are many details that must be acquired in the actualities of the school situation.

It can be helpful to the student to have opportunities to talk with school personnel with whom he may be expected to work a year hence —the principal, the attendance officer, the school psychologist or visiting teacher. Where there are several students in the school, group conferences for such purposes can often be set up, perhaps by releasing the students from their classrooms. It can also be very helpful for a student to sit in on conferences regarding an individual child so that he can have firsthand experience with some of the problems of working cooperatively faced by parents, cooperating teacher, and perhaps the principal, psychologist, or social worker.

Conferences can also serve to help the student look a year ahead, especially in areas where his school or his class tend to be atypical. The number of pupils in his room may have been unusually large, or unusually small. How would one work if next year's situation were different? The children may have been exceptionally cooperative or the student may have joined the group after patterns of classroom behavior were established. How would one go about securing good work habits in the early fall? And what would one do if three or four children proved to be facing difficult problems of adjustment? The youngsters may be very bright and have a wealth of experiential background. What adjustments would one have to make if one's first assignment were to a community where youngsters had more limited resources? Using the day-by-day experiences in the present classroom as a starting point, cooperating teachers can often give students valuable, realistic help in facing contrasting situations.

Conferences regarding teaching procedures should help to build feelings of security. How to plan cooperatively with a student teacher, how to acquaint him with over-all school policies, and how to help him become aware of problems he may face next year are aspects of conferring with students that cause cooperating teachers very little concern. Such problems are objective. It is a challenge to share one's professional insights. But how does one go about helping a student to face up to his own strengths and weaknesses in classroom performance? Will he be unduly discouraged if the inadequacies of a lesson are pointed out? How does one conduct such conferences so that they are of maximum value?

Students will have been urged in college classes to seek help—to consider their student-teaching experience as a time to make mistakes and an opportunity to grow through constructive criticism. Nevertheless, each comes with his own particular necessity to be successful, his own concept of the ideal teacher he would like to be, and his own personal feelings of security. No two students will react to supervisory conferences in exactly the same way. While certain general principles can be suggested as a guide to such conferences, exact procedures will depend on the personal relationships between each student and his cooperating teacher. Whatever the specific procedures, the student should come away from the conference feeling that he has received help and a little more confident about assuming his leadership responsibilities in the classroom.

Perhaps the most important guide line for conducting a conference in which the student's teaching is to be analyzed is that he, like all of us, needs to know where he is succeeding as well as where he needs to improve. Occasionally, in his zeal to help an individual acquire a new technique, a cooperating teacher forgets to point to other aspects of the day that went extremely well, assuming that the beginner will recognize these for himself. Even the most adept and seemingly most secure student, however, does not always realize when he has done a good job. In fact, like the talented experienced teacher whose insights always lead him to see more possibilities than he can execute, the skillful beginner is quite likely to underrate his performance. Conferences should be conducted, then, so that the student has specific reassurance about aspects of his work that were successful.

Conferences should do more than dwell on a student's strengths, although with an insecure student who seems unduly discouraged by suggestions as to how he might improve, the emphasis in early conferences might, for the most part, stress successes rather than failures. The typical student, however, knows that he has much to learn; he can grow uneasy if his cooperating teacher seems never to mention his inadequacies. Perhaps the cooperating teacher feels that he can't take criticism? or is it that he's so poor he is not worth assisting? or perhaps his cooperating teacher is just too busy to help? Cooperating teachers should not hesitate to analyze quite frankly with students the rough spots in the day's work.

The cooperative planning sessions of the first few weeks when the cooperating teacher's successes and failures are often the focus of discussion can help to establish ways of identifying and analyzing difficulties that can be utilized later when the student's efforts are evaluated. The student should be encouraged to offer his reactions to the way various activities unfolded. He can be involved in watching an individual child or a special group to pick up clues as to why they are having trouble. He can, with the cooperating teacher, examine a plan that did not work and learn firsthand that experienced teachers themselves do not always have successful days. It is also possible to take a first step toward self-criticism by asking the student to report on his efforts to help individuals.

MR. JOHNSON

That little group I had in the corner was really having trouble. I'm not sure our plans were clear. How did your group come along?

SANDRA KANE

All right, I think. At least they seemed to go right ahead, so I think the plans made sense to them. But then Barbie asked me if she could go off on a project on her own. I said I thought she should stay with the group, and she just bothered them from then on. Was I right?

MR. JOHNSON

You might like to keep an eye on Barbie for the next day or so. I'm not sure anything we've done for her could be called exactly "right." Did you try to help her see how she could fit in?

SANDRA

Well, no, I guess I just told her. I was afraid to give her much chance to argue. . . .

It is helpful, as the student begins to assume more teaching responsibility, to encourage him to take the lead in explaining his plans and raising questions. This procedure tends to forestall any tendency to say "Well, how did it go?" or "I was terrible, wasn't I?" and then to wait meekly for criticism. Some students may need to be urged to take responsibity for initiating requests for help, especially if they are not yet quite at ease in the situation. One does not, after all, ask a question that might reveal naïvete unless the listener is trusted. Once two or three questions, however trivial they may seem, are analyzed thoughtfully and with due respect to the student's desire to know, the ice tends to be broken. Cooperating teachers, of course, will certainly sense, and need to raise, problems of which the student is blissfully unaware. Starting a conference with the concerns uppermost in the student's mind does not preclude the discussion of other topics.

The cooperating teacher's attitude toward an activity that goes poorly can do much to help the student accept and profit from his difficulties. It is reassuring to realize that mistakes are expected. Sometimes, in spite of all his preceding college discussions, the student thinks of his teaching as testing experience, a situation in which he must demonstrate complete competence no matter what he attempts. As a matter of fact, a lesson that misses fire can sometimes contribute considerably more to increased teaching skill than one that goes perfectly, provided it is properly analyzed. Elizabeth Parker plunges into an art lesson without thinking through how she is going to distribute the needed materials. In order to make one last point, John Anderson carries a discussion fifteen minutes beyond the time when his sixth-graders are obviously becoming restless. Janie Sampson assumes, without looking, that the map in the social studies text will serve her purposes and suddenly has forty bewildered fourth-graders asking for help at once. Sarah Welsh says rashly to her first grade, "If I hear one more crayon drop we'll just put our Thanksgiving cards for our mothers away and not finish them"—and a whole box of crayons topples off shy little Sandy's desk with a clatter. These are situations that should lead a cooperating teacher to say quite sincerely, "I'm so glad that happened this year while you had someone to help you analyze it," and a student to say equally sincerely, "I certainly learned something today."

Students frequently need to be helped to identify the outside influences that can cause the best of lessons to go awry. A conscientious student (and sometimes an earnest cooperating teacher, too) often desires from children a level of self-control and cooperation that would tax the most mature adult. A rainy day does make a difference. So does Christmas, or Halloween, or the noontime discussion about Janice's birthday party. It's natural to relax a little while papers are being passed, or to reach the point where one must wiggle even if the lesson is still going on. Then, there are in most classrooms one or more youngsters who are facing unusually difficult problems of personal adjustment—who desperately need recognition, even though it is a scolding, or whose span of attention is unusually short. It can be reassuring to students to be helped to distinguish between situations such as these and situations where the basic difficulty lies in their own lack of skill. Not that an experienced teacher merely blames the situation under such circumstances—actually, he makes all the adjustments in his program and methods that he thinks will help. He also sets his expectations realistically, however, and does not call himself a failure if his best efforts do not succeed completely. "I thought I'd lose my mind trying to figure out what I was suddenly doing wrong," reported Jane Adams just before Christmas, "until I went down to lunch and listened to everybody else. I guess you just have to decide to enjoy Christmas even if you don't get anything else done."

Students also need to be helped to realize that increasing the complexity of their responsibility also increases the possibilities of difficulty. This is a fact that cooperating teachers may also need to recognize, especially if they are concerned about the reactions of the college supervisor. Dictating a spelling list is not fraught with nearly the possibilities for error that are inherent in guiding the plans for a unit of work. Far from working toward a day that his cooperating teacher would call perfect, the student teacher who is gaining skill works toward more challenging situations in which to try his wings. His activities, therefore, offer increased opportunities to analyze with him the fine points of skilled teaching—to point out possible refinements in his techniques. This is a point of view that is not always easily achieved. Some students state quite frankly that years of working toward an *A* or a perfect paper make it very difficult to accept the fact that in their chosen profession further growth is always possible. "I'm beginning to see what you mean," said Nancy Smith. "A really creative teacher never stops wanting help in doing a better job. Why, even Mrs. Jones says she always learns many new things from us, and she's taught for years."

Unnecessary feelings of frustration and insecurity can develop because students do not realize how long it sometimes takes to make new ways of working automatic. For their own sense of security, cooperating teachers also need to know that achieving the smooth coordination of all the skills that make up the complex act of teaching is a lengthy process. Often the student's concentration on achieving one goal will cause him to lose sight of another. It may seem as though the same problem has to be discussed many times over before it is solved successfully. Beginners may also need aid and reassurance in facing the fact that some types of errors cannot be eliminated overnight. This is especially true in the general area of human relationships. Fifteen minutes of clear explanation can probably correct an error of fact in geography, but a discussion pattern in which it has been quite permissible for the pupils to chorus answers, shout for attention, and conduct side arguments will not be changed so easily. A beginner can become very discouraged when the new technique does not "pay off." Often, perhaps without expressing his disappointment, he abandons a procedure long before it has had time to become effective. ("I *did* try waiting for them to be quiet, but it didn't seem to help much." "We did some planning together so that they would know what to do next, but they just made silly suggestions, so I stopped it.") Once a problem has been identified with a student, the cooperating teacher needs to be alert to evidences of improvement, however slight, and to draw attention to these. Succeeding conferences can be used to point to this improvement, to analyze new difficulties, and to suggest next steps as the student seems able to execute them.

Conferences should help students to understand basic educational principles. The student who can analyze in general terms what went wrong in a situation is not always able to make a concrete suggestion regarding what to do next. The suggestions made in conference should be specific enough to give the student a sense of direction. Merely suggesting a new procedure, however, is not always of sufficient help. The student needs to know why the alternative is recommended. There is a vast difference between a situation in which a technique is used by an expert who understands what he is doing and one in which the same technique is mimicked blindly by the beginner who does not understand its purpose. One of the most challenging aspects of working with student teachers often proves to be the stimulation offered to cooperating teachers to think through why they teach as they do.

The young adult who is learning to teach, like any other learner, builds his generalizations gradually. It is not always immediately apparent to him that the principles discussed in his college classes apply in the situation in which he now finds himself or that the procedure which worked well yesterday can also be used in a slightly different situation today. He must be helped to employ many of the same processes of inductive reasoning in arriving at new generalizations for himself that would be characteristic of younger learners. It should be possible, however, for the cooperating teacher to short-cut the reasoning process somewhat in the light of the student's maturity and background:

JOHN ARTHUR
They always seem so restless, even when I ask them to cooperate.

MR. MAXWELL
I wonder if you realize how infrequently you do ask for the atmosphere you want. I timed you today, and during Peter's report you let the group

in the corner talk among one another for a full ten minutes before you tried to pull them back.

JOHN
You mean I should be harder on them. I know I should, but it seems so mean.

MR. MAXWELL
Take that a little further. What do you mean by being hard on them?

JOHN
Well, scolding them or threatening to keep them in to make up the wasted time, or something else to show them I'm the boss. But I hate to throw my weight around.

MR. MAXWELL
Have you ever stopped to think why you want them to listen? Is it only to show you're boss?

JOHN
Well, no, they make it hard for everyone around them to hear, to say nothing of how little they learn. It's impolite, too, to the speaker, I suppose.

MR. MAXWELL
What would you do if it were a fraternity committee?

JOHN
Use the gavel.

MR. MAXWELL
Would you feel mean? Would you be throwing your weight around?

JOHN
No, that's the chairman's job. Say, is this what you've been driving at?

MR. MAXWELL
That's the general idea. It takes time; you're getting their attention when you're teaching much more smoothly now. These informal situations are the rough ones. What about it? Do you think you'd feel differently about asking for order if you saw yourself as a chairman rather than a boss?

JOHN
I guess I might.

MR. MAXWELL
Let's make it concrete. What might you say as a class chairman that would not sound as though you're just throwing your weight around?

JOHN

Well, you always say, "Are you ready?" And I've seen you stop the speaker and say, "Let's wait until everyone is listening." And I guess I haven't used our "good audience" rules very consistently. We could look at them. I suppose if I began to hear voices, I'd have to ask for quiet again.

MR. MAXWELL

Yes. You've given that group in the corner quite a bit of experience in being impolite. It's going to take some time to teach them a new habit. Shall I try particularly to analyze what they do tomorrow?

JOHN

That'd help, I think. Time me again, too, will you? I think I get so wound up in the reports that I don't always see what's going on.

This discussion assisted John in identifying some basic principles of effective democratic leadership. Mr. Maxwell contributed illustrations which helped to sharpen the issues, but he led John to arrive at his own generalizations. It is important to note, also, that he did not stop when the generalization was identified; he encouraged John to make the practical application that provided him with some specific classroom procedures. And he guarded against discouragement by pointing out that the children's behavior might not be changed instantly.

Conferences should help students to grow toward self-understanding. The excerpt of a conference just cited indicates another important kind of growth that all teachers need to be helped to achieve—growth in self-understanding. John didn't want to "throw his weight around"; he "felt mean." Seeing himself in the neutral role as a class chairman was a new idea to him. If teachers are to grow in their ability to understand others, they must gain increased understanding of themselves. Oftentimes the student's association with his cooperating teacher is one of the closest of all his college contacts. The discussions of specific classroom events offer many opportunities to help him to grow in understanding himself.

It can be enlightening to students to analyze the leadership roles they are assuming in the classroom.[1] They can profitably be helped to examine their day-by-day classroom reactions for the light that these throw upon the roles that are being played. Which behavior from pupils proves the most irritating? At which points is there the highest tolerance for pupils' inadequacies? Why? Are there types of children

[1] Chapter 5, pages 150-153, provides a discussion of the implications of various teacher roles for interpersonal relationships in the classroom.

to whom the student feels drawn? some by whom he feels repelled? What seems to be the reason for this? What is the nature of the student's leadership in situations involving problems of behavior? How does he feel after he has had to speak firmly? What is his reaction in situations where pupils do not follow his directions instantly? What is the pronoun when the student is playing a leadership role, *I* or *we*? If it's *we*, is it truly a *we* situation? ("I think it would be fun," said Alice Jay, "if we each wrote five sentences about our spelling words for homework.") Helping a student to identify clearly the role he is now playing is an important first step in assisting him to assume more effective roles.

A student's attitudes toward success and failure can have a marked influence upon his progress toward professional competence. Parents and previous teachers may have put such a high premium on success that supervisory suggestions are much more of a threat than they would appear to be on the surface. On the other hand, previous experiences with failure may have resulted in timidity, unwillingness to try out new ideas, clinging to the cooperating teacher's pattern. Students can be helped to look at their reactions to days that go poorly and to opportunities to try their wings. What is the response to a rugged day?—tears? a sleepless night? an optimistic change of plans? How much of the conference period seems to be devoted to letting the student justify why he proceeded as he did? to hearing complaints? What is the reaction to Ricky if he muffs an obvious question while the principal or college supervisor is in the room? to the group of boys who choose this time to show off? Are there delays or snags in situations where the student is to take over a new responsibility?—not quite enough time to start today? one more day needed to collect books? a problem in an area where the student is more secure that really should be attacked first? Ultimately a teacher must find challenges both in trying out new ideas and in analyzing failures or his chosen profession will offer him few satisfactions. A student can be helped to take a major step toward becoming a professional person if he can learn to evaluate his work objectively.

Student teachers are often working closely with two supervisors. It can be important to help them look objectively at their attitudes toward supervisory suggestions. These will be compounded of a multitude of factors, many of which the student teacher may not be consciously aware. For some, previous contacts with others in supervisory positions—parents, teachers, college personnel—will have developed attitudes and expectancies leading to easy cooperation. For others, these early experiences may have built habits of unquestioning obedience. In a few, the last vestiges of adolescent rebellion may crop up in a "don't tell me, I'll work it out for myself" attitude. In some cases, the cooperating teacher or supervisor may resemble beloved Miss Jacobson who has represented for years the ideal teacher the student hopes to become. It is also possible, however, that something in the cooperating teacher's manner will hint of one of the student's previous teachers who aroused feelings of anxiety or failure. To all the attitudes stemming from previous experiences with older persons in authority roles must be added a host of impressions—many positive, some negative—contributed by other student teachers whose comments their peers are not always equipped to interpret. Every student has a very natural desire to succeed, to be thought well of by the cooperating teacher. It is important for cooperating teachers (who, themselves, take a very natural pride in their skill in building effective human relationships) to realize that such varied attitudes toward supervision can exist. It is even more important for students to begin to understand why they react as they do toward supervisory assistance.

Cooperating teachers are not trained counselors. Students can expect, however, the same help in understanding themselves that an experienced teacher would give to a pupil. The comments which the cooperating teacher might make in conferences would be designed to help the student to take a look at aspects of his behavior that are near the surface, not to pry. "Have you ever wondered why Bobby seems to worry you so much more than Jim?" "You seem to expect every day to be perfect. Are you by any chance a student who never settled for anything but top grades?" "Teachers can feel under the weather, too. You need to know how to guard against your own fatigue so that children don't suffer."

In his need to grow in self-understanding, the beginning teacher does not differ much from the rest of us. We carry into our professional relationships with colleagues, pupils, parents, administrators, and supervisors equally complex expectations of which we are equally unaware. Certainly, cooperating teachers bring to the student-teaching relationship their own expectations, attitudes, and feelings of competence. These will influence their attitudes toward students' successes and failures, strengths and weaknesses, and toward their relationships with college personnel just as students' expectations and fears affect their relationships with children.

USING RECORDS EFFECTIVELY

Objective evidence is a valuable aid to supervision. Experienced supervisors and cooperating teachers know very well how many things happen in a classroom in a single busy day. In the confusion of all that there is to remember it can be helpful to have details in black and white so that they can be reviewed and thought over at leisure.

Several types of records will be needed in supervising students. Among the most useful are the records of the student's classroom performance. Sometimes conferences may be a week or more apart, or they may be postponed over the week end with its numerous interfering activities. If this happens, many of the details that would help to explain why a lesson went well or poorly tend to become fuzzy and indistinct. Yet in the details—the precise sequence of comments by the student or the exact steps that led to the breakdown of discipline—often lies the key to effective improvement.

It is not enough to keep records of what goes on in the classroom while the student is teaching. Some sort of record ought to be maintained by both student and cooperating teacher of the conference itself. By the end of a typical conference where problems have been raised, difficulties thrashed out, and plans reviewed and agreed upon, it is not always easy to be sure whether all is well or what the next steps are to be unless some memorandum is kept by the persons concerned.

Keeping records, of course, is not a one-sided proposition. The student must be prepared, even if not always required, to share his written materials with the cooperating teacher. Plans can be more constructively appraised if they are written out in detail. Not only this, but the fact that they are written out makes oral explanation easier and more precise. The student should also be expected to keep notes of his special concerns. If conferences are to be successful, his problems and questions should be written out, not left to the chance of recall on the spur of the moment.

The kinds of reports required by the teacher-education institution will vary from one institution to another. Depending on the nature of the supervisory plan and the comprehensiveness of the record system, they may range from a simple statement to a complex and elaborate series of check lists, evaluations, and written reports. In general, it may be anticipated that the less frequent the visits of the college supervisor, the more necessary it may be for him to keep himself informed by means of fairly extensive records and reports. In all probability, both cooperating teacher and student will be involved in this process.

No two people keep records in exactly the same way. It is safe to say, however, that the longer the time lapse between conferences, the more important it is to note specific details. It is safe to suggest, also, that only those types of records should be made which prove useful either to the specific cooperating teacher and student teacher team or to the teacher-education institution. Neither cooperating teacher nor student has the time to devote to elaborate recording devices that do not serve the ultimate purpose—helping the student to grow.

Notes on the day's work can be useful. Cooperating teachers have devised a number of ways of keeping records of the day's work. On problems where a previous conference has helped to establish general principles and the student is relatively secure in what he is doing, brief memos—jotted down on whatever small bits of paper are handy—can often be useful. These are particularly helpful if time to chat during the day is limited. Sometimes the memo refers to an error in fact or to a confusion at a point where the cooperating teacher feels that interrupting the lesson would be unwise. Sometimes it points to something that worked particularly well. Sometimes it calls attention to a problem in personal relationships of which the student needs to be aware. Typical of such memos are the following:

I wonder if they are all clear on what *zone* means? Would it be good to check again tomorrow to be sure?

There are several books in our library that will help Andy's group. Ask me for them.

Did you notice how much Ricky has grown in his ability to analyze words? Let's talk about giving him a more advanced book.

Sandy has interrupted every committee. Let's talk about how to help him.

Much smoother transition today. Keep it up!

Some cooperating teachers have used more complete and more consecutive notes in a log of the day which combines a record of what went on, reactions to it, and questions for further discussion. This is often kept in a notebook so that the full record is available at any time. The student is free to read the record at the close of the day; points of major concern may become the foci of conferences. This kind of a record can be useful in orienting the college supervisor to the responsibilities being assumed by the student and the help he is being given.

Tuesday, November 12.

9:00 You remembered to wait until you had your audience today. Did you notice how well they are beginning to settle down now that you are working at it consistently?

9:10 Planning—nice job of using youngsters' ideas on crucial points today. Barnie was quibbling!

9:20 Spelling practice—much more pointed teaching today. Should you have plunged into possessives when you saw how vague they were? Let's talk about this—perhaps plan some language activities?

9:40 Library trip—should we do something special to encourage those who don't take books? Perhaps some individualized reading experiences? Any ideas?—This could be a nice unit for you. Could you be thinking ahead on this?

10:30 * * * * * *

At points where it is important for a student to be given help in concrete detail, a running record of what went on, as nearly complete as the cooperating teacher's writing speed will allow, can provide valuable data for a conference. Whereas logs such as the sample just cited often contain advice, questions, and problems to discuss, the running record of activities will be more useful if it is an objective picture of what happened. When such notes are intended for a permanent file, a stenographer's notebook provides a convenient means of making a carbon for the student. Complete verbatim transcripts cannot be made unless shorthand is used, but it is at least possible to record the key comments that influenced the trend of the discussion, or if the problem is one of how to work with a particular youngster, to secure enough detail to make it possible to analyze his behavior. Because such notes contain few supervisory suggestions they usually require further analysis in conference to be of value to the student.

In order to incorporate supervisory suggestions within their running records of classroom activities, some supervisors and cooperating teachers have divided the page using the left hand side for notes of what went on and the right hand margin for an occasional comment. The following are a supervisor's running notes on a student teacher's planning session at a point in the student's growth where his concept of how to involve pupils in setting up the schedule for the day was merely to have them go through the motions of naming typical activities and voting upon a desired sequence. The student teacher's comments are recorded in full, but to save time in writing, the supervisor has adopted the device of putting the children's comments in parentheses without indicating names. The supervisor's evaluative comments appear at the right.

While Mamie collects the tax stamps, let's put our agenda on the board.	
(Spelling.) (Sharing.)	Need you take time to have them list routine aspects of the schedule?
(Can we have social studies?) Yes, we have our reports to finish.	Are you helping them do any real thinking about what *needs* to be done today?
(More dictionary exercises?) No, we didn't think you needed any more practice for a while.	Guesses like this suggest they don't have the needed background to make intelligent suggestions.
(Can we have health?)	
Well, we have our papers to collect, do we not?	
(Could we see that movie?)	
No, that has to go back; it wasn't for our group. Now what shall we do first?	
(Spelling?)	
You want your spelling first, then? [Vote] (Social studies?) [Vote]	Subdued cheer after each vote. Order depends entirely on group choice? No other reasons?

The running notes that follow helped a student to see why her planning session at the beginning of a unit on Explorers went off on a tangent. The group had seen a movie about Columbus, and the supervisor's notes up to the point where this record begins show an extensive and challenging list of questions posed by the youngsters. The student's preoccupation with the end product which the children in their immaturity could not envision became obvious to her when the notes were reviewed in conference. The abbreviations in the original notes are given.

We're going to stop here—this list just a jumping-off point—you'll have a lot of reading to do to get all this information—now let's think of some way of organizing it.	Wonder if they have the background to decide?
(We could answer these questions.)	
Yes, but this'll only be a small part—how could we *organize* all we learn?	Organize!
(Well, in science last year we worked in groups.)	
Good, but we are trying to decide how to *organize* this information.	Leading them into something?
(Everyone could take 2 questions.)	
(Could we do a booklet on certain things?)	
Carry your idea a little further.	
(Each could do one . . . or we could do skits.)	
(Yes, skits . . . skits last year . . . could use a box for a boat.)	
Just a minute. You did skits last year—so you don't want to do something new?	
(Well, yes . . . but a skit could . . . more reactions in a chorus.)	
Can I throw out an idea? Wouldn't it be better to read and *organize* our material first?	Organize! Can they decide intelligently until *after* they've read?
(You mean we can't do skits?)	

Cooperating teachers occasionally hesitate to do as much writing as these records suggest while the student is teaching. Much depends on the contents of the record. Probably most disturbing is the policy of taking notes only when something is going wrong. When the student, however, has had some satisfying experiences of being helped by brief memos or running notes and realizes that positive as well as negative comments are being made, the flying pencil is soon forgotten. Most cooperating teachers talk over with the student the type of notes they would like to take and ask for a frank reaction if the note-taking process ever proves disturbing.

There are also possibilities of making tape recordings of the student at work. This would probably take a few days of preliminary experience so that pupils as well as the student could become used to the microphone. However, it could prove valuable in analyzing the trend of a discussion and perhaps also in helping the student to appraise his voice and to identify any undesirable mannerisms.

When the college supervisor is making extensive notes similar to those just discussed, it is often helpful if the student shares the carbon copy with the cooperating teacher. In this case the carbon provides a second person's analysis of the situation. It may suggest problems upon which student and cooperating teacher may work for further improvement or points at which the student needs help in applying the supervisor's general suggestion to specifics of the classroom—specifics of which the supervisor may not be aware because of his infrequent visits. Often, too, a problem already identified by the cooperating teacher will be recorded in slightly different words which may help to sharpen the nature of the difficulty for the student. Even more important, however, such sharing of records helps the two persons supervising the student to coordinate their efforts in his behalf.

Students' records can be analyzed. Students' plans and logs of their teaching experience may be helpful supervisory aids. These are perhaps most frequently used in conferences preceding the actual teaching experience, but they can also be helpful in evaluation. Bill Anderson's game ends in a riot because his rules were not clear. What do his plans show?—did he think through the rules in detail? had he listed alternatives if the youngsters failed to have the basic skills he assumed? Janice Simpson's first-graders mill about in complete confusion while she tries to work with a reading group. How carefully did she think through her plans for them?—did she list the materials they would need? had she thought about how detailed their directions should be? had she allowed any time for individual help? Problems such as these can be used by the cooperating teacher to document the value of detailed planning and to show the type of detail that is most useful.

In some cases, college supervisors will ask for logs of the student-teaching experience in order to keep in touch with the situation and perhaps to sense common problems for group conferences. Such logs usually contain a running record of the activities undertaken, together with the student's evaluation of his work and the questions on which he would like further help. Cooperating teachers have sometimes hesitated to add such an obligation to the student's regular classroom activities, since they are able to observe for themselves progress from day to day. However, such logs can prove useful for conference purposes.

Monday, October 12

Conducted the sharing period today. Miss Anderson was called out for fifteen minutes, but the children did not seem to notice. I think they regard me as their teacher now. Think I did better today in helping shy children talk, but Jonathan still doesn't respond.

Question: Should a sharing period be for anything but developing language skills? Six-year-olds never seem to share much that really teaches anyone anything.

Also, what do you do if a shy child uses *ain't*? If he's not corrected now, when will he be?

Tried using the pictures to interest my reading group in the story; got much better attention.

Trying to plan ahead myself for Halloween. Have some ideas for art from class last year. Spent an hour in library looking for stories.

Question: Can youngsters this age tell stories? Would like to have some creative language work in this unit.

This kind of brief diary might be read by the cooperating teacher ahead of the regular conference period. The conference could then be focused on the most urgent of the student's questions or perhaps used to allow the cooperating teacher to match his evaluation of the experiences recorded against the reactions of the student.

Appraisal blanks can help in evaluation. Typically, the teacher-education institution will request one or more written appraisals of the student from the cooperating teacher. These forms, and similar ones from school systems to which students are applying for positions, can be helpful supervisory instruments when properly used.

Often it is both reassuring and helpful to the student to talk over the evaluation blank near the beginning of his student-teaching experience, indicating the types of evidence that might be used in deciding how to check specific items. Such procedure can relieve anxieties regarding how work is to be appraised, and it can often provide an objective way of pointing out the importance of types of behavior of which the student has not been aware. For example, in spite of preceding discussions, some students may not realize that promptness—in arriving at school, in completing assignments, in supplying reports requested—is an attribute about which an administrator is much concerned. It may also startle the subject-oriented student, to realize that the school system to which he applies is concerned about his ability to develop democratic relations with pupils and his ability to help them to think for themselves.

Cooperating teachers have also used rating blanks successfully in evaluative conferences at a midpoint in the student-teaching period and, again, at a concluding conference. Often the student is provided with a duplicate form on which he is asked to rate himself. His rating can then be compared with those of the cooperating teacher and discrepancies be analyzed. In a midterm conference, plans can be developed for experiences in areas of weaknesses or in areas where evidence is not yet available. At a final conference, the discussion may be pointed toward the following year—resources likely to be available for further growth, weaknesses of which the student should be especially conscious, perhaps types of schools or classes for which he seems best suited.

WORKING COOPERATIVELY WITH COLLEGE PERSONNEL

Accepting responsibility for a student teacher involves cooperative relationships with college personnel. The nature of these relationships will depend on the particular institution and the personality of the college supervisor. Policies in making supervisory assignments vary greatly from place to place. In some situations the responsibility for the student's growth will be left almost entirely to the cooperating teacher, with occasional brief visits from the college supervisor; in others college personnel will have schedules permitting them to visit frequently and to stay for a substantial block of time when they arrive.

A cooperating teacher's reactions to a visit from a college supervisor will undoubtedly be influenced by previous experiences with supervision and possibly by memories of his own student-teaching days. Actually, the concept of supervision, whatever the level, has changed in recent years. No longer is it a matter of inspection for rating purposes.

The days of the prepared lesson kept on tap for emergencies and the messenger with the scissors or some other time-honored system of warning are a thing of the past. College supervisors are anxious to be of service. Whether their visits are long or short, frequent or infrequent, there are at least four attitudes that can be assumed. First, the college supervisor will view his responsibility in terms of facilitating the work of the cooperating teacher and student in whatever ways they deem his services to be most useful. Second, his aim will be to help the student operate as effectively as possible in the situation as he finds it, not to mold either student or classroom into a preconceived pattern of his own. Third, he will wish to be as sensitive as is the cooperating teacher to the needs of the student, his uncertainties, his aspirations, and his reactions to failure. Fourth, far from having all the answers with regard to how to work with children, the typical college supervisor will be most grateful for the contacts with actual classroom situations that his supervisory responsibilities provide.

It helps to see the classroom as it normally exists. How does a cooperating teacher make the most effective use of college supervisory help? One basic suggestion is that the college supervisor needs to see the classroom situation as it is normally. This is true both of the total classroom experiences and of the student's specific responsibilities. Sometimes cooperating teachers are tempted to make changes in the program when the supervisor arrives, either in a well-meant effort to show the supervisor a more interesting aspect of the day or to help the student appear to advantage. There may be occasions, of course, when the typical program should be reversed because the college supervisor's time is limited and there are specific aspects of the student's work about which the cooperating teacher and student desire advice. A sudden change in plans, however, can be disturbing both to student teacher and to children.

Actually, every aspect of the day can be helpful to the college supervisor. If he is to be of assistance to the student, he faces the difficult problem of becoming well acquainted with the particular group of boys and girls and with the cooperating teacher's methods. A quiet work period can afford time to observe individuals. A lesson taught by the cooperating teacher can help him to sense the ways of working with youngsters with which the student is becoming acquainted. Watching a program evolve, or the ground work for a committee's activities being laid, often reveals professional problems important to consider in college classes.

By the same token, every aspect of the student teacher's work can yield worth-while information. Observing the student at work in a situation that is difficult for him can often provide more clues to points where help is needed than watching him in a situation where he is proficient. Seeing how the student handles a rehearsal for a play will sometimes reveal much more clearly his skill in working with children than watching the finished production. The student's adjustment to an upset day or to the youngster who is having trouble frequently provides more information regarding his strengths as a teacher than does the smooth and eventless day.

Cooperating teachers are occasionally anxious lest the ragged parts of the day will not be understood by the college supervisor and will reflect unfavorably either on their work or the student's. It is important for both cooperating teacher and student to realize that the college supervisor brings considerable sophistication in classroom problems. He knows that a series of three or four rainy days can be reflected in pupil behavior, that the one youngster who loves the limelight may choose the occasion of his visit to monopolize a discussion, that a democratic planning session can lead to some unforeseen proposals, that a beginner's normal anxiety to do well can cause him to seem tense in situations he typically handles very well. One of the procedures most helpful to the student as well as to the college supervisor (and for that matter, to the cooperating teacher, also) is to make the college visitor a part of the classroom as rapidly as possible. One way to do this is to explain to the class who the supervisor is, why he is there, and then to bring him into the regular class activities. The supervisor, too, has a responsibility here. His task is to blend inconspicuously into the situation as he finds it.

Problems need to be raised frankly. The college supervisor comes to help both cooperating teacher and student. This he will not be able to do effectively if he does not know their immediate concerns. Although he can see for himself what problems the student is facing at the time of his visit, there may be other difficulties that the course of a single day does not reveal. Cooperating teachers sometimes hesitate to indicate these, lest the information reflect undesirably upon the student's general competence. It ought to be taken for granted that the college supervisor is as anxious as the cooperating teacher to see the student do well, and just as unwilling to have the difficulty of the moment become part of the student's permanent record. He, like the cooperating teacher, wishes to use his time to advantage in the student's best interests.

Often it can be very helpful to ask a third person, in this case the college supervisor, to study particularly a problem that has concerned a student and his cooperating teacher. There are times when it is not easy for either cooperating teacher or student who are close to the situation to spot exactly what is causing the trouble, although they can identify the area in which they are dissatisfied. Someone new to the room often catches a detail that the persons familiar with the setting have missed. From his varied experiences with beginners the college supervisor can often suggest helpful "hunches" regarding what typically causes similar problems. He knows, too, perhaps with somewhat more assurance than the cooperating teacher whether most beginners are likely to trip over the same problem or whether this student's difficulty is unique. Then, too, the way in which a new person phrases a suggestion may vary just enough from what the cooperating teacher has been saying to clarify the issue. It is often highly desirable, then, for the college supervisor to see those aspects of the program in which student and cooperating teacher feel least secure.

Out of deference to the college, cooperating teachers may also hesitate to raise questions which seem to imply criticism of the college program or counseling system. It may be that the course load or schedule are making it very difficult for the student to meet his full obligations in the school classroom. A student may also come lacking certain basic skills which the cooperating teacher believes could have been readily taught in college classes. College personnel should be made aware of such problems. It may be that the difficulty is unique with the particular student, or that it is one which only practical classroom experience can remedy. On the other hand, an effective change in college procedure may be brought about.

Frankness is also essential if the rating sheets and requests for recommendations for placement papers are to be truly useful. Neither the college nor the employing officer receives much guidance in working with a student if the typical rating is high no matter what the student's performance has been. Some colleges have relieved the cooperating teacher of the responsibility of recommending a final grade for the student-teaching experience partly because it is difficult to do this fairly and objectively when working with only one person and partly because it can be destructive of the cooperating teacher's relationships with the student. Where grades must be given, or the cooperating teacher's rating sheet is to serve as one of the bases for the grade, it is essential for cooperating teacher and college supervisor to have talked together so that the rating system is clear and the bases for the cooperating teacher's ratings understood.

Three-way conferences should be utilized. One of the problems faced by both cooperating teacher and college supervisor is how to coordinate their efforts to help the student. Typically, the suggestions and the problems of the person who is working with the student day after day should have priority and the efforts of the college supervisor should be directed toward supporting the cooperating teacher. The college supervisor has, of course, a responsibility for sharing problems he senses or for suggesting other ways of working he deems will be helpful. Often, with the best of intentions, one person can misunderstand and misquote another, and the student who goes from a conference with his cooperating teacher to one with his supervisor can be trapped in the misunderstanding. Whenever time permits, therefore, three-way conferences can be helpful. Here issues can be pursued until all persons are agreed upon desirable next steps. Such conferences can sometimes be used for a cooperative analysis of the student's activities that have just been observed. If the student has been having particular difficulty, it can be helpful to have the advice of a third person on how best to proceed. The reactions of the college supervisor to plans for the student's future experiences can also be secured. Where three-way conferences are not possible, both cooperating teacher and college supervisor need to keep the student informed regarding their discussions about him. Conversely, as he confers with either individual alone, the student has a responsibility to share the suggestions made by the other. In other words, every possible means should be utilized for coordinating and integrating the supervisory efforts of those most concerned with the student's growth.

College resources should be utilized. Cooperating teachers should expect help from the teacher-education institution over and above that given by the college supervisor. Often there will be a student-teaching handbook describing the program and offering concrete suggestions. Sometimes such handbooks are written mainly for students, but even these can prove useful in alerting cooperating teachers to the orientation the student brings to his assignment. Frequently, the student teacher will be attending a seminar focused on his student teaching. Sometimes, too, he will have been in one or more professional classes centered in teaching problems. The bibliographies and mimeographed teaching aids from such classes can acquaint the cooperating teacher with the general nature of the student's background. Where such materials are not supplied systematically, the student can be requested to ask for duplicates. Often this process has worked in reverse and cooperating teachers have supplied special book lists or teaching aids that have been very helpful to college personnel.

Depending on the institution, there may also be special meetings for cooperating teachers—workshops, seminars, or college courses. In some places participation in such training sessions is considered to be essential before a teacher is invited to become a cooperating teacher. Sometimes such groups have prepared student-teaching handbooks in which they share their insights regarding an effective student-teaching experience. Certainly the common problems faced by cooperating teachers are many and meetings where ways of proceeding are shared can be of much help. The cooperating teacher, then, ought to feel that the college is offering its resources to him, and the college has a heavy responsibility in making him a part of its teacher-education program.

The cooperative relationships developed between elementary and secondary schools and teacher-education institutions offer unparalleled opportunities to send into tomorrow's classrooms teachers with depth of insight into the needs of children and good judgment regarding how to meet them. This affiliation should do more. It should bring the resources of the teacher-education institution to bear on the professional problems of teachers. Even more important, the cooperative relationships among experienced teachers, college personnel, and beginners should make more vital and realistic the program for boys and girls. Parents, teachers, administrators, members of college faculties, the children themselves—each has a unique responsibility and a special contribution to make. In our cooperative endeavors lies the hope for the schools of tomorrow.

BOOKS YOU SHOULD KNOW

Cottrell, Donald P. (Editor). *Teacher Education for a Free People.* Oneonta, N.Y.: The American Association of Colleges for Teacher Education, 1956. Pp. xiii + 415.

Curtis, Dwight K., and Andrews, Leonard O. *Guiding Your Student Teacher.* Englewood Cliffs, N.J.: Prentice-Hall, 1954. Pp. xvi + 384.

Four Went to Teach. Thirty-fifth Yearbook of the Association for Student Teaching. Lock Haven, Pa.: The Association, 1956. Pp. xvii + 173.

Milner, Ernest J. *You and Your Student Teacher.* New York: Bureau of Publications, Teachers College, Columbia University, 1954. Pp. v + 42.

Stratemeyer, Florence B., and Lindsey, Margaret. *Working with Student Teachers.* New York: Bureau of Publications, Teachers College, Columbia University, 1958. Pp. x + 502.

Cooperating teachers will also find helpful the professional bulletins of The Association for Student Teaching, The Association, Lock Haven, Pa.

Index